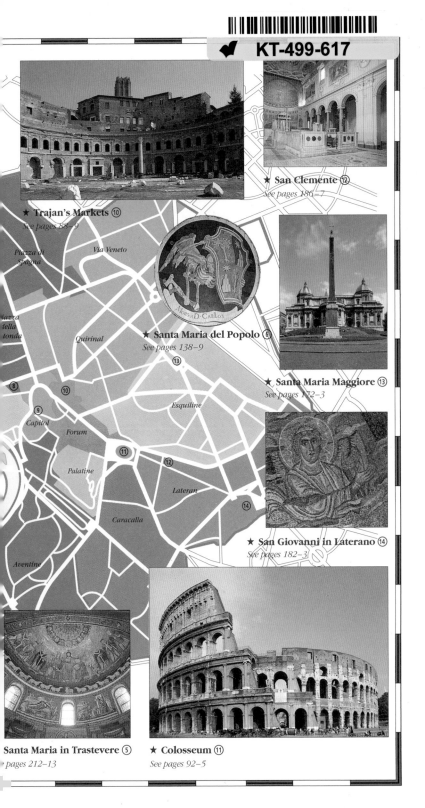

★ Trajan's Markets ⑩
See pages 88–9

★ San Clemente ⑫
See pages 186–7

Plazza di
Spagna

Via Veneto

iazza
ella
tonda

Quirinal

★ Santa Maria del Popolo ⑥
See pages 138–9

Esquiline

★ Santa Maria Maggiore ⑬
See pages 172–3

⑧

⑩

⑨

Capitol

Forum

Palatine

⑪

⑫

Lateran

★ San Giovanni in Laterano ⑭
See pages 182–3

Caracalla

Aventine

Santa Maria in Trastevere ⑤
pages 212–13

★ Colosseum ⑪
See pages 92–5

EYEWITNESS *TRAVEL GUIDES*

ROME

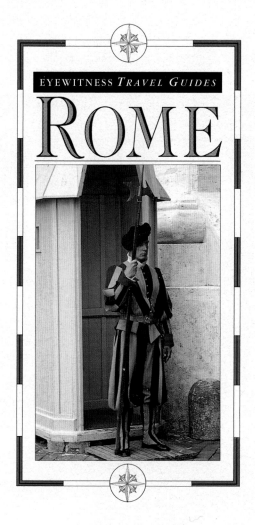

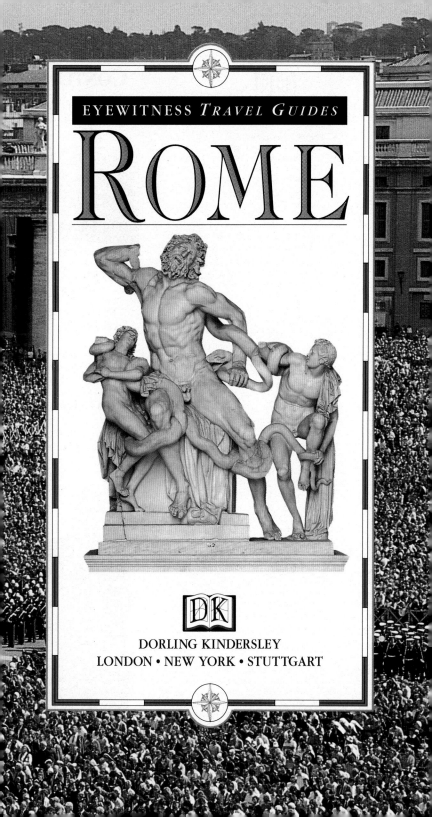

EYEWITNESS *TRAVEL GUIDES*

ROME

DORLING KINDERSLEY
LONDON • NEW YORK • STUTTGART

A DORLING KINDERSLEY BOOK

PROJECT EDITOR Fiona Wild
ART EDITOR Annette Jacobs
EDITORS Ferdie McDonald, Mark Ronan, Anna Streiffert
DESIGNER Lisa Kosky
DESIGN ASSISTANT Marisa Renzullo

MANAGING EDITOR Douglas Amrine
MANAGING ART EDITOR Geoff Manders
SENIOR EDITOR Georgina Matthews
SERIES DESIGN CONSULTANT Peter Luff
EDITORIAL DIRECTOR David Lamb
ART DIRECTOR Anne-Marie Bulat

PRODUCTION CONTROLLER Hilary Stephens
PICTURE RESEARCH Catherine O'Rourke
RESEARCH IN ROME Sam Cole
DTP EDITOR Siri Lowe

MAIN CONTRIBUTORS
Olivia Ercoli, Ros Belford, Roberta Mitchell

MAPS
Andrew Heritage, James Mills-Hicks, John Plumer,
Chez Picthall (Dorling Kindersley Cartography)

PHOTOGRAPHERS
John Heseltine, Mike Dunning, Kim Sayer

ILLUSTRATORS
Studio Illibill, Kevin Jones Associates,
Martin Woodward, Robbie Polley

•

This book was produced with the assistance of
Websters International Publishers.

Film outputting bureau PLS (London)
Reproduced by Colourscan (Singapore)
Printed and bound by Graphicom (Italy)

First published in Great Britain in 1993
by Dorling Kindersley Limited
9 Henrietta Street, London WC2E 8PS
Reprinted 1994

A CIP CATALOGUE RECORD IS AVAILABLE FROM THE BRITISH LIBRARY.

ISBN 0-7513-0008-X

•

Every effort has been made to ensure that the information in this
book is as up-to-date as possible at the time of going to press.
However, details such as telephone numbers, opening hours,
prices, gallery hanging arrangements and travel information are
liable to change. The publishers cannot accept responsibility for
any consequences arising from the use of this book.

We would be delighted to receive any corrections and
suggestions for incorporation in the next edition. Please write to
the Managing Editor, Eyewitness Travel Guides
Dorling Kindersley
9 Henrietta Street, London WC2E 8PS.

CONTENTS

HOW TO USE
THIS GUIDE 6

Colosseum

INTRODUCING ROME

PUTTING ROME
ON THE MAP 10

THE HISTORY OF
ROME 14

ROME
AT A GLANCE 40

ROME THROUGH
THE YEAR 58

**Moses by Michelangelo in
San Pietro in Vincoli**

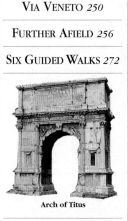

HOW TO USE THIS GUIDE

THIS EYEWITNESS TRAVEL GUIDE helps you get the most from your stay in Rome with the minimum of practical difficulty. The opening section, *Introducing Rome*, locates the city geographically, sets modern Rome in its historical context and explains how Roman life changes through the year. *Rome at a Glance* is an overview of the city's attractions. The main sightseeing section, *Rome Area by Area*, starts on page 62. It describes all the important sights with maps, photographs and detailed illustrations. In addition, six planned walks take you to parts of Rome you might otherwise miss.

Carefully researched tips for hotels, shops and markets, restaurants and cafés, sports and entertainment are found in *Travellers' Needs*, and the *Survival Guide* has advice on everything from posting a letter to catching the Metro.

ROME AREA BY AREA

The chapters covering the 16 central sightseeing areas are indicated by colour-coded bars. Each chapter opens with a portrait of the area and a list of the sights to be covered. These are located by numbers on an *Area Map*. This is followed by a large-scale *Street-by-Street Map* focusing on the most interesting part of the area. The main body of the chapter consists of detailed descriptions of all the sights. Finding your way about the chapter is made simple by a consistent numbering system used throughout for the sights. This refers to the order in which they are described in the chapter.

Sights at a Glance lists the sights in the area by category: Churches and Temples, Museums and Galleries, Historic Streets and Piazzas, Historic Buildings, Arches and Gates, Columns, Obelisks and Statues, Fountains, Ancient Sites and Parks and Gardens.

The area covered in greater detail on the *Street-by-Street Map* is shaded red.

Numbered circles pinpoint all the listed sights on the *Area Map*. Palazzo Doria Pamphilj, for example, is **❻**.

1 Area Map

For easy reference, the sights in each area are numbered and located on a map of the area. To help the visitor, the map also shows Metro stations and parking areas.

Photographs of distinctive details of buildings help you to identify the sights.

Colour-coding on each page makes the area easy to find in the book.

2 Street-by-Street Map

This gives a bird's eye view of the heart of each sightseeing area. To help you locate and identify important sights as you walk around, these are picked out in stronger colour.

A locator map shows you exactly where you are in relation to surrounding areas. The area shown in the *Street-by-Street Map* is marked in red.

Palazzo Doria Pamphilj ❻ is shown on this map as well.

A suggested route for a walk takes in the most interesting and attractive streets in the area.

Red stars indicate the sights that no visitor should miss.

Travel tips help you to reach the area quickly.

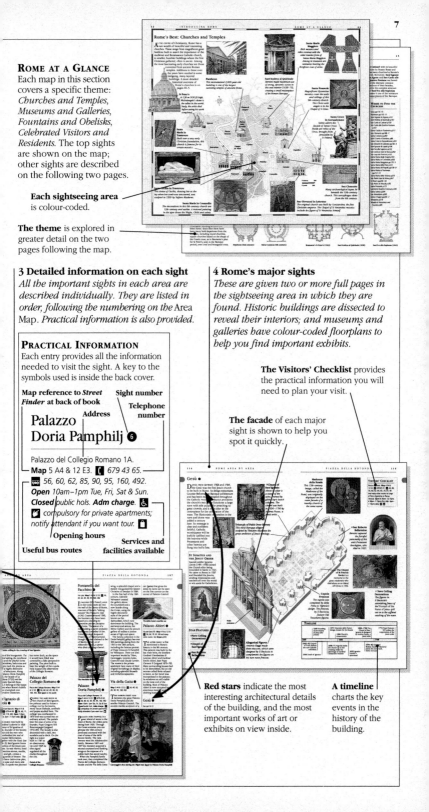

ROME AT A GLANCE
Each map in this section covers a specific theme: *Churches and Temples, Museums and Galleries, Fountains and Obelisks, Celebrated Visitors and Residents.* The top sights are shown on the map; other sights are described on the following two pages.

Each sightseeing area is colour-coded.

The theme is explored in greater detail on the two pages following the map.

3 Detailed information on each sight
All the important sights in each area are described individually. They are listed in order, following the numbering on the Area Map. *Practical information is also provided.*

PRACTICAL INFORMATION
Each entry provides all the information needed to visit the sight. A key to the symbols used is inside the back cover.

Map reference to *Street Finder* **at back of book**   **Sight number**

Address   **Telephone number**

Palazzo Doria Pamphilj 6

Palazzo del Collegio Romano 1A.
Map 5 A4 & 12 E3. 679 43 65.
 56, 60, 62, 85, 90, 95, 160, 492.
Open 10am–1pm Tue, Fri, Sat & Sun.
Closed public hols. **Adm charge.**
 compulsory for private apartments; notify attendant if you want tour.

Opening hours

Useful bus routes   **Services and facilities available**

4 Rome's major sights
These are given two or more full pages in the sightseeing area in which they are found. Historic buildings are dissected to reveal their interiors; and museums and galleries have colour-coded floorplans to help you find important exhibits.

The Visitors' Checklist provides the practical information you will need to plan your visit.

The facade of each major sight is shown to help you spot it quickly.

Red stars indicate the most interesting architectural details of the building, and the most important works of art or exhibits on view inside.

A timeline charts the key events in the history of the building.

INTRODUCING
ROME

Putting Rome on the Map

Since its foundation 2,700 years ago on seven hills near the banks of the River Tiber, Rome has grown into a city of three million people covering 1,500 sq km (580 sq miles) of southern Italy. Within this area is the independent Vatican City State. Rome was made capital of the newly united Italy in 1870. It is about 28 km (17 miles) from the sea and has good rail and road links to many other historic Italian towns and cities.

KEY

☐	Rome and Environs
—	Main railway
✈	Airport
▬	Motorway
▬	A road

0 kilometres   50

0 miles   25

Pisa

Livorno

Firenze (Florence)

Arno

Siena

Arezz

Isola d'Elba

Lago di Bolsena

Vite

Tarqu

Civitavecchia

(Vatican City) Cit

N

Aerial view looking north over Isola Tiberina

M A R

T I R R E

(TYRRHENIAN S

Europe
Rome is in southern Europe, on the same line of latitude as New York. It has two airports and is about 3 hours' flying time from London. Rome is also linked to the rest of Europe by road and rail. It is about 15 hours from Paris by train. It is also at the centre of Italy's main road network, parts of which follow the routes of ancient Roman roads.

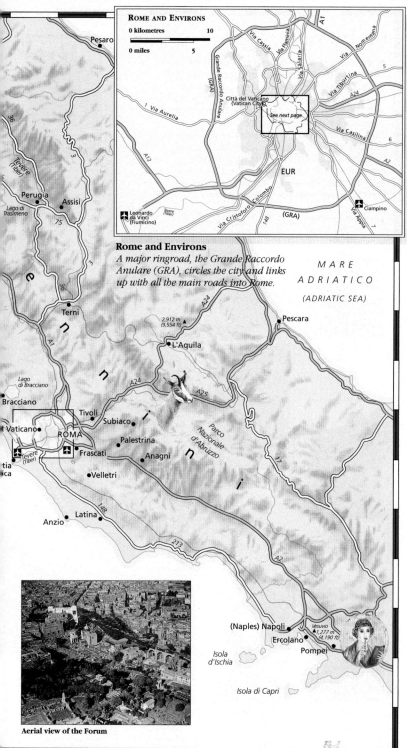

ROME AND ENVIRONS

0 kilometres 10

0 miles 5

Città del Vaticano
(Vatican City)

See next page

Via Cassia

Via Flaminia

Via Salaria

Via Nomentana

A1

Via Tiburtina

A24

Via Casilina

Via Aurelia

Grande Raccordo Anulare (GRA)

A12

Via Cristoforo Colombo

Via Appia

EUR

(GRA)

Leonardo
da Vinci
(Fiumicino)

Ciampino

Rome and Environs

*A major ringroad, the Grande Raccordo
Anulare (GRA), circles the city and links
up with all the main roads into Rome.*

MARE
ADRIATICO
(ADRIATIC SEA)

Pesaro

Perugia

Assisi

Lago di
Trasimeno

Terni

Lago
di Bracciano

Bracciano

Vaticano

ROMA

tia
ica

Tevere
(Tiber)

Tivoli

Subiaco

Palestrina

Frascati

Anagni

Velletri

Anzio

Latina

2,912 m
(9,554 ft)

L'Aquila

Parco
Nazionale
d'Abruzzo

Pescara

(Naples) Napoli

Ercolano

Pompei

Vesuvio
1,277 m
(4,190 ft)

Isola
d'Ischia

Isola di Capri

Aerial view of the Forum

Central Rome

Most of the sights described in this book lie within the old city wall in 16 areas shown on the map below. Each of the areas has its own chapter. If you are on a short visit, you may have to restrict yourself to just a few of the central areas: the Forum to see ancient Rome; the Capitol, Piazza della Rotonda and Piazza Navona for the historic centre of the city; Campo de' Fiori for its grand Renaissance palazzi; Piazza di Spagna for its reminders of the 18th-century Grand Tour and its smart modern shops; and the Vatican to see St Peter's and the centre of Roman Catholicism.

PAGES 128–41
Street Finder maps
4, 5

0 metres 500
0 yards 500

Vatican

PAGES 222–49
Street Finder maps
3, 4

Piazza Spagna

Piazza della Rotonda

Piazza Navona

Campo de' Fiori

PAGES 116–27
Street Finder maps
4, 11, 12

Janiculum

Trastevere

PAGES 142–53
Street Finder maps
4, 8, 11, 12

PAGES 214–21
Street Finder maps
3, 4, 7, 11

PAGES 206–13
Street Finder maps
4, 7, 8, 11

PAGES 102–15
Street Finder maps
4, 5, 12

PAGES 198–205
Street Finder maps
7, 8, 12

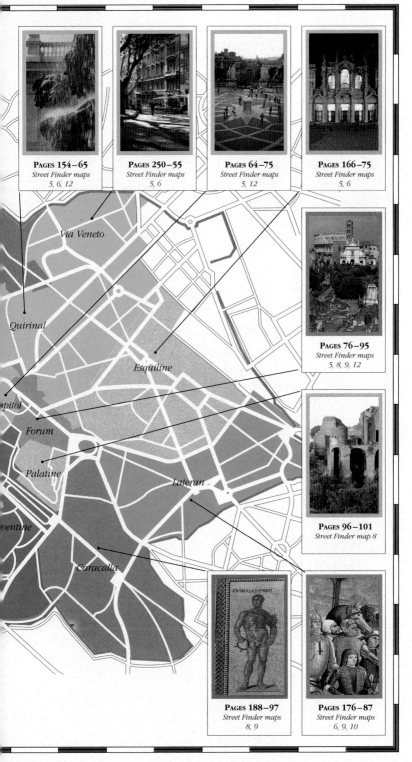

PAGES 154–65
*Street Finder maps
5, 6, 12*

PAGES 250–55
*Street Finder maps
5, 6*

PAGES 64–75
*Street Finder maps
5, 12*

PAGES 166–75
*Street Finder maps
5, 6*

PAGES 76–95
*Street Finder maps
5, 8, 9, 12*

PAGES 96–101
Street Finder map 8

PAGES 188–97
*Street Finder maps
8, 9*

PAGES 176–87
*Street Finder maps
6, 9, 10*

Via Veneto

Quirinal

Esquiline

Capitol

Forum

Palatine

Lateran

Aventine

Caracalla

THE HISTORY OF ROME

ONE OF THE most ancient cities in Europe, Rome was founded over 2,700 years ago. Since then it has been continuously inhabited, and, as the headquarters first of the Roman Empire and then of the Catholic Church, it has had an immense impact on the world. Many European languages are based on Latin; many political and legal systems follow the ancient Roman model; and buildings all round the world utilize styles and techniques perfected in ancient Rome. The city itself retains layers of buildings spanning over two millennia. Not surprisingly, all this history can seem a little overwhelming.

Rome began as an Iron Age hut village, founded in the mid-8th century BC. In 616, the Romans' sophisticated Etruscan neighbours seized power, but were ousted in 509, when Rome became a Republic. It conquered most of the rest of Italy, then turned its attentions overseas, and by the 1st century BC, ruled Spain, North Africa and Greece. The expansion of the Empire provided opportunities for power-hungry individuals, and the clashing of egos led to the collapse of democracy. Julius Caesar ruled for a time as dictator, and his nephew Octavian became Rome's first emperor, assuming the title Augustus. During the reign of Augustus, Christ was born, and though Christians were persecuted until the 4th century, the new religion took hold and Rome became its main centre.

Even though it was the seat of the papacy, during the Middle Ages Rome went into decline. The city recovered spectacularly in the mid-15th century, and for over 200 years was embellished by the greatest artists of the Renaissance and the Baroque. Finally, in 1870, Rome became the capital of the newly unified Italy.

Roman eagle (2nd century AD)

15th-century map of Rome from the north

Detail from 2nd-century AD Roman mosaic from the Temple of Fortune in Palestrina

Rome's Early Development

ACCORDING TO THE HISTORIAN Livy, Romulus founded Rome in 753 BC. Sometime later, realizing his tribe was short of females, he invited the neighbouring Sabines to a festival, and orchestrated the mass abduction of their women. Although Livy's account is pure legend, there is evidence that Rome was founded around the middle of the 8th century BC, and that the Romans and Sabines united shortly afterwards. Historical evidence also gives some support to Livy's claim that after Romulus's death Rome was ruled by a series of kings, and that in the 7th century BC it was conquered by the Etruscans and ruled by the Tarquin family. Last of the dynasty was Tarquinius Superbus (Tarquin the Proud). His despotic rule led to the Etruscans being expelled and the founding of a Republic run by two annually elected consuls. The uprising was led by Lucius Junius Brutus, the model of the stern, patriotic Roman Republican.

EXTENT OF THE CITY

| | 750 BC | | Today |

Ceremonial trumpets

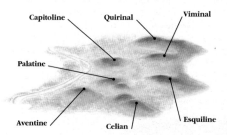

Capitoline Quirinal Viminal

Palatine

Aventine Celian Esquiline

The Seven Hills of Rome
By the 8th century BC, shepherds and farmers lived on four of Rome's seven hills. As the population grew, huts were built in the marshy valley later occupied by the Forum.

Iron Age Hut
Early settlers lived in wattle and daub huts. Traces of their foundations have been found on the Palatine.

Augur, digging foundation

TEMPLE OF JUPITER
This Renaissance painting by Perin del Vaga shows Tarquinius Superbus founding the Temple of Jupiter on the Capitol, the sacred citadel of Rome.

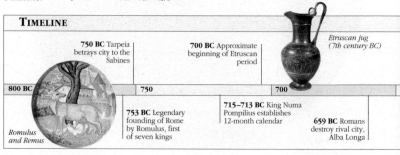

TIMELINE

Etruscan jug (7th century BC)

750 BC Tarpeia betrays city to the Sabines

700 BC Approximate beginning of Etruscan period

| 800 BC | 750 | 700 |

Romulus and Remus

753 BC Legendary founding of Rome by Romulus, first of seven kings

715–713 BC King Numa Pompilius establishes 12-month calendar

659 BC Romans destroy rival city, Alba Longa

Rome's Early Development

The Legend of the She-Wolf
The evil King of Alba threw his baby nephews, Romulus and Remus, into the Tiber but they were washed ashore, and suckled by a she-wolf.

Raven, guardian of the citadel

Apollo of Veio
Etruscan culture and religion were influenced by the Greeks. This 5th- or 6th-century statue of the Greek god Apollo comes from Veio, a powerful, wealthy Etruscan city.

King Tarquin, holding stone worshipped as a thunderbolt

The Legend of Aeneas
Some Roman legends make the Trojan hero Aeneas the grandfather of Romulus and Remus.

WHERE TO SEE ETRUSCAN ROME
The Cloaca Maxima sewer still functions, but there are few other traces of Etruscan Rome. Most finds come from Etruscan sites outside Rome like Tarquinia, with its tomb paintings of sumptuous banquets *(see p271)*, but there are good collections in the Villa Giulia *(pp262–3)* and Vatican Museums *(p238)*. The most famous object, however, is a bronze statue of the legendary she-wolf in the Capitoline Museums *(p73)*. The Antiquarium Forense *(p87)* displays objects from the necropolis which once occupied the site of the Roman Forum.

Funeral urns shaped like huts were used for cremation from the mid-8th century BC.

Etruscan jewellery, like this 7th-century BC gold filigree brooch, was lavish. Treasures of this kind have given the Etruscans a reputation for luxurious living.

578 BC Servius Tullius Etruscan King

600 BC Possible date of construction of Cloaca Maxima sewer

565 BC Traditional date of the Servian Wall around Rome's seven hills

Statue of Jupiter

510 BC Temple of Jupiter consecrated on Capitoline

600 | **550** | **500**

616 BC Tarquinius Priscus, first Etruscan king. Forum and Circus Maximus established

534 BC King Servius murdered

509 BC L J Brutus expels Etruscans from Rome and founds the Republic

L J Brutus

507 BC War against Etruscans. Horatius defends wooden bridge across Tiber

Kings, Consuls and Emperors

Rome had over 250 rulers in the 1,200 years between its foundation by Romulus and AD 476, when the last emperor was deposed by the German warrior, Odoacer. Romulus was the first of seven kings, overthrown in 509 BC when Rome became a Republic. Authority was held by two annually elected consuls, but provision was made for the appointment of a dictator in times of crisis. In 494 BC, the office of Tribune was set up to protect the plebeians from injustice at the hands of their patrician rulers. Roman democracy, however, was always cosmetic. It was discarded completely in 27 BC, when absolute power was placed in the hands of the emperor.

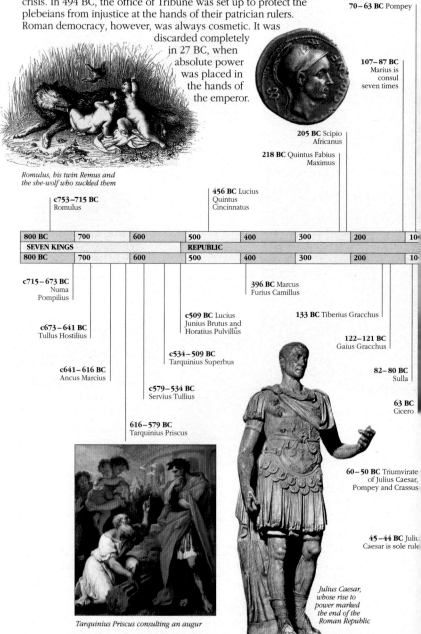

70–63 BC Pompey

107–87 BC Marius is consul seven times

205 BC Scipio Africanus

218 BC Quintus Fabius Maximus

Romulus, his twin Remus and the she-wolf who suckled them

456 BC Lucius Quintus Cincinnatus

c753–715 BC Romulus

800 BC	700	600	500	400	300	200	10
SEVEN KINGS			REPUBLIC				
800 BC	700	600	500	400	300	200	10

c715–673 BC Numa Pompilius

396 BC Marcus Furius Camillus

c673–641 BC Tullus Hostilius

c509 BC Lucius Junius Brutus and Horatius Pulvillus

133 BC Tiberius Gracchus

122–121 BC Gaius Gracchus

c641–616 BC Ancus Marcius

c534–509 BC Tarquinius Superbus

82–80 BC Sulla

c579–534 BC Servius Tullius

63 BC Cicero

616–579 BC Tarquinius Priscus

60–50 BC Triumvirate of Julius Caesar, Pompey and Crassus

45–44 BC Julius Caesar is sole ruler

Julius Caesar, whose rise to power marked the end of the Roman Republic

Tarquinius Priscus consulting an augur

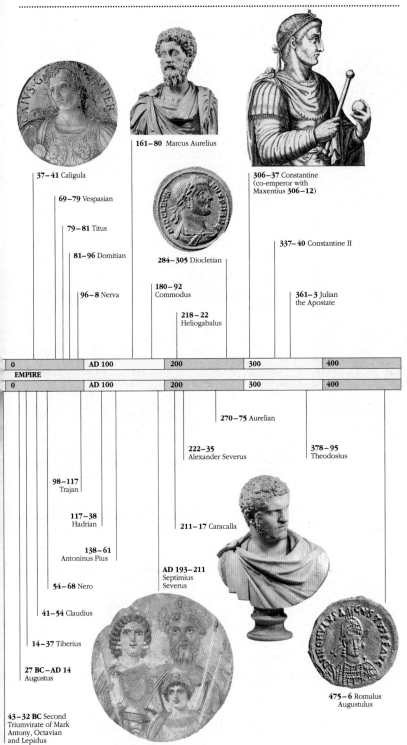

37–41 Caligula

69–79 Vespasian

79–81 Titus

81–96 Domitian

96–8 Nerva

161–80 Marcus Aurelius

284–305 Diocletian

180–92 Commodus

218–22 Heliogabalus

306–37 Constantine
(co-emperor with
Maxentius **306–12**)

337–40 Constantine II

361–3 Julian
the Apostate

| 0 | AD 100 | 200 | 300 | 400 |

EMPIRE

| 0 | AD 100 | 200 | 300 | 400 |

270–75 Aurelian

222–35
Alexander Severus

378–95
Theodosius

98–117
Trajan

117–38
Hadrian

138–61
Antoninus Pius

211–17 Caracalla

AD 193–211
Septimius
Severus

54–68 Nero

41–54 Claudius

14–37 Tiberius

27 BC–AD 14
Augustus

43–32 BC Second
Triumvirate of Mark
Antony, Octavian
and Lepidus

Septimius Severus and family

475–6 Romulus
Augustulus

The Roman Republic

Bronze coin, showing Temple of Vesta (c57 BC)

BY THE MID-2ND CENTURY BC, Rome controlled the west Mediterranean, policing and defending it with massive armies. The troops had more loyalty to the generals than to distant politicians, giving men like Marius, Sulla, Pompey and Caesar the muscle to seize political power. Meanwhile, peasants, whose land had been destroyed during the invasion of Hannibal in 219 BC, had flooded into Rome. They were followed by slaves and freedmen from conquered lands such as Greece, swelling the population to half a million. There was plenty of work for immigrants, constructing roads, aqueducts, markets and temples, financed by taxes on Rome's expanding trade.

EXTENT OF THE CITY

☐ 400 BC   ☐ Today

Cut stone blocks

Covered water channels

Arch spanning road

The gradient of an aqueduct was about 1 in 1,000.

How an Aqueduct Worked

Water from a spring in the hills was collected in a reservoir to build up pressure and ensure a steady supply to the city.

High ground

Cleaning vent

Reservoir

Underground water channel

Arches carrying water across low ground

Cicero Denounces Catiline

In 62 BC Catiline planned a coup. Cicero discovered the plot and persuaded the Senate to condemn the conspirators to death.

TIMELINE

499 BC Battle against Latin tribes; Temple of Castor and Pollux built to commemorate the victory

Via Appia

380 BC Servian Wall rebuilt

396 BC Definitive victory over rival Etruscan city, Veio

312 BC Construction of Via Appia and Rome's first aqueduct, the Aqua Appia

500 BC	450 BC	400 BC	350 BC	300 B

Relief of Capitoline geese

390 BC Rome invaded by Celtic Gauls: quacking geese on Capitoline hill warn of impending attack

264–241 BC First Punic War (against Carthage)

☐ **Roman Republic**

Roman Street
In the 1st century BC, most buildings in Rome were made from brick and concrete. Only a few public buildings used marble.

AQUEDUCT (2ND CENTURY BC)
Rome owed much of her prosperity to her skilled civil engineers. When the city's wells were no longer sufficient, aqueducts were built to bring water from surrounding hills. Some were over 80 km (50 miles) long.

Arches for maintaining a constant gradient over low-lying land

Temple of Juno
The ruins of this 197 BC temple are embedded in the church of San Nicola in Carcere (see p152). Romans consulted their gods before all important ventures.

Scipio Africanus
In 202 BC the Roman general Scipio defeated Hannibal. Rome replaced Carthage as master of the Mediterranean.

WHERE TO SEE REPUBLICAN ROME

This fresco depicting a gang of slaves building a wall can be seen at the Museo Nazionale Romano *(see p163)*.

The Temple of Saturn, first built in 497 BC, now consists of eight majestic columns overlooking the Forum at the end of the Via Sacra *(see p83)*.

Rome's loveliest Republican buildings are the two Temples of the Forum Boarium *(see p203)*. Four more temples can be seen in the Area Sacra of Largo Argentina *(p150)*. Most monuments from this period, however, lie underground. Only a few, like the Tomb of the Scipios *(p195)*, have been excavated. One of the bridges leading to Tiber Island *(p152)*, the Ponte Fabricio, dates from the 1st century BC and is still used by pedestrians.

220 BC Via Flaminia built, linking Rome to the Adriatic coast	**168 BC** Victory in Macedonian War completes Roman conquest of Greece	**133–120 BC** Gracchi brothers killed for trying to introduce land reforms	*Ponte Fabricio, built in 62 BC* **51 BC** Caesar conquers Gaul
250 BC	**200 BC**	**150 BC**	**100 BC**
218–202 BC Second Punic War; Scipio Africanus defeats Carthaginians *Hannibal*		**149–146 BC** Third Punic War; Carthage destroyed	**71 BC** Spartacus's slave revolt crushed by Crassus and Pompey **60 BC** Rome has three joint rulers: Pompey, Crassus and Caesar

Imperial Rome

In 44 BC Caesar became dictator for life, only to be assassinated a month later. The result was 17 years of civil war, which ended only in 27 BC when Augustus became Rome's first emperor. The Empire expanded in fits and starts, but by the late 3rd century was so huge that Diocletian decided to share it between four emperors. Thanks to trade and taxes from its vast domains, Rome was the most magnificent city in the world, studded with the lavish buildings of emperors keen to advertise their civic munificence and military triumphs.

Statue of Bacchus, god of wine

EXTENT OF THE CITY

☐ AD 250   ☐ Today

Cross-vaulted ceiling with mosaic decoration

Natatio (swimming pool)

Apotheosis of Augustus
The first and perhaps the greatest Roman emperor, Augustus ruled for 27 years and was deified by the Senate after his death.

ROMA CAPVT MVNDI

The baths could hold up to 3,000 people. They met to gossip in the central *frigidarium* (cold room).

Area for exercise and gymnastics

The Roman Empire under Trajan
By the 2nd century AD, the Roman Empire stretched from Britain to Syria, and Rome was known as the Caput Mundi, *the head of the world.*

TIMELINE

49 BC Caesar crosses the Rubicon and takes Rome

27 Augustus becomes first emperor

Emperor Nero

64 Fire during Nero's rule destroys much of city

65 First persecution of Christians under Nero

72 Colosseum begun

50 BC | **0** | **AD 50** | **100**

44 Caesar becomes dictator for life, and is murdered by Brutus and Cassius

13 Ara Pacis is erected to celebrate the peace Augustus has secured in the Empire

AD 42 St Peter the Apostle comes to Rome

67 St Peter is crucified and St Paul executed in Rome

Statue of St Peter in San Paolo fuori le Mura

☐ **Imperial Rome**

Roman Revelry
Banquets could last for ten hours, with numerous courses. In order to continue eating, guests would retire to a small room to vomit between courses.

WHERE TO SEE IMPERIAL ROME

There are relics of Imperial Rome throughout the city centre, some hidden below churches and palazzi, others like the Forum *(see pp76–87)*, the Palatine *(pp97–101)* and the Imperial Fora *(pp88–91)*, fully excavated. The magnificence of the era, however, is best conveyed by the Pantheon *(pp110–11)* and the Colosseum *(pp92–5)*.

BATHS OF DIOCLETIAN (AD 298)

Rome's public baths were not just places to keep clean. They also had bars, libraries, barbers' shops, brothels and sports facilities.

The Arch of Titus *(p87)*, erected in the Forum in AD 81, commemorates Emperor Titus's Sack of Jerusalem in AD 70.

Tepidarium **(warm room)**

Virgil (70–19 BC)
Virgil was Rome's greatest epic poet. His most famous work is the Aeneid, *the story of the Trojan hero, Aeneas's journey to the future site of Rome.*

A relief of Mithras, a popular Persian god (3rd century AD), can be seen beneath the church of San Clemente *(pp186–7)*.

164–180 Plague rages in Roman Empire

212 Citizenship granted to virtually all inhabitants of the Empire

270 Aurelian Wall begun

Section of Aurelian Wall

150　　　　　**200**　　　　　**250**

125 Hadrian redesigns the Pantheon

216 Baths of Caracalla completed

247 Rome's Millennium is celebrated

284 Empire divided into West and East

Mosaic from the Baths of Caracalla

Early Christian Rome

Crucifixion in Santa Maria Antiqua

IN THE 1ST CENTURY AD, during the reign of Tiberius, a rebellious pacifist was crucified in a distant corner of the Empire. This was nothing unusual, but within a few years Jesus Christ and his teachings became notorious in Rome, his followers were perceived as a threat to public order, and many were executed. This was no deterrent, and the new religion spread through all levels of Roman society. When the Apostles Peter and Paul arrived in Rome there was already a small Christian community, and in spite of continued persecution by the state, Christianity flourished. In AD 313 the Emperor Constantine issued an edict granting freedom of worship to Christians, and soon after founded a shrine on the site of St Peter's tomb. This secured Rome's position as a centre of Christianity, but in the 5th century the political importance of Rome declined and the city fell to Goths and other invaders.

EXTENT OF THE CITY

AD 395 ☐ Today

Santo Stefano Rotondo
This 17th-century engraving shows how a Roman temple (top) might have been transformed (above) into the 5th-century round church of Santo Stefano.

St Paul

Youthful, beardless representation of Christ

Classical-style border decorated with fruit

4TH-CENTURY MOSAIC, SANTA COSTANZA
Beautiful mosaics, often with palm trees and other oriental motifs suggesting Jerusalem, helped spread the message of early Christianity.

The Good Shepherd
The pagan image of a shepherd sacrificing a lamb became a Christian symbol.

TIMELINE

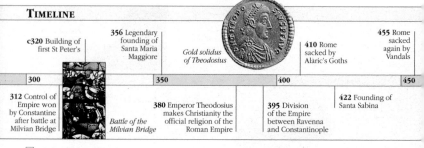

c320 Building of first St Peter's

356 Legendary founding of Santa Maria Maggiore

Gold solidus of Theodosius

410 Rome sacked by Alaric's Goths

455 Rome sacked again by Vandals

| 300 | 350 | 400 | 450 |

312 Control of Empire won by Constantine after battle at Milvian Bridge

Battle of the Milvian Bridge

380 Emperor Theodosius makes Christianity the official religion of the Roman Empire

395 Division of the Empire between Ravenna and Constantinople

422 Founding of Santa Sabina

☐ **Early Christian Rome**

Epigraph of Peter and Paul
This is one of hundreds of early Christian graffiti housed in the Lapidary Gallery of the Vatican (see p237).

Crucifixion, Santa Sabina
This 5th-century panel on the door of Santa Sabina (see p204) is one of the earliest known representations of the Crucifixion. Interestingly, Christ's cross is not actually shown.

St Peter receiving peace from the Saviour

Lambs symbolizing the Christian flock

Constantine's Cross
Constantine's vision of the True Cross during the Battle of the Milvian Bridge made him convert to Christianity.

WHERE TO SEE EARLY CHRISTIAN ROME

There are traces of early Christianity all over Rome. Many ancient churches were built over early Christian meeting places and sites of martyrdoms: among them San Clemente *(see pp186–7)*, Santa Pudenziana *(p171)* and Santa Cecilia *(p211)*. Outside the walls of the old city are miles of underground catacombs *(pp265–6)*, many decorated with Christian frescoes, while the Vatican's Pio-Christian Museum *(p240)* has the best collection of early Christian art.

This statuette, carved out of bone, is embedded in the rock of the Catacombs of San Panfilo, just off the Via Salaria (**map** 2 F4).

The Cross of Justin, in the Treasury of St Peter's *(p232)*, was given to Rome by the Emperor Justin in AD 578.

475 Fall of Western Roman Empire; Byzantium becomes seat of Empire

A Byzantine image of St Paul

609 Pantheon is consecrated as a Christian church

500

550

600

496 Anastasius II is first pope to assume title *Pontifex Maximus*

590–604 Pope Gregory the Great strengthens the papacy

630 Sant'Agnese fuori le Mura is built in Roman Byzantine style

The Papacy

THE POPE is considered Christ's representative on earth, claiming his authority from St Peter, the first Bishop of Rome. Though some popes have been great thinkers and reformers, the role has rarely been purely spiritual. In the Middle Ages, many popes were involved in power struggles with the Holy Roman Emperor. Renaissance popes like Julius II and Leo X, the patrons of Raphael and Michelangelo, lived as luxuriously as any secular prince. The popes listed here include all those who exercised significant political or religious influence, up as far as the end of the Counter Reformation, when the power of the papacy began to wane.

St Ludovic Kneels before Boniface VIII *by Simone Martini*

314–35 St Sylvester I

222–30 St Urban I

217–22 St Callixtus I

590–604 St Gregory the Great

496–8 St Anastasius II

Gregory the Great leading a procession to end the plague

931–5 John XI

891–6 Formosus

955–64 John XII

1227–41 Gregory IX

1216–27 Honorius III Savelli

0	200	400	600	800	1000	1200

PAPACY BASED IN ROME

0	200	400	600	800	1000	1200

336–7 St Mark

352–66 Liberius

90–9 St Clement

42–67 St Peter

579–90 Pelagius II

608–15 St Boniface IV

731–41 St Gregory III

772–95 Adrian I

1047–8 Benedict IX

1073–85 St Gregory VII

1099–1118 Paschal II

1130–43 Innocent II

1154–9 Adrian IV

847–55 St Leo IV

817–24 St Paschal I

1198–1216 Innocent III

St Peter, *from a mosaic in Santa Prassede (see p171)*

795–816 St Leo III

Innocent III's Vision of the Church, *from a fresco by Giotto*

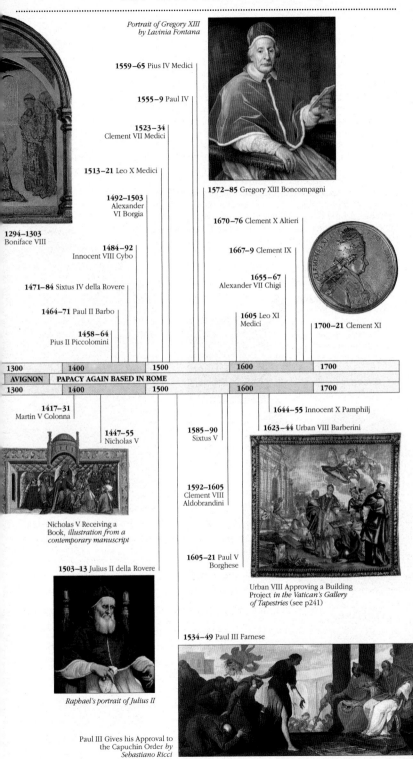

Portrait of Gregory XIII
by Lavinia Fontana

1559–65 Pius IV Medici

1555–9 Paul IV

1523–34
Clement VII Medici

1513–21 Leo X Medici

1492–1503
Alexander
VI Borgia

1572–85 Gregory XIII Boncompagni

1670–76 Clement X Altieri

1294–1303
Boniface VIII

1484–92
Innocent VIII Cybo

1667–9 Clement IX

1471–84 Sixtus IV della Rovere

1655–67
Alexander VII Chigi

1464–71 Paul II Barbo

1605 Leo XI
Medici

1700–21 Clement XI

1458–64
Pius II Piccolomini

1300	1400	1500	1600	1700
AVIGNON	PAPACY AGAIN BASED IN ROME			
1300	1400	1500	1600	1700

1417–31
Martin V Colonna

1644–55 Innocent X Pamphilj

1447–55
Nicholas V

1585–90
Sixtus V

1623–44 Urban VIII Barberini

Nicholas V Receiving a
Book, illustration from a
contemporary manuscript

1592–1605
Clement VIII
Aldobrandini

1503–13 Julius II della Rovere

1605–21 Paul V
Borghese

Urban VIII Approving a Building
Project in the Vatican's Gallery
of Tapestries (see p241)

Raphael's portrait of Julius II

1534–49 Paul III Farnese

Paul III Gives his Approval to
the Capuchin Order by
Sebastiano Ricci

Medieval Rome

Mosaic, San Clemente

Supplanted by Constantinople as capital of the Empire in the 4th century, Rome was reduced to a few thousand inhabitants by the early Middle Ages; its power was just a memory, its monuments little more than weed-covered ruins. In the 8th and 9th centuries, the growing importance of the papacy revived the city and made it once more a centre of power. But continual conflicts between the pope and the Holy Roman Emperor soon weakened the papacy. The 10th, 11th and 12th centuries were among the bleakest in Roman history: violent conflict with invaders left Rome poverty-stricken and the constantly warring local barons tore apart what remained of the city. In 1309 the papacy was forced to move to Avignon, leaving Rome to slide into further squalor and strife.

EXTENT OF THE CITY

▨ 1300	☐ Today

Charlemagne Crowned in St Peter's
On Christmas Day in 800, Charlemagne was made emperor of the Holy Roman Empire, a new Christian dominion to replace that of ancient Rome.

San Giovanni in Laterano

Aurelian Wall

Column of Trajan

Column of Marcus Aurelius

Madonna and Child Mosaic
The Chapel of St Zeno (817–24) in the church of Santa Prassede (see p171) has some of the best examples of Byzantine mosaics in Rome.

MEDIEVAL PLAN OF ROME
Maps like this one, illustrating the principal features of the city, were produced for pilgrims, the tourists of the Middle Ages.

TIMELINE

700	800	900	100
725 King Ine of Wessex founds the first hostel for pilgrims in the Borgo	**852** The Vatican is fortified with walls following a raid by Saracens	*Emperor Otto I*	**961** King Otto the Great becomes first German Holy Roman Emperor
778 Charlemagne, King of the Franks, conquers Italy	**800** Charlemagne crowned emperor in St Peter's	**880–932** Rome is ruled by two women, Theodora and then her daughter, Marozia	

☐ Medieval Rome

Stefaneschi Triptych *(1315)*
Giotto and his pupils painted this triptych for Cardinal Stefaneschi as an altarpiece for St Peter's. It is now in the Vatican Museums (see p240).

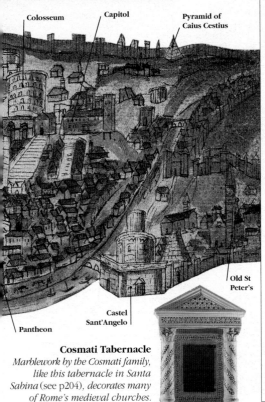

Colosseum   Capitol   **Pyramid of Caius Cestius**

Old St Peter's

Castel Sant'Angelo

Pantheon

Cosmati Tabernacle
Marblework by the Cosmati family, like this tabernacle in Santa Sabina (see p204), decorates many of Rome's medieval churches.

WHERE TO SEE MEDIEVAL ROME

Among the most interesting churches of the period are San Clemente, with a fine apse mosaic and Cosmati floor *(see pp186–7)*, Santa Maria in Trastevere *(pp212–13)* and Santa Maria sopra Minerva, Rome's only Gothic church *(p108)*. Santa Cecilia in Trastevere *(p211)* has a Cavallini fresco, and there is fine Cosmati work in Santa Maria in Cosmedin *(p202)*.

Charlemagne's Dalmatic in the Treasury of St Peter's *(p232)* was supposedly worn by the Holy Roman Emperor at his coronation. In fact the richly embroidered vestment probably dates from the 14th century.

Santa Sabina *(p204)* on the Aventine Hill has a medieval bell-tower.

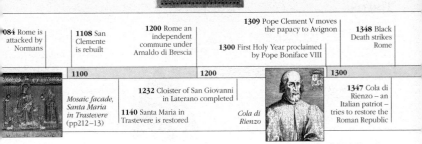

084 Rome is attacked by Normans

1108 San Clemente is rebuilt

1200 Rome an independent commune under Arnaldo di Brescia

1309 Pope Clement V moves the papacy to Avignon

1300 First Holy Year proclaimed by Pope Boniface VIII

1348 Black Death strikes Rome

1100   **1200**   **1300**

Mosaic facade, Santa Maria in Trastevere (pp212–13)

1232 Cloister of San Giovanni in Laterano completed

1140 Santa Maria in Trastevere is restored

Cola di Rienzo

1347 Cola di Rienzo – an Italian patriot – tries to restore the Roman Republic

Renaissance Rome

POPE NICHOLAS V came to the throne in 1447 determined to make Rome a city fit for the papacy. Among his successors, men like Julius II and Leo X eagerly followed his lead, and the city's appearance was transformed. The Classical ideals of the Renaissance inspired artists, architects and craftsmen, such as Michelangelo, Bramante, Raphael and Cellini, to build and decorate the churches and palaces of a newly confident Rome.

Detail of Botticelli's *Youth of Moses* (1480s)

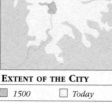

EXTENT OF THE CITY

☐ 1500 ☐ Today

Hemispherical dome

Balustrade of small columns

Classical colonnade of 16 Doric columns

School of Athens by Raphael
In this fresco (see p243) Raphael complimented many of his peers by representing them as ancient Greek philosophers. The building shown is based on a design by Bramante.

THE TEMPIETTO
The Tempietto (1502) at San Pietro in Montorio (see p219) was one of Bramante's first works in Rome. A simple, perfectly proportioned miniature Classical temple, it is a model of High Renaissance architecture.

Cosmati-style mosaic floor

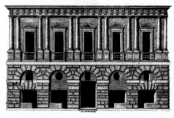

Palazzo Caprini
Bramante's design had a strong influence on later Renaissance palazzi. Parts of the building survive in Palazzo dei Convertendi (see p227).

TIMELINE

1377 Papacy returns to Rome from Avignon under Pope Gregory XI

1409–15 Papacy moves to Pisa

1452 Demolition of old St Peter's basilica begins

1444 Birth of Bramante

1350

1400

1

1378–1417 The Great Schism, a division in the papacy in Avignon

1417 Pope Martin V ends the Great Schism in the papacy

Pope Martin V, reigned 1417–31

☐ **Renaissance Rome**

Sack of Rome
In 1527, the unruly troops of Charles V of Spain pillaged the city, destroying countless works of art. Pope Clement VII took refuge in Castel Sant'Angelo.

Pope Nicholas V
Nicholas ordered the demolition of the old St Peter's.

Statue of St Peter, believed to have been crucified on this site

Underground chapel

WHERE TO SEE RENAISSANCE ROME

The Campo de' Fiori area *(see pp142–53)* is full of grand Renaissance palazzi, especially along Via Giulia *(pp276–7)*. Across the river stands the delightful Villa Farnesina *(pp220–21)*. The most typical church of the period is Santa Maria del Popolo *(pp138–9)*, and the best collection of Renaissance art is in the Vatican Museums *(pp234–47)*. These include the Sistine Chapel *(pp244–7)* and the Raphael Rooms *(pp242–3)*.

The Madonna di Foligno by Raphael (1511–12) is one of the fine Renaissance paintings in the Vatican Pinacoteca *(p241)*.

The Pietà, commissioned for St Peter's in 1501, was one of Michelangelo's first sculptures executed in Rome *(p233)*.

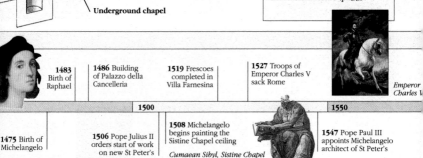

| **1483** Birth of Raphael | **1486** Building of Palazzo della Cancelleria | **1519** Frescoes completed in Villa Farnesina | **1527** Troops of Emperor Charles V sack Rome | Emperor Charles V |

1500   1550

1475 Birth of Michelangelo

1506 Pope Julius II orders start of work on new St Peter's

1508 Michelangelo begins painting the Sistine Chapel ceiling

Cumaean Sibyl, Sistine Chapel

1547 Pope Paul III appoints Michelangelo architect of St Peter's

Baroque Rome

Baroque putto

BY THE 16TH CENTURY, the Catholic Church had become immensely rich – one of the chief criticisms of the Protestant reformers. The display of grandeur and extravagance by the papal court contrasted sharply with the poverty of the people, and wealthy Roman society was characterized by sumptuous luxury and a ceaseless round of entertainment. To make the Catholic faith more appealing than Protestantism, scores of churches were built and monuments and fountains were erected to glorify the Holy See. The finest architects in the ornate, dramatic style of the Baroque were Bernini and Borromini.

EXTENT OF THE CITY

▨ *1645*   ☐ *Today*

Ceiling portraying heavenly scenes

Monument to Pope Alexander VII
This Bernini tomb in St Peter's (pp230–33) includes a skeleton brandishing an hour glass.

Gian Lorenzo Bernini *(1598–1680)*
The favourite artist of the papacy, Bernini transformed Rome with his churches, palaces, statues and fountains.

Holy Family fresco

Tapestry of Pope Urban VIII
Bernini's most devoted patron, Pope Urban VIII Barberini (1623–44), is shown here receiving the homage of the nations.

A marble rose marks the best place to stand to appreciate the illusion of space created by the artist.

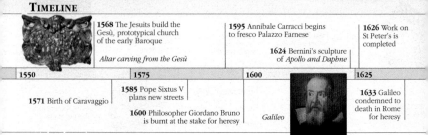

TIMELINE

1568 The Jesuits build the Gesù, prototypical church of the early Baroque

Altar carving from the Gesù

1595 Annibale Carracci begins to fresco Palazzo Farnese

1624 Bernini's sculpture of *Apollo and Daphne*

1626 Work on St Peter's is completed

1550	1575	1600	1625

1571 Birth of Caravaggio

1585 Pope Sixtus V plans new streets

1600 Philosopher Giordano Bruno is burnt at the stake for heresy

Galileo

1633 Galileo condemned to death in Rome for heresy

☐ **Baroque Rome**

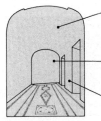

Illusionistic beams in ceiling

Chapel painted on flat slanting wall

Figures painted to be viewed from an angle

Queen Christina of Sweden
In a coup for Catholicism, Christina renounced Protestantism and abdicated her throne. In 1655 she moved to Rome, where she became the centre of a lively literary and scientific circle.

St Ignatius, founder of the Jesuits

San Carlo alle Quattro Fontane
One of Borromini's most influential designs was this tiny oval church (see p161) on the Quirinal hill.

Francesco Borromini
(1599–1667)
In the many churches he built in Rome, Borromini made use of revolutionary geometric forms.

POZZO CORRIDOR
The use of perspective to create an illusion of depth and space was a favourite Baroque device. Andrea Pozzo painted this illusionistic corridor in the 1680s in the Rooms of St Ignatius near the Gesù (see pp114–15).

1651 Bernini redesigns much of Piazza Navona *Bernini's Fontana dei Fiumi in Piazza Navona*	**1694** Palazzo di Montecitorio is completed	**1735** Spanish Steps are designed **1732** Works start on Trevi Fountain	
1650	**1675**	**1700**	**1725**
1657 Borromini completes Sant'Agnese in Agone **1656** Work starts on Bernini's colonnade for St Peter's square	*Bonnie Prince Charlie, pretender to the throne of England*	**1721** Bonnie Prince Charlie is born in Rome	**1734** Clement XII makes Palazzo Nuovo world's first public museum

Understanding Rome's Architecture

Arch of Titus

THE ARCHITECTURE of Imperial Rome kept alive the Classical styles of ancient Greece, at the same time developing new, uniquely Roman forms based on the arch, the vault and the dome. The next important period was the 12th century, when many Romanesque churches were built. The Renaissance saw a return to Classical ideals, inspired by the example of Florence, but in the 17th century Rome found a style of its own again in the flamboyance of the Baroque.

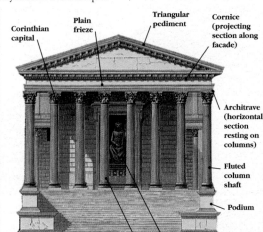

The entablature above these columns has both straight and arched sections (Hadrian's Villa).

CLASSICAL ROME

Most Roman buildings were of concrete faced with brick, but from the 1st century BC, the Romans started to imitate earlier Greek models, using marble to decorate temples and other public buildings.

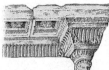

Caryatids were sculpted columns, usually in the form of a female figure. Roman caryatids, like this one in the Forum of Augustus, were often copied in detail from earlier Greek examples.

Corinthian capital

Plain frieze

Triangular pediment

Cornice (projecting section along facade)

Architrave (horizontal section resting on columns)

Fluted column shaft

Podium

Roman temples were usually built on a raised dais or podium, to make them prominent. Many were fronted by a portico, a roofed porch with columns.

Cella (inner sanctuary)

Colonnade enclosing portico

The orders of Classical architecture were building styles, each based on a different column design. The three major orders were borrowed by the Romans from the Greeks.

Aedicules were small shrines, framed by two pillars, usually containing a statue of a god.

Doric order   Ionic order   Corinthian order

Coffers were decorative sunken panels that reduced the weight of domed and vaulted ceilings.

EARLY CHRISTIAN AND MEDIEVAL ROME

The first Christian churches in Rome were based on the basilica: oblong, with three naves, each usually ending in an apse. From the 10th to the 13th century, most churches were built in the Romanesque style, which used the rounded arches of ancient Rome.

The triumphal arch divides the nave of a church from the apse. Here, in San Paolo fuori le Mura, it is decorated with mosaics.

Basilicas in Rome have, in most cases, kept their original rectangular shape. The nave of San Giovanni in Laterano retains its 4th-century floorplan.

RENAISSANCE AND BAROQUE ROME

Renaissance architecture (15th–16th centuries) drew its inspiration directly from Classical models. It revived the use of strict geometric proportions. The Baroque age (late 16th–17th centuries) broke many established rules, favouring grandiose decoration over pure Classical forms.

A baldacchino is a canopy, supported on columns, rising over the main altar. This Baroque example is in St Peter's.

Putti were a popular decorative feature in the Baroque. A putto is a painting or a sculpture of a child like a Cupid or cherub.

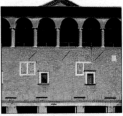

A loggia is an open-sided gallery or arcade. It may be a separate structure or part of a building, as here at San Saba.

Rusticated masonry decorates the exterior of many Renaissance palazzi. It consists of massive blocks divided by deep joints.

A tabernacle is used to house the Sacrament for the mass. This 13th-century Gothic wall tabernacle is in San Clemente.

COSMATESQUE SCULPTURE AND MOSAICS

The Cosmati family, active in Rome during the 12th and 13th centuries, have given their name to a particularly Roman style of decoration. They worked in marble, producing all kinds of fittings for churches, including cloisters, episcopal thrones, tombs, pulpits, fonts and candlesticks. These were often decorated with

Cosmatesque floor, Santa Maria in Cosmedin

bands of colourful mosaic. They also left many fine floor mosaics, usually of white marble with an inlay of red and green porphyry. Ancient Roman columns were cut up to provide the materials. Several other families of stonemasons used a similar style, and their work is also described as Cosmatesque.

Rome during Unification

U NDER NAPOLEON, Italy had a brief taste of unity, but by 1815 it was once more divided into many small states and papal rule was restored in Rome. Over the next 50 years, patriots, led by Mazzini, Garibaldi and others, struggled to create an independent, unified Italy. In 1848 Rome was briefly declared a Republic, but Garibaldi's forces were driven out by French troops. The French continued to protect the pope, while the rest of Italy was united as a kingdom under Vittorio Emanuele of Savoy. In 1870, troops stormed the city, and Rome became capital of Italy.

Garibaldi in his distinctive red shirt

EXTENT OF THE CITY
▨ 1870   ☐ Today

Porta Pia

Tricoloured flag of the new Italian kingdom

Plumed hat of the Bersaglieri, crack troops from Savoy

Allegory of Italy's Liberty
This patriotic poster from 1890 shows the king, his chief minister Cavour, Garibaldi and Mazzini. The woman in red represents Italy.

Vittorio Emanuele II
Vittorio Emanuele, King of Piedmont, became the first King of Italy in 1861.

ROYALISTS STORM PORTA PIA
On 20 September 1870, troops of the kingdom of Italy put an end to the papal domination of Rome. They breached the city walls near Porta Pia; the pope retreated and Rome was made the Italian capital.

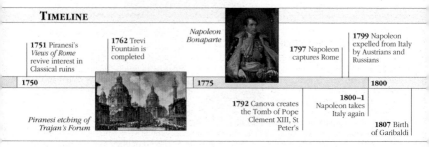

TIMELINE

Napoleon Bonaparte

1751 Piranesi's *Views of Rome* revive interest in Classical ruins

1762 Trevi Fountain is completed

1797 Napoleon captures Rome

1799 Napoleon expelled from Italy by Austrians and Russians

1750 — 1775 — 1800

Piranesi etching of Trajan's Forum

1792 Canova creates the Tomb of Pope Clement XIII, St Peter's

1800–1 Napoleon takes Italy again

1807 Birth of Garibaldi

☐ **Rome during Unification**

Garibaldi and Rome

The charismatic leader Giuseppe Garibaldi had taken much of Italy from foreign rule by 1860. Rome still remained a crucial problem. Here he declares "O Roma o morte" (Rome or Death).

Villa Paolina

Giuseppe Verdi (1813–1901)

Verdi, the opera composer, supported unification and in 1861 became a member of Italy's first national parliament.

Breach in Aurelian Wall

A Freed City

This marble plaque was set up at Porta Pia to commemorate the liberation of Rome.

Victor Emmanuel Monument

A vast monument to Italy's first king (see p74) stands at the end of Via del Corso.

S · P · Q · R
VRBE · ITALIAE · VINDICATA
INCOLIS · FELICITER · AVCTIS
GEMINOS · FORNICES · CONDIDIT

1816 Work begins on Piazza del Popolo

Fountain in Piazza del Popolo

1848 Nationalist uprising in Rome. Pope flees and a Republic is formed

1860 Garibaldi and his 1,000 followers take Sicily and Naples

1870 Royalist troops take Rome, completing the unification of Italy

1825

1850

1820 Revolts throughout Italy

1821 Keats dies in Piazza di Spagna

1849 Pope is restored to power, protected by a French garrison

Pope Pius IX

1861 Kingdom of Italy founded with capital in Turin

Twentieth-Century Rome

World Cup mania

THE FASCIST DICTATOR, Mussolini, dreamed of recreating the immensity, order and power of the old Roman Empire: "Rome", he said, "must appear wonderful to the whole world." He planned to build a massive Palace of Fascism by the Forum. This came to nothing, though he did begin to build a grandiose new complex, EUR, in the suburbs, and razed 15 churches and many medieval houses to create space for wide new roads. Fortunately most of the old centre has survived, leaving the city with one of Europe's most picturesque historic cores.

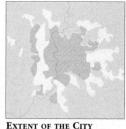

EXTENT OF THE CITY

▨ *1960s*   ▢ *Today*

Mussolini's Plans for Rome
This propaganda poster reflects Mussolini's grandiose projects such as Via dei Fori Imperiali in the Forum area (see p76), and EUR (p267).

Placido Domingo | José Carreras | Luciano Pavarotti

Pope John Paul II
John Paul II is the first non-Italian pope since the 1520s. A traditionalist, he exerts a tremendous influence on the lives of the world's Catholics.

THREE TENORS CONCERT (1990)
Combining Italy's love for music and football, this opera recital at the Baths of Caracalla was broadcast live during the World Cup.

TIMELINE

1900	1912	1925	1938

1915 Italy enters World War I

1926 Opposition parties banned

1946 National referendum establishes Italy as a Republic; King Umberto II exiled

1944 Allies liberate Rome from Germans

1911 Victor Emmanuel Monument is completed

1922 Fascists march on Rome. Mussolini becomes Prime Minister

1929 Lateran Treaty creates a separate Vatican state

Poster for EUR

1940 Italy enters World War II; work begins on EUR zone

▢ **Twentieth-Century Rome**

Religion in the 20th Century
Rome has attracted pilgrims for centuries, and they continue to come, especially at Easter and for the ever more frequent beatifications. The city also hosts a large, cosmopolitan religious community.

Conductor Zubin Mehta

Poster for La Dolce Vita
In the 1950s and '60s Rome was Europe's Hollywood. Ben Hur, Quo Vadis? and Cleopatra *were made at the Cinecittà studios, as well as Italian films like Fellini's* La Dolce Vita.

Valentino Model
While not as important as Milan for fashion, Rome is still home to some of the industry's leading designers.

City-Centre Traffic
Rome's streets are congested, and many buildings have been damaged by pollution. There are plans to close the historic centre to traffic.

1960 Olympic Games are held in Rome

1978 Premier Aldo Moro kidnapped, then killed by Red Brigades; Karol Wojtyla is elected Pope John Paul II

1981 Assassination attempt on Pope John Paul II in St Peter's Square

| 1950 | 1962 | 1975 | 1988 |

1957 Treaty of Rome initiates European Common Market

1962 Second Vatican Council brings about Church reforms

1990 World Cup is held in Rome

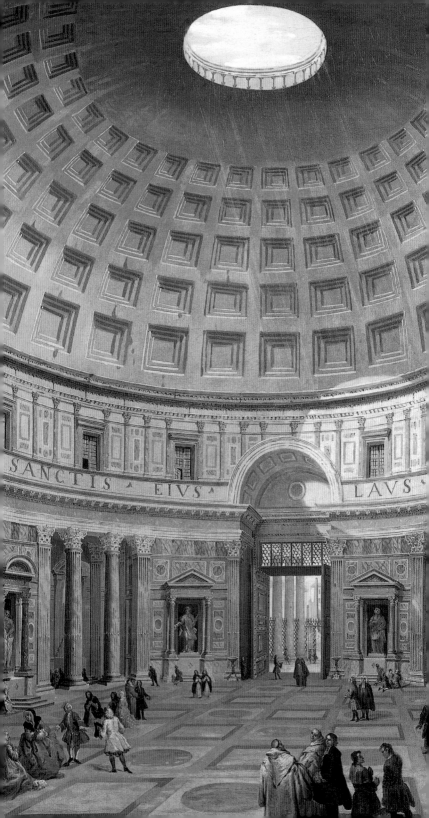

ROME AT A GLANCE

ROM ITS EARLY DAYS as a settlement of shepherds on the Palatine hill, Rome grew to rule a vast empire stretching from northern England to North Africa. Later, after the empire had collapsed, Rome became the centre of the Christian world and artists and architects flocked to work for the popes. The legacy of this history can be seen all over the city. The following pages are a time-saving summary of some of the best Rome has to offer. There are sections on churches, museums and galleries, fountains and obelisks, and celebrated visitors and residents in Rome. Below are the top attractions that no visitor should miss.

ROME'S TOP TOURIST ATTRACTIONS

Capitoline Museums
See pp70–73.

Colosseum
See pp92–5.

Sistine Chapel
See pp244–7.

Spanish Steps
See p134.

Raphael Rooms
See pp242–3.

Trevi Fountain
See p159.

Castel Sant'Angelo
See pp248–9.

Pantheon
See pp110–11.

St Peter's
See pp230–33.

Roman Forum
See pp78–87.

Piazza Navona
See p120.

Interior of the Pantheon, by Giovanni Paolo Pannini (1691–1765)

Rome's Best: Churches and Temples

A S THE CENTRE of Christianity, Rome has a vast wealth of beautiful and interesting churches. These range from magnificent great basilicas built to assert the importance of the medieval and Renaissance Catholic church, to smaller, humbler buildings where the first Christians gathered, often in secret. Among the most fascinating early churches are those converted from ancient Roman temples. Additions to these over the years have resulted in some intriguing, many-layered buildings. A more detailed historical overview of Rome's churches is on pages 44–5.

Pantheon
This monumental 2,000-year-old building is one of the largest surviving temples of ancient Rome.

St Peter's
At 136 m (450 ft) high, Michelangelo's dome is the tallest in the world. Sadly, the artist died before seeing his work completed.

Santa Maria in Trastevere
Built over a very early Christian foundation, this church is famous for its ornate mosaics.

Vatican

Piazza di Spagna

Piazza della Rotonda

Piazza Navona

Janiculum

Campo de' Fiori

Cap

Trastevere

Santa Cecilia in Trastevere
This statue of Cecilia, showing her as she lay when her tomb was uncovered, was sculpted in 1599 by Stefano Maderno.

Santa Maria in Cosmedin
The decorations in this 6th-century church are 12th-century and earlier. A restored painting in the apse shows the Virgin, Child and saints.

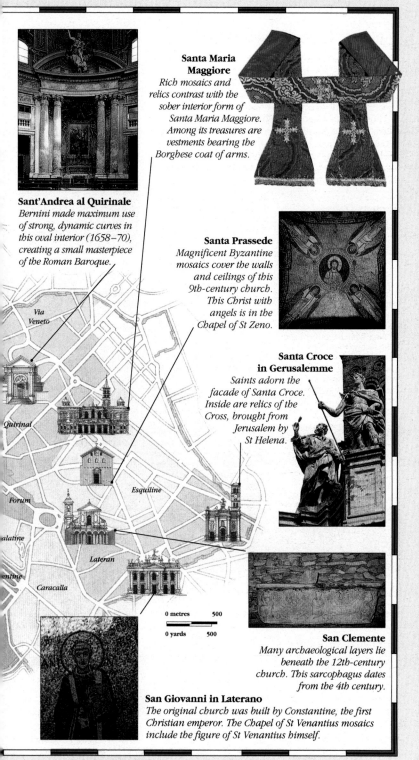

Sant'Andrea al Quirinale
Bernini made maximum use of strong, dynamic curves in this oval interior (1658–70), creating a small masterpiece of the Roman Baroque.

Santa Maria Maggiore
Rich mosaics and relics contrast with the sober interior form of Santa Maria Maggiore. Among its treasures are vestments bearing the Borghese coat of arms.

Santa Prassede
Magnificent Byzantine mosaics cover the walls and ceilings of this 9th-century church. This Christ with angels is in the Chapel of St Zeno.

Santa Croce in Gerusalemme
Saints adorn the facade of Santa Croce. Inside are relics of the Cross, brought from Jerusalem by St Helena.

Via Veneto

Quirinal

Forum

Esquiline

Palatine

Lateran

Caelentine

Caracalla

0 metres 500

0 yards 500

San Clemente
Many archaeological layers lie beneath the 12th-century church. This sarcophagus dates from the 4th century.

San Giovanni in Laterano
The original church was built by Constantine, the first Christian emperor. The Chapel of St Venantius mosaics include the figure of St Venantius himself.

Exploring Churches and Temples

THERE ARE MORE CHURCHES in Rome than there are days of the year, so you'll have to be selective. Catholic pilgrims have always been drawn to the seven major basilicas: **St Peter's**, the heart of the Roman Catholic church, **San Giovanni in Laterano**, **San Paolo fuori le Mura**, **Santa Maria Maggiore**, **Santa Croce in Gerusalemme**, **San Lorenzo fuori le Mura** and **San Sebastiano**. These have a wealth of relics, tombs and magnificent works of art from many different periods. Smaller churches can be equally fascinating, especially those that have preserved their original character.

13th-century fresco by Pietro Cavallini in Santa Cecilia

ANCIENT TEMPLES

ONE PAGAN TEMPLE survives virtually unaltered since it was erected in the 2nd century AD. The **Pantheon**, "Temple of all the Gods", has a domed interior quite different in structure from any other church in Rome. It was reconsecrated as a Christian church in the 7th century.

Other Roman temples have been incorporated into Christian churches at various times. Two of these are in the Forum; **Santi Cosma e Damiano** was established in the Temple of Romulus in 526, while San Lorenzo in Miranda was built on to the ruins of the **Temple of Antoninus and Faustina** in the 11th century. The Baroque facade, built in 1602, looms behind the columns of the temple.

Another church that clearly shows its ancient Roman origins is **Santa Costanza**, built as a mausoleum for Constantine's daughter. It is a round church with some splendid 4th-century mosaics.

EARLY CHRISTIAN AND MEDIEVAL CHURCHES

SOME EARLY BASILICAS, the 5th-century **Santa Maria Maggiore** and **Santa Sabina** for example, retain much of their original structure. Other, even earlier churches such as the 4th-century **San Paolo fuori le Mura** and **San Giovanni in Laterano** still preserve their original basilica shape. San Paolo was rebuilt after a fire in 1823 destroyed the original building, and the San Giovanni of today dates from a 1646 reconstruction by Borromini. Both these churches still have their medieval cloisters.

Santa Maria in Trastevere and **Santa Cecilia in Trastevere** were built over houses where the earliest Christian communities met and worshipped in secret, to avoid persecution. One church where the different layers of earlier structures can clearly be seen is **San Clemente**. At its lowest level, it has a Mithraic temple of the 3rd century AD. Other early churches include **Santa Maria in Cosmedin,** with its impressive Romanesque bell tower, and the fortified convent of **Santissimi Quattro Coronati**. Many Roman churches, most notably **Santa Prassede**, contain fine early Christian and medieval mosaics.

The impressive domed interior of the Pantheon, which became a church in 609

Cloister of San Giovanni in Laterano

UNUSUAL FLOORPLANS

The design of Rome's first churches was based on the ancient basilica, a rectangular building divided into three naves. Since then there have been many bold departures from the this plan, including round churches, square churches based on the shape of the Greek cross, as in Bramante's plan for St Peter's, and, in the Baroque period, even oval and hexagonal ones.

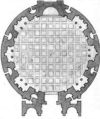

Pantheon (2nd century)

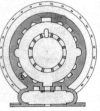

Santa Costanza (4th century)

RENAISSANCE

The greatest undertaking of the Renaissance popes was the rebuilding of **St Peter's**. Disagreements on the form it should take meant that, although work started in 1506, it was not completed until well into the 17th century. Fortunately, this did not prevent the building of Michelangelo's great dome. As well as working on St Peter's, Michelangelo also provided the **Sistine Chapel** with its magnificent frescoes.

On a completely different scale, another key work of Renaissance architecture is Bramante's tiny **Tempietto** (1499) on the Janiculum. **Santa Maria della Pace** has a Bramante cloister, some frescoes by Raphael and a charming portico by Pietro da Cortona. Also of interest is Michelangelo's imaginative use of the great vaults of the Roman Baths of Diocletian in the church of **Santa Maria degli Angeli**.

There are other churches worth visiting for the sake of

Michelangelo's dramatic dome crowning the interior of St Peter's

their outstanding paintings and sculptures. **Santa Maria del Popolo**, for example, has two great paintings by Caravaggio, the Chigi Chapel designed by Raphael, and a series of 15th-century frescoes by Pinturicchio. **San Pietro in Vincoli**, besides having the chains with which St Peter was bound in prison, also has Michelangelo's awe-inspiring statue of Moses, while **San Luigi dei Francesi** has three Caravaggios depicting St Matthew and frescoes by Domenichino.

BAROQUE

Interior of Rosati's dome in San Carlo ai Catinari (1620)

THE COUNTER REFORMATION inspired the exuberant, lavish style of churches such as the **Gesù** and **Sant' Ignazio di Loyola**. The best-loved examples of Roman Baroque are the later works associated with Bernini, such as the great colonnade and baldacchino he built for **St Peter's**. Of the smaller churches he designed, perhaps the finest is **Sant' Andrea al Quirinale**, while **Santa Maria della Vittoria** houses his truly astonishing Cornaro Chapel with its sculpture of the *Ecstasy of St Teresa*. The late Baroque was not all Bernini, however. You should also look out for churches such as **San Carlo**

ai Catinari with its beautiful dome by Rosato Rosati and the many churches by Bernini's rival, Borromini. **Sant'Agnese in Agone** and **San Carlo alle Quattro Fontane** are famed for the dramatic concave surfaces of their facades, while the complex structure of **Sant'Ivo alla Sapienza** makes it one of the miniature masterpieces of the Baroque.

Bramante's St Peter's (1503)

Sant'Andrea al Quirinale (1658)

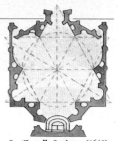

Sant'Ivo alla Sapienza (1642)

Rome's Best: Museums and Galleries

THE MUSEUMS OF ROME are among the richest in the world; the Vatican alone contains incomparable collections of Egyptian, Etruscan, Greek, Roman and Early Christian artefacts, as well as frescoes by Michelangelo and Raphael, priceless manuscripts and jewels. Excavations in the 19th century added treasures from ancient Rome which are now on show in museums throughout the city. The finest Etruscan collections in the world can be enjoyed in the Villa Giulia. More details of Rome's museums and galleries are given on pages 48–9.

Villa Giulia
Etruscan treasures from Rome's early history are displayed in this beautiful Renaissance villa.

Vatican Museums
The galleries and long corridors hold priceless artefacts such as this 9th-century mosaic showing scenes from the life of Christ.

N

0 metres   500

0 yards   500

Piazza Spag

Piazza delle Roton

Vatican

Piazza Navona

TIBER

Galleria Spada
This collection's strength lies in its 17th- and 18th-century paintings. Earlier works include a Visitation *by Andrea del Sarto (1486–1530).*

Campo de' Fiori

Janiculum

Trastevere

Palazzo Corsini
Included here are works by Caravaggio, Rubens and Van Dyck, as well as a painting of the Baroque sculptor Bernini – a rare portrait by Il Baciccia (1639–1709).

Galleria Doria Pamphilj
Most of the great names of the Renaissance are represented on this gallery's crowded walls. Titian (1485–1576) painted Salomé *early in his career.*

Museo Borghese
The ground floor galleries house sculpture from ancient Greece and Rome as well as early Bernini masterpieces such as his David *(1619).*

Museo Nazionale Romano
This fresco, from Livia's Villa (1st century AD) outside Rome, is one of a huge collection of finds from archaeological sites throughout the city.

Palazzo Barberini
The works of art here date mainly from the 13th to the 16th centuries. This figure of Providence comes from Pietro da Cortona's The Triumph of Divine Providence *(1633–9).*

Palazzo Venezia
The highlights of Rome's most important museum of decorative arts are its Byzantine and medieval collections, including this Byzantine enamel of Christ dating from the 13th century.

Via Veneto

Quirinal

Esquiline

tol

Forum

Palatine

Caracalla

Lateran

tine

Capitoline Museums: Palazzo dei Conservatori
Pietro da Cortona's Rape of the Sabine Women *(1629) is one of many Baroque paintings in the picture gallery.*

Capitoline Museums: Palazzo Nuovo
Among the sculptures is this head of Giulia Domna (wife of Septimius Severus) from the 2nd century AD.

Exploring Museums and Galleries

Etruscan clay head, Villa Giulia

Rome's MUSEUMS and galleries have two major strengths: Greek and Roman archaeological treasures, and paintings and sculptures of the Renaissance and the Baroque. The Vatican Museums have superb collections of both, as do, on a smaller scale, the Capitoline Museums. Fine paintings can also be found scattered throughout Rome in museums, galleries and churches *(see pp44–5).*

ETRUSCAN ARTEFACTS

5th-century BC Etruscan gold plate with inscription, Villa Giulia

THE ETRUSCANS inhabited an area stretching from Florence to Rome from the 8th century BC, and governed Rome from the late 7th century BC *(see pp16–17).* It was the Etruscan custom to bury the dead along with their possessions, and as a result Etruscan artefacts have been excavated from tombs all over central Italy. Three main collections can be seen in Rome. The **Villa Giulia** has been the home of the Museo Nazionale Etrusco since 1889. The villa, designed by Vignola for Pope Julius III for summer outings, is one of Rome's prettiest Renaissance buildings. In addition to the collections, the villa gardens contain a reconstructed Etruscan temple. Not all of the finds are Etruscan; some of the pottery, statuettes and other artefacts are relics of the Faliscans, Latins and other tribes who inhabited central Italy before the Romans.

The Gregorian Etruscan Museum in the **Vatican Museums** was opened in 1837 to house Etruscan finds from tombs on church-owned land. The Museo Barracco in the **Piccola Farnesina** has statues from the much older civilizations of ancient Egypt and Assyria.

ANCIENT ROMAN ART

THE ARCHAEOLOGICAL zone in Rome forms a huge open-air museum of evidence of ancient Roman life, while the porticoes and cloisters of the city's churches are filled with ancient sarcophagi and fragments of statuary. The largest important collection can be seen in the **Museo Nazionale Romano** at the Baths of Diocletian in front of the station. The museum's many ancient artefacts include, most notably, a sarcophagus from Livia's Villa at Prima Porta just north of Rome. Much of this extensive collection is in store while the rooms are being reorganized. The most important statues are in the **Vatican Museums**, which also have the best of the great Greek works, such as the *Laocoön*, brought to Rome around the 1st century AD. It had tremendous influence on the subsequent

Victory banner, Museo della Civiltà Romana

development of Roman art. Splendid copies of Greek originals can be seen in the **Capitoline Museums**.

In the Forum, occupying two floors of the church of Santa Francesca Romana, is the small but worthwhile **Antiquarium Forense**. For those who enjoy history, the large scale model at the **Museo della Civiltà Romana** in EUR gives an excellent idea of what ancient Rome looked like in the 4th century AD.

Centurion's breast-plate, Museo della Civiltà Romana

ART GALLERIES

Muses in Raphael's *Parnassus* (1508–11), Vatican Museums

IN THE PAST, many of Rome's great aristocratic families owned magnificent private collections of paintings and sculpture. Some of these are still housed in ancestral palazzi, which are open to the public. One is the **Galleria Doria Pamphilj**, which has the greatest concentration of paintings of any palazzo in Rome. It's well worth searching through the dimly lit rooms to find the pearls of the collection, which include works by Raphael, Filippo Lippi, Caravaggio, Titian and Claude Lorrain, as

well as a portrait of Pope Innocent X Pamphilj by the Spanish artist Velázquez. The collection of the **Galleria Spada**, begun by Bernardino Spada in 1632, is still in the fine original gallery built for it. The paintings demonstrate 17th-century Roman taste: Rubens, Caravaggio, Guido Reni, Guercino, Domenichino and Jan Brueghel the Elder. The **Galleria Colonna** houses a collection of art from the same period.

Hellenistic faun, Museo Borghese

Other old family residences are now showcases for state art collections. The Galleria Nazionale d'Arte Antica is divided between **Palazzo Barberini** and **Palazzo Corsini**. Palazzo Barberini, built between 1625 and 1633 by Bernini and others for the Barberini family, houses paintings from the 13th to the 16th centuries. It also has *objets d'art* acquired by the state from various private collections. At some future date, the 17th- and 18th-century paintings exhibited in the Palazzo Corsini, on the south side of the Tiber, will be transferred to join the Palazzo Barberini collection.

Another wonderful private collection was that of the Borghese family, also now managed by the state. The **Museo Borghese** is under repair and only the sculpture on the ground floor can be seen. But it's worth going to see the technically amazing *Apollo and Daphne* by the youthful genius Bernini and the famous statue of Pauline Borghese by Canova.

The **Capitoline Museums** hold collections that were gifts of the popes to the people of Rome. The Pinacoteca (art gallery) in the **Palazzo dei Conservatori** contains works by Titian, Guercino and Van Dyck. There is an art gallery at the **Vatican Museums**, but lovers of Renaissance art will head straight for the Sistine Chapel and the Raphael Rooms. Rome's main modern art collection is in the **Galleria Nazionale d'Arte Moderna**.

SMALLER MUSEUMS

THE MOST IMPORTANT of the smaller collections is the beautifully laid-out medieval museum in **Palazzo Venezia**, which has exhibits ranging from ceramics to sculpture. Rome has a wealth of small, specialist museums including a **Museum of Musical Instruments**, a **Museo del Folklore**, with tableaux showing life in Rome during the last century, and the **Burcardo Theatre Museum**.

For those with an interest in the English Romantic poets who lived in Rome in the 19th century, there is the **Keats-Shelley Memorial House**, a museum in the house where John Keats died. If you're keen on the French Empire, the **Museo Napoleonico** has relics and paintings of Napoleon and members of his family, many of whom lived in Rome. Finally, for

Laocoön **(1st century AD) in the Vatican's Pio-Clementine Museum**

those with a taste for the macabre there is a waxworks, the **Museo delle Cere**.

Portrait of Pauline Borghese painted by Kinson (c1805), now in the Museo Napoleonico

---

WHERE TO FIND THE MUSEUMS AND GALLERIES

The Deposition (1604) by Caravaggio, the Vatican

Rome's Best: Fountains and Obelisks

ROME HAS SOME of the loveliest fountains in the world. Many of them are the work of the greatest sculptors of the Renaissance and Baroque. Some fountains are flamboyant displays, others restful trickles of water. Many are simply drinking fountains, while a few cascade from the sides of buildings. Obelisks date from far earlier in the city's history. Although some of them were commissioned by Roman emperors, many are even older and were brought to Rome by triumphant, conquering armies. A more detailed overview of Rome's fountains and obelisks is on pages 52–3.

Piazza San Pietro
Twin fountains give life to the splendid monumental piazza of St Peter's. Maderno designed the one on the Vatican side in 1614; the other was later built to match.

Piazza del Popolo
Nineteenth-century marble lions and fountains surround an ancient obelisk in the centre of the piazza.

Fontana dei Fiumi
The figures in the fountain of the four rivers by Bernini represent the Ganges, the Plate, the Danube and the Nile.

Obelisk of Santa Maria sopra Minerva
The Egyptian obelisk, held up by Bernini's marble elephant, dates from the 6th century BC.

Fontana delle Tartarughe
One of Rome's more secret fountains, this jewel of Renaissance sculpture shows youths helping tortoises into a basin.

Fontana della Barcaccia
This elegant fountain of 1627 is probably the work of Pietro Bernini, father of the more famous Gian Lorenzo.

N

0 metres 500

0 yards 500

Trevi Fountain
The Trevi, inspired by Roman triumphal arches, was designed by Nicola Salvi in 1762. Tradition has it that a coin thrown into the water guarantees a visitor's return to Rome.

izza
agna Via Veneto

Quirinal

Esquiline

pitol

Forum

Palatine

Lateran

Caracalla

ventine

Fontana delle Naiadi
When this fountain was unveiled in 1901, the realistically sensual bronze nymphs caused a storm of protest.

Obelisk of Piazza San Giovanni in Laterano
The oldest obelisk in Rome dates from the 15th century BC. It came to Rome in AD 357, brought here on the orders of Constantine II.

Piazza della Bocca della Verità Fountain
In this 18th-century fountain, built by Carlo Bizzaccheri for Pope Clement XI, water spills over a craggy rock formation where two Tritons hold aloft a large shell.

Exploring Fountains and Obelisks

Fountain of the Amphorae (1920s)

THE POPES who restored the ancient Roman aqueducts used to build fountains to commemorate their deeds of munificence. As a result, fountains of all sizes and shapes punctuate the city, drawing grateful crowds on hot summer evenings. Ancient obelisks provide powerful reminders of the debt Roman civilization owed to the Egyptians. Architects have learnt to incorporate them into Roman piazzas in fascinating ways.

FOUNTAINS

THE TREVI FOUNTAIN is one of the most famous of all. It is a *mostra*, a monumental fountain built to mark the end of an aqueduct – in this case the Acqua Vergine, built by Marcus Agrippa in 19 BC, although the Trevi itself was not erected until 1762. Other *mostre* are the **Fontana Paola,** built for Pope Paul V in 1612 on the Janiculum, and the less magnificent **Moses Fountain**, commemorating the opening of the Acqua Felice by Pope Sixtus V in 1587.

Almost all Rome's famous piazzas have fountains. In **Piazza San Pietro** there is a matching pair of powerful fountains. Piazza Navona has Bernini's wonderful Baroque **Fontana dei Fiumi** (fountain of the rivers) as its main attraction. The fountain's four figures each represent one of the four principal rivers then known. To the south of this is the smaller **Fontana del Moro** (the Moor), also by Bernini, showing an Ethiopian struggling with a dolphin. At the north end, Neptune wrestles with an octopus on a

19th-century fountain. In Piazza Barberini is the magnificent Bernini creation of 1642–3: the **Fontana del Tritone** with its sea god blowing through a shell.

More recently, large piazzas have been redesigned around fountains. Valadier's great design for **Piazza del Popolo** (1816–20) has marble lions and fountains surrounding the central obelisk plus two more

Fountain of the Four Tiaras located behind St Peter's

The Pantheon Fountain

fountains on the east and west sides of the square. The turn of the century saw the opening of the **Fontana delle Naiadi** (nymphs), in Piazza della Repubblica; its earthy figures caused great scandal at the time. The highly original **Fountain of the Amphorae** (map 8 D2) was erected in Piazza dell' Emporio during the 1920s. The same designer, Pietro Lombardi, also created the **Fountain of the Four Tiaras** (map 3 C3) behind the colonnade of St Peter's.

The city also has a number of smaller, and often very charming, fountains. At the foot of the Spanish Steps is the **Fontana della Barcaccia** (the leaking boat) of 1627; the **Fontana delle Tartarughe**

Fontana dei Cavalli Marini

THE TREVI FOUNTAIN

Appropriately for a fountain resembling a stage set, the theatrical Trevi has been the star of many films set in Rome, including romantic films like *Three Coins in a Fountain* and *Roman Holiday*, but also *La Dolce Vita*, Fellini's satirical portrait of Rome in the 1950s. Whatever liberties Anita Ekberg took then, paddling in the fountains of Rome is now forbidden, however tempting it could be in the summer heat.

Anita Ekberg in *La Dolce Vita* (1960)

(the tortoise fountain) has been in the tiny Piazza Mattei since 1581, and by Santa Maria in Domnica is the **Fontana della Navicella** (little boat), created out of an ancient Roman sculpture in the 16th century. In the forecourt of **Santa Sabina** (map 8 D2) water gushes from a huge mask set in an ancient basin. The **Pantheon Fountain** (map 4 F4), from 1575, is by Jacopo della Porta. **Le Quattro Fontane** (four fountains) have stood at the Quirinal hill crossroads since 1593.

Fountains in parks and gardens include the **Galleon Fountain** (1620–21) at the Vatican, and the **Fontana dei Cavalli Marini** (seahorses), of 1791, at Villa Borghese. The somewhat decayed 16th-century terraced gardens of the **Villa d'Este,** with their display of over 500 fountains, are still worth the journey.

Piazza Navona with Fontana dei Fiumi, by Pannini (1691–1765)

time of Augustus and also erected in the Circus Maximus. The slightly smaller **Obelisk of Piazza Montecitorio** was another of Augustus's trophies.

Other obelisks, such as the one at the top of the Spanish Steps, are Roman imitations of Egyptian originals. The **Obelisk of Piazza dell' Esquilino** and the one in **Piazza del Quirinale** (map 5 B4) first stood at the entrance to the Mausoleum of Augustus. When re-erected, most obelisks were mounted on decorative bases, often with statues and fountains at their foot. Others became integral parts of sculptures. Bernini was responsible for the marble elephant balancing the Egyptian **Obelisk of Santa Maria sopra Minerva** on its back, and for the **Fontana**

dei Fiumi, with an obelisk from the Circus of Maxentius. Another obelisk was added to the remodelled Pantheon Fountain in 1711. The obelisk in **Piazza San Pietro** is Egyptian but does not have the usual hieroglyphics.

The **Obelisk of Axum** was brought by Mussolini's army from Ethiopia in 1937 as a war trophy. It now stands by the United Nations building near the Circus Maximus.

Wall fountain at Villa d'Este

The Ovato Fountain at Villa d'Este

OBELISKS

THE MOST ANCIENT and tallest of Rome's obelisks is the **Obelisk of Piazza di San Giovanni in Laterano**. Built of red granite, 31 m (100 ft) high, it came from the Temple of Ammon at Thebes, erected in the 15th century BC. It was brought to Rome in AD 357 by the order of Constantine II and put up in the Circus Maximus. In 1587 it was rediscovered, broken into three pieces, and was re-erected in the following year. Next in age is the obelisk in **Piazza del Popolo**, from the 12th or 13th century BC. It was brought to Rome in the

Obelisk in Piazza del Popolo

WHERE TO FIND THE FOUNTAINS AND OBELISKS

Celebrated Visitors and Residents

ROME EXERTS a powerful fascination and foreigners throughout history have succumbed to its charms, often staying for long periods or even taking up permanent residence. The list of famous visitors is almost endless: painters, sculptors and architects from Rome's very earliest days; writers, poets, musicians, exiles, pilgrims, religious teachers, philosophers, aesthetes, archaeologists – all have passed through. Their orchestral works, operas, paintings, drawings, drama and literary journals testify to Rome's inspirational effect.

J W von Goethe *(1749–1832)*
The German poet, philosopher, artist, playwright, botanist and courtier lived at No. 20 Via del Corso, now a museum.

Martin Luther *(1483–1546)*
The religious reformer from Germany came to the convent at Santa Maria del Popolo in 1511. His horror at the corruption he saw led to the Reformation.

Sant'Ignazio di Loyola *(1491–1556)*
He came to Rome from Spain in 1537 and founded the Jesuits near what is now the Gesù, the first Jesuit church.

Queen Christina *(1626–89)*
The Swedish queen abdicated in 1654, and came to live in Palazzo Corsini on Via Lungara.

St Dominic *(1170–1221)*
Founder of the Dominican order, St Dominic was born in Spain. The order's headquarters were at Santa Sabina on the Aventine.

Vatican

Piazza del Popolo

Piazza della Rotonda

Piazza Navona

Janiculum

Campo de' Fiori

Trastevere

Jean Auguste Ingres *(1780–1867)*
The 19th-century French painter, leader of the Neo-Classical tradition, lived in Rome from 1806 until 1820. He returned in 1834 as director of the French Academy at Villa Medici.

Pauline Borghese
(1780–1825)
Napoleon's sister was the subject of scandal in 1805, when she posed semi-nude for a statue by Canova, which is now in Villa Borghese.

Via Veneto

The Exiled Stuarts
James Stuart (1688–1766), unsuccessful claimant to the British throne, came to Rome as an exile. He was presented with Palazzo Balestra by Pope Clement XI and died here.

Quirinal

Esquiline

itol

Forum

Lateran

Palatine

Caracalla

ventine

Lord Byron *(1788–1824)*
Though the English poet's stay in the city was brief, the influence on his work was long-lasting. Stanzas in Childe Harold's Pilgrimage *and* Manfred *were inspired by seeing the Colosseum in moonlight.*

Percy Bysshe Shelley
(1792–1822)
The great English Romantic poet wrote his drama Prometheus Unbound *in the calm of the ruined Baths of Caracalla in 1819.*

0 metres 500

0 yards 500

Artists and Writers Inspired by Rome

ARTISTS AND WRITERS have been attracted to Rome since Classical times. Many came to work for the emperors; the poets Catullus, Horace, Virgil and Ovid, for example, all enjoyed the patronage of Emperor Augustus. Later on, especially in the Renaissance and Baroque periods, the greatest artists and architects came to Rome to compete for commissions from the popes. However, patronage was not the only magnet. Since the Renaissance, Rome's Classical past and its picturesque ruins have drawn artists, architects and writers from all over Italy and abroad.

The prolific love poet Ovid (43 BC–AD 17)

Self-portrait by the 18th-century artist Angelica Kauffmann, c1770

PAINTERS, SCULPTORS AND ARCHITECTS

Diego Velázquez, one of many great 17th-century artists to visit Rome

IN THE EARLY 16th century, artists and architects were summoned from all parts of Italy to realize the grandiose building projects of the popes. From Urbino came Bramante (1444–1514) and Raphael (1483–1520); from Perugia Perugino (1450–1523); from Florence Michelangelo (1475–1564) and many others. They worked in the Vatican, on the new St Peter's and the decoration of the Sistine Chapel. Artists were often well rewarded, but they also lived in dangerous times. Florentine sculptor and goldsmith Benvenuto Cellini (1500–71) helped defend Castel Sant' Angelo *(see pp248–9)* during the Sack of Rome (1527), but was later imprisoned there and made a dramatic escape. His memoirs tell the story.

Towards the end of the 16th century church patronage was generous to the

Milanese-born Caravaggio (1571–1610) despite his violent character and unruly life. The Carracci family from Bologna also flourished – especially brothers Annibale (1560–1609) and Agostino (1557–1602).

The work of Gian Lorenzo Bernini (1598–1680) can be seen all over Rome. He succeeded Carlo Maderno (1556–1629) as architect of St Peter's, and created its great bronze baldacchino, the splendid colonnade *(see pp230–31)* and numerous fountains, churches and sculptures. His rival for the title of leading architect of the Roman Baroque was Francesco Borromini (1599–1667), whose highly original genius can be appreciated in many Roman churches and palazzi.

In the 17th century it became more common for artists from outside Italy to come and work in Rome. Diego Velázquez (1599–1660), King Philip IV of Spain's court painter, came in 1628 to study

the art treasures of the Vatican. Rubens (1577–1640) came from Antwerp to study, and carried out various commissions. The French artists Nicolas Poussin (1594–1665) and Claude Lorrain (1600–82) lived here for many years.

The Classical revival of the 18th century attracted artists to Rome in unprecedented numbers. From Britain came the Scottish architect Robert Adam (1728–92) and the Swiss artist Angelica Kauffmann (1741–1807), who settled here and was buried with great honour in Sant'Andrea delle Fratte. After the excesses of the Baroque, sculpture also turned to the simplicity of Neo-Classicism. A leading exponent of this movement was Antonio Canova (1757–1821). Sculptors from all over Europe were influenced by him, including the Dane Bertel Thorvaldsen (1770–1844) who lived in Rome for many years.

Claude Lorrain's view of the Forum, painted in Rome in 1632

WRITERS

DANTE (1262–1321) visited Rome during his exile from Florence and in the *Inferno* describes the great influx of pilgrims for the first Holy Year (1300). The poet Petrarch (1304–74), born in Arezzo, came to the city in much happier circumstances to be crowned with laurels on the Capitol in 1341. The poet Torquato Tasso (1544–95), from Sorrento, was invited to receive a similar honour, but died soon after his arrival. He is buried in Sant'Onofrio *(see p219)* on the Janiculum.

Two of the first writers from abroad to visit Rome were the French essayist Montaigne (1533–92) and English poet John Milton (1608–74). Then, by the early 18th century, writers seemed to flock to Rome. Edward Gibbon (1737–94) was inspired to write *Decline and Fall of the Roman Empire* when he heard the monks singing the Angelus outside Santa Maria in Aracoeli *(see p69)*. German visitors included J J Winckelmann (1717–68)

Torquato Tasso

who wrote influential studies of ancient art, and the poet J W von Goethe (1749–1832).

In the Romantic period Rome teemed with English writers: poets Keats, Shelley and Byron, followed by the Brownings and the novelist Charles Dickens. Travel writers in the 19th century included Augustus Hare (1834–1903) and the German historian Ferdinand Gregorovius (1821–91). Much of *The Portrait of a Lady* by American Henry James (1843–1916) is set in Rome.

Modern life in Rome is brilliantly captured by the Roman-born novelist and short-story writer Alberto Moravia (1907–90).

Portrait of the poet John Keats painted by his friend Joseph Severn in 1819

MUSICIANS

GIOVANNI LUIGI da Palestrina (1525–94), from the town of that name, became choirmaster and organist to the Vatican and composed some of the greatest unaccompanied choral music ever written. In 1770 the 14-year-old Mozart heard Gregorio Allegri's unpublished *Miserere* in the Sistine Chapel and wrote it down from memory. Arcangelo

Corelli (1653–1713), the great violinist and composer of the Baroque age, worked in Rome under the patronage of Cardinal Ottoboni. One of his first commissions was to provide a festival of music for Queen Christina of Sweden.

During the 19th century the Prix de Rome brought many French musicians to study here at the Villa Medici *(see p135)*. Hector Berlioz (1803–69) owed the inspiration for his popular *Roman Carnival,* the overture to his opera *Benvenuto Cellini,* to his two-year stay in Rome. Georges Bizet (1838–75) and Claude Debussy (1862–1918) were also Prix de Rome winners. Franz Liszt (1811–86), after his 50th year, settled in Rome, took minor orders and became known as Abbé Liszt. He wrote *Fountains of the Villa d'Este* while staying at the villa in Tivoli.

Giacomo Puccini

More recent, 20th-century musical associations with Rome include the popular works by Ottorino Respighi (1870–1936): *The Fountains of Rome* and *The Pines of Rome,* while Giacomo Puccini (1858–1924) used Roman settings when creating his dramatic, tragic opera *Tosca.*

ROMAN CINEMA

The Cinecittà studios, built in 1937 just outside Rome, are most famous for the films made here in the 1940s, classics of Italian Neo-Realism such as Roberto Rossellini's *Roma Città Aperta* and Vittorio De Sica's *Sciùscià* and *Ladri di Bicicletta.* In the 1950s Cinecittà became a centre for international productions, including the epics *Ben Hur* and *Spartacus.*

The director most strongly associated with Roman cinema is Federico Fellini, whose films *La Dolce Vita* (1960) and *Roma* (1972) present a highly idiosyncratic portrait of the follies of the city. Of all the Roman-born filmmakers, perhaps the most famous is the controversial writer Pier Paolo Pasolini (1922–75), who became internationally known with his films *Teorema* (1968) and *Il Decamerone* (1971).

Pier Paolo Pasolini

ROME THROUGH THE YEAR

THE BEST TIMES to visit Rome are spring and autumn when the weather is usually warm, and sometimes even hot enough to sunbathe and swim at the beaches and lakes outside the city. November is best avoided as the weather tends to be grey and extremely rainy, while in high summer, most people (including Romans, who leave the city in their droves) find the heat unbearable.

Easter and Christmas are obviously very special in Rome, but there are other religious festivals worth seeing at other times in the year, as well as some enjoyable secular events like the Festa de Noantri in Trastevere and the Flower Festival in Genzano. In villages outside Rome, local celebrations are held to welcome new crops such as strawberries and beans in the spring, and grapes and truffles in the autumn.

SPRING

EASTER, falling in March or April, marks the official beginning of the tourist season in Rome. Catholics from all over the world flock into the city to make their pilgrimages to the main basilicas and to hear the pope's Easter Sunday address outside St Peter's, while the less devout come simply to take advantage of the mild weather. Meanwhile, Romans pile into their cars and head for the coast and countryside, so you can expect the roads, beaches, and the restaurants of the Castelli Romani and Lake Bracciano to be busy.

Temperatures tend to be around 18° C (66° F), but can hit 28° C (82° F), so by mid-May it's usually possible to lunch and dine outside. However, there can still be sudden downpours and temperature swings, so do bring warm clothes and an umbrella.

Crowds gathering in St Peter's square at Easter

In April tubs full of colourful azaleas are ranged on the Spanish Steps and along Via Veneto, and once the roses start to flower in the city's Rose Garden overlooking the Circus Maximus, it is opened to the public.

For a fortnight from mid-May Via dei Coronari is lit by candles, lined with plants and hung with banners for the street's antiques fair, while Via Margutta hosts an outdoor art

show. In the first week of May the International Horse Show is held in the Villa Borghese, and towards the end of the month many world-class tennis players flock to Rome to compete in the International Tennis Championships held at the Foro Italico.

EVENTS

Festa di Santa Francesca Romana (9 March), Santa Francesca Romana. Blessing of the city's cars, buses and trams (see p87).
Festa di San Giuseppe (19 March), in the Trionfale area. St Joseph's (and Father's) Day celebrated with street stalls, cream puffs and music.
Good Friday (March/April), Colosseum. Procession of the Cross at 9pm led by the pope.
Easter Sunday (March/April), St Peter's square. Address made by the pope (see p231).
Rome's Birthday (Sunday before 21 April), Piazza del Campidoglio.
Festa della Primavera (March/April), Spanish Steps and Trinità dei Monti. Azaleas in the street and concerts.
Art exhibition (April/May), Via Margutta (see p339).
International Horse Show (early May), Villa Borghese (see p350).
Antiques Fair (mid–late May), Via dei Coronari (see p324).
International Tennis Championships (late May), Foro Italico (see p350).

Flowers for sale on the Piazza del Popolo

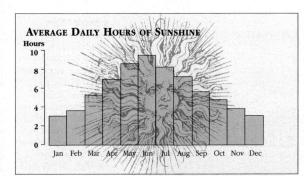

AVERAGE DAILY HOURS OF SUNSHINE

Hours

Jan Feb Mar Apr May Jun Jul Aug Sep Oct Nov Dec

Sunshine Chart
Rome is famous for its light. June is the sunniest month; but it is also very dry, and without the odd shower the bright heat can feel intense. In autumn, Rome's southerly position means that the sun can still be enjoyably warm at midday.

SUMMER

IN JUNE a summer season of concerts begins, with performances in some of the city's most beautiful palaces, churches and courtyards. In July and August opera is usually staged in the Baths of Caracalla and classical drama at Ostia Antica. Throughout the summer there are also contemporary cultural events – film, music of all kinds, dance and theatre – staged as part of the Cineporto and Massenzio film festivals *(see p346)* and RomaEuropa. On midsummer evenings there are stalls and amusements on the Tiber embankments by Castel Sant'Angelo, while in the last two weeks of July

Flower-carpeted streets in Genzano

when the temperature often soars to over 40° C (104° F), virtually all Romans flee the city for the seaside, and many cafés, shops and restaurants close for the month.

EVENTS

Flower Festival *(June, the Sunday after Corpus Domini)*, Genzano, Castelli Romani, south of Rome. Streets are carpeted with flowers.
Festa di San Giovanni *(23–24 June)*, Piazza di Porta San Giovanni. Celebrated with meals of snails in tomato sauce, suckling pig, a fair and firework display.
RomaEuropa *(late June–late July)*, mainly in Villa Medici. Films, dance, theatre and concerts *(see p341)*.
Festa di San Pietro *(29 June)*, many churches. Celebrations mark the feast of St Peter.

Expo Tevere *(end June–mid-July)*, along the Tiber. Arts and crafts, food and wine stalls, folk music and fireworks *(see p339)*.
Festa de Noantri *(last two weeks in July)*, the streets of Trastevere. Feasting, processions and entertainment *(see p339 and p341)*.
Arts outdoors *(July/August)*, Baths of Caracalla, Villa Ada, Ostia Antica, by the Tiber, in parks. Opera, concerts, drama and film *(see p341)*.
Festa della Madonna della Neve *(5 August)*, Santa Maria Maggiore. Legendary 4th-century fall of snow re-enacted with showers of white flower petals *(see p172)*.
Ferragosto *(15 August)*, Santa Maria in Trastevere. Midsummer Roman holiday. Almost everything closes down. Celebrations are held for the Feast of the Assumption.

Summer vegetables

Trastevere becomes an open-air party as the Noantri festival is celebrated with trinket stalls, dining in the street and fireworks. Mid-July is good for shoppers as the sales *(saldi)* begin.

Many Romans leave the city at the end of June, when schools close, but as June and July are peak tourist months, hotels, cafés, restaurants and sights are packed. In August,

The heat of an August afternoon in front of St Peter's

AVERAGE MONTHLY RAINFALL

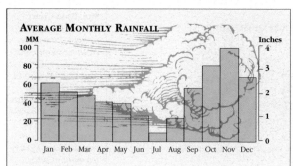

Rainfall Chart
Autumn is Rome's rainiest season, with heavy downpours, sometimes lasting for days, especially in November. Rain in summer tends to come in violent – but often extremely refreshing – 'storms. In winter and early spring expect a few dull, drizzly days.

AUTUMN

SEPTEMBER AND OCTOBER are the best – and among the most popular – months to visit Rome. The fiery heat of July and August will have cooled a little, but midday can be very hot, and you can still eat and drink outside without feeling chilly until late at night. Visiting Rome in November is not recommended: it is the wettest month of the year and Roman rainstorms are often very strong and heavy.

At the beginning of October an artisans' fair is held on Via dell'Orso and adjacent streets, while nearby the antiques galleries of Via dei Coronari hold open house. There are also October antiques fairs in Orvieto and Perugia, two of the loveliest Umbrian hill towns, which are about an hour's drive north of Rome. In November, there's yet another prestigious antiques fair at the papal palace of Viterbo, 65 km (40 m) north of Rome (*see p271*).

Autumn is, of course, the season of harvest festivals, and it can be fun to head out to the small towns around Rome to sample local cheeses, sausages, chestnuts

A roast chestnut stall in autumn

and mushrooms. Perhaps the most spectacular of these is the wine festival in Marino (in the Castelli Romani, south of Rome) where wine flows freely from the fountain in the central piazza. In Rome itself, there's a grape festival in early September, the Sagra dell'Uva, held in the Basilica of Constantine in the Forum, where there are grapes for sale as well as street entertainment. Throughout the autumn and winter, freshly roasted chestnuts can be bought from vendors on street corners, and there is usually a stall on Campo de' Fiori where you can sample the new season's wine, *vino novello*, for free.

On All Souls and All Saints days, which fall on 1 and 2 November, the Romans make pilgrimages to the tombs of relatives who are buried in the cemeteries of Prima Porta and Verano. Chrysanthemums are then traditionally placed on their graves and for this reason they should definitely not be given to friends, hosts and hostesses as thank you presents for their hospitality. On a much happier note, the classical concert and opera seasons begin again in October and November. Details of performances can be found in *Trovaroma (see p340)* and on posters dotted around the city.

EVENTS

Art fair *(September)*, Via Margutta *(see p339)*.
Sagra dell'Uva *(early September)*, Basilica of Constantine. Harvest festival with grapes selling at bargain prices and lots of folksy street entertainment.
Crafts fair *(last week September/first week October)*, Via dell'Orso, near Piazza Navona *(see p339)*.
Marino Wine Festival *(first Sunday in October)*, Marino. Celebrations include tastings, street entertainment and wine spouting from the fountain in the main piazza.
Antiques Fair *(mid-October)*, Via dei Coronari *(see p339)*.
Festa di Santa Cecilia *(22 November)*, Santa Cecilia in Trastevere and Catacombs of San Callisto.
Vino Novello tasting *(late November)*, Campo de' Fiori.

Autumn in the Villa Doria Pamphilj park

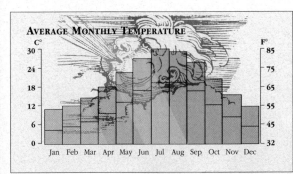

Temperature Chart
The chart shows the average minimum and maximum monthly temperatures. July and August can be unbearably hot, making sightseeing a chore. The fresher days of spring and autumn are ideal to visit Rome, but there are some dull and rainy spells.

WINTER

DURING THE WINTER Rome is bracingly chilly but the temperature rarely drops below freezing. Not all buildings are centrally heated so if you're staying in a small hotel bring warm clothes and request extra blankets as soon as you arrive, as they are often in short supply. Warm up in cafés with hot chocolate and frothy cappuccino.

The run-up to Christmas is great fun in Rome, especially if you have children. Manger scenes, *presepi*, are set up in many churches, piazzas and public places and from mid-

Rome during one of its rare snowfalls

The Befana on Piazza Navona

December to Twelfth Night Piazza Navona hosts the Befana, a Christmas market where you can buy manger scenes, decorations and toys. Unless you have friends in Rome, Christmas itself can be rather lonely, as it is very much a family event. On New Year's Eve, however, everyone is out on the street to drink sparkling wine and let off fireworks. Watch out for flying wardrobes as there's a tradition of throwing out old furniture in the New Year.

The Carnival season runs from late January through to

February, celebrated largely by children with fancy-dress parties and parades along Via Nazionale, Via Cola di Rienzo and the Pincio. Keep out of the way of teenagers with shaving cream spray cans and water-filled balloons.

EVENTS

Festa della Madonna Immacolata *(8 December)*, Piazza di Spagna. Firemen climb up a ladder to place a wreath on the statue of the Virgin Mary.
Befana *(mid-December– mid-January)*, Piazza Navona. Christmas and children's market *(see p120)*.
Nativity scenes *(mid-December–mid-January)*, many churches. Life-size scene in St Peter's square, collection at Santi Cosma e Damiano.
Midnight Mass *(24 December)*, at most churches.
Christmas Day *(25 December)*, St Peter's square. Blessing by the pope.
New Year's Eve *(31 December)*, all over city. Firework displays, furniture thrown out.

PUBLIC HOLIDAYS
New Year's Day (1 Jan)
Epiphany (6 Jan)
Easter Monday
Liberation Day (25 April)
Labour Day (1 May)
Ferragosto (15 Aug)
All Saints (1 November)
Immaculate Conception (8 December)
Christmas Day (25 December)
Santo Stefano (26 December)

Via Condotti at Christmas

ROME AREA BY AREA

CAPITOL

THE TEMPLE OF JUPITER on the Capitol, the southern summit of the Capitoline hill, was the centre of the Roman world. Reached by a zig-zag path up from the Forum, the temple was the scene of all the most sacred religious and political ceremonies. The hill and its temple came to symbolize Rome's authority as *caput mundi*, head of the world, and the concept of a "capital" city is derived from the Capitol. Throughout the city's history, the Capitol, or Campidoglio as it is called in Italian, has remained the seat of municipal government.

Hand of colossal statue in Palazzo dei Conservatori

Today's city council, the Comune di Roma, meets in the Renaissance splendour of Palazzo Senatorio. Rome's position as a modern capital is forcefully expressed in the enormous white Victor Emmanuel Monument, which unfortunately blots out the view of the Capitol from Piazza Venezia. The present arrangement of the buildings on the hill dates from the 16th century, when Michelangelo created a beautiful piazza reached by a dramatic flight of steps, the Cordonata. Two of the three buildings around the piazza are now home to the Capitoline Museums.

SIGHTS AT A GLANCE

Churches and Temples
Santa Maria in Aracoeli **7**
Temple of Jupiter **8**
San Marco **12**

Museums and Galleries
Capitoline Museums:
Palazzo Nuovo pp70–71 **1**
Capitoline Museums:
Palazzo dei Conservatori
pp72–3 **2**
Palazzo Venezia
and Museum **11**

Historic Buildings
Roman Insula **5**

Historic Streets and Piazzas
Piazza del Campidoglio **3**
Cordonata **4**
Aracoeli Staircase **6**

Ancient Sites
Tarpeian Rock **9**

Monuments
Victor Emmanuel
Monument **10**

GETTING THERE
All the sights in this area are within walking distance of Piazza Venezia. Bus routes converge here from all parts of the city, as do many thousands of motorists. From Termini station you can catch the 64, 65, 70, 75 or 170; from Piazza Barberini the 56, 60 or 492. From St Peter's and the Vatican the only bus is the 64. Other useful routes include the 44, 46, 57, 90 and 90b.

KEY

Street-by-Street map

0 metres 200
0 yards 200

N

SEE ALSO
• *Street Finder*, maps 5, 12

Michelangelo's Piazza del Campidoglio

Street-by-Street: The Capitol and Piazza Venezia

THE CAPITOL, citadel of ancient Rome, is a must for every visitor. A broad flight of steps (the Cordonata) leads up to Michelangelo's spectacular Piazza del Campidoglio. This is flanked by the Palazzo Nuovo and Palazzo dei Conservatori, housing the Capitoline Museums with their fine collections of sculpture and paintings. The absence of cars makes the hill a welcome retreat from the squeal of brakes below, but you should brave the traffic to visit Palazzo Venezia and its museum.

Victor Emmanuel Monument
This huge white marble monument to Italy's first king was completed in 1911 ⑩

San Marco
The church of the Venetians in Rome has a fine 9th-century apse mosaic ⑫

Palazzo Venezia
The museum's finest exhibits, such as this 13th-century gilded angel decorated with enamel, date from the late Middle Ages ⑪

Roman Insula
This is a ruined apartment block dating from Imperial Rome ⑤

Aracoeli Staircase
When it was built in 1348, the staircase became a centre for political debate ⑥

Cordonata
Michelangelo's great staircase changed the orientation of the Capitol towards the west ④

PIAZZA VENEZIA

PIAZZA VENEZIA

PIAZZA VENEZIA

VIA DEL TEATRO DI MARC

KEY

– – – Suggested route

0 metres   75

0 yards   75

★ **Palazzo dei Conservatori**
In this part of the Capitoline Museums a fine series of reliefs from the Temple of Hadrian (see p106) is displayed in the courtyard ②

**Santa Maria
in Aracoeli**
*The treasures hidden
behind the church's
brick facade include
this 15th-century
fresco of the* Funeral
of St Bernardino *by
Pinturicchio* ❼

LOCATOR MAP
See Central Rome Map pp12–13

★ **Palazzo Nuovo**
*This bust of Augustus in the
Hall of the Emperors is one of
many fine Classical sculptures
in the Capitoline Museums* ❶

Palazzo Senatorio was used by
the Roman Senate from about the
12th century. It now houses the
offices of the mayor.

★ **Piazza del
Campidoglio**
*Michelangelo
designed both
the geometric
paving and the
facades of the
buildings* ❸

**Temple of
Jupiter**
*This artist's
impression
shows the gold
and ivory statue
of Jupiter that
stood in the
temple* ❽

Tarpeian Rock
*In ancient Rome
traitors were
thrown to their
death from this cliff
on the Capitol* ❾

STAR SIGHTS
★ **Piazza del Campidoglio**
★ **Palazzo dei Conservatori**
★ **Palazzo Nuovo**

Capitoline Museums: Palazzo Nuovo ❶

See pp70–71.

Capitoline Museums: Palazzo dei Conservatori ❷

See pp72–3.

Piazza del Campidoglio ❸

Map 5 A5 & 12 F5. 🚌 *See Getting There p65.*

WHEN EMPEROR Charles V visited Rome in 1536, Pope Paul III Farnese was so embarrassed by the muddy state of the Capitol that he asked Michelangelo to draw up plans for repaving the piazza, and for renovating the facades of the Palazzo dei Conservatori and Palazzo Senatorio.

Michelangelo came up with the idea of a third building, the Palazzo Nuovo, to form a piazza in the shape of a trapezium, embellished with Classical sculptures chosen for their relevance to Rome. Building started in 1546 but progressed so slowly that Michelangelo only lived to oversee the double flight of steps at the entrance of Palazzo Senatorio.

The piazza was completed in the 17th century, the design remaining largely faithful to the original. Pilasters two storeys high and balustrades interspersed by statues link the buildings thematically. The piazza faces west towards St Peter's, the Christian equivalent of the Capitol and site of other great commissions executed by Michelangelo for Pope Paul III.

Cordonata ❹

Map 5 A5 & 12 F5. 🚌 *See Getting There p65.*

FROM PIAZZA VENEZIA, the Capitol is approached by a gently rising, subtly widening ramp – the Cordonata. At the foot is a pair of granite Egyptian lions, and on the left a 19th-century monument to Cola di Rienzo, close to where the dashing 14th-century tyrant was executed. The top of the ramp is guarded by restored Classical statues of the Dioscuri, Castor and Pollux.

Roman Insula ❺

Piazza d'Aracoeli. **Map** 5 A5 & 12 F4. 📞 *67 10 30 65.* 🚌 *See Getting There p65.* **Open** by appt only: apply to Ripartizione X (see p367).

TWO THOUSAND YEARS ago the urban poor of Rome used to make their homes in *insulae* – apartment blocks.

One of the statues of the Dioscuri at the top of the Cordonata

These were often badly maintained by landlords, and expensive to rent in a city where land costs were high. This 2nd-century AD tenement block, of barrel-vault construction, is the only survivor in Rome from that era. The fourth, fifth and part of the sixth storey remain above current ground level.

In the Middle Ages, a section of these upper storeys was converted into a church; its bell tower and 14th-century Madonna in a niche are visible from the street.

During the Fascist years, the area was cleared, and three lower floors emerged. Some 380 people may have lived in the tenement, in the squalid conditions described by the 1st-century AD satirical writers Martial and Juvenal. The latter mentions that he had to climb 200 steps to reach his garret.

This *insula* may once have had more storeys. The higher you lived, the more dismal the conditions, as the poky spaces of the building's upper levels testify.

The Cordonata in an 18th-century painting by Antonio Canaletto

Aracoeli Staircase ❻

Piazza d'Aracoeli. **Map** 5 A5 & 12 F4. 🚌 *See Getting There p65.*

THE ARACOELI Staircase numbers 124 marble steps (122 if you start from the right) and was completed in 1348, some say in thanks for the passing of the Black Death, but probably in view of the 1350 Holy Year.

The 14th-century tribune-turned-tyrant Cola di Rienzo used to harangue the masses from the Aracoeli Staircase; in the 17th century foreigners used to sleep on the steps, until Prince Caffarelli, who lived on the hill, scared them off by rolling barrels filled with stones down them.

Popular belief has it that by climbing the steps on your knees you can win the national lottery. From the top there is a good view of Rome, with the domes of Sant' Andrea della Valle and St Peter's slightly to the right.

Aracoeli Staircase

Santa Maria in Aracoeli ❼

Piazza d'Aracoeli (entrances via Aracoeli Staircase and door behind Palazzo Nuovo). **Map** 5 A5 & 12 F4. 📞 679 81 55. 🚌 *See Getting There p65.* **Open** 7am–noon, 4pm–6pm (Jun–Sep: 6.30pm) daily.

DATING FROM AT LEAST the 6th century, the church of Santa Maria in Aracoeli, or St Mary of the Altar in the Sky, stands on the northern summit of the Capitoline, on

Ceiling commemorating Battle of Lepanto in nave of Santa Maria in Aracoeli

the site of the ancient temple to Juno. Its 22 columns were taken from various ancient buildings; the inscription on the third column to the left tells us that it comes *"a cubiculo Augustorum"* – from the bedroom of the emperors.

The church of the Roman senators and people, Santa Maria in Aracoeli has been used to celebrate many triumphs over adversity. Its ceiling, with naval motifs, commemorates the Battle of Lepanto (1571), and was built under Pope Gregory XIII Boncompagni, whose family crest, the dragon, can be seen towards the altar end.

Many other Roman families and individuals are honoured by memorials in the church. To the right of the entrance door, the tombstone of archdeacon Giovanni Crivelli, rather than being set into the floor of the church, stands eternally to attention, partly so that the signature "Donatelli" (by Donatello) can be read at eye-level.

The frescoes in the first chapel on the right, painted by Pinturicchio in the 1480s in the beautifully clear style of the early Renaissance, relate the life and death of St Bernardino of Siena. On the left-hand wall, the perspective of *The Burial of the Saint* slants to the right, taking into account the position of the viewer from just outside the chapel.

The church is most famous, however, for the *Santo Bambino*, an olive-wood figure of the Christ Child dating from the 15th century. It was carved by a Franciscan monk out of a tree from the garden of Gethsemane. The figure's miraculous powers are supposed to include resurrecting the dead, and it is sometimes called out to the bedsides of the gravely ill. If it can do the trick its lips go purple, if not they turn pale.

At Christmas the Christ Child takes its place in the centre of a picturesque crib (second chapel to the left) but is usually to be found in the sacristy, as is the panel of the *Holy Family* from the workshop of Giulio Romano.

The miraculous olive-wood Christ Child at Santa Maria in Aracoeli

Capitoline Museums: Palazzo Nuovo ❶

A COLLECTION of Classical statues has been kept on the Capitoline hill since the Renaissance. The first group of bronze sculptures was given to the city by Pope Sixtus IV in 1471 and more additions were made by Pope Sixtus V in 1586. The Palazzo Nuovo was designed by Michelangelo as part of the renovation of the Piazza del Campidoglio, and after its completion in 1654, a number of the statues were transferred there. In 1734 Pope Clement XII Corsini decreed that the building be turned into the world's first public museum.

Hall of the Philosophers
The hall contains a rich mix of portraits of Greek politicians, scientists and literary figures. They are Roman copies that decorated the libraries, villas and gardens of the wealthy in ancient times.

MUSEUM GUIDE

The two floors of the Palazzo Nuovo are devoted chiefly to sculpture. Most of the finest works, such as the Capitoline Venus, are Roman copies of Greek masterpieces. There are also two collections of busts assembled in the 18th century for visitors keen to identify all the philosophers and poets of ancient Greece and the rulers of ancient Rome. The price of entry includes admission to the Palazzo dei Conservatori, which is directly opposite.

Portrait of a Flavian Lady
The woman wears the fanciful and elaborate hairstyle popular among the female aristocracy of the 1st century AD.

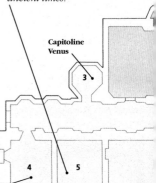

Capitoline Venus

First floor

Courtyard

★ Marcus Aurelius
This bronze equestrian statue of the emperor dates from the 2nd century AD. It used to stand on a pedestal in the centre of the Campidoglio, but has now been restored and is housed in the Palazzo Nuovo.

Ground floor

The facade of Palazzo Nuovo was designed by Michelangelo, but the work was actually finished in 1654 by the brothers Carlo and Girolamo Rainaldi.

STAR SCULPTURES

★ **Marcus Aurelius**

★ **Discobolus**

★ **Dying Galatian**

KEY TO FLOORPLAN

▨ Non-exhibition space

☐ Exhibition space

Mosaic of the Doves
This charming, naturalistic mosaic once decorated the floor of Hadrian's Villa at Tivoli (see p269). It shows doves drinking water from a vase.

★ **Discobolus**
The twisted torso was part of a Greek statue of a discus thrower. An 18th-century French sculptor, Monnot, made the additions that turned him into a wounded warrior.

Stairs to ground floor

Red Faun
Found at Tivoli, the famous red marble satyr is a 2nd-century AD version of a Greek original – an example of Hadrian's fondness for all things Greek.

2

7   8

3

Stairs to first floor

★ **Dying Galatian**
Great compassion is conveyed in this Roman copy of an original Greek work of the 3rd century BC.

9   8   7

Alexander Severus as Hunter
In this marble of the 3rd century AD, the emperor's pose is a pastiche of Perseus, holding up the head of Medusa the Gorgon after he had killed her in her sleep.

Main entrance

Capitoline Museums: Palazzo dei Conservatori ❷

THE PALAZZO DEI CONSERVATORI was the seat of the city's magistrates during the late Middle Ages. Its frescoed halls are still used occasionally for political meetings and the ground floor houses the municipal registry office. The palazzo was built by Giacomo della Porta who carried out Michelangelo's designs for the Piazza del Campidoglio in the mid-16th century. While much of the palazzo is given over to sculpture, the art galleries on the second floor hold works by Veronese, Guercino, Tintoretto, Rubens, Caravaggio, Van Dyck and Titian.

Facade of Palazzo dei Conservatori
Work began on this Michelangelo design in 1563, the year before his death.

MUSEUM GUIDE
The rooms on the first floor are remarkable for their original 16th-and 17th-century decoration and for a number of the Classical statues. The second-floor art gallery houses paintings and a collection of porcelain in room 6. Both the Museo Nuovo and Braccio Nuovo sections are now closed.

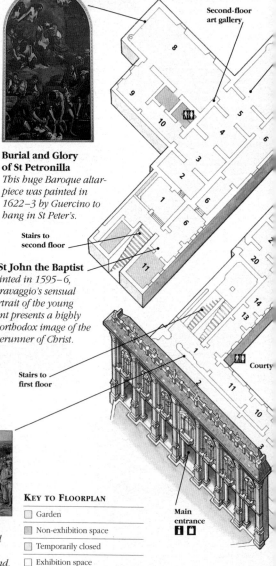

Burial and Glory of St Petronilla
This huge Baroque altar-piece was painted in 1622–3 by Guercino to hang in St Peter's.

Stairs to second floor

★ **St John the Baptist**
Painted in 1595–6, Caravaggio's sensual portrait of the young saint presents a highly unorthodox image of the forerunner of Christ.

Stairs to first floor

Second-floor art gallery

Courty

Main entrance

The Horatii and Curatii
D'Arpino's fresco was painted in 1613 and depicts a duel taken from early Roman legend.

KEY TO FLOORPLAN
- ☐ Garden
- ☐ Non-exhibition space
- ☐ Temporarily closed
- ☐ Exhibition space

Endymion
*The youth doomed
to sleep forever by
the goddess Diana
was painted by Pier
Francesco Mola
(1612–66) who
studied under
Cavalier d'Arpino.*

VISITORS' CHECKLIST

See p71.

STAR EXHIBITS

★ **She-Wolf**

★ **St John the Baptist by Caravaggio**

★ **Spinario**

Braccio Nuovo

Esquiline Venus
*The 1st-century
BC figure was
associated with
the cult of Isis.*

Museo Nuovo

Roman Garden

Constantine II
*The head of a colossal
4th-century AD statue
of the emperor has survived,
along with a hand and
other odd fragments.*

First floor

★ **She-Wolf**
*The Etruscan bronze of the
wolf dates from the early 5th
century BC. The legendary
twins, Romulus and Remus
(see pp16–17), were probably
added in the 15th century.*

★ **Spinario**
*This is a charming bronze
sculpture from the 1st
century BC of a boy
trying to remove a
thorn from his foot.*

Temple of Jupiter ❽

Via del Tempio di Giove. **Map** 5 A5 & 12 F5. 🚌 See **Getting There** p65.

THE TEMPLE of Jupiter, the most important in ancient Rome, was founded in honour of the arch-god around 590 BC on the southern summit of the Capitoline hill. From the few traces that remain, archaeologists have been able to reconstruct the rectangular, Greek appearance of the temple as it once stood. In places you can see remnants of its particularly Roman feature, the podium. Most of this lies beneath the Museo Nuovo wing of the Capitoline Museums *(see pp72–3)*.

By walking around the site, from the podium's south-western corner in Via del Tempio di Giove to its south-eastern corner in Piazzale Caffarelli, you can see that the temple was about the same size as the Pantheon.

Ancient coin showing the Temple of Jupiter

Tarpeian Rock ❾

Via di Monte Caprino and Via del Tempio di Giove. **Map** 5 A5 & 12 F5. 🚌 See **Getting There** p65.

THE SOUTHERN TIP of the Capitoline is called the Tarpeian Rock (Rupe Tarpea), after Tarpeia, the young daughter of Spurius Tarpeius, defender of the Capitol in the 8th-century BC Sabine War.

The Sabines, bent on vengeance for the rape of their women by Romulus and

Sabine soldiers crushing the treacherous Tarpeia with their shields

his men, bribed Tarpeia to let them up on to the Capitol. As the Augustan historian Livy records, the Sabines used to wear heavy gold bracelets and jewelled rings on their left hands, and Tarpeia's reward for her treachery was to be "what they wore on their shield-arms".

The Sabines kept to the letter of the bargain if not to its spirit – they repaid Tarpeia not with their jewellery but by crushing her to death between their shields. Tarpeia was possibly the only casualty of her act of treachery – as the invading warriors met the Roman defenders, the Sabine women leapt between the two opposing armies, forcing a reconciliation. Traitors and other condemned criminals were subsequently executed by being thrown over the sheer face of the rock.

The place is still considered dangerous, and at present is fenced off, while surveying work is carried out.

Victor Emmanuel Monument ❿

Piazza Venezia. **Map** 5 A5 & 12 F4. 🚌 See **Getting There** p65. **Not open** to the public.

KNOWN AS Il Vittoriano, this monument was begun in 1885 and inaugurated in 1911 in honour of Victor Emmanuel II of Savoy, the first king of a unified Italy. The king is depicted here in a gilt bronze equestrian statue, over-sized like the monument itself – the statue is 12 m (39 ft) long.

The edifice contains a museum of the Risorgimento, the events that led to unification *(see pp36–7)*. It has, however, been closed since the early 1980s. Built in austere white Brescian marble, the "wedding cake" or "typewriter" (two of the many insulting nicknames given to this unloved white elephant) will never mellow into the ochre tones of surrounding buildings. It is widely held to be the epitome of self-important, insensitive architecture.

Victor Emmanuel Monument in Piazza Venezia

Palazzo Venezia and Museum ⑪

Via del Plebiscito 118. **Map** 5 A4 &
12 E4. 【 679 88 65. ■ See
Getting There *p65.* **Open** *9am–2pm*
Tue–Sat, 9am–1pm Sun (last adm: 30
mins before closing). **Closed** *public*
hols. **Adm charge.** ◙ &
Temporary exhibitions*.*

O NE OF THE first Renaissance
civic buildings in Rome,
the palazzo's arched windows
and doors are so
harmonious that the
facade was once
attributed to the
great Humanist
architect Leon
Battista Alberti
(1404–72). It
was more
probably
built by
Giuliano da

Pope Paul II

Maiano, who is
known to have carved the
fine doorway on to the piazza.
 Palazzo Venezia was built in
1455 for the Venetian cardinal
Pietro Barbo, who later became
Pope Paul II. It was at times a
papal residence, at other times
the Venetian Embassy to Rome,
before passing into Austrian
hands in 1797. Since 1916 it
has belonged to the state, and
in the Fascist era Mussolini
used it as his headquarters,
addressing crowds from the
central balcony.
 The interior is best seen on
a visit to the Museo del
Palazzo Venezia, Rome's most
underrated museum, which
holds first-class collections of
early Renaissance painting;
painted wood sculptures and
Renaissance chests from all
over Italy; tapestries from all
over Europe; majolica; silver;
Neapolitan ceramic figurines;
Renaissance bronzes; arms
and armour; Baroque
terracotta sculptures by Bernini,
Algardi and others; and 17th-
and 18th-century Italian
painting. There is a marble
screen from the Aracoeli
convent, which was destroyed
to make way for the Victor
Emmanuel Monument, and a
bust of Paul II, showing him to
rank with Martin V and Leo X
among the fattest-ever popes.
The building also houses the
national art library (closed).

Palazzo Venezia with Mussolini's balcony in the centre

San Marco ⑫

Piazza San Marco 48. **Map** 5 A4 &
12 F4. 【 679 52 05. ■ See **Getting**
There *p65.* **Open** *Apr–Sep: 7am–*
12.30pm, 5pm–7.30pm; Oct–Mar:
8am–1pm, 4pm–7pm daily. 🚻 Ø

T HE CHURCH of San Marco
was founded in 336 by
St Mark, the then pope, in
honour of St Mark the
Evangelist. The relics of Pope
Mark lie under the altar. The
church was restored
by Pope Gregory IV
in the 9th century –
the magnificent
apse mosaics date
from this period.
 Further major
rebuilding took
place in 1455–71,
when Pope Paul II
Barbo made San
Marco the church of
the Venetian

**Coat of arms of
Pope Paul II**

community in Rome. The blue
and gold coffered ceiling is
decorated with Pope Paul's
heraldic crest, the lion
rampant, recalling the lion of
St Mark, the patron saint of
Venice. The appearance of the
rest of the interior, with its
colonnades of Sicilian jasper,
was largely the creation of
Filippo Barigioni in the 1740s.
Complemented by an
interesting array of funerary
monuments in the aisles, the
taste is typical of the
late Roman Baroque.
 Leon Battista
Alberti, whose name
is also mentioned
tentatively in
connection with
Palazzo Venezia,
may have been the
architect of the
elegant travertine
arcade and loggia
of the facade.

San Marco's apse mosaic of Christ, with Gregory IV on the far left

FORUM

THE FORUM was the centre of political, commercial and judicial life in ancient Rome. The largest buildings were the basilicas, where legal cases were heard. According to the playwright Plautus, the area teemed with "lawyers and litigants, bankers and brokers, shopkeepers and strumpets, good-for-nothings waiting for a tip from the rich". As Rome's population boomed, the Forum became too small. In 46 BC Julius Caesar built a new one, setting a precedent that was followed by emperors from Augustus to Trajan. As well as the Imperial Fora, emperors also erected triumphal arches to themselves, and just to the east Vespasian built the Colosseum, centre of entertainment after the business of the day.

Figure of barbarian on the Arch of Constantine

SIGHTS AT A GLANCE

Churches and Temples
Temple of Saturn **5**
Temple of Castor and Pollux **8**
Temple of Vesta **9**
Temple of Antoninus and Faustina **11**
Temple of Romulus and Santi Cosma e Damiano **12**
Santa Francesca Romana **14**
Temple of Venus and Rome **17**

Historic Buildings
Basilica Aemilia **1**
Curia **2**
Basilica Julia **7**

House of the Vestal Virgins **10**
Basilica of Constantine and Maxentius **13**
Trajan's Markets pp88–9 **18**
Torre delle Milizie **20**
Casa dei Cavalieri di Rodi **21**
Mamertine Prison **24**
Colosseum pp92–5 **27**

Museums
Antiquarium Forense **15**

KEY

| Tour of the Forum maps |
| **M** Metro station |

Arches and Columns
Arch of Septimius Severus **4**
Column of Phocas **6**
Arch of Titus **16**
Column of Trajan **19**
Arch of Constantine **26**

Ancient Sites
Rostra **3**
Forum of Augustus **22**
Forum of Caesar **23**
Forum of Nerva **25**

GETTING THERE
The simplest way to reach the area is by Metro to Colosseo on line B. The main entrance to the Forum is on Via dei Fori Imperiali, served by buses 11, 27, 81, 85, 87 and 186. Many more routes go to Piazza Venezia. For Trajan's Markets, the best buses are ones such as the 64, 65, 70 and 75 which stop in Via IV Novembre.

SEE ALSO

• *Street Finder*, maps 5, 8, 9, 12

• *Where to Stay* pp294–5

• *Triumphal Arches Walk* pp278–9

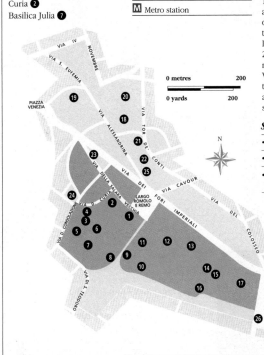

| 0 metres | 200 |
| 0 yards | 200 |

View of the Forum with the Colosseum rising behind the bell tower of Santa Francesca Romana

A Tour of the Roman Forum: West

To APPRECIATE THE LAYOUT of the Forum before visiting its confusing patchwork of ruined temples and basilicas, it is best to view the whole area from above, from the back of the Capitol. From there you can make out the Via Sacra (the Sacred Way), the route followed through the Forum by religious and triumphal processions towards the Capitol. Up until the 18th century when archaeological excavations began, the Arch of Septimius Severus and the columns of the Temple of Saturn lay half buried underground. Excavation of the Forum continues, and the ruins uncovered date from many different periods of Roman history.

The Temple of Vespasian
was the point from where Piranesi made this 18th-century engraving of the Forum. Its three columns were then almost completely buried.

Temple of Concord

Portico of the Dii Consentes

Temple of Saturn
The eight surviving columns of this temple stand close by the three columns of the Temple of Vespasian ❺

Rostra
These are the ruins of the platform used for public oratory in the Forum ❸

Basilica Julia
Named after Julius Caesar, who ordered its construction, the basilica housed important law courts ❼

Column of Phocas
One of the very last monuments erected in the Forum, this single column dates from AD 608 ❻

★ **Arch of Septimius Severus**
A 19th-century engraving shows the arch after the Forum was first excavated ❹

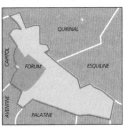

LOCATOR MAP
See Central Rome Map pp12–13

Santi Luca e Martina was an early medieval church, but was completely rebuilt in 1640 by Pietro da Cortona.

Curia
A modern reconstruction has been built on the site of the chamber of the Roman Senate ❷

STAR SIGHTS

★ **Arch of Septimius Severus**

KEY

- - - Suggested route

| 0 metres | 75 |
| 0 yards | 75 |

Basilica Aemilia
This large meeting hall was razed to the ground in the 5th century AD ❶

Entrance to Forum

The Temple of Julius Caesar was erected in his memory by Augustus on the spot where Caesar's body was cremated after his assassination in 44 BC.

Julius Caesar

To Roman Forum: East
See pp80–81

Temple of Castor and Pollux
A temple to the twin sons of Jupiter stood on this spot from the 5th century BC. This section of cornice and the columns supporting it date from the rebuilding of AD 6 ❽

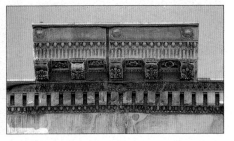

A Tour of the Roman Forum: East

THE EASTERN END of the Roman Forum is dominated by the massive barrel-vaulted ruins of the Basilica of Constantine. To picture the building as it was in the 4th century AD, you must imagine marble columns, floors and statues, and glittering tiles of gilt bronze. The remains of the other important buildings are scanty, though the garden and ponds in the centre of the House of the Vestal Virgins make it a very attractive spot. The two churches in this part of the Forum cannot be reached from within the archaeological area, but are accessible from the road outside.

The Regia was the office of the Pontifex Maximus, the chief priest of ancient Rome.

To Forum entrance

Temple of Antoninus and Faustina
The portico of this temple, built in AD 141, has been incorporated in the church of San Lorenzo in Miranda ⓫

VIA SACRA

An early Iron Age necropolis was found here in 1902. Finds from it, such as this burial urn, are on view in the Antiquarium.

Temple of Vesta
Partly reconstructed, this tiny temple to the goddess of the hearth was one of ancient Rome's most sacred shrines ❾

Temple of Romulus
This domed building from the 4th century AD has survived as part of the church of Santi Cosma e Damiano ⓬

★ House of the Vestal Virgins
The priestesses who tended the sacred flame in the Temple of Vesta lived here. The house was a large rectangular building around a central garden ❿

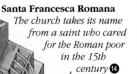

★ Basilica of Constantine
The stark remains of the basilica's huge arches and ceilings give some idea of the original scale and grandeur of the Forum's public buildings ⑬

LOCATOR MAP
See Central Rome Map pp12–13

Santa Francesca Romana
The church takes its name from a saint who cared for the Roman poor in the 15th century ⑭

Antiquarium Forense
A small museum houses archaeological finds made in the Forum. They include this frieze of Aeneas and the Founding of Rome *from the Basilica Aemilia* ⑮

Colonnade surrounding Temple of Venus and Rome

VIA DEI FORI IMPERIALI

Temple of Venus and Rome
These extensive ruins are of a magnificent temple, built here in AD 135 by the Emperor Hadrian, largely to his own design ⑰

VIA SACRA

Ruined Baths

Arch of Titus
This 19th-century reconstruction shows how the arch may have looked when it spanned the flagstoned roadway of the Via Sacra ⑯

STAR SIGHTS

★ **Basilica of Constantine**

★ **House of the Vestal Virgins**

KEY

– – – Suggested route

0 metres	75
0 yards	75

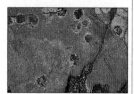

**Melted coins embedded in the
floor of the Basilica Aemilia**

Basilica Aemilia ❶

See Visitors' Checklist.

ORIGINALLY this building was
a rectangular colonnaded
hall, with a multicoloured
marble floor and a bronze-
tiled roof. It was built by the
consuls Marcus Aemilius
Lepidus and Marcus Fulvius
Nobilor in 179 BC. The two
consuls, who were elected
annually, exercised supreme
power over the Republic.

Basilicas in ancient Rome
served no religious purpose;
they were meeting halls for
politicians, moneylenders and
publicani (businessmen
contracted by the state to
collect taxes). A consortium
agreed to hand over a specified
sum to the state, but its
members were allowed to
collect as much as they

could and keep the difference.
This is why tax-collectors in
the Bible were so loathed.

The basilica was
rebuilt many times; it
was finally burned
down when the Goths
sacked Rome in AD
410. Business seems
to have carried on
until the last moment,
for the pavement is
splashed with tiny
lumps of coins that
melted in the fire.

Curia ❷

See Visitors' Checklist.

A MODERN REPLICA has been
built over the ruins of the
hall where Rome's Senate
(chief council of state) used
to meet. The first Curia stood
on the site now occupied
by the church of Santi
Luca e Martina, but
after the building
was destroyed by
fire in 52 BC, Julius
Caesar built a new
Curia at the edge
of the Forum. This
was restored by
Domitian in AD 94
and, after another
fire, rebuilt by
Diocletian in the 3rd
century. The replica you see
today is based on Diocletian's
Curia. Inside are two relief
panels commissioned by
Trajan to decorate the Rostra.
One shows Trajan destroying
records of unpaid taxes to
free citizens from debt; in the
other he sits on a throne
receiving a mother and child.

Ruins of the Imperial Rostra

Rostra ❸

See Visitors' Checklist.

SPEECHES WERE delivered from
this dais, the most famous –
thanks to Shakespeare –
being Mark Antony's "Friends,
Romans, Countrymen" oration
after the assassination of Julius
Caesar in 44 BC. Caesar
himself had just reorganized
the Forum and this speech
was made from the newly-
sited Rostra, where the
ruins now stand.
In the following
year the head and
hands of Cicero
were put on show
here after he had
been put to death
by the second
Triumvirate
(Augustus, Mark
Antony and Marcus
Lepidus). Fulvia,
Mark Antony's
wife, stabbed the great
orator's tongue with a hairpin.
It was also here that Julia,
Augustus's daughter, was said
to have played the prostitute –
one of many scandalous acts
that led to her banishment.

The dais took its name from
the ships' prows *(rostra)* with
which it was decorated.
Sheathed in iron (for ramming
enemy ships), these had been
captured at the Battle of
Antium in the 4th century BC.

Replica of the Curia

**Honorary
statue**

**Relief panel
in balustrade,
showing
Trajan's acts
of charity**

**Prows of ships
(rostra)**

ROSTRA
*This reconstruction
shows the platform for
public speaking in the Forum,
as it looked in Imperial times.*

Arch of Septimius Severus ❹

See Visitors' Checklist.

THIS TRIUMPHAL ARCH, one of the most striking and best preserved monuments of the Forum, was erected in AD 203 to celebrate the tenth anniversary of the accession of Septimius Severus. The relief panels – largely eroded – celebrate the emperor's victories in Parthia (modern-day Iraq and Iran) and Arabia.

Barbarian captives, Arch of Severus

Originally, the inscription along the top of the arch was to Septimius and his two sons, Caracalla and Geta, but after Septimius died Caracalla murdered Geta, and had his brother's name removed. Even so the holes into which the letters of his name were pegged are still visible.

During the Middle Ages the central arch, half buried in earth and debris, was used to shelter a barber's shop.

Triumphal arch of the Emperor Septimius Severus

Temple of Saturn ❺

See Visitors' Checklist.

THE MOST PROMINENT of the ruins in the fenced-off area between the Forum and the Capitoline hill is the Temple of Saturn. It consists of a high platform, eight columns and a section of entablature. There was a temple dedicated to

Ionic capitals on the surviving columns of the Temple of Saturn

Saturn here as early as the 5th century BC, but it had to be rebuilt many times and the current remains date only from the 4th century AD.

Saturn was the mythical god-king of Italy, said to have presided over a prosperous and peaceful Golden Age from which slavery, private property, crime and war were absent. As such, he appealed particularly to the lower and slave classes. Every year, between 17 December and 23 December, Saturn's reign was remembered in a week of sacrifices and feasting, known as the Saturnalia.

As long as the revels lasted, the normal social order was turned upside down. Slaves were permitted to drink and dine with (and sometimes even be served by) their masters. Senators and other high-ranking Romans would abandon the aristocratic togas that they usually wore to distinguish them from the lower classes and put on more democratic, loose-fitting gowns. During the holidays all the law courts and schools in the city were closed. No prisoner could be punished, and no war could be declared.

People also celebrated the Saturnalia in their own homes: they exchanged gifts, in particular special wax dolls and wax tapers, and played light-hearted gambling games, the stakes usually being nuts, a symbol of fruitfulness. Much of the spirit and many of the rituals of the festival have been preserved in the Christian celebration of Christmas.

Column of Phocas ❻

See Visitors' Checklist.

THIS COLUMN, 13.5 m (44 ft) high, is one of the few to have remained upright since the day it was put up. Until 1816, when an inquisitive Englishwoman, Lady Elizabeth Foster, widow of the fifth Duke of Devonshire, decided to excavate its pedestal, nobody knew what it was. It turned out to be the youngest of the Forum's monuments, erected in AD 608 in honour of the Byzantine emperor, Phocas, who had just paid a visit to Rome. The column may have been placed here as a mark of gratitude to Phocas for giving the Pantheon to the pope (*see pp110–11*).

Slender, fluted Column of Phocas

Remains of the Basilica Julia, a Roman court of civil law

Basilica Julia **7**

See Visitors' Checklist, p82.

THIS IMMENSE basilica, which occupied the area between the Temple of Saturn and the Temple of Castor and Pollux, was begun by Julius Caesar in 54 BC and completed after his death by his great nephew Augustus. It was damaged by fire almost immediately afterwards in 9 BC, but was subsequently repaired and dedicated to the emperor's grandsons, Gaius and Lucius.

After numerous sackings and pilferings, only the steps, pavement and column stumps remain. Nevertheless the ground plan is fairly clear. The basilica had a central hall, measuring 82 m by 18 m

(260 ft by 59 ft), surrounded by a double portico. The hall was on three floors, while the outer portico had only two.

The Basilica Julia was the seat of the *centumviri*, a body of 180 magistrates who tried civil law cases. They were split into four chambers of 45 men, and unless a case was particularly complicated they would all sit separately.

The four courts were, however, divided only by screens or curtains, and the voices of lawyers and cheers and boos of spectators in the upper galleries echoed through the building. Lawyers used to hire crowds of spectators, who would applaud every time the lawyer who was paying them made a point and jeer at his opponents. The clappers and booers must have had a good deal of time on their hands: scratched into the steps are chequerboards where they played dice and other gambling games to while away the time between cases.

Temple of Castor and Pollux **8**

See Visitors' Checklist, p82.

THE THREE SLENDER fluted columns of this temple form one of the Forum's most beautiful ruins. The first temple here was probably dedicated in 484 BC in honour of the mythical twins and patrons of horsemanship, Castor and Pollux. During the battle of Lake Regillus (496 BC) against the ousted Tarquin kings, the Roman dictator Postumius promised to build a temple to the twins if the Romans were victorious. Some said the twins appeared on the battlefield, helped the Romans to victory and then materialized in the Forum – the temple marks the spot – to announce the news.

The temple, like most buildings in the Forum, was rebuilt many times. The three surviving columns date from the last occasion on which it was rebuilt – by the future Emperor Tiberius after a fire in 12 BC. For a long period the temple housed the city's office of weights and measures, and it was also used at times by a number of bankers.

Corinthian columns of the Temple of Castor and Pollux

Temple of Vesta **9**

See Visitors' Checklist, p82.

THE FORUM'S most elegant temple, a circular building originally surrounded by a ring of 20 fine fluted columns, dates from the 4th century AD, though there had been a temple on the site for far longer. It was partially reconstructed in 1930.

The cult of the Vestals was one of the oldest in Rome, and centred on six Vestal Virgins, who were required to

TEMPLE OF VESTA
The temple preserved the shape of an original primitive structure made of wooden posts with a thatched roof.

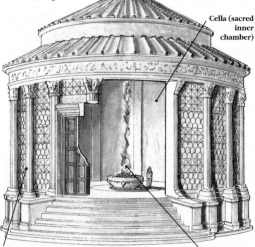

Cella (sacred inner chamber)

Ring of Corinthian columns

Sacred flame

keep alight the sacred flame of Vesta, the goddess of the hearth. This responsibility was originally entrusted to the daughters of the king, but it then passed to the Vestals, the only group of women priests in Rome. It was no easy task, as the flame was easily blown out by the wind. Any Vestal who allowed the flame to die was whipped by the high priest (*Pontifex Maximus*) and dismissed.

The girls, who had to belong to noble families, were selected when they were between six and ten years old. They served for 30 years: the first ten were spent learning their duties, the next ten performing them and the final ten teaching novices. They enjoyed high status and financial security, but were compelled to remain virgins. The penalty for transgressing was to be buried alive, although only ten Vestals are recorded as ever having suffered this fate. The men concerned were whipped to death. When Vestals retired, they were free to live the rest of their lives as ordinary citizens. If they wished they could marry, but few ever did.

Another of the Vestals' duties was to guard the Palladium, a sacred statue of the goddess Pallas Athenae. The irreverent Emperor Heliogabalus burgled the temple in the 3rd century AD. He thought he had succeeded in stealing the Palladium, but the Vestals had been warned of his intention and had replaced it with a replica.

Central courtyard of the House of the Vestal Virgins

House of the Vestal Virgins ⑩

See Visitors' Checklist, p82.

As soon as a girl became a Vestal she came to live in the House of the Vestal Virgins. Originally this was an enormous complex with about 50 rooms on three storeys. The only substantial remains today are some of the rooms around the central courtyard. This space is perhaps the most evocative part of the Forum. Overlooking ponds of water lilies and plump goldfish is a row of eroded, and mostly headless, statues of senior Vestals, dating from the 3rd and 4th centuries AD. The better-preserved examples were transferred to the Museo Nazionale Romano *(see p163)*. On one of the pedestals the inscription has been removed because the Vestal in question suffered some disgrace. It is thought she may have been a certain Claudia, known to have betrayed the cult by converting to Christianity.

Though many of the rooms surrounding the courtyard are well-preserved – some even retain flights of steps leading to an upper floor – you are not allowed inside them. If you peep into the series of rooms along the south side, however, you might be able to see the remains of a mill,

Honorary statue of a Vestal Virgin

used for grinding the grain with which the Vestals made a special sacrificial cake. The bakery was next door.

Temple of Antoninus and Faustina ⑪

See Visitors' Checklist, p82.

One of the forum's oddest sights is the Baroque facade of the church of San Lorenzo in Miranda rising above the porch of a Roman temple. First dedicated in AD 141 by the Emperor Antoninus Pius to his late wife Faustina, the temple was rededicated to them both on the death of the emperor. In the 11th century it was converted into a church because it was thought San Lorenzo (St Lawrence) had been condemned to death there. The current church, dating from the 17th century, is closed to the public.

Restored section of Temple of Vesta

Temple of Antoninus and Faustina

Temple of Romulus and Santi Cosma e Damiano ⑫

See Visitors' Checklist, p82. **Santi Cosma e Damiano** 📞 699 15 40. **Open** *7am–1pm, 3pm–7pm daily.* **Adm charge** *for crib.* ✝ 📷 ♿

N O-ONE IS SURE to whom the so-called Temple of Romulus was dedicated, but it wasn't to Romulus, the founder of Rome, or to the son of the Emperor Maxentius.

The temple is a circular brick building, topped by a cupola, with two rectangular side rooms and a concave porch. The heavy, dull bronze doors are original.

Since the 6th century the temple has acted as a vestibule to the church of Santi Cosma e Damiano, which itself occupies an ancient building – a hall in Vespasian's Forum of Peace. The entrance to the church is on Via dei Fori Imperiali. The beautiful carved figures of its 18th-century Neapolitan *presepio* (crib or

Nativity scene) are not on view at the moment, but the church has a vivid Byzantine apse mosaic with Christ pictured against orange clouds.

Roof of the Temple of Romulus

Basilica of Constantine and Maxentius ⑬

See Visitors' Checklist, p82.

T HE BASILICA'S three vast, coffered barrel vaults are powerful relics of what was the largest building in the Forum. Work began in the early 4th century under the Emperor Maxentius. When he was deposed by Constantine after the Battle of the Milvian Bridge in AD 312, work on the massive project continued under the new regime. The building, which, like other Roman basilicas, was used for

the administration of justice and for carrying on business, is often referred to simply as the Basilica of Constantine.

The area covered by the basilica was roughly 100 m by 65 m (330 ft by 215 ft). It was originally designed to have a long nave and aisles running from east to west, but Constantine switched the axis around to create three short broad aisles with the main entrance in the centre of the long south wall. The height of the building was 35 m (115 ft). In the apse at the western end, where it could be seen from all over the building, stood

a 12-m (39-ft) statue of the emperor, made partly of wood and partly of marble. The giant head, hand and foot are on display in the courtyard of the Palazzo dei Conservatori *(see pp72–3).* The roof of the basilica glittered with gilded tiles until the 7th century when they were stripped off to cover the roof of the old St Peter's.

The three barrel-vaulted aisles of the basilica were used as law courts.

The octagonal coffers in the vaulted ceiling were originally faced with marble.

The main entrance was added by Constantine in AD 313.

The roof was supported by eight massive Corinthian columns. One now stands in Piazza Santa Maria Maggiore *(see p173).*

Santa Francesca Romana

Piazza di Santa Francesca Romana. **Map**
5 B5. ☎ 679 55 28. ▦ 11, 27, 81, 85,
87, 186. Ⓜ Colosseo. **Open** 9.30am–
1pm, 4pm–7pm daily. ✝ ◎ ⌂

EVERY YEAR on 9 March
devout Roman drivers try
to park as close as possible to
this Baroque church with
a pleasant Romanesque
bell tower. The aim of
their strange pilgrimage
is to have their vehicles
blessed by Santa
Francesca Romana, the
patron saint of
motorists.
Francesca was
a 15th-century
wife and
mother from
Trastevere who
founded a
society of
pious women

Bell tower of devoted to
Santa Francesca helping the
poor and sick. After she had
been canonized in 1608 the
church, which was originally
called Santa Maria Nova, was
rededicated to Francesca.

The most curious sight
inside the church is a flagstone
with what are reputed to be
the imprints of the knees of
St Peter and St Paul. The story
goes that a magician, Simon
Magus, decided to prove that
his powers were superior to
those of the Apostles by
levitating himself above the
Forum. As Simon was in mid-
air, Peter and Paul fell to their
knees and prayed fervently
that God would show who
was boss. Simon immediately
plummeted to his death.

Antiquarium Forense ⓭

See Visitors' Checklist, p82.

THE FORMER CONVENT of
Santa Francesca Romana is
now occupied by the offices
in charge of the excavations
of the Forum and a small
museum. The latter is currently
being reorganized, and only
a couple of rooms are open.
They contain Iron Age burial
urns, graves and their skeletal

Dedication to Titus and Vespasian on the Arch of Titus

occupants along with some
ancient bric-a-brac exhumed
from the Forum's drains.
When the reorganization is
complete you should be able
to see fragments of statues,
capitals, friezes and other
architectural decoration taken
from the Forum's buildings.

Frieze of Aeneas in the Antiquarium Forense

Arch of Titus ⓰

See Visitors' Checklist, p82.

THIS TRIUMPHAL ARCH was
erected in AD 81 by the
Emperor Domitian in honour
of the victories of his brother,
Titus, and his father, Vespasian,
in Judaea. In AD 68 the Jews,
weary of being exploited by
unscrupulous Roman officials,
rebelled. A bitter war broke
out which ended two years
later in the fall of Jerusalem
and the Jewish Diaspora.

Although the reliefs
inside the arch are
badly eroded, you can
make out a triumphant
procession of Roman
soldiers carrying off
spoils from the Temple
of Jerusalem. The
booty includes the
altar, silver trumpets
and a golden seven-
branched candelabrum.

Temple of Venus and Rome ⓱

See Visitors' Checklist, p82.

THE EMPEROR Hadrian
designed this temple to
occupy what had been the
vestibule to Nero's
Golden House. Many
of the columns have
been re-erected, and
though there is no
access, there is a good
view as you leave the
Forum and from the
upper tiers of the
Colosseum. The temple,
the largest in Rome,
was dedicated to Roma,
the personification of the city,
and to Venus because she was
the mother of Aeneas, father
of Romulus and Remus. Each
goddess had her own cella
(shrine). When the architect
Apollodorus pointed out that
the seated statues in the
niches were too big (had they
tried to "stand" their heads
would have hit the vaults),
Hadrian had him put to death.

Statue of   **Porphyry
goddess**   **column**

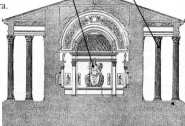
Cross-section of Temple of Venus and Rome

Trajan's Markets ®

ORIGINALLY CONSIDERED among the wonders of the Classical world, Trajan's Markets now show only a hint of their former splendour. Emperor Trajan and his architect, Apollodorus of Damascus, built this visionary new complex of 150 shops and offices (probably used for administering the corn dole) in the early 2nd century AD. It was the ancient Roman equivalent of the modern shopping centre, selling everything from silks and spices imported from the Middle East to fresh fish, fruit and flowers.

The Markets Today
Above the façade stands the 13th-century Torre delle Milizie, built for defensive purposes.

Cross vaulting

Trajan
The emperor was a benevolent ruler and a successful general.

Main Hall
Twelve shops were built on two floors, and the corn dole was shared out on the upper storey. This was a free corn ration given to Roman men to prevent hunger.

Via Biberatica
The main street which runs through the market may have been lined with inns and shops selling pepper and spices.

Small semicircle of shops

Staircase

TIMELINE

AD 100–112 Building of Trajan's Markets	**472** Invasion by Ricimer the Suevian. Some of his Germanic troops stationed here	**1200s** Torre delle Milizie built on top of the markets	**1572** Convent of Santa Caterina da Siena built over part of markets	**1924** Many medieval houses demolished	
AD 100	**AD 500**	**1000**	**1300**	**1800**	**1950**
AD 117 Death of Trajan **AD 98** Trajan succeeds Nerva as emperor	**552** Byzantine takeover of Rome. Markets occupied and fortified by the army	**1300s** Annibaldi and Caetani families vie for control of the area	**1828** First tentative excavations, but value of site not recognized	**1911–14** Convent demolished **1930–33** Markets finally excavated	

VISITORS' CHECKLIST

Mercati Traianei, Via IV Novembre.
Map 5 B4. **[** 67 10 36 13. **▦**
57, 64, 65, 70, 75, 170 to Via IV
Novembre and many routes to
Piazza Venezia. **Open** 9am–1pm
Tue–Sat, 9am–12.30pm Sun;
Apr–Sep: 9am–6pm Thu & Sat
(last adm: 30 mins before closing).
Closed Mon, public hols. **Adm**
charge. ◙ ₺ to main hall only.

The Markets in the 16th Century
*This fanciful fresco depicts a gladiatorial
combat taking place in front of the partly-buried
remains of Trajan's Markets.*

A Market Shop
*Shops were built with
arched entrances, with
jambs and lintels
creating rectangular
portals and windows.
A wooden mezzanine
was used for storage.*

Upper Corridor
*Shops on this upper level
were thought to have sold
wine and oil as a number
of storage jars were
discovered here.*

**Large hall with
semidomed
ceiling**

**Wall dividing
market area from
Forum of Trajan**

Shops on the ground floor of
the large curving semicircle
were smaller than those on
the upper storeys. They were
also cooler and probably sold
vegetables, fruit and flowers.

The terrace
over the archway
spanning Via
Biberatica has
a good view of
the Forum of
Trajan below.

MARKET SHOPPING

Shops opened early and closed about
noon. The best ones were decorated
with mosaics of the goods they sold.
Almost all the shopping was done
by men, though women visited the
dressmaker and cobbler. The
tradesmen were almost all male.
In employment records for the
period AD 117–193, the only
female shopkeepers mentioned
are three wool-sellers, two
jewellers, a greengrocer
and a fishwife.

Fish mosaic

Trajan's Markets ⑱

See pp88–9.

Column of Trajan ⑲

Via dei Fori Imperiali. **Map** 5 A4 &
12 F4. *See Visitors' Checklist for
Trajan's Markets, p89.*

Detail of Trajan's Column

THIS ELEGANT marble column
was inaugurated by Trajan
in AD 113, and celebrates his
two campaigns in Dacia
(Romania) in AD 101–2 and
AD 105–6. The column, base
and pedestal are 40 m (131 ft)
tall – precisely the same height
as the spur of the Quirinal hill
which was excavated to make
room for Trajan's Forum.
Spiralling up the column are
minutely detailed scenes from
the campaigns, beginning with
the Romans preparing for war
and ending with the Dacians
being ousted from their
homeland. The column is
pierced with small windows
to illuminate its internal spiral
staircase (closed to the public).
If you wish to see the reliefs
in detail there is a complete
set of casts in the Museo
della Civiltà Romana at EUR
(see p267).
   When Trajan died in AD 117
his ashes, along with those of
his wife, Plotina, were placed
in a golden urn in the column's
hollow base. The column's
survival was largely thanks to
the intervention of Pope
Gregory the Great (reigned
590–604). He was so moved
by a relief showing Trajan
helping a woman whose son
had been killed that he
begged God to release the
emperor's soul from hell. God

duly appeared to the pope to
say that Trajan had been
rescued, but requested him
not to pray for the souls of
any more pagans.
   According to legend, when
Trajan's ashes were exhumed
his skull and tongue were not
only intact, but his tongue
told of his release from hell.
The land around the column
was then declared sacred and
the column itself was spared.
The statue of Trajan remained
on top of the column until
1587, when it was replaced
with one of St Peter.

Torre delle Milizie ⑳

Mercati Traianei, Via IV Novembre.
Map 5 B4. ***Closed*** for restoration.

FOR CENTURIES this massive
brick tower was thought to
have been the one in which
Nero stood watching Rome
burn, after he had set it alight
in order to clear the city's
slums. It is uncertain whether
arson was among Nero's
crimes, but it is certain that he
did not watch the fire from
this tower – it was built in the
13th century.

Casa dei Cavalieri di Rodi ㉑

Piazza del Grillo 1. **Map** 5 B5.
[67 10 24 75. 🚌 11, 27, 81, 85,
87, 186. ***Open*** by appt only.

Loggia, Casa dei Cavalieri di Rodi

SINCE THE 12TH CENTURY the
crusading order, the Knights
of St John, also known as the
Knights of Rhodes (Rodi) or
Malta, have had their priorate
in this medieval house above
the Forum of Augustus. If you
are lucky enough to get
inside, ask to see the beautiful
Cappella di San Giovanni
(Chapel of St John).

Forum of Augustus ㉒

Piazza del Grillo 1. **Map** 5 B5 & 12 F5.
[67 10 24 75. 🚌 11, 27, 81, 85,
87, 186. ***Open*** by appt only.

**Podium of the Temple of Mars in
the Forum of Augustus**

THE FORUM of Augustus
was built to celebrate
Augustus's victory over Julius
Caesar's assassins, Brutus and
Cassius, at the Battle of
Philippi in 41 BC. The temple
in its centre was dedicated to
Mars the Avenger. The forum
stretched from a high wall at
the foot of the sleazy Suburra
quarter to the edge of the
Forum of Caesar. At least half
of it is now concealed below
Mussolini's Via dei Fori
Imperiali. The temple is easily
identified, with its cracked
steps and four Corinthian
columns. Originally it had a
statue of Mars which looked
very like Augustus. In case
anyone failed to notice the
resemblance, a giant statue of
Augustus himself was placed
against the Suburra wall.

Forum of Caesar ㉓

Via del Carcere Tulliano. **Map** 5 A5.
[67 10 30 65. 🚌 11, 27, 81, 85,
87, 186. ***Open*** by appt only.

THE FIRST of Rome's Imperial
fora was built by Julius
Caesar. He spent a fortune –
most of it booty from his
conquest of Gaul – buying up
and demolishing houses on
the site. Pride of place went
to a temple dedicated in 46
BC to the goddess Venus
Genetrix, from whom Caesar
claimed descent. The temple
contained statues of Caesar
and Cleopatra as well as of
Venus. All that remains of this
temple to vanity is a platform
and three Corinthian columns.

The forum was enclosed by a double colonnade which sheltered a row of shops, but this burnt down in AD 80 and was rebuilt by Domitian and Trajan. Trajan also added the Basilica Argentaria (an important financial exchange) and a heated public lavatory. The forum is not open to the public, but parts of it are visible from above in Via dei Fori Imperiali.

Mamertine Prison ㉔

Clivo Argentario 1. **Map** 5 A5.
🅲 679 29 02. 🚌 81, 85, 87, 186.
Open Apr–Sep: 9am–12.30pm, 2.30pm–6pm; Oct–Mar: 9am–noon, 2pm–5pm. **Donation** expected. 📷 🅰

19th-century engraving of guards visiting prisoners in the Mamertine

BELOW THE 16th-century church of San Giuseppe dei Falegnami (St Joseph of the Carpenters) is a dank dungeon in which, according to Christian legend, St Peter was imprisoned. He is said to have caused a spring to bubble up into the cell, and used the water to baptize the two prison guards.

The prison was in an old cistern with access to the city's main sewer (the Cloaca Maxima). The lower cell, the Tullianum, was used for executions and bodies were thrown into the sewer. Among the enemies of Rome to be executed here was the Gaulish leader Vercingetorix, defeated by Julius Caesar in 52 BC.

17th-century view of the ruined Forum of Nerva

Forum of Nerva ㉕

Piazza del Grillo 1 (reached through Forum of Augustus). **Map** 5 B5.
🅲 67 10 30 65. 🚌 11, 27, 81, 85, 87, 186. **Closed** for excavations.

THE FORUM of Nerva was begun by his predecessor, Domitian, and completed in AD 97. Little more than a long corridor with a colonnade along the sides and a Temple of Minerva at one end, it was also known as the Forum Transitorium because it lay between the Forum of Peace built by the Emperor Vespasian in AD 70 and the Forum of Augustus. Vespasian's forum is almost completely covered by Via dei Fori Imperiali, as is much of the Forum of Nerva itself. Excavations have unearthed Renaissance shops and taverns, but only part of the forum can be seen, including the base of the temple and two columns that were part of the original colonnade. These support a relief of Minerva above a frieze of young girls learning to sew and weave.

Arch of Constantine ㉖

Between Via di San Gregorio and Piazza del Colosseo. **Map** 8 F1.
🚌 11, 15, 27, 81, 85, 87, 118, 186, 673. 🚃 13, 30b. Ⓜ Colosseo.

THIS TRIUMPHAL ARCH was dedicated in AD 315 to celebrate Constantine's victory three years before over his co-emperor, Maxentius. Constantine claimed he owed his victory to a vision of Christ, but there is nothing Christian about the arch – in fact, most of the medallions, reliefs and statues were scavenged from earlier monuments.

There are statues of Dacian prisoners taken from Trajan's Forum and reliefs of Marcus Aurelius, including one where he distributes bread to the poor. Inside the arch are reliefs of Trajan's victory over the Dacians. These were probably by the artist who worked on the Column of Trajan.

Medallion on the Arch of Constantine

Colosseum ㉗

See pp92–5.

North side of the Arch of Constantine, facing the Colosseum

Colosseum ㉗

ROME'S GREATEST amphitheatre was commissioned by the Emperor Vespasian in AD 72 on the marshy site of a lake in the grounds of Nero's palace, the Domus Aurea *(see p175)*. Deadly gladiatorial combats and wild animal fights were staged free of charge by the emperor and wealthy citizens for public viewing.

Outer Wall of the Colosseum
Stone plundered from the facade in the Renaissance was used to build several palaces, bridges and parts of St Peter's.

The Colosseum was built to a practical design, with its 80 arched entrances allowing easy access to 55,000 spectators, but it is also a building of great beauty. The drawing here shows how it looked in AD 80. It was one of several similar amphi-theatres built in the Roman Empire, and some survive at El Djem in North Africa, Nîmes and Arles in France and Verona in northern Italy. Despite being damaged over the years by neglect and theft, it remains a majestic sight to this day.

The Founder of the Colosseum
Vespasian was a professional soldier who became emperor in AD 69, founding the Flavian dynasty.

The outer walls are made of travertine.

FLORA OF THE COLOSSEUM
By the 19th century the Colosseum was heavily overgrown. Different micro-climates in various parts of the ruin had created an im-pressive variety of herbs, grasses and wild flowers. Several botanists were inspired to study and catalogue them and two books were published, one listing 420 different species. **Borage, a herb**

The bollards anchored the velarium.

The velarium was a huge awning which shaded spectators from the sun. Supported on poles fixed to the upper storey of the building, it was then hoisted into position with ropes anchored to bollards outside the stadium.

TIMELINE

80 Vespasian's son, Titus, stages inaugural festival in the amphitheatre. It lasts 100 days

AD 70	100
72 Emperor Vespasian begins work on the Colosseum	**81–96** Amphi-theatre completed in reign of Domitian

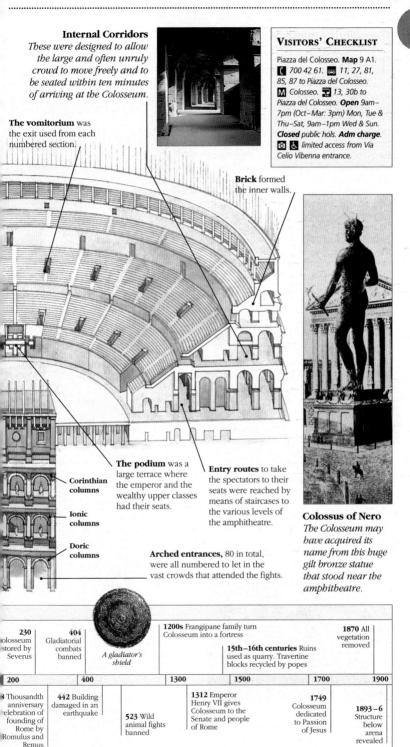

Internal Corridors
These were designed to allow the large and often unruly crowd to move freely and to be seated within ten minutes of arriving at the Colosseum.

The vomitorium was the exit used from each numbered section.

VISITORS' CHECKLIST

Piazza del Colosseo. **Map** 9 A1.
📞 700 42 61. 🚌 11, 27, 81, 85, 87 to Piazza del Colosseo.
Ⓜ Colosseo. 🚊 13, 30b to Piazza del Colosseo. **Open** 9am–7pm (Oct–Mar: 3pm) Mon, Tue & Thu–Sat, 9am–1pm Wed & Sun. **Closed** public hols. **Adm charge.**
📷 ♿ limited access from Via Celio Vibenna entrance.

Brick formed the inner walls.

Corinthian columns

Ionic columns

Doric columns

The podium was a large terrace where the emperor and the wealthy upper classes had their seats.

Entry routes to take the spectators to their seats were reached by means of staircases to the various levels of the amphitheatre.

Arched entrances, 80 in total, were all numbered to let in the vast crowds that attended the fights.

Colossus of Nero
The Colosseum may have acquired its name from this huge gilt bronze statue that stood near the amphitheatre.

		A gladiator's shield	1200s Frangipane family turn Colosseum into a fortress			1870 All vegetation removed
230 olosseum stored by Severus	**404** Gladiatorial combats banned			**15th–16th centuries** Ruins used as quarry. Travertine blocks recycled by popes		

200	**400**		**1300**	**1500**	**1700**	**1900**
8 Thousandth anniversary elebration of founding of Rome by Romulus and Remus	**442** Building damaged in an earthquake	**523** Wild animal fights banned	**1312** Emperor Henry VII gives Colosseum to the Senate and people of Rome		**1749** Colosseum dedicated to Passion of Jesus	**1893–6** Structure below arena revealed

How Fights were Staged in the Arena

THE EMPERORS HELD shows here which often began with animals performing circus tricks. Then on came the gladiators, who fought each other to the death. When one was killed, attendants dressed as Charon, the mythical ferryman of the dead, carried his body off on a stretcher, and sand was raked over the blood ready for the next bout. A badly-wounded gladiator would surrender his fate to the crowd. The "thumbs up" sign from the emperor meant he could live, "thumbs down" that he die, and the victor became an instant hero. Animals were brought here from as far away as North Africa and the Middle East. The games held in AD 248 to mark the 1,000th anniversary of the founding of Rome saw the death of a host of lions, elephants, hippos, zebras and elks.

Beneath the Arena
Late 19th-century excavations exposed the network of underground rooms where the animals were kept.

Interior of the Colosseum
The stadium was built in the form of an ellipse, with tiers of seats around a vast central arena.

Emperor's entrance

Emperor's box

Layout of underground passages

Tiers of seats

Consul's box

Consul's entrance

Gladiators' entrance

A complex of rooms, passages and lifts lie underneath the arena.

Roman Gladiators
These were usually slaves, prisoners of war or condemned criminals. Most were men, but there were a few female gladiators.

Dramatic Entrances
Below the sand was a wooden floor through which animals, men and scenery appeared in the arena.

The Colosseum by Antonio Canaletto
This 18th-century view of the Colosseum shows the Meta Sudans fountain (now demolished). Water "sweated" from a metal ball on top of its brick cone.

Metal fencing kept animals penned in, while archers stood by just in case any escaped.

Seating was tiered, and different social classes were segregated.

A winch brought the animal cages up to arena level when they were due to fight.

A ramp and trap door enabled the animal to reach the arena after walking along a corridor.

Cages were like three-sided lifts which went up to the next level where the animals were released.

SEA BATTLES IN THE ARENA
The historian Dion Cassius, writing in the 4th century AD, relates how, 150 years earlier, the Colosseum's arena was flooded to stage a mock sea battle. Scholars now believe that he was mistaken. The spectacle probably took place in the Naumachia of Augustus, a water-filled arena situated across the Tiber in Trastevere.

PALATINE

ACCORDING TO LEGEND, Romulus and Remus were brought up here by a wolf in a cave. Traces of Iron Age huts, dating from the 8th century BC, have been found on the Palatine hill, providing archaeological support for the area's legendary links with the founding of Rome. The Palatine was a very desirable place to live, becoming home to some of the city's most famous inhabitants. The great orator Cicero had a house here, as did the lyric poet Catullus. Augustus was born on the hill and continued to live here in very modest circumstances even when he became emperor. The two buildings identified as the House of Augustus and the House of Livia, his wife, are among the best preserved here. The first emperor's example of frugality was ignored by his successors, Tiberius, Caligula and Domitian, who all built extravagant palaces here. The ruins of Tiberius's palace lie beneath the 16th-century Farnese Gardens. The most extensive ruins are those of the Domus Augustana and Domus Flavia, the two wings of Domitian's palace, and the later extension built by Septimius Severus.

Fresco of mask in the House of Augustus

SIGHTS AT A GLANCE

Temples
Temple of Cybele ❻

Historic Buildings
Domus Flavia ❶
Domus Augustana ❸
House of Livia ❺

Ancient Sites
Cryptoporticus ❷
Stadium ❹
Huts of Romulus ❼

Parks and Gardens
Farnese Gardens ❽

SEE ALSO
• *Street Finder*, map 8

GETTING THERE
There are two ways of getting on to the Palatine hill; either through the Roman Forum (from Via dei Fori Imperiali) or through the entrance in Via di San Gregorio. One ticket is valid for both Forum and Palatine. The best buses are the 11, 27, 81, 85, 87, 186; all stop in Via dei Fori Imperiali near the main entrance. Colosseo Metro station (*see p77*) is also handy.

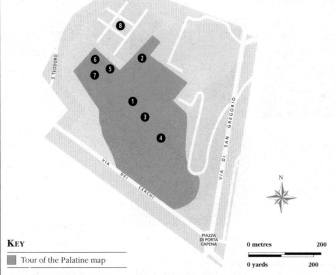

KEY

▢ Tour of the Palatine map

0 metres 200
0 yards 200

Towering ruins of the Palace of Septimius Severus on the Palatine hill

A Tour of the Palatine

SHADED ON ITS LOWER SLOPES with pines, and scattered
in spring with wild flowers, the Palatine is the most
pleasant and relaxing of the city's ancient sites. You can
reach the hill by walking up from
the Roman Forum *(see pp76–7).*
The area is dominated by the
ruins of the Domus Flavia and
the Domus Augustana, two
parts of Domitian's huge
palace built at the end of the
1st century AD. What you
are able to see depends
on where excavations are
taking place at the time.

Huts of Romulus
*These are traces of an
8th-century BC village
on the Palatine* **7**

**To Farnese
Gardens**
See p101

**House of
Augustus**

Temple of Cybele
*Also known as the Temple of the
Magna Mater, this was the centre
of an important fertility cult* **6**

★ **House of Livia**
*Many of the wall paintings
have survived in the house
where Augustus lived with
his wife Livia* **5**

STAR SIGHTS

★ **Domus Flavia**

★ **House of Livia**

KEY

--- --- ---   Suggested route

0 metres	75
0 yards	75

N

★ **Domus Flavia**
*This oval fountain was
designed to be seen from the
dining hall of the palace* **1**

Domus Augustana
*The Roman emperors lived
in this part of the palace, whi
the Domus Flavia was used f
public functions* **3**

Cryptoporticus
In this long underground gallery, built by Nero, the stuccoes that decorated the walls and vault have been replaced with copies ❷

LOCATOR MAP
See Central Rome Map pp12–13

Octagonal fountain of the Domus Flavia

The Palatine Museum is housed in a former convent, but has been closed for many years.

Stadium
Part of the Imperial palace, this enclosure may have been used by the emperors as a private garden ❹

To Forum entrance

The exedra of the Stadium may have housed a balcony for emperors to view races.

Baths of Septimius Severus

The Palace of Septimius Severus (reigned AD 193–211) was an extension of the Domus Augustana. It projected beyond the hillside, requiring enormous arched supports.

Substructure of palace

Domus Flavia ❶

See Visitors' Checklist.

Marble pavement in the courtyard of the Domus Flavia

In AD 81 DOMITIAN, the third of the Flavian dynasty of emperors, decided to build a splendid new palace on the Palatine hill. But the western peak, the Germalus, was covered with houses and temples, while the eastern peak, the Palatium, was very steep. So the emperor's architect, Rabirius, flattened the Palatium and used the soil to fill in the cleft between the two peaks, burying (and preserving) a number of Republican-era houses.

The palace had two wings – one official (the Domus Flavia), the other private (the Domus Augustana). It was the main Imperial palace for 300 years. At the front of the Domus Flavia, the surviving stubs of columns and fragments of walls trace the shapes of three adjoining rooms. In the first of these, the Basilica, Domitian dispensed his personal brand of justice.

The central Aula Regia was a throne room decorated with 12 black basalt statues. The third room (now covered with corrugated plastic) was the Lararium, a shrine for the household gods known as Lares (usually the owner's ancestors). It may have been used for official ceremonies or by the palace guards.

Fearing assassination, Domitian had the walls of the courtyard covered with shiny marble slabs designed to act as mirrors so that he could see anyone lurking behind him. In the event, he was assassinated in his bedroom, possibly on the orders of his wife, Domitia. The courtyard is now a pleasant place to pause; the flower beds in the centre follow the maze pattern of a sunken fountain pool.

Cryptoporticus ❷

See Visitors' Checklist.

THE CRYPTOPORTICUS, a series of underground corridors, was built by Nero to connect his Golden House *(see p175)* with the palaces of earlier emperors on the Palatine. A further branch leading to the Palace of Domitian was added later. Its vaults are decorated with delicate stucco reliefs – copies of originals now kept in the Palatine's closed museum.

Domus Augustana ❸

See Visitors' Checklist.

THIS PART of Domitian's palace was called the Domus Augustana because it was the private residence of the "august" emperors. On the upper level a high brick

wall remains, and you can make out the shape of its two courtyards. The far better preserved lower level is closed to the public, though you can look down on its sunken courtyard with the geometric foundations of a fountain in its centre. Sadly, you can't see the stairs linking the two levels (once lit by sunlight falling on a mirror-paved pool), nor the surrounding rooms, paved with coloured marble.

Stadium ❹

See Visitors' Checklist.

Stadium viewed from the south

THE STADIUM on the Palatine was laid out at the same time as the Palace of Domitian. It is not clear whether it was a public stadium, a private track for exercising horses, or simply a large garden. The alcove in the eastern wall looks as though it may have held a box from which the emperor could have watched races. It is, however, known that the Stadium was used for foot races by the Ostrogothic king, Theodoric, in the 6th century – he added the small oval-shaped enclosure at the southern end of the site.

Remains of the Domus Augustana and the Palace of Septimius Severus

House of Livia ❺

See Visitors' Checklist. If closed, apply to custodian.

Fresco in the House of Livia

THIS HOUSE dating from the 1st century BC is one of the best preserved on the Palatine. It was probably part of the house in which the Emperor Augustus and his wife Livia lived. Compared with later Imperial palaces, it is a relatively modest home. According to Suetonius, the biographer of Rome's early emperors, Augustus slept in the same small bedroom for 40 years on a low bed which had "a very ordinary coverlet". He wore home-made clothes (woven by Livia, his sister Octavia and daughter Julia), but he was vain enough to wear shoes with extremely thick soles to conceal the fact that he was rather short.

Detail of floor mosaic

The ground level of the Palatine is now above the house, so you walk down a flight of steps and along a mosaic-paved corridor into a courtyard. Its imitation marble wall frescoes have been detached in order to preserve them, but they still hang in situ. Though they are very faded, you can still make out the veining patterns. Leading off the courtyard are three small reception rooms. The frescoes in the central one include a faded scene of Hermes coming to the rescue of Zeus's beloved Io, who is guarded by the 100-eyed Argos. In the left-hand room you can make out frescoed figures of griffins and other beasts, while the decor in the right-hand room includes landscapes and cityscapes.

Temple of Cybele ❻

See Visitors' Checklist.

OTHER THAN a platform with a few column stumps and capitals, there is little to see of the Temple of Cybele, a popular fertility goddess imported to Rome from Asia. The priests of the cult castrated themselves in the belief that if they sacrificed their own fertility it would guarantee that of the natural world. The annual festival of Cybele, from March 22–4, culminated with frenzied eunuch-priests slashing their bodies to offer blood to the goddess, and the ceremonial castration of novice priests.

Statue of the goddess Cybele

Huts of Romulus ❼

See Visitors' Checklist.

ACCORDING TO LEGEND, after killing his brother Remus, Romulus founded a village on the Palatine. In the 1940s a series of holes was found filled with earth lighter in colour than the surrounding soil. Archaeologists deduced that these holes must originally have held the supporting poles of three Iron Age huts – the first foundations of Rome *(see pp16–17).*

Farnese Gardens ❽

See Visitors' Checklist.

IN THE MID-16TH century Cardinal Alessandro Farnese, grandson of Pope Paul III, bought the ruins of Tiberius's palace on the Palatine. He filled in the ruined building and had Vignola, architect of the interior of the Gesù church, design a garden for him. The result was one of the first botanical gardens in Europe, its terraces linked by steps stretching from the House of Vestal Virgins in the Forum to the Palatine's Germalus peak. The gardeners introduced a number of plants to Italy and Europe, among them *Acacia farnesiana*. Farnese was at the centre of a glittering set which included a number of courtesans, so the parties here are likely to have been somewhat unholy.

The area was dug up during the excavation of the Palatine and re-landscaped afterwards. Nevertheless the tree-lined avenues, rose gardens and glorious views still make it an ideal place to unwind.

Farnese pavilions, relics of the age when the Palatine was a private garden

PIAZZA DELLA ROTONDA

THE PANTHEON, one of the great buildings in the history of European architecture, has stood at the heart of Rome for nearly 2,000 years. The historic area around it has seen uninterrupted economic and political activity throughout that time. Palazzo di Montecitorio, built for Pope Innocent X as a papal tribunal in 1697,

Bitter-style apéritif, popular in Roman cafés

is now the Italian parliament and many nearby buildings are government offices. This is also the main financial district of Rome with banking headquarters and the stock exchange. Not many people live here, but in the evenings, Romans stroll in the narrow streets and fill the lively restaurants and cafés that make this a focus for the city's social life.

SIGHTS AT A GLANCE

Churches and Temples
Temple of Hadrian ❶
Sant'Ignazio di Loyola ❸
Gesù pp114–15 ❾
Santa Maria sopra Minerva ⓫
Pantheon pp110–11 ⓭
Sant'Eustachio ⓮
La Maddalena ⓯
Santa Maria in
Campo Marzio ⓲
San Lorenzo in Lucina ⓴

Historic Streets and Piazzas
Piazza di Sant'Ignazio ❷
Via della Gatta ❼

Historic Buildings
Palazzo del Collegio
Romano ❹
Palazzo Doria Pamphilj ❻
Palazzo Altieri ❽
Palazzo Baldassini ⓱
Palazzo Borghese ⓳
Palazzo di Montecitorio ㉑
Palazzo Capranica ㉔

Columns, Obelisks and Statues
Pie' di Marmo ❿
Obelisk of Santa Maria
sopra Minerva ⓬
Obelisk of Montecitorio ㉒
Column of Marcus Aurelius ㉓

Fountains
Fontanella del Facchino ❺

Cafés and Restaurants
Caffè Giolitti ⓰

KEY
▨ Street-by-Street map
Ⓟ Parking

GETTING THERE
The area has no Metro station, but is about 15 minutes' walk from Spagna or Barberini Metro stops. There are some convenient bus stops in Via del Plebiscito, served by the 56, 64, 70, 90, 492 and many other routes. Piazza Colonna is served by the 56, 60, 85 and all buses that go up Via del Corso. The only bus that passes through the narrow streets of the area is the 119 electric minibus, which stops right outside the Pantheon.

| 0 metres | 200 |
| 0 yards | 200 |

SEE ALSO

The immense granite columns of the Pantheon

Street-by-Street: Piazza della Rotonda

IF YOU WANDER THROUGH this area, sooner or later you will
emerge into Piazza della Rotonda with its jumble of
open-air café tables in front of the Pantheon. The refreshing
splash of the fountain makes it a welcome resting place. In
this warren of narrow streets, it can be hard to realize just how
close you are to some of Rome's finest
sights. The magnificent art collection of
Palazzo Doria Pamphilj and the Baroque
splendour of the Gesù are just a few
minutes' walk from the Pantheon. At night
there is always a lively buzz of activity, as
people dine in style or enjoy
the coffee and ice creams for
which the area is famous.

Temple of Hadrian
*The columns of this
Roman temple now
form the façade of the
stock exchange* ❶

**Piazza di
Sant'Ignazio**
*The square is a
rare example of
stylish domestic
architecture
from the early
18th century* ❷

La Tazza d'Oro enjoys a
reputation for the wonderful
coffee consumed on its
premises as well as for
its freshly-ground coffee
to take away. *(See p319.)*

**Santa Maria
sopra Minerva**
*The rich decoration
of Rome's only Gothic
church was added in
the 19th century* ⓫

★ **Pantheon**
*The awe-inspiring interior of
Rome's best-preserved ancient
temple is only hinted at
from the outside* ⓭

**Obelisk of Santa Maria
sopra Minerva**
*In 1667 Bernini dreamed up
the idea of mounting a recently
discovered obelisk on the back
of a marble elephant* ⓬

LOCATOR MAP
See Central Rome Map pp12–13

★ **Sant'Ignazio di Loyola**
Andrea Pozzo painted this glorious Baroque ceiling (1685) to celebrate St Ignatius and the Jesuit order ❸

Fontanella del Facchino
The water in this small 16th-century fountain spurts from a barrel held by a porter ❺

Palazzo del Collegio Romano
Up until 1870, the college educated many leading figures in the Catholic Church ❹

★ **Palazzo Doria Pamphilj**
Among the masterpieces in the art gallery of this magnificent family palazzo is this portrait of Pope Innocent X by Velázquez (1650) ❻

Via della Gatta
The street is named after the statue of a cat ❼

Palazzo Altieri
This enormous 17th-century palazzo is decorated with the arms of Pope Clement X ❽

★ **Gesù**
The design of the first-ever Jesuit church had a great impact on religious architecture ❾

PIAZZA DEL COLLEGIO ROMANO

VIA DELLA GATTA

VIA DEL PLEBISCITO

GESÙ

KEY

– – – Suggested route

STAR SIGHTS

★ Pantheon

★ Palazzo Doria Pamphilj

★ Gesù

★ Sant'Ignazio di Loyola

Pie' di Marmo
This marble foot is a stray fragment from a gigantic Roman statue ❿

| 0 metres | 75 |
| 0 yards | 75 |

Temple of Hadrian ❶

La Borsa, Piazza di Pietra. **Map** 4 F3 &
12 E2. 🚌 *56, 60, 71, 81, 85, 90,
119, 492.* **Not open** to the public.

THIS TEMPLE, built to honour
the Emperor Hadrian as a
god, was dedicated by his
successor Antoninus Pius in
AD 145. The remains of
the temple are visible on the
southern side of Piazza di
Pietra, incorporated in a
17th-century building. This
was originally a papal customs
house, completed by Carlo
Fontana and his son in the
1690s. Today the building
houses the Roman stock
exchange (La Borsa).

Eleven marble Corinthian
columns 15 m (49 ft) high
stand on a base of *peperino*,
a volcanic rock quarried from
the Alban hills to the south of
Rome. The columns
decorated the northern flank
of the temple enclosing its
inner shrine, the *cella*. The
peperino wall of the *cella* is
still visible behind the columns,
as is part of the coffered
portico ceiling.

A number of reliefs from
the temple, representing
conquered Roman provinces,
are now in the courtyard of
the Palazzo dei Conservatori
(see pp72–3). They reflect the
mostly peaceful foreign policy
of Hadrian's reign.

Remains of Hadrian's Temple

Piazza di Sant'Ignazio ❷

Map 4 F4 & 12 E3. 🚌 *56, 60, 71,
81, 85, 90, 119, 492.*

ONE OF THE MAJOR works of
the Roman Rococo, the
piazza (1727–8) is Filippo
Raguzzini's masterpiece. It
offsets the imposing facade of
the church of Sant'Ignazio
with the intimacy of the

Illusionistic ceiling in the crossing of Sant'Ignazio

houses of the bourgeoisie. The
theatrical setting, the curvilinear
design and the playful forms
of its windows, balconies and
balusters mark the piazza as
one of a highly distinctive
group of structures. Along
with Palazzo Doria Pamphilj
(1731), the facade of La
Maddalena (1735) and the
aristocratic Spanish Steps
(1723), it belongs to that happy
moment when Rome's bubbly
Rococo triumphed over
conservative Classicism.

Sant'Ignazio di Loyola ❸

Piazza di Sant'Ignazio. **Map** 4 F4 &
12 E3. 📞 *679 44 06.* 🚌 *56, 60, 71,
81, 85, 90, 119, 492.* **Open** *7.30am–
12.30pm, 4pm–7.15pm daily.* 📷 ✝

THE CHURCH was built by
Cardinal Ludovisi in 1626
in honour of St Ignatius of
Loyola, founder of the Society
of Jesus and the man who
most embodied the zeal of
the Counter Reformation.

Together with the Gesù *(see
pp114–15),* Sant'Ignazio forms
the nucleus of the Jesuit area
in Rome. Its vast interior, lined
with precious stones, marble,
stucco and gilt, creates a
thrilling sense of theatre. The
church has a Latin-cross plan,
with an apse and many side
chapels. A cupola was planned

but never built, so the space
it would have filled was
covered by a fake perspective
painting. The piers built to
bear the weight of the cupola
help support the observatory
of the Collegio Romano.

Palazzo del Collegio Romano ❹

Piazza del Collegio Romano. **Map** 5 A4
& 12 E3. 🚌 *56, 60, 62, 85, 90, 95,
160, 492.* **Not open** to the public.

SHARING THE SAME BLOCK as
the church of Sant'Ignazio,
the palazzo used to house a
college run by the Jesuits;
many future bishops, cardinals
and popes studied here. The
college was confiscated in
1870 and was turned into an
ordinary school. The portals
bear the coat of arms of its
founder, Pope Gregory XIII
Boncompagni (reigned
1572–85). The facade is also
decorated with a bell, two
sundials and a clock. On the
right is a tower
built in 1787 as
an observatory.
Up until 1925 its
time signal
regulated all the
clocks throughout
the city.

**Portal of the
Collegio Romano**

Fontanella del Facchino 🟤

Via Lata. **Map** 5 A4 & 12 E3. 🚌 *56, 60, 62, 85, 90, 95, 160, 492.*

IL FACCHINO (the Porter), once in the Corso, now set into the wall of the Banco di Roma, was one of Rome's "talking statues" like Pasquino *(see p124)*. Created around 1590, the fountain may have been based on a drawing by Florentine painter Jacopino del Conte. The statue of a man holding a barrel probably represents a member of the Università degli Acquaroli (Fraternity of Watercarriers), though it is also claimed to be of Martin Luther, or of Abbondio Rizzio, a porter who died carrying a barrel.

The Facchino drinking fountain

Palazzo Doria Pamphilj 🟤

Piazza del Collegio Romano 1A. **Map** 5 A4 & 12 E3. 📞 *679 43 65*. 🚌 *56, 60, 62, 85, 90, 95, 160, 492.* **Open** *10am–1pm Tue, Fri, Sat & Sun.* **Closed** *public hols.* **Adm charge.** 🦽 🎧 *compulsory for private apartments; notify attendant if you want tour.* 📷

PALAZZO DORIA PAMPHILJ is a great island of stone in the heart of Rome, the oldest parts dating from 1435. Through the Corso entrance you can glimpse the 16th-century porticoed courtyard with the coat of arms of the della Rovere family. The next owners were the Aldobrandini family. Between 1601 and 1647 the mansion acquired a second courtyard and flanking wings at the expense of a public bath that stood nearby.

When the Pamphilj family took over, they completed the Piazza del Collegio Romano facade and the Via della Gatta

wing, a splendid chapel and a theatre inaugurated by Queen Christina of Sweden in 1684.

In the first half of the 18th century, Gabriele Valvassori created the gallery above the courtyard and a new facade along the Corso, using the highly decorative style of the period known as the *barocchetto*, which now dominates the building. The stairways and salons, the Mirror Gallery and the picture gallery all radiate a joyous sense of light and space.

The family collection in the Doria Pamphilj gallery has over 400 paintings dating from the 15th to the 18th century, including the famous portrait of Pope Innocent X Pamphilj by Velázquez. There are also important works by Titian, Caravaggio, Lorenzo Lotto, Guercino and Claude Lorrain. The rooms in the private apartment have many of their original furnishings on display, including splendid Brussels and Gobelins tapestries.

Via della Gatta 🟤

Map 5 A4 & 12 E3. 🚌 *56, 60, 62, 85, 90, 95, 160, 492.*

THIS NARROW STREET runs between the great Palazzo Doria Pamphilj and the smaller Palazzo Grazioli. The ancient marble sculpture of a

cat *(gatta)* that gives the street its name can be seen on the first cornice on the corner of Palazzo Grazioli.

Via della Gatta's marble cat

Palazzo Altieri 🟤

Via del Gesù 93. **Map** 4 F4 & 12 E3. 🚌 *56, 64, 70, 81, 90 and many other routes. See* **Shops** *p333.*

THE ALTIERI FAMILY is first mentioned in Rome's history in the 9th century. This palazzo was built by the last male heirs, the brothers Cardinal Giambattista di Lorenzo Altieri and Cardinal Emilio Altieri, later Pope Clement X (reigned 1670–76). Many surrounding houses had to be demolished, but an old woman called Berta refused to leave, so her hovel was incorporated in the palazzo. Its windows are still visible on the west end of the building. Most of Palazzo Altieri is now occupied by the enormous material and clothing business, Bises.

Gesù 🟤

See pp114–15.

Caravaggio's *Rest during the Flight into Egypt* in Palazzo Doria Pamphilj

Marble foot from a Roman statue

Pie' di Marmo ⑩

Via di Santo Stefano del Cacco.
Map 4 F4 & 12 E3. 56, 64, 70,
81, 90, 90b, 119.

IT WAS POPULARLY believed in
the Middle Ages that half
the population of ancient
Rome must have been made
up of bronze, golden and
marble statues. Fragments of
these giants, usually gods or
emperors, are scattered over
the city. This piece, a marble
foot *(pie' di marmo)*, comes
from an area dedicated to the
Egyptian gods Isis and Serapis
and was probably part of a
statue in one of the temples.
These statues were painted
and covered with jewels and
clothes given by the faithful –
a great fire hazard with
unattended burning tapers.

Santa Maria sopra Minerva ⑪

Piazza della Minerva 42. **Map** 4 F4 &
12 E3. 67 92 80. 56, 64, 70,
81, 90, 119. **Open** 7am–noon, 4pm–
7pm daily. **Cloister open** 8am–1pm,
3.30pm–7.30pm daily.
Concerts.

FEW OTHER CHURCHES can
display such a complete
and impressive record of
Italian art. Dating from the
13th century, the Minerva is
one of the very few examples
of Gothic architecture in
Rome. It was the traditional
stronghold of the Dominicans,
whose anti-heretical zeal
earned them the punning
nickname of *Domini Canes*
(the hounds of the Lord).
   Built on ancient ruins,
supposed to have been the
Temple of Minerva, the
simple T-shaped vaulted
building acquired rich chapels
and works of art by which its

many patrons wished to be
remembered. Note the
Cosmatesque 13th-century
tombs and the exquisite
works of 15th-century Tuscan
and Venetian artists. Native
Roman talent of the period
can be admired in Antoniazzo
Romano's *Annunciation*,
featuring Cardinal Juan de
Torquemada, uncle of the
infamous Spanish Inquisitor.
   The more monumental style
of the Roman Renaissance is
well represented in the tombs
of the 16th-century Medici
popes, Leo X and his cousin
Clement VII, and in the richly
decorated Aldobrandini
Chapel. Near the steps of
the choir is the celebrated
sculpture of the *Risen Christ*,
started by Michelangelo but
completed by Raffaele da
Montelupo in 1521.
   There are also splendid
works of art from the
Baroque period, including
a tomb and a bust by
Bernini. The church is
visited not only for its
art, but also because it
contains the tombs of
many famous Italians:
St Catherine of Siena,
who died here in 1380;
the Venetian sculptor
Andrea Bregno (died
1506); the Humanist
Cardinal Pietro Bembo
(died 1547); and Fra
Angelico, the Dominican
friar and painter, who
died in Rome in 1455.

Obelisk of Santa Maria sopra Minerva ⑫

Piazza della Minerva. **Map** 4 F4 &
12 D3. 56, 64, 70, 81, 90, 119.

ORIGINALLY MEANT to decorate
Palazzo Barberini as a kind
of joke, this exotic elephant
and obelisk sculpture is typical
of Bernini's inexhaustible
imagination. (The elephant
was actually sculpted by Ercole
Ferrata to Bernini's design.)
The old obelisk was found
in the garden of the
monastery of Santa Maria
sopra Minerva, and the friars
wanted the monument
erected in their piazza. The
elephant was provided with
its enormous saddle-cloth
because of a friar's
insistence that the gap
under the animal's
abdomen would
undermine its stability.
Bernini knew better: you
need only look at
the Fontana dei
Fiumi *(see p120)*
in Piazza Navona
to appreciate his
use of empty space.
The elephant, an
ancient symbol of
intelligence and piety,
was chosen as the
embodiment of the
Bernini's Egyptian   virtues on which
obelisk and   Christians should
marble elephant   build true wisdom.

Nave of Santa Maria sopra Minerva

Pantheon ⑬

See pp110–11.

Sant'Eustachio ⑭

Piazza Sant'Eustachio. **Map** 4 F4 & 12 D3. **📞** 686 53 34. **🚌** 70, 81, 87, 90, 90b, 119, 186, 492. **Open** 4pm–7.30pm daily. **✝** **📷**

THE ORIGINS of this church go back to early Christian times, when it was a centre for offering succour to the poor. In medieval times many charitable brotherhoods elected Sant' Eustachio as their patron and had chapels in the church.

The dumpy Romanesque bell tower is one of the few surviving parts of the medieval church, which was totally redecorated in the 17th and 18th centuries.

Bell tower of Sant'Eustachio

La Maddalena ⑮

Piazza della Maddalena. **Map** 4 F3 & 12 D2. **📞** 679 77 96. **🚌** 70, 81, 87, 90, 90b, 186, 492. **Open** 7.30am– 7pm daily. **✝** **📷**

SITUATED IN a small piazza near the Pantheon, the Maddalena's Rococo facade, built in 1735, epitomizes the love of light and movement of the late Baroque. Its curves are reminiscent of Borromini's San Carlo alle Quattro Fontane *(see p161)*. The facade has been lovingly restored, despite the protests of diehard Neo-Classicists who dismiss its painted stucco as icing sugar.

The small size of the Maddalena did not deter the 17th- and 18th-century

The old-fashioned *salone* of the Caffè Giolitti

decorators who filled the interior with ornament from the floor to the top of the elegant cupola. The organ loft and choir are particularly powerful examples of the Baroque's desire to fire the imagination of the faithful.

Many of the paintings and sculptures employ the new Christian imagery of the Counter Reformation. In the niches of the nave, for example, the statues are personifications of virtues such as Humility and Simplicity. There are also scenes from the life of San Camillo, who died in the adjacent convent in 1614. The church belonged to his followers, the Camillians, a preaching order active in Rome's hospitals. Like the Jesuits, they commissioned powerful works of art to convey the force of their religious message.

La Maddalena's stuccoed facade

Caffè Giolitti ⑯

Via degli Uffici del Vicario 40. **Map** 4 F3 & 12 D2. **📞** 679 42 06. **🚌** 56, 60, 90, 119, 492. **Open** 7am–1.30am Tue–Sun.

FOUNDED IN 1900, the Caffè Giolitti is the heir to the glittering *Belle Epoque* cafés that lined the nearby Corso in Rome's first days as capital of the new Italian state. Its spacious *salone* accommodates tourists in summer, Roman families at weekends, and on weekdays a varied crowd of office workers, construction workers and officials from the nearby parliament in Palazzo di Montecitorio.

Palazzo Baldassini ⑰

Via delle Coppelle 35. **Map** 4 F3 & 12 D2. **🚌** 70, 81, 90, 90b, 119. **Not open** to the public.

MELCHIORRE BALDASSINI built his home in the style of the Florentine Renaissance, skilfully adapted to the more austere surroundings of Rome. With its cornices marking the different floors and wrought-iron window grilles, this is one of the best examples of a Roman palazzo of the early 16th century. It stands in the part of Rome still known as the Renaissance Quarter, which grew up around the long straight streets such as Via di Ripetta and Via della Scrofa built at the time of Pope Leo X (reigned 1513–21).

Pantheon ⑬

IN THE MIDDLE AGES the Pantheon, the Roman "temple of all the gods", became a church; in time this magnificent building with its awe-inspiring domed interior became a symbol of Rome itself. The rectangular portico screens the vast hemispherical dome: only from inside can its true scale and beauty be appreciated. The rotunda's height and diameter are equal: 43.3 m (140 ft). The hole at the top of the dome, the *oculus*, provides the only light. We owe this marvel of Roman engineering to the Emperor Hadrian (AD 118–125), who designed it to replace an earlier temple built by Marcus Agrippa, son-in-law of Augustus. The shrines that now line the wall of the Pantheon range from the Tomb of Raphael to those of the kings of modern Italy.

★Interior of Dome
The dome was cast by pouring concrete mixed with tufa and pumice over a temporary wooden framework.

The walls of the drum supporting the dome are 6 m (19 ft) thick.

The portico, enclosed by granite columns

The immense portico is built on the foundations of Agrippa's temple.

STAR FEATURES

★ **Interior of Dome**

★ **Tomb of Raphael**

Bell Towers
This 18th-century view by Bernardo Bellotto shows Bernini's much-ridiculed turrets, which were removed in 1883.

Floor Patterning
The marble floor, restored in 1873, preserves the original Roman design.

RAPHAEL AND LA FORNARINA

Raphael, at his own request, was buried here when he died in 1520. He had lived for years with his model, La Fornarina (*see p210*), seen here in a painting by Giulio Romano, but she was excluded from the ceremony of his burial. On the right of his tomb is a memorial to his fiancée, Maria Bibbiena, niece of the artist's patron, Cardinal Dovizi di Bibbiena.

VISITORS' CHECKLIST

Piazza della Rotonda. **Map** 4 F4 & 12 D3. 68 30 02 30. 119 to Piazza della Rotonda; 64, 70, 75 & other routes to Largo di Torre Argentina. **Open** 9am–6pm (Oct–Mar: 5pm) Mon–Sat; Sun 9am–1pm. **Closed** 15 Aug, 25 & 26 Dec. Concerts.

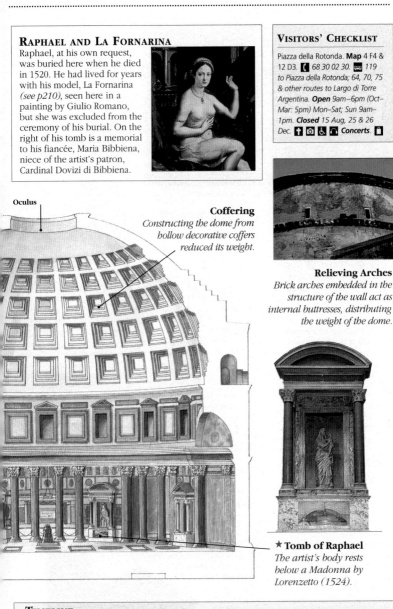

Oculus

Coffering
Constructing the dome from hollow decorative coffers reduced its weight.

Relieving Arches
Brick arches embedded in the structure of the wall act as internal buttresses, distributing the weight of the dome.

★ **Tomb of Raphael**
The artist's body rests below a Madonna by Lorenzetto (1524).

TIMELINE

27–25 BC Marcus Agrippa builds first Pantheon	*M·AGRIPPA* *Inscription on pediment*	**735** Gregory III roofs the Pantheon in lead	**1305–77** While papal seat is in Avignon, Pantheon is used as fortress and poultry market	**1888** Tomb of King Vittorio Emanuele II completed
30 BC	**AD 100**	**600**	**1100**	**1600**
AD 118 Hadrian builds new Pantheon	**609** Pope Boniface IV consecrates Pantheon as church of Santa Maria ad Martyres	**663** Byzantine Emperor Constans II strips gilded tiles from the roof	**1632** Urban VIII melts down bronze from portico for Bernini's baldacchino in St Peter's	

Bernini's curving southern facade of Palazzo di Montecitorio

Santa Maria in Campo Marzio ⑱

Piazza in Campo Marzio 45. **Map** 4 F3 & 12 D2. **(** 678 70 21. 📟 56, 60, 90, 90b, 119, 492. **Open** 4.30pm–6.30pm daily. **Closed** Aug. 🕇 ⬚

AROUND the courtyard through which you enter the church, there are fascinating remnants of medieval houses, once the property of the original monastery. The church itself was rebuilt in 1685 by Antonio de Rossi, using a square Greek-cross plan with a cupola. Above the altar is a 12th-century painting of the Madonna, which gives the church its name.

Palazzo Borghese ⑲

Largo della Fontanella di Borghese. **Map** 4 F3 & 12 D1. 📟 70, 81, 90, 90b, 119. **Not open** to the public.

THE PALAZZO was acquired in about 1605 by Cardinal Camillo Borghese, just before he became Pope Paul V. Flaminio Ponzio was hired to enlarge the building and give it the grandeur appropriate to the residence of the pope's family. He added a wing overlooking Piazza Borghese and the delightful porticoed courtyard inside. Subsequent enlargements included the building and decoration of a great *nympheum* known as the Bath of Venus. For more than two centuries this palazzo housed the Borghese family's renowned collection of paintings, which was bought

by the Italian state in 1902 and transferred to the Villa Borghese *(see pp260–61).*

Pope Paul V, who commissioned Palazzo Borghese for his family

San Lorenzo in Lucina ⑳

Via in Lucina 16A. **Map** 4 F3 & 12 E1. **(** 687 14 94. 📟 70, 81, 90, 90b, 119. **Open** 8am–noon, 5pm–8pm daily. 🕇 ⬚

THE CHURCH is one of Rome's oldest Christian places of worship, and was probably built on a well sacred to Juno, protectress of women. It was rebuilt in the 12th century, and today's external appearance is typical of the period: a portico

with re-used Roman columns, crowned by medieval capitals, a plain triangular pediment and a Romanesque bell tower with coloured marble inlay.

In contrast, the interior of the church was totally rebuilt in the 17th century. The old basilical plan was destroyed and the two side naves were replaced by richly-decorated Baroque chapels. Don't miss the fine busts in the Fonseca Chapel, designed by Bernini, or the *Crucifixion* by Guido Reni above the main altar. There is also a 19th-century monument honouring French painter Nicolas Poussin, who died in Rome in 1655 and was buried in the church.

Palazzo di Montecitorio ㉑

Piazza di Montecitorio. **Map** 4 F3 & 12 E2. 📟 56, 60, 85, 90, 90b, 119, 492. **Not open** to the public.

THE PALAZZO's first architect, Bernini, got the job after he presented a silver model of his design to the wife of his patron, Prince Ludovisi. The building was completed in 1697 by Carlo Fontana and became the Papal Tribunal of Justice. In 1871 it was chosen to be Italy's new Chamber of Deputies and by 1918 it had doubled in size with a second grand facade. The 630 members of parliament are elected by a system of proportional representation that ensures that no single party ever gains an overall majority.

The church of San Lorenzo in Lucina

Emperor Augustus's obelisk

Obelisk of Montecitorio ㉒

Piazza di Montecitorio. **Map** 4 F3 & 12 E2. 🚌 56, 60, 85, 90, 119, 492.

THE MEASUREMENT of time in ancient Rome was always a rather hit-and-miss affair: for many years the Romans relied on an imported (and therefore inaccurate) sundial, a trophy from the conquest of Sicily. In 10 BC the Emperor Augustus laid out an enormous sundial in the Campus Martius. Its centre was roughly in today's Piazza di San Lorenzo in Lucina. The shadow was cast by an enormous granite obelisk that he had brought back from Heliopolis in Egypt. Unfortunately this sundial too became inaccurate after only 50 years, possibly as a result of subsidence.

The obelisk was still in the piazza in the 9th century, but then disappeared until it was rediscovered lying under medieval houses in the reign of Pope Julius II (1503–13). The pope was intrigued, because Egyptian hieroglyphs were thought to hold the key to the wisdom of Adam before the Fall, but it was only under Pope Benedict XIV (reigned 1740–58) that the obelisk was finally unearthed. It was erected in its present location in 1787 by Pope Pius VI.

Column of Marcus Aurelius ㉓

Piazza Colonna. **Map** 5 A3 & 12 E2. 🚌 56, 60, 85, 90, 90b, 119, 492.

CLEARLY AN IMITATION of the Column of Trajan (see p90), this monument was erected after the death of Marcus Aurelius in AD 180 to commemorate his victories over the barbarian tribes of the Danube. The 80-year lapse between the two works produced a great artistic change: the wars of Marcus Aurelius are rendered with simplified pictures in stronger relief, sacrificing Classical proportions for the sake of clarity and immediacy. The spirit of the work is more akin to the 4th-century Arch of Constantine (see p91) than to Trajan's monument. Gone are the heroic qualities of the Roman soldiers, by now mostly barbarian mercenaries, and a sense of respect for the vanquished. A new emphasis on the supernatural points to the end of the Hellenistic tradition and the beginning of the Christian culture.

Composed of 28 drums of marble, the column was restored in 1588 by Domenico Fontana on the orders of Pope Sixtus V. The emperor's statue on the summit was replaced by a bronze of St Paul. The 20 spirals of the low relief chronicle the German war of AD 171–3, and (above) the Sarmatic war of AD 174–5. The column is almost 30 m (100 ft) high and 3.7 m (12 ft) in diameter. An internal spiral staircase leads to the top. The easiest way to appreciate the sculptural work, however, is to visit the Museo della Civiltà Romana at EUR (see p267) and study the casts of the reliefs.

Palazzo Capranica ㉔

Piazza Capranica. **Map** 4 F3 & 12 D2. 🚌 56, 60, 85, 90, 90b, 119, 492.

Windows of Palazzo Capranica

ONE OF ROME'S small number of surviving 15th-century buildings, the palazzo was commissioned by Cardinal Domenico Capranica both as his family residence and as a college for higher education. Its fortress-like appearance is a patchwork of subsequent additions, not unusual in the late 15th century, when Rome was still hovering between medieval and Renaissance taste. The Gothic-looking windows on the right of the building show the cardinal's coat of arms and the date 1451 is inscribed on the doorway underneath. The palazzo is now a shell housing a popular cinema.

Relief of the emperor's campaigns on the Column of Marcus Aurelius

Gesù 🟒

DATING FROM BETWEEN 1568 and 1584, the Gesù was the first Jesuit church to be built in Rome. Its design epitomizes Counter Reformation Baroque architecture and has been much imitated throughout the Catholic world. The layout proclaims the church's two major functions: a large nave with side pulpits for preaching to great crowds, and a main altar as the centrepiece for the celebration of the mass. The illusionistic decoration in the nave and dome was added a century later. Its message is clear and confident: faithful, Catholic worshippers will be joyfully uplifted into the heavens while Protestants and other heretics are flung into hell's fires.

★ Chapel of Sant'Ignazio
Above its altar is a statue of the saint, framed by gilded lapis lazuli columns. The chapel was built in 1696–1700 by Andrea Pozzo, a Jesuit artist.

Triumph of Faith Over Heresy
This vivid Baroque allegory sculpted by Théudon illustrates the great ambition of Jesuit theology.

ST IGNATIUS AND THE JESUIT ORDER

Spanish soldier Ignatius Loyola (1491–1556) joined the Church after being wounded in battle in 1521. He came to Rome in 1537 and founded the Jesuits, sending missionaries and teachers all over the world to win souls for Catholicism.

Main entrance

STAR FEATURES

★ **Nave Ceiling Decorations**

★ **Chapel of Sant'Ignazio**

★ **San Roberto Bellarmino**

Allegorical Figures
Antonio Raggi made these stuccoes, which were designed by Il Baciccia to complement the figures on his own nave frescoes.

Madonna della Strada
This 15th-century image, called the Madonna of the Road, was originally displayed on the outer facade of a nearby church of the same name.

★ San Roberto Bellarmino
Bernini captured the forceful personality of this anti-Protestant theologian, who died in 1621.

The Chapel of St Francis Xavier is a memorial to the great missionary who died alone on an island off China in 1552.

★ Nave Ceiling Decorations
The figures in Il Baciccia's astonishing fresco of the Triumph of the Name of Jesus *spill out on to the coffered vaulting of the nave.*

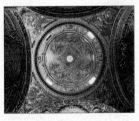

Cupola Frescoes
The cupola was completed by della Porta to Vignola's design. The frescoes, by Il Baciccia, feature Old Testament figures.

TIMELINE

	1500	1600	1700
	1540 Founding of the Society of Jesus (the Jesuits)	**1571** Giacomo della Porta's design chosen for the facade	**1696–1700** The Chapel of Sant' Ignazio is designed by Andrea Pozzo, a Jesuit artist	**1773** Pope Clement XIV orders the suppression of the Jesuit order
		1584 Church's consecration		
1545–63 Council of Trent defines the new Catholic orthodoxy		**1568–71** Vignola builds the church up to the crossing under the patronage of Cardinal Alessandro Farnese	**1670–83** Giovanni Battista Gaulli (Il Baciccia) paints the nave vault, dome and apse	
1556 Death of Ignatius		**1622** Ignatius Loyola is canonized		

PIAZZA NAVONA

Lion on Fontana dei Fiumi

HE FOUNDATIONS of the buildings surrounding the elongated oval of Piazza Navona were the ruined grandstands of the vast Stadium of Diocletian. The piazza today still provides a dramatic spectacle with the obelisk of the Fontana dei Fiumi in front of the church of Sant' Agnese in Agone as its focal point.

The predominant style of the area is Baroque, many of its finest buildings dating from the reign of Innocent X Pamphilj (1644–55), patron of Bernini and Borromini. Of special interest is the complex of the Chiesa Nuova, headquarters of the Filippini, the order founded by San Filippo Neri, the 16th-century "Apostle of Rome".

SIGHTS AT A GLANCE

Churches and Temples
Sant'Agnese in Agone ④
Santa Maria dell'Anima ⑤
Santa Maria della Pace ⑥
San Luigi dei Francesi ⑦
Sant'Ivo alla Sapienza ⑨
Sant'Andrea della Valle ⑩
Chiesa Nuova ⑮
Oratorio dei Filippini ⑯
San Salvatore in Lauro ㉑
Sant'Apollinare ㉕

Museums
Palazzo Braschi ⑫
Museo Napoleonico ㉒

Historic Buildings
Palazzo Pamphilj ③
Palazzo Madama ⑧
Palazzo Massimo alle Colonne ⑪
Torre dell'Orologio ⑰
Palazzo del Banco di Santo Spirito ⑱
Palazzo Gaddi ⑲
Palazzo Altemps ㉓

Fountains and Statues
Fontana dei Fiumi ①
Pasquino ⑬

Historic Streets and Piazzas
Piazza Navona ②
Via del Governo Vecchio ⑭
Via dei Coronari ⑳

Restaurants
Hostaria dell'Orso ㉔

SEE ALSO

GETTING THERE
This central area is within walking distance of many parts of the city. Much of the area itself is closed to traffic, but it is easily reached by bus. The principal routes along Corso Vittorio Emanuele II are the 64 from Termini station to St Peter's and the 46. Corso del Rinascimento, which runs parallel to Piazza Navona, is served by several useful routes, including the 70, 81, 90 and 492.

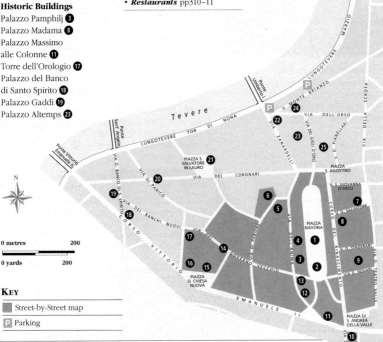

KEY

◼ Street-by-Street map

Ⓟ Parking

Piazza Navona, with the Fontana del Moro and church of Sant'Agnese in Agone

Street-by-Street: Piazza Navona

NO OTHER PIAZZA in Rome can rival the theatricality of Piazza Navona. Day and night there is always something going on in the pedestrian area around its three flamboyant fountains. The Baroque is also represented in many of the area's churches. To discover an older Rome, walk along Via del Governo Vecchio to admire the facades of its Renaissance buildings and browse in the fascinating antiques shops.

Oratorio dei Filippini
The musical term oratorio comes from this place of informal worship **16**

Torre dell' Orologio
This clock tower by Borromini (1648) is part of the Convent of the Filippini **17**

Chiesa Nuova
This church was rebuilt in the late 16th century for the order founded by San Filippo Neri **15**

To Corso Vittorio Emanuele II

Via del Governo Vecchio
This street preserves a large number of fine Renaissance houses **14**

Santa Maria della Pace
The medallion shows Pope Alexander VII, who had the church restored by Pietro da Cortona in 1656 **6**

Pasquino
Romans hung satirical verses and dialogues on this weatherbeaten statue **13**

Palazzo Pamphilj
This grand town house was built for Pope Innocent X and his family in the mid-17th century **3**

Palazzo Braschi
A late 18th-century building with a splendid balcony, the palazzo houses the Museo di Roma **12**

Palazzo Massimo alle Colonne
The magnificent curving colonnade (1536) is by Baldassarre Peruzzi **11**

STAR SIGHTS

★ **Sant'Andrea della Valle**

★ **San Luigi dei Francesi**

★ **Piazza Navona**

KEY

— — — Suggested route

| 0 metres | 75 |
| 0 yards | 75 |

Sant'Agnese in Agone
Borromini's startling concave facade (1657) dominates one side of Piazza Navona ❹

Santa Maria dell'Anima
For four centuries this has been the German church in Rome ❺

Palazzo Madama
A spread-eagled stone lionskin decorates the central doorway of the palazzo, now the Italian Senate ❽

LOCATOR MAP
See Central Rome Map pp12–13

Fontana dei Fiumi
Bernini designed this fountain supporting an obelisk ❶

★ **San Luigi dei Francesi**
An 18th-century statue of St Louis stands in a niche in the facade ❼

★ **Piazza Navona**
This unique piazza owes its shape to a Roman race track and its stunning decor to the genius of the Roman Baroque ❷

The Fontana del Moro was remodelled in 1653 by Bernini, who designed the central sea god.

Sant'Ivo alla Sapienza
This tiny domed church is one of Borromini's most original creations. He worked on it between 1642 and 1660 ❾

★ **Sant'Andrea della Valle**
The church, with its grandiose facade by Carlo Rainaldi (1665), has gained fame outside Rome as the setting of the first act of Puccini's Tosca ❿

To Campo de' Fiori

Fontana dei Fiumi ❶

Piazza Navona. **Map** 4 E4 & 11 C3.
🚌 70, 81, 87, 90, 90b, 186, 492.

BUILT FOR POPE Innocent X Pamphilj, this magnificent fountain in the centre of Piazza Navona was unveiled in 1651. The pope's coat of arms, the dove and the olive branch, decorate the bold pyramid rock formation supporting the Egyptian obelisk, which once stood in the Circus of Maxentius on the Appian Way. Bernini designed the fountain, which was paid for by means of highly unpopular taxes on bread and other staples. The great rivers then known – the Ganges, the Danube, the Nile and the River Plate – are represented by four giants.

The Nile's veiled head symbolizes the river's unknown source, but there is also a legend that the veil conveys Bernini's dislike for the nearby Sant'Agnese in Agone, designed by his rival Borromini. Similarly, the

View of Palazzo Pamphilj across Piazza Navona

athletic figure of the River Plate, cringing with arm upraised, is supposed to express Bernini's fear that the church will collapse. Sadly these widely-believed stories can have no basis in fact: Bernini had completed the fountain before Borromini started work on the church.

Piazza Navona ❷

Map 4 E3 & 11 C2. 🚌 46, 62, 64, 70, 81, 87, 90, 90b, 186, 492.

ROME'S MOST beautiful Baroque piazza follows the shape of Domitian's Stadium, which once stood on this site – some of its arches are still visible below the church of Sant'Agnese in Agone. The *agones* were athletic contests held in the 1st-century stadium, which could seat 33,000. The word "Navona" is thought to be a corruption of *in agone*. The piazza's unique appearance and atmosphere were created in the 17th century with the addition of the Fontana dei Fiumi. The other

fountains, the Fontana di Nettuno and the Fontana del Moro, date from the previous century but have been altered several times since. The figure known as Il Moro is a late work by Bernini.

Up until the 19th century, Piazza Navona was flooded during August by stopping the fountain outlets. The rich would splash around in carriages, while street urchins paddled after them. Today the piazza is a favourite in all seasons, especially in winter when it fills with colourful stalls selling toys and sweets for the feast of the Befana.

Palazzo Pamphilj ❸

Piazza Navona. **Map** 4 E4 & 11 C3.
🚌 46, 62, 64, 70, 81, 87, 90, 90b, 186, 492. **Not open** to the public.

Family dove and olive branch on facade of Palazzo Pamphilj

IN 1644 Giovanni Battista Pamphilj became pope, assuming the name of Innocent X. During his 10-year reign, he heaped riches on his own family, especially his domineering sister-in-law, Olimpia Maidalchini. The "talking statue" Pasquino *(see p124)* gave her the nickname "Olim-Pia", Latin for "formerly virtuous". She lived in the grand Palazzo Pamphilj, which has frescoes by Pietro da Cortona and a gallery by Borromini. The building is now the Brazilian embassy.

Symbolic figure of the River Ganges in Bernini's Fontana dei Fiumi

Sant'Agnese in Agone ❹

Piazza Navona. **Map** 4 E4 & 11 C3.
📞 679 44 35. 🚌 70, 81, 87, 90,
90b, 186, 492. **Open** 5pm–6.30pm
Mon–Sat, 10am–1pm Sun & public
hols. 🚻 📷 ♿

THE CHURCH IS believed to have been founded on the site of the brothel where, in AD 304, the young St Agnes was exposed naked to force her to renounce her faith. A marble relief in the crypt shows the miraculous growth of her hair, which fell around her body to protect her modesty. She was martyred on this site and is buried in the catacombs that bear her name along the Via Nomentana *(see p264).*

Today's church was commissioned by Pope Innocent X in 1652. The first architects were father and son, Girolamo and Carlo Rainaldi, but they were replaced by Borromini who worked on the church from 1653 to 1657. He stuck more or less to the Rainaldi scheme except for the concave facade designed to emphasize the dome. A statue of St Agnes on the facade is said to be reassuring the Fontana dei Fiumi's statue of the River Plate that the church is stable.

Statue of St Agnes on facade of Sant' Agnese in Agone

Carlo Saraceni's *Miracle of St Benno and the Keys of Meissen Cathedral*

Santa Maria dell'Anima ❺

Via della Pace 20. **Map** 4 E4 & 11 C2.
📞 683 37 29. 🚌 70, 81, 87, 90, 90b,
186, 492. **Open** 7.30am–7pm Mon–
Sat (exc Jul & Aug 1–3pm), 8am–1pm,
3pm–7pm Sun. 🚻 📷 ♿

POPE ADRIAN VI (reigned 1522–3), son of a ship-builder from Utrecht, was the last non-Italian pope before John Paul II. He would have disapproved of his superb tomb by Baldassarre Peruzzi in Santa Maria dell'Anima. It stands to the right of Giulio Romano's damaged altarpiece and is redolent of the pagan Renaissance spirit the pope had so condemned during his brief, rather gloomy reign, when patronage of the arts ground to a halt. Santa Maria dell'Anima is the German church in Rome and some of its paintings, such as the *Miracle of St Benno* by Carlo Saraceni (1618), illustrate events connected with the history of Germany.

Santa Maria della Pace ❻

Vicolo del Arco della Pace 5. **Map**
4 E3 & 11 C2. 📞 686 11 56. 🚌 70,
81, 87, 90, 90b, 186, 492. **Closed** for
restoration. 🚻 📷 ♿ 2 steps.

A DRUNKEN SOLDIER allegedly pierced the breast of a painted Madonna on this site, causing it to bleed. Pope Sixtus IV della Rovere (reigned 1471–84) placated the Virgin by ordering Baccio Pontelli to build her a church if she would bring the war with Turkey to an end. Peace was restored and the church was named Santa Maria della Pace (St Mary of Peace).

The cloister was added by Bramante in 1504. As in his famous Tempietto *(see p219)* he scrupulously followed Classical rules of proportion to produce a thoroughly original result, achieving a monumental effect in a relatively small space.

Pietro da Cortona may have had Bramante's Tempietto in mind when he added the church's charming semi-circular portico in 1656. The interior, a short nave ending under an octagonal cupola, houses Raphael's famous frescoes of four *Sybils*, and four *Prophets* by his pupil Timoteo Viti, painted for the banker Agostino Chigi in 1514. Baldassarre Peruzzi also did some work in the church (fresco in the first chapel on the left), as did the architect Antonio da Sangallo the Younger, who designed the second chapel on the right.

San Luigi dei Francesi ❼

Via Santa Giovanna d'Arco.
Map 4 F4 & 12 D2. 683 38 18.
70, 81, 87, 90, 90b, 186, 492.
Open 8am–12.30pm, 3.30pm–7pm
daily. **Closed** Thu pm.

THE FRENCH national church
was founded in 1518, but
it took until 1589 to be
finished, with contributions
by Giacomo della Porta and
Domenico Fontana. Visitors
are drawn to the church by
the many well-known
Frenchmen buried here and
by the three Caravaggios in
the fifth chapel on the left,
dedicated to St Matthew.

Painted between 1597 and
1602, these were Caravaggio's
first great religious works: the
Calling of St Matthew, the
Martyrdom of St Matthew and
St Matthew and the Angel.
The first version of this last
painting was rejected because
of its vivid realism: never
before had a saint been
shown as a tired old man
with dirty feet, and
a second version
had to be
painted. All
three works
display very
disquieting
realism and
highly dramatic
use of light.

Caravaggio, whose paintings of St Matthew hang in San Luigi dei Francesi

**Shield linking symbols of France
and Rome on facade of San Luigi**

Palazzo Madama ❽

Corso del Rinascimento. **Map** 4 F4 &
12 D3. 70, 81, 87, 90, 90b, 186,
492. **Adm** by written appt only.

THIS 16TH-CENTURY palazzo
was built for the Medici
family, who had owned a bank
here in the previous century.
It was the residence of the
Medici cardinals, the cousins
Giovanni and Giuliano. Both
later became pope, Giovanni
as Leo X and Giuliano as
Clement VII. Caterina de'
Medici, Clement VII's niece,
also lived here before she was
married to Henry, son of King
Francis I of France in 1533.

The palazzo takes its name
from Madama Margherita of

Austria, illegitimate daughter
of Emperor Charles V, who
married Alessandro de' Medici
and, after his death, Ottavio
Farnese. This caused the
fabulous art collection of the
Florentine Medici family to be
broken up; part was inherited
by the Roman Farnese family.

The spectacular facade was
built in the 17th century by
Paolo Maruccelli. He gave it
an ornate cornice and
whimsical decorative details
on the roof. Since 1871 the
palazzo has been the seat of
the Senate, the upper house
of the Italian parliament.

Cornice of Palazzo Madama

Sant'Ivo alla Sapienza ❾

Corso del Rinascimento 40.
Map 4 F4 & 12 D3. 70, 81, 87,
90, 90b 186, 492. **Open** for mass
10am–noon Sun. **Closed** Jul,
Aug.

THE CHURCH'S lantern
is crowned with a
cross on top of a
dramatic twisted
spiral – a highly
distinctive landmark
from Rome's roof
terraces. Seen
from close by,
this Borromini
church is
even more   **Lantern and spire**
striking. No   **of Sant'Ivo**
other Baroque
church is quite like it. Based
on a ground design of
astonishing geometrical
complexity, the walls are a
breathtaking combination of
concave and convex surfaces.
The church stands in the
small courtyard of the Palazzo
della Sapienza, seat of the old
University of Rome from the
15th century until 1935.

Sant'Andrea della Valle ❿

Piazza Sant'Andrea della Valle.
Map 4 E4 & 12 D4. 686 13 39.
46, 62, 64, 70, 81, 87, 90, 90b,
186, 492. **Open** 7.30am–noon,
4.30pm–7.30pm.

Dome of Sant'Andrea della Valle

The church is the scene of the first act of Puccini's opera *Tosca*, though opera fans will not find the Attavanti chapel, a poetic invention. The real church has much to recommend it – the recently restored facade shows the flamboyant Baroque style at its best. Inside, a golden light filters through high windows, showing off the gilded interior. Here lie the two popes of the Sienese Piccolomini family: on the left of the central nave is the tomb of Pius II, the first Humanist pope (reigned 1458–64); Pope Pius III lies opposite – he reigned for less than a month in 1503.

The church is famous for its beautiful dome, the largest in Rome after St Peter's. It was built by Carlo Maderno in 1622–5 and was painted with splendid frescoes by Domenichino and Giovanni Lanfranco. The latter's extravagant style, to be seen in the dome fresco *Glory of Paradise*, won him most of the commission, and the jealous Domenichino is said to have tried to kill his colleague. He failed, but Domenichino's jealousy was unnecessary, as shown by his two beautiful paintings of

scenes from the life of St Andrew around the apse and altar. In the Strozzi Chapel, built in the style of Michelangelo, the altar has copies of the *Leah* and *Rachel* by Michelangelo in San Pietro in Vincoli *(see p170)*.

Palazzo Massimo alle Colonne ⓫

Corso Vittorio Emanuele II 141.
Map 4 F4 & 11 C3. 46, 62, 64,
70, 81, 87, 90, 186, 492. **Open**
7am–1pm 16 Mar every year.

Roman column, Palazzo Massimo

During the last two years of his life, Baldassarre Peruzzi built this palazzo for the Massimo family, whose home had been destroyed in the Sack of Rome in 1527. Peruzzi displayed great ingenuity in dealing with an awkwardly shaped site. The previous building had stood on the ruined Theatre of Domitian, which created a curve in the great processional Via Papalis. Peruzzi's convex colonnaded facade follows the line of the street. His originality is also evident in the small square upper windows, the courtyard and the stuccoed vestibule. The Piazza de' Massimi entrance has a Renaissance-style, frescoed facade. A single column from the theatre has been set up in the piazza.

The Massimo family traced its origins to Quintus Fabius Maximus, conqueror of Hannibal in the 3rd

century BC, and their proud coat of arms is borne by an infant Hercules. Over the years the family produced many great Humanists, and in the 19th century, it was a Massimo who negotiated peace with Napoleon. On 16 March each year the palazzo opens to the public to commemorate young Paolo Massimo's resurrection from the dead by San Filippo Neri in 1538.

Palazzo Braschi ⓬

Piazza San Pantaleo 10. **Map** 4 E4 &
11 C3. 686 56 96. 46, 62, 64,
70, 81, 87, 90, 186, 492. **Museo di
Roma closed** for restoration.

On one side of Piazza San Pantaleo is the last Roman palazzo to be built for the family of a pope. Palazzo Braschi was built in the late 18th century for Pope Pius VI Braschi's nephews by the architect Cosimo Morelli. He gave the building its imposing facade which looks out on to the piazza.

The palazzo now houses the municipal Museo di Roma, at present being restored. It holds collections of pictures, drawings and everyday objects illustrating life in the city from medieval times until the last century.

Angel with raised wing by Ercole Ferrata, flanking the facade of Sant'Andrea della Valle

Pasquino ⑬

Piazza di Pasquino. **Map** 4 E4 & 11 C3. 🚌 *46, 62, 64, 70, 81, 87, 90, 186, 492.*

Pasquino, the most famous of Rome's satirical "talking statues"

THIS ROUGH CHUNK of marble is all that remains of a Hellenistic group, probably representing the incident in Homer's *Iliad* in which Menelaus shields the body of the slain Patroclus. For years it lay as a stepping stone in a muddy medieval street until it was erected on this corner in 1501, near the shop of an outspoken cobbler named Pasquino. Freedom of speech was not encouraged in papal Rome, so the cobbler wrote out his satirical comments on current events and attached them to the statue.

Other Romans were quick to follow suit, hanging their maxims and verses on the statue by night to escape punishment. Despite the wrath of the authorities, the sayings of the "talking statue" (renamed Pasquino) were part of popular culture right up until the 19th century. Other statues started to "talk" in the same satirical vein; Pasquino used to conduct dialogues with another statue known as Marforio that stood in Via del Campidoglio and is now in the courtyard of Palazzo Nuovo *(see pp70–71)*. Rome's only English-language cinema, which is in Trastevere, is called the Pasquino *(see p347)*.

Via del Governo Vecchio ⑭

Map 4 E4 & 11 B3. 🚌 *46, 62, 64.*

THE STREET TAKES its name from Palazzo del Governo Vecchio, the seat of papal government in the 17th and 18th centuries. Once part of the Via Papalis, which led from the Lateran to St Peter's, the street is lined with 15th- and 16th-century houses and small workshops. Particularly interesting are the 15th-century houses at No. 104 and No. 106. The small palazzo at No. 123 was once thought to have been the home of Bramante. Opposite is Palazzo del Governo Vecchio. It is also known as Palazzo Nardini, from the name of its founder, which is inscribed on the first-floor windows along with the date 1477.

Via del Governo Vecchio

Chiesa Nuova ⑮

Piazza della Chiesa Nuova. **Map** 4 E4 & 11 B3. 📞 *687 52 89.* 🚌 *46, 62, 64.* **Open** *8am–noon, 4.30pm–7pm daily.* ✝ 📷

Facade of the Chiesa Nuova

SAN FILIPPO NERI (St Philip Neri) is the most appealing of the Counter Reformation saints. A highly unconventional reformer, he required his noble Roman followers to humble themselves in public. He made aristocratic young men parade through the streets of Rome in rags or even with a fox's tail tied behind them, and set noblemen to work as labourers building his church. With the help of Pope Gregory XIII, his church was built in place of an old medieval church, Santa Maria in Vallicella, and it has been known ever since as the Chiesa Nuova (new church).

Begun in 1575 by Matteo da Città di Castello and continued by Martino Longhi the Elder, it was consecrated in 1599 (although the facade, by Fausto Rughesi, was only finished in 1606). Against San Filippo's wishes, the interior was decorated after his death; Pietro da Cortona frescoed the nave, dome and apse, taking nearly 20 years. There are also three paintings by Rubens: *Madonna and Angels* above the altar, *Saints Domitilla, Nereus and Achilleus* on the right of the altar, and *Saints Gregory, Maurus and Papias* on the left. San Filippo is buried in his own chapel, to the left of the altar.

Borromini's facade of the Oratorio

Oratorio dei Filippini ⑯

Piazza della Chiesa Nuova. **Map** 4 E4 & 11 B3. **(** 686 93 74. **᠁** 46, 62, 64. **Open** most mornings, but phone to check. **᠗ Concerts.**

WITH THE ADJOINING church and convent, the oratory formed the centre of Filippo Neri's religious order, founded in 1575. Its members are commonly known as Filippini. The musical term "oratorio" (a religious text sung by solo voices and chorus) derives from the services held here.

Filippo Neri came to Rome aged 18 to work as a tutor. The city was undergoing a period of religious strife and an economic slump after the Sack of Rome in 1527. There was also an outbreak of the plague. It was left to newcomers like Neri and Ignazio di Loyola to revive the spiritual life of the city.

Neri formed a brotherhood of laymen who worshipped together and helped pilgrims and the sick *(see Santissima Trinità dei Pellegrini p146)*. He founded the Oratory as a centre for religious discourse. Its conspicuous curving brick facade was built by Borromini in 1637–43.

Torre dell' Orologio ⑰

Piazza dell'Orologio. **Map** 4 E4 & 11 B3. **᠁** 46, 62, 64.

BORROMINI BUILT this clock tower to decorate one corner of the Convent of the Oratorians of San Filippo Neri in 1647–8. It is typical of Borromini in that the front and rear are concave and the sides convex. The mosaic of the Madonna beneath the clock is by Pietro da Cortona, while on the corner of the building is a small tabernacle to the Madonna flanked by angels in the style of Bernini.

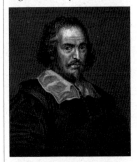

Pietro da Cortona (1596–1669)

Palazzo del Banco di Santo Spirito ⑱

Via del Banco di Santo Spirito. **Map** 4 D4 & 11 A2. **᠁** 41, 46, 62, 64, 982. **Open** normal banking hours.

FORMERLY THE MINT of papal Rome, this palazzo is often referred to as the Antica Zecca (old mint). The upper storeys of the facade, built by Antonio da Sangallo the Younger in the 1520s, are in the shape of a Roman triumphal arch. Above it stand two Baroque statues symbolizing Charity and Thrift, and in the centre of the arch above the main entrance an inscription records the founding of the Banco di Santo Spirito by Pope Paul V Borghese in 1605.

Pope Paul was a very shrewd financier and he encouraged Romans to deposit their money at the bank by offering the vast estates of the Hospital of Santo Spirito *(see p226)* as security. The system catered only for the rudimentary banking requirements of the population, but business was brisk as people deposited money here safe in the knowledge that they could get it out simply by presenting a chit. The hospital coffers also gained from the system. The Banco di Santo Spirito still exists, but is now part of the Banco di Roma.

Facade of the Banco di Santo Spirito, built to resemble a Roman arch

Palazzo Gaddi ⑲

Via del Banco di Santo Spirito 42.
Map 4 D3 & 11 A2. 🚌 *41, 46, 62, 64, 280.* **Not open** to the public.

Portrait of Michelangelo in his old age by Jacopino del Conte

TRADITIONALLY attributed to the Florentine Jacopo Sansovino, Palazzo Gaddi was owned by Florentine families for many generations. Cardinal Gaddi, himself born into a famous Florentine family, the Altoviti, built the palazzo in the 16th century during the reign of Pope Clement VII de' Medici, when the Tuscan colony in Rome flourished. Michelangelo is known to have lived at the palazzo; close by is the place where the Sienese banker Agostino Chigi set up his first bank in Rome. For years Chigi kept the papal tiara in safe keeping as security against a loan made to Pope Julius II.

Via dei Coronari ⑳

Map 4 D3 & 11 B2. 🚌 *46, 62, 64, 70, 81, 87, 90, 90b, 186, 492.*

LARGE NUMBERS of medieval pilgrims making their way to St Peter's walked along this street to cross over the Tiber at Ponte Sant'Angelo. Of the businesses that sprang up to try to part the pilgrims from their money, the most enduring was the selling of rosaries, and the street is still named after the rosary sellers *(coronari)*.

The street followed the course of the ancient Roman Via Recta (straight street), which originally ran from today's Piazza Colonna to the Tiber.

Making one's way through the vast throng of people in Via dei Coronari could be extremely hazardous. In the Holy Year of 1450, some 200 pilgrims died, crushed by the crowds or drowned in the Tiber. Following the tragedy, Pope Nicholas V demolished the Roman triumphal arch that stood at the entrance to Ponte Sant'Angelo. In the late 15th century, Pope Sixtus IV encouraged the building of private houses and palaces along the street.

Although the rosary sellers have been replaced by antiques dealers, the street still has many original buildings from the 15th and 16th centuries. One of the earliest, at Nos. 156–7, is known as the House of Fiammetta, the mistress of Cesare Borgia.

Antiques shop, Via dei Coronari

San Salvatore in Lauro ㉑

Piazza San Salvatore in Lauro 15.
Map 4 E3 & 11 B2. 📞 *687 51 87.*
🚌 *46, 62, 64, 280.* **Open** 10am–noon (exc Thu), 4.30pm–7pm daily. ✝

THE CHURCH is named "in Lauro" after the laurel grove that grew here in ancient times. Today's church was built at the end of the 16th century by Ottaviano

Cloister, San Salvatore in Lauro

Mascherino. The bell tower and sacristy were 18th-century additions by Nicola Salvi, famous for the Trevi Fountain *(see p159)*. The church contains the first great altarpiece by the 17th-century artist Pietro da Cortona, *The Birth of Jesus*, in the first chapel to the right.

The adjacent San Giorgio convent, to the left, has a pretty Renaissance cloister, a frescoed refectory and the monument to Pope Eugenius IV (reigned 1431–47), moved here when old St Peter's was pulled down. An extravagant Venetian, he spent thousands of ducats on his gold tiara, but requested a "simple, lowly burial place" near his predecessor Pope Eugenius III. His portrait, by Salviati, is in the refectory.

In 1669 the church became the seat of a pious association, the Confraternity of the Piceni, inhabitants of the Marche region. Fanatically loyal to the pope, the Piceni were traditionally employed as papal soldiers and tax-collectors.

Facade of San Salvatore in Lauro

Museo Napoleonico ㉒

Piazza di Ponte Umberto 1.
Map 4 E3 & 11 C1. 68 80 62 86.
70, 81, 87, 90, 90b, 186, 280, 492.
Closed for restoration until Jan '94.
Adm charge.

Entrance to Museo Napoleonico

THIS MUSEUM contains memorabilia and portraits of Napoleon Bonaparte and his family. Personal relics of Napoleon himself include an Indian shawl he wore during his exile on St Helena.

After his death in 1821, the pope allowed many of the Bonaparte family to settle in Rome, including his formidable mother Letizia, who lived in Palazzo Misciattelli on Via del Corso, and died there in 1836. Of her other children, the most intriguing is the flighty Pauline, who married the Roman Prince Camillo Borghese. The museum has a cast of her right breast, made by Canova in 1805 as a preparatory study for his statue of her as a reclining Venus, now in the Museo Borghese (see p260–61). Portraits and personal effects of

many other members of the family are on display, including court dresses, uniforms, and even a penny-farthing bicycle that belonged to Prince Eugène, the son of Emperor Napoleon III.

The last male of the Roman branch of the family was Napoleon Charles, portrayed in a late 19th-century painting by Guglielmo de Sanctis. The collection was assembled in 1927 by the Counts Primoli, the sons of Charles's sister, Carlotta Bonaparte.

Palazzo Altemps ㉓

Via Sant'Apollinare 8. **Map** 4 E3 & 11 C2. 70, 81, 87, 90, 90b, 186, 280, 492. **Not open** to the public.

THE PALAZZO was built for Girolamo Riario, nephew of Pope Sixtus IV, and the Riario coat of arms can still be seen in the janitor's room. In the popular uprising that followed the pope's death in 1484, the building was sacked and Girolamo fled the city.

In 1568 the palazzo was bought by Cardinal Marco Sittico Altemps. His family was of German origin – the name is an Italianization of Hohenems – and extremely influential in the church. In 1565, when the cardinal's brother married San Carlo Borromeo's sister, Ortensia, Pope Pius IV marked the day with the last great tournament to be held in the Vatican's Belvedere Courtyard (see pp234–5). The palazzo was renovated in

Belvedere of Palazzo Altemps

the 1570s by Martino Longhi the Elder, who added the great belvedere, crowned with obelisks and a marble unicorn. The Altemps were ostentatious collectors; the courtyard and the staircase leading from it are lined with ancient sculptures. The palazzo is now a seminary.

Hostaria dell' Orso ㉔

Via dei Soldati 25. **Map** 4 E3 & 11 C2. 686 42 50. 70, 81, 87, 90, 90b, 186, 280, 492. **Open** 12.30pm–3pm, 7.30pm–11pm Mon–Sat.

NOW A RESTAURANT, this ancient inn has a 15th-century portico and loggia built with columns taken from Roman ruins. Legend has it that Dante once stayed here. Later visitors to Rome known to have used the inn include the 16th-century French writers Rabelais and Montaigne.

Dante Alighieri (1265–1321)

Sant'Apollinare ㉕

Piazza Sant'Apollinare 49. **Map** 4 E3 & 11 C2. 68 30 37. 70, 81, 87, 90, 90b, 186, 492. **Open** 7.30am–noon, 4pm–7.30pm daily.

FOUNDED IN medieval times, the church was rebuilt by Ferdinando Fuga in the 18th century. It is dedicated to the saint said to have accompanied St Peter from Antioch to Rome, who later became the first Bishop of Ravenna. At a special service held every Sunday, Gregorian chants are sung by the priests.

Piazza di Spagna

BY THE 16th century, the increase in numbers of visiting pilgrims and ecclesiastics was making life in Rome's already congested medieval centre unbearable. A new triangle of roads was built, still in place today, to help channel pilgrims as quickly as possible from the city's north gate, the Porta del Popolo, to the Vatican. By the 18th century hotels had sprung up all over

Lion fountain in Piazza del Popolo

the district. Today this attractive area offers much more: the superb works of Renaissance and Baroque art in Santa Maria del Popolo and Sant' Andrea delle Fratte, the magnificent reliefs of the restored Ara Pacis, art exhibitions in the Villa Medici, fine views of the city from the Spanish Steps and the Pincio Gardens and Rome's most famous shopping streets, centred around Via Condotti.

SIGHTS AT A GLANCE

Churches
Sant'Andrea delle Fratte ❶
Trinità dei Monti ❿
All Saints ⓬
Santa Maria dei Miracoli and
Santa Maria in Montesanto ⓮
Santa Maria del
Popolo pp138–9 ⓱
San Rocco ㉑
Santi Ambrogio e Carlo
al Corso ㉒

Museums and Galleries
Keats-Shelley
Memorial House ❼
Casa di Goethe ⓭

Historic Buildings
Collegio di Propaganda
Fide ❷
Villa Medici ⓫

Arches, Gates and Columns
Colonna dell'Immacolata ❸
Porta del Popolo ⓲

Historic Streets and Piazzas
Via Condotti ❹
Piazza di Spagna ❻

Spanish Steps ❾
Piazza del Popolo ⓰

Monuments and Tombs
Ara Pacis ⓳
Mausoleum of Augustus ⓴

Parks and Gardens
Pincio Gardens ⓯

Cafés and Restaurants
Caffè Greco ❺
Babington's Tea Rooms ❽

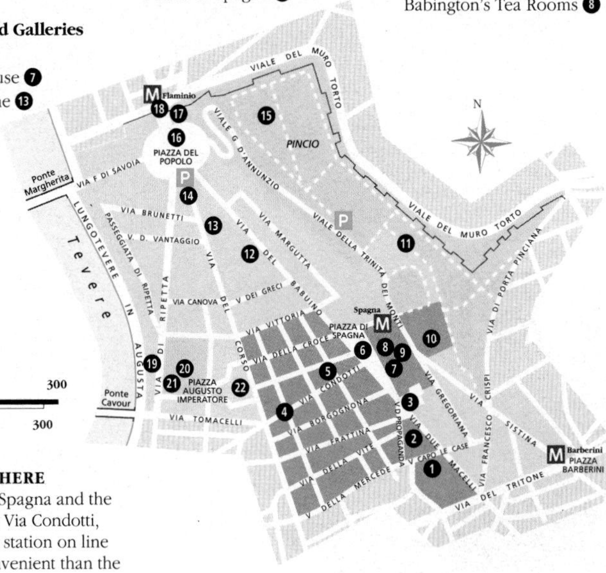

GETTING THERE

For Piazza di Spagna and the shops around Via Condotti, Spagna Metro station on line A is more convenient than the main bus routes along Via del Corso and Via del Tritone. Stay on until Flaminio Metro if you wish to visit Piazza del Popolo. For getting around locally, the 119 minibus, which goes up Via del Babuino, is very handy.

KEY

▨	Street-by-Street map
Ⓜ	Metro station
Ⓟ	Parking
—	City Wall

SEE ALSO

- *Street Finder*, maps 4, 5
- *Where to Stay* pp294–5
- *Restaurants* pp310–11
- *Shops* pp322–37

The Spanish Steps leading up to the church of Trinità dei Monti

Street-by-Street: Piazza di Spagna

THE NETWORK of narrow streets between Piazza di Spagna and Via del Corso is one of the liveliest areas in Rome, drawing throngs of tourists and Romans to its discreet and elegant shops. In the 18th century the area was full of hotels for frivolous English aristocrats doing the Grand Tour, but there were also artists, writers and composers, who took the city's history and culture more seriously.

Caffè Greco
Busts and portraits recall the café's former artistic patrons **5**

★ **Piazza di Spagna**
For almost three centuries the square with its curious Barcaccia fountain in the centre has been the chief meeting place for visitors to Rome **6**

Via delle Carrozze took its name from the carriages of wealthy tourists that used to queue up there for repairs.

Via Condotti
This shadowy, narrow street has the smartest shops in one of the smartest shopping areas in the world **4**

Bulgari sells very expensive jewellery behind an austere shopfront in Via Condotti.

| 0 metres | 75 |
| 0 yards | 75 |

KEY

– – – Suggested route

Ⓜ Metro station

Trinità dei Monti
This 16th-century church has a spectacular setting and some of the finest views in Rome ⑩

Babington's Tea Rooms
English tourists are catered for in the style of the 1890s ⑧

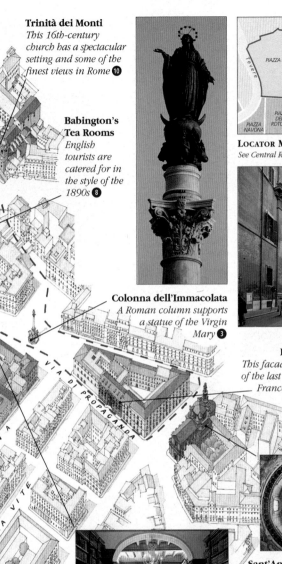

LOCATOR MAP
See Central Rome Map pp12–13

Colonna dell'Immacolata
A Roman column supports a statue of the Virgin Mary ③

Collegio di Propaganda Fide
This facade (1665) was one of the last works of the great Francesco Borromini ②

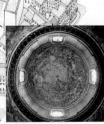

Sant'Andrea delle Fratte
Pasquale Marini painted The Redemption *to decorate the interior of Borromini's high dome in 1691* ①

★ Keats-Shelley Memorial House
The library is part of the small museum established in the house where the English poet Keats died in 1821 ⑦

★ Spanish Steps
Even obscured by crowds, the steps are one of the glories of late Baroque Rome ⑨

STAR SIGHTS
★ Piazza di Spagna
★ Keats-Shelley Memorial House
★ Spanish Steps

Sant'Andrea delle Fratte ❶

Via Sant'Andrea delle Fratte 1.
Map 5 A3. ⓒ 679 31 91. 🚌 119.
Ⓜ Spagna. **Open** 6.30am–12.45pm,
4pm–7.30pm daily. ✝ 📷 ♿

W HEN SANT'ANDREA delle Fratte was built in the 12th century, this was the northernmost edge of Rome. Though the church is now firmly embedded in the city, its name (*fratte* means thickets) recalls its original setting.

The church was completely rebuilt in the 17th century, partly by Borromini. His bell tower and dome, best viewed from the higher ground further up Via Capo le Case, are remarkable for the complex arrangement of concave and convex surfaces. The bell tower is particularly fanciful, with angel caryatids, flaming torches resembling ice cream cones, and exaggerated scrolls like semi-folded hearts supporting a spiky crown.

In 1842, the Virgin Mary appeared in the church to a Jewish banker, who promptly converted to Christianity and became a missionary. Inside, the chapel of the Miraculous Madonna is the first thing you notice. The church is better known, however, for the angels that Borromini's rival, Bernini, carved for the Ponte Sant'Angelo. Pope Clement IX declared they were too lovely to be exposed to the weather, so they remained with Bernini's family until 1729, when they were moved to the church.

Collegio di Propaganda Fide ❷

Via di Propaganda 1. **Map** 5 A2.
ⓒ 679 69 41. 🚌 119. Ⓜ Spagna.
Open to individuals on written request.

B UILT FOR the Jesuits in 1662 when they were at the height of their power, the Collegio di Propaganda Fide (College for the Propagation of the Faith) was Borromini's last work. The headquarters of the Jesuits had to be a remarkable building, but the extraordinary facade (now thickly coated with grime) must have outstripped even their expectations. It is striped with broad pilasters, between which the first-floor windows bend in, and the central bay bulges out. A rigid band divides ground and first floors, and the cornice above the convex central bay swerves inwards. The more you look at it, the more restless it seems. The unhappy architect committed suicide shortly after completing it.

Entrance to the Jesuit College

Colonna dell'Immacolata ❸

Piazza Mignanelli. **Map** 5 A2.
🚌 119. Ⓜ Spagna.

I NAUGURATED IN 1857, the column commemorates Pope Pius IX's proclamation of the doctrine of the Immaculate Conception, holding that the Virgin Mary was the only human being ever to have been born "without the stain of original sin". The column itself dates from ancient Rome. Now crowned with a statue of the Virgin Mary, it is one of the many pagan monuments in the city to have been converted to Christian use.

**Angel by Bernini,
Sant'Andrea delle Fratte**

**Portrait of Pope Pius IX
(reigned 1846–78)**

Via Condotti ➍

Map 5 A2. 🚌 81, 90, 90b, 119.
Ⓜ Spagna. See *Shops and Markets*
pp322–33.

NAMED AFTER the conduits
that carried water to the
Baths of Agrippa near the
Pantheon, Via Condotti is
now home to the most
traditional of Rome's designer
clothes shops. It is also
extremely popular for early
evening strolls, when elegant,
perfumed ladies and men in
immaculate suits and flowing
trench coats mingle with
tourists in shorts and trainers.
The most famous shops here
are Beltrami (for leather),
Ferragamo (for exquisitely
crafted and often fantastical
shoes), Hermès and Gucci.

Slightly younger designers
such as Laura Biagiotti,
Gianfranco Ferrè, Gianni
Versace and the Fendi sisters
have shops on parallel Via
Borgognona. Valentino's
shops are on Via Maria dei
Fiori and Via Bocca di Leone,
which cross Via Condotti just
below Piazza di Spagna, and
Giorgio Armani and Emporio
Armani are on nearby Via del
Babuino, among the discreet
art galleries, exclusive antique
shops and furnishing stores.

**View along Via Condotti towards
the Spanish Steps**

Caffè Greco ➎

Via Condotti 86. Map 5 A2.
📞 679 17 00. 🚌 81, 90, 90b, 119.
Ⓜ Spagna. Open 8am–8.45pm Mon–
Sat. Closed public hols, 1–21 Aug. ♿

THIS CAFE was opened by a
Greek (hence *greco*) in
1760, and throughout the 18th
century it was a favourite

The 230-year-old Caffè Greco

meeting place for foreign
artists. Writers such as
Keats, Byron and
Goethe and composers
like Liszt, Wagner and
Bizet all breakfasted
and drank here. So too
did Casanova, and
mad King Ludwig of
Bavaria. Today, Italians
stand in the crowded
foyer to sip espresso
coffee, and foreigners
sit at tables in a
cramped, cosy back
room, against plush
walls studded with the
portraits of the café's famous
former customers.

**Pope Urban VIII's arms,
with the Barberini bees**

Piazza di Spagna ➏

Map 5 A2. 🚌 119. Ⓜ Spagna.

SHAPED LIKE a crooked bow
tie and surrounded by tall
shuttered houses painted in
muted shades of ochre, cream
and russet, Piazza di Spagna
(Spanish square) is crowded
all day and (in summer) most
of the night. It is the most
famous square in Rome, and
has long been the haunt of
foreign visitors and expatriates.

In the 17th century Spain's
ambassador to the Holy See
had his headquarters on the
square, and the area around it
was deemed to be Spanish
territory. Foreigners who
unwittingly trespassed were
liable to be dragooned into
the Spanish army. In the 18th
and 19th centuries Rome was
almost as popular with
visitors as it is today, and the

square stood at the heart of
the city's main hotel district.
Some of the travellers came in
search of knowledge and
artistic inspiration, but most
were more interested in
gambling, collecting ancient
statues to adorn their family
homes, and conducting love
affairs with Italian women.

Not surprisingly, the
wealthy travellers attracted
hordes of beggars, who were
usually supplied with tear-
jerking letters by scribes who
worked in the square.

The Fontana della Barcaccia
in the square is the least
showy of Rome's Baroque
fountains, and it is often
completely screened from
view by
people resting
on its rim. It
was designed
either by the
famous Gian
Lorenzo
Bernini or by
his father
Pietro.
Because the
pressure from
the aqueduct
that feeds the
fountain is
extremely low there are no
spectacular cascades or spurts
of water. Instead, Bernini
constructed a leaking boat –
barcaccia means useless,
old boat – which lies half
submerged in a shallow pool.

The bees and suns that
decorate the Fontana della
Barcaccia are taken from the
family coat of arms of Pope
Urban VIII Barberini, who
commissioned the fountain.

**The Fontana della Barcaccia at
the foot of the Spanish Steps**

Bust of Shelley by Moses Ezekiel

Keats-Shelley Memorial House ❼

Piazza di Spagna 26. **Map** 5 A2.
📞 678 42 35. 🚌 119. Ⓜ *Spagna.*
Open 9am–1pm, 3pm–6pm (Oct–Mar: 2.30pm–5.30pm) Mon–Fri.
Closed public hols. **Adm charge.** Ⓟ
🖼 book in advance. 📷

IN NOVEMBER 1820 the English poet John Keats came to stay with his friend, the painter Joseph Severn, in a dusty pink house, the Casina Rossa, on the corner of the Spanish Steps. Suffering from consumption, Keats had been sent to Rome by his doctor, in the hope that the mild, dry climate would help the young man's recovery. Depressed because of scathing criticism of his work and tormented by his unrequited love for a young girl named Fanny Brawne, Keats died the following February aged 25.

His death inspired his friend and fellow poet, Percy Bysshe Shelley, to write the poem *Mourn not for Adonais*. In July 1822 Shelley himself was drowned in a boating accident in the Gulf of La Spezia off the coast of Tuscany. Keats, Shelley and Severn are all buried in Rome's Protestant Cemetery (*see p205*).

In 1906 the house was bought by an Anglo-American association and preserved as a memorial and library in honour of English Romantic poets. The relics include a lock of Keats's hair, some fragments of Shelley's bones in a tiny urn and a garish carnival mask picked up by Lord Byron as a souvenir of a trip to Venice. You can visit the room where Keats died, though all the original furniture was burnt after his death, on papal orders.

Babington's Tea Rooms ❽

Piazza di Spagna 23. **Map** 5 A2.
📞 678 60 27. 🚌 119. Ⓜ *Spagna.*
Open Sep–Jun: 9am–8.15pm Wed–Mon; Jul & Aug: 9am–8.15pm Tue–Sat. **Closed** public hols. ♿

THESE AUGUST, old-fashioned tea rooms were opened in 1896 by two Englishwomen, Anna Maria and Isabel Cargill Babington, to serve homesick British tourists with scones, jam and pots of Earl Grey tea. The food remains homely – shepherd's pie and chicken supreme for lunch, muffins and cinnamon toast for tea – though these days the menu offers pancakes with maple syrup for breakfast as well as the traditional bacon and egg.

Purveyors of English breakfasts to homesick exiles since 1896

Spanish Steps ❾

Scalinata della Trinità dei Monti, Piazza di Spagna. **Map** 5 A2. 🚌 119.
Ⓜ *Spagna.*

IN THE 17TH century the French owners of Trinità dei Monti decided to link the church with Piazza di Spagna by building a magnificent new flight of steps. They also planned to place an equestrian statue of King Louis XIV at the top. Pope Alexander VII Chigi was not too happy at the

The Spanish Steps in spring with azaleas in full bloom

prospect of erecting a statue of a French monarch in the papal city, and the arguments continued until the 1720s when an Italian architect, Francesco de Sanctis, produced a design that satisfied both the French and the papacy. The steps, completed in 1726, combine straight sections, curves and terraces to create one of the city's most dramatic and distinctive landmarks.

When the Victorian novelist Charles Dickens visited Rome, he reported that the Spanish Steps were the meeting place for artists' models, who would dress in colourful traditional costumes, hoping to catch the attention of a wealthy artist. The steps are now a popular place to sit, write postcards, take photos, flirt, busk or just watch the passers-by.

Trinità dei Monti ⓾

Piazza della Trinità dei Monti.
Map 5 A2. 679 41 79. 119.
Ⓜ *Spagna.* **Open** *10am–12.30pm, 4pm–6pm daily.*

Trinità dei Monti's bell towers

THE VIEWS of Rome from the platform in front of the twin bell towered facade of Trinità dei Monti are so beautiful that the church itself is often ignored. It is, however, unusual for Rome, for it was founded by the French in 1495, and although it was later badly damaged, there are still traces of attractive late Gothic latticework in the vaults of the transept. The interconnecting side chapels are decorated with Mannerist paintings, including two fine works by Daniele da Volterra.

19th-century engraving of the inner facade of the Villa Medici

A pupil of Michelangelo, Volterra had to paint clothes on the nudes in the *Last Judgment* in the Sistine Chapel, in response to the objections of Pope Pius IV.

Michelangelo's influence is obvious in the powerfully muscled bodies shown in the *Deposition* (second chapel on the left). The circles of gesturing figures and dancing angels surrounding the Virgin Mary in the *Assumption* (third chapel on the right), have more in common with the graceful style of Raphael.

Villa Medici ⓫

Accademia di Francia a Roma, Viale della Trinità dei Monti 1. **Map** 5 A2. 676 11 or 679 83 81. 119.
Ⓜ *Spagna.* **Accademia open** *irregularly, so phone first.* **Exhibitions, concerts. Gardens closed** *for restoration.* **Adm charge.**

SUPERBLY POSITIONED on the Pincio hill above Piazza di Spagna, this 16th-century villa has kept the name it assumed when Cardinal Ferdinando de' Medici bought it in 1576. From the terrace you can look across the city to Castel Sant'Angelo, from where Queen Christina of Sweden is said to have fired the large cannon ball which now sits in the basin of the fountain.

The villa is now home to the French Academy. This

The 17th-century French painter Nicolas Poussin

was founded by Louis XIV in 1666 to give a few select painters the chance to study in Rome. Nicolas Poussin was one of the first advisers to the Academy, Ingres was a director and ex-students include Fragonard and Boucher.

After 1803 when the French Academy moved to the Villa Medici, musicians were also admitted; both Berlioz and Debussy came to Rome as students of the Academy.

All Saints ⓬

Via del Babuino 153B. **Map** 4 F2.
679 43 57. 90, 90b, 119.
Open *mornings daily.*

IN 1816 THE POPE gave English residents and visitors the right to hold Anglican services in Rome, but it wasn't until the early 1880s that they acquired a site to build their own church. The architect chosen for the job was G E Street, best known in Britain for his Neo-Gothic churches and the London Law Courts. All Saints is also built in Victorian Neo-Gothic, and the interior, though splendidly decorated with different coloured Italian marbles, has an unmistakably English air. It has an apse mosaic designed by the British Pre-Raphaelite artist, Edward Burne-Jones, ceramic tiles in a pattern by William Morris (once Street's assistant), and an organ from Huddersfield.

Casa di Goethe ⓭

18–20 Via del Corso. **Map** 4 F1.
🚌 90, 90b, 119, 926. **Not open** to
the public.

THE GERMAN POET, dramatist
and novelist Johann
Wolfgang von Goethe (1749–
1832) lived in this house from
1786 until 1788, working on
the journal that eventually
formed part of his travel book
The Italian Journey. Rome's
noisy street life irritated him,
especially during Carnival
time, and he was a little
perturbed by the number of
murders in his neighbourhood,
but Rome rejuvenated him
and his book became one of
the most influential ever to be
written about Italy.

Santa Maria dei Miracoli and Santa Maria in Montesanto ⓮

Piazza del Popolo. **Map** 4 F1. 🚌 90,
90b, 95, 119, 926. Ⓜ Flaminio. **Santa
Maria dei Miracoli** 📞 361 02 50.
Open 6am–1pm, 5pm–7pm
Mon–Sat, 8am–1pm, 5pm–7pm Sun,
public hols. 🚪 📷 ♿ **Santa Maria
in Montesanto** 📞 361 05 94. **Open**
5pm–8pm (Nov–Mar: 4pm–7pm)
Mon, Wed, Fri. 🚪 📷

THE TWO CHURCHES at the
south end of Piazza del
Popolo were designed by the
Baroque architect Carlo
Rainaldi (1611–91), proof that
he could be as ingenious as his
more famous contemporaries
Bernini and Borromini.
   To provide a focal point for
the piazza, the churches had
to look symmetrical, but
the site on the

Portrait of Goethe in the Roman countryside by Tischbein (1751–1821)

left was narrower than that on
the right. Rainaldi solved the
problem by giving Santa Maria
dei Miracoli (on the right) a
circular dome and Santa Maria
in Montesanto an oval one,
cleverly squeezing it into the
narrower site, while the sides
of the supporting drums that
face the piazza are identical.

Pincio Gardens ⓯

Il Pincio. **Map** 4 F1. 🚌 90, 90b, 95,
119, 926. Ⓜ Flaminio. ♿

THE PINCIO GARDENS lie
above Piazza del Popolo,
on a hillside that has been so
skilfully terraced and richly
planted with trees that, from
below, the zig-zagging road
climbing to the gardens is
virtually invisible.
   There were magnificent
gardens on the Pincio hill
in ancient Roman times,
but the present gardens
were designed in the early
19th century by Giuseppe
Valadier (who also re-
designed the
Piazza del
Popolo).

The Pincio Gardens water clock

The broad avenues, lined
with umbrella pines, palm
trees and evergreen oaks
soon became a fashionable
place to stroll, and even this
century such diverse characters
as Gandhi and Mussolini,
Richard Strauss and King
Farouk of Egypt patronized
the Casina Valadier, an
exclusive café and restaurant
in the grounds.
   From the Pincio's main
square, Piazzale Napoleone I,
the panoramic views of Rome
stretch from the Monte Mario
to the Janiculum. For full
effect, approach the gardens
from the grounds of Villa
Borghese (*see pp258–9*)
above the Pincio, or along
Viale della Trinità dei Monti.

**The twin churches of Santa Maria di Montesanto (left) and Santa Maria
dei Miracoli in a 19th-century view of Piazza del Popolo**

The panorama is particularly beautiful at sunset, the traditional time for tourists to take a stroll in the gardens.

One of the most striking features of the park itself is an Egyptian-style obelisk which Emperor Hadrian erected on the tomb of his favourite, the beautiful male slave Antinous. After the slave's premature death (according to some accounts he died saving the emperor's life), Hadrian deified him.

The 19th-century water clock on Via dell'Orologio was designed by a Dominican monk. It was displayed at the Paris Exhibition of 1889.

The Casina Valadier restaurant in the Pincio Gardens

Piazza del Popolo **16**

Map 4 F1. ![bus] 90, 90b, 95, 119, 926.
M Flaminio.

A VAST COBBLED OVAL standing at the apex of the triangle of roads known as the Trident, Piazza del Popolo forms a grand symmetrical antechamber to the heart of Rome. Twin Neo-Classical facades stand on either side of the Porta del Popolo; an Egyptian obelisk rises in the centre; and the matching domes and porticoes of Santa Maria dei Miracoli and Santa Maria di Montesanto flank the beginning of Via del Corso.

Although it is now one of the most unified squares in Rome, Piazza del Popolo evolved gradually over the centuries. In 1589 the great town-planning pope, Sixtus V, had the obelisk erected in the centre by Domenico Fontana.

Traditional carnival band in Piazza del Popolo

Over 3,000 years old, the obelisk was originally brought to Rome by Augustus to adorn the Circus Maximus after the conquest of Egypt. Almost a century later Pope Alexander VII commissioned Carlo Rainaldi to build the twin Santa Marias.

In the 19th century the piazza was turned into a grandiose oval by Giuseppe Valadier, the designer of the Pincio Gardens. He also encased Santa Maria del Popolo in a Neo-Classical shell to make its south facade fit in better with the overall appearance of the piazza.

In contrast to the piazza's air of ordered rationalism, many of the events staged here were barbaric. In the 18th and 19th centuries, public executions were held in Piazza del Popolo, often as part of the celebration of Carnival. Condemned men were sometimes hammered to death by repeated blows to the temples. The last time a criminal was executed in this way was in 1826, even though the guillotine had by then been adopted as a more scientific means of execution.

The riderless horse races from the piazza down Via del Corso were scarcely more humane: the performance of the runners was enhanced by feeding the horses stimulants, wrapping them in nail-studded ropes, and letting off fireworks at their heels.

Santa Maria del Popolo **17**

See pp138–9.

Porta del Popolo **18**

Between Piazzale Flaminio and Piazza del Popolo. **Map** 4 F1. ![bus] 90, 90b, 95, 119, 926. **M** Flaminio.

T HE VIA FLAMINIA, built in 220 BC to connect Rome with Italy's Adriatic coast, enters the city at Porta del Popolo, a grand 16th-century gate built on the orders of Pope Pius IV Medici. The architect, Nanni di Baccio Bigio, modelled it on a Roman triumphal arch. The outer face has statues of St Peter and St Paul on either side of the arch and a huge Medici coat of arms above.

A century later, Pope Alexander VII commissioned Bernini to decorate the inner face to celebrate the arrival in Rome of Queen Christina of Sweden. Lesser visitors were often held up while customs officers rifled their luggage. The only way to speed things up was with a bribe.

Porta del Popolo's central arch

Santa Maria del Popolo ⑰

ONE OF ROME'S greatest stores of artistic treasures, this early Renaissance church was commissioned by Pope Sixtus IV della Rovere in 1472. Among the artists who worked on the building were Andrea Bregno and Pinturicchio. Later additions were made by Bramante and Bernini. Many illustrious families have chapels here, all decorated with appropriate splendour. The Della Rovere Chapel has delightful Pinturicchio frescoes, the Cerasi Chapel has two Caravaggio masterpieces, the *Conversion of St Paul* and the *Crucifixion of St Peter*, but the finest of all is the Chigi Chapel designed by Raphael for his patron, the banker Agostino Chigi. The most striking of the church's many Renaissance tombs are the two by Andrea Sansovino behind the main altar.

★ Chigi Chapel
Raphael designed this chapel, which has an altarpiece by Sebastiano del Piombo. Niches on either side of the altar house sculptures by Bernini and Lorenzetto. Mosaics in the dome show God as creator of the seven heavenly bodies.

Kneeling Skeleton
This floor mosaic of the figure of death was added to the Chigi Chapel in the 17th century.

NERO'S GHOST

Nero lived on in the imagination of the people long after the fall of the Roman Empire. In the Middle Ages a legend arose that a walnut tree growing here on the spot where his ashes were buried was haunted by the emperor. Ravens roosting in the tree were thought to be demons tormenting him for his hideous crimes. When the first church was built here in 1099 by Pope Paschal II, the tree was cut down, supposedly putting an end to the supernatural events that had terrified local people.

Entrance

Cybo Chapel

STAR FEATURES

★ Chigi Chapel

★ Caravaggio Paintings in Cerasi Chapel

★ Delphic Sibyl

Della Rovere Chapel
Pinturicchio painted the frescoes in the lunettes and the Adoration *above the altar in 1485–9.*

The altarpiece of *The
Assumption* is by Annibale
Carracci (1540–1609).

**★ Caravaggio Paintings
in Cerasi Chapel**
*One of two Caravaggios
in the Cerasi Chapel,* The
Crucifixion of St Peter
*uses dramatic fore-
shortening to highlight
the sheer effort involved
in turning the saint's
crucifix upside down.*

Stained Glass
*In 1509 French
artist Guillaume de
Marcillat was invited to
provide Rome's first two
stained-glass windows.*

The Tomb of Ascanio
Sforza, who died in 1505,
is by Andrea Sansovino.

★ Delphic Sibyl
*This is one of a series of frescoes by
Pinturicchio, some Classical and
others Biblical, painted in 1508–9 to
decorate the ceiling of the apse.*

The altar
houses the 13th-
century painting
known as the
*Madonna del
Popolo.*

The Tomb of Giovanni
della Rovere (1483) is by
pupils of Andrea Bregno.

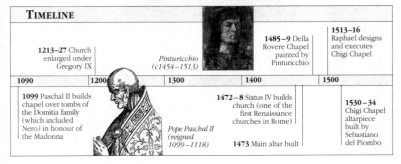

TIMELINE

				1513–16 Raphael designs and executes Chigi Chapel
			1485–9 Della Rovere Chapel painted by Pinturicchio	
1213–27 Church enlarged under Gregory IX	*Pinturicchio (c1454–1513)*			
1090	1200	1300	1400	1500
1099 Paschal II builds chapel over tombs of the Domitia family (which included Nero) in honour of the Madonna	*Pope Paschal II (reigned 1099–1118)*	1472–8 Sixtus IV builds church (one of the first Renaissance churches in Rome) 1473 Main altar built		1530–34 Chigi Chapel altarpiece built by Sebastiano del Piombo

Ara Pacis ⑲

Via di Ripetta. **Map** 4 F2.
📞 67 10 24 75. 🚌 81, 90, 90b,
119, 926. **Open** 9am–1.30pm
Tue–Sat, 9am–1pm Sun; also Apr–Sep:
4pm–7pm Tue & Sat (last adm: 30 mins
before closing). **Adm charge.** 📷

Frieze on south wall showing procession with the family of Augustus

RECONSTRUCTED at great
expense over a period of
many years, the Ara Pacis
(Altar of Peace) is one of the
most significant monuments
of ancient Rome. It celebrates
the peace created throughout
the Mediterranean area by the

Marcus Agrippa (right)

Emperor Augustus after
victorious campaigns in Gaul
and Spain. The monument
was commissioned by the
Senate in 13 BC and completed
four years later. It is a square
enclosure on a low platform
with the altar in the centre.
All the surfaces are decorated
with magnificent friezes and
reliefs carved in Carrara
marble. Their high quality
indicates that the
craftsmen must have
been Greek. The reliefs
on the north and south
walls depict a procession
that took place on 4 July
13 BC, in which the

members of the emperor's
family can be identified,
ranked by their position in the
succession. Heir apparent at
the time was Marcus Agrippa,
husband of Augustus's
daughter Julia. All the
portraits in the relief are
carved with astonishing
realism, even the toddler
clinging to his mother's skirts.
    The tale of the rediscovery
of the Ara Pacis dates back to
the 16th century, when the
first panels were unearthed.
One section ended up in
Paris, another in Florence.
Further finds were made in
the late 19th century, when
archaeologists finally realized

just what they had discovered.
What we see today has all
been pieced together since
1938. The reconstruction, in
part original, in part facsimile,
is enshrined in a large glass
hangar creating a wonderful
spectacle when lit up at night.

**Livia (right), Augustus's wife and
the mother of Tiberius, with an
unidentified member of the family**

**Augustus's young
grandson, Lucius**

South wall

East wall

The altar was used
once a year for a
sacrifice on the
anniversary of the
monument's
inauguration.

West wall

North wall

An acanthus frieze
runs around the
lower half of the
outside wall.

Mausoleum of Augustus 20

Piazza Augusto Imperatore. **Map** 4 F2.
🚌 81, 90, 90b, 119, 926. **Adm** by
written permission only: apply to
Ripartizione X, Piazza Campitelli 7.
📞 67 10 38 19.

Now just a weedy mound, ringed with cypresses and sadly strewn with litter, this was once the most prestigious burial place in Rome. Augustus had the mausoleum built in 28 BC, the year he became sole ruler, as a tomb for himself and his descendants. The circular building was 87 m (270 ft) in diameter with two obelisks (now in Piazza del Quirinale and Piazza dell' Esquilino) at the entrance.

Inside were four concentric passageways (linked by corridors) where the urns containing the ashes of the Imperial family were placed. The first to be buried there was Augustus's favourite nephew, Marcellus, who had married Julia, the emperor's daughter. He died in 23 BC, possibly poisoned by Augustus's second wife Livia, who felt that her son, Tiberius, would make a more reliable emperor. When Augustus died in AD 14, his ashes were placed in the mausoleum, Tiberius duly became emperor, and dynastic poisonings continued to fill the family vault with urns.

This sinister monument was later used as a medieval fortress, a vineyard, a private garden, and even, in the 18th century, as a bullring.

Augustus, the first Roman emperor

Madonna, San Rocco and Sant'Antonio with Victims of the Plague by Il Baciccia (1639–1709)

San Rocco 21

Largo San Rocco 1. **Map** 4 F2.
📞 686 39 55. 🚌 81, 90, 90b, 119.
Open 7.30am–10am, 6pm–7.30pm
(Oct–Mar: 5pm–8pm) daily. **Closed**
17–31 Aug. 🔲 📷

This church, with a restrained Neo-Classical facade by Giuseppe Valadier, the designer of Piazza del Popolo, began life as the chapel of a 16th-century hospital with beds for 50 men – San Rocco was a healer of the plague-stricken. A maternity wing was added for the wives of Tiber bargees to save them from having to give birth in the insanitary conditions of a boat. The hospital came to be used by unmarried mothers, and one section of the hospital was set aside for women who did not wish to give their names. They were even permitted to wear a veil for the duration of their stay. Unwanted children were sent to an orphanage, and if any mothers or children died they were buried in anonymous graves.

The hospital was abandoned at the turn of the century, and demolished in the 1930s during the excavation of the Mausoleum of Augustus. The church has an interesting Baroque altarpiece by Il Baciccia, the artist who decorated the ceiling of the Gesù (see pp114–15).

Santi Ambrogio e Carlo al Corso 22

Via del Corso 437. **Map** 4 F2.
📞 687 83 32. 🚌 81, 90, 90b, 119.
Open 7.30am–12.30pm, 5pm–
7pm (Oct–Mar: 7.30pm) daily. Ring
porter's door to left of church
if closed. 📷

This church belonged to the Lombard community in Rome, and is dedicated to two canonized bishops of Milan, Lombardy's capital. In 1471, Pope Sixtus IV gave the Lombards a church which they dedicated to Sant'Ambrogio, who died in 397. Then in 1610, when Carlo Borromeo was canonized, the church was rebuilt in his honour. Most of the new church was the work of father and son, Onorio and Martino Longhi, but the fine dome is by Pietro da Cortona. The altarpiece by Carlo Maratta (1625–1713) is the *Gloria dei Santi Ambrogio e Carlo*. An ambulatory leads behind the altar to a chapel housing the heart of San Carlo in a richly decorated reliquary.

Statue of San Carlo by Attilio Selva (1888–1970) behind the apse of Santi Ambrogio e Carlo

CAMPO DE' FIORI

ETWEEN Corso Vittorio Emanuele II and the Tiber, the city displays many distinct personalities. The open-air market of Campo de' Fiori preserves the lively, bohemian atmosphere of the medieval inns that once flourished here, while the area also contains Renaissance palazzi, such as Palazzo Farnese and Palazzo Spada, where powerful Roman families built

18th-century Madonna in Campo de' Fiori

their fortress-like houses near the route of papal processions. Close by, overlooking the picturesque Tiber Island, lies the old Jewish Ghetto, where many traces of daily life from past centuries can still be seen. The Portico of Octavia and the Theatre of Marcellus are spectacular examples of the city's many-layered history, built up over the half-ruined remains of ancient Rome.

SIGHTS AT A GLANCE

Churches and Temples
Santissima Trinità
dei Pellegrini ❹
Santa Maria dell'Orazione
e Morte ❻
San Girolamo della Carità ❽
Sant'Eligio degli Orefici ❾
Santa Maria di Monserrato ❿
San Carlo ai Catinari ⓱
Santa Maria in Campitelli ⓳
San Nicola in Carcere ㉒
San Giovanni dei Fiorentini ㉘

Museums and Galleries
Palazzo Spada ❺

Piccola Farnesina ⓭
Burcardo Theatre Museum ⓮

Historic Buildings
Palazzo Pio Righetti ❷
Palazzo del Monte di Pietà ❸
Palazzo Farnese ❼
Palazzo Ricci ⓫
Palazzo della Cancelleria ⓬
Palazzo Cenci ㉕
Casa di Lorenzo Manilio ㉖

Fountains
Fontana delle Tartarughe ⓲

Historic Streets and Piazzas
Campo de' Fiori ❶
Tiber Island ㉓
Ghetto and Synagogue ㉔
Via Giulia ㉗

Ancient Sites
Area Sacra ⓰
Theatre of Marcellus ⓴
Portico of Octavia ㉑

Famous Theatres
Teatro Argentina ⓯

GETTING THERE
Most of the streets around Campo de' Fiori are too narrow for buses, but many routes converge on Largo Argentina, a useful starting point for exploring. The 90 and 90b will also take you to Via del Teatro di Marcello. Only three buses, the 46, 62 and 64, go the full length of Corso Vittorio Emanuele II.

SEE ALSO

• **Street Finder**, maps 4, 8, 11, 12

• **Where to Stay** pp294–5

• **Restaurants** pp310–11

• **Via Giulia Walk** pp276–7

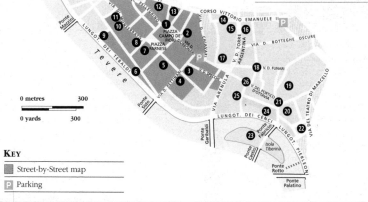

0 metres   300
0 yards   300

KEY

Street-by-Street map

P Parking

Fruit stalls beneath the statue of Giordano Bruno in the Campo de' Fiori market

Street-by-Street: Campo de' Fiori

THIS FASCINATING PART of Renaissance Rome is also an exciting area for shopping and night life, centred on the market square of Campo de' Fiori. Its stalls supply many nearby restaurants and young people shop for clothes in Via dei Giubbonari. Popular reasonably-priced restaurants and pizzerias keep the area alive late into the night. By day there are great buildings to admire, though few are open to the public. Two exceptions are the Piccola Farnesina with its collection of Classical statues and Palazzo Spada, home to many important paintings.

Sant'Eligio degli Orefici
A small Renaissance church designed by Raphael is concealed behind a later facade ❾

Palazzo Ricci
Painted Classical scenes were a favourite form of decoration for the facades of Renaissance houses ⓫

San Girolamo della Carità
The chief attraction of this church is Borromini's fabulous Spada Chapel ❽

Santa Maria di Monserrato
This church, which has strong connections with Spain, houses a Bernini bust of Cardinal Pedro Foix de Montoya ❿

Santa Maria dell'Orazione e Morte
A pair of dramatic winged skulls flank the doorway to this church dedicated to the burial of the dead ❻

KEY

— — — Suggested route

| 0 metres | 75 |
| 0 yards | 75 |

Palazzo Farnese
Michelangelo and other great artists helped create this monumental Renaissance palazzo ❼

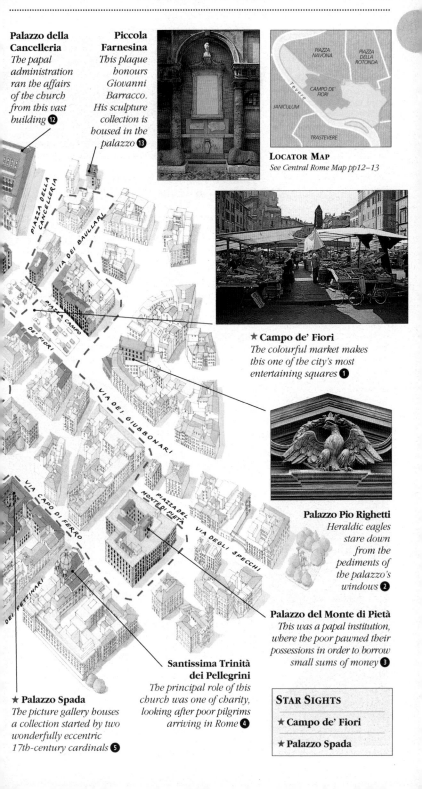

Palazzo della Cancelleria
The papal administration ran the affairs of the church from this vast building ⑫

Piccola Farnesina
This plaque honours Giovanni Barracco. His sculpture collection is housed in the palazzo ⑬

LOCATOR MAP
See Central Rome Map pp12–13

★ **Campo de' Fiori**
The colourful market makes this one of the city's most entertaining squares ①

Palazzo Pio Righetti
Heraldic eagles stare down from the pediments of the palazzo's windows ②

Palazzo del Monte di Pietà
This was a papal institution, where the poor pawned their possessions in order to borrow small sums of money ③

Santissima Trinità dei Pellegrini
The principal role of this church was one of charity, looking after poor pilgrims arriving in Rome ④

★ **Palazzo Spada**
The picture gallery houses a collection started by two wonderfully eccentric 17th-century cardinals ⑤

STAR SIGHTS

★ **Campo de' Fiori**

★ **Palazzo Spada**

Campo de' Fiori ❶

Piazza Campo de' Fiori. **Map** 4 E4 & 11 C4. 🚌 46, 62, 64, 70, 81, 87, 90, 90b, 186, 492, 926. See **Markets** p338.

THE CAMPO DE' FIORI (field of Flora), once a meadow, occupies the site of the open space facing the Theatre of Pompey. Cardinals and noblemen used to rub shoulders with fishmongers and foreigners in the piazza's market, making it one of the liveliest areas of medieval and Renaissance Rome. Today's market retains much of the traditional lively atmosphere.

In the centre of the square is a statue of a hooded figure. This is the philosopher Giordano Bruno, who was burnt at the stake for heresy on this spot in 1600 – a grim reminder of the executions that were held here.

The piazza was surrounded by inns for pilgrims and other travellers. Many of these were once owned by the successful 15th-century courtesan, Vannozza Catanei, mistress of Pope Alexander VI Borgia. On the corner between the piazza and Via del Pellegrino you can see Catanei's shield, which she had decorated with her own coat of arms and those of her husband and her lover, the Borgia pope.

Market stalls in Campo de' Fiori

Window pediment with heraldic lion and pine cones, Palazzo Pio Righetti

Palazzo Pio Righetti ❷

Piazza del Biscione 89. **Map** 4 E5 & 11 C4. 🚌 46, 62, 64, 70, 81, 87, 90, 186, 492. **Not open to the public.**

THE VAST 17th-century Palazzo Pio Righetti was built over the ruined Theatre of Pompey. The windows of the palazzo are decorated with lions and pine cones from the coat of arms of the Pio da Carpi family who lived here.

The curve of the Theatre of Pompey, completed in 55 BC, is followed by Via di Grotta Pinta. This was Rome's first permanent theatre built of stone and concrete. In places, for example the basement of the Pancrazio restaurant, you can see early examples of *opus reticulatum* – small square blocks of tufa (porous rock) set diagonally as a facing for a concrete wall.

Palazzo del Monte di Pietà ❸

Piazza del Monte di Pietà 33. **Map** 4 E5 & 11 C4. 📞 51 72 66 95. 🚌 44, 56, 60, 65, 75, 170, 710. **Chapel open** 7.40am–6pm Tue–Fri, 7.40am–noon Sat. **Closed** public hols. **Adm** by appt or on request to porter.

THE MONTE, as it is known, is a public institution, founded in 1539 by Pope Paul III Farnese as a pawnshop to staunch the usury then rampant in the city. The building still has offices and auction rooms for the sale of unredeemed goods.

The stars with diagonal bands on the huge central plaque decorating the facade are the coat of arms of Pope Clement VIII Aldobrandini,

added when Carlo Maderno enlarged the palace in the 17th century. The clock on the left was added later.

Within, the chapel is a jewel of Baroque architecture, adorned with gilded stucco, marble panelling and reliefs. The decoration makes a perfect setting for the sculptures by Domenico Guidi – a bust of San Carlo Borromeo and a relief of the *Pietà*. There are also splendid reliefs by Giovanni Battista Théudon and Pierre Legros of Biblical scenes illustrating the charitable nature of the institution.

Relief by Théudon of *Joseph Lending Grain to the Egyptians* in Palazzo del Monte di Pietà

Santissima Trinità dei Pellegrini ❹

Piazza della Trinità dei Pellegrini. **Map** 4 E5 & 11 C5. 📞 656 84 57. 🚌 44, 56, 60, 65, 75, 170, 710 and many other routes. **Closed** for restoration.

THE CHURCH WAS donated in the 16th century to a charitable organization founded by San Filippo Neri to care for the poor and the sick, in particular the

Guido Reni's *Holy Trinity*

thousands of paupers who flocked in pilgrimage to Rome during the special holy years known as Jubilees.

The 18th-century facade has niches with statues of the Evangelists by Bernardino Ludovisi. The interior, with Corinthian columns, ends in a horseshoe vault and apse, dominated by Guido Reni's striking altarpiece of the *Holy Trinity* (1625). The frescoes in the lantern are also by Reni.

Other interesting paintings include *St Gregory the Great Freeing Souls from Purgatory*, by Baldassarre Croce (third chapel to the left); Cavalier d'Arpino's *Virgin and Saints* (second chapel to the left); and a painting by Borgognone (1677), showing the Virgin and recently canonized saints, including San Carlo Borromeo and San Filippo Neri. In the sacristy are depictions of the nobility washing the feet of pilgrims, a custom started by San Filippo.

Fresco in the dome of Sant-issima Trinità

Palazzo Spada ❺

Piazza Capo di Ferro 13. **Map** 4 E5 & 11 C4. 686 11 58. 44, 46, 62 64, 65, 70, 87, 90, 186, 492 and many other routes. **Gallery open** 9am–7pm Tue–Sat, 9am–1pm Sun. **Adm charge**. **Adm** to other rooms by request to Ufficio Personale, Consiglio di Stato 677 71.

THIS MAJESTIC PALAZZO, built around 1540 for Cardinal Capo di Ferro, has an elegant stuccoed courtyard and facade decorated with reliefs evoking Rome's glorious past.

Cardinal Bernardino Spada, who lived here in the 17th century with his brother Virginio (also a cardinal), hired Bernini and Borromini to work on the building. The brothers' whimsical delight in false perspectives resulted in a colonnaded gallery by Borromini that appears four times longer than it really is.

The cardinals also amassed a superb private collection of paintings. These are now displayed in the Galleria Spada together with some Classical statues and 18th-century furniture. The wide range of artists represented includes Rubens, Dürer and Guido Reni. Works to look out for by lesser artists include *The Visitation* by Andrea del Sarto (1486–1530), *Cain and Abel* by Giovanni Lanfranco (1582–1647) and *The Death of Dido* by Guercino (1591–1666).

Santa Maria dell'Orazione e Morte ❻

Via Giulia. **Map** 4 E5 & 11 B4. 23, 65, 280. **Open** for mass 6pm Sun, public hols.

A PIOUS CONFRATERNITY was formed here in the 16th century to collect the bodies of the unknown dead and give them a Christian burial. The theme of death is stressed in this church, dedicated to St Mary of Prayer and Death. The doors and windows of Ferdinando Fuga's dramatic Baroque facade are decorated with winged skulls. Above the central entrance there is a *clepsydra* (an ancient hourglass) – symbolic of death.

Offertory box in Santa Maria dell'Orazione e Morte

Palazzo Farnese ❼

Piazza Farnese. **Map** 4 E5 & 11 B4. 46, 62, 64, 70, 71, 87, 90, 186, 492, 926. **Not open** to the public.

AN IMPOSING building that became the prototype for many princely palaces, Palazzo Farnese was originally built for Cardinal Alessandro Farnese, who commissioned the greatest artists of the time to work on its design.

After the cardinal became Pope Paul III in 1534, the building was redesigned by Antonio da Sangallo the Younger. He was assisted in this by Michelangelo, who contributed the great cornice and central window of the main facade, and the third level of the courtyard.

Michelangelo had a plan for the Farnese gardens to be connected by a bridge to the Farnese home in Trastevere, Villa Farnesina *(see pp220–21)*. The elegant arch spanning Via Giulia belongs to this sadly unrealized scheme. The palazzo was finally completed in 1589, on a less ambitious scale, by Giacomo della Porta. It is now the home of the French Embassy.

Majestic facade of Palazzo Farnese

Spada Chapel in San Girolamo

San Girolamo della Carità ⓗ

Via di Monserrato 62A. **Map** 4 E5 & 11 B4. [687 97 86. ▦ 23, 46, 62, 64, 65, 280. **Open** 7.40am–noon Mon–Sat, 10.45am–noon Sun. 🚹 ◙

THE CHURCH was built on the site of the home of San Filippo Neri, the 16th-century saint from Tuscany. This warm, patient character renewed Rome's spiritual and cultural life by his friendly, open approach to religion. He would have loved the frolicking putti shown surrounding his statue, in his chapel, reminding him of the Roman urchins he had cared for during his lifetime.

The breathtaking Spada Chapel was designed by Borromini, and is unique both

Statue of San Filippo Neri by Pierre Legros

as a work of art and as an illustration of the spirit of the Baroque age. All architectural elements are concealed so that the space of the chapel's interior is defined solely by decorative marblework and statues. Veined jasper and precious multicoloured marbles are sculpted to imitate flowery damask and velvet hangings. Even the altar rail is a long swag of jasper drapery held up by a pair of kneeling angels with wooden wings.

Although there are memorials to former members of the Spada family, oddly there is no indication as to which of the Spadas was responsible for endowing the chapel. It was probably art-lover Cardinal Virginio Spada, a follower of San Filippo Neri.

Sant'Eligio degli Orefici ⓘ

Via di Sant'Eligio 8A. **Map** 4 D4 & 11 B4. [686 82 60. ▦ 23, 41, 46, 62, 64, 65, 280. **Open** 10am–noon Mon–Sat. When closed ring at No. 9 Via di Sant'Eligio. **Closed** Aug & Sep. 🚹 ◙

THE NAME of the church still records the fact that it was commissioned by a rich corp-oration of goldsmiths (orefici) in the early 16th century. The original design was by Raphael, who, like his master Bramante, had acquired a sense of the grandiose from the remains of Roman antiquity. The influence of some of Bramante's works, such as the choir of Santa Maria del Popolo (see p138–9), is evident in the simple way the arches and pilasters define the structure of the walls.

The cupola of Sant' Eligio is attributed to Baldassarre Peruzzi, while the facade was added in the early 17th century by Flaminio Ponzio. Among the various 16th-century painters who decorated the interior was Taddeo Zuccari, who worked on Palazzo Farnese (see p147).

Santa Maria di Monserrato ⓙ

Via di Monserrato. **Map** 4 E4 & 11 B3. [686 58 61. ▦ 23, 41, 46, 62, 64, 65, 280. **Closed** to the public except by special permission: apply only in writing to the address above. 🚹 ◙

An early bust by Bernini of Cardinal Pedro Foix de Montoya

THE ORIGINS of this, the Spanish national church in Rome, go back to 1506, when a hospice for Spanish pilgrims was begun by a brotherhood dedicated to the Virgin of Montserrat in Catalonia. Don't miss Bernini's bust of Pedro Foix de Montoya, the church's benefactor, and Annibale Carracci's painting of *San Diego de Alcalá*. There is also a copy of a Sansovino statue of St James in the third chapel on the left and some beautiful 15th-century tombs by Andrea Bregno and Luigi Capponi in the courtyard and side chapels.

San Diego by Annibale Carracci

Palazzo Ricci ⓫

Piazza de' Ricci. **Map** 4 D4 & 11 B4.
23, 46, 62, 64, 65, 280.
Not open to the public.

Palazzo Ricci was famous
for its frescoed facade –
now rather faded – originally
painted in the 16th century
by Polidoro da Caravaggio, a
follower of Raphael.

In Renaissance Rome it
was common to commission
artists to decorate the outsides
of their houses with heroes of
Classical antiquity. A fresco
by a leading artist such as
Polidoro, reputedly the
inventor of this style of
painting, was a conspicuous
status symbol. Decorative
schemes like this required
inventiveness to outshine the
other palazzi, a mastery of
perspective and, above all,
great dexterity as the painting
on wet plaster had to be
completed before it dried.

Palazzo della Cancelleria ⓬

Piazza della Cancelleria. **Map** 4 E4 &
11 C3. 69 82. 44, 46, 62, 64,
70, 81, 87, 90, 90b, 186, 492, 926.
Open 4pm–8pm Mon–Sat with
permit only.

The palazzo, a supreme
example of the confident
architecture of the Early
Renaissance, was begun in
1485. It was financed partly
with the gambling winnings
of Cardinal Raffaele Riario.
Roses, the emblem of the
Riario family, adorn the vaults
and capitals of the beautiful
Doric courtyard. The palazzo's
interior was decorated after
the Sack of Rome in 1527.
Giorgio Vasari boasted that he
had completed work
on one enormous
room in just 100 days;
Michelangelo allegedly
retorted: "It looks like
it." Other Mannerist
artists, Perin del Vaga
and Francesco Salviati,
frescoed the rooms of
the cardinal in charge
of the Papal Chancellery, the
office that gave the palazzo
its name when it was
installed here by Pope Leo X.

**Lily on facade
of the Piccola
Farnesina**

Part of the frescoed facade of Palazzo Ricci

On the right of the main
entrance is the unobtrusive
church of San Lorenzo in
Damaso, founded by Pope
Damasus (reigned 366–384).
Its surrounding porticoes
housed libraries which held
the first Papal Archives.

Piccola Farnesina ⓭

Corso Vittorio Emanuele II 166.
Map 4 E4 & 11 C3. 68 80 68 48.
46, 62, 64, 70, 81, 87, 90, 90b,
186, 492, 926. **Open** 9am–1.30pm
Tue–Sun, 5pm–8pm Tue, Thu.
Adm charge.

This delightful miniature
palazzo acquired its name
from the lilies decorating
its cornices. These were
mistakenly identified as part
of the Farnese family crest. In
fact they were part of the coat
of arms of a French clergyman,
Thomas Leroy, for whom the
palazzo was built in 1523.

The entrance is in a new
facade built to overlook
Corso Vittorio Emanuele II
when the road was constructed
at the turn of the century.
The original facade on the
left of today's entrance is
attributed to Antonio da
Sangallo the Younger.
Note the asymmetrical
arrangement of its
windows and ledges.
The elegant central
courtyard also retains
its original appearance.
The Piccola Farnesina
now houses the Museo
Barracco, a collection
of ancient sculpture assembled
during the last century by the
politician Baron Giovanni
Barracco. A bust of the baron

can be seen in the courtyard.
The collection includes
Assyrian, Egyptian, Greek and
Etruscan works as well as
Roman ones. Some of the
exhibits are rather fragmentary,
but in the setting of this fine
Renaissance building they
make an attractive display.

Inner courtyard, Piccola Farnesina

Burcardo Theatre Museum ⓮

Via del Sudario 44. **Map** 4 F4 & 12 D4.
68 80 67 55. 44, 46, 56, 60,
62, 64, 70, 81, 90, 90b, 492, 926.
Open 9am–1.30pm Mon–Fri,
9am–5.30pm Thu. **Closed** Aug.

This late 15th-century house
belonged to Johannes
Burckhardt, chamberlain to
Pope Alexander VI Borgia and
author of a diary describing
Rome under the Borgias. His
house now holds Rome's most
complete collection of theatre
literature, with over 30,000
books, plus Chinese puppets
and comic masks from the
various regions of Italy.

Teatro Argentina ⓯

Via di Torre Argentina. **Map** 4 F4 & 12 D4. **[** 68 80 46 01. **📞** 44, 46, 56, 60, 62, 64, 70, 81, 90, 90b, 94, 492, 926. **Plays** performed Oct–Jun. See **Entertainment** pp346–7.

O NE OF ROME'S most important theatres was founded by the powerful Sforza Cesarini family in 1730, though the facade dates from a century later. Many famous operas were first performed here. In 1816, for example, the theatre saw the ill-fated début of Rossini's *Barber of Seville*, during which the composer insulted the unappreciative audience, who then pursued him, enraged, through the streets of Rome. Many of Verdi's masterpieces were first produced here.

Detail of facade, Teatro Argentina

Area Sacra ⓰

Largo di Torre Argentina. **Map** 4 F4 & 12 D4. **📞** 44, 46, 56, 60, 62, 64, 70, 81, 90, 90b, 94, 492, 926. Apply for permit to: Ripartizione X (see p367).

T HE REMAINS of four temples were discovered here during rebuilding in the 1920s. They date from the era of the Republic, and are among the oldest to have been found in Rome. For the purpose of identification, they are known as A, B, C and D. The oldest (temple C) dates back to the 4th century BC. It was placed on a high platform preceded by an altar and is typical of Italic temple plans as opposed to the Greek model. Temple A is from the 3rd century BC. In medieval times the small church of San Nicola was built over its podium. The remains of its two apses are still visible.

The column stumps to the north belonged to a great

San Carlo at Prayer by Guido Reni

portico, known as the Hecatostylum (portico of 100 columns). In Imperial times two marble lavatories were built here – the remains of one are visible behind temple A. Behind temples B and C are remains of a great platform of tufa blocks. These have been identified as part of the Curia of Pompey, a rectangular building housing a statue of Pompey, where the Senate met and where Julius Caesar was assassinated on 15 March 44 BC.

Area Sacra, with circular ruins of temple B in the foreground

San Carlo ai Catinari ⓱

Piazza B Cairoli. **Map** 4 F5 & 12 D4. **[** 689 38 74. **📞** 44, 56, 60, 65, 75, 170, 710, 926. **Open** 7am–noon, 4pm–8pm. **Closed** May, Jun. **✝** **📷**

I N 1620 ROME'S Milanese congregation decided to honour the new saint, their countryman Cardinal Carlo

Borromeo, with this great church. It is called "ai Catinari" on account of the bowl-makers' *(catinari)* shops in the area. The solemn travertine facade was completed in 1638 by the Roman architect Soria. The 16th-century basilical plan is flanked by chapels. The St Cecilia chapel was designed and decorated by Antonio Gherardi, who added a family portrait.

The church's paintings and frescoes by Pietro da Cortona and Guido Reni are confident, mature works of the Counter Reformation, depicting the life and acts of the recently canonized San Carlo. Make sure you also see the ornate crucifix, inlaid with marble, glass and mother-of-pearl, by the 16th-century sculptor Algardi on the sacristy altar.

Sacristy altar, San Carlo ai Catinari

Fontana delle Tartarughe ⓲

Piazza Mattei. **Map** 4 F5 & 12 D4. **📞** 44, 56, 60, 65, 75, 170, 710, 926.

T HE DELIGHTFUL Fontana delle Tartarughe – *tartarughe* are tortoises – was commissioned by the Mattei family to decorate "their" piazza between 1581 and 1588. The design was by Giacomo della Porta, but the fountain owes much of its grace and charm to the four slender bronze youths each resting one foot on the head of a dolphin, sculpted by Taddeo Landini. Nearly a century later an unknown sculptor was inspired to add the struggling tortoises to complete the composition.

Della Porta's graceful Fontana delle Tartarughe

Santa Maria in Campitelli 🄳

Piazza di Campitelli. **Map** 4 F5 & 12E5. **[** 68 80 39 78. **🚌** 57, 90, 90b, 92, 94, 95, 716. **Open** 7am–noon, 4pm–7pm daily. ✝ 🄿 ♿

Cherubs, Santa Maria in Campitelli

IN 17TH-CENTURY ROME the plague could still strike fiercely and there were no reliable, effective remedies. Many Romans simply prayed for a cure to a sacred medieval icon of the Virgin, the Madonna del Portico. When a particularly lethal outbreak of plague abated in 1656, popular gratitude was so strong that a new church was built to house the icon in appropriate splendour.

The church, designed by Bernini's pupil, Carlo Rainaldi, was completed in 1667. The main elements of the lively Baroque facade are the graceful columns, symbolizing the supporters of the true faith.

Inside the church a fabulous gilded altar tabernacle with spiral columns was designed by Giovanni Antonio de Rossi to contain the image of the Virgin. The side chapels are decorated by some of Rome's

finest Baroque painters: Sebastiano Conca, Giovanni Battista Gaulli (known as Il Baciccia) and Luca Giordano.

Theatre of Marcellus 🄴

Via del Teatro di Marcello. **Map** 4 A5 & 12 E5. **[** 481 48 00. **🚌** 57, 90, 90b, 92, 94, 95, 716. **Closed** except for concerts. See **Entertainment** p343.

THE CURVED OUTER WALL of this vast amphitheatre has supported generations of Roman buildings. It was built by the Emperor Augustus, who dedicated it to Marcellus, his nephew and son-in-law, who had died aged 19 in 23 BC. By the 13th century the theatre had been converted into the fortress of the Savelli family. In the 16th century Baldassarre Peruzzi built a great palace on the theatre ruins for the Orsini family, including a garden facing the Tiber. The lower arches were later occupied by humble dwellings and workshops.

Close to the theatre stand three beautiful Corinthian columns and a section of frieze. These belonged to the Temple of Apollo, which housed many works of art plundered by the Romans from Greece in the 2nd century BC.

Lavish altar tabernacle in Santa Maria in Campitelli

The Theatre of Marcellus by Thomas Hartley Cromek (1809–73)

Portico of Octavia 🄵

Via del Portico d'Ottavia. **Map** 4 F5 & 12 E5. **🚌** 57, 90, 90b, 92, 94, 95, 716.

BUILT IN HONOUR of Augustus's sister Octavia (the abandoned wife of Mark Antony), this is the only surviving portico of what used to be the monumental piazza of Circus Flaminius.

The rectangular portico enclosed temples dedicated to Jupiter and Juno, decorated with bronze statues. The part we see today is the great central atrium originally covered by marble facings.

In the Middle Ages a great fish market and a church, Sant'Angelo in Pescheria, were built in the ruins of the portico. As the church was associated with the fishing activities of the nearby river port, aquatic flora and fauna feature in many of its inlays. Links with the Tiber are also apparent in the stucco facade on the adjacent Fishmonger's Oratory, built in 1689. The church has a detached fresco of the Madonna and angels painted by the school of Benozzo Gozzoli.

San Nicola in Carcere ❷

Via del Teatro di Marcello 46. **Map** 5 A5 & 12 E5. [📞] 686 99 72. [🚌] 57, 90, 90b, 92, 94, 95, 716. **Open** 7.30am–noon, 4pm–7pm Mon–Sat, 10am–1pm Sun. **Closed** Aug–mid-Sep. [🛗] [📷]

THE MEDIEVAL CHURCH of San Nicola in Carcere stands on the site of three Roman temples of the Republican era which were converted into a prison in the Middle Ages (*carcere* means prison). The temples of Juno, Spes and Janus faced a city gate leading from the Forum Holitorium, the city's vegetable and oil market, to the road down to the port on the Tiber. The columns embedded in the walls of the church belonged to two flanking temples whose platforms are now marked by grass lawns.

The church was rebuilt in 1599 and restored in the 19th century, but the bell tower and Roman columns are part of the original design.

Facade and medieval bell tower of San Nicola in Carcere

Tiber Island ❷

Isola Tiberina. **Map** 8 D1 & 12 D5. [🚌] 15, 23, 97, 774, 780.

IN ANCIENT TIMES the island, which lay opposite the city's port, had large structures of white travertine at either end built to resemble the stern and prow of a ship.

Since 293 BC, when a temple was dedicated here to Aesculapius, the god of healing and protector against the plague, the island has been associated with the sick. There is still a hospital on the

Tiber Island, with Ponte Cestio linking it to Trastevere

island. San Bartolomeo, the church in the island's central piazza, was built on the ruins of the Temple of Aesculapius in the 10th century. Its Romanesque bell tower is a useful landmark, clearly visible from the banks of the Tiber.

From the Ghetto area you can reach the island by a footbridge, the Ponte Fabricio. The oldest original bridge over the Tiber still in use, it was built in 62 BC. In medieval times the Pierleoni, and then the Caetani, two powerful families, controlled this strategic point by means of a tower, still in situ. The other bridge to the island, the Ponte Cestio, is inscribed with the names of the Byzantine emperors associated with its restoration in AD 370.

Ghetto and Synagogue ❷

Synagogue, Lungotevere dei Cenci. **Map** 4 F5 & 12 E5. [📞] 687 50 51. [🚌] 23, 44, 56, 60, 65, 75, 170, 710, 774. **Open** 9.30am–2pm, 3pm–5pm. **Closed** Sat. [Ø] [🚻] [🛗] **Ghetto**, main street is Via del Portico d'Ottavia.

EVEN THOUGH they were first brought to Rome as slaves by Pompey the Great, Jews were much appreciated for their financial and medical skills during the time of the Roman Empire. In the Middle Ages their relative freedom continued; in fact, the anti-Pope Anacletus came from a converted Jewish family.

It was not until the 16th century that there was any systematic persecution. From 25 July 1556 all the Jews of Rome were forced to live inside a high-walled enclosure erected on the orders of Pope

Paul IV. The Ghetto was in a particularly unhealthy part of Rome. Inhabitants were allowed out during the day, but at night the gates were locked. On Sundays they were driven into the church of Sant'Angelo in Pescheria to listen to Christian sermons – a practice abolished only in 1848. Persecution started again under Fascism, when hundreds were sent to German concentration camps.

Today many Jews still live here and the medieval streets, with shops selling typical Roman kosher food, retain much of their old character. The imposing Synagogue on Lungotevere was built in 1874.

Synagogue overlooking the Tiber

Palazzo Cenci ❷

Vicolo dei Cenci. **Map** 4 F5 & 12 D5. [🚌] 44, 56, 60, 65, 75, 170, 710. **Not open** to the public.

PALAZZO CENCI belonged to the family of Beatrice Cenci, who was accused, together with her brothers and stepmother, of witchcraft and the murder of her tyrannical father. She was condemned to death and beheaded at Ponte Sant'Angelo in 1599.

Most of the original medieval palazzo has been demolished, and the building you see today dates back to the 1570s, though its rather forbidding appearance seems medieval.

Heraldic half-moons decorate the main facade on Via del Progresso while pretty balconies open on the opposite side where a medieval arch joins the palace to Palazzetto Cenci, designed by Martino Longhi the Elder. Inside is a traditional courtyard with an Ionic-style loggia; many of the rooms retain the original 16th-century decoration that the unfortunate Beatrice would have known as a child.

Balcony of Palazzo Cenci

Casa di Lorenzo Manilio ㉖

Via del Portico d'Ottavia 1D. **Map** 4 F5 & 12 D5. 🚌 *44, 56, 60, 65, 75, 170, 710.* **Not open** to the public.

Bᴇꜰᴏʀᴇ ᴛʜᴇ ʀᴇɴᴀɪꜱꜱᴀɴᴄᴇ, most Romans had only vague, confused ideas of their city's glorious past, but after the 15th-century revival of interest in the philosophy and arts of antiquity, some even encouraged to build houses recalling the splendour of ancient Rome. In 1468 a certain Lorenzo Manilio built a great house for his family, decorating it with an elegant Classical plaque. The Latin inscription dates the building according to the ancient Roman method – 2,221 years

after the foundation of the city – and mentions the owner's name. Original reliefs are embedded in the facades as well as a fragment of an ancient sarcophagus. The Piazza Costaguti facade features windows patriotically inscribed with the legend *Have Roma* (Hail Rome).

Row of Roman busts decorating the Casa di Lorenzo Manilio

Via Giulia ㉗

Map 4 D4 & 11 A3. 🚌 *23, 65, 280.*

Tʜɪꜱ ᴘɪᴄᴛᴜʀᴇꜱQᴜᴇ 16th-century street was built by Bramante for Pope Julius II della Rovere. Lined with aristocratic palazzi dating from the 16th–18th centuries as well as churches and antique shops, Via Giulia makes a fascinating walk *(see pp276–7).*

Mask fountain in Via Giulia

San Giovanni dei Fiorentini ㉘

Via Acciaioli 2. **Map** 4 D4 & 11 A2. 🇮 *687 08 86.* 🚌 *23, 46, 62, 64, 65, 280.* **Open** *7am–11am, 5pm–7.30pm (Oct–Mar: 4.30pm–7pm) daily.* 🛉

Tʜᴇ ᴄʜᴜʀᴄʜ of St John of the Florentines was built for the large Florentine community living in this area. Pope Leo X wanted it to be an expression of the cultural superiority of Florence over Rome. Started in the early 16th century, the church took over a century to build. The principal architect was Antonio da Sangallo the Younger, but many others contributed before Carlo Maderno's elongated cupola was finally completed in 1614. The present facade, recently cleaned and restored, was added in the 18th century.

The church was decorated mainly by Tuscan artists. One interesting exception is the 15th-century statue of San Giovannino by the Sicilian Mino del Reame in a niche above the sacristy. The spectacular high altar houses a marble group by Antonio Raggi, the *Baptism of Christ*. The altar itself is by Borromini, who is buried in the church along with Carlo Maderno.

This is the only church in Rome where animals are welcomed: the faithful can bring their pets, and an annual Easter lamb-blessing ceremony takes place here.

Antonio Raggi's *Baptism of Christ* in San Giovanni dei Fiorentini

QUIRINAL

ONE OF THE original seven hills of Rome, the Quirinal was a largely residential area in Imperial times. To the east of the hill were the vast Baths of Diocletian, still standing today in front of what is now the main rail station. Abandoned during the Middle Ages, the district returned to favour in the late 16th century. The

1st-century BC stucco in the Museo Nazionale Romano

prime site was taken by the popes for the Palazzo del Quirinale. Great families such as the Colonna and the Aldobrandini had their palazzi lower down the hill. With the end of papal rule in 1870, the Quirinal became the residence of the kings of Italy, and the surrounding area, especially along the Via Nazionale, was redeveloped.

SIGHTS AT A GLANCE

Churches
Santi Apostoli ❹
San Marcello al Corso ❻
Santa Maria in Trivio ❽
Santi Vincenzo e Anastasio ❿
Sant'Andrea al Quirinale ⓫
San Carlo alle Quattro Fontane ⓬
San Bernardo alle Terme ⓮
Santa Maria degli Angeli ⓱
Santa Maria dei Monti ㉑
Sant'Agata dei Goti ㉒
Santi Domenico e Sisto ㉔

Museums and Galleries
Museo delle Cere ❺
Accademia Nazionale di San Luca ❾

Museo Nazionale Romano ⓲
Palazzo delle Esposizioni ⓴

Historic Piazzas
Piazza della Repubblica ⓳

Historic Buildings
Palazzo del Quirinale ❷
Palazzo Colonna ❸
Baths of Diocletian ⓰

Fountains and Statues
Castor and Pollux ❶
Trevi Fountain ❼
Le Quattro Fontane ⓭
Moses Fountain ⓯

Parks and Gardens
Villa Aldobrandini ㉓

GETTING THERE
The area has Metro stops at Repubblica and Cavour. Useful buses include the 64, 65, 70 and 75 along Via Nazionale and the 71 and 81, which go under the Quirinal through the Traforo Umberto I tunnel. There is no bus to the top of the Quirinal, however. You have to walk up Via XXIV Maggio.

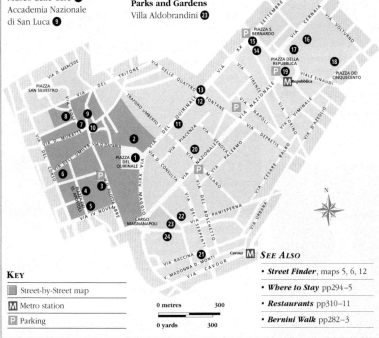

KEY

▨	Street-by-Street map
Ⓜ	Metro station
Ⓟ	Parking

0 metres   300
0 yards   300

SEE ALSO

Fontana delle Naiadi in Piazza della Repubblica

Street-by-Street: The Quirinal Hill

EVEN THOUGH Palazzo del Quirinale is closed to the public, it is well worth walking up the hill to the palace to see the giant Roman statues of Castor and Pollux in the piazza and enjoy fine views of the city below. Come down the hill by way of the narrow streets and stairways that lead to one of Rome's unforgettable sights, the Trevi Fountain. Many small churches lie hidden away in the back streets. Towards Piazza Venezia there are grand palazzi, including that of the Colonna, one of Rome's most ancient and powerful families.

Santa Maria in Via is famous for its medieval well and miraculous 13th-century icon of the Madonna.

Santa Maria in Trivio
The attractive facade of this tiny church conceals a rich Baroque interior **8**

Accademia Nazionale di San Luca
The art academy has works by famous former members, such as Canova and Angelica Kauffmann **9**

★ **Trevi Fountain**
Rome's grandest and best-known fountain almost fills the tiny Piazza di Trevi **7**

Santi Vincenzo e Anastasio
The grand facade of this small Baroque church is on a corner facing the Trevi Fountain **10**

San Marcello al Corso
This stark Crucifixion by Van Dyck hangs in the sacristy of the church **6**

Palazzo Odescalchi has a Bernini facade from 1664, with a balustrade and richly decorated cornice. The building faces Santi Apostoli.

Museo delle Cere
The emphasis of this wax museum, opened in 1953, is on horror **5**

To Piazza Venezia

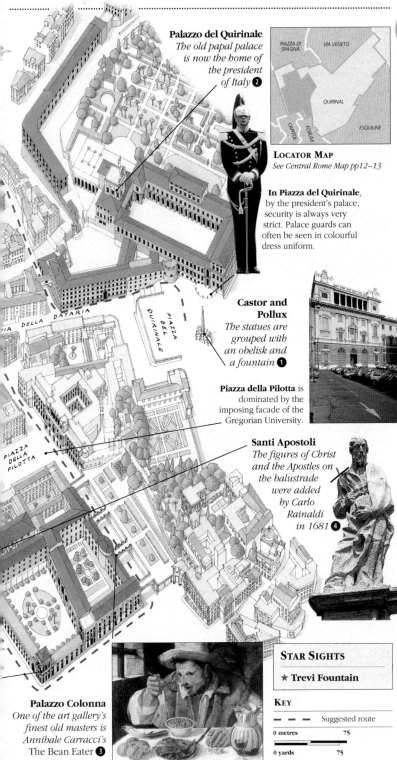

Palazzo del Quirinale
The old papal palace is now the home of the president of Italy ❷

LOCATOR MAP
See Central Rome Map pp12–13

In Piazza del Quirinale, by the president's palace, security is always very strict. Palace guards can often be seen in colourful dress uniform.

Castor and Pollux
The statues are grouped with an obelisk and a fountain ❶

Piazza della Pilotta is dominated by the imposing facade of the Gregorian University.

Santi Apostoli
The figures of Christ and the Apostles on the balustrade were added by Carlo Rainaldi in 1681 ❹

Palazzo Colonna
One of the art gallery's finest old masters is Annibale Carracci's The Bean Eater ❸

STAR SIGHTS

★ Trevi Fountain

KEY

– – – Suggested route

| 0 metres | 75 |
| 0 yards | 75 |

Castor and Pollux ❶

Piazza del Quirinale. **Map** 5 B4.
🚌 52, 53, 56, 60, 61, 62, 71, 81, 95, 119, 492 and many other routes.

Quirinal fountain and obelisk with Roman statues of Castor and Pollux

CASTOR AND POLLUX – the patrons of horsemanship – and their prancing horses stand in splendour in the Piazza del Quirinale. Over 5.5 m (18 ft) high, these statues are huge Roman copies of 5th-century BC Greek originals. They once stood at the entrance to the nearby Baths of Constantine. Pope Sixtus V had them restored and placed here in 1588. Formerly known as the "horse tamers", they gave the square its familiar name of Monte Cavallo (horse hill).

The obelisk which stands between them was brought here in 1786 from the Mausoleum of Augustus. In 1818 the composition was completed by the addition of a massive granite basin, once a cattle trough in the Forum.

Palazzo del Quirinale ❷

Piazza del Quirinale. **Map** 5 B3.
🚌 52, 53, 56, 60, 61, 62, 71, 81, 95, 119, 492 and many other routes.
Not open to the public.

BY THE 1500s, the Vatican had a reputation as an unhealthy location because of the high incidence of malaria, so Pope Gregory XIII chose this superb site on the highest

of Rome's seven hills as a summer residence for the popes. Work began in 1574. The Piazza del Quirinale has buildings on three sides while the fourth is open, giving a splendid view over the city to the great dome of St Peter's in the distance.

Many great architects worked on the palace, before it assumed its present form in the 1730s. Domenico Fontana designed the main facade, Carlo Maderno the huge chapel and Bernini the narrow wing that runs the length of Via del Quirinale.

Following the unification of Italy in 1870, it became the official residence of the king, then in 1947 of the president of the republic. For security reasons, the palace and gardens have been closed to the public since 1979.

Canova's monument to Pope Clement XIV in Santi Apostoli, with figures of Humility and Modesty

Palazzo del Quirinale, official residence of the president of Italy

Palazzo Colonna ❸

Via della Pilotta 17. **Map** 5 A4 & 12 F3. 📞 679 43 62. 🚌 57, 64, 65, 70, 75, 81, 170, 492, 710 and many other routes. **Open** 9am–12.30pm Sat only (last adm: noon). **Closed** Aug. **Adm charge.** 🚫 📷 on request.

POPE MARTIN V Colonna (reigned 1417–31) began building the palazzo, but most of the structure dates from the 18th century. The art gallery, built by Antonio del Grande between 1654 and 1665, is the only part open to the public. The pictures are numbered but unlabelled, so pick up a guide on the way in. Go up the stairs and through the antechamber

leading to a series of three gleaming marble rooms with prominent yellow columns, the Colonna family emblem (*colonna* means column).

The ceiling frescoes celebrate Marcantonio Colonna's victory over the Turks at the Battle of Lepanto (1571). On the walls are 16th- to 18th-century paintings, including Annibale Carracci's *Bean Eater (see p157)*. The room of landscape paintings, many by Poussin's brother-in-law Gaspare Dughet, reflects the 18th-century taste of Cardinal Girolamo Colonna. Beyond is a room with a ceiling fresco of the *Apotheosis of Martin V*. The throne room has a chair reserved for visiting popes and a copy of Pisanello's portrait of the portly Martin V.

The gallery also offers a fine view of the private palace garden, site of the ruined Temple of Serapis.

Santi Apostoli ❹

Piazza dei Santi Apostoli. **Map** 5 A4 & 12 F3. 📞 679 73 35. 🚌 56, 60, 64, 65, 70, 75, 85, 90, 170, 492 and many other routes. **Open** 6.30am–noon, 4pm–7.15pm daily. ✝️ 📷

THE ORIGINAL 6th-century church on this site was rebuilt in the 15th century by Popes Martin V Colonna and

Sixtus IV della Rovere, whose oak tree crest decorates the capitals of the late 15th-century portico. Inside the portico on the left is Canova's 1807 memorial to the engraver Giovanni Volpato. The church itself contains a much larger monument by Canova, his Tomb of Clement XIV (1789).

The Baroque interior by Francesco and Carlo Fontana was completed in 1714. Note the 3-D effect of Giovanni Odazzi's painted *Rebel Angels*, who really look as though they are falling from the sky. A huge 18th-century altarpiece by Domenico Muratori shows the martyrdom of the Apostles James and Philip, whose tombs are in the crypt.

Museo delle Cere ❺

Piazza dei Santi Apostoli 67. **Map** 5 A4 & 12 F3. **📞** 679 64 82. **🚌** 56, 60, 64, 65, 70, 75, 85, 90, 170, 492 and many other routes. **Open** 9am–8pm daily. **Adm charge**.

Facade of Rome's wax museum

EXHIBITS in Rome's wax museum include politicians and a recreation of Mussolini's last cabinet meeting. For the ghoulishly inclined, it also boasts a vintage electric chair.

San Marcello al Corso ❻

Piazza San Marcello 5. **Map** 5 A4 & 12 F3. **📞** 678 08 88. **🚌** 56, 60, 62, 70, 85, 90, 95, 492. **Open** 6.30am–noon, 4pm–7pm daily. **✝ 📷**

THIS CHURCH was originally one of the first places of Christian worship in Rome, which were known as *tituli*. A later Romanesque building

burned down in 1519, and was rebuilt by Jacopo Sansovino with a single nave and many richly-decorated private chapels on either side.

The third chapel on the right has fine frescoes of scenes from the life of the Virgin Mary by Francesco Salviati. The decoration of the next chapel was interrupted by the Sack of Rome in 1527. Raphael's follower Perin del Vaga fled, leaving the ceiling frescoes to be completed by Daniele da Volterra and Pellegrino Tibaldi when peace returned to the city.

In the nave stands a splendid Venetian-style double tomb by Sansovino, a memorial to Cardinal Giovanni Michiel (victim of a Borgia poisoning in 1503) and his nephew, Bishop Antonio Orso.

Trevi Fountain ❼

Fontana di Trevi. **Map** 5 A3 & 12 F2. **🚌** 52, 53, 58, 60, 61, 62, 71, 95, 492 and many other routes.

MOST VISITORS assume that it has always been there, but by the standards of the Eternal City, the Trevi Fountain is a fairly recent creation.

Rome's grandest fountain, the Trevi

Nicola Salvi's theatrical design for Rome's largest and most famous fountain was completed only in 1762. The central figures are Neptune, flanked by two Tritons. One struggles to master a very unruly "sea-horse", the other leads a far more docile animal. These symbolize the two contrasting moods of the sea.

The site originally marked the terminal of the Aqua Virgo aqueduct built in 19 BC. One of the first-storey reliefs shows a young girl (the legendary virgin after whom the aqueduct was named) pointing to the spring from which the water flows.

Chapel in San Marcello al Corso, decorated by Francesco Salviati

Santa Maria in Trivio ⑧

Piazza dei Crociferi 49. **Map** 5 A3 & 12 F2. **(** 679 52 53. ➡ *52, 53, 58, 60, 61, 62, 71, 95, 492 and many other routes.* **Open** *8.10am–noon, 4pm–7pm daily (phone first).* ✝ ◎

Facade of Santa Maria in Trivio at the turn of the century

IT HAS BEEN SAID that Italian architecture is one of facades, and nowhere is this clearer than in the 1570s facade of Santa Maria in Trivio, delightfully stuck on to the building behind it. Note the false windows. There is illusion inside too, particularly in the ceiling frescoes, which show scenes from the New Testament by Antonio Gherardi (1644–1702).

The name of the tiny church probably means "St Mary-at-the-meeting-of-three-roads". The word Trivio has been corrupted to Trevi, hence the name of the famous fountain.

Accademia Nazionale di San Luca ⑨

Piazza dell'Accademia di San Luca 77. **Map** 5 A3 & 12 F2. **(** 679 88 50. ➡ *52, 53, 56, 58, 60, 61, 62, 71, 81, 95, 119, 492.* **Open** *9am–1pm Mon, Wed, Fri and last Sun of month (last adm: 12.15pm).* **Closed** *Jul, Aug, public hols.* ◎ ♿ *apply to custodian.*

ST LUKE IS supposed to have been a painter, hence the name of Rome's academy of fine arts. Appropriately, the gallery contains a painting of

St Luke Painting a Portrait of the Virgin by Raphael and his followers. The academy's heyday was in the 17th and 18th centuries, when many members made gifts of their work to the collection. Canova, for example, donated a model for his famous marble group, the *Three Graces*.

Of particular interest are three fascinating self-portraits by women: the 17th-century Italian Lavinia Fontana; the 18th-century Swiss Angelica Kauffmann, whose painting is copied from a portrait of her by Joshua Reynolds; and Elisabeth Vigée-Lebrun, the French painter of the years before the 1789 Revolution.

Santi Vincenzo e Anastasio ⑩

Vicolo dei Modelli 73. **Map** 5 A3 & 12 F2. **(** 678 30 98. ➡ *52, 53, 58, 60, 61, 62, 71, 95, 492 and many other routes.* **Open** *6.45am–11am, 4pm–7pm daily.* ✝ ◎

OVERLOOKING the Trevi Fountain is one of the most over-the-top Baroque facades in Rome. Its thickets of columns are crowned by

the huge coat of arms of Cardinal Raimondo Mazzarino, who commissioned Martino Longhi the Younger to build the church in 1650. The female bust above the door is of one of the cardinal's famous nieces, either Louis XIV's first love, Maria Mancini (1639–1715), or her younger sister, Ortensia. In the apse, memorial plaques record the popes whose *praecordia* (a part of the heart) are enshrined behind the wall. This gruesome tradition was started at the end of the 16th century by Pope Sixtus V. It continued until Pius X put a stop to it in the early years of this century.

Facade of Santi Vincenzo e Anastasio by Martino Longhi

Self-portrait by Lavinia Fontana in the Accademia Nazionale di San Luca

Interior of Bernini's oval Sant'Andrea al Quirinale

Sant'Andrea al Quirinale ⓫

Via del Quirinale 29. **Map** 5 B3.
📞 *474 48 01.* 🚌 *56, 64, 65, 70,
75, 94, 170.* **Open** *8am–noon, 4pm–
7pm Wed–Mon.* **Closed** *Aug.*
Gratuity *expected by sacristan for
showing St Stanislas's rooms.* 🔌 📷

K NOWN AS the "Pearl of the
Baroque" because of its
beautiful roseate marble
interior, Sant'Andrea was
designed by Bernini and
executed by his assistants
between 1658 and 1670. It was
built for the Jesuits, hence
the many IHS emblems (*Jesus
Hominum Salvator* – Jesus
Saviour of Mankind).

The site for the church was
wide but shallow, so Bernini
took the innovative step of
pointing the long axis of his
oval plan not towards the altar,
but towards the sides; he
then leads the eye round to
the altar end. Here he ordered
works of art in various media
which function not in
isolation, but together. The

crucified St Andrew (Sant'
Andrea) of the altarpiece
looks up at a stucco version
of himself, who in turn
ascends towards the lantern
and the Holy Spirit.

Do not miss the rooms of
St Stanislas Kostka. The
quarters of the Jesuit novice,
who died in 1568 aged 19,
reflect not his own spartan
taste, but the richer style of
the 17th-century Jesuits. The
Polish saint has been brilliantly
immortalized in marble by
Pierre Legros (1666–1719).

San Carlo alle Quattro Fontane ⓬

Via del Quirinale 23. **Map** 5 B3.
📞 *488 32 61.* 🚌 *52, 53, 56, 60,
61, 62, 95, 492.* **Open** *9am–1pm
Mon–Sat; 4pm–6pm Mon–Fri.* 🔌 📷

I N 1634, the Spanish
Trinitarians, an order whose
role was to pay the ransom of
Christian hostages to the Arabs,
commissioned Borromini to
design a church and convent
at the Quattro Fontane
crossroads. The church, so
small it would fit inside one
of the piers of St Peter's, is
also known as "San Carlino".

Although dedicated to Carlo
Borromeo, the 16th-century
Milanese cardinal canonized
in 1620, San Carlo is as much
a monument to Borromini.
Both the facade and the
interior employ bold, fluid
curves that give light and life
to a small, cramped site. The
oval dome and tiny lantern
are particularly ingenious. The
undulating lines of the facade
are decorated with angels and
a statue of San Carlo. Finished
in 1667, the facade is one of
Borromini's very last works.

There are further delights in
the playful inverted shapes in
the cloister and the stucco
work in the refectory (now
the sacristy), which houses a
painting of San Carlo by
Orazio Borgianni (1611).

In a small room off the
sacristy hangs a portrait of
Borromini himself wearing the
Trinitarian cross. Borromini
committed suicide in 1667,
and in the crypt (which may
soon be opened to the public)
a small curved chapel reserved
for him remains empty.

Dome of San Carlo alle Quattro Fontane, lit by concealed windows

Le Quattro Fontane ⑬

Intersection of Via delle Quattro Fontane and Via del Quirinale. **Map** 5 B3. 🚌 *56, 60, 61, 64, 65, 70, 75, 95, 119, 492.* Ⓜ *Barberini.*

Fountain of Strength (or Juno)

THESE FOUR small fountains are attached to the corners of the buildings at the inter-section of two narrow, busy streets. They date from the great redevelopment of Rome in the reign of Sixtus V (1585–90). Each fountain has a statue of a reclining deity. The river god accompanied by the she-wolf is clearly the Tiber; the other male figure may be the Nile or the Aniene. The female figures represent Strength and Fidelity or the goddesses, Juno and Diana.

The crossroads is at the highest point of the Quirinal hill and commands splendid views of three distant landmark obelisks: those placed by Sixtus V in front of Santa Maria Maggiore and Trinità dei Monti, and the one that stands in Piazza del Quirinale.

San Bernardo alle Terme ⑭

Via Torino 94. **Map** 5 C3. 📞 *488 21 22.* 🚌 *60, 61, 62, 65, 492.* Ⓜ *Repubblica.* **Open** *6am–6.30pm daily.* 🏛 📷 ♿

THE CHURCH is on the southern side of the piazza of the same name. It was once one of four round

towers which stood at the corners of the ruined Baths of Diocletian (Terme di Diocleziano). Like a miniature Pantheon, the church has a dome with octagonal coffering and a small opening at the top to light the interior. In the great circular wall supporting the dome there are eight niches, housing huge plaster statues of saints by Camillo Mariani (1567–1611).

It was only in 1598 that Countess Caterina Nobili Sforza had the idea of transforming this tower into a church. She lies buried beneath one of the fine 18th-century marble altars.

Moses Fountain ⑮

Fontana dell'Acqua Felice, Piazza San Bernardo. **Map** 5 C2. 🚌 *60, 61, 62, 65, 492.* Ⓜ *Repubblica.*

Fontana's Moses Fountain

OFFICIALLY KNOWN as the Fontana dell'Acqua Felice, this fountain owes its popular name to the grotesque

statue of Moses in the central niche. The massive structure with its three elegant arches was designed by Domenico Fontana to mark the terminal of the Acqua Felice aqueduct, so-called because it was one of the many great improvements commissioned by Felice Peretti, Pope Sixtus V. Completed in 1586, it brought clean piped water to this quarter of Rome for the first time.

Pope Sixtus V, the great town-planner

The notorious statue of Moses striking water from the rock is larger than life and the proportions of the body are obviously wrong. Sculpted either by Prospero Bresciano or Leonardo Sormani, it is a clumsy attempt at recreating the awesome appearance of Michelangelo's Moses in the church of San Pietro in Vincoli *(see p170).* As soon as it was unveiled, it was said to be frowning at having been brought into the world by such an inept sculptor.

The side reliefs also illustrate water stories from the Old Testament: Aaron leading the Israelites to water and Joshua pointing the army towards the Red Sea. The fountain's four lions are copies of Egyptian originals (now in the Vatican Museums), which Sixtus V had put there for public "convenience" and "delight".

Fidelity (or Diana) with her attendant dog, one of the Quattro Fontane

over a hectare (2.5 acres) of ground between the present Piazza dei Cinquecento and Piazza della Repubblica. The baths, the most extensive in Rome, could accommodate up to 3,000 bathers at a time. The best-preserved areas have been adapted to house the church of Santa Maria degli Angeli and the Museo Nazionale Romano.

Santa Maria degli Angeli ⓱

Via Cernaia 9. **Map** 6 D3. 488 08 12. 57, 65, 75, 170, 492, 910 and many other routes. Repubblica, Termini. **Open** 10.30am–noon, 4pm–7pm Mon–Sun.

INCORPORATED into the ruined Baths of Diocletian by Michelangelo in 1563, the church was so altered in the 18th century by Luigi Vanvitelli it has lost most of its original character. The most striking works of art are a fresco of the *Martyrdom of St Sebastian* by Domenichino and a gigantic statue of St Bruno by Jean-Antoine Houdon. An exhibition in the sacristy gives a detailed account of Michelangelo's original design.

Museo Nazionale Romano ⓲

Viale Enrico de Nicola 79. **Map** 6 D2. 48 90 35 07. 57, 65, 75, 170, 492, 910 and many other routes. Repubblica, Termini. **Open** 9am–2pm Tue–Sat, 9am–1pm Sun & public hols (last adm: 30 min before closing). **Adm charge.**

FOUNDED IN 1889, the Museo Nazionale holds most of the antiquities found in Rome since 1870. It has also absorbed pre-existing collections, notably that of the Ludovisi family, to become one of the world's leading museums of Classical art. It occupies the part of the Baths of Diocletian not taken up by the church of Santa Maria degli Angeli, including the former Carthusian monastery, which

Part of the Museo Nazionale Romano in the Baths of Diocletian

Baths of Diocletian ⓰

Terme di Diocleziano, Piazza della Repubblica. **Map** 6 D3. 57, 65, 75, 170, 492, 910 and many other routes. Repubblica, Termini.

BUILT IN AD 298–306 under the infamous Emperor Diocletian, who was responsible for thousands of Christian deaths, the baths *(see pp22–3)* occupied well

Gold coin with head of the Emperor Diocletian (AD 285–305)

Egyptian relief showing head crowned with symbolic cobra in the Museo Nazionale Romano

has a cloister designed by Michelangelo when he was working on Santa Maria.

Unfortunately, the museum is an extreme example of the malaise afflicting many Roman museums. The majority of its rooms, which contain many first-class sarcophagi, mosaics and detached frescoes, are closed to the public. As an end in itself, a visit to the museum therefore gives more frustration than pleasure. However, if you have an hour to kill while waiting for a train from Termini station, it is well worth popping across Piazza dei Cinquecento to see the disorderly but evocative array of sculptural fragments on display around the central Renaissance courtyard.

Plans for the future include the opening of a whole new section of the museum in the former Palazzo Massimo in Piazza dei Cinquecento.

Piazza della Repubblica ⑲

Map 5 C3. 🚌 *4, 16, 36, 38, 60, 61, 62, 65, 75, 192, 492 and many other routes.* Ⓜ *Repubblica.*

Romans often refer to the piazza by its old name, Piazza Esedra, so-called because it follows the shape of an *exedra* (a semicircular recess) that was part of the Baths of Diocletian. The piazza was part of the great redevelopment undertaken when Rome became capital of a unified Italy. Under its sweeping 19th-century colonnades there were once elegant shops, but they have been ousted by banks, travel agencies and cafés.

In the middle of the piazza stands the Fontana delle Naiadi. Mario Rutelli's four naked bronze nymphs caused something of a scandal when they were unveiled in 1901. Each reclines on an aquatic creature symbolizing water in its various forms: a sea-horse for the oceans, a water snake for rivers, a swan for lakes, and a curious frilled lizard for subterranean streams. The figure in the middle, added in 1911, is of the sea god Glaucus, who represents man victorious over the hostile forces of nature.

Piazza della Repubblica and the Fontana delle Naiadi

Palazzo delle Esposizioni ⑳

Via Nazionale 194 (second entrance in Via Milano). **Map** 5 B4. 📞 *488 54 65.* 🚌 *56, 64, 65, 70, 75, 94, 170.* **Open** *10am–9pm Wed–Mon (last adm: 8.30pm).* **Closed** *public hols.* **Adm charge.** 🚫 ♿ *Via Milano entrance only.* **Concerts**, **lectures**, **films**. *See* **Entertainment** *pp346–7.* 🍴 💻 📷

Facade of the Palazzo delle Esposizioni

This somewhat grandiose building, with wide steps, Corinthian columns and statues, was designed as an exhibition centre by the architect Pio Piacentini and built by the city of Rome in 1882 during the reign of Umberto I. The main entrance looks like a triumphal arch.

The exhibition space has recently been modernized. Exhibitions change every three months, with paintings, sculpture, live performances and films on offer. Foreign films are usually shown in the original language. The palazzo also houses the Galleria Comunale d'Arte Moderna, closed to the public since the early 1980s.

Santa Maria dei Monti ㉑

Via Madonna dei Monti 41. **Map** 5 B4. 📞 *48 55 31.* 🚌 *11, 27, 81.* Ⓜ *Cavour.* **Open** *7am–noon, 5pm– 7.30pm Mon–Sat, 8.30am–1.30pm Sun, public hols.* ✝ 📷 ♿

Designed by Giacomo della Porta, this church, dating from 1580, has a particularly splendid dome. Over the high altar is a medieval painting of the Madonna, patroness of this quarter of Rome. The altar in the left transept houses the tomb and effigy of the unworldly French saint Benoit-Joseph Labre, who died here in 1783, having spent his life as a solitary pilgrim. While in Rome he slept rough in the ruins of the Colosseum, gave away any charitable gifts he received, and came regularly to Santa Maria dei Monti to worship. Still in his mid-thirties, he collapsed and died outside the church. The foul rags he wore are preserved as relics.

One of the bronze nymphs of the fountain in Piazza della Repubblica

Sant'Agata dei Goti 🄜

Via Mazzarino 16 and Via Panisperna.
Map 5 B4. **(** 488 19 94. 🚌 57,
64, 65, 70, 81, 170. **Open** 7am–9am,
5.30pm–7pm Mon–Sat, 7am–11am
Sun (phone first). 🚹 📷 🚻

T HE GOTHS who gave their
name to this church (*Goti*
are Goths) occupied Rome in
the 6th century AD. They
were Arian heretics who
denied the divinity of Christ.
The church was founded
shortly before the main
Gothic invasions, between
AD 462 and 470, and the
beautiful granite columns date
from this period. The main
altar has a well-preserved
12th-century Cosmatesque
tabernacle, but the most
delightful part of the church
is the charming 18th-century
courtyard built around an
ivy-draped well.

Villa Aldobrandini 🄝

Via Panisperna. Entrance to gardens:
Via Mazzarino 1. **Map** 5 B4.
🚌 57, 64, 65, 70, 75, 170.
Gardens open dawn–dusk daily.
Villa not open to the public.

B UILT IN the 16th century for
the Dukes of Urbino and
acquired for his family by Pope
Clement VIII Aldobrandini
(reigned 1592–1605), the
villa is now government
property and houses an
international law library.

The villa itself, decorated
with the family's six-starred
coat of arms, is closed to the
public, but the gardens and
terraces, hidden behind a
high wall that runs along Via
Nazionale, can be reached
through an iron gate in Via
Mazzarino. Steps lead up past
2nd-century AD ruins into the
recently renovated gardens,
highly recommended as an
oasis of tranquillity in the
centre of the city. Gravel
paths lead between formal
lawns and clearly marked
specimen trees, and benches
are provided for the weary.
Since the garden is raised
some 10 m (30 ft) above street
level, the views are excellent.

18th-century courtyard of Sant'Agata dei Goti

Santi Domenico e Sisto 🄞

Largo Angelicum 1. **Map** 5 B4.
(670 22 08. 🚌 57, 64, 65, 70, 75,
170. **Open** by appt only. **Closed**
Jul–Sep. 📷

Chapel in Santi Domenico e Sisto

T HE CHURCH has a tall,
slender Baroque facade
rising above a steep flight of
steps. This divides into two
curving flights that sweep up
to the terrace in front of the
entrance. The pediment of the
facade is crowned by eight
flaming candlesticks.

The interior has a vaulted
ceiling with a large fresco
of the *Apotheosis of
St Dominic* by
Domenico Canuti
(1620–84). The
first chapel on
the right was
decorated by
Bernini, who
may also have
designed the
sculpture of Mary
Magdalene
meeting
the risen Christ
in the Garden of
Gethsemane.
This fine marble
group was
executed by

Facade of Santi Domenico e Sisto

Antonio Raggi (1649). Above
the altar is a 15th-century
terracotta plaque of the
Madonna and Child. On the
left over a side altar is a large
painting of the Madonna from
the same period, attributed to
Benozzo Gozzoli (1420–97), a
pupil of Fra Angelico.

ESQUILINE

T HE ESQUILINE is the largest and highest of Rome's seven hills. In Imperial Rome the western slopes overlooking the Forum housed the crowded slums of the Suburra. On the eastern side there were a few villas belonging to wealthy citizens like Maecenas, patron of the arts and adviser to Augustus. The essential character of the place has persisted through two millennia; it is still one of the poorer quarters

Michelangelo's *Rachel* in San Pietro in Vincoli

of the city. The area is now heavily built up, except for a rather seedy park on the Colle Oppio, a smaller hill to the south of the Esquiline, where you can see the remains of the Baths of Titus, the Baths of Trajan and Nero's Golden House. The area's main interest, however, lies in its churches. Many of these were founded on the sites of private houses where Christians met to worship secretly in the days when the religion was banned.

SIGHTS AT A GLANCE

Churches

San Martino ai Monti ❶
San Pietro in Vincoli ❷
Santa Pudenziana ❸
*Santa Maria Maggiore
pp172–3* ❹
Santa Prassede ❺
Santa Bibiana ❼

Museums

Museo Nazionale d'Arte
Orientale ❾

Historic Piazzas

Piazza Vittorio Emanuele II ❽

Ancient Sites

Auditorium of Maecenas ❿
Nero's Golden House ⓫

Arches

Arch of Gallienus ❻

GETTING THERE

This area is close to Termini station and has several other Metro stops: Vittorio Emanuele and Manzoni on line A, Cavour and Colosseo on line B. Bus routes here are a little confusing. Among the most useful are the 93 and 93b from Termini to Santa Maria Maggiore and then along Via Merulana.

SEE ALSO

• *Street Finder*, maps 5, 6

• *Restaurants* pp310–11

• *Mosaics Walk* pp280–81

KEY

▨	Street-by-Street map
FS	Railway station
M	Metro station
P	Parking

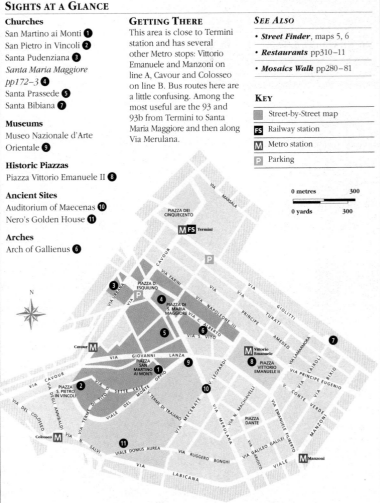

0 metres   300
0 yards   300

Southern facade of Santa Maria Maggiore by night

Street-by-Street: The Esquiline Hill

T HE SIGHT that draws most people to this rather scruffy part of Rome is the great basilica of Santa Maria Maggiore. But it is also well worth searching out some of the smaller churches on the Esquiline: Santa Pudenziana and Santa Prassede with their celebrated mosaics, and San Pietro in Vincoli, home to one of Michelangelo's most famous sculptures. To the south, in the Colle Oppio park, are the scattered remains of the Baths of Trajan.

Santa Pudenziana
The apse of this ancient church has a magnificent 4th-century mosaic of Christ surrounded by the Apostles ❸

Piazza dell'Esquilino
was furnished with an obelisk in 1587 by Pope Sixtus V. This helped to guide pilgrims coming from the north to the important church of Santa Maria Maggiore.

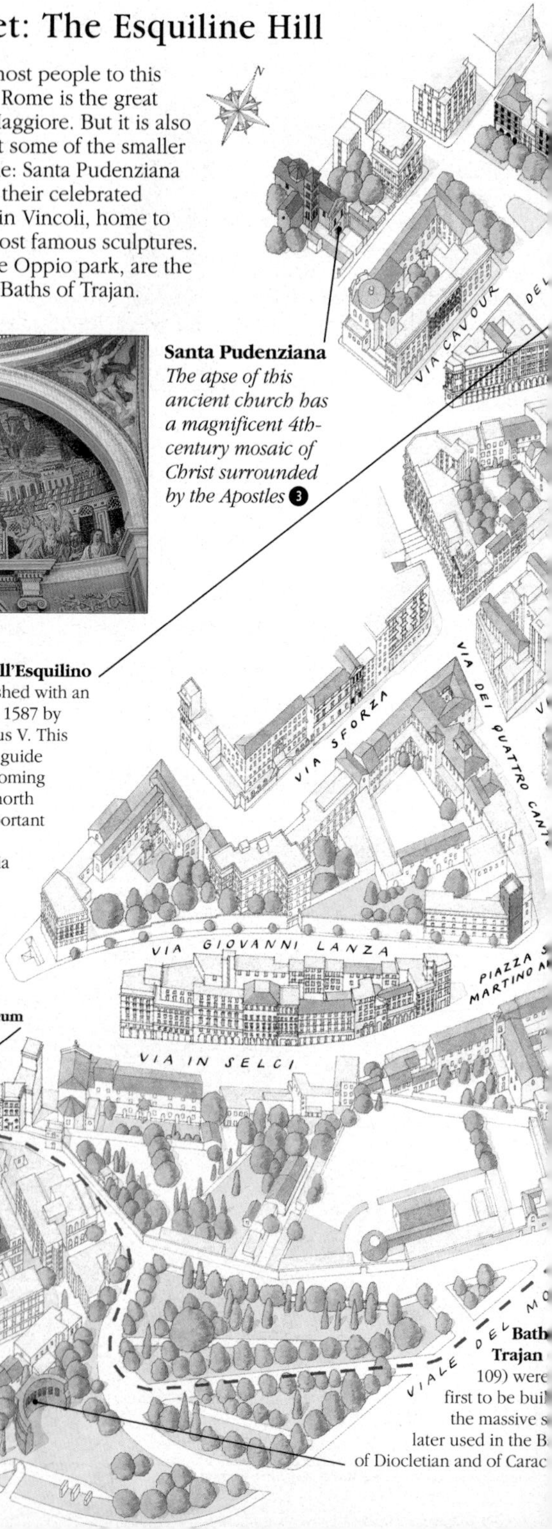

To the Colosseum

★ **San Pietro in Vincoli**
The church's treasures include Michelangelo's Moses *and the chains that bound St Peter* ❷

**Bath
Trajan**
109) were
first to be buil
the massive s
later used in the B
of Diocletian and of Carac

★ **Santa Maria Maggiore**
This imposing rear facade was added by Baroque architect Carlo Rainaldi in 1673. Santa Maria's interior is one of the most richly decorated in Rome ④

LOCATOR MAP
See Central Rome Map pp12–13

The Tomb of Pius V (died 1572) by Domenico Fontana stands in this less well-known Sistine Chapel, under the northeast dome of Santa Maria Maggiore.

VIA DELL'ESQUILINO

PIAZZA DI SANTA MARIA MAGGIORE

VIA CARLO ALBERTO

VIA MERULANA

Arch of Gallienus
This was built in the 3rd century AD to replace an entrance in the old Servian Wall ⑥

To Vittorio Emanuele Metro

★ **Santa Prassede**
The 9th-century mosaics in the Chapel of San Zeno are among the finest in Rome ⑤

The Torre dei Capocci, a restored medieval tower, is one of the area's most distinctive landmarks.

San Martino ai Monti
The frescoes include 17th-century Roman landscapes and scenes from the life of Elijah by Gaspare Dughet ①

KEY

– – – Suggested route

0 metres   75

0 yards   75

STAR SIGHTS

★ Santa Maria Maggiore

★ San Pietro in Vincoli

★ Santa Prassede

San Martino ai Monti ●

Viale del Monte Oppio 28. **Map** 6 D5.
📞 486 31 26. 🚌 11, 16, 27, 70, 71,
81, 93, 93b, 613. Ⓜ Cavour, Vittorio
Emanuele. **Open** 7am–noon, 4.30pm–
7pm (Oct–Mar: 4.30pm–6.30pm)
daily. 🕇 📷 ♿

**Fresco of old San Giovanni in
Laterano in San Martino ai Monti**

CHRISTIANS have been
worshipping on the site
of this church since the 3rd
century, when they used to
meet in the house of a man
named Equitius. In the 4th
century, after Constantine had
legalized Christianity, Pope
Sylvester I built a church, one
of very few things he did
during his pontificate. In fact
he was so insignificant that
in the 5th century a more
exciting life was fabricated
for him – which included
tales of him converting
Constantine, curing him of
leprosy and forcing him to
close all pagan temples. Pope
Sylvester's fictional life was
further enhanced in the 8th
century, with the forgery of
a document in which
Constantine offered him
the Imperial crown.
Pope Sylvester's church
was replaced in about
AD 500 by St Symmachus,
rebuilt in the 9th century
and then transformed
completely in the 1650s.
Consequently, the only
immediate signs of its age are
the ancient Corinthian
columns dividing the nave
and aisles. The most
interesting features of the
interior are a series of
frescoed landscapes of the
Campagna (the countryside

around Rome) by the 17th-
century French artist Gaspare
Dughet, Poussin's brother-in-
law, in the right aisle. The
frescoes by Filippo Gagliardi,
at either end of the left aisle,
show old St Peter's and the
interior of San Giovanni in
Laterano before Borromini's
redesign. If you can find the
sacristan, you can go beneath
the church to see the remains
of Equitius's house.

San Pietro in Vincoli ●

Piazza di San Pietro in Vincoli 4A.
Map 5 C5. 📞 488 28 65. 🚌 11, 27,
81. Ⓜ Colosseo. **Open** 7am–12.30pm,
3.30pm–7pm (Oct–Mar: 6pm) Mon–Sat,
8.45am–11.45am Sun. 🕇 📷 ♿ 🕇

ACCORDING TO TRADITION, the
two chains (vincoli) used
to shackle St Peter while he
was being held in the depths

Reliquary with St Peter's chains

of the Mamertine Prison (see
p91) were subsequently taken
to Constantinople. In the 5th
century, Empress Eudoxia
deposited one in a church in
Constantinople and sent the
other to her daughter Eudoxia
in Rome. She in turn gave hers
to Pope Leo I, who had this
church built to house it. Some
years later the second chain
was brought to Rome,
where it linked miraculously
with its partner.
The chains are still here,
displayed below the high
altar, but the church is now
best known for Michelangelo's
Tomb of Pope Julius II. When
it was commissioned in 1505,
Michelangelo spent eight
months searching for perfect
blocks of marble at Carrara in
Tuscany, but Pope Julius
became more interested in
the building of a new St
Peter's and the project
was laid aside. After the
pope's death in 1513,
Michelangelo resumed
work on the tomb, but
had only finished the
statues of *Moses* and
the *Dying Slaves* when Pope
Paul III persuaded him to
start work on the Sistine
Chapel's *Last Judgment*.
Michelangelo had
planned a vast monument
with over 40 statues, but
the tomb that was built –
mainly by his pupils –
is simply a facade with
six niches for statues. The
Dying Slaves are in Paris
and Florence, but the
tremendous bearded
Moses is here. The horns
on Moses' head should
really be beams of light
– they are the result
of the Hebrew original
from the Old Testament
being wrongly translated.

Michelangelo's *Moses* in San Pietro

Apse mosaics in Santa Prassede, showing the saint with St Paul

Santa Pudenziana ❸

Via Urbana 160. **Map** 5 C4.
📞 481 46 22. 🚌 16, 70, 71, 93,
93b, 613. Ⓜ Cavour. **Open** 8am–
noon, 4pm–7pm (Oct–Mar: 3pm–
6pm) daily. ✝ 📷

IN THE NORMAL COURSE of
events, churches tend to be
dedicated to existing saints.
In this case, the church,
through a linguistic accident,
created a brand new saint. In
the 1st century AD a Roman
senator called Pudens lived
on this site and, according to
legend, allowed St Peter to
lodge with him. In the 2nd

century a bath house was
built on this site and in the
4th century a church was
established inside the baths.
This was known as the
Ecclesia Pudentiana (the
church of Pudens). In time it
was assumed that "Pudentiana"
was a woman's name and a
life was created for her – she
became the sister of Prassede
and was credited with caring
for Christian victims of
persecution. In 1969 both
saints were declared invalid,
though their churches both
kept their names.

The 19th-century façade of
the church retains an 11th-
century frieze depicting both
Prassede and Pudenziana

dressed as crowned Byzantine
empresses – the Church's way
of asserting that it was as
important as the temporal
authority of Byzantium.

The apse has a remarkable
4th-century mosaic, clearly
influenced by Classical pagan
art in its use of subtle colours.
The Apostles are represented
as Roman senators in togas.
Unfortunately, a clumsy
attempt at restoration in the
16th century destroyed two of
the Apostles and left other
figures without their legs.

Santa Maria Maggiore ❹

See pp172–3.

Santa Prassede ❺

Via Santa Prassede 9A. **Map** 6 D4.
📞 488 24 56. 🚌 16, 93, 93b, 613.
Ⓜ Vittorio Emanuele. **Open** 7.30am–
noon, 4pm–6.30pm daily. ✝ 📷 ♿

9th-century mosaics, Santa Prassede

THE CHURCH was founded
by Pope Paschal II in the
9th century on the site of a
2nd-century oratory. Artists
from Byzantium decorated the
church with glittering, jewel-
coloured mosaics. Those in
the apse and choir depict
stylized white-robed elders,
the haloed elect looking down
from the gold and blue walls
of heaven, spindly-legged
lambs, feather-mop palm trees
and bright red poppies. In the
apse, Santa Prassede and
Santa Pudenziana stand on
either side of Christ, with the
fatherly arms of St Paul and St
Peter on their shoulders. There
are also beautiful mosaics in
the Chapel of St Zeno, built
as a mausoleum for Pope
Paschal's mother, Theodora.

11th-century frieze and medallions on the façade of Santa Pudenziana

Santa Maria Maggiore ❹

O F ALL THE GREAT Roman basilicas, Santa Maria has the most successful blend of different architectural styles. Its colonnaded triple nave is part of the original 5th-century building. The Cosmatesque marble floor and delightful Romanesque bell tower, with its blue ceramic roundels, are medieval. The Renaissance saw a new coffered ceiling, and the Baroque gave the church twin domes and its imposing front and rear facades. The mosaics are Santa Maria's most famous feature. From the 5th century come the Biblical scenes in the nave and the spectacular mosaics on the triumphal arch. Medieval highlights include a 13th-century enthroned Christ in the loggia.

★ **Cappella Paolina**
Flaminio Ponzio designed this richly decorated chapel (1611) for Pope Paul V Borghese.

Obelisk in Piazza dell'Esquilino
The Egyptian obelisk was erected by Pope Sixtus V in 1587 as a landmark for pilgrims.

LEGEND OF THE SNOW

In 352, Pope Liberius had a dream in which the Virgin told him to build a church on the spot where he found snow. When it fell on the Esquiline, on the morning of 5 August in the middle of a baking Roman summer, he naturally obeyed. The miracle of the snow is commemorated each year by a service during which thousands of white petals float down from the ceiling of Santa Maria. Originally roses were used, but nowadays the petals are more usually taken from dahlias.

Coffered Ceiling
The gilded ceiling, possibly by Giuliano da Sangallo, was a gift of Alexander VI Borgia at the end of the 15th century. The gold is said to be the first brought from America by Columbus.

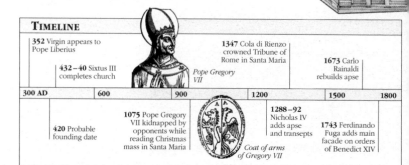

TIMELINE

352 Virgin appears to Pope Liberius			**1347** Cola di Rienzo crowned Tribune of Rome in Santa Maria	**1673** Carlo Rainaldi rebuilds apse
	432–40 Sixtus III completes church	*Pope Gregory VII*		
300 AD	**600**	**900**	**1200**	**1500** **1800**
	420 Probable founding date	**1075** Pope Gregory VII kidnapped by opponents while reading Christmas mass in Santa Maria	**1288–92** Nicholas IV adds apse and transepts *Coat of arms of Gregory VII*	**1743** Ferdinando Fuga adds main facade on orders of Benedict XIV

VISITORS' CHECKLIST

Piazza di Santa Maria Maggiore.
Map 6 D4. ℂ *48 31 95.*
🚌 *16, 27, 70, 71, 93, 93b to
Piazza di Santa Maria Maggiore
& many routes to Piazza dei
Cinquecento.* 🚃 *14.* Ⓜ *Termini,
Cavour.* **Open** *7am–8pm
(Oct–Mar: 7pm) daily (last adm:
15 mins before closing).* ✝ 📷

★ Coronation of the Virgin Mosaic
This is the central image of a series
of wonderful apse mosaics of the
Virgin by Jacopo Torriti (1295).

Baldacchino *(1740s)*
Its columns of red
porphyry and bronze
were the work of
Ferdinando Fuga.

**★ Tomb of
Cardinal
Rodriguez**
The Gothic
tomb (1299)
contains
magnificent
Cosmatesque
marblework.

★ Cappella Sistina
The chapel was built for
Pope Sixtus V (1585–90) by
Domenico Fontana and
houses the pope's tomb.

**Column in Piazza
Santa Maria Maggiore**
A bronze of the Virgin and Child was
added to this ancient marble column
in 1615. The column came from the
Basilica of Constantine in the Forum.

STAR FEATURES

★ **Cappella Sistina**

★ **Coronation of the
Virgin Mosaic**

★ **Cappella Paolina**

★ **Tomb of Cardinal
Rodriguez**

Arch erected in memory of Emperor Gallienus

Arch of Gallienus 6

Via Carlo Alberto. **Map** 6 D4. 🚌 4, 9, 16, 70, 71. Ⓜ Vittorio Emanuele.

Squashed between two buildings just off Via Carlo Alberto is the central arch of an originally three-arched gate erected in memory of Emperor Gallienus, who was assassinated by his Illyrian officers in AD 262. It was built on the site of the old Esquiline Gate in the Servian Wall, parts of which are visible nearby.

Santa Bibiana 7

Via Giovanni Giolitti 154.
Map 6 F4. 🅒 731 33 62. 🚌
11, 70, 71. Ⓜ Vittorio Emanuele.
Open 7am–10am, 4.30pm–7.30pm
(Oct–Mar: 7pm) daily. 🚻 📷 ♿

The deceptively simple facade of Santa Bibiana was Bernini's first foray into architecture. It is a clean, economic design with superimposed pilasters and deeply shadowed archways. The church itself was built on the site of the palace belonging to Bibiana's family. This is where the saint was buried

after being flogged to death with leaded cords during the brief persecution of the Christians that took place in the reign of Julian the Apostate (361–3). Just inside the church is a small column against which Bibiana is said to have been whipped. Her remains, along with those of her mother Dafrosa and her sister Demetria, who also suffered martyrdom, are preserved in an alabaster urn below the altar. In a niche above the altar stands a statue of Santa Bibiana by Bernini – the first fully-clothed figure he ever sculpted. He depicts her standing beside a column, holding the cords with which she was whipped, apparently on the verge of a deadly swoon.

Early sculpture by Bernini of the martyr Santa Bibiana (1626)

Piazza Vittorio Emanuele II 8

Map 6 E5. 🚌 4, 9, 11, 70, 71, 105. 🚆 14, 516, 517. Ⓜ Vittorio Emanuele.
See **Markets** p338.

Piazza Vittorio, as it is called for short, is one of the city's main open-air food markets. The huge arcaded square was built in the grand urban development undertaken after the unification of Italy in 1870. It was named after Italy's first king, but there is nothing regal about its appearance today. The arcades are very shabby, sheltering shops and stalls selling all sorts of cheap shoes and clothes, from trainers to wedding dresses.

The equally neglected garden area in the centre of the square contains a number of mysterious ruins, including a large mound, the remains of a Roman fountain from the 3rd century AD and the Porta Magica, a curious 17th-century doorway inscribed with alchemical signs and formulae.

Museo Nazionale d'Arte Orientale 9

Via Merulana 248. **Map** 6 D5.
🅒 73 59 46. 🚌 4, 9, 16, 70, 71, 93, 93b, 613. Ⓜ Vittorio Emanuele.
Closed for restoration.

The museum occupies part of the late 19th-century Palazzo Brancaccio, which became the home of the Italian Institute of the Middle and Far East in 1957. The collection ranges from prehistoric Iranian ceramics, sculpture from Afghanistan, Nepal, Kashmir and India to 18th-century Tibetan paintings on vellum. From the Far East there are collections of Japanese screen paintings and Chinese jade.
The most unusual exhibits are the finds from the Italian excavation of the ancient civilization of Swat in

4th-century relief from Kashmir

**Nepalese Bodhisattva in the
Museo Nazionale d'Arte Orientale**

northeast Pakistan. This
fascinating culture lasted from
the 3rd century BC to about
the 10th century AD. Its
wonderfully exotic, sensual
reliefs show an unusual
combination of Hellenistic,
Buddhist and Hindu influences.

Auditorium of
Maecenas ⑩

Largo Leopardi. **Map** 6 D5.
🚌 4, 9, 16, 70, 71, 81, 93, 93b,
613. Ⓜ Vittorio Emanuele. **Open**
9am–1.30pm Tue–Sun; also Apr–Sep:
4pm–7pm Thu, Sat. 🚫 ♿

Mᴀᴇᴄᴇɴᴀѕ, dandy dresser,
gourmet and patron of
the arts, was also an astute,
lifelong adviser and colleague
of the Emperor Augustus. He
was fabulously rich, and
spent some of his wealth
creating a fantastic villa and
gardens on the Esquiline hill,
most of which has long
disappeared beneath the
modern city. The partially
reconstructed auditorium,
isolated on a traffic island, is
all that remains.

Inside, a semicircle of tiered
seats suggests that it may
have been a place for
readings and performances. If
it was, then Maecenas would
have been entertained here
by his protégés, the lyric poet
Horace and Virgil, author of
the *Aeneid*, reading their
latest works. However, water
ducts have also been
discovered and it may well
have been a *nympheum* – a

kind of summerhouse – with
fountains. Traces of frescoes
remain on the walls: you can
make out garden scenes and
a procession of miniature
figures – including one of a
drunken Dionysus being
propped upright by a satyr.

Nero's Golden
House ⑪

Domus Aurea, Via Labicana 136. **Map**
5 C5. 📞 699 01 10. 🚌 15, 81, 85,
87, 186. **Closed** for restoration;
phone the Soprintendenza
Archeologica at the above number
(8am–1.30pm) to arrange a visit.

**Frescoed room in the ruins of
Nero's Golden House**

Aꜰᴛᴇʀ ᴀʟʟᴇɢᴇᴅʟʏ setting fire
to Rome in AD 64, Nero
decided to build himself an
outrageous new palace. It
occupied part of the Palatine,
and most of the Celian and
Esquiline hills – an area
approximately 25 times the

size of the Colosseum. The
vestibule on the Palatine side
of the complex contained a
colossal gilded statue of Nero.
There was an artificial lake,
with gardens and woods
where imported wild beasts
were allowed to roam.
According to Suetonius in his
life of Nero, the palace walls
were adorned with gold and
mother-of-pearl, rooms were
designed with ceilings that
showered guests with flowers
or perfumes, the dining hall
rotated and the baths were
fed with both sulphurous
water and sea-water.

Tacitus described Nero's
debauched garden parties,
with banquets served on
barges and lakeside brothels
serviced by aristocratic women,
though as Nero killed himself
in AD 68, he did not have
long to enjoy his new home.

Nero's successors, anxious
to distance themselves from
the monster-emperor, did
their utmost to erase all traces
of the palace. Vespasian
drained the lake and built
the Colosseum (see pp92–5)
in its place, Titus and Trajan
each erected a complex of
baths over the palace, and
Hadrian placed the Temple of
Venus and Rome (see p87)
over the vestibule.

Rooms from one wing of
the palace have survived,
buried beneath the ruins of
the Baths of Trajan on the
Oppian hill. A number of
wall-paintings can still be
seen, but the underground
chambers are damp and
dangerous. They have been
closed to the public since a
landslide in 1984.

18th-century artist's impression of Nero's Golden House

LATERAN

I N THE MIDDLE AGES the Lateran Palace was the residence of the popes, and the basilica of San Giovanni beside it rivalled St Peter's in splendour. After the return of the popes from Avignon at the end of the 14th century, the area declined in importance. Pilgrims still continued to visit San Giovanni and Santa

Cherub from San Giovanni in Laterano

Croce in Gerusalemme, but the area remained sparsely inhabited. Ancient convents slumbered amid gardens and vineyards until Rome became capital of Italy in 1870 and a network of residential streets was laid out here to house the influx of newcomers. Archaeological interest lies chiefly in the Aurelian Wall and the ruins of the Aqueduct of Nero.

SIGHTS AT A GLANCE

Churches
San Giovanni in Laterano pp182–3 ❶
Santa Croce in Gerusalemme ❺
Santi Quattro Coronati ⓫
San Clemente pp186–7 ⓬
Santo Stefano Rotondo ⓭

Shrines
Scala Santa and Sancta Sanctorum ❷

Arches and Gates
Porta Asinaria ❸
Porta Maggiore ❼

Ancient Sites
Amphiteatrum Castrense ❹
Baker's Tomb ❽
Aqueduct of Nero and the Freedmen's Tombs ❾

Museums
Museum of Musical Instruments ❻

Historic Buildings
Villa Wolkonsky ❿

SEE ALSO

GETTING THERE
San Giovanni Metro station on line A is just outside the city wall, but handy for many of the sights in the area. The 16, 85, 87, 93 and 93b are among the many buses to Piazza di San Giovanni in Laterano. This can also be reached by the 13 and 30b trams. These are slow, but their routes make them useful for exploring this part of Rome.

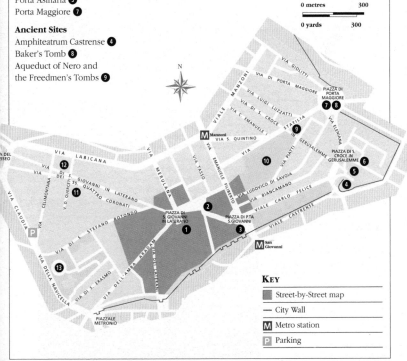

KEY
	Street-by-Street map
—	City Wall
M	Metro station
P	Parking

15th-century apse fresco in Santa Croce in Gerusalemme

Street-by-Street: Piazza di San Giovanni

BOTH THE BASILICA of San Giovanni and the Lateran Palace look out over a huge open area, the Piazza di San Giovanni, laid out at the end of the 16th century with an Egyptian obelisk, the oldest in Rome, in the centre. Sadly the traffic streaming in and out of the city through Porta San Giovanni tends to detract from its grandeur. Across the square is the building housing the Scala Santa (the Holy Staircase), one of the most revered relics in Rome and the goal for many pilgrims. The area is also a venue for political rallies, and the feast of St John on 23 June is celebrated with a fair at which Romans consume vast quantities of snails.

The Chapel of Santa Rufina, originally the portico of the baptistry, has a 5th-century mosaic of spiralling foliage in the apse.

VIA DI SANTO S

VIA DELL'AMBA ARADAM

VIA DEI LATERANI

The Cloister of San Giovanni fortunately survived the two fires that destroyed the early basilica. A 13th-century masterpiece of mosaic work, the cloister now houses fragments from the medieval basilica.

Piazza di San Giovanni in Laterano boasts an ancient obelisk and parts of Nero's Aqueduct. This 18th-century painting by Canaletto shows how the piazza once looked.

STAR SIGHTS

★ San Giovanni in Laterano

KEY

— — — Suggested route

0 metres   75

0 yards   75

The Chapel of San Venanzio is decorated with a series of 7th-century mosaics on a gold background. This detail from the apse shows one of the angels flanking the central figure of Christ. San Venanzio was an accomplished 6th-century Latin poet.

LOCATOR MAP
See Central Rome Map pp12–13

The Lateran Palace, residence of the popes until 1309, was rebuilt by Domenico Fontana in 1586.

★ **San Giovanni in Laterano**
Borromini's interior dates from the 17th century, but the grand facade by Alessandro Galilei, with its giant statues of Christ and the Apostles, was added in 1735 ❶

Scala Santa
This door at the top of the staircase leads to the Sancta Sanctorum, the pope's private chapel ❷

PIAZZA DI SAN GIOVANNI IN LATERANO

VIA D. FONTANA

PIAZZA DI PORTA SAN GIOVANNI

The Triclinio Leoniano is a piece of wall and a mosaic from the dining hall of 8th-century Pope Leo III.

Porta Asinaria
This minor gateway, no longer in use, is as old as the Aurelian Wall, dating back to the 3rd century AD ❸

San Giovanni in Laterano ❶

See pp182–3.

Scala Santa and Sancta Sanctorum ❷

Piazza di San Giovanni in Laterano 14.
Map 9 C1. 70 49 44 89. *4, 15, 16, 81, 85, 87, 186 and many other routes.* 13, 30b. San Giovanni. **Open** Apr–Sep: 6am–noon, 2.30pm–6.30pm; Oct–Mar: 6am–12.30pm, 3pm–7pm daily.

Devout Christians climbing the Scala Santa on their knees

O N THE EAST SIDE of Piazza di San Giovanni in Laterano, a building designed by Domenico Fontana (1589) houses two surviving parts of the old Lateran Palace. One is the pope's private chapel, the Sancta Sanctorum, the other the holy staircase, the Scala Santa. The 28 steps, said to be those that Christ ascended in Pontius Pilate's house during his trial, are supposed to have been brought from Jerusalem by St Helena, mother of the Emperor Constantine. This belief, however, cannot be traced back any earlier than the 7th century.

The steps were moved to their present site by Pope Sixtus V (reigned 1585–90) when the old Lateran Palace was destroyed. No foot may touch the holy steps, so they are covered by wooden boards. They may only be climbed by the faithful on their knees, a penance that is performed especially on

Good Friday. In the vestibule there are various 19th-century sculptures including an *Ecce Homo* by Giosuè Meli (1874).

The Scala Santa and two side stairways lead to the Chapel of St Lawrence or Sancta Sanctorum (Holy of Holies), built by Pope Nicholas III in 1278. Decorated with fine Cosmatesque marble-work, the chapel contains many important relics, the most precious being an image of Jesus – the *Acheiropoeton* or "picture painted without hands", said to be the work of St Luke, assisted by an angel. The image was taken on procession in medieval times to ward off plagues.

Porta Asinaria ❸

Between Piazza di Porta San Giovanni and Piazzale Appio. **Map** 10 D2. *4, 15, 16, 81, 85, 87.* 13, 30b. San Giovanni. See **Markets** p339.

T HE PORTA ASINARIA (Gate of the Donkeys) is one of the minor gateways in the Aurelian Wall *(see p196)*. Twin circular towers were added and a small enclosure built around the entrance; the remains are still visible today. From outside the walls you can see the gate's white travertine facade and two rows of small windows, giving light to two corridors built into the wall above the gateway. In

Porta Asinaria from inside the wall

AD 546 treacherous barbarian soldiers serving in the Roman army opened this gate to the hordes of the Goth Totila, who mercilessly looted the city. In 1084 the Holy Roman Emperor Henry IV entered Rome via Porta Asinaria with the antipope Guibert to oust Pope Gregory VII. The gateway was badly damaged later that year by the pope's rescuer, the Norman Robert Guiscard, who set the whole area around San Giovanni in Laterano on fire.

The area close to the gate, especially in the Via Sannio, is the home of a popular flea-market. During the week, the streets fill with stalls selling cheap clothes, both new and second-hand, shoes and camping equipment, and bargains can often be found.

Amphiteatrum Castrense ❹

Between Piazza di Santa Croce in Gerusalemme and Viale Castrense. **Map** 10 E1. *9.* 13, 30b. **Not open** to the public.

Columns and bricked-up arches of the Amphiteatrum Castrense

T HIS SMALL 3rd-century amphitheatre was used for games and baiting animals. It owes its preservation to the fact that it was incorporated in the Aurelian Wall *(see p196)*, which included several existing high buildings in its fortifications. The graceful arches framed by brick semicolumns were blocked up. The amphitheatre is best seen from outside the walls, from where there is also a good view of the bell tower of Santa Croce in Gerusalemme.

Discovery and Triumph of the Cross, attributed to Antoniazzo Romano, in Santa Croce in Gerusalemme

Santa Croce in Gerusalemme **5**

Piazza di Santa Croce in Gerusalemme 12. **Map** 10 E1. **701 47 69.** 9. 13, 30b. **Open** 6am–12.30pm, 3.30pm–7.30pm (Oct–Jun: 6.30pm) daily.

EMPEROR CONSTANTINE'S mother St Helena founded this church in AD 320 in the grounds of her private palace. Although the church stood at the edge of the city, the relics of the Crucifixion that St Helena had brought back from Jerusalem made it a centre of pilgrimage. Most important were the pieces of Christ's Cross (*croce* means cross) and part of Pontius Pilate's inscription in Latin, Hebrew and Greek: "Jesus of Nazareth King of the Jews".

In the crypt is a Roman statue of Juno, found at Ostia *(see pp270–71)*, transformed into a statue of St Helena by replacing the head and arms and adding a cross. The 15th-century apse fresco shows the medieval legends that arose around the Cross. Helena is shown holding it over a dead youth and restoring him to life. Another episode shows its recovery from the Persians by the Byzantine Emperor Heraclitus after a bloody battle. In the centre of the apse is a magnificent tomb by Jacopo Sansovino made for Cardinal Quiñones, Emperor Charles V's confessor (died 1540).

Museum of Musical Instruments **6**

Museo degli Strumenti Musicali, Piazza di Santa Croce in Gerusalemme. **Map** 10 E1. **701 47 96.** 9. 13, 30b. **Open** 9am–2pm (last adm: 1pm) Mon–Sat. **Closed** public hols. **Adm charge.**

ONE OF ROME'S lesser-known museums, the building stands on the site of the Sessorianum, the great Imperial villa belonging to Empress St Helena, later included in the Aurelian Wall. Opened in 1974, the museum has a collection of over 3,000 instruments from all over the world. It includes instruments typical of the various regions of Italy, and wind, string and percussion instruments of all ages (including Egyptian, Greek and Roman). There are also sections dedicated to church and military music.

The greater part of the collection is composed of Baroque instruments: don't miss the gorgeous Barberini harp, remarkably well-preserved, on the first floor in Room 13. There are spinets, harpsichords and clavichords of many different kinds, and one of the first pianos ever made, dating from 1722.

18th-century statue of St Helena on the facade of Santa Croce

Art Nouveau entrance to the Museum of Musical Instruments

San Giovanni in Laterano ●

Early in the 4th century, the Laterani family were disgraced and their land taken by Emperor Constantine to build Rome's first Christian basilica. Today's church retains the original shape, but has been destroyed by fire twice and rebuilt several times. Borromini undertook the last major rebuild of the interior in 1646, and the main facade is an 18th-century addition. Before the pope's move to Avignon in 1309, the adjoining Lateran Palace was the official papal residence, and until 1870 all popes were crowned in the church. The pope is the Bishop of Rome and here in the city's main cathedral he celebrates Maundy Thursday mass and attends the annual blessing of the people.

Cappella di San Venanzio
This chapel is attached to the baptistry and is decorated with 7th-century mosaics.

Entrance to museum

Apse

Papal Altar
Only the pope can celebrate mass at this altar. The Gothic baldacchino, decorated with frescoes, dates from the 14th century.

★ Cloisters
Built by the Vassalletto family in about 1220, the cloisters are remarkable for their twisted twin columns and inlaid marble mosaics.

TIMELINE

AD 313 Constantine gives Laterani site to Pope Melchiades for a church	**896** Church damaged in earthquake	**1144** Church dedicated to San Giovanni in Laterano	**1377** Return of popes from Avignon	**1646** Borromini rebuilds interior
314–18 Five-aisled basilical church is built		**1309** Papacy moves to Avignon		

AD 300	800	1000	1400	
324 Basilica consecrated by Pope Sylvester I and dedicated to the Redeemer	**904–911** Church rebuilt under Pope Sergius III	**1300** First Holy Year proclaimed	**1360** Church burnt down for second time	**1586** Domenico Fontana builds north facade
		1308 Church destroyed by fire	**1730–40** Alessandro Galilei constructs main facade	

★ Baptistry
Though much restored, the domed baptistry dates back to Constantine's time. It assumed its present octagonal shape in AD 432 and the design has served as the model for baptistries throughout the Christian world.

VISITORS' CHECKLIST

Piazza di San Giovanni in Laterano 4. **Map** 9 C2. 69 88 64 33. 4, 15, 16, 85, 87, 93, 93b and other routes to Piazza San Giovanni. San Giovanni. 13, 30b. **Church and Cloister open** 7am–7pm (Oct–Mar: 6pm) daily. **Baptistry closed** for restoration work. **Museum open** 9am–1pm, 3pm–5pm Mon–Fri. **Adm charge** for cloister and museum.

STAR FEATURES

★ **Baptistry**

★ **Cloisters**

North Facade
This was added by Domenico Fontana in 1586. The pope gives his blessing from the upper loggia.

The original Lateran Palace was almost destroyed by the fire of 1308 which devastated San Giovanni. Pope Sixtus V commissioned Fontana to replace it in 1586.

Statues of Christ and the Apostles

Boniface VIII Fresco
This fragment showing the pope proclaiming the Holy Year of 1300 is attributed to Giotto.

A side door is opened once every 25 years for Holy Year.

Main entrance on east facade

TRIAL OF A CORPSE
Fear of rival factions led the early popes to extraordinary lengths. An absurd case took place at the Lateran Palace in 897 when Pope Stephen VI tried the corpse of his predecessor, Formosus, for disloyalty to the Church. The corpse was found guilty, its right hand was mutilated and it was thrown into the Tiber.
Pope Formosus

Corsini Chapel
This chapel was built in the 1730s for Pope Clement XII. The altarpiece is a mosaic copy of Guido Reni's painting of Sant'Andrea Corsini.

Porta Maggiore ❼

Piazza di Porta Maggiore. **Map** 6 F5.
🚌 *105.* 🚋 *13, 14, 19, 19b, 516, 517.*

Originally the two arches of Porta Maggiore were not part of the city wall, but part of an aqueduct built by the Emperor Claudius in AD 52. They carried the water of the Aqua Claudia over the Via Labicana and Via Prenestina, two of ancient Rome's main southbound roads. You can still see the original roadway beneath the gate. In the large slabs of basalt – a hard volcanic rock used in all old Roman roads – note the great ruts created by generations of cartwheels. On top of the arches separate conduits carried the water of two aqueducts: the Aqua Claudia, and its offshoot, the Aqueduct of Nero. They bear inscriptions from the time of the Emperors Vespasian and Titus, who restored them in AD 71 and AD 81. In all, six aqueducts from different water sources entered the city at Porta Maggiore.

The Aqua Claudia was 68 km (43 miles) long, with more than 15 km (9 miles) above ground. Its majestic arches are a distinctive feature of the Roman countryside, and a popular brand of mineral water still bears its name. One stretch of the Aqua Claudia had its arches bricked up when it was incorporated into the 3rd-century Aurelian Wall *(see p196).*

Relief showing breadmaking on the tomb of the baker Eurysaces

Baker's Tomb ❽

Piazzale Labicano. **Map** 6 F5. 🚌 *105.*
🚋 *13, 14, 19, 19b, 516, 517.*

In the middle of the tram junction near Porta Maggiore stands the tomb of the rich baker Eurysaces and his wife Atistia, built in 30 BC. Roman custom forbade burials within city walls, and the roads leading out of cities became lined with tombs and monuments for the middle and upper classes. This tomb is shaped like a baking oven: a low-relief frieze at the top shows Eurysaces presiding over his slaves in the various phases of breadmaking. The inscription proudly asserts his origins and reveals him as a freed slave, probably of Greek origin. Many men like him saved money from their meagre slave salaries to earn their freedom and set up businesses, becoming the backbone of Rome's economy.

Relief on the Tomb of the Statilii freedmen

Aqueduct of Nero and the Freedmen's Tombs ❾

Intersection of Via Statilia and Via di Santa Croce in Gerusalemme.
Map 10 D1. 🚌 *9, 105.* 🚋 *13, 14, 19, 19b, 30b.* **Apply** for permit: Ripartizione X, (see p367).

The aqueduct was built by Nero in the 1st century AD as an extension of the Aqua Claudia. It was later extended to supply the Imperial residences on the Palatine. Partly incorporated into later buildings, the imposing arches make their way via the Lateran to the Celian hill. Along the first section of the aqueduct, in Via Statilia, is a small tomb in the shape of a house, dating from the 1st century BC, bearing the names and likenesses of a small group of freed slaves. Their name, Statilii, indicates that they had been freed by the noble Statilii, the family of Claudius's notorious wife Messalina. Servants of families often pooled funds in this way to pay for a dignified burial in a common resting place.

Porta Maggiore, a city gate formed by the arches of an aqueduct

Well-preserved section of Nero's Aqueduct near San Giovanni

Villa Wolkonsky ⑩

Via Conte Rosso. **Map** 10 D1.
🚋 *4, 81.* 🚐 *13, 30b.* **Not open** to
the public.

NOW THE RESIDENCE of the
British ambassador, the
villa has a beautiful garden
strewn with Roman remains,
including arches of the Aqua
Claudia and a columbarium,
or collective grave, of the 2nd
century AD. Sadly, garden
parties for British residents
are no longer given here on
the Queen's official birthday.

Santi Quattro Coronati ⑪

Via dei Santi Quattro Coronati 20. **Map**
9 B1. 📞 *73 53 21.* 🚋 *15, 81, 85, 87,
118.* 🚐 *13, 30b.* **Open** *9.30am–
noon, 3.30pm–6pm (Oct–Mar:
9.30am–noon) Mon–Sat.* 🏛 📷 ♿

Cloister of Santi Quattro Coronati

THE NAME of this fortified
convent (Four Crowned
Saints) refers to four Christian
soldiers martyred after they
refused to worship a pagan
god. For centuries it was the
bastion of the pope's
residence, the Lateran Palace.
Its high apse still looms over
the houses below, while a
Carolingian tower dominates
the entrance. Erected in the
4th century AD, it was rebuilt
after the invading Normans
set fire to the neighbourhood
in 1084. Hidden within is the
garden of the delightful inner
cloister (admission on request),
one of the earliest of its kind,
built around 1220.
  The remains of medieval
frescoes can be seen in the
Chapel of Santa Barbara, but
the convent's main feature is
the Chapel of St Sylvester – its
remarkable frescoes (1246)
recount the legend of the
conversion to Christianity of

the Emperor Constantine by
Pope Sylvester I (reigned 314–
35), then living as a hermit on
Monte Soratte, north of Rome.
  Stricken by the plague,
Constantine is prescribed a
bath in children's blood, to
the horror of the matrons of
Rome. Unable to bring himself
to obey, Constantine is
visited in a dream by St Peter
and St Paul. They advise him
to find Sylvester, who cures
him and baptizes him. The
final scene shows the emperor
kneeling before the pope.
The implied idea of the pope
as heir to the Roman Empire
would affect the whole course
of medieval European history.

San Clemente ⑫

See pp186–7.

Santo Stefano Rotondo ⑬

Via di Santo Stefano 7. **Map** 9 B2.
📞 *70 49 37 17.* 🚋 *15, 118, 673.*
Open *9am–noon Mon–Fri.* 🚫

ONE OF ROME'S earliest
Christian churches, Santo
Stefano Rotondo was built
between 468 and 483. It has
an unusual circular plan with
four chapels jutting out in the
shape of a cross. The round
inner area was surrounded by

**Distinctive circular outline
of Santo Stefano Rotondo**

concentric corridors with 22
Ionic columns providing
support. The high drum in
the centre is 22 m (72 ft) high
and just as wide. It is lit by 22
high windows, a few of them
restored or blocked by
restorations carried out under
Pope Nicholas V (reigned
1447–55), who consulted the
Florentine architect Leon
Battista Alberti. The archway
supported on two high
columns in the centre of the
church may have been added
during this period, when the
outer corridor was eliminated.
  In the 16th century the
church walls were frescoed
by Niccolò Pomarancio, with
particularly gruesome
illustrations of the martyrdom
of innumerable saints. Some
of the medieval decor
remains in the chapels: in the
first chapel to the left of the
entrance is a 7th-century
mosaic of Christ with San
Primo and San Feliciano.

Fresco of St Sylvester and Constantine in Santi Quattro Coronati

San Clemente ⑫

SAN CLEMENTE PROVIDES an opportunity to travel back through three layers of history. At street level, there is a 12th-century church; underneath this lies a 4th-century church; and below that are ancient Roman buildings, including a Temple of Mithras. Mithraism, an all-male fertility cult imported from Persia in the 1st century BC, was a rival to Christianity during the age of Imperial Rome.

The upper levels are dedicated to St Clement, the fourth pope, who was exiled to the Crimea and martyred by being tied to an anchor and drowned. His life is illustrated in some of the frescoes in the 4th-century church. The site was taken over in the 17th century by Irish Dominicans, who still continue the excavating work begun by Father Mullooly in 1857.

Entrance to the church is through a door in Via di San Giovanni in Laterano.

Paschal Candlestick
This 12th-century spiralling candlestick, striped with glittering mosaic, is a magnificent example of Cosmati work.

18th-Century Facade
Twelfth-century columns were used in the arcade.

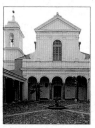

★ **Cappella di Santa Caterina**
The restored frescoes by the 15th-century Florentine artist, Masolino, show scenes from the life of the martyred St Catherine of Alexandria.

12th-century church

4th-century church

Piscina
This deep pit was discovered in 1967. It could have been used as a font or fountain.

1st–3rd-century temple and buildings

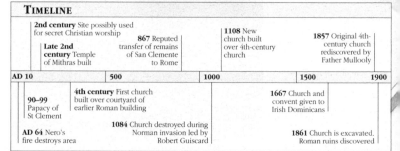

TIMELINE

2nd century Site possibly used for secret Christian worship

Late 2nd century Temple of Mithras built

867 Reputed transfer of remains of San Clemente to Rome

1108 New church built over 4th-century church

1857 Original 4th-century church rediscovered by Father Mullooly

AD 10	500	1000	1500	1900

90–99 Papacy of St Clement

4th century First church built over courtyard of earlier Roman building

1667 Church and convent given to Irish Dominicans

AD 64 Nero's fire destroys area

1084 Church destroyed during Norman invasion led by Robert Guiscard

1861 Church is excavated. Roman ruins discovered

★ Apse Mosaic
The 12th-century
Triumph of the
Cross *includes
beautifully detailed
animals and
acanthus leaves.*

Schola Cantorum
The 6th-century
enclosure for the
choir was retained
for the new church,
built in 1108.

**Temple of
Mithras**

Catacomb
Discovered in
1938 and dating
from the 5th or 6th
century, it contains
16 wall tombs
known as loculi.

VISITORS' CHECKLIST

Via di San Giovanni in Laterano.
Map 9 B1. 70 45 10 18.
81, 85, 87, 93, 186 to Via
Labicana. Colosseo. 13,
30b to Colosseo. **Open** 9am–
12.30pm, 3.30pm–6.30pm
(Oct–Mar: 6pm) daily. **Adm
charge** to excavations.

**★ Triclinium and
Altar of Mithras**
The altar, with a
relief of Mithras
slaying the bull,
stands in the
triclinium, *a room
used for ritual
banquets.*

**★ 11th-
Century
Frescoes**
Commissioned by
the de Rapiza family,
one shows the story of a boy
found alive in St Clement's
tomb beneath the Black Sea.

STAR FEATURES

★ **Apse Mosaic**

★ **Cappella di Santa
Caterina**

★ **11th-Century
Frescoes**

★ **Triclinium and Altar
of Mithras**

IOVINVSALVMNVS

CARACALLA

T HE CELIAN HILL over-
looks the Colosseum,
and takes its name
from Caelius Vibenna, the
legendary hero of Rome's
struggle against the Tarquins
(see pp16–17). In Imperial
Rome this was a fashionable
place to live, and some of
its vanished splendour is
still apparent in the vast ruins of the
Baths of Caracalla. Today, thanks to

**Capital from ruins of
Baths of Caracalla**

the Archaeological Zone
established at the turn of
the century, it is a delightfully peaceful area, a green
wedge from the Aurelian
Wall to the heart of the city.
Through it runs the cobbled
Via di Porta San Sebastiano,
part of the old Via Appia.
This road leads to Porta San
Sebastiano, one of the best-preserved
gates in the ancient city wall.

SIGHTS AT A GLANCE

Churches
Santi Giovanni e Paolo ❶
San Gregorio Magno ❷
Santa Maria in Domnica ❹
San Sisto Vecchio ❻
Santi Nereo e Achilleo ❼
San Cesareo ❽
San Giovanni a Porta Latina ❾
San Giovanni in Oleo ❿
Santa Balbina ⓰

Arches and Gates
Arch of Dolabella ❸
Arch of Drusus ⓭
Porta San Sebastiano
and the Aurelian Wall ⓮
Sangallo Bastion ⓯

Historic Buildings
UN Food and Agriculture
Organization ⓱
Baths of Caracalla ⓲

Tombs
Columbarium of
Pomponius Hylas ⓫
Tomb of the Scipios ⓬

Parks and Gardens
Villa Celimontana ❺

GETTING THERE
Circo Massimo Metro station is
handy if you are visiting the
churches and parks on the
Celian hill. For the Baths of
Caracalla and other sights
closer to Porta San Sebastiano,
take the 90 or 118 along Viale
delle Terme di Caracalla.
Other buses, such as the 93,
97 and 613, go to Piazzale
Numa Pompilio, a useful
central starting point for
exploring the area.

SEE ALSO

• *Street Finder*, maps 8, 9

• *Where to Stay* pp294–5

• *Restaurants* pp310–11

KEY
◼ Street-by-Street map
— City Wall
Ⓜ Metro station
Ⓟ Parking

Mosaic of an athlete from the Baths of Caracalla

Street-by-Street: The Celian Hill

I**N THE COURSE OF A MORNING** exploring the green
slopes of the Celian hill, you will see a fascinating
assortment of archaeological remains and beautiful
churches. A good starting point is the church of San
Gregorio Magno, from where the Clivo di Scauro leads
up to the top of the hill. The steep narrow street passes
the ancient porticoed church of Santi Giovanni e Paolo
with its beautiful Romanesque bell tower soaring above
the surrounding medieval monastery buildings. Of the
parks on the hill, the best kept and most peaceful is the
Villa Celimontana with its formal walks and avenues.
It is a good place for a
picnic, as there
are few bars or
restaurants
in the area.

Clivo di Scauro, the
Roman *Clivus Scauri*, leads
up to Santi Giovanni e
Paolo, passing under
the flying buttresses
that support
the church.

VIA DI SAN GREGORIO

CLIVO DI SCAURO

La Vignola is a
delightful Renaissance
pavilion, reconstructed
here in 1911 after it
had been demolished
during the creation of
the Archaeological
Zone around the
Baths of Caracalla.

**To Circo
Massimo
Metro**

San Gregorio Magno

*A monastery and
chapel were
founded here by
Pope Gregory the
Great at the end of
the 6th century* ❷

★ **Santi Giovanni e Paolo**
*The nave of the church, lit by a blaze
of chandeliers, has been restored
many times, assuming its present
appearance in the 18th century* ❶

★ **Villa Celimontana**
*The delightful 16th-
century villa built for the
Mattei family is now the
centre of a public park* ❺

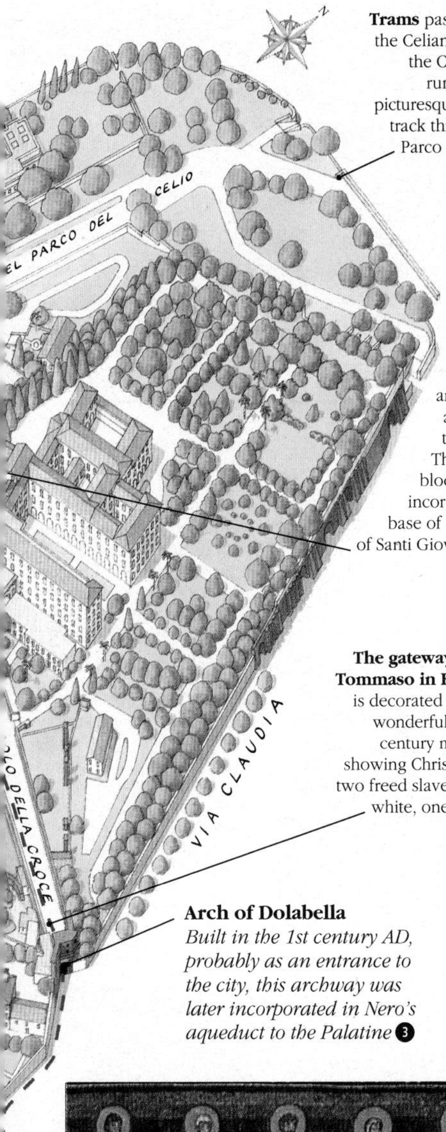

Trams passing over the Celian hill from the Colosseum rumble up a picturesque narrow track through the Parco del Celio.

LOCATOR MAP
See Central Rome Map pp12–13

Ruins of the Temple of Claudius are visible over a large area of the Celian hill. These travertine blocks have been incorporated in the base of the bell tower of Santi Giovanni e Paolo.

The gateway of San Tommaso in Formis is decorated with a wonderful 13th-century mosaic showing Christ with two freed slaves, one white, one black.

Arch of Dolabella
Built in the 1st century AD, probably as an entrance to the city, this archway was later incorporated in Nero's aqueduct to the Palatine ❸

★ **Santa Maria in Domnica**
This church is famed for its 9th-century mosaics. These Apostles appear on the triumphal arch above the apse, flanking a medallion containing the figure of Christ ❹

STAR SIGHTS

★ **Santi Giovanni e Paolo**

★ **Santa Maria in Domnica**

★ **Villa Celimontana**

KEY

– – – Suggested route

0 metres 75
0 yards 75

Santi Giovanni e Paolo ❶

Piazza Santi Giovanni e Paolo 13.
Map 9 A1. 700 57 45. 11, 15, 27, 90, 118, 673. 13, 30b.
Colosseo or Circo Massimo. **Open** 8.30am–noon, 4pm–5.30pm Sat–Thu. church only (not Roman house).

SANTI GIOVANNI E PAOLO is dedicated to two martyred Roman officers whose house stood on this site. Giovanni (John) and Paolo (Paul) had served the first Christian emperor, Constantine. When they were later called to arms by the pagan emperor, Julian the Apostate, they refused and were beheaded in their own house in AD 362.

Built towards the end of the 4th century, the church retains many elements of its original structure. The Ionic portico dates from the 12th century, and the apse and bell tower were added by Nicholas Breakspeare, the only English pope, who reigned as Adrian IV (1154–9). The base of the superb 13th-century bell tower was part of the Temple of Claudius that stood on this site. In common with many Romanesque bell towers, it has inlaid marble and ceramic roundels decorating the brickwork.

The interior, remodelled in 1718, has granite piers and columns. A tomb slab in the nave marks the burial place of the martyrs, whose relics are preserved in an urn under the high altar. In a tiny room near the altar, a magnificent 13th-century fresco depicts the figure of Christ flanked by his Apostles (ask the sacristan to unlock the door for you).

Excavations beneath the church have revealed two Roman houses, of the 2nd and 3rd centuries, united and used as a Christian burial place. The two-storeyed construction, with 20 rooms and a labyrinth of corridors, has well-preserved pagan and Christian paintings. The arches to the left of the church were part of a 3rd-century street of shops.

Fresco of Christ and the Apostles in Santi Giovanni e Paolo

San Gregorio Magno ❷

Piazza di San Gregorio. **Map** 8 F2.
700 82 87. 11, 15, 27, 118, 673. 13, 30b. Circo Massimo.
Open 9am–1pm, 4pm–7pm daily.

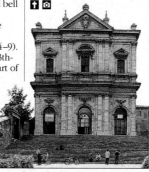

Facade of San Gregorio Magno

TO THE ENGLISH, this is one of the most important churches in Rome, for it was from here that St Augustine was sent on his mission to convert England to Christianity. The church was founded in AD 575 by San Gregorio Magno (St Gregory the Great), who turned his family home on this site into a monastery. It was rebuilt in medieval times and restored in 1629–33 by Giovanni Battista Soria. To reach the church you ascend a flight of steps from the street.

The forecourt contains some interesting tombs. To the left is that of Sir Edward Carne, who came to Rome several times between 1529 and 1533 as King Henry VIII's envoy to gain the pope's consent to the annulment of Henry's marriage to Catherine of Aragon.

The interior, remodelled by Francesco Ferrari in the mid-18th century, is typically Baroque, except for the fine mosaic floor and some ancient columns. At the end of the right aisle is the chapel of St Gregory. Leading off it, another small chapel, believed to have been the saint's own cell, houses his episcopal throne – a Roman chair of sculpted marble. The Salviati Chapel on the left contains a picture of the Virgin said to have spoken to St Gregory.

Outside, amid the cypresses to the left of the church, stand three small chapels, dedicated to St Andrew, St Sylvia (Gregory the Great's mother) and St Barbara.

Marble throne of Gregory the Great from the 1st century BC

Arch of Dolabella ❸

Via di San Paolo della Croce.
Map 9 A2. 🚌 *15, 118, 673.*

THE ARCH was built in AD 10 by the consuls Cornelius Dolabella and Caius Junius Silanus, possibly on the site of one of the gateways of the old Servian Wall. Made of solid travertine blocks, it was subsequently used to support Nero's extension of the Claudian aqueduct, built to supply the Imperial palace on the Palatine hill.

The restored Arch of Dolabella

Santa Maria in Domnica ❹

Piazza della Navicella 12. **Map** 9 A2.
📞 *700 15 19.* 🚌 *15, 118, 673.*
Open *8.30am–noon, 3.30pm–7pm (Oct–Mar: 6pm) daily.* 🚻 📷 ♿

THE CHURCH overlooks the Piazza della Navicella (little boat), which takes its name from the 16th-century fountain there. It was made from an ancient stone galley, probably a temple offering made by a Roman traveller on his safe return to the city. The church dates from the 9th century; in the 16th century Pope Leo X added the portico and the coffered ceiling.

In the apse behind the slightly incongruous modern altar is a superb 9th-century mosaic commissioned by Pope Paschal I. Wearing the square halo of the living, the pope appears at the feet of the Virgin and Child. The Virgin, surrounded by a throng of angels, holds a handkerchief in the manner of a fashionable lady at a Byzantine court.

Villa Celimontana ❺

Piazza della Navicella. **Map** 9 A2.
🚌 *15, 81, 85, 87, 90, 118, 673.*
Park open *7am–dusk daily.*

THE DUKES OF MATTEI bought this land in 1553 and transformed the vineyards that covered the hillside into a formal garden. As well as palms and other exotic trees, the garden even has its own Egyptian obelisk. Villa Mattei, built in the 1580s, is now known as Villa Celimontana and houses the Italian Geographical Society.

The Mattei family used to open the park to the public on the day of the Visit of the Seven Churches, an annual event instituted by San Filippo Neri in 1552. Starting from the Chiesa Nuova *(see p124)*, Romans went on foot to the city's seven major churches.

When they reached Villa Mattei, they were given a meal of bread, wine, salami, cheese, an egg and two apples. The garden, now owned by the city of Rome, still makes an ideal place for a picnic.

Park of Villa Celimontana

San Sisto Vecchio ❻

Piazzale Numa Pompilio 8. **Map** 9 A3.
📞 *77 51 74.* 🚌 *90, 93, 97, 118, 613, 671.* **Open** *9am–11am daily.*
Closed *Aug.* 🚫

THIS SMALL CHURCH is of great historical interest as it was granted to St Dominic in 1219 by Pope Honorius III. The founder of the Dominican order soon moved his own headquarters to Santa Sabina *(see p204)*, San Sisto becoming the first home of the order of Dominican nuns. The best feature of the church itself is the 13th-century bell tower.

Apse mosaic of the Virgin and Child in Santa Maria in Domnica

Santi Nereo e Achilleo ⑦

Via di Porta San Sebastiano 4.
Map 9 A3. █ 575 79 96. ▦ 90,
93, 118, 613, 671. **Open** 10am–
noon, 4pm–6pm Sat–Thu. ◙ &

A CCORDING to legend, St
Peter, after escaping
from prison, was
fleeing the city
when he lost a
bandage from
his wounds. The
original church
was founded
here in the 4th
century on the
spot where the
bandage fell, but
later on it was
rededicated to　　　**Detail of mosaic,**
the 1st-century　　**Santi Nereo e Achilleo**
AD martyrs St
Nereus and St Achilleus.

Restored at the end of the
16th century, the church has
retained many medieval
features, including some fine
9th-century mosaics on the
triumphal arch. A magnificent
pulpit rests on an enormous
porphyry pedestal which was
found nearby in the Baths
of Caracalla. The walls of the
side naves are decorated
with a series of rather grisly
16th-century frescoes by
Niccolò Pomarancio, showing
in clinical detail how each of
the Apostles was martyred.

**Fresco by Niccolò Pomarancio of the *Martyrdom
of St Simon* in Santi Nereo e Achilleo**

San Cesareo ⑧

Via di Porta San Sebastiano.
Map 9 A3. █ 53 01 40. ▦ 118.
Closed for restoration.

T HIS SPLENDID old church,
built over Roman ruins of
the 2nd century AD, has been
closed since 1988. You can
still admire Giacomo della
Porta's fine Renaissance
facade, but if the
workmen will let you
in, you can also see
Cosmatesque mosaic
work and carving to
rival that of any
church in Rome. The
episcopal throne, altar
and pulpit are decorated
with delightful birds
and beasts. The church
was restored in the
16th century by Pope
Clement VIII, whose coat of
arms decorates the ceiling.

San Giovanni a Porta Latina ⑨

Via di San Giovanni a Porta Latina.
Map 9 B3. █ 70 49 17 77. ▦ 4,
90, 118. **Open** 8am–12.30pm,
3pm–7pm daily. **Donation** expected.
✝ ◙ &

T HE CHURCH of "St John at
the Latin Gate" was
founded in the 5th century,
rebuilt in 720 and restored in
1191. This is one
of the most
picturesque of
the old Roman
churches. Classical
columns support
the medieval
portico, and the
12th-century bell
tower is superb.
A tall cedar tree
shades an ancient
well standing in
the forecourt. The
interior has
recently been
restored, but it
preserves the rare
simplicity of its
early origins with
ancient columns
of varying styles
lining the aisles.
Traces remain of
early medieval
frescoes. There are

12th-century frescoes showing
46 different scenes from both
the Old and New Testaments,
which are among the finest
of their kind in Rome.

Fresco, San Giovanni a Porta Latina

San Giovanni in Oleo ⑩

Via di Porta Latina. **Map** 9 C4. ▦ 4,
90, 118. ***Closed*** for restoration.

Frieze of San Giovanni in Oleo

T HE NAME of this charming
octagonal Renaissance
chapel means "St John in Oil".
The tiny building marks the
spot where, according to
legend, St John was boiled in
oil – and came out unscathed,
or even refreshed. An earlier
chapel is said to have existed
on the site; the present one
was built in the early 16th
century. The design has been
attributed to Bramante or
Antonio da Sangallo the
Younger. It was restored by
Borromini, who altered the
roof, crowning it with a cross
supported by a sphere
decorated with roses. He also
added a terracotta frieze of
roses and palm leaves. The
wall paintings inside the
chapel include one of St John
in a cauldron of boiling oil.

Niches for funerary urns in the Columbarium of Pomponius Hylas

Columbarium of Pomponius Hylas ⓫

Via di Porta Latina 10. **Map** 9 B4.
🚌 4, 90, 118. **Open** by appt only:
apply to Ripartizione X, Via del
Portico d'Ottavia 29 or phone
67 10 38 19.

KNOWN AS a columbarium because it resembles a dovecote (*columba* is the Latin word for dove), this kind of vaulted tomb was normally built by rich Romans to house the cremated remains of their freedmen. Many similar tombs have been uncovered in this part of Rome, which up until the 3rd century AD lay outside the city wall. This one, excavated in 1831, dates from the 1st century AD. An

Mosaic inscription in the
Columbarium of Pomponius Hylas

inscription informs us that it is the Tomb of Pomponius Hylas and his wife, Pomponia Vitalinis. Above her name is a "V" which indicates that she was still living when the inscription was made. The tomb was probably a commercial venture. Niches in the interior walls of the columbarium were sold to people who could not afford to build vaults of their own.

Tomb of the Scipios ⓬

Via di Porta San Sebastiano 9.
Map 9 B4. 📞 70 49 00 53. 🚌 4,
90, 118. **Closed** for restoration.

THE SCIPIOS were a family of conquering generals. Southern Italy, Corsica, Algeria, Spain and Asia Minor all fell to their victorious Roman armies. The most famous of all was Publius Cornelius Scipio Africanus, who defeated the great Carthaginian general Hannibal at the Battle of Zama in 202 BC. Scipio Africanus himself was not buried here in the family tomb, but at Liternum near Naples, where he owned a favourite villa. The Tomb of the Scipios was discovered in 1780. It contained various sarcophagi,

statues and niches with terracotta burial urns. Many of the originals have now been moved to the Vatican Museums and copies stand in their place.

The earliest sarcophagus was that of Cornelius Scipio Barbatus, consul in 298 BC, for whom the tomb was built. Members of his illustrious family continued to be buried here up to the middle of the 2nd century BC. Excavations in the area have revealed many other archaeological finds: a columbarium similar to that of Pomponius Hylas, a Christian catacomb and a three-storey house dating from the 3rd century AD, which was built over the Tomb of the Scipios.

Arch of Drusus ⓭

Via di Porta San Sebastiano.
Map 9 B4. 🚌 118.

**Arch of Drusus, part of the Aqua
Antoniniana aqueduct**

ONCE MISTAKENLY identified as a triumphal arch, the so-called Arch of Drusus merely supported the branch aqueduct that supplied the Baths of Caracalla. It was built in the 3rd century AD, so had no connection with Drusus, a stepson of the Emperor Augustus. Its monumental appearance was due to the fact that it carried the aqueduct across the important route, Via Appia. The arch still spans the old cobbled road, just 50 m (160 ft) short of the gateway Porta San Sebastiano.

Fortified gateway of Porta San Sebastiano

Porta San Sebastiano and the Aurelian Wall

Museo delle Mura, Via di Porta San Sebastiano 18. **Map** 9 B4. **(** 70 47 52 84. **(** 118. **Open** 9am–1.30pm Tue–Sat, 9am–1pm Sun; also Apr– Sep: 4pm–7pm Tue, Thu, Sat (last adm: 30 mins before closing). **Closed** public hols. **Adm charge.** ✗

MOST OF the Aurelian Wall, begun by the Emperor Aurelian (AD 270–75) and completed by his successor Probus (AD 276–82), has survived. Aurelian ordered its construction as a defence against marauding Germanic tribes, whose raids were penetrating deeper and deeper into Italy. Some 18 km (11 miles) round, with 18 gates and 381 towers, the wall took in all the seven hills of Rome. It was raised to almost twice its original height by Maxentius (AD 306–12).

Porta San Sebastiano, the gate that leads to the Via Appia Antica (see p284) is the largest and best-preserved gateway in the wall. It was rebuilt by the Emperor Honorius in the 5th century AD. Originally the Porta Appia, in Christian times it gradually became known as the Porta San Sebastiano, because the Via Appia led to the Basilica and Catacombs of San Sebastiano, which were popular places of pilgrimage.

It was at this gate that the last triumphal procession to enter the city by the Appian Way was received in state –

that of Marcantonio Colonna after the victory of Lepanto over the Turkish fleet in 1571. Today the gate's towers house a museum containing prints and models illustrating the history of the walls. The views are spectacular, especially out over the unchanging land-scape of the Via Appia.

The wall continued to be Rome's main defence until 1870, when it was breached by Italian artillery just by Porta Pia, close to today's British Embassy. Many of the gates are still in use, and although the city has spread, most of its noteworthy sights still lie within the walls.

Sangallo Bastion

Viale di Porta Ardeatina. **Map** 9 A4. **(** 93, 94, 160, 613, 671. **Closed** for restoration.

Pope Paul III Farnese

HAUNTED BY the memory of the Sack of Rome in 1527 and fearing attack by the Turks, Pope Paul III asked Antonio

da Sangallo the Younger to reinforce the Aurelian Wall. Work on the huge projecting bastion began in 1537. For the moment its massive bulk can be admired from outside.

Santa Balbina

Piazza di Santa Balbina 8. **Map** 8 F3. **(** 578 02 07. **(** 160. **M** Circo Massimo. **Open** 8am–6pm daily. ✝

OVERLOOKING the Baths of Caracalla, this isolated church framed by cypresses is dedicated to Santa Balbina, a 2nd-century virgin martyr. Dating back to the 4th century, this is one of the oldest churches in the city. Inside stands the magnificent sculpted and inlaid tomb of Cardinal Stefanus de Surdis, signed by Giovanni di Cosma and dated 1303.

UN Food and Agriculture Organization

Viale delle Terme di Caracalla. **Map** 8 F2. **(** 57 97 37 32. **(** 11, 15, 27, 90, 118, 673. **(** 13, 30b. **M** Circo Massimo. **Closed** to public.

Obelisk of Axum (4th century AD)

THE FOOD and Agriculture Organization of the United Nations is based here in a modern building completed in 1951. Before it stands the obelisk of Axum, looted from Ethiopia by Mussolini, who commissioned the building originally to house the Ministry of Italian Africa.

Baths of Caracalla ⑱

Viale delle Terme di Caracalla 52.
Map 9 A3. 🛈 575 86 26. 🚌 90, 93, 118, 160. **Open** 9am–6pm (Oct–Mar: 3pm) Tue–Sat, 9am–1pm Sun, Mon. **Closed** public hols. **Adm charge.** 📷 ♿ **Concerts** 🛈 575 83 02.

Cᴏᴍᴘʟᴇᴛᴇᴅ by the Emperor Caracalla in AD 217, the baths functioned for about 300 years, until the plumbing was destroyed by invading Goths. Over 1,500 bathers at a time could enjoy the facilities. A Roman bath was a long and complicated business, beginning with a sort of Turkish bath, followed by a spell in the *calidarium*, a large hot room with pools of water to moisten the atmosphere. Then came the lukewarm *tepidarium*, a visit to the large central meeting place, known as the *frigidarium*, and finally a plunge into the *natatio*, an open-air swimming

Fragment of mosaic pavement

pool. For the rich, this was followed by a rub-down with scented woollen cloth. As well as the baths, there were spaces for exercise, libraries, art galleries and gardens – a true leisure centre. Most of the rich marble decorations of the baths were removed by the Farnese family in the 16th century to adorn the interior of Palazzo Farnese *(see p147)*.

Part of one of the gymnasia in the Baths of Caracalla

In August open-air operas are staged in the ruins. Despite the over-bright lights and chirping crickets, the unparalleled setting makes the productions a great attraction *(see pp38–9)*.

Kᴇʏ

🔲 Calidarium (very hot)
🔲 Tepidarium (lukewarm)
🔲 Frigidarium (cold)
⬜ Natatio (pool)
🔲 Garden

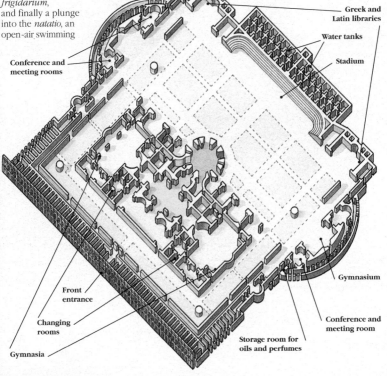

Conference and meeting rooms

Greek and Latin libraries

Water tanks

Stadium

Front entrance

Changing rooms

Gymnasia

Storage room for oils and perfumes

Gymnasium

Conference and meeting room

AVENTINE

THIS IS ONE of the most peaceful areas within the walls of the city. Although it is largely residential, there are some unique historic sights. From the top of the Aventine hill, crowned by the magnificent basilica of Santa Sabina, there are fine views across the river to Trastevere and St Peter's. At the foot of the hill, ancient Rome is preserved in the two tiny Temples of the Forum Boarium and the Circus Maximus. The liveliest streets are in Testaccio, which has shops, restaurants and clubs, while to the south, beside Rome's solitary pyramid, the Protestant Cemetery is another oasis of calm.

Mask fountain in courtyard of Santa Sabina

SIGHTS AT A GLANCE

Churches and Temples
Santa Maria in Cosmedin ❶
San Giorgio in Velabro ❸
San Teodoro ❹
Santa Maria della Consolazione ❺
San Giovanni Decollato ❻
Temples of the Forum Boarium ❽
Santa Sabina ❾
Santi Bonifacio e Alessio ❿
San Saba ⓯

Historic Buildings
Casa dei Crescenzi ❼

Arches
Arch of Janus ❷

Historic Streets and Piazzas
Piazza dei Cavalieri di Malta ⓫

Ancient Sites
Monte Testaccio ⓬
Circus Maximus ⓰

Monuments and Tombs
Protestant Cemetery ⓭
Pyramid of Caius Cestius ⓮

GETTING THERE
The quickest way is by Metro line B to Piramide or Circo Massimo. For a more interesting trip, take a tram – the 13 or 30b. Several buses go down Viale Aventino to Piramide, but the only bus to the top of the Aventine hill is the 94.

KEY

▨	Street-by-Street map
—	City Wall
Ⓜ	Metro station
Ⓟ	Parking

SEE ALSO
• **Street Finder**, maps 7, 8, 12
• **Where to Stay** pp294–5
• **Restaurants** pp310–11

0 metres   300
0 yards   300

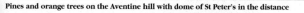

Pines and orange trees on the Aventine hill with dome of St Peter's in the distance

Street-by-Street: Piazza della Bocca della Verità

THE AREA ATTRACTS VISITORS eager to place their hands inside the Bocca della Verità (the Mouth of Truth) in the portico of Santa Maria in Cosmedin. There are many other sights to see in this quiet corner of the city beside the Tiber, which was the site of ancient Rome's first port and its busy cattle market. Substantial Classical remains include two small temples from the Republican age and the Arch of Janus from the later Empire. In the 6th century the area became home to a Greek community from Byzantium, who founded the churches of San Giorgio in Velabro and Santa Maria in Cosmedin.

Sant'Omobono, a late 16th-century church, now stands in isolation in the middle of an important archaeological site. The remains of sacrificial altars and two temples from the 6th century BC have been discovered.

Casa dei Crescenzi
This 11th-century building used columns and capitals from ancient Roman temples **7**

Ponte Rotto, as this forlorn ruined arch in the Tiber is called, means simply "broken bridge". Built in the 2nd century BC, its original name was the Pons Aemilius.

★ **Temples of the Forum Boarium**
The tiny round Temple of Hercules and its neighbour, the Temple of Portunus, are the best preserved of Rome's Republican temples **8**

LUNGOTEVERE DEI PIERLEONI

TEVERE

PONTE PALATINO

KEY

- - - Suggested route

0 metres   75
0 yards   75

STAR SIGHTS

★ Santa Maria in Cosmedin

★ Temples of the Forum Boarium

★ **Santa Maria in Cosmedin**
This medieval church has a fine marble mosaic floor and a Gothic baldacchino **1**

Santa Maria della Consolazione
This 16th-century church used to serve a hospital nearby ⑤

San Teodoro
The 15th-century portal of this ancient round church is decorated with the arms of Pope Nicholas V ④

LOCATOR MAP
See Central Rome Map pp12–13

San Giovanni Decollato
The plain Renaissance facade was completed in about 1504 ⑥

San Giorgio in Velabro
The simple 12th-century portico of Ionic columns was destroyed by a bomb in 1993 ③

Arch of Janus
This square structure with arches on each side dates from the 4th century AD ②

The Arco degli Argentari, dedicated to the Emperor Septimius Severus in AD 204, is decorated with scenes of religion and war.

The Fontana dei Tritoni by Carlo Bizzaccheri was built here in 1715. The style shows the powerful influence of Bernini.

Bocca della Verità

Santa Maria in Cosmedin ❶

Piazza della Bocca della Verità 18.
Map 8 E1. 678 14 19. 15, 23, 57, 90, 92, 94, 95, 160, 716. **Open** 9am–1pm, 3pm–6pm daily.

THIS BEAUTIFUL unadorned church was built in the 6th century on the site of the ancient city's food market. The elegant Romanesque bell tower and portico were added during the 12th century. In the 19th century a Baroque facade was removed and the church restored to its original simplicity. It contains many fine examples of Cosmati work, in particular the mosaic pavement, the raised choir, the bishop's throne and the canopy over the main altar.

Set into the wall of the portico is the Bocca della Verità (Mouth of Truth). This may have been a drain cover, dating back to before the 4th century BC. Medieval tradition had it that the formidable jaws would snap shut over the hand of those who told lies – a useful trick for testing the faithfulness of spouses.

Arch of Janus ❷

Via del Velabro. **Map** 8 E1. 15, 57, 90, 92, 95, 160, 716.

PROBABLY DATING from the reign of Constantine, this imposing four-faced marble arch stood at the bustling crossroads on the edge of the Forum Boarium, near the ancient docks. It was an ideal place for merchants and customers to do business in the shade. On the keystones above the four arches you can see small figures of the goddesses Roma, Juno, Ceres and Minerva. In medieval times the arch used to form the base of a tower fortress. It was restored to its original shape in 1827.

San Giorgio in Velabro ❸

Via del Velabro 19. **Map** 8 E1.
679 33 35. 15, 57, 90, 90b, 92, 94, 95, 160, 716, 774, 780.
Closed for restoration.

San Giorgio in Velabro before the 1993 bombing

IN THE HOLLOW of the street named after the Velabrum, the swamp where Romulus and Remus are said to have been found by the she-wolf, is a small church dedicated to St George, whose bones lie under the altar. The 7th-century basilica has suffered over the centuries from periodic floods, but has been restored to its original appearance, with a double row of assorted granite and marble columns (taken from ancient Roman temples) dividing the triple nave. The austerity of the cool grey interior is relieved by golden frescoes in the apse (attributed to Pietro Cavallini, 1295). The facade and the bell tower date from the 12th century.

Recent testimony to the church's low-lying location is given by the high water-level mark of 1870 in the portico.

San Teodoro ❹

Via di San Teodoro. **Map** 8 E1.
678 66 24. 15, 57, 90, 92, 95, 160, 716. **Closed** to public.
Prayer meeting Mon 5.30pm–7pm.

IF YOU HAPPEN to be in the area at about 5.30pm on a Monday, you will find this small round 6th-century church at the foot of the Palatine open for a weekly prayer meeting. It is well worth going inside – the 6th-century mosaics in the apse are breathtaking, as is the Florentine cupola (1454). The pretty outer courtyard is by Carlo Fontana (1705).

The church of San Teodoro, one of Rome's hidden treasures

The Arch of Janus, where cattle dealers sheltered from the midday sun

Facade of Santa Maria della Consolazione

Santa Maria della Consolazione ⑤

Piazza della Consolazione 84.
Map 5 A5. 🕻 678 46 54. 🚌 57, 64, 90, 92, 94, 95, 160, 716.
Open 7am–noon, 5pm–7pm (Oct–Mar: 4pm–6pm) daily. **Closed** Aug. 🕇 🖻 🕹

THE CHURCH STANDS near the foot of the Tarpeian Rock, which was the site of numerous public executions.

In 1385, Giordanello degli Alberini, a condemned nobleman, paid two gold florins for an image of the Virgin Mary to be placed here, to provide some consolation to prisoners in their final moments. Hence the name of the church that was built here in 1470. It was reconstructed between 1583 and 1606 by Martino Longhi who provided the early Baroque facade.

The church's 11 side-chapels are owned by noble families and local crafts guild members. In the presbytery is the famed image of Mary, attributed to Antoniazzo Romano.

San Giovanni Decollato ⑥

Via di San Giovanni Decollato 22.
Map 8 E1. 🕻 678 94 48.
🚌 15, 57, 90, 92, 95, 160, 716.
Closed for restoration.

THE MAIN ALTAR is dominated by Giorgio Vasari's *Beheading of St John* (1553) from which the church takes its name, San Giovanni

Decollato. In 1490 Pope Innocent VIII gave this site to build a church for a very specialized Florentine confraternity. Ghoulishly attired in black robes and hoods, their task was to encourage condemned prisoners to repent and to give them a decent burial after they had been hanged. In the cloisters there are seven manholes (one of them reserved for women), which received the bodies.

The oratory contains a cycle of frescoes describing the life of St John the Baptist by the leading Florentine Mannerists, Jacopino del Conte and Francesco Salviati. In style the figures resemble some of those in the Sistine Chapel.

Casa dei Crescenzi ⑦

Via Luigi Petroselli. **Map** 8 E1. 🚌 15, 23, 57, 90, 92, 94, 95, 160, 716.

STUDDED WITH archaeological fragments, the house is what remains of a 12th-century tower fortress. It was built by the powerful Crescenzi family in order to keep an eye on the old docks of Rome (today the site of the Anagrafe or Public Records Office) and on the bridge where the family collected a toll.

Ancient Roman fragments in the Casa dei Crescenzi

Temples of the Forum Boarium ⑧

Piazza della Bocca della Verità.
Map 8 E1. 🚌 15, 23, 57, 90, 92, 94, 95, 160, 716.

Temple of Portunus

THESE MIRACULOUSLY well-preserved Republican temples are particularly appealing by moonlight, in their grassy enclave under the umbrella pines beside the Tiber. They date from the 2nd century BC and were saved for posterity when they were reconsecrated as Christian churches in the Middle Ages. They offer rare examples of combined elements from Greek and Roman architecture.

The rectangular temple (formerly known as the Temple of Fortuna Virilis) was in fact dedicated to Portunus, the god of rivers and ports – a reference to the nearby port of ancient Rome. Set on a podium, it has four Ionic travertine columns fluted at the front and 12 half-columns, embedded in the tufa wall of the *cella* – the room that housed the image of the god. Nearby is the small circular Temple of Hercules. It is often referred to as the Temple of Vesta because of its similarity to the one in the Forum.

Luminous interior of Santa Sabina

Santa Sabina ❾

Piazza Pietro d'Illiria 1. **Map** 8 E2.
📞 574 35 73. 🚌 94. **Open** 7am–
12.30pm, 3.30pm–6pm daily. 📷 ♿

H IGH ON the Aventine stands a perfect early Christian basilica, founded by Peter of Illyria in AD 422 and restored to its original simplicity early this century. Light filters through high 9th-century windows on to a wide nave framed by white Corinthian columns supporting an arcade decorated with a marble frieze. Over the main door is a 5th-century blue and gold mosaic dedicatory inscription; the pulpit, carved choir and bishop's throne are from the 9th century.

The church was given to the Dominicans in the 13th century and in the nave is the magnificent mosaic tombstone of one of the first leaders of the order, Muñoz de Zamora (died 1300). The side portico has 5th-century panelled doors carved from cypress wood, representing scenes from the Bible, including one of the earliest Crucifixions in existence.

Santi Bonifacio e Alessio ❿

Piazza di Sant'Alessio 23. **Map** 8 D2.
📞 574 34 46. 🚌 94. **Open**
8.30am–noon, 3.30 pm–6.30pm
(Oct–Mar: 5pm) daily. 📷 ♿

T HE CHURCH is dedicated to two early Christian martyrs, whose remains lie under the main altar. Legend has it that Alessio, son of a rich senator living on the site, fled to the East to become a pilgrim and avoid an impending marriage. Returning home after many years, he died as a servant, unrecognized, under the stairs of the family entrance hall, clutching the manuscript of his story for posterity.

The original 5th-century church has undergone substantial changes over the centuries. Noteworthy are the 18th-century facade with its five arches, the restored Cosmati doorway and pavement, and the magnificent Romanesque five-storey bell tower (1217). An 18th-century Baroque chapel by Andrea Bergondi houses part of the famous staircase. Other relics include the well from Alessio's family home and the glowing Byzantine Madonna of the Intercession brought to Rome from Damascus at the end of the 10th century.

Piazza dei Cavalieri di Malta ⓫

Map 8 D2. 🚌 23, 57, 94, 95, 716.

S URROUNDED BY cypress trees, this ornate walled piazza decorated with obelisks and military trophies was designed by Piranesi in 1765. It is named after the Order of the Knights of Malta (Cavalieri di Malta) whose priory (at No. 3) is famous for the bronze keyhole through which there is a miniature view of St Peter's, framed by a tree-lined avenue. The priory church, Santa Maria del Priorato, restored and decorated in Neo-Classical style by Piranesi in the 18th century, can be visited with permission from the headquarters of the Order. At the southwest corner of the square is the international Benedictine church of Sant'Anselmo, where the strains of Gregorian chant may be heard on Sunday mornings at 9.30am.

Doorway of the Priory of the Knights of Malta

Monte Testaccio ⓬

Via Galvani. **Map** 8 D4. 🚌 27, 92.
Closed to public.

F ROM ABOUT 140 BC to AD 250 this hill was created by the dumping of millions of *testae* (hence Testaccio) – fragments of the amphorae used to carry goods to the nearby warehouses. The artificial hill is 36 m (120 ft) high, but its full archaeological significance was not realized until the late 18th century.

Facade of Santi Bonifacio e Alessio

Protestant Cemetery

Via Caio Cestio 6. **Map** 8 D4.
📞 574 11 41. 🚌 11, 23, 27, 57, 94,
95, 716. 🚊 13, 30b. Ⓜ Piramide.
Open 8am–11.30am, 3.20pm–5.30pm
(Oct–Feb: 2.20pm–4.30pm)
Thu–Tue. **Donation** expected. 📷 ♿

T HE PEACE of this well-tended
cemetery beneath the
Aurelian Wall is profoundly
moving. Non-Catholics, mainly
English and German, have
been buried here since 1738.

In the oldest part are
the graves of John
Keats (died 1821),
whose epitaph reads:
"Here lies One
Whose Name was
writ in Water", and
his friend Joseph
Severn (died 1879);
not far away are the
ashes of Percy
Bysshe Shelley
(died 1822).
Goethe's son
Julius is also
buried here.

**Tombstone
of John Keats**

Pyramid of Caius Cestius

Piazzale Ostiense. **Map** 8 E4. 🚌 11, 23,
57, 94, 95. 🚊 13, 30b. Ⓜ Piramide.

Memorial pyramid of Caius Cestius

C AIUS CESTIUS, a wealthy
praetor (senior Roman
magistrate), died in 12 BC.
His one claim to fame is his
tomb, an imposing pyramid
faced in white marble set in
the Aurelian Wall near Porta
San Paolo. It stands 27 m
(89 ft) high and, according to
an inscription, took 330 days
to build. Unmistakable as a
landmark, it must have looked
almost as incongruous when
it was built as it does today.

**Detail of carving on sarcophagus
in the portico of San Saba**

San Saba

Via di San Saba. **Map** 8 F3.
📞 574 33 52. 🚌 11, 27, 94, 673.
🚊 13, 30b. **Open** 7am–noon,
4pm–6.30pm daily. ✝ 📷 ♿

T UCKED AWAY in a residential
street on the Little Aventine
hill, San Saba began life as an
oratory for Palestinian monks
fleeing from Arab invasions in
the 7th century. The existing
church dates from the 10th
century and has undergone
much restoration. The portico
houses a fascinating collection
of archaeological remains.

The church has three naves
in the Greek style and a short
fourth 11th-century nave to
the left with vestiges of 13th-
century frescoes of the life of
St Nicholas of Bari. Particularly
intriguing is a scene of three
naked young ladies lying in
bed, who are saved from
penury by the gift of a bag of
gold from St Nicholas, the
future Santa Claus. The
beautiful marble inlay in the
main door, the floor and the
remains of the choir are all
13th-century Cosmati work.

Circus Maximus

Via del Circo Massimo. **Map** 8 F2.
🚌 11, 15, 27, 90, 94, 118, 673.
🚊 13, 30b. Ⓜ Circo Massimo.

W HAT WAS ONCE ancient
Rome's largest stadium is
today little more than a long
grassy esplanade. Set in the
valley between the Palatine
and Aventine hills, the Circus
Maximus was continually
embellished and expanded
from the 4th century BC until
AD 549 when the last races
were held. The grandstands
held some 250,000 spectators,
cheering wildly at the horse
and chariot races, athletic
contests and wild animal fights,
betting furiously throughout.

The Circus had a central
dividing barrier *(spina)* with
seven large egg-shaped objects
on it used for counting the
laps of a race. These were
joined in 33 BC by seven
bronze dolphins that served a
similar purpose. In 10 BC
Augustus built the Imperial
box under the Palatine and
decorated the *spina* with the
obelisk that now stands in the
centre of Piazza del Popolo
(see p137). A second obelisk,
which was added in the 4th
century by Constantius II, is
now in Piazza di San Giovanni
in Laterano *(see pp178–9)*.

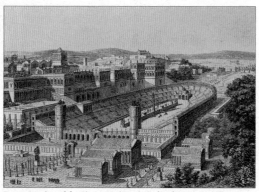

Reconstruction of the Circus Maximus in its heyday

TRASTEVERE

THE PROUD and aggressively independent inhabitants of Trastevere, the area "across the Tiber", consider themselves the most authentic Romans. In one of the most picturesque old quarters of the city, it is still possible to glimpse scenes of everyday life that seem to belong to bygone centuries. There are, however, signs that much of the earthy, proletarian character of the place may soon be destroyed by the proliferation of fashionable restaurants, clubs and

Romanesque bell tower

boutiques. Some of Rome's most fascinating medieval churches lie hidden away in the patchwork of narrow, cobbled back-streets, the only clue to their location an occasional glimpse of a Romanesque bell tower. Santa Cecilia was built on the site of the martyrdom of the patron saint of music, San Francesco a Ripa commemorates St Francis of Assisi's visit to Rome, and Santa Maria in Trastevere is the traditional centre of the spiritual and social life of the area.

SIGHTS AT A GLANCE

SEE ALSO

KEY

▨	Street-by-Street map
—	City Wall
🅿	Parking

GETTING THERE

Nearly all the bus routes that serve this area go along the broad, central Viale di Trastevere. The 75 and 170 are convenient if you are coming from Termini station or Piazza Venezia. From the Via Veneto area, take the 56 or 60, both of which have their terminus *(capolinea)* in Piazza Sonnino. From the Vatican it is best to take a 23 or 280 along Lungotevere.

0 metres   300

0 yards   300

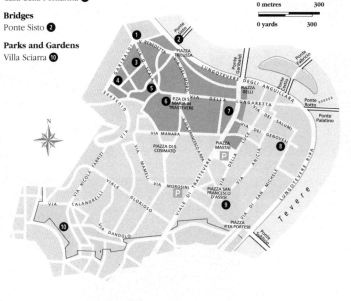

A typical *vicolo* (narrow alleyway) between the densely-packed buildings of Trastevere

Street-by-Street: Trastevere

ALL YEAR ROUND TRASTEVERE is a major attraction both for its restaurants, clubs and cinemas, and for its picturesque maze of narrow cobbled alleyways. On summer evenings the streets are packed with jostling groups of pleasure-seekers, especially during the noisy local festival, the Festa de Noantri *(see p59)*. Everywhere café and restaurant tables spill out over pavements, especially around Piazza di Santa Maria in Trastevere and outside the pizzerias along Viale di Trastevere. There are also kiosks selling slices of watermelon and *grattachecca*, a mixture of syrup and grated ice. It is usually easier to appreciate the antique charm of Trastevere's narrow streets in the more tranquil atmosphere of the early morning.

Casa della Fornarina
Raphael's beautiful mistress is said to have lived here. There is now a flourishing restaurant in the back garden ❶

Santa Maria dei Sette Dolori
This church (1643) is a minor work by Borromini ❹

Santa Maria della Scala
The church's unassuming facade conceals a rich Baroque interior ❸

Sant'Egidio and Museo del Folklore
This 17th-century fresco of Sant' Egidio by Pomarancio decorates the left-hand chapel in the church. The convent next door is a museum of Roman life and customs ❺

★ Santa Maria in Trastevere
The church is famous for its 12th-century mosaics by Pietro Cavallini. This detail is from a mosaic of the prophet Isaiah to the left of the apse ❻

STAR SIGHTS

★ **Santa Maria in Trastevere**

KEY

– – – Suggested route

0 metres   75

0 yards   75

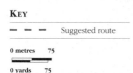

The fountain of Piazza di Santa Maria in Trastevere by Carlo Fontana (1692) is a popular meeting place. At night it is floodlit and dozens of young people sit on the steps around its octagonal base.

Ponte Sisto
This bridge was built on the orders of Sixtus IV in 1474 to link Trastevere to central Rome **2**

LOCATOR MAP
See Central Rome Map pp12–13

Piazza Belli is named after Giuseppe Gioacchino Belli (1791–1863), who wrote satirical sonnets in Roman dialect rather than academic Italian. At the centre of the piazza stands a statue of the poet (1913).

Vicolo del Piede is one of the picturesque narrow streets lined with restaurant tables leading off Piazza di Santa Maria in Trastevere.

The Torre degli Anguillara (13th century) is the only survivor of the many medieval towers that once dominated the Trastevere skyline. The building is home to a society devoted to the study of Dante.

San Crisogono
The Romanesque bell tower dates from the early 12th century. The plain portico is a later addition (1626), but is in keeping with the spirit of this ancient church **7**

**Restaurant at the rear of
La Fornarina's house**

Casa della Fornarina ❶

Via di Santa Dorotea 20. **Map** 4 D5 &
11 B5. ▐ 581 82 84. 🚌 23, 65,
280. See **Restaurants** p316.

NOTHING IS REALLY known
about Raphael's model
and lover, La Fornarina, yet
over the centuries she has
acquired a name and even a
brief biography. She was called
Margherita, her father was a
Sienese baker (*La Fornarina*
means the baker's girl) and
his shop was here in Trastevere
conveniently near Raphael's
frescoes in the Villa Farnesina
(*see pp220–21*). Behind the
house there is now a successful
restaurant, Da Romolo.

Margherita's longstanding
liaison with Raphael earned
her a reputation as a "fallen
woman". Worse, Raphael,
wishing to be absolved before
dying, turned her away from
his deathbed. Four months
after his death he supposedly
took refuge in the convent of
Santa Apollonia in Trastevere.

She is generally assumed to
have been the model for
Raphael's famous portrait of
La Donna Velata (woman
with a veil) in the Palazzo
Pitti in Florence.

Ponte Sisto ❷

Map 4 E5 & 11 B5. 🚌 23, 65, 280.

NAMED AFTER Pope Sixtus IV
della Rovere (reigned
1471–84), who commissioned
it, this bridge was built by his
architect, Baccio Pontelli, to
replace an ancient Roman

bridge. Pope Sixtus IV also
built the Sistine Chapel (*see
pp244–7*) and the Hospital of
Santo Spirito (*see p226*), and
restored many churches and
monuments. The pope's
enterprising spirit had to
contend with great financial
difficulties: his predecessor's
collection of precious gems
and his own silver plate had
to be sold or mortgaged in
order to finance his projects.

Pope Sixtus IV probably
raised the money he needed
to build the bridge by levying
a tax on the city's
prostitutes.
Several popes
are known
to have used
this very
unpopular
form of
taxation.

**Pope
Sixtus IV**

Santa Maria della Scala ❸

Via della Scala. **Map** 4 D5 & 11 B5.
▐ 58 06 23 30. 🚌 23, 65, 280.
Open 6.30am–noon, 4pm–7pm
(Oct–Mar: 6.15pm) Mon–Sat, 6.45am–
12.15pm Sun and public hols. 🔋

Santa Maria della Scala's altar

THIS CHURCH belongs to a
time of great building
activity that lasted about 30
years from the end of the 16th
to the early 17th century. Its
rather simple facade contrasts
with a rich interior decorated
with multicoloured marbles
and a number of spirited
Baroque altars and reliefs.

Santa Maria dei Sette Dolori ❹

Via Garibaldi 27. **Map** 7 B1.
▐ 589 73 27. 🚌 23, 65, 280.
Closed to public.

BORROMINI DESIGNED this
church, begun in the early
1640s and, like many of his
projects, left incomplete. The
rough brick facade and the
convex and concave surfaces
are typical of his work.
Rounded corners and the
impressive columns accentuate
the church's small proportions.

Sant'Egidio and Museo del Folklore ❺

Piazza Sant'Egidio 1. **Map** 7 C1.
🚌 23, 56, 60, 65, 280.
Museo del Folklore ▐ 581 37 17.
Open 9am–1pm Tue–Sun; also
5pm–7pm Tue & Thu (last adm: 30
mins before closing). **Adm charge.**
Church open for services only.
🔋 8.30pm daily.

BUILT IN 1630, Sant'Egidio
was the church of the
adjoining Carmelite convent,
one of many founded in the
area to shelter the poor and
destitute. The convent is now
a folklore museum, containing
a wealth of material relating
to the festivals, pastimes,
superstitions and customs of
the Romans when they lived
under papal rule. There are
old paintings and prints of the
city and tableaux showing
scenes of everyday life in
18th- and 19th-century Rome,
including reconstructions of
shops and a tavern. The
museum also has manuscripts
by the much-loved local dialect
poets Belli and Trilussa.

**Watercolour of public scribe
(1880) in the Museo del Folklore**

Santa Maria in Trastevere ⑥

See pp212–13.

San Crisogono ⑦

Piazza Sonnino 44. **Map** 7 C1. **☎** 581 82 25. **🚌** 56, 60, 75, 170, 710. **Open** 7.30am–11.30am, 4pm–7pm Mon– Sat, 7am–1pm Sun. **Adm charge** for excavations. 🕇 📷 🔇

THIS CHURCH was built on the site of one of the city's oldest *tituli* (private houses used for Christian worship). An 8th-century church with 11th-century frescoes can still be seen beneath the present church. This dates from the early 12th century, a period of intense building activity in the popular quarters of Rome. San Crisogono was decorated by Pietro Cavallini – the apse mosaic by his school remains.

Most of the columns were taken from previous buildings, including the great porphyry ones of the triumphal arch. The mosaic floor is the result of recycling precious marble from various Roman ruins.

Apse mosaic in San Crisogono

Santa Cecilia in Trastevere ⑧

Piazza di Santa Cecilia. **Map** 8 D1. **☎** 589 92 89. **🚌** 56, 60, 75, 710. **Open** 10am–noon, 4pm–6pm daily. **Adm charge** for excavations. **Cavallini fresco** can be seen 10am–11.30am Tue and Thu (donation expected).

ST CECILIA, ARISTOCRAT and patron saint of music, was martyred here in AD 230. After an unsuccessful attempt

at scalding her to death, she was beheaded. A church was founded – perhaps in the 4th century – on the site of the saint's house (still to be seen beneath the church, with the remains of a Roman tannery). For a long time her body went missing, but it turned up again in the Catacombs of San Callisto (*see p265*). In the 9th century it was reburied here by Pope Paschal I, who rebuilt the church. A fine apse mosaic survives from this period.

The altar canopy by Arnolfo di Cambio and the fresco of *The Last Judgment* by Pietro Cavallini, reached through the adjoining convent, date from the 13th century, one of the few periods when Rome had a distinctive artistic style of its own. In front of the altar is a statue of St Cecilia by Stefano Maderno, who used her miraculously preserved remains as a model when she was briefly disinterred in 1599.

San Francesco a Ripa ⑨

Piazza San Francesco d'Assisi 88. **Map** 7 C2. **☎** 581 90 20. **🚌** 44, 75, 170, 710. **Open** 7am–noon, 4pm–7pm daily. 🕇 📷 🔇

ST FRANCIS OF ASSISI lived here in a hospice when he visited Rome in 1219 and his stone pillow and crucifix are preserved in his cell. The church was rebuilt by his follower, the nobleman Rodolfo Anguillara, who is portrayed on his tombstone wearing the Franciscan habit.

Entirely rebuilt in the 1680s by Cardinal Pallavicini, the church is rich in sculptures. Particularly flamboyant are the 18th-century Rospigliosi and Pallavicini monuments in the transept chapel. Not to be missed in the Altieri chapel (fourth on the left, along the nave) is Bernini's breathtaking sculpture, the *Ecstasy of Beata Ludovica Albertoni.*

Detail of 13th-century fresco by Pietro Cavallini in Santa Cecilia

Villa Sciarra ⑩

Via Calandrelli 35. **Map** 7 B2. **🚌** 44, 75, 710. **Park open** 9am–sunset daily. **House closed** for restoration. 🔇

IN ROMAN TIMES the site of this small, attractive public park was a nymph's sanctuary. It is especially picturesque in spring, when its cherry trees and wisterias are in full bloom. The paths through the park are decorated with Romantic follies, fountains and statues, and there are splendid views of the city over the Janiculum bastions.

Bernini's *Ecstasy of Beata Ludovica Albertoni* (1674) in San Francesco a Ripa

Santa Maria in Trastevere ❻

PROBABLY THE FIRST official Christian place of worship to be built in Rome, this basilica became the focus of devotion to the Virgin Mary. According to legend, the church was founded by Pope Callixtus I in the 3rd century, when Christianity was still a minority cult. Today's church is largely a 12th-century building, remarkable for its mosaics, in particular those by Pietro Cavallini. The 22 granite columns in the nave were taken from the ruins of ancient Roman buildings. Despite some 18th-century Baroque additions, Santa Maria has retained its medieval character. This friendly church has strong links with the local community.

Piazza Santa Maria in Trastevere
The piazza in front of the church is the traditional heart of Trastevere. Today it is surrounded by lively bars and restaurants. Carlo Fontana built the octagonal fountain in the late 17th century.

The floor, relaid in the 1870s, is a recreation of the Cosmatesque mosaic floor of the 13th century.

The bell tower was built in the 12th century. At the top is a small mosaic of the Virgin.

★ Facade Mosaics
The 12th-century mosaic shows Mary feeding the baby Jesus and ten women holding lamps. Eight of the lamps are lit, symbolizing virginity; the veiled women whose lamps have gone out are probably widows.

STAR FEATURES

★ **Cavallini Mosaics**

★ **Facade Mosaics**

MODEST DONORS
Many of Rome's mosaics include a portrait of the pope or cardinal responsible for the building of the church. Often the portrait is dwarfed by the rest of the picture, which glorifies the saint to whom the church is dedicated. On the facade of Santa Maria, two tiny unidentified figures kneel at the Virgin's feet. Were they to stand up, the men would barely reach her knees.

Facade mosaic, detail

The portico was remodelled in 1702 by Carlo Fontana. Statues of four popes decorate the balustrade above.

Front entrance

15th-century wall tabernacle by Mino del Reame

Apse Mosaic
The 12th-century mosaic in the basin of the apse shows the Coronation of the Virgin. She sits on Christ's right hand, surrounded by saints.

VISITORS' CHECKLIST

Piazza Santa Maria in Trastevere.
Map 7 C1. 581 48 02.
44, 56, 60, 75, 97, 170, 280, 710, 718, 719, 774, 780 to Viale di Trastevere (Piazza Sidney Sonnino); 23, 65 to Lungotevere Raffaello Sanzio. **Open** 7.30am– 1pm, 4pm–7pm daily. 6pm daily.

★ **Cavallini Mosaics**
The details in the six mosaics of the Life of the Virgin (1291) display a touching realism.

Madonna della Clemenza
The life-size icon probably dates from the 7th century. A replica is displayed above the altar of the Cappella Altemps.

Tomb of Cardinal Pietro Stefaneschi
The last of his line, Pietro Stefaneschi died in 1417. His tomb is by an otherwise unknown sculptor called Paolo.

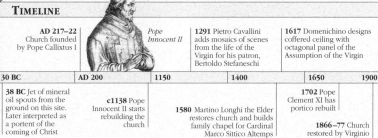

TIMELINE

AD 217–22 Church founded by Pope Callixtus I	*Pope Innocent II*	**1291** Pietro Cavallini adds mosaics of scenes from the life of the Virgin for his patron, Bertoldo Stefaneschi	**1617** Domenichino designs coffered ceiling with octagonal panel of the Assumption of the Virgin

30 BC	AD 200	1150	1400	1650	1900

38 BC Jet of mineral oil spouts from the ground on this site. Later interpreted as a portent of the coming of Christ

c1138 Pope Innocent II starts rebuilding the church

1580 Martino Longhi the Elder restores church and builds family chapel for Cardinal Marco Sittico Altemps

1702 Pope Clement XI has portico rebuilt

1866–77 Church restored by Virginio Vespignani

JANICULUM

VERLOOKING THE TIBER on the Trastevere side of the river, the Janiculum hill has often played its part in the defence of the city. The last occasion was in 1849 when Garibaldi held off the attacking French troops. The park at the top of the hill is filled with monuments to Garibaldi and his men. A popular place for walks, the park provides a welcome escape from the densely-packed streets of Trastevere.

Puppets in the park at the top of the Janiculum hill

You will often find puppet shows and other kinds of amusements for children. In medieval times most of the hill was occupied by monasteries and convents. Bramante built his miniature masterpiece, the Tempietto, in the convent of San Pietro in Montorio. The Renaissance also saw the development of the riverside area along Via della Lungara, where the rich and powerful built beautiful houses such as the Villa Farnesina.

SIGHTS AT A GLANCE

Churches and Temples
Sant'Onofrio ⑥
San Pietro in Montorio ⑦
Tempietto ⑧

Museums and Galleries
Palazzo Corsini and Galleria
Nazionale d'Arte Antica ②

Historic Buildings
Villa Farnesina
pp220–21 ①

Fountains
Fontana Paola ⑨

Monuments
Garibaldi Monument ⑤

Arches and Gates
Porta Settimiana ③

Parks and Gardens
Botanical Gardens ④

SEE ALSO
• *Street Finder*, maps 3, 4, 7, 11
• *Where to Stay* pp294–5
• *Restaurants* pp310–11

GETTING THERE

The Janiculum (Il Gianicolo) is not the easiest part of Rome to reach by public transport. It can be approached either from the Vatican area *(see p223)* or from Trastevere *(see p207)*. There is only one bus, the 41, that goes up to the top of the hill, but the 44, 75 or 710 will take you from Piazza Venezia to a convenient point to start your walk. For sights along Via della Lungara, take the 23, 65 or 280, which go along Lungotevere.

0 metres   300
0 yards   300

KEY

▨ Tour of the Janiculum map
— City Wall

The staircase fountain in the Botanical Gardens

A Tour of the Janiculum

THE LONG HIKE to the top of the Janiculum is rewarded by wonderful views over the city. The park's monuments include a lighthouse and statues of Garibaldi and his wife Anita. There is also a cannon which is fired off at noon each day. In Via della Lungara, between the Janiculum and the Tiber, stand Palazzo Corsini with its national art collection and the Villa Farnesina, decorated by Raphael for his friend and patron, the fabulously wealthy banker Agostino Chigi.

Tasso's Oak is a memorial to the poet Torquato Tasso, who liked to sit here in the days before he died in 1595. The tree was struck by lightning in 1843.

The Manfredi Lighthouse, built in 1911, was a gift to the city of Rome from Italians in Argentina.

The Monument to Anita Garibaldi by Mario Rutelli was erected in 1932. The great patriot's Brazilian wife lies buried beneath the statue.

The view from Villa Lante, a beautiful Renaissance summer residence, gives a magnificent panorama of the whole city.

Garibaldi Monument
The inscription on the base of the equestrian statue means "Rome or Death" ❺

Botanical Gardens
These were established in 1883 when part of the grounds of Palazzo Corsini was given to the University of Rome ④

★ **Palazzo Corsini**
This 15th-century triptych by Fra Angelico hangs in the Galleria Nazionale d'Arte Antica ②

LOCATOR MAP
See Central Rome Map pp12–13

★ **Villa Farnesina**
The suburban villa of the banker Agostino Chigi is celebrated for its frescoes by Raphael, Baldassarre Peruzzi and other Renaissance masters ①

VICOLO DELLA PENITENZA

VIA DELLA PENITENZA

VIA DELLA LUNGARA

VIA DEI RIARI

VIA CORSINI

VIA G. GARIBALDI

Porta Settimiana
Looking through this Renaissance gateway from Via della Lungara, you catch a glimpse of Trastevere's warren of narrow streets ③

KEY

– – – Suggested route

0 metres 75
0 yards 75

STAR SIGHTS

★ **Villa Farnesina**

★ **Palazzo Corsini and Galleria Nazionale d'Arte Antica**

Villa Farnesina ①

See pp220–21.

Palazzo Corsini and Galleria Nazionale d'Arte Antica ②

Via della Lungara 10. **Map** 4 D5 &
11 A5. 68 80 23 23. 23, 41,
65, 280. **Open** 9am–2pm Tue–Sat,
9am–1pm Sun & public hols (last
adm: 30 mins before closing).
Closed 15 Aug, 25 Dec and 1 Jan.
Adm charge.

Queen Christina's bedroom in the Palazzo Corsini

THE HISTORY of Palazzo
Corsini is intimately
entwined with that of Rome.
Built for Cardinal Domenico
Riario in the late 15th century,
it has boasted among its many
distinguished guests Bramante,
the young Michelangelo,
Erasmus and Queen Christina
of Sweden, who died here in
1689. The old palazzo was
completely rebuilt for Cardinal
Neri Corsini by Ferdinando
Fuga in 1736. As Via della
Lungara is too narrow for a
good frontal view, Fuga
designed the facade so it could
be viewed from an angle.
  Palazzo Corsini now houses
the Galleria Nazionale d'Arte
Antica. This outstanding
collection includes paintings
by Rubens, Van Dyck, Murillo,
Caravaggio and Guido Reni,
together with 17th- and 18th-
century Italian regional art.
The palazzo is also home to
the Accademia dei Lincei, a
learned society founded in

1603, which once included
Galileo among its members.
  In 1797 Palazzo Corsini was
the backdrop to momentous
events: French General Duphot
(the fiancé of Napoleon's
sister Pauline) was killed here
in a skirmish between papal
troops and Republicans. The
consequent French occupation
of the city and the deportation
of Pope Pius VI led to the
proclamation of a short-lived
Roman Republic (1798–9).

Porta Settimiana ③

Between Via della Scala and Via della
Lungara. **Map** 4 D5 & 11 B5. 23,
65, 280.

THIS GATE was built in 1498
by Pope Alexander VI
Borgia to replace a minor
passageway in the Aurelian
Wall. The Porta Settimiana
marks the start of Via della
Lungara, a long straight road
built in the early 16th century.

Botanical Gardens ④

Largo Cristina di Svezia 24, off Via
Corsini. **Map** 4 D5. 686 61 93.
23, 65, 280. **Open** 9am–7pm
(Oct-Mar: 6pm) Mon–Sat, 10am–5pm
Sun. **Closed** public hols.

SEQUOIAS, PALM TREES and
splendid collections of
orchids and bromeliads are
housed in Rome's Botanical
Gardens *(Orto Botanico)*. The
gardens contain more than
7,000 plant species from all
over the world. Indigenous
and exotic species are grouped

to illustrate their botanical
families and their adaptation
to different climates and
eco-systems. There are also
several interesting examples
of plants like the gingko that
have survived virtually
unchanged from earlier eras.
The gardens were originally
part of the Palazzo Corsini,
but since 1883 have belonged
to the University of Rome.

Garibaldi Monument ⑤

Piazzale Giuseppe Garibaldi.
Map 3 C5. 41, 44, 75, 710.

Base of the Garibaldi Monument

THIS HUGE equestrian statue
is part of a commemorative
park, recalling the heroic
events witnessed on the
Janiculum when the French
army attacked the city in 1849.
Garibaldi's Republicans fended
off the greatly superior French
forces for weeks, until the
Italians were overwhelmed.
Garibaldi and his men escaped.
The monument, erected in
1895, was the work of Emilio
Gallori. Around the pedestal
are four smaller sculptures in
bronze showing battle scenes
and allegorical figures.

Steps and tiered fountains at the Botanical Gardens

Courtyard of Sant'Onofrio

Sant'Onofrio ⑥

Piazza di Sant'Onofrio 2. **Map** 3 C4.
📞 *686 44 98.* 🚌 *41.* **Open** *10am–
noon Sun for mass; otherwise adm by
appt only.* **Closed** *Aug, except saint's
feast day on 12 Aug.* 📷 ✚
Museum open *by appt only.*

Beato nicola da Forca Palena, whose tombstone guards the entrance, founded this church in 1419 in honour of the hermit Sant'Onofrio. It retains the flavour of the 15th century in the simple shapes of the portico and the cloister. In the early 17th century the portico was decorated with frescoes by Domenichino.

The monastery next to the church houses a small museum dedicated to the 16th-century poet Torquato Tasso, who died here in one of the cells.

San Pietro in Montorio ⑦

Piazza San Pietro in Montorio 2.
Map 7 B1. 📞 *581 39 40.* 🚌 *41,
44, 75, 710.* **Open** *9am–noon,
4pm–6pm daily. If closed, ring bell at
door to right of church.* 📷 ✚

San pietro in montorio – the church of St Peter on the Golden Hill – was founded in the Middle Ages near the spot where St Peter was presumed to have been crucified. It was rebuilt by order of Ferdinand and Isabella of Spain at the end of the 15th century, and decorated by outstanding artists of the Renaissance.

The facade is typical of a time when clean, geometric shapes derived from Classical architecture were in vogue. The single nave ends in a deep apse that once contained Raphael's *Transfiguration*, now in the Vatican. Two wide chapels, one on either side of the nave, were decorated by some of Michelangelo's most famous pupils. The left-hand chapel was designed by one of the few artists Michelangelo openly admired, Daniele da Volterra, also responsible for the altar painting, the *Baptism of Christ*. The chapel on the right was the work of Giorgio Vasari, who included a self-portrait (in black, on the left) in his altar painting, the *Conversion of St Paul*.

The first chapel to the right of the entrance contains a powerful *Flagellation*, by the Venetian artist Sebastiano del Piombo (1518); Michelangelo is said to have provided the original drawings. Work by Bernini and his followers can be seen in the second chapel on the left and in the flanking De Raymondi tombs.

Tempietto ⑧

Via Garibaldi 33 (in courtyard of San
Pietro in Montorio). **Map** 7 B1.
📞 *581 39 40.* 🚌 *41, 44, 75, 710.*
Open *9am–noon, 4pm–6pm daily.*
See **The History of Rome** *pp30–31.*

In 1502 bramante completed what many consider to be the first true Renaissance building in Rome – the Tempietto. The name means simply "little temple". Its circular shape echoes early Christian *martyria*, chapels built on the site of a saint's martyrdom. This was believed to be the place where St Peter was crucified.

Bramante chose the Doric order for the 16 columns surrounding the domed chapel. Above the columns is a Classical frieze and a delicate balustrade. Though the scale of the Tempietto is tiny, Bramante's masterly use of Classical proportions creates a satisfyingly harmonious whole.

The Tempietto illustrates the great Renaissance dream that the city of Rome would once again relive its ancient glory.

Fontana Paola ⑨

Via Garibaldi. **Map** 7 B1. 🚌 *41, 44,
75, 710.*

Fontana Paola, built for Pope Paul V

This monumental fountain commemorates the reopening in 1612 of an aqueduct originally built by Emperor Trajan in AD 109. The aqueduct was renamed the Acqua Paola after Paul V, the Borghese pope who ordered its restoration. When it was first built, the fountain had five small basins, but in 1690 Carlo Fontana altered the design, adding the huge basin you can see today. Despite many laws intended to deter them, generations of Romans used this convenient pool of fresh water for bathing and washing their vegetables.

Bramante's round chapel, the Tempietto

Villa Farnesina ●

T HE WEALTHY SIENESE BANKER Agostino Chigi, who had established the headquarters of his far-flung financial empire in Rome, commissioned the villa in 1508 from his compatriot Baldassarre Peruzzi. The simple, harmonious design, with a central block and projecting wings, made this one of the earliest true Renaissance villas. The decoration was carried out between 1510 and 1519 and this has recently been restored. Peruzzi frescoed some of the interiors himself. Later, Sebastiano del Piombo, Raphael and his pupils added more elaborate works. The frescoes illustrate Classical myths, and the vault of the main hall, the Sala di Galatea, is adorned with astrological scenes showing the position of the stars at the time of Chigi's birth. Artists, poets, cardinals, princes and the pope himself were entertained here in magnificent style by their wealthy and influential host. In 1577 the villa was bought by Cardinal Alessandro Farnese. Since then, it has been known as the Villa Farnesina.

North Facade
The Loggia of Cupid and Psyche looks out on formal gardens that were used for parties and putting on plays.

Entrance

The Wedding of Alexander and Roxanne by Sodoma
Cherubs are shown helping the bride Roxanne to prepare for her marriage.

★ Triumph of Galatea by Raphael
The beautiful sea nymph Galatea was one of the 50 daughters of the god Nereus.

The Gabinetto delle Stampe
sometimes holds exhibitions of rare prints.

Frescoes in the Room of Galatea
Perseus beheads Medusa in a scene from one of Peruzzi's series of mythological frescoes.

THE ARCHITECT

Baldassarre Peruzzi, painter and architect, arrived in Rome from Siena in 1503 aged 20 and became Bramante's chief assistant. Although his architectural designs were typical of Classicism, his painting owes more to Gothic influences, as his figurework is very highly stylized. On Raphael's death, he became Head of Works at St Peter's, but was captured in the Sack of Rome (*see p31*), exiled to Siena until 1535, and died in 1536.

Baldassarre Peruzzi

★ Salone delle Prospettive
Peruzzi's frescoes create the illusion of looking out at views of 16th-century Rome through a marble colonnade.

VISITORS' CHECKLIST

Via della Lungara 230.
Map 4 D5 & 11 A5. ▇ 23, 65, 280 to Lungotevere Farnesina.
◖ 68 80 17 67. **Open** 9am–1pm Mon–Sat. ◢ ◪ ◫
Gabinetto delle Stampe *(rare print collection)* ◖ 68 80 56 57.
Open 9am–1pm Tue–Sat for occasional exhibitions. ◢

Fresco from the Salone delle Prospettive
This scene shows the Torre delle Milizie (see p90) as it looked in the 1500s.

★ Loggia of Cupid and Psyche
The model for the figure on the left in Raphael's painting of The Three Graces *was Agostino Chigi's mistress, the courtesan Imperia.*

Lunette in the Room of Galatea
This giant monochrome head by Peruzzi was once attributed to Michelangelo.

STAR FEATURES

★ **Triumph of Galatea by Raphael**

★ **Loggia of Cupid and Psyche**

★ **Salone delle Prospettive**

VATICAN

Nuns in St Peter's Square

A S THE SITE where St Peter was martyred and buried, the Vatican became the residence of the popes who succeeded him. Decisions taken here have shaped the destiny of Europe, and the great basilica of St Peter's draws pilgrims from all over the Christian world. The papal palaces beside St Peter's house the Vatican Museums. With the added attractions of Michelangelo's Sistine Chapel and the Raphael Rooms, their wonderful collections of Classical sculpture make them the finest museums in Rome. The Vatican's position as a state within a state was guaranteed by the Lateran Treaty of 1929, marked by the building of a new road, the Via della Conciliazione. This leads from St Peter's to Castel Sant' Angelo, a monument to a far grimmer past. Built originally as the Emperor Hadrian's mausoleum, this papal fortress and prison has witnessed many fierce battles for control of the city.

SIGHTS AT A GLANCE

Churches and Temples
St Peter's pp230–33 ❶
Santo Spirito in Sassia ❹
Santa Maria in Traspontina ❾

Museums and Galleries
Vatican Museums pp234–47 ❷

Historic Buildings
Hospital of Santo Spirito ❺
Palazzo del Commendatore ❻
Palazzo dei Convertendi ❼
Palazzo dei Penitenzieri ❽

Palazzo Torlonia ⓬
Castel Sant'Angelo pp248–9 ⓭
Palazzo di Giustizia ⓮

Gates
Porta Santo Spirito ❸

Historic Streets and Piazzas
The Borgo ❿
Vatican Corridor ⓫

GETTING THERE
The quickest way to reach the area is by Metro line A to Ottaviano. This is especially convenient when visiting the Vatican Museums. The 64 bus runs regularly from Piazza dei Cinquecento, in front of Termini station. Other routes that serve the area include the 23, 81 and 492, which stop in Piazza del Risorgimento. There is a regular shuttle bus between St Peter's and the Vatican Museums.

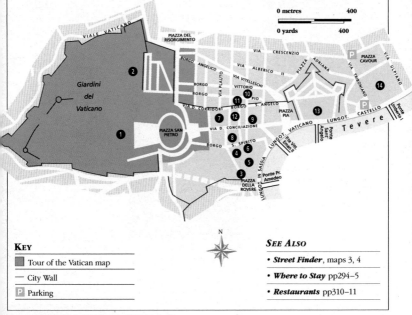

| 0 metres | 400 |
| 0 yards | 400 |

KEY

▨	Tour of the Vatican map
—	City Wall
🅿	Parking

SEE ALSO

Dome of St Peter's dominating the Vatican skyline

A Tour of the Vatican

THE VATICAN, a centre of power for Catholics all over the world and a sovereign state since February 1929, is ruled by the pope. About 1,000 people live here, staffing the Vatican's facilities. There is a post office and shops, Vatican radio, broadcasting to the world in over 20 languages, a daily newspaper (l'Osservatore Romano), Vatican offices and a publishing house.

The Madonna of Guadalupe shows the miraculous image of the Madonna which appeared on the cloak of a Mexican Indian in 1531.

Papal heliport

The Grotto of Lourdes is a replica of the grotto in the southwest of France, where in 1858 the Virgin appeared to St Bernadette.

The Vatican Railway Station, opened in 1930, connects with the line from Rome to Viterbo, but is now used only for freight.

Radio Vatican is broadcast from this tower, part of the Leonine Wall built in 847.

The Papal Audience Chamber, by Pier Luigi Nervi, was opened in 1971. It seats up to 12,000.

The information office gives details of tours of the Vatican Gardens.

★ **St Peter's**
The Chapel of St Peter is in the Grottoes under the basilica. The rich marble decoration was added by Clement VIII at the end of the 16th century ❶

Piazza San Pietro was laid out by Bernini between 1656 and 1667. The narrow space in front of the church opens out into an enormous ellipse flanked by colonnades.

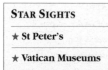

STAR SIGHTS
★ St Peter's
★ Vatican Museums

The obelisk was erected here in 1586 with the help of 150 horses and 47 winches.

The Eagle Fountain was built to celebrate the arrival of water from the Acqua Paola aqueduct at the Vatican. The eagle is the Borghese crest.

LOCATOR MAP
See Central Rome Map pp12–13

The Casina of Pius IV is a delightful summerhouse in the Vatican Gardens built by Pirro Ligorio in the mid-16th century.

Entrance to Vatican Museums

★ Vatican Museums
Raphael's Madonna of Foligno (1513) is just one of the Vatican's many Renaissance masterpieces **2**

The Galleon Fountain is a perfect scale model of a 17th-century ship in lead, brass and copper. It was made by a Flemish artist for Pope Paul V.

The Cortile della Pigna is mostly the work of Bramante. The niche for the pine cone, once a Roman fountain, was added by Pirro Ligorio in 1562.

KEY

- – – – Suggested route

0 metres   75

0 yards   75

To Via della Conciliazione

St Peter's **1**

See pp230–33.

Vatican Museums **2**

See pp234–47.

Porta Santo Spirito **3**

Via dei Penitenzieri. **Map** 3 C3.
🚌 *23, 34, 49, 64, 81, 492.*

THIS GATE stands at what was the southern limit of the "Leonine City", the area enclosed within walls by Pope Leo IV as a defence against the Saracens who had sacked Rome in AD 845. The walls measure 3 km (2 miles) in circumference.

Work on the walls started in AD 846. Pope Leo supervised the huge army of labourers personally, and thanks to his encouragement, the job was completed in four years. He then led a solemn procession to consecrate his massive feat of construction.

Since the time of Pope Leo the walls have needed much reinforcement and repair. The gateway visible today at Porta Santo Spirito was built by the architect Antonio da Sangallo the Younger in 1543–4. It is framed by two huge bastions that were added in 1564 by

Pope Pius IV Medici. Sadly, Sangallo's design for a monumental entrance to the Vatican was never completed; the principal columns come to an end somewhat abruptly in a modern covering of cement.

Santo Spirito in Sassia **4**

Borgo Santo Spirito 4. **Map** 3 C3.
📞 *687 93 10.* 🚌 *23, 34, 41, 46, 64.*
Open *7am–12.30pm, 4pm–8pm daily.* 🕇 📷 ♿

Nave of Santo Spirito in Sassia

BUILT ON THE SITE of a church erected by King Ine of Wessex, who died in Rome in the 8th century, the church is the work of Antonio da Sangallo the Younger. It was rebuilt (1538–44) after the

Sack of Rome had left it in ruins in 1527. The facade was added under Pope Sixtus V (1585–90). The nave and side chapels are decorated with a series of light, lively frescoes. The pretty bell tower is earlier, dating from the reign of Sixtus IV (1471–84). It was probably the work of the pope's architect Baccio Pontelli, who also built the nearby Hospital of Santo Spirito, and the Ponte Sisto *(see p210)* further down the River Tiber.

Sixtus V's arms over door of Santo Spirito

Hospital of Santo Spirito **5**

Borgo Santo Spirito 2. **Map** 3 C3.
🚌 *23, 34, 41, 46, 64.* **Octagonal chapel open** *8.30am–2pm daily.*

THE HOSPITAL is said to have been founded as a result of a nightmare experienced by Pope Innocent III (reigned 1198–1216). In the dream, an angel showed him the bodies of Rome's unwanted babies dredged up from the Tiber in fishing nets. The pope hastened to build a hospice for sick paupers.

In 1475 the hospital was reorganized by Pope Sixtus IV

Fresco of an angel in the octagonal chapel of the Hospital of Santo Spirito

to care for the influx of poor pilgrims expected for the Holy Year. For its day, Sixtus's hospital was a revolutionary building. Cloisters separated the different categories of patient. One is still reserved for orphans and their nurses.

Unwanted infants were passed through a revolving barrel-like contraption known as the *rota*, still visible to the left of the central entrance in Borgo Santo Spirito. This was to guarantee anonymity. Martin Luther, who came here in 1511, was scandalized by the number of abandoned children he saw, believing them to be "the sons of the pope himself".

In the centre, under the hospital's conspicuous drum, is an octagonal chapel, where mass was said for patients. This room can be visited; the rest of the building still functions as a hospital.

Rusticated doorway of the Palazzo dei Convertendi

The *rota* of Santo Spirito, where mothers left unwanted babies

Palazzo del Commendatore ❻

Borgo Santo Spirito 3. **Map** 3 C3.
🚌 *23, 34, 41, 46, 64.* **Courtyard only open** *to the public.*

As DIRECTOR of the Hospital of Santo Spirito, the Commendatore not only ran the hospital, he was also responsible for its estates and revenues. This important post was originally given to members of the pope's family.

The palazzo, built next door to the hospital, has a spacious 16th-century frescoed loggia appropriate to the dignity and sobriety of its owners. The frescoes represent the story of the founding of the Hospital of Santo Spirito. To the left of the entrance is the Spezieria, or Pharmacy. This still has the wheel used for grinding the bark of the cinchona tree to produce the drug quinine, first introduced here in 1632 by Jesuits from Peru as a cure for malaria.

Above the courtyard is a splendid clock (1827). The dial is divided into six; it was not until 1846 that the familiar division of the day into two periods of 12 hours was introduced in Rome by Pope Pius IX.

Della Rovere arms

Palazzo dei Convertendi ❼

Via della Conciliazione 43.
Map 3 C3. 🚌 *23, 34, 41, 46, 64.*
Not open *to the public.*

With THE BUILDING of Via della Conciliazione in the 1930s, Palazzo dei Convertendi was taken down and later moved to this new site nearby. The house, which is partly attributed to the architect Bramante, is where the artist Raphael died in 1520.

Palazzo dei Penitenzieri ❽

Via della Conciliazione 33. **Map** 3 C3.
📞 *686 54 35.* 🚌 *23, 34, 41, 46, 64.* See **Where to Stay** *p295.*

The PALAZZO owes its name to the fact that the place was once home to the confessors *(penitenzieri)* of St Peter's. Their place has now been taken by tourists, as the building has been converted into the Hotel Columbus. Originally built by Cardinal Domenico della Rovere in 1480, the palazzo still bears the family's coat of arms, the oak tree (*rovere* means oak), on its graceful courtyard well-head. On the cardinal's death, the palazzo was acquired by Pope Julius II della Rovere's favourite, Cardinal Francesco Alidosi. Suspected of treason, the cardinal was murdered in 1511 by the pope's nephew, the Duke of Urbino, who also took possession of his palazzo. A few of the rooms still contain beautiful frescoes.

View of the Tiber and the Borgo between Castel Sant'Angelo and St Peter's by Gaspare Vanvitelli (1653–1736)

Santa Maria in Traspontina ⑨

Via della Conciliazione 14.
Map 3 C3. 📞 *68 30 00 63.*
🚌 *23, 34, 41, 46, 64.* **Open**
*6.30am–noon, 4pm–7.30pm
daily.* 🕀 📷 ♿

**The facade of the Carmelite church
of Santa Maria in Traspontina**

THE CHURCH occupies the site of an ancient Roman pyramid, believed in the Middle Ages to have been the Tomb of Romulus. The pyramid was destroyed by Pope Alexander VI Borgia, but representations of it survive in the bronze doors at the entrance to St Peter's and in a Giotto triptych in the Vatican Pinacoteca *(see p240).*

The present church was begun in 1566 to replace an earlier one which had been in the line of fire of the cannons defending Castel Sant'Angelo during the Sack of Rome in 1527. The papal artillery officers insisted that the dome of the new church should be as low as possible, so it was built without a supporting drum. The first chapel to the right is dedicated to the gunners' patron saint, Santa Barbara, and is decorated with warlike motifs. In the third chapel on the left are two columns, said to be those to which St Peter and Paul were bound before martyrdom.

The Borgo ⑩

Map 3 C3. 🚌 *23, 34, 41, 46, 64.*

THE WORD BORGO derives from the German *burg*, meaning town. Rome's Borgo is where the first pilgrims to St Peter's were housed in hostels and hospices, often for quite lengthy periods. The first of these foreign colonies, called "schools", was founded in AD 725 by a Saxon, King Ine of Wessex, who wished to live a life of penance and to be buried near the Tomb of St Peter. These days hotels and

hostels have made the Borgo a colony of international pilgrims once again. Much of the area's character was destroyed by redevelopment in the 1930s, but it is still enjoyable to explore the old narrow streets on either side of Via della Conciliazione.

Vatican Corridor ⑪

Castel Sant'Angelo to the Vatican.
Map 3 C3. 🚌 *23, 34, 41, 46, 64.*

**Clement VII, who used the Vatican
Corridor to evade capture in 1527**

LOCALLY KNOWN as the Passetto (small corridor), this long passageway was built into the fortifications during medieval times. Meant to link the Vatican with the fortress of Castel Sant'Angelo, it constituted a fortified escape route which could also be used to control the strategic Borgo area. Arrows and other missiles could be fired from its bastions on to the streets and houses below. The corridor was used in 1494 by Pope Alexander VI Borgia when Rome was invaded by King Charles VIII of France. In 1527 it enabled Pope Clement VII to take refuge in Castel Sant'Angelo, as the troops commanded by the Constable of Bourbon began the Sack of Rome.

Palazzo Torlonia ⑫

Via della Conciliazione 30. **Map** 3 C3.
🚌 23, 34, 41, 46, 64. **Not open** to the public.

THE PALAZZO was built in the late 15th century by the wealthy Cardinal Adriano Castellesi, in a style closely resembling Palazzo della Cancelleria (see p149). The cardinal was a much-travelled rogue, who collected vast revenues from the bishopric of Bath and Wells which he was given

Palazzo Torlonia (1496), unaffected by changes to the surrounding area

Pope Leo X

by his friend King Henry VII of England. In return he gave Henry his palazzo for use as the seat of the English ambassador to the Holy See. Castellesi was finally stripped of his cardinalate by Pope Leo X Medici and disappeared from history.

Since then the palazzo has had many owners and tenants. In the 17th century it was rented for a time by Queen Christina of Sweden. The Torlonia family, who acquired the building in 1820, owed its fortune to the financial genius of shopkeeper-turned-banker Giovanni Torlonia. He lent money to the impoverished Roman nobility and bought up their property during the Napoleonic Wars.

Castel Sant'Angelo ⑬

See pp248–9.

Palazzo di Giustizia ⑭

Piazza Cavour. **Map** 4 E3. 🚌 34, 49, 70, 87, 186, 280, 492, 990. **Not open** to the public.

THE MONUMENTAL Palazzo di Giustizia (Palace of Justice) was built between 1889 and 1910 to house the national law courts. Its riverside facade is crowned with a bronze chariot and fronted by giant statues of the great men of Italian law.

The building was supposed to embody the new order replacing the injustices of papal rule, but it has never endeared itself to the Romans. It was soon dubbed the Palazzaccio (roughly, "the ugly old palazzo") both for its appearance and for the nature of its business. By the 1970s the building was collapsing under its own weight and may prove impossible to repair.

The ornate travertine facade of the Palazzo di Giustizia

St Peter's ●

Tᴴᴇ ᴄᴇɴᴛʀᴇ of the Roman
Catholic faith, St Peter's
draws pilgrims from all
over the world. Few are
disappointed when they
enter the sumptuously
decorated basilica beneath
Michelangelo's vast dome.

A shrine was erected on
the site of St Peter's tomb
in the 2nd century and the
first great basilica, ordered
by the Emperor Constantine,
was completed around AD
349. By the 15th century it
was falling down, so in
1506 Pope Julius II laid the
first stone of a new church.
It took more than a century to build and all
the great architects of the Roman Renaissance
and Baroque had a hand in its design.

★ **Dome of St Peter's**
*Designed by Michelangelo,
though not finished in his
lifetime, the spectacular
cupola, 132.5 m (435 ft)
high, gives unity to the
majestic interior of the
basilica.*

The nave
is 211.5 m
(690 ft) long.

Papal Altar
*The present altar dates from
the reign of Clement VIII
(1592–1605). The plain
slab of marble found in the
Forum of Nerva stands
under Bernini's
baldacchino, over-
looking the well of the
confessio, the crypt
where St Peter's body
is reputedly buried.*

Baldacchino
*This magnificent canopy of
gilded bronze, supported on
spiral columns 20 m (66 ft)
high, was designed by
Bernini in the 17th century.*

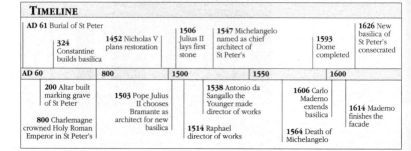

TIMELINE

AD 61 Burial of St Peter			1506 Julius II lays first stone	1547 Michelangelo named as chief architect of St Peter's		1626 New basilica of St Peter's consecrated
	324 Constantine builds basilica	**1452** Nicholas V plans restoration			**1593** Dome completed	

AD 60	800	1500		1550	1600	
200 Altar built marking grave of St Peter		**1503** Pope Julius II chooses Bramante as architect for new basilica	**1538** Antonio da Sangallo the Younger made director of works		**1606** Carlo Maderno extends basilica	**1614** Maderno finishes the facade
800 Charlemagne crowned Holy Roman Emperor in St Peter's			**1514** Raphael director of works		**1564** Death of Michelangelo	

★ View from the Dome
The superb symmetry of Bernini's colonnade can be appreciated from the dome.

The two minor cupolas at the corners of the transept are by Vignola.

Pope Urban VIII's Keys
At the base of the columns of the baldacchino, the coat of arms of Pope Urban VIII features the keys to the Kingdom of Heaven.

VISITORS' CHECKLIST

Piazza San Pietro. **Map** 3 B3.
698 44 66, 698 48 66.
64 to Piazza San Pietro or 23, 32, 49, 81, 492, 991 to Piazza del Risorgimento. Connecting bus from Vatican Museums.
19 to Piazza del Risorgimento.
Ottaviano. **Basilica open** 7am–7pm (Oct–Mar: 6pm).
Treasury open 9am–6pm (Oct–Mar: 5pm). **Vatican Grottoes open** 7am–6pm (Oct–Mar: 5pm). **Dome open** 8am–6pm (Oct–Mar: 4.45pm). **Adm charge** to Treasury and Dome.
Papal audiences: Regular public audiences, usually at 11am on Wed in Papal Audience Chamber, but sometimes in Piazza San Pietro. Tickets (free) from Prefecture of Pontifical Household (north side of piazza). **Open** 9am–1pm Mon & Tue, or write to: Prefettura della Casa Pontificia, 00120 Città del Vaticano. Appearances also at noon on Sundays at the library window to bless the crowd in Piazza San Pietro below.

Facade by Carlo Maderno (1614)

Stairs to the dome

Filarete Door
Finished in 1445, Antonio Averulino's bronze door came from the original basilica.

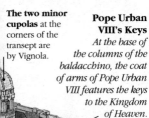

Entrances

STAR FEATURES
★ Dome of St Peter's
★ View from the Dome

Piazza San Pietro
On special religious occasions the pope appears on a balcony above the square to bless the crowds.

A Guided Tour of St Peter's

THE BASILICA is 187 m (615 ft) long and its vast marble-encrusted interior contains 11 chapels and 45 altars in addition to a wealth of precious works of art. Some were salvaged from the original basilica and others commissioned from late Renaissance and Baroque artists, but much of the elaborate decoration is owed to Bernini's work in the mid-17th century. The two side aisles are 76 m (250 ft) long and converge under Michelangelo's enormous dome. The central focus of the building is the Papal Altar beneath Bernini's great baldacchino, filling the space between four massive piers which support the dome. From the basilica you can visit the Grottoes, the Treasury and St Peter's Sacristy, or climb up to the terrace for panoramic views.

⑤ **Baldacchino by Bernini**
Commissioned by Pope Urban VIII in 1624, the extravagant Baroque canopy dominates the nave and crowns the Papal Altar, at which only the pope may celebrate mass.

Bernini's Monument to Urban VIII

④ **Throne of St Peter in Glory**
In the domed apse, look up to the window above Bernini's Baroque sculpture of 1666. It lights the image of the Holy Spirit, shown as a dove amid clouds, rays of sunlight and flights of angels.

Entrance to Treasury and Sacristy

Entrance to Necropolis

HISTORICAL PLAN OF THE BASILICA OF ST PETER'S

St Peter was buried in AD 64 in a necropolis near his crucifixion site at the Circus of Nero. Constantine built a basilica on the burial site in AD 324. In the 15th century the old church was found to be unsafe and had to be demolished. It was rebuilt in the 16th and 17th centuries. By 1614 the facade was ready, and in 1626 the new church was consecrated.

KEY

■	Circus of Nero
■	Constantinian
■	Renaissance
■	Baroque

③ **Monument to Pope Alexander VII**
Bernini's last work was finished in 1678 and is in an alcove on the left of the transept. The pope sits among the figures of Truth, Justice, Charity and Prudence.

② **Monument to Leo XI**
On the left beneath the aisle arch is Alessandro Algardi's white marble 1650 monument to Leo XI, whose reign as pope lasted only 27 days.

KEY

– – – Tour route

⑥ Angelo della Navicella

A fragment of Giotto's beautiful 13th-century mosaic, salvaged from the old basilica, is now in the Grottoes. A later copy of the entire mosaic of Jesus and St Peter fishing on Lake Tiberias decorates the atrium.

⑦ St Peter

Until recently this famous 13th-century statue, now attributed to Arnolfo di Cambio, was thought to be a late Roman work. Situated at the end of the nave, it is sculpted in bronze with a delicate filigree halo.

Entrance to Grottoes

The Tabernacle by Bernini is made of gilt bronze in the shape of a temple.

Chapel of St Sebastian

Stuart Monument by Canova

The Porta Santa (Holy Door) is opened only in Holy Years.

⑧ Pietà

This famous marble sculpture was finished in 1499 when Michelangelo was only 25. It stands in a chapel to one side of the nave, protected by glass since being damaged in 1972.

Filarete Door

Navicella Mosaic

Atrium by Carlo Maderno

① Tomb of Maria Sobieski

The first impressions of the interior of the basilica are of the vast scale and perfect symmetry. Near the entrance is Filippo Barigioni's 18th-century monument to the wife of James Stuart, the Old Pretender.

Vatican Museums ❷

THE BUILDINGS that house one of the world's most important art collections were originally papal palaces built for Renaissance popes such as Sixtus IV, Innocent VIII and Julius II. The long courtyards and galleries, linking Innocent VIII's Belvedere Palace to the other buildings, are by Donato Bramante and were commissioned for Julius II in 1503. Most of the later additions to the buildings were made in the 18th century, when priceless works of art accumulated by earlier popes were first put on show. This complex of museums also houses the Sistine Chapel and the Raphael Rooms, and should not be missed.

★ Atrium of the Four Gates
Built by Camporese in 1792–3, this vast domed edifice was the original entrance to the Vatican Museums.

The Belvedere Palace was commissioned in the late 15th century by Pope Innocent VIII.

★ Cortile della Pigna
This huge bronze pine cone, part of an ancient Roman fountain, once stood in the courtyard of old St Peter's. Its niche was designed by Pirro Ligorio.

Cortile della Biblioteca

Cortile del Belvedere

Apartment of Pius V

Sistine Chapel

Borgia Tower

Borgia Apartment

Raphael Loggia

Cortile di San Damaso

STAR FEATURES

★ Cortile della Pigna

★ Atrium of the Four Gates

★ Bramante Stairway

Spiral Ramp
The spectacular stairway up to the museums from the street was designed by Giuseppe Momo in 1932.

Entrance

VISITORS' CHECKLIST

Città del Vaticano. Entrance in Viale Vaticano. **Map** 3 B2.
69 88 33 33. 23, 81, 492 to Piazza del Risorgimento or 64 to St Peter's. Connecting bus between St Peter's and museums.
Ottaviano. 19 to Piazza del Risorgimento. **Open** 8.45am–1pm Mon–Sat, 8.45am–1pm last Sun of month; Jul–Sep and Easter: 8.45am–4pm Mon–Fri, 8.45am–1pm Sat. **Closed** public & religious hols. Special permit required for Raphael Loggia, Vatican library, Lapidary Gallery and Vatican Archives. **Adm charge**, free last Sun of month. special routes.
Temporary exhibitions, lectures, films.

Simonetti Stairway
Built in the 1780s with a vaulted ceiling, the stairs were part of the conversion of the Belvedere Palace into the Pio-Clementine Museum.

Cortile Ottagonale
The inner court of the Belvedere Palace was given its octagonal shape in 1773.

Braccio Nuovo

★ Bramante Stairway
Pope Julius II built the spiral staircase within a square tower as an entrance to the palace. The staircase could be ridden up on horseback in case of emergency.

TIMELINE

1000	1500	1600	1700	1800
1198 Innocent III creates papal palace	**1503** Bramante lays out Belvedere Courtyard	**1655** Bernini designs Scala Regia	**1756** Foundation of Christian Museum	**1800–23** Chiaramonti Museum founded **1837** Etruscan Museum founded
	1509 Raphael begins work on Rooms			
1473 Pope Sixtus IV builds Sistine Chapel	**1503–13** Pope Julius II starts Classical sculpture collection	*Bramante (1444–1514)*	**1758** Museum of Pagan Antiquities founded **1776–84** Pius VI enlarges museum	**1822** Braccio Nuovo is opened **1970** Pope Paul VI opens Gregorian Museum of Pagan Antiquities

Exploring the Vatican Museums

FOUR CENTURIES of papal patronage
and connoisseurship have resulted
in one of the world's great collections
of Classical and Renaissance art. The
Vatican houses many of the great
archaeological finds of central
Italy including the *Laocoön*
group, discovered in 1506 on
the Esquiline, the *Apollo del
Belvedere* and the Etruscan
bronze known as the *Mars of
Todi*. During the Renaissance,
parts of the museums were
decorated with wonderful
frescoes commissioned for the Sistine
Chapel, the Raphael Rooms and the
Borgia Apartment.

*Mars of
Todi*

**Gallery of the
Candelabra**
*Once an open
loggia, this gallery
of Greek and
Roman sculpture
has a fine view
of the Vatican
Gardens.*

Siege of Malta
*The Gallery of Maps is
an important record of
16th-century history
and cartography.*

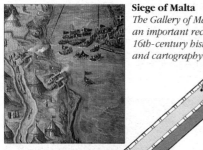

**Gallery of
Tapestries**

**Etruscan
Museum**

**Gallery of
Tapestries**

Roo
the

**Upper
floor**

**Raphael
Loggia**

**Modern
Religious Art**

**Sistine
Chapel**

**Raphael
Rooms**

GALLERY GUIDE

*Visitors have to follow a
one-way system. It is best
to concentrate on a single
collection or to choose one
of the suggested itineraries.
These are colour-coded so
that you can follow them throughout the
museums. They vary in length from 90
minutes to five hours. If you are planning
a long visit, make sure you allow plenty
of time for resting. Conserve your
stamina for the Sistine Chapel and the
Raphael Rooms; they are 20–30 minutes'
walk from the entrance, without allowing
for any viewing time along the way.*

Sala dei Misteri
*This is one of the rooms
of the Borgia Apartment,
richly decorated with
Pinturicchio frescoes.*

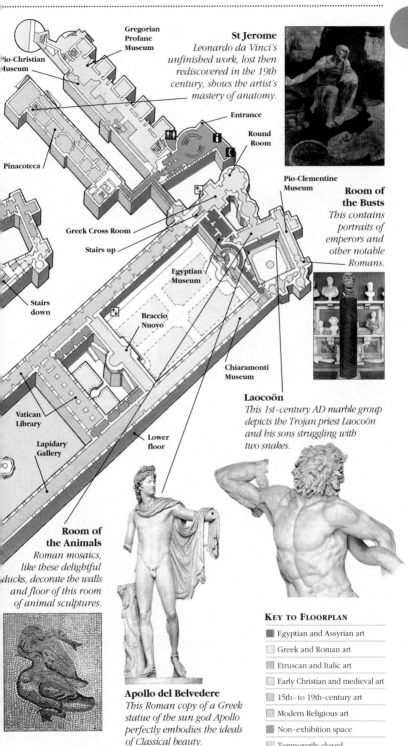

Gregorian Profane Museum

Pio-Christian Museum

St Jerome
Leonardo da Vinci's unfinished work, lost then rediscovered in the 19th century, shows the artist's mastery of anatomy.

Entrance

Round Room

Pinacoteca

Pio-Clementine Museum

Room of the Busts
This contains portraits of emperors and other notable Romans.

Greek Cross Room

Stairs up

Egyptian Museum

Stairs down

Braccio Nuovo

Chiaramonti Museum

Vatican Library

Lapidary Gallery

Lower floor

Laocoön
This 1st-century AD marble group depicts the Trojan priest Laocoön and his sons struggling with two snakes.

Room of the Animals
Roman mosaics, like these delightful ducks, decorate the walls and floor of this room of animal sculptures.

Apollo del Belvedere
This Roman copy of a Greek statue of the sun god Apollo perfectly embodies the ideals of Classical beauty.

KEY TO FLOORPLAN

- ■ Egyptian and Assyrian art
- □ Greek and Roman art
- ■ Etruscan and Italic art
- ▨ Early Christian and medieval art
- ■ 15th- to 19th-century art
- ■ Modern Religious art
- ▨ Non-exhibition space
- ▨ Temporarily closed

Exploring the Vatican's Collections

THE VATICAN'S GREATEST TREASURES are its Greek and Roman antiquities. These have been on display since the 18th century. The 19th century saw the addition of exciting discoveries from Etruscan tombs and excavations in Egypt. In the Pinacoteca (art gallery) there is a small, choice collection of paintings, including works by Raphael, Titian and Leonardo. Works by great painters and sculptors are also on view throughout the older parts of the museums in the form of sumptuous decorations commissioned by the Renaissance popes.

Coloured bas-relief from an Egyptian tomb (c2400 BC)

EGYPTIAN AND ASSYRIAN ART

THE EGYPTIAN COLLECTION contains finds from 19th- and 20th-century excavations in Egypt and statues which were brought to Rome in Imperial times. There are also Roman imitations of Egyptian art from Hadrian's Villa (see p269) and from the Campus Martius district of ancient Rome. Egyptian-style statuary from Hadrian's Villa was used to decorate the Greek Cross Room, the entrance to the new wing built in 1780 by Michelangelo Simonetti.

The genuine Egyptian works, exhibited on the lower floor of the Belvedere Palace, include statues, mummies, mummy cases and funerary artefacts. There is also a large collection of documents written on papyrus, the paper the ancient Egyptians made from reeds. Among the main treasures is a colossal granite statue of Queen Tuia, the mother of Rameses II, found on the site of the Horti Sallustiani gardens (see p251) in 1714. The statue, which dates from the 13th century BC, may have been brought to Rome by the Emperor Caligula (reigned AD 37–41), who had an unhealthy interest in pharaohs and in his own mother, Agrippina.

Also noteworthy are the head of a statue of Mentuhotep IV (21st century BC), the beautiful mummy case of Queen Hetep-heret-es, and the tomb of Iri, the guardian of the Pyramid of Cheops (22nd century BC).

The Assyrian Stairway is decorated with fragments of reliefs from the palaces of the Kings of Nineveh (8th century BC). These depict the military exploits of King Sennacherib and his son Sargon II, and show scenes from Assyrian and Chaldean mythology.

ETRUSCAN AND OTHER PRE-ROMAN ART

THIS COLLECTION comprises artefacts from pre-Roman civilizations in Etruria and Latium, from Neolithic times to the 1st century BC, when these ancient populations were assimilated into the Roman state. Pride of place in the Gregorian Etruscan Museum goes to the objects found in the Regolini-Galassi tomb, excavated in 1836 at the necropolis of Cerveteri (see p271). The tomb was found intact and yielded numerous everyday household objects, plus a throne, a bed and a funeral cart, all cast in bronze, dating from the 7th century BC. Beautiful black vases, delightful terracotta figurines and bronze statues such as the famous *Mars of Todi*, displayed in the Room of the Bronzes, show the Etruscans to have been a highly civilized, sophisticated people.

A number of Greek vases that were found in Etruscan tombs are on display in the Vase Collection. The Room of the Italiot Vases contains only vases produced locally in the Greek cities of Southern Italy and in Etruria itself. These date from the 3rd to the 1st century BC.

Etruscan gold clasp (fibula) from the 7th century BC

Head of an athlete in mosaic from the Baths of Caracalla

GREEK AND ROMAN ART

THE GREATER PART of the Vatican Museums is dedicated to Greek and Roman art. Exhibits line connecting corridors and vestibules; walls and floors display fine mosaics; and famous sculptures decorate the main courtyards.

The first serious organization of the collection took place in the reign of Julius II (1503–13) around Bramante's Belvedere Courtyard. The prize pieces form the nucleus of the 18th-century Pio-Clementine Museum. In the pavilions of the Octagonal Courtyard and in the surrounding rooms are sculptures considered among the greatest achievements of Western art. The *Apoxyomenos* (an athlete wiping his body after a race) and the *Apollo del Belvedere* are high-quality Roman copies of Greek originals of about 320 BC. The magnificent *Laocoön*, sculpted by three artists from Rhodes, had long been known to exist from a description by Pliny the Elder. It was rediscovered near the ruins of Nero's Golden House *(see p175)* in 1506. Classical works such as these had a profound influence on Michelangelo and other Renaissance artists.

The much smaller Chiaramonti Museum, named after Pope Pius VII Chiaramonti, was laid out by Canova in the early 19th century. It includes a striking colossal head of the goddess Athene. The Braccio Nuovo, an extension of the Chiaramonti, decorated with Roman floor mosaics, contains a statue of Augustus from the villa of his wife Livia at Prima Porta. Its pose is based on the famous *Doryphoros* by the Greek sculptor Polyclitus, of which there is a Roman copy on display opposite.

Exhibits in the Vase Rooms range from the Greek geometric style (8th century BC) to black-figure vases from Corinth, such as the famous vase by Exekias, with Achilles and Ajax playing a game similar to draughts (530 BC), and the later red-figure type, such as the *kylix* (a wide shallow cup) with Oedipus and the Sphinx from the 5th century BC. A stairway links this section to the Gallery of the Candelabra and the Room of the Biga (a two-horse chariot). The horses and harness were added in the 18th century.

The Gregorian Profane Museum, housed in a new wing, charts the evolution of Roman art from dependence upon Greek models to a recognizably Roman style.

Original Greek works include large marble fragments from the Parthenon in Athens. There is also a Roman copy of *Athene and Marsyas* by Myron, which was part of the decoration of the Parthenon. Totally Roman in character are two reliefs known as the Rilievi della Cancelleria,

Marble relief of the Emperor Vespasian

because they were discovered beneath the Palazzo della Cancelleria *(see p149)* in the 1930s. They show military parades of the Emperor Vespasian and his son Domitian. This section also has fine Roman floor mosaics. There are two from the Baths of Caracalla *(see p197)*, depicting athletes and referees. They date from the 3rd century AD. Most striking of all is a mosaic that creates the impression of an unswept floor, covered with debris after a meal. Away from the main Classical collections, in one of the rooms of the Vatican Library, is the *Aldobrandini Wedding*, a beautiful Roman fresco of a bride being prepared for her marriage, dating from the 1st century AD.

The *Doryphoros* or spear-carrier, a Roman copy in marble of an original Greek bronze

Floor mosaic from the Baths of Otricoli in Umbria, in the Round Room

altarpieces. The outstanding work is Giotto's altarpiece dating from about 1300, known as the *Stefaneschi Triptych*. It expresses much the same theme as the early Christian works: the continuity between the Classical world of the Roman Empire and the new order of Christian Europe. The crucifixion of St Peter takes place between two landmarks of ancient Rome, the Pyramid of Caius Cestius *(see p205)*, and the pyramid known in the Middle Ages as the Tomb of Romulus, which stood near the Vatican. The triptych, which decorated the main altar of old St Peter's, includes portraits of Pope St

Detail from Giotto's *Stefaneschi Triptych*

EARLY CHRISTIAN AND MEDIEVAL ART

THE MAIN COLLECTION of early Christian antiquities is in the Pio-Christian Museum, founded in the last century by Pope Pius IX and formerly housed in the Lateran Palace. It contains inscriptions and sculpture from catacombs and early Christian basilicas. The sculpture consists chiefly of reliefs decorating sarcophagi, though the most striking work is a free-standing 4th-century statue of the *Good Shepherd*. The sculpture's chief interest lies in the way it blends Biblical episodes with pagan mythology. Christianity adopted Classical images so that its doctrines could be understood in clear visual terms. The idealized pastoral figure of the shepherd, for example, became Christ himself, while bearded philosophers turned into the Apostles. At the same time, Christianity laid claim to be the spiritual and cultural heir of the Roman Empire.

The first two rooms of the Pinacoteca are dedicated to late medieval art, mostly wooden panels painted in tempera which served as

Celestine V (reigned 1294–6), and of the donor, Cardinal Jacopo Stefaneschi, shown offering the triptych to St Peter.

The Vatican Library has a number of medieval treasures exhibited rather haphazardly in showcases; these include woven and embroidered cloths, reliquaries, enamels and icons. One of the aims of the 18th-century reorganization of the Vatican collections was to glorify Christian works by contrasting them with earlier pagan creations. In the long Lapidary Gallery over 3,000 stone tablets with Christian and pagan inscriptions are displayed on opposite walls. The world's greatest collection of its kind, it may be visited only with special permission.

15TH- TO 19TH-CENTURY ART

THE RENAISSANCE POPES, many of whom were cultured connoisseurs of the arts, considered it their duty to sponsor the leading painters, sculptors and goldsmiths of

***Pietà* by the Venetian artist Giovanni Bellini (1430–1516)**

the age. The galleries around the Cortile del Belvedere were all decorated by great artists between the 16th and the 19th centuries. The Gallery of Tapestries is hung with tapestries woven in Brussels to designs by students of Raphael; the Apartment of Pope Pius V has beautiful 15th-century Flemish tapestries; and the Gallery of Maps is frescoed with 16th-century maps of ancient and contemporary Italy. When you go to visit the Raphael Rooms *(see pp242–3)*, you should not overlook the nearby Room of the Chiaroscuri and Pope Nicholas V's tiny private chapel, frescoed by Fra Angelico between 1447 and 1451. Similarly, before reaching the Sistine Chapel *(see pp244–7)*, visit the Borgia Apartment, frescoed in a decorative, flowery style by Pinturicchio and his students in the 1490s. The contrast with Michelangelo's Sistine Chapel ceiling, begun in 1508, could hardly be greater. Another set of fascinating frescoes decorates the Loggia of Raphael, but this requires special permission to visit.

Many important works by Renaissance masters are on show in the Pinacoteca (art gallery). Highlights among the works by 15th-century painters are a fine *Pietà* by the Venetian Giovanni Bellini and Leonardo da Vinci's unfinished *St Jerome*. Of the

great 16th-century works, do not miss the fine altarpiece by Titian, the *Crucifixion of St Peter* by Guido Reni, the *Deposition* by Caravaggio and the *Communion of St Jerome* by Domenichino. Raphael has a whole room dedicated to his work. It contains the beautiful *Madonna of Foligno* and the *Transfiguration* as well as eight tapestries made to his designs.

Lunette of the *Adoration of the Magi* by Pinturicchio in the Room of the Mysteries in the Borgia Apartment

MODERN RELIGIOUS ART

MODERN ARTISTS exhibited in the Vatican Museums face daunting competition from the great works of the past. Few modern works are displayed conspicuously, the exceptions being Momo's spiral staircase of 1932, which greets visitors as they enter the museums, and Giò Pomodoro's abstract sculpture in the centre of the Cortile della Pigna.

In 1973 a contemporary art collection was inaugurated by Pope Paul VI. Housed in the Borgia Apartment, it includes over 800 exhibits by modern artists from all over the world, donated by collectors or the artists themselves. Works in a great variety of media show many contrasting approaches to religious subjects. There are paintings, drawings, engravings and sculpture by 19th- and 20th-century artists, as well as mosaics, stained glass, ceramics and tapestries. Well-known modern painters such as Georges Braque, Paul Klee, Edvard Munch and Graham Sutherland are all represented. There are also drawings by Henry Moore, ceramics by Picasso and stained glass by Fernand Léger. Projects for modern church ornaments include Matisse's decorations for the church of St Paul de Vence, Luigi Fontana's models for the bronze doors of Milan cathedral, and Emilio Greco's panels for the doors of Orvieto cathedral.

***Town with Gothic Cathedral* by Paul Klee (1879–1940)**

Raphael Rooms

POPE JULIUS II'S PRIVATE APARTMENTS were built above those of his hated predecessor, Alexander VI, one of the Borgias, who died in 1503. Julius was impressed with Raphael's work and chose him to redecorate the four rooms *(stanze)*. Raphael and his pupils began the task in 1508, replacing existing works by several better-known artists, including Raphael's own teacher, Perugino. The work took over 16 years and Raphael himself died before its completion. The frescoes express the religious and philosophical ideals of the Renaissance. They quickly established Raphael's reputation as an artist in Rome, putting him on a par with Michelangelo, then working on the ceiling of the Sistine Chapel.

Detail from *The Expulsion of Heliodorus from the Temple*, showing Pope Julius II watching the scene from his litter

Cortile del Belvedere

KEY TO FLOORPLAN

① Hall of Constantine

② Room of Heliodorus

③ Room of the Segnatura

④ Room of the Fire in the Borgo

HALL OF CONSTANTINE ①

THE FRESCOES in this room were started in 1517, three years before Raphael's death, but Raphael himself probably had little hand in their execution. As a result they are not held in the same high regard as those in the other rooms. The work was completed in 1525 in the reign of Pope Clement VII by Giulio Romano and two other former pupils of Raphael, Giovanni Francesco Penni and Raffaellino del Colle.

The theme of the decoration is the triumph of Christianity over paganism. The four major frescoes show scenes from the life of Constantine and include his *Vision of the Cross* and his victory over his rival Maxentius at *The Battle of the Milvian Bridge*, for which Raphael had provided a preparatory sketch. In both *The Baptism of Constantine* and *The Donation of Constantine*, the figure of Pope Sylvester *(see p170)* was given the features of Clement VII.

ROOM OF HELIODORUS ②

THIS PRIVATE antechamber was decorated by Raphael between 1512 and 1514. The main frescoes show the miraculous protection granted to all the Church's ministers, doctrines and property. The room's name refers to the fresco on the right, *The Expulsion of Heliodorus from the Temple*. This shows a story from Jewish history, in which a thief called Heliodorus is felled

Swiss guards waiting with papal chair in *The Mass at Bolsena*

by a horseman as he tries to make off with the treasure from the Temple of Jerusalem. The scene is witnessed by the pope, borne on a litter by courtiers. The incident is also a thinly-veiled reference to Julius II's success in driving foreign armies out of Italy. In *The Meeting of Leo I and Attila* Raphael pays a similar compliment to the pope's political skill. Pope Leo was originally given the face of Julius II, but after his death, Raphael substituted the features of Julius's successor, Leo X.

The Mass at Bolsena depicts a miracle that occurred in 1263. A priest

***The Battle of the Milvian Bridge*, completed by one of Raphael's assistants**

The Liberation of St Peter, a three-part composition, shows the saint asleep in his cell in the middle section, led out of prison by an angel on the right, while, on the left, the prison guards cower in terror

who doubted that the bread and wine really were the body and blood of Christ suddenly saw the host bleed while he was celebrating mass. Julius II appears in this fresco, accompanied by a colourful group of Swiss guards.

Julius appears yet again as St Peter in *The Liberation of St Peter*. This fresco is remarkable for its dramatic lighting effects, achieved despite the painting's awkward shape and its position above a window.

ROOM OF THE SEGNATURA ③

THE NAME is derived from a special council which met in this room to sign official documents. The frescoes here were completed between 1508 and 1511. The scheme Raphael followed was dictated by Pope Julius II. It reflects the Humanist belief that there could be perfect harmony between Classical culture and Christianity in their mutual search for truth.

The Dispute over the Holy Sacrament, the first fresco completed by Raphael for Pope Julius, represents the triumph of religion and spiritual truth. The consecrated host is shown at the centre of the painting. This links the group of learned scholars, who discuss its significance, to the Holy Trinity and the saints floating on clouds up above.

On the opposite wall, *The School of Athens (see p30)* is a bustling scene

centred around the debate on the search for truth between Greek philosophers Plato and Aristotle. It also features portraits of many of Raphael's contemporaries, including Leonardo da Vinci, Bramante and Michelangelo. The other works include a portrait of the bearded Pope Julius II, who in 1511 vowed not to shave until he managed to rid Italy of all usurpers.

ROOM OF THE FIRE IN THE BORGO ④

THIS WAS ORIGINALLY the dining room, but when the decoration was completed under Pope Leo X, it became a music room. All the frescoes exalt the reigning pope by depicting events in the lives of his namesakes, the 9th-century popes Leo III and IV. The main frescoes were finished by two of Raphael's assistants between 1514 and 1517,

following their master's own plans. The most famous, *The Fire in the Borgo*, was painted from Raphael's designs and reflects his maturity as an artist. It celebrates the miracle that took place in 847, when Pope Leo IV extinguished a fire raging in the Borgo *(see p228)* by making the sign of the cross. The incident is likened to the flight of Aeneas from Troy described by Virgil. The figure of Aeneas appears in the foreground carrying his father on his back. This borrowing of an event from Classical legend shows a new willingness to experiment on the part of Raphael. Sadly, his pupils did not always follow his designs faithfully and this, combined with some poor restoration, has spoilt the work.

Detail from *The Fire in the Borgo*, showing Aeneas, the Trojan hero, with his father on his back, fleeing from the fire

The Dispute over the Holy Sacrament, the first fresco completed in the Rooms

Sistine Chapel: The Walls

THIS IS the main chapel in the Vatican Palace, named Cappella Sistina after its founder, Pope Sixtus IV. Its massive walls were frescoed by some of the finest artists of the 15th and 16th centuries, including Michelangelo, Perugino and Botticelli. The 12 paintings on the side walls show parallel episodes from the lives of Moses and of Christ. The decoration of the chapel walls was completed by Michelangelo, who added the great altar wall fresco, *The Last Judgment*.

KEY TO THE FRESCOES: ARTISTS AND SUBJECTS

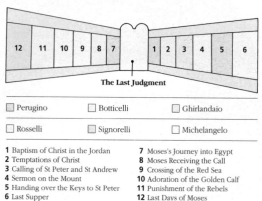

| 12 | 11 | 10 | 9 | 8 | 7 | | 1 | 2 | 3 | 4 | 5 | 6 |

The Last Judgment

☐ Perugino ☐ Botticelli ☐ Ghirlandaio

☐ Rosselli ☐ Signorelli ☐ Michelangelo

1 Baptism of Christ in the Jordan
2 Temptations of Christ
3 Calling of St Peter and St Andrew
4 Sermon on the Mount
5 Handing over the Keys to St Peter
6 Last Supper
7 Moses's Journey into Egypt
8 Moses Receiving the Call
9 Crossing of the Red Sea
10 Adoration of the Golden Calf
11 Punishment of the Rebels
12 Last Days of Moses

THE LAST JUDGMENT BY MICHELANGELO

Detail showing figure of Christ

AMONG MICHELANGELO's last works in the refurbished Sistine Chapel, *The Last Judgment* was completed in 1541 and is considered the masterpiece of his mature years. Commissioned by Pope Paul III Farnese, the work required the destruction of some earlier frescoes and the removal of two windows above the altar. A new wall was erected which slanted inwards to stop the dust settling on it. Michelangelo worked unassisted on the fresco for seven years.

The painting depicts the souls of the dead rising up to face the wrath of God, a subject rarely used for an altar decoration. It was chosen by the pope as a warning to Catholics to adhere to their faith in the turmoil of the Reformation. In fact the work conveys the artist's own tormented attitude to his faith.

The huge fresco offers none of the soothing certainties of Christian orthodoxy, nor the ordered world view of Classicism. In a dynamic, emotional composition, the figures are caught up in a swirling vortex of motion. The dead are torn from their graves and hauled up to face Christ the Judge, whose athletic, muscular figure is the focus of all the painting's movement.

Christ shows little sympathy for the agitated saints who surround him, clutching the instruments of their martyrdom. Neither is any pity shown towards the damned, hurled downwards to the demons in hell. Here Charon, pushing people off his boat into the depths of Hades, and the infernal judge Minos, are taken

Looking towards *The Last Judgment*

from Dante's *Inferno*. Minos is given a pair of ass's ears, and is actually a portrait of courtier Biagio da Cesena, who had objected to the nude figures in the fresco. Michelangelo's self-portrait can be spotted on the skin held by the martyr St Bartholomew. The painting illustrates the artist's belief that suffering is vital in finding faith in God.

St Bartholomew with his skin, bearing the face of Michelangelo

WALL FRESCOES

Detail from Botticelli's fresco
Temptations of Christ

WHEN THE Sistine Chapel was built, the papacy was a strong political power with vast accumulated wealth. In 1475 Pope Sixtus IV was able to summon some of the greatest painters of his day to decorate the chapel. Among the artists employed were Perugino, who was Raphael's master and is often credited with overseeing the project, Sandro Botticelli, Domenico Ghirlandaio, Cosimo Rosselli and Luca Signorelli. Their work on the chapel's frescoes took from 1481 to 1483.

Although frequently overlooked by visitors who concentrate on Michelangelo's work, the frescoes along the side walls of the chapel include some of the finest works of 15th-century Italian art. The two cycles of frescoes represent scenes from the lives of Moses and Christ. Above them in the spaces between the windows are portraits of the earliest popes, painted by various artists, including Botticelli.

The fresco cycles start at the altar end of the chapel, with the story of Christ on the right-hand wall and that of Moses on the left. Originally there were two paintings, *The Birth of Christ* and *The Finding of Moses*, on the wall behind the altar, but these were both destroyed to make way for Michelangelo's *The Last Judgment*.

The final paintings of the two cycles are also lost. They were on the entrance wall, which collapsed during the 16th century. When the wall was restored, they were replaced with poor substitutes.

As was customary at the time, each fresco contains a series of scenes, linked thematically to the central episode. Hidden meanings and symbols connect each painting with its counterpart on the opposite wall, and there are also many allusions to contemporary events.

The elaborate architectural details in the frescoes include familiar Roman monuments. The Arch of Constantine *(see p91)* provides the backdrop for the *Punishment of the Rebels* by Botticelli, the fifth panel in the cycle of Moses, in which the artist himself appears as the last figure but one on the right. Two similar arches appear in the painting opposite, Perugino's *Handing over the Keys to St Peter*.

Moses was both spiritual and temporal leader of his people. He called down the wrath of God on those who challenged his decisions, thus

The crowd of onlookers in the *Calling of St Peter and St Andrew* by Ghirlandaio

setting a precedent for the power exercised by the pope. In *Handing over the Keys to St Peter*, Christ confers spiritual and temporal authority on St Peter by giving him the keys to the Kingdoms of Heaven and Earth. The golden-domed building in the centre of the vast piazza represents both the Temple of Jerusalem and the Church, as founded by Peter, the first pope. The fifth figure on the right is thought to be a self-portrait by Perugino.

Botticelli's *Temptations of Christ* includes a view of the

The central episode in Botticelli's *Punishment of the Rebels*

Hospital of Santo Spirito, rebuilt in 1475 by Sixtus IV *(see p226)*. Here the devil is disguised in the habit of a Franciscan monk. Portraits of both Botticelli and Filippino Lippi are visible in the left hand corner. A portrait of the pope's nephew, Girolamo Riario, appears in the painting of the *Crossing of the Red Sea* by Rosselli, in which the sea is literally red. This painting also commemorates the papal victory at Campomorto in 1482.

Perugino's *Handing over the Keys to St Peter*

Sistine Chapel: The Ceiling

MICHELANGELO FRESCOED the chapel ceiling for Pope Julius II between 1508 and 1512. Refusing assistance, he worked alone on specially designed scaffolding. The subjects are from the Old Testament – except for the Classical Sibyls, who appear because they were said to have prophesied the birth of Christ. The main picture here shows the ceiling before its recent restoration; the smaller details show the colours revealed after cleaning.

The Creation of Adam
A powerful but tender study of hands shows Adam receiving spiritual grace and intellectual strength from God.

Creation of the Sun and Moon
On the third day the dynamic figure of God the Creator commands the sun to shed its light on the earth.

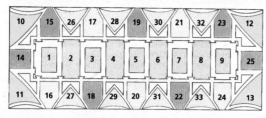

KEY

10	15	26	17	28	19	30	21	32	23	12
14	1	2	3	4	5	6	7	8	9	25
11	16	27	18	29	20	31	22	33	24	13

☐ **GENESIS 1** God Dividing Light from Darkness; **2** Creation of the Sun and Moon; **3** Separating Waters from Land; **4** Creation of Adam; **5** Creation of Eve; **6** Original Sin; **7** Sacrifice of Noah; **8** The Deluge; **9** Drunkenness of Noah.

☐ **ANCESTORS OF CHRIST 26** Solomon with his Mother; **27** Parents of Jesse; **28** Rehoboam with Mother; **29** Asa with Parents; **30** Uzziah with Parents; **31** Hezekiah with Parents; **32** Zerubbabel with Parents; **33** Josiah with Parents.

☐ **PROPHETS 14** Jonah; **15** Jeremiah; **18** Daniel; **19** Ezekiel; **22** Isaiah; **23** Joel; **25** Zechariah.

☐ **SIBYLS 16** Libyan Sibyl; **17** Persian Sibyl; **20** Cumaean Sibyl; **21** Erythrean Sibyl; **24** Delphic Sibyl.

☐ **OLD TESTAMENT SCENES OF SALVATION 10** Punishment of Haman; **11** Moses and the Brazen Serpent; **12** David and Goliath; **13** Judith and Holofernes.

The Creation of Eve
God has just created Eve from one of the sleeping Adam's ribs. The shape of the tree suggests Christ's Cross.

Original Sin shows the tasting of the Tree of Knowledge and the expulsion of Adam and Eve from the Garden of Eden.

The Ignudi are athletic male nudes that frame the main scenes on the ceiling.

Delphic Sibyl
The beautiful prophetess of the Greek Oracle of Delphi is portrayed in a moment of intense inspiration.

The Deluge concentrates on the figures of the people stranded by the flood.

Castel Sant'Angelo ⑬

THE MASSIVE FORTRESS of Castel Sant'Angelo takes its name from the statue of the Archangel Michael on its summit. It began life in AD 139 as the Emperor Hadrian's mausoleum. Since then it has had many roles: as part of the Emperor Aurelian's city wall, as a medieval citadel and prison, and as the residence of the popes in times of political unrest. From the dank cells in the lower levels to the fine apartments of the Renaissance popes above, a 58-room museum covers all aspects of the castle's history.

Mausoleum of Hadrian
This artist's impression shows the tomb before Aurelian fortified its walls in AD 270–75.

Courtyard of Honour
Heaps of stone cannonballs decorate the courtyard, once the castle's ammunition store.

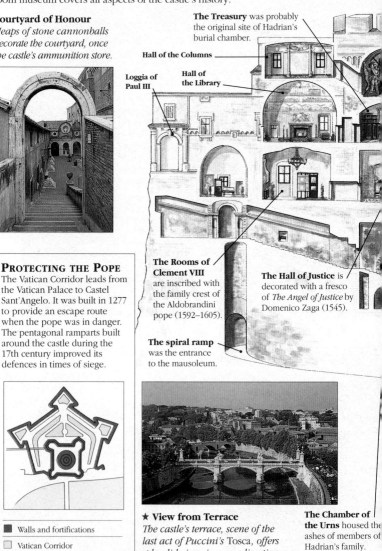

The Treasury was probably the original site of Hadrian's burial chamber.

Hall of the Columns

Loggia of Paul III

Hall of the Library

The Rooms of Clement VIII are inscribed with the family crest of the Aldobrandini pope (1592–1605).

The Hall of Justice is decorated with a fresco of *The Angel of Justice* by Domenico Zaga (1545).

The spiral ramp was the entrance to the mausoleum.

PROTECTING THE POPE
The Vatican Corridor leads from the Vatican Palace to Castel Sant'Angelo. It was built in 1277 to provide an escape route when the pope was in danger. The pentagonal ramparts built around the castle during the 17th century improved its defences in times of siege.

■ Walls and fortifications

☐ Vatican Corridor

★ **View from Terrace**
The castle's terrace, scene of the last act of Puccini's Tosca, offers splendid views in every direction.

The Chamber of the Urns housed the ashes of members of Hadrian's family.

STAR FEATURES

★ Sala Paolina

★ View from Terrace

★ Staircase of
Alexander VI

Bronze Angel
*The gigantic statue of the
Archangel Michael is
by the 18th-century
Flemish sculptor
Pieter Verschaffelt.*

VISITORS' CHECKLIST

Lungotevere Castello. **Map** 4 D3
& 11 A1. ☎ 687 50 36. 🚌 23,
64, 87, 280 to Lungotevere
Castello; 34, 49, 70, 81, 186,
926, 990 to Piazza Cavour.
Ⓜ Lepanto. **Open** 9am–2pm,
Tue–Sat; 9am–1pm Sun; 2pm–
7pm (Oct–Mar: 4.30pm) Mon
(last adm: 1 hr before closing).
Closed public hols. **Adm charge.**
📷 🎦 10.30am Sun only. 🚻
📷 **Exhibitions**.

The Round Hall houses the original model
from which Verschaffelt's angel was cast.

★ **Sala Paolina**
*The illusionistic frescoes
by Perin del Vaga and
Pellegrino Tibaldi
(1544–7) include one
of a courtier entering
the room through a
painted door.*

Hall of Apollo
*The room is frescoed
with scenes from
mythology attributed
to the pupils of Perin
del Vaga (1548).*

**Ventilation
shaft**

★ **Staircase of
Alexander VI**
*This staircase cuts
right through
the heart of the
building.*

Bridge

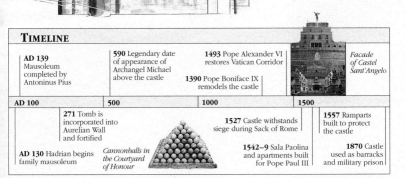

TIMELINE

AD 139 Mausoleum completed by Antoninus Pius	**590** Legendary date of appearance of Archangel Michael above the castle	**1493** Pope Alexander VI restores Vatican Corridor		*Facade of Castel Sant'Angelo*
		1390 Pope Boniface IX remodels the castle		

| AD 100 | 500 | 1000 | 1500 | |

271 Tomb is incorporated into Aurelian Wall and fortified		**1527** Castle withstands siege during Sack of Rome	**1557** Ramparts built to protect the castle
AD 130 Hadrian begins family mausoleum	*Cannonballs in the Courtyard of Honour*	**1542–9** Sala Paolina and apartments built for Pope Paul III	**1870** Castle used as barracks and military prison

VIA VENETO

I N IMPERIAL ROME, this was a suburb where rich families owned luxurious villas and gardens. Ruins from this era can be seen in the excavations in Piazza Sallustio, named after the most extensive gardens in the area, the Horti Sallustiani.

Film director Federico Fellini

After the Sack of Rome in the 5th century, the area reverted to open countryside. Not until the 17th century did it recover its lost splendour, with the building of Palazzo Barberini and the now-vanished Villa Ludovisi.

When Rome became capital of Italy in 1870, the Ludovisi sold their land for development. They kept a plot for a new house, but tax on the profits from the sale was so high, they had to sell that too. By 1900, Via Veneto had become a street of smart modern hotels and cafés. It featured prominently in Fellini's 1960 film *La Dolce Vita*, a scathing satire on the lives of film stars and idle rich, but since then has lost its position as the meeting place of the famous.

SIGHTS AT A GLANCE

Churches and Temples
Santa Maria della Concezione ❸
Santa Susanna ❼
Santa Maria della Vittoria ❽

Historic Buildings
Casino dell'Aurora ❷
Palazzo Barberini ❻

Famous Streets
Via Veneto ❶

Fountains
Fontana delle Api ❹
Fontana del Tritone ❺

SEE ALSO

• *Street Finder*, map 5
• *Where to Stay* pp294–5
• *Restaurants* pp310–11

0 metres   200
0 yards   200

N

GETTING THERE
This is one of the easiest parts of Rome to reach by public transport. Barberini and Repubblica Metro stations on line A are very handy, and Stazione Termini is only 10–15 minutes' walk away. The Via Veneto itself starts at Piazza Barberini, well served by buses from all parts of the city. The 95 goes the whole length of Via Veneto to Porta Pinciana. Other useful routes include the 52, 53, 56, 58 and 60 along Via del Tritone.

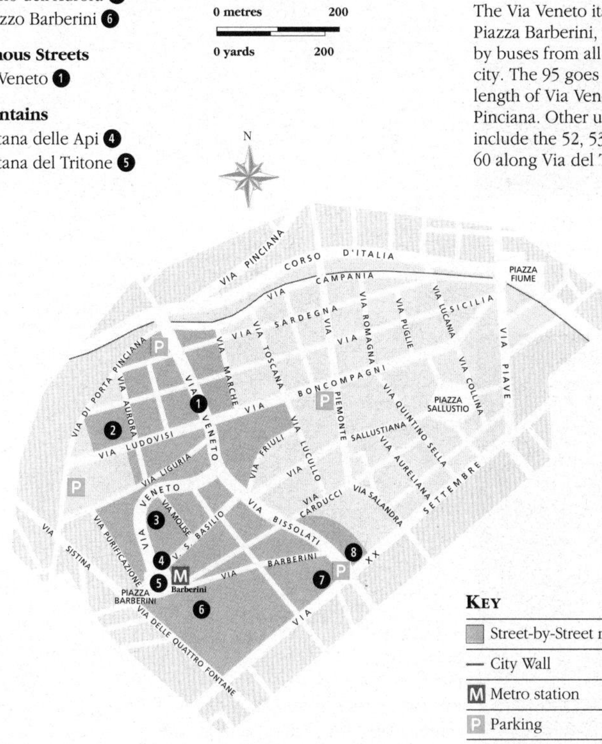

KEY

▨	Street-by-Street map
—	City Wall
Ⓜ	Metro station
Ⓟ	Parking

The onset of autumn in Via Veneto

Street-by-Street: Via Veneto

T HE STREETS AROUND VIA VENETO, though within the
walls of ancient Rome, contain little dating from
before the unification of Italy in 1870. With its hotels,
restaurants, bars and travel agencies, the area is the
centre of 20th-century tourism in the way that Piazza di
Spagna was the hub of the tourist trade in the Rome of
the 18th-century Grand Tour. However, glimpses of the
old city can be seen among the modern streets. These
include Santa Maria della Concezione, the church of the
Capuchin friars, whose convent once stood in its own
gardens. In the 17th century Palazzo Barberini was built
here for the powerful papal family. Bernini's Fontana
del Tritone and Fontana delle Api have stood in Piazza
Barberini since it was the meeting place of cart tracks
                        entering the city from
                        surrounding vineyards.

Casino dell'Aurora
*A pavilion is all that
remains of the great
Ludovisi estate that
once occupied most of
this quarter of Rome* ❷

**Santa Maria della
Concezione**
*This church is best
known for the
macabre collection of
bones in its crypt* ❸

Fontana delle Api
*Bernini's drinking
fountain is decorated
with bees, emblem
of his Barberini
patrons* ❹

Fontana del Tritone
*Bernini's muscular sea god
has been spouting water
skywards for 350 years* ❺

★ **Palazzo
Barberini**
*Pietro da Cortona
worked on his spectacular
ceiling fresco* The Triumph of Divine
Providence *between 1633 and 1639* ❻

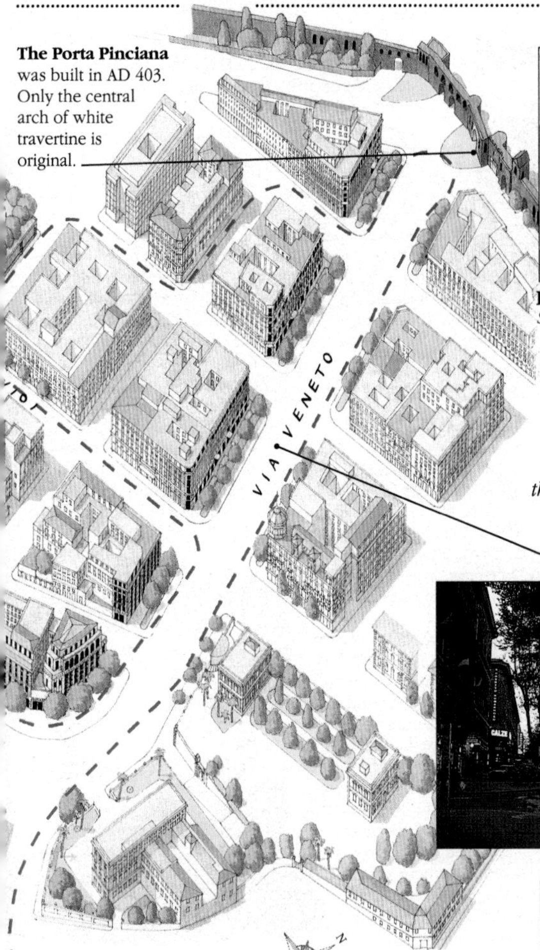

The Porta Pinciana
was built in AD 403.
Only the central
arch of white
travertine is
original.

LOCATOR MAP
See Central Rome Map pp12–13

Via Veneto
*Built during the
redevelopment of Rome at
the end of the 19th century,
this street of smart hotels and
spacious pavement cafés
enjoyed its heyday during
the 1950s and 1960s* ❶

Santa Susanna
*This church is
dedicated to a
martyr executed
during Diocletian's
persecution of
Christians in the
3rd century AD* ❼

STAR SIGHTS

★ **Santa Maria
della Vittoria**

★ **Palazzo Barberini**

KEY

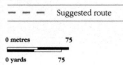

— — — Suggested route

| 0 metres | 75 |
| 0 yards | 75 |

★ **Santa Maria
della Vittoria**
*The highlight of this
Baroque church is
the Cornaro Chapel,
designed to resemble a
theatre. The centre of
the stage is occupied
by Bernini's thrilling
sculpture of the
Ecstasy of St Teresa* ❽

Pavement café in Via Veneto

Via Veneto ❶

Map 5 B1. 🚌 52, 53, 56, 58, 58b, 95, 490, 495 and many other routes. Ⓜ *Barberini*.

V IA VENETO descends in a lazy curve from the Porta Pinciana to Piazza Barberini, lined in its upper reaches with exuberant turn-of-the-century hotels and canopied pavement cafés. It was laid out in 1879 over a large estate sold by the Ludovisi family in the great building boom of Rome's first years as capital of Italy. Palazzo Margherita, intended to be the new Ludovisi family palazzo, was completed in 1890. It now houses the American embassy.

In the 1960s this was the most glamorous street in Rome, its cafés patronized by film stars and plagued by the *paparazzi*. Most of the people drinking in the cafés today are tourists, as film stars now seem to prefer the livelier bohemian atmosphere of Trastevere.

Palazzo Margherita, the US embassy

Casino dell'Aurora ❷

Via Lombardia 46. **Map** 5 B2. 🅲 48 39 42. 🚌 52, 53, 56, 58. **Open** by appt only.

T HE CASINO (a stately country residence) was a summerhouse in the grounds of the Ludovisi palace. It was built by Cardinal Ludovisi in the 17th century, and frescoed by Guercino. The subject of the ceiling fresco is Aurora, the goddess of dawn. It is a dizzying work creating the impression that the Casino has no roof, but lies open to a cloudy sky, across which horses pull Aurora's carriage away from the darkness of night towards the light of day.

Santa Maria della Concezione ❸

Via Veneto 27. **Map** 5 B2. 🅲 487 11 85. 🚌 52, 53, 56, 58, 58b, 490, 495 and many other routes. Ⓜ *Barberini*. **Open** 7am–noon, 3.45pm–7.30pm daily. **Crypt open** 9am–noon, 3pm–6.20pm (Oct–Mar: 6pm). **Donation** expected. 🚻 📷

P OPE URBAN VIII's brother, Antonio Barberini was a cardinal and a Capuchin friar. In 1626 he founded this plain, unassuming church at what is now the foot of the Via Veneto. When he died he was buried not, like most cardinals, in a grand marble sarcophagus, but below a simple flagstone close to the altar, where you can read the bleak epitaph in Latin: "Here lies dust, ashes, nothing".

The grim reality of death is illustrated even more graphically in the crypt beneath the church, where generations of Capuchin friars have decorated the walls of the five vaulted chapels with the bones and skulls of their departed brethren. In all, some 4,000 skeletons were used to create this macabre *memento mori*. Some of the bones are wired together to form Christian symbols such as crowns of thorns, sacred hearts and crucifixes. There are also a number of complete skeletons, including one of a Barberini princess who died as a child. At the exit, an inscription in Latin reads: "What you are, we used to be. What we are, you will be."

Pope Urban VIII

Fontana delle Api ❹

Piazza Barberini. **Map** 5 B2. 🚌 52, 53, 56, 58, 58b, 490, 495 and many other routes. Ⓜ *Barberini*.

T HE FOUNTAIN of the bees – *api* are bees, symbol of the Barberini family – is one of Bernini's more modest works. Tucked away in a corner of Piazza Barberini, it is quite easy to miss. Dating from 1644, it pays homage to Pope Urban VIII Barberini, and features rather crab-like bees which appear to be sipping the water as it dribbles down into the basin. A Latin inscription informs us that the water is for the use of the public and their animals.

Bernini's Fontana delle Api

Fontana del Tritone ❺

Piazza Barberini. **Map** 5 B3. 🚌 52, 53, 56, 58, 58b, 490, 495 and many other routes. Ⓜ *Barberini*.

I N THE CENTRE of busy Piazza Barberini is one of Bernini's liveliest fountains, the Triton Fountain. It was created for Pope Urban VIII Barberini in 1642, shortly after the completion of his palace on the ridge above. Acrobatic dolphins stand on their heads, twisting their tails together to support a huge scallop shell on which the sea god Triton kneels, blowing a spindly column of water up into the air through a conch shell. Entwined artistically among the dolphins' tails are the papal tiara, the keys of St Peter and the Barberini coat of arms.

The Triton and his conch shell in Bernini's Fontana del Tritone

Palazzo Barberini ⬤

Via delle Quattro Fontane 13. **Map** 5 B3. 📞 *481 45 91 or 482 41 84.* 🚌 *52, 53, 56, 58, 58b, 490, 495 and many other routes.* Ⓜ *Barberini.* **Open** *9am–7pm Tue–Sun (last adm: 30 mins before closing).* **Adm charge.** 📷

WHEN MAFFEI BARBERINI became Pope Urban VIII in 1623 he decided to build a grand palace for his family. The site he chose was then on the fringes of the city, overlooking a ruined temple. The architect, Carlo Maderno, designed it as a typical rural villa, with wings extending into the surrounding gardens. Maderno died in 1629, shortly after the foundations had been laid, and Bernini took over, assisted by Borromini. The peculiar pediments on some of the top floor windows, and the oval staircase inside, are almost certainly by Borromini.

Of the many sumptuously decorated rooms, the most striking is the Gran Salone, with a dazzling illusionistic ceiling fresco by Pietro da Cortona. The palazzo also houses paintings from the 13th to the 16th centuries, part of the Galleria Nazionale d'Arte

Antica, with important works by Filippo Lippi, El Greco and Caravaggio. There is also a Holbein portrait of King Henry VIII of England dressed for his wedding to Anne of Cleves. Of greater local significance are Guido Reni's *Beatrice Cenci*, the young woman executed for planning her father's murder *(see p150)*, and *La Fornarina*, traditionally identified as a portrait of Raphael's mistress *(see p212)*, although not painted by the artist himself.

Santa Susanna ⬤

Piazza San Bernardo. **Map** 5 C2. 📞 *482 75 10.* 🚌 *16, 36, 37, 60, 61, 62, 910 and many other routes.* Ⓜ *Repubblica.* **Open** *10am-noon Sun.*

Facade of Santa Susanna

SANTA SUSANNA'S most striking feature is its vigorous Baroque facade by Carlo Maderno, finished in 1603. Christians have worshipped on the site since at least the 4th century. In the nave, there are four huge frescoes by Baldassarre Croce (1558–1628), painted to resemble tapestries. These depict scenes from the life of Susanna, an obscure Roman saint who was martyred here, and the rather better-known life of the Old Testament Susanna, who was spotted bathing in her husband's garden by two lecherous judges.

When it has been restored, Santa Susanna will resume its function as the Catholic church for Americans in Rome.

Santa Maria della Vittoria ⬤

Via XX Settembre 17. **Map** 5 C2. 📞 *482 61 90.* 🚌 *16, 36, 37, 60, 61, 62, 910 and many other routes.* Ⓜ *Repubblica.* **Open** *6.30am–noon, 4.30pm–6pm daily.* 📷 🚫

SANTA MARIA della Vittoria is an intimate Baroque church with a lavishly decorated candlelit interior. It contains one of Bernini's most ambitious sculptural works, the *Ecstasy of St Teresa* (1646), centrepiece of the Cornaro Chapel, built to resemble a miniature theatre. It even has an audience: sculptures of the chapel's benefactor, Cardinal Federico Cornaro, and his ancestors sit in boxes, as if watching and discussing the scene played out in front of them.

Visitors may be shocked or thrilled by the apparently physical nature of St Teresa's ecstasy. She lies on a cloud, her mouth half open and her eyelids closed, with rippling drapery covering her body. Looking over her with a smile, which from different angles can appear either tender or cruel, is a curly-haired angel holding an arrow with which he is about to pierce the saint's body for a second time. The marble figures are framed and illuminated by rays of divine light materialized in bronze.

Bernini's astonishing *Ecstasy of St Teresa*

FURTHER AFIELD

THE MORE INQUISITIVE visitor to Rome may wish to try a few excursions to the large parks and some of the more isolated churches on the outskirts of the city. With a day to spare, you can explore the villas of Tivoli and the ruins of the ancient Roman port of Ostia. Traditional haunts of the

Dish (3rd century BC) in Villa Giulia

Grand Tour *(see p130)*, such as the catacombs and the ruined aqueducts of Parco Appio Claudio, still offer glimpses of the rapidly vanishing Campagna, the countryside around Rome. More modern sights include the suburb of EUR, built in the Fascist era, and the memorial at the Fosse Ardeatine.

SIGHTS AT A GLANCE

Towns and Areas
EUR ⓮
Tivoli ⓱

Historic Roads
Via Appia Antica ❼

Churches
Santa Costanza ❹
Sant'Agnese fuori le Mura ❺
San Lorenzo fuori le Mura ❻
San Paolo fuori le Mura ⓯

Museums and Galleries
Museo Borghese pp260–61 ❷
Villa Giulia pp262–3 ❸

Parks and Gardens
Villa Borghese ❶
Parco Appio Claudio ⓭
Villa Doria Pamphilj ⓰
Villa d'Este ⓲
Villa Gregoriana ⓳

Ancient Sites
Hadrian's Villa ⓴
Ostia Antica ㉑

Tombs and Catacombs
Catacombs of San Callisto ❽
Catacombs of San Sebastiano ❾
Catacombs of Domitilla ❿
Fosse Ardeatine ⓫
Tomb of Cecilia Metella ⓬

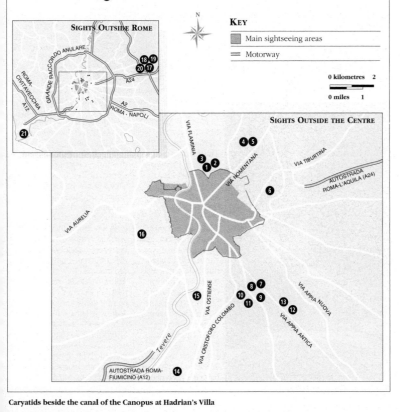

N

KEY

▨ Main sightseeing areas

═ Motorway

0 kilometres 2
0 miles 1

SIGHTS OUTSIDE ROME

SIGHTS OUTSIDE THE CENTRE

Caryatids beside the canal of the Canopus at Hadrian's Villa

Villa Borghese ➊

Map 2 E5. ▤ *3, 4, 52, 53, 57, 95, 490, 495, 910.* ▣ *19, 19b, 30b.*
Park open *dawn to sunset.* **Zoo** Viale del Giardino Zoologico. **Map** 2 E4.
▣ *321 65 64.* ▤ *3, 52, 910.* ▣ *19, 19b, 30b.* **Open** *8.30am–5pm (last adm: 4pm) Mon–Fri, 8.30pm– 6pm (last adm: 5 pm) Sat & Sun.* **Closed** *Mon pm, 1 May.* ⊙ ▦ ⅋ ⅋ ■ ▯
Galleria Nazionale d'Arte Moderna Viale delle Belle Arti 131. **Map** 2 D4.
▣ *322 41 52.* ▣ *19, 19b, 30b.*
Open *9am–7pm Tue–Sat; 9am–1pm Sun (last adm: 30 mins before closing).* ⅋ ⅋ ⅋ ■ ▯

British School at Rome, designed by Edwin Lutyens in 1911

T HE VILLA and its park were designed in 1605 for Cardinal Scipione Borghese, nephew of Pope Paul V. The park was the first of its kind in Rome. It contained 400 newly-planted pine trees, garden sculpture by Bernini's father, Pietro, and dramatic waterworks built by Giovanni Fontana. The layout of the formal gardens was imitated by other prominent Roman families at Villa Ludovisi and Villa Doria Pamphilj, but the cardinal's 18th-century successors preferred a more natural-looking park.

In the early 19th century Prince Camillo Borghese assembled the family's magnificent art collection in the Casino Borghese, now the home of the Galleria and Museo Borghese.

In 1902 the park became the property of the Italian state. Within its 6-km (4-mile) circumference there are now museums and galleries, foreign academies and schools of archaeology, a zoo, a riding school, a grassy amphitheatre, an artificial lake, an aviary and an array of summer houses, fountains, Neo-Classical statuary and exotic follies.

There are several ways into the park, including a monumental entrance on Piazzale Flaminio, built for Prince Camillo Borghese in 1825 by Luigi Canina. Other conveniently-sited entrances are at Porta Pinciana at the end of Via Veneto and from the Pincio Gardens *(see p136).* The main attraction of Italian gardens in hot weather is shade, so the long avenues are lined with hedges and trees. Piazza di Siena, a pleasantly open, grass-covered amphitheatre surrounded by tall umbrella pines, was the inspiration for Ottorino Respighi's famous symphonic poem *The Pines of Rome*, written in 1924. Near Piazza di Siena are the so-called Casina di Raffaello, said to have been owned by Raphael, and the

Statue of the English poet Byron by Thorvaldsen

18th-century Palazzetto dell'Orologio. These were summerhouses from which people enjoyed the beautiful vistas across the park.

Many buildings in the park were originally surrounded by formal gardens: the Casino Borghese and the nearby 17th-century Casino della Meridiana and its aviary (the Uccelliera) have both kept their geometrical flowerbeds. Throughout the park the inter-sections of paths and avenues are marked by fountains and statues. West of Piazza di Siena is the Fontana dei Cavalli Marini (the Fountain of the Seahorses) added during the villa's 18th-century remodelling. Walking through the park you will encounter statues of Byron, Goethe and Victor Hugo, and a gloomy equestrian King Umberto I.

Dotted about the park are picturesque temples made to look like ruins, including a circular Temple of Diana between Piazza di Siena and Porta Pinciana, and a Temple of Faustina, wife of Emperor Antoninus Pius, on the hill north of Piazza di Siena. The nearby medieval-looking Fortezzuola by Canina contains the works of the sculptor Pietro Canonica, who lived in the building and died there in 1959. In the garden stands Canonica's *Monument to the Alpino and his Mule*, which honours the humblest

Neo-Classical Temple of Diana

Ionic temple dedicated to Aesculapius, built on the lake island

protagonists in Italy's alpine battles against Austria in World War I.

In the centre of the park is the Giardino del Lago, its main entrance marked by an 18th-century copy of the Arch of Septimius Severus.

The garden has an artificial lake complete with an Ionic Temple to Aesculapius, the god of health, by the 18th-century architect Antonio Asprucci. Rowing boats and ducks make the lake a favourite with children, banana trees and bamboo grow around the shore, and clearings are studded with sculptures.

Surrounded by flowerbeds south of the lake is the Art Nouveau Fontana dei Fauni, one of the garden's prettiest sculptures. In a clearing close to the entrance on Viale Pietro Canonica are the original Tritons of the Fontana del Moro in Piazza Navona *(see p120)* – they were moved here and replaced by copies in the 19th century.

From the northwest the park is entered by the Viale delle Belle Arti, where the Galleria Nazionale d'Arte Moderna houses a fairly uninspiring collection of 19th- and 20th-century paintings. The Art Nouveau character of the area dates from the International Exhibition held here in 1911, for which pavilions were built by many nations, the most impressive being the British School at Rome, by Edwin Lutyens,

with a facade adapted from the upper west portico of St Paul's Cathedral in London. Originally a School of Archaeology, the school now offers the chance to study literature, fine arts and history. The statues close by are equally international: they include Simon Bolivar and other liberators of Latin America, and the great Persian poet Firdusi.

Beyond the art gallery, in the northeastern corner of the park, lie a rather depressing Zoo and the Museo Zoologico. A far greater attraction is the pretty 16th-century Villa Giulia with its world-famous collection of Etruscan and other pre-Roman remains.

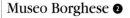

GIARDINO ZOOLOGICO

Zoo entrance

Another Renaissance building of importance is the Palazzina of Pius IV, close to the Via Flaminia entrance. It was designed by the architect Vignola in 1552 and then transformed into an elegant apartment for Pius IV's nephew Carlo Borromeo. It is now the home of the Italian Embassy to the Holy See.

Museo Borghese **2**

See pp260–61.

Villa Giulia **3**

See pp262–3.

A stone lion guarding the ornate entrance to the Zoo

Museo Borghese ❷

T HE VILLA AND PARK were laid out by
Cardinal Scipione Borghese, favourite
nephew of Paul V, who had the house
designed for pleasure and entertainment.
The hedonistic cardinal was also an
extravagant patron of the arts and he
commissioned sculptures from the young
Bernini which now rank among his most
famous works. Scipione also opened his
pleasure park to the public. Today the
villa houses the superb private Borghese
collection of sculptures and paintings in
the Museo and
Galleria Borghese.

Facade of the Villa Borghese
*This painting (1613) by the villa's Flemish
architect Jan van Santen shows the highly
ornate facade of the original design.*

MUSEUM GUIDE
*The museum is
divided into two
sections: the sculpture
collection (Museo
Borghese) occupies
the entire ground
floor and the picture
gallery (Galleria
Borghese) is on the
upper floor. The
Galleria Borghese has
reopened to the public
after extensive
restoration work.*

★ Pluto and Persephone
*One of Bernini's finest works,
the sculpture shows Pluto
carrying off his bride. The
sculptor's astonishing
skill with marble
can be clearly
seen in the
twisting
figures.*

**Sleeping
Hermaphrodite**
*Dated around 150
BC, this is a bronze
Roman copy of the
Greek original by
Polycles. The head and
mattress were added
by Andrea Bergondi
in the 17th century.*

The Egyptian Room
*Frescoes show episodes in
Egyptian history and
Egyptian motifs.*

TIMELINE

	1613 15-year-old Bernini sculpts *Aeneas and Anchises*	**Early 1800s** Statues and reliefs are considered too ornate and stripped from the villa's facade	**1809** Much of the collection is sold by Prince Camillo Borghese to France and goes to Louvre	**1902** Villa, grounds and collection bought by the state
	1621–5 Bernini sculpts *Pluto and Persephone*			
1625		**1725**		**1825**
	1622–5 Bernini sculpts *Apollo and Daphne*		**1805** Canova sculpts the semi-nude, reclining Pauline Borghese	**Early 1900s** Balustrade round the forecourt is bought by Lord Astor for the Cliveden estate in England
	1613–15 The Flemish architect Jan van Santen designs and builds Villa Borghese	*Daphne's fingers turning into leaves*		

Rear entrance

★ Apollo and Daphne
Bernini's most famous masterpiece depicts the nymph Daphne fleeing the sun god Apollo at the moment of Daphne's dramatic transformation into a tree.

★ David
Modelling David's face on his own, the 25-year-old Bernini captured the moment before David threw the stone that slew Goliath.

★ Pauline Borghese
Napoleon's sister Pauline posed as Venus for the sculptor Canova. Once the statue was completed, Pauline's husband Camillo Borghese kept it locked away, even denying Canova access.

Front entrance

STAR SCULPTURES

★ **Pauline Borghese by Canova**

★ **Apollo and Daphne by Bernini**

★ **David by Bernini**

★ **Pluto and Persephone by Bernini**

Gladiator Mosaic
The floor is decorated with the fragments of a 4th-century AD mosaic from a villa in Torrenova.

KEY TO FLOORPLAN

☐ Exhibition space

▨ Non-exhibition space

Villa Giulia ③

THIS VILLA was built as a country retreat for Pope Julius III, and was designed for entertaining rather than as a permanent home. It once housed an impressive collection of statues – 160 boatloads were sent to the Vatican after the pope died in 1555. The gardens, pavilions and fountains were designed by exceptional architects: Vignola (designer of the Gesù), the biographer Vasari, and the sculptor Ammannati. Michelangelo also contributed. The villa's main features are its facade, the courtyard and garden and the *nympheum*. Since 1889 Villa Giulia has housed the Museo Nazionale Etrusco, with its outstanding collection of pre-Roman antiquities from central Italy.

Faliscan Crater of the Dawn
This ornate vase, painted in the free style of the 4th century BC, shows Dawn rising in a chariot.

Chigi Vase
Battle and hunting scenes adorn this Corinthian vase from the 6th century BC

First floor

★ Husband and Wife Sarcophagus
This 6th-century BC masterpiece, from Cerveteri, shows a dead couple at the eternal banquet.

MUSEUM GUIDE
This is the most important Etruscan museum in Italy, housing artefacts from most of the major excavations in Tuscany and Lazio. Rooms 1–10 and 23–34 are arranged by site and include Vulci, Todi, Veio and Cerveteri, while private collections are in rooms 11–22.

Votive Offering
The religious Etruscans made artefacts, such as this model of a boy feeding a bird, in their gods' honour.

TIMELINE

1550 Work begins on Villa Giulia under Pope Julius III	**1655** Queen Christina of Sweden stays in villa as Vatican guest	**1889** Etruscan museum founded		**1919** Castellani private collection donated to museum
		Late 1700s First large-scale studies of Etruscan artefacts		

1550	1650	1750	1850	1950

Late 1500s First, chance finds of Etruscan artefacts raise some scholastic interest		**1908** Barberini private collection bought by the state	**1972** Pesciotti private collection bought by the state
1555 Villa completed	*Corner decoration of bronze chariot used to burn incense*		

Facade

The villa's facade dates from 1552–3. The entrance is designed in the form of a triumphal arch.

VISITORS' CHECKLIST

Piazzale di Villa Giulia 9.
Map 1 C4. 322 65 71.
52, 926 to Viale Bruno
Buozzi, 95, 490, 495 to Viale
Washington. 19, 19b, 30b
to Piazza Thorwaldsen. **Open**
9am–7pm (Oct–Mar: 2pm)
Tue–Sun. **Closed** 1 Jan, 1 May,
25 Dec. **Adm charge.**
with seven days notice.
Concerts: "Notturno Etrusco"
evenings held at the Ninfeo
(Nympheum) on Saturdays
throughout July & August.
Lectures, films.

★ Reconstruction of an Etruscan Temple

Count Adolfo Cozza built the Temple of Alatri here in 1891. He based his design on the accounts of Vitruvius and 19th-century excavations.

Nympheum

Literally, the "area dedicated to the nymphs", this is a sunken courtyard decorated with Classical mosaics, statues and fountains.

STAR EXHIBITS

- ★ **Husband and Wife Sarcophagus**
- ★ **Ficoroni Cist**
- ★ **Reconstruction of an Etruscan Temple**

KEY TO FLOORPLAN

☐	Exhibition space
☐	Non-exhibition space
☐	Temporarily closed
☐	Gardens
☐	Nympheum pool

Main entrance

Ground floor

★ Ficoroni Cist

Engraved and beautifully illustrated, this fine bronze marriage coffer dates from the 4th century BC.

Santa Costanza ④

Via Nomentana 349. ☎ 861 08 40.
🚌 36, 36b, 37, 60, 136, 137. **Open**
9am–noon, 4pm–6pm Mon & Wed–
Sat, 4pm–6pm Sun and public hols.
Adm charge. 📷 ♿ 📹

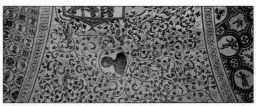

Part of the 4th-century mosaic in the ambulatory of Santa Costanza

Circular interior of 4th-century
church of Santa Costanza

THE ROUND CHURCH of Santa
Costanza was originally
built in the early 4th century
as a mausoleum for Emperor
Constantine's daughters
Constantia and Helena. The
dome and its drum are
supported by a circular arcade
which rests on 12 magnificent
pairs of granite columns. The
ambulatory that runs around
the outside of the central
arcade has a barrel-vaulted
ceiling decorated with
wonderful 4th-century mosaics
of fruit, flowers, animals and
birds and even charming
scenes of a Roman grape
harvest. In a niche on the far
side of the church from the
entrance is a replica of
Constantia's ornately carved
porphyry sarcophagus. The
original was moved to the
Vatican Museums in 1790.

Constantia's sanctity is
somewhat debatable – she
was described by the historian Marcellinus as a fury
incarnate, constantly goading
her equally unpleasant
husband Hannibalianus to
violence. Her canonization
was probably the result of
some confusion with a saintly
nun of the same name.

Sant'Agnese fuori le Mura ⑤

Via Nomentana 349. ☎ 861 08 40.
🚌 36, 36b, 37, 60, 136, 137. **Open**
9am–noon, 4pm–6pm Mon & Wed–
Sat, 4pm–6pm Sun and public hols.
Adm charge to catacombs. 📷 ♿ 📹

THE CHURCH OF Sant'Agnese
stands among a group of
early Christian buildings which
includes the ruins of a covered
cemetery, some extensive
catacombs and the crypt where
the 13-year-old martyr St Agnes
was buried in AD 304. Agnes
was exposed naked by order
of Emperor Diocletian, furious
that she should have rejected
the advances of a young man
at his court, but her hair
miraculously grew to protect
her modesty. The church is
said to have been built at the
request of the Emperor
Constantine's daughter,
Constantia, after she had
prayed at the Tomb of St Agnes
for delivery from leprosy.

Though much altered over
the centuries, the form and
much of the structure of the
4th-century basilica remain
intact. In the 7th-century apse
mosaic St Agnes appears as a

bejewelled Byzantine empress
in a stole of gold and a violet
robe. According to tradition
she appeared like this eight
days after her death holding a
white lamb. Every year on 21
January two lambs are blessed
on the church altar and a
vestment called the *pallium* is
woven from their wool. Every
newly-appointed archbishop
is sent a *pallium* by the pope.

Steps leading down to Sant'Agnese

San Lorenzo fuori le Mura ⑥

Piazzale del Verano 3. ☎ 49 15 11.
🚌 11, 71, 492. 🚋 19, 19b, 30b.
Open 7am–noon, 4pm–7pm (Oct–
Mar: 6.30pm) daily. 📷 ♿

JUST OUTSIDE the eastern wall
of the city, set off by the
cypresses of the Campo
Verano cemetery, stands the

Apse mosaic in Sant'Agnese, showing the saint flanked by two popes

church of San Lorenzo. Roasted slowly to death in AD 258, San Lorenzo was one of the most revered of Rome's early Christian martyrs. The first basilica erected over his burial place by Constantine was largely rebuilt in 576 by Pope Pelagius II. Close by stood a 5th-century church dedicated to the Virgin Mary. The intriguing two-levelled church we see today is the result of these two churches being knocked into one. This process, started in the 8th century, was completed in the 13th century by Pope Honorius III, when the nave, the portico and much of the decoration were added. The remains of San Lorenzo are in the choir of the 6th-century church (beneath the 13th-century high altar).

The church was restored after it was badly damaged by Allied bombers in an air raid during World War II.

Romanesque bell tower of San Lorenzo

Via Appia Antica 🄼

118, 218. See **Walks** pp284–5.

THE FIRST PART of the Via Appia was built in 312 BC by the Censor Appius Claudius Caecus. When it was extended to the ports of Benevento, Taranto and Brindisi in 190 BC, the road became Rome's link with its expanding empire in the East. It was the route taken by the funeral processions of the dictator Sulla (78 BC) and Emperor Augustus (AD 14) and it was along this road that St Paul was led a prisoner to Rome in AD 56.

Gradually abandoned during the Middle Ages, the road was restored in the mid-16th century by Pope Pius IV. It is lined with ruined family tombs and the collective burial places known as columbaria, while beneath the fields on

12th-century cloister of San Lorenzo fuori le Mura

either side lies a vast maze of catacombs. Today the road starts at Porta San Sebastiano (see p196). Major Christian sights include the church of Domine Quo Vadis?, built on the spot where St Peter is said to have met Christ while fleeing from Rome, and the Catacombs of San Callisto and San Sebastiano. Among the tombs lining the road are those of Cecilia Metella (see p266) and of Romulus, son of the Emperor Maxentius, who died in AD 309.

Catacombs of San Callisto 🄼

Via Appia Antica 110. 513 67 25. 118, 218. **Open** 8.30am–noon, 2.30pm–5.30pm (Oct–Mar: 5pm) Thu–Tue. **Closed** public hols. **Adm charge**.

IN BURYING their dead in underground cemeteries outside the city walls, the early Christians were simply obeying the laws of the time. They were not forced to use them because of persecution. Because so many saints were buried there, the catacombs later became shrines and places of pilgrimage.

The vast Catacombs of San Callisto are on four different levels and only partly explored. The rooms and connecting passageways are hewn out of volcanic tufa. The dead were

placed in niches, known as loculi, which held two or three bodies. The most important rooms were decorated with stucco and frescoes. The area that can be visited includes the Crypt of the Popes, where many of the early popes were buried, and the Crypt of Santa Cecilia, where the saint's body was discovered in 820 before being moved to her church in Trastevere (see p211).

Catacombs of San Sebastiano 🄼

Via Appia Antica 136. 788 70 35. 118, 218. **Open** 9am–noon, 2.30pm–5.30pm (Oct–Mar: 5pm) Fri–Wed. **Closed** Dec. **Adm charge**.

THE 17TH-CENTURY church of San Sebastiano, above the catacombs, occupies the site of a basilica from the age of Constantine. Preserved at the entrance to the catacombs is the triclia, a building that once stood above ground and was used by parties of mourners for taking funeral refreshments. Its walls are covered with graffiti invoking St Peter and St Paul, whose remains may have been moved here during one of the periods when the Christians were persecuted by the Roman authorities.

Cypresses lining the Via Appia

Catacombs of Domitilla ⑩

Via delle Sette Chiese 282.
📞 511 03 42. 🚌 94, 218, 613.
Open 8.30am–noon, 2.30pm–
5.30pm (Oct–Mar: 5pm) Wed–Mon.
Closed Jan. **Adm charge.** 🚫 📷

THIS NETWORK of catacombs is the largest in Rome. Many of the tombs from the 1st and 2nd centuries AD have no Christian connection. In the burial chambers that can be visited there are frescoes of both Classical and Christian scenes, including one of the earliest depictions of Christ as the *Good Shepherd*. Above the catacombs stands the basilica of Santi Nereo e Achilleo. After rebuilding and restoration, little remains of the original 4th-century church.

Fosse Ardeatine ⑪

Via Ardeatina 174. 📞 513 67 42.
🚌 218. **Open** 8.30am–6pm
(Oct–Mar: 4pm) daily (last adm:
30 mins before closing). 📷

ON THE EVENING of 24 March 1944, Nazi forces took 335 prisoners to this abandoned quarry south of Rome and shot them at point blank range. The execution was in reprisal for a bomb attack that had killed 32 German soldiers. The victims included various political prisoners, 73 Jews and ten other civilians, among them a priest and a 14-year-old boy. The Germans blew up the tunnels where the massacre had taken place, but a local peasant had witnessed the scene and later helped

find the corpses. The site is now a memorial to the values of the Resistance against the Germans, which gave birth to the modern Italian Republic. A forbidding bunker-like monument houses the rows of identical tombs containing the victims. Beside it is a museum of the Resistance. Interesting works of modern sculpture include *The Martyrs*, by Francesco Coccia, and the gates shaped like a wall of thorns by Mirko Basaldella.

Bronze entrance gates to the Fosse Ardeatine by Mirko Basaldella

Tomb of Cecilia Metella ⑫

Via Appia Antica, III Miglio.
📞 780 24 65. 🚌 118. **Open** 9am–
1 hr before sunset (Oct–Mar: 2pm)
Tue–Sat, 9am–2pm Mon & Sun.
Closed public hols. 📷

ONE OF THE most famous landmarks on the Via Appia Antica is the huge drum-shaped tomb built for the noble Cecilia Metella. Her father and husband were rich patricians and successful generals of late Republican Rome, but hardly anything is known about the

Fragments of marble relief on the Tomb of Cecilia Metella

woman herself. Byron muses over her unknown destiny in his poem *Childe Harold*. In 1302 Pope Boniface VIII gave the tomb to his family, the Caetani, who incorporated it in a fortified castle that blocked the Via Appia, allowing them to control the traffic on the road and exact high tolls. The marble facing of the tomb was pillaged by Pope Sixtus V at the end of the 16th century.

Parco Appio Claudio ⑬

Via Lemonia. 🚌 118, 557, 558, 650,
663, 664, 765. **Open** 24 hrs daily.

THE PARK covers a large expanse of land between the Via Appia Nuova and the Via Tuscolana. One day it may become part of one vast archaeological park stretching from here to the Colosseum and the Forum. Its main features are the remains of three aqueducts, the Aqua Marcia dating from 140 BC, the Aqua Claudia, completed in AD 52 by the Emperor Claudius, and the Felice

Ruins of the Aqua Claudia aqueduct (1st century AD) in the Parco Appio Claudio

Aqueduct built by Sixtus V in the 16th century. The arches of Roman aqueducts carried water in separate conduits from two or three different sources (see pp20–21). The area is an excellent place to enjoy uninterrupted views of the Roman Campagna and the Alban hills to the south.

EUR ⑭

93, 97, 197, 293, 493, 765, 771, 791. **M** EUR Fermi, EUR Palasport.
Museo della Civiltà Romana
Piazza G. Agnelli. **(** 592 61 35.
Open 9am–1.30pm Tue–Sat, 9am–1pm Sun and public hols; also 4pm–7pm Tue & Thu. **Adm charge**.

EUR's Palazzo della Civiltà del Lavoro, the "Square Colosseum"

THE ESPOSIZIONE Universale di Roma (EUR), a suburb to the south of the city, was built originally for an international exhibition, a kind of "Work Olympics", that was planned for 1942, but never took place because of the war. The architecture was intended to glorify Fascism and to modern eyes the style of the public buildings is very overblown and rhetorical. The Palazzo della Civiltà del Lavoro (the Palace of the Civilization of Work) is an unmistakable landmark for people arriving from Fiumicino airport.

The scheme was completed in the 1950s. In terms of town planning, EUR has been quite successful and people are still keen to live here. The great marble halls house a number

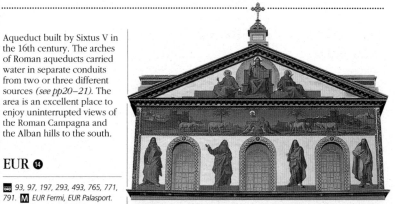

19th-century mosaic on facade of San Paolo fuori le Mura

of government offices and museums. The Museo della Civiltà Romana has a vast scale model of Rome at the time of Constantine and casts of the reliefs on the Column of Trajan. To the south is a lake and park, and the huge domed Palazzo dello Sport built for the 1960 Olympics.

San Paolo fuori le Mura ⑮

Via Ostiense 186. **(** 541 03 41.
23, 93b, 170, 223, 673. **M** San Paolo. **Open** 7.30am–7pm (Sep–Mar: 6pm) daily (last adm: 15 mins before closing).

TODAY'S CHURCH is a faithful if somewhat soulless reconstruction of the great 4th-century basilica destroyed by fire on the night of 15 July 1823. A few fragments of the original church survived. The triumphal arch over the nave is decorated on one side with much-restored 5th-century mosaics. On the other side are mosaics by Pietro Cavallini, originally on the facade. The splendid Venetian apse mosaics (1220) represent the figures of Christ with St Peter, St Andrew, St Paul and St Luke.

The fine marble canopy over the high altar is signed by the sculptor Arnolfo di Cambio (1285) "together with his partner Pietro", who may have been Pietro Cavallini. Below the altar is the *confessio*, the tomb of St Paul, whose body was

supposed to have been buried here. To the right is an impressive Paschal candlestick by Nicolò di Angelo and Pietro Vassalletto.

The one part of San Paolo spared completely by the fire was the cloister with its pairs of colourful inlaid columns, some octagonal, some spiral, supporting the arcade. Built largely by the Vassalletto family and completed around 1214, it is considered one of the most beautiful in Rome.

Villa Doria Pamphilj ⑯

Via di San Pancrazio. 41, 75, 144.
Park open dawn–dusk daily.

ROME'S LARGEST public park, the Villa Doria Pamphilj, was laid out in the mid-17th century for Prince Camillo Pamphilj. His uncle Pope Innocent X paid for the magnificent summer residence, the Casino del Bel Respiro, and numerous fountains and summerhouses, some of which still survive. Today the park is a popular meeting place for joggers and dog lovers.

Casino del Bel Respiro, Villa Doria Pamphilj

Day Trips around Rome

Tivoli, a favourite place to escape the heat of the Roman summer

Tivoli ⑰

Town is 31 km (20 miles) northeast of Rome. **FS** *from Roma Termini or Tiburtina.* 🚌 *ACOTRAL from Rebibbia (on Metro line B).*

T IVOLI HAS BEEN a popular summer resort since the days of the Roman Republic. Among the famous men who owned villas here were the poets Catullus and Horace, Caesar's assassins Brutus and Cassius, and the Emperors Trajan and Hadrian. Tivoli's main attractions were its clean air and beautiful situation on the slopes of the Tiburtini hills, its healthy sulphur springs and the waterfalls of the Aniene – the Emperor Augustus said these had cured him of insomnia. The Romans' luxurious lifestyle was revived in Renaissance times by the owners of the Villa d'Este,

Detail of Fontana dell'Organo at Villa d'Este

the town's most famous sight.

In the Middle Ages Tivoli suffered frequent invasions as its position made it an ideal base for an advance on Rome. In 1461 Pope Pius II built a fortress here, the Rocca Pia, declaring: "It is easier to regain Rome while possessing Tivoli, than to regain Tivoli while possessing Rome."

After suffering heavy bomb-damage in 1944, Tivoli's main buildings and churches were speedily restored. The town's cobbled streets are still lined with medieval houses. The Duomo (cathedral) houses a beautiful 13th-century life-size wooden group representing the *Deposition from the Cross*.

Villa d'Este ⑱

Piazza Trento, Tivoli. **C** *0774-220 70.* **FS** *Tivoli, then 30 mins walk or local bus (many routes).* **Open** *9am–1 hr before sunset Tue–Sun.* **Closed** *public hols.* **Adm charge.** 📷

T HE VILLA OCCUPIES the site of an old Benedictine convent. In the 16th century the estate was developed by Cardinal Ippolito d'Este, son of Lucrezia Borgia. A palace was designed by Pirro Ligorio to make the most of its hilltop situation, but the villa's fame rests more on the terraced gardens and fountains laid out by Ligorio and Giacomo della Porta.

Though the gardens have suffered over the centuries from neglect, the grottoes and fountains still give a vivid impression of the frivolous luxury enjoyed by the princes of the church. From the great loggia of the palace you descend through the privet-lined paths to the Grotto of Diana and Bernini's Fontana del Bicchierone. Below to the right is the Rometta (little Rome), a model of Tiber Island with allegorical figures and the legendary she-wolf.

The Rometta is at one end of the Viale delle Cento Fontane. Its 100 fountains are in the shape of grotesques, obelisks, ships and the eagles of the d'Este coat of arms, now overgrown with moss. Other fountains have also lost much of their former glory. The Fontana dell'Organo was a water-organ, in which the force of the water pumped air through the pipes, but it has long been silent. The garden's lowest level has flower beds, fountains and splendid views out over the plain below.

Terrace of 100 Fountains in the gardens of Villa d'Este

Villa Gregoriana ⑲

Largo Massimo, Tivoli. **FS** *Tivoli, then short walk.* **Open** *Jun–Aug: 10am–7.30pm; Sep–May: 9.30am–1 hr before sunset daily.* **Adm charge.**

T HE MAIN ATTRACTIONS of this steeply sloping wooded park are the waterfalls and grottoes created over the centuries by the River Aniene. The park is named after Pope Gregory XVI, who in the 1830s ordered the building of a tunnel to put an end to the danger of flooding. This created a new waterfall, the Grande Cascata, which plunges 108 m (350 ft) into the valley behind the town.

The Canopus, extensively restored, with replicas of its original caryatids lining the bank of the canal

Hadrian's Villa ⓴

Villa Adriana, Via Tiburtina. Site is 6 km (4 miles) southwest of Tivoli. 📞 0774-53 02 03. 🚆 Tivoli, then local bus No. 4. 🚌 ACOTRAL from Rebibbia (on Metro line B). **Open** 9am–90 mins before sunset daily (last adm: 1 hr before closing). **Closed** public hols. **Adm charge.** 📷 📱

Built as a private summer retreat between AD 118 and 134, Hadrian's Villa was a vast open-air museum of the finest architecture of the Roman world. The grounds of the Imperial palace covered an area of 120 hectares (300 acres) and were filled with full-scale reproductions of the emperor's favourite buildings from Greece and Egypt. Although excavations began in the 16th century, many of the ruins lying scattered in the surrounding fields have yet to be identified with any certainty. The grounds of the

villa make a very picturesque site for a picnic, with scattered fragments of columns lying among olive trees and cypresses.

For an idea of how the whole complex would have looked in its heyday, study the scale model in the building beside the car park. The most important buildings are signposted and several have been partially restored or reconstructed. One of the most impressive is the so-called Maritime Theatre. This is a round pool with an island in the middle, surrounded by columns. The island, reached by means of a swing bridge, was probably Hadrian's private studio, where he withdrew from the cares of the Empire to indulge in his two favourite pastimes, painting and architecture. There were also theatres, Greek and Latin libraries, two bath houses, extensive housing for guests and the palace staff, and formal gardens with fountains, statues, pools.

Hadrian was a lover of Greek philosophy as well as architecture. One part of the gardens is thought to have been Hadrian's reproduction of the Grove of Academe, where Plato lectured to his

Fragment of marble mosaic pavement in the Imperial palace

students. He also had a replica made of the Stoà Poikile, a beautiful painted colonnade in Athens, from which the Stoic philosophers took their name. Hadrian's copy of the Poikile enclosed a great piazza with a central pool. The so-called Hall of the Philosophers close to the Poikile was probably a library.

The most ambitious of Hadrian's replicas was the Canopus, a sanctuary of the god Serapis near Alexandria. For this a canal 185 metres (200 yards) long was dug and Egyptian statues were imported to decorate the temple and its grounds. This impressive piece of engineering has been restored and the banks of the canal are lined with caryatids.

Another picturesque spot in the grounds is the Vale of Tempe, the legendary haunt of the goddess Diana with a stream representing the river

Pair of Ionic columns in the vaulted baths of Hadrian's Villa

Peneios. Below ground the emperor even built a fanciful recreation of the underworld, Hades, reached through underground tunnels, of which there were many linking the various parts of the villa.

Plundered by barbarians who camped here in the 6th and 8th centuries, the villa fell into disrepair. Its marble was burnt to make lime for cement and Renaissance antiquarians contributed further to its destruction. Statues unearthed in the grounds are on show in museums around Europe. The Vatican's Egyptian Collection (see p238) has many fine works that were found here.

Ostia Antica

Viale dei Romagnoli 717. Site is 25 km
(16 miles) southwest of Rome. 565
00 22 or 565 14 05. Magliana on
line B, then train to Ostia Antica.
Excavations open 9am–about 1 hr
before sunset daily (last adm: 1 hr
before closing). **Closed** 1 May.
Museum open 9am–1pm daily.
Closed public hols. **Adm charge**.

IN REPUBLICAN TIMES Ostia was
Rome's main commercial
port and a military base
defending the coastline and
the mouth of the Tiber. The
port continued to flourish
under the Empire, despite the
development of Portus, a new
port slightly to the northwest,
in the 2nd century AD. Ostia's
decline began in the 4th
century, when a reduction in
trade was followed by the
gradual silting up of the
harbour. Worse was to come
when malaria became endemic
in the area and the city, whose
population is reckoned to
have been nearly 100,000 at its
peak, was totally abandoned.

Buried for centuries by
sand, the city is remarkably
well preserved. The site is
less spectacular than Pompei
or Herculaneum because
Ostia died a gradual death,
but it gives a more complete
picture of life under the
Roman Empire. People of all
social classes and from all
over the Mediterranean lived
and worked here.

Visitors can understand the
layout of Ostia's streets almost
at a glance. The main road
through the town, the
Decumanus Maximus, would
have been filled with hurrying
slaves and citizens, avoiding
the jostling carriages and
carts, while tradesmen

Ruins of shops, offices and houses near Ostia's theatre

pursued their business under
the porticoes lining the street.
The floorplans of the public
buildings along the road are
very clear. Many were bath
houses, such as the Baths of
the Cisiarii (carters) and the
grander Baths of Neptune,
named after their fine black-
and-white floor mosaics.
Beside the restored theatre,
three large masks, originally
part of the decoration of the
stage, have been mounted
on large blocks of tufa.
Beneath the great brick
arches that supported the
semicircular tiers of seats
were taverns and shops.
Classical plays are put on
here in the summer.

The Tiber's course has
changed considerably since
Ostia was the port of Rome. It
once flowed past just to the
north of Piazzale delle

**Mask decorating
the theatre**

Corporazioni, the square
behind the theatre. The
corporations were the guilds
of the various trades involved
in fitting out and
supplying ships:
tanners and rope-
makers, ship
builders and
timber merchants,
ships' chandlers
and corn weighers.
There were some
60 or 70 offices
around the square.
Mosaics showing
scenes of everyday
life in the port and
the names and
symbols of the
corporations can
still be seen.

There were also offices used
by ship-owners and their
agents from places as far apart
as Tunisia and the south of
France, Sardinia and Egypt. In
one office, belonging to a
merchant from the town of
Sabratha in North Africa,
there is a delightful mosaic
of an elephant.

The main cargo coming into
Rome was grain from Africa.
Much of this was distributed
free to prevent social unrest.
Although only men received
this *annona* or corn dole, at
times over 300,000 were
eligible. In the centre of the
square was a temple, probably

Mural from Ostia of merchant ship being loaded with grain

dedicated to Ceres, goddess of the harvest. Among the buildings excavated are many large warehouses in which grain was stored before it was shipped on to Rome.

The Decumanus leads to the Forum and the city's principal temple, erected by Hadrian in the 2nd century AD and dedicated to Jove, Juno and Minerva. In this rather romantic, lonely spot, it is hard to imagine the Forum as a bustling centre, where justice was dispensed and officials

Floor mosaic of Nereid and sea monster in the House of the Dioscuri

Detail of floor mosaic in the Piazzale delle Corporazioni

met to discuss the city's affairs. In the 18th century it was used as a sheepfold.

Away from the main street are the buildings where Ostia's inhabitants lived. The great majority were housed in rented apartments in blocks three or four storeys high known as *insulae*. These varied considerably in their comfort and decoration. The House of Diana was one of the smarter ones, with a balcony around the second floor, a private bath house and a central courtyard with a cistern where tenants came to collect their water. Around the ground floor of the block were shops, taverns and bars selling snacks and drinks. In the bar at the House of Diana you can see the marble counter used by customers buying their sausages and hot wine sweetened with honey.

For the wealthy there were detached houses *(domus)* such as the House of the Dioscuri, which has fine coloured mosaics, and the House of Cupid and Psyche, named after a charming statue found there. This is now in the site's small museum, along with other sculptures and reliefs found in Ostia.

Among the houses and shops there are other fascinating buildings including a laundry and the firemen's barracks. The religions practised in Ostia reflect the cosmopolitan nature of the port. There are also no fewer than 18 temples dedicated to the Persian god Mithras, as well as a Jewish Synagogue dating from the 1st century AD and a Christian basilica. A plaque records the death of St Augustine's mother in a hotel here in AD 387.

ALSO WORTH SEEING

Anagni FS *from Termini (c50 min).* Picturesque hill-town with papal palace and famous Romanesque cathedral.

Bracciano FS *from Termini or Tiburtina (c90 min).* 🚇 *from Lepanto, on Metro line A (bus c90 min).* Volcanic lake with villages and wooded hills. Nice for walks or a visit to Orsini Castle. Swimming in summer.

Cerveteri FS *from Termini, Tiburtina or Ostiense to Cerveteri-Ladispoli, then local bus (c70 min).* 🚇 *from Via Lepanto, on Metro line A (bus c80 min).* One of the greatest Etruscan cities. Necropolis with complete streets and houses.

Nemi FS *from Cinecittà, on Metro line A (bus c60 min).* Charming village at volcanic lake in the Castelli Romani. Famous for its wine and strawberries.

Palestrina FS *from Rebibbia, on Metro line B (bus c70 min).* Impressive Roman sanctuary to goddess Fortuna. Museum and the Mosaic of the Nile.

Pompei FS *from Termini. Express train to Pompei (c160 min) or any train to Naples, then change to local train (c170 min).* 🚌 *Special bus tours from tourist agents.* Excavations of the wealthy Roman city where the busy daily life was put to an end by the eruption of Vesuvius in AD 79.

Subiaco FS *from Rebibbia, on Metro line B (bus c120 min).* Birthplace of St Benedict. Two monasteries to visit.

Tarquinia FS *from Tiburtina or Ostiense (c180 min).* 🚇 *from Via Lepanto, on Metro line A. Change at Civitavecchia (c150 min).* Outstanding collection of Etruscan objects and frescoes from Tarquinia's necropolis.

Viterbo FS *from Termini (c150 min) or ACOTRAL train from Roma Nord, Piazzale Flaminio, on Metro line A (c120 min).* 🚇 *from Saxa Rubra reached by the ACOTRAL train above (bus c90 min).* Medieval quarter, papal palace and archaeological museum within 13th-century walls.

SIX GUIDED WALKS

ROME IS an excellent city for walking. The distances between major sights in the historic centre are easily covered on foot and many streets are pedestrianized. When you get tired, there are plenty of pavement cafés in wonderful settings, such as Piazza Navona and Campo de' Fiori. If you are interested in archaeology, then a walk across the Forum *(see pp76–87)* and over the Palatine *(see pp96–101)* takes you away from the roaring traffic of modern Rome to a different world of scattered ruins and shady pine trees.

The first of the six suggested walks takes in picturesque quarters on either side of the Tiber, the river that has played such an important part in the city's development. The second walk, along the perfectly straight Via

Bernini angel on Ponte Sant'Angelo

Giulia, gives a vivid impression of the Renaissance city. The next three walks each follow a particular theme. For visitors who wish to savour the glory of ancient Rome, there is a walk taking in the surviving triumphal arches of the emperors. For those who prefer the Middle Ages, there is a tour of early Christian churches with well-preserved mosaics, and for those who enjoy the Roman Baroque there is a walk concentrating on the great contribution of Bernini to the appearance of the city.

The Romans were famous for the straightness of their roads. The final walk is outside the central sightseeing area along the best-known of all Roman roads, the Via Appia Antica, parts of which are still intact after more than 2,000 years of use.

CHOOSING A WALK

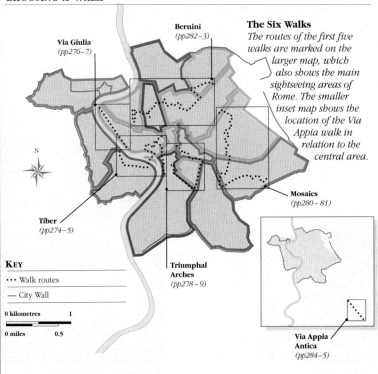

Via Giulia
(pp276–7)

Bernini
(pp282–3)

The Six Walks
The routes of the first five walks are marked on the larger map, which also shows the main sightseeing areas of Rome. The smaller inset map shows the location of the Via Appia walk in relation to the central area.

N

Tiber
(pp274–5)

Mosaics
(pp280–81)

Triumphal Arches
(pp278–9)

KEY

••• Walk routes

— City Wall

0 kilometres   1

0 miles   0.5

Via Appia Antica
(pp284–5)

Pedestrians strolling across Ponte Sant'Angelo

A Two-Hour Walk by the River Tiber

ROME OWES ITS VERY EXISTENCE to the Tiber; the city grew up around an easy fording point where a market place developed. The river could also be a hazard; shallow and torrent-like, it flooded the city every winter up to 1870, when work began on the massive Lungotevere embankments that run along both sides of the river. These provide many fine views from points along their avenues of plane trees. The walk also explores the neighbourhoods along the riverside, in particular the Jewish Ghetto and Trastevere, which have preserved much of their character from earlier periods in the colourful history of Rome.

Santa Maria in Cosmedin ①

From the old port of Rome to Via dei Funari

Starting from the church of Santa Maria in Cosmedin ① (see p202), cross the piazza to the Temples of the Forum Boarium ② (see p203). This was the cattle market that stood near the city's river port. The river here has preserved two less obvious structures from ancient Rome: the mouth of the Cloaca Maxima ③, the city's great sewer, and one arch of a ruined bridge, known as the Ponte Rotto ④. In Via di Ponte Rotto stands the extraordinary medieval Casa dei Crescenzi ⑤ (see p203), decorated with fragments of Roman temples. Passing the modern Anagrafe (public records office) ⑥, built on the site of the old Roman port, you come to San Nicola in Carcere ⑦ (see p152).

You are now in the Foro Olitorio, Rome's ancient vegetable market. To the east stand the ruins of a Roman portico and the medieval house of the Pierleoni family. Head for the massive Theatre

Arch of the Ponte Rotto ④

of Marcellus ⑧ (see p151), and look for the three Corinthian columns of the Temple of Apollo beside it. Turn into Piazza Campitelli and walk up to Santa Maria in Campitelli ⑨ (see p151). The church honours a miraculous image of the Virgin credited with halting the plague in 1656. The 16th-century piazza was the home of Flaminio Ponzio, its architect, who lived at No. 6. Take Via dei Delfini to Piazza Margana where you should look up at the 14th-century tower of the Margani family ⑩. Retrace your steps, then go up Via dei Funari (Street of the Ropemakers) to the 16th-century facade of Santa Caterina dei Funari ⑪.

The Ghetto

From Piazza Lovatelli take Via Sant'Angelo in Pescheria, which leads to the ruined Portico of Octavia ⑫ (see p151) in the Jewish Ghetto (see p152). The Roman portico, once Rome's fish market, houses the church of Sant'Angelo in Pescheria. Find the marble plaque on the facade: fish longer than this slab were given to the city's conservatori (governors). Turn into the Ghetto: two column stumps belonging to the Portico stand in front of a patched-up doorway made of fragments of Roman sculpture. The cramped buildings and streets around Via del Portico

Main altar of Santa Maria in Campitelli ⑨

d'Ottavia are typical of old Rome: see the Casa di Lorenzo Manilio ⑬ (see p153), and turn down Via delle Cinque Scole, past Palazzo Cenci ⑭ (see p152), towards the river. On Lungotevere walk past the Synagogue ⑮ (see p152) to the small church of San Gregorio ⑯. Here stood the gates of the Ghetto, which were locked at sundown.

Across the river to Trastevere

Crossing to Tiber Island (see p152) by Ponte Fabricio, with its two ancient

Classical relief of Medusa above the doorway of Palazzo Cenci ⑭

much of the spirit of old Trastevere. Walk up to the start of Viale di Trastevere at Piazza Belli. After crossing the road look back

Santa Maria in Trastevere, don't miss the old-fashioned chemist's shop at No. 7. The piazza itself, in front of the magnificent church of Santa Maria in Trastevere ㉒ (see pp212–13), has a cheerful atmosphere, and the fountain steps are a favourite meeting place. Go back a little way to Via del Moro. This leads to Piazza Trilussa, dominated by the fountain of the Acqua Paola ㉓, where you emerge on to the bank of the river again. Note the life-like statue, near the fountain, of Roman poet Trilussa, who wrote in the local dialect. From Ponte Sisto ㉔ (see p210), look back to Tiber Island and, beyond it, to the medieval bell tower of Santa Maria in Cosmedin, set against the pine trees on the summit of the Palatine.

[Map showing walk route with numbered points including PIAZZA MARGANA ⑩, ⑪, VIA DEI FUNARI, ⑬, PIAZZA CAMPITELLI ⑨, ⑫, VIA PORT. D'OTTAVIA, EI CENCI ⑮, ⑯ PIAZZA MONTE SAVELLO ⑦, ⑧, Isola Tiberina, Ponte Fabricio, ⑰, ⑱, Ponte Cestio, ⑥, ⑤, ④, PIAZZA D. BOCCA DELLA VERITÀ ②, Ponte Palatino, ③, ①, TEATRO DI MARCELLO, VIA D. CONSOLAZIONE, ZZA IN CINULA ⑲, ULLARA]

The western tip of Tiber Island

```
0 metres                    250
0 yards                     250
```

stone heads on the parapet, you can enjoy a good view of the river in both directions. On the island itself, you should not miss the Pierleoni Tower ⑰ or the church of San Bartolomeo all'Isola ⑱.

Trastevere

As you cross into Trastevere, you can see the medieval house of the powerful Mattei family ⑲, with its fragments of ancient sculpture. Beyond it, Piazza in Piscinula and the surrounding streets retain

KEY

— Walk route

⚡ Good viewing point

at the medieval tower of the Anguillara ⑳ and the statue honouring the poet Gioacchino Belli ㉑ (see p209). As you go down Via della Lungaretta to Piazza

Piazza in Piscinula, old Trastevere

A One-Hour Walk along Via Giulia

L AID OUT BY BRAMANTE for Pope Julius II in the early 16th century, Via Giulia was the first Renaissance street to slice through Rome's jumble of medieval alleys. The original plan included new law courts in a central piazza, but this project was abandoned for lack of cash. The street is now occupied mainly by antiques shops and furniture restorers. On summer evenings the street is lit with hundreds of oil lamps, and cloisters and courtyards provide romantic settings for a special season of concerts.

Baroque capital on the facade of Sant'Eligio degli Orefici ⑦

From Lungotevere to Largo della Moretta

Starting from Lungotevere dei Tebaldi ① at the eastern end of Via Giulia, you will see ahead of you an archway ② spanning the road. This was the start of Michelangelo's unrealized project linking Palazzo Farnese and its gardens *(see p147)* with the Villa Farnesina *(see pp220–21)* on the other side of the river.

Just before you reach the archway, you will see to your left the curious Fontana del Mascherone ③, in which an ancient grotesque mask and granite basin were combined to create a Baroque fountain.

Beyond the Farnese archway on the left is the lively Baroque facade of the church of Santa Maria dell'Orazione e Morte ④ *(see p147)*. A bit further along on the same side of the road stands Palazzo Falconieri ⑤, enlarged by Borromini in 1650. Note its two stone falcons glowering at each other across the width of the facade. On the other side of the road you pass the yellowish facade of Santa Caterina da Siena ⑥, church of the Sienese colony in Rome, which has pretty 18th-century reliefs. The figures of Romulus and Remus symbolize Rome

Relief of Romulus and Remus on Santa Caterina da Siena ⑥

and Siena – there is a legend that the city of Siena was founded by the less fortunate of the twins. After passing the short street that leads down to Sant'Eligio degli Orefici ⑦ *(see p148)* and the facade of Palazzo Ricci ⑧ *(see p149)*, you come to an area of half-demolished buildings around the ruined church of San Filippo Neri ⑨, called Largo della Moretta. If you look to the left down to the river, you can see

Fontana del Mascherone ③

Ponte Mazzini and the huge prison of Regina Coeli on the other side of the Tiber. At this point you may like to make a small detour to the right to the beginning of Via del Pellegrino, where there is an inscription ⑩, defining the *pomerium*, or boundary, of the city in the time of the Emperor Claudius.

From Largo della Moretta to the Sofas of Via Giulia

Further on, facing the narrow Vicolo del Malpasso are the imposing prisons, the Carceri

Nuove ⑪, built by Pope Innocent X Pamphilj in 1655. When first opened, they were a model of humane treatment of prisoners, but were replaced by the Regina Coeli prison across the river at the end of the 19th century. The buildings now house offices of the Ministry of Justice and a small Museum of Crime.

At the corner of Via del Gonfalone, a small side street running down to the river,

KEY

— Walk route

๊ Good viewing point

0 metres	250
0 yards	250

Farnese archway across Via Giulia, built to a design by Michelangelo ②

you can see part of the foundations of Julius II's planned law courts. Just down the street stands the small Oratorio di Santa Lucia del Gonfalone ⑫, which is often used for concerts.

The next interesting facade is Carlo Rainaldi's 17th-century Santa Maria del Suffragio ⑬ on the left. On the same side is San Biagio degli Armeni ⑭, the Armenian church in Rome. It is often referred to by local people as San Biagio della Pagnotta (of the loaf of bread). The nickname originates from

the traditional distribution of bread to the poor that took place on the saint's feast day.

On the corner there are more travertine blocks belonging to the foundations of Julius II's projected law courts, known because of their curious shape as the "Sofas of Via Giulia".

The Florentine Quarter

Your next stop should be the imposing Palazzo Sacchetti at No. 66 ⑲. Originally this was the house of Antonio da Sangallo the Younger, the architect of Palazzo Farnese, but it was greatly enlarged by later owners. The porticoed courtyard houses a 15th-century Madonna and a striking Roman relief of the 3rd century AD. Just opposite Palazzo Sacchetti, note the beautiful late Renaissance portal of Palazzo Donarelli ⑯. The 16th-century house at No. 93 is richly decorated with stuccoes and coats of arms ⑰. No. 85 is another typical Renaissance palazzo with a heavily rusticated ground floor ⑱. There is a tradition

Plaque honouring Antonio da Sangallo on Palazzo Sacchetti ⑮

that, like many houses of the period, it once belonged to Raphael. Palazzo Clarelli ⑲ was built by Antonio da Sangallo the Younger as his own house. The inscription above the doorway bears the name of Duke Cosimo II de' Medici, whose family later bought the palazzo.

This whole area used to be inhabited by a flourishing Florentine colony, which had its own water-mills built on pontoons along the Tiber. Their national church is San Giovanni dei Fiorentini ⑳ (see p153), the final great landmark at the end of Via Giulia. Many Florentine artists and architects had a hand in its design, including Sangallo and Jacopo Sansovino.

Coat of arms of Pope Paul III Farnese on the facade of Via Giulia No. 93 ⑰

Detail on the side of the door of Santa Maria del Suffragio ⑬

TIPS FOR WALKERS

Starting point: Lungotevere dei Tebaldi, by Ponte Sisto.
Length: 1 km (1,100 yds).
Getting there: Take either a 46, 62 or 64 to Corso Vittorio Emanuele II, then walk down Via dei Pettinari or a 23, 65 or 280 along Lungotevere.
Best time for walk: On summer evenings the street is lit by oil lamps. At Christmas, there are cribs on display in shop windows.
Stopping-off points: There are bars in Via Giulia, at Nos. 21 and 84. Campo de' Fiori has better bars, with outdoor tables, and a wide choice of places to eat. These include a Chinese restaurant in Via dei Giubbonari and a fried fish restaurant in Piazza Santa Barbara dei Librai (closed Sun).

A 90-Minute Tour of Rome's Triumphal Arches

Rome's greatest gift to architecture was the arch and the Roman people's highest tribute to its victorious generals was the triumphal arch. In Imperial times, arches were erected to honour an emperor's campaign victories almost as a matter of course, promoting his personal cult and ensuring his subsequent deification. Spectacular processions passed through these arches. Conquering generals, cheered by rapturous crowds, rode in their chariots to the Capitol, accompanied by their legions bearing spoils from their campaigns.

Part of the Via Sacra, once spanned by the Arch of Augustus ③

Arches of the Forum

This walk through the Forum and around the base of the Palatine takes in Rome's three great surviving triumphal arches and two arches of more

Relief of barbarian captives on the Arch of Septimius Severus ①

humble design that were used simply as places of business. It starts from the Arch of

TIPS FOR WALKERS

Starting point: The Roman Forum, entrance Largo Romolo e Remo, on Via dei Fori Imperiali.
Length: 2.5 km (1½ miles).
Getting there: The nearest Metro stations is Colosseo on line B. Buses 11, 27, 81, 85, 87, 186 stop in Via dei Fori Imperiali, near the Forum entrance.
Best time for walk: Any time of day during Forum opening hours (see p82) is suitable.
Stopping-off points: Several bars and restaurants overlook the Colosseum. There is a small bar in Via dei Cerchi and a smarter one behind San Giorgio in Velabro, in Piazza San Giovanni Decollato (closed Sun). For a meal, try Alvaro al Circo Massimo (closed Mon) in Via di San Teodoro.

Emperor Septimius Severus ① and his sons Geta and Caracalla (see p83) in the Forum. Erected in AD 203, it celebrates a successful campaign in the Middle East. Eight years later when Caracalla had his brother killed, all mention of Geta was removed from the inscription.

Look up at the reliefs showing phases of the campaigns. Set in tiers, they are probably the sculptural counterparts of the paintings illustrating the general's feats that were borne aloft in the triumphal procession. On the right, the inhabitants of a fortified city surrender to the Romans' siege machines. Below are smaller friezes showing the triumphal procession itself.

Heading east, make your way through the Forum to the ruins of the Temple of Julius Caesar ②. The temple was built by Augustus in 42 BC, on the site where Caesar's body was cremated after Mark Antony's famous funerary oration. A nearby sign marks the ruins of the Arch of Augustus ③, spanning the Via Sacra between the Temple of Castor and Pollux ④ (see p84) and the Temple of Caesar. This arch, erected after Augustus had defeated Mark Antony and Cleopatra, was demolished in 1545, and its materials were used in the

Capital from Temple of Castor and Pollux ④

new St Peter's. From here, proceed uphill towards the elegant Arch of Titus ⑤ (see p87). Compared with Septimius Severus's arch, it shows an earlier, simpler style. Look up at the beautiful lettering of the inscription before you examine the inner bas-reliefs. These show

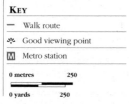

KEY

— Walk route

☀ Good viewing point

Ⓜ Metro station

0 metres	250
0 yards	250

Arch of Titus in a 19th-century watercolour by the English artist Thomas Hartley Cromek ⑤

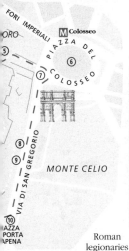

MONTE CELIO

through the arch would have been carrying building materials quarried from the Forum's various ruins.

Arch of Constantine

Leave the Forum by heading down the hill towards the Colosseum ⑥ *(see pp92–5)* and the nearby Arch of Constantine ⑦ *(see p91)*. This arch, hastily built to commemorate the emperor's victory over his rival Maxentius in AD 312, is a patchwork of reliefs from different periods. Stand on the Via di San Gregorio side and compare the earlier panels at the top (AD 180–193) with the hectic battle scenes just above the

Arches of Domitian's extension to the Claudian Aqueduct ⑨

smaller arches, sculpted in AD 315. In the curious dwarf-like soldiers, you can see the transition from Classicism to a cruder medieval style of sculpture.

Now take Via di San Gregorio, which runs along the valley between the Palatine and Celian hills. This was the ancient route taken by most triumphal processions. Passing the entrance to the Palatine ⑧ and

Roman legionaries carrying the spoils looted from the conquest of Jerusalem, heralds holding plaques with the names of vanquished peoples and cities, and Titus riding in triumph in his chariot.

The medieval Frangipane family turned the Colosseum into a vast impregnable stronghold and incorporated the Arch of Titus into their fortifications. Notice the wheelmarks scratched on the inside walls of the arch by generations of carts; they indicate the steady rise in the level of the Forum before it was eventually excavated in the 18th and 19th centuries. Many of the carts that passed

the well-preserved arches of the Claudian Aqueduct ⑨ on the right, you come to Piazza di Porta Capena ⑩, named after the gate that stood here to mark the beginning of the Via Appia *(see p284)*. After rounding the back of the Palatine, follow Via dei Cerchi, which runs alongside the grassy area that preserves the oval outline of the Circus Maximus ⑪ *(see p205)*.

Arches of the Forum Boarium

When you reach the church of Sant'Anastasia ⑫, turn right up Via di San Teodoro, then first left down Via del Velabro. Straddling the street is the four-sided Arch of Janus ⑬ *(see p202)*, erected in the 3rd century AD. This is not a triumphal arch but a covered area where merchants could take shelter from the sun or rain when discussing business. Like the Arch of Titus, it became part of a fortress built by the Frangipane family during the Middle Ages.

Tucked away beside the nearby church of San Giorgio in Velabro ⑭ *(see p202)* is what looks like a large rectangular doorway. This is the Arco degli Argentari, or Moneychangers' Arch ⑮. Look up at the inscription, which says that it was erected by local silversmiths in honour of Septimius Severus and his family in AD 204. As in the emperor's triumphal arch, the name of Geta has been obliterated by his brother and murderer, Caracalla. Geta's figure has also been removed from among the portraits on the panels inside the arch. Triumph in Imperial Rome could be very short-lived.

Four-sided Arch of Janus ⑬

A Three-Hour Tour of Rome's Best Mosaics

IN IMITATION of the audience chambers of Imperial palaces, Rome's early Christian churches were decorated with colourful mosaics. These were pieced together from cubes of marble, coloured stone and fragments of glass. To create a golden background, gold leaf was placed between pieces of glass. These were then heated so that they fused. The glorious colours and subjects portrayed gave the faithful a glimpse of the heavenly court of the King of Kings. This walk concentrates on a few of the churches decorated in this wonderful medium.

Apse mosaic in the Chapel of Santa Rufina ③

San Giovanni

Start from Piazza di Porta San Giovanni, where you can visit the heavily-restored mosaic which was originally in the banqueting hall of Pope Leo III (reigned 795–816) ①, showing Christ among the Apostles. On the left are Pope Sylvester and the Emperor Constantine, on the right, Pope Leo and Charlemagne just before he was crowned

Obelisk and side facade of San Giovanni in Laterano ②

Holy Roman Emperor in AD 800. Inside the church of San Giovanni in Laterano ② (see pp182–3), the 13th-century apse mosaic shows Christ as he appeared miraculously during the consecration of the church. In the panels by the windows, look for the small figures of two Franciscan friars; these are the artists Jacopo Torriti (left) and Jacopo de Camerino (right). Leave by

the exit on the right near the splendid 16th-century organ and head for the octagonal Baptistry of San Giovanni ③, where the Chapel of Santa Rufina has a beautiful apse mosaic in green, azure and gold, dating from the 5th century. In the neighbouring Chapel of San Venanzio, there are golden 7th-century mosaics, showing the strong influence of the Eastern Church at this time.

Santo Stefano Rotondo to San Clemente

Leave the piazza by the narrow road that leads to the round church of Santo Stefano Rotondo ④ (see p185). One of its chapels contains a 7th-century Byzantine mosaic honouring two martyrs buried here. Further on, in Piazza della Navicella, is the church of Santa Maria in Domnica ⑤ (see p193). It houses the superb mosaics commissioned by Pope Paschal I, who gave new impetus to Rome's mosaic production in the 9th century. He is represented kneeling beside the Virgin. On leaving the church, notice the facade of San Tommaso in Formis ⑥, which has a charming mosaic of Christ flanked by two freed slaves, one black and one white, dating from the 13th

Ceiling mosaic, Baptistry of San Giovanni ③

Interior of Baptistry of San Giovanni ③

acanthus leaves. San Clemente also has a fine 12th-century Cosmatesque mosaic floor.

The Colle Oppio
Passing the old entrance to the church, cross Via Labicana and walk up the hill to the small Colle Oppio park ⑨. This has fine views of the Colosseum and contains the ruins of Nero's Golden House ⑩ *(see p175)* and the Baths of

century. From here, head up the steep hill, past the forbidding apse of Santi Quattro Coronati ⑦ *(see p185)*, to the fascinating church of San Clemente ⑧ *(see pp186–7)*. Its 12th-century apse mosaic shows the cross set in a swirling pattern of

Trajan ⑪. Across the park lie San Martino ai Monti ⑫ *(see p170)*, which has a 6th-century mosaic portrait of Pope St Sylvester in the crypt, and Santa Prassede ⑬ *(see p171)*. Here the Chapel of St Zeno contains the most important Byzantine mosaics in Rome, reminiscent of the fabulous mosaics of Ravenna. Pope Paschal I erected the chapel as a mausoleum for his

14th-century facade mosaics by Filippo Rusuti. Inside, the 5th-century mosaics in the nave depict Old Testament stories, while the triumphal arch has scenes relating to the birth of Christ, including one of the Magi wearing striped stockings. In the apse there is a Coronation of the Virgin by Jacopo Torriti (1295).

On leaving Santa Maria, pass the obelisk ⑮ in the piazza behind the church and go downhill to Via Urbana and Santa Pudenziana ⑯ *(see p171)*. The figures in the apse mosaic, one of the oldest in Rome (AD 390), are remarkable for their naturalism. The two women with crowns are traditionally identified as Santa Prassede and Santa Pudenziana.

Mosaic saint in Santa Prassede ⑬

When you leave the church, you can either retrace your steps to Santa Maria Maggiore or walk down Via Urbana to Via Cavour Metro station.

11th-century frieze above the doorway of Santa Pudenziana ⑯

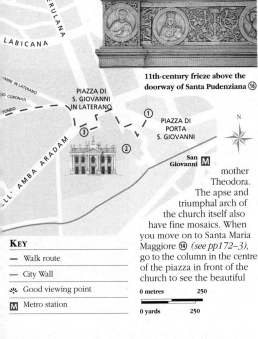

mother Theodora. The apse and triumphal arch of the church itself also have fine mosaics. When you move on to Santa Maria Maggiore ⑭ *(see pp172–3)*, go to the column in the centre of the piazza in front of the church to see the beautiful

KEY

— Walk route

— City Wall

🔆 Good viewing point

Ⓜ Metro station

0 metres 250

0 yards 250

TIPS FOR WALKERS

Starting point: Piazza di Porta San Giovanni.
Length: 3.5 km (2 miles).
Getting there: The nearest Metro station is San Giovanni, on line A, in Piazzale Appio, just outside Porta San Giovanni. The 81, 85, 87 buses and the 13 and 30b trams stop in front of San Giovanni in Laterano.
Best time for walk: It is advisable to go in the morning, in order to to appreciate the mosaics in the best possible light.
Stopping-off points: The bars and restaurants in Piazza del Colosseo are popular with artists, who like to draw the Colosseum on the paper tablecloths. In the Parco del Colle Oppio there is a small café kiosk with tables. There are several bars around Santa Maria Maggiore, some with outdoor tables.

A Two-Hour Walk around Bernini's Rome

Gian Lorenzo Bernini (1598–1680) is the artist who probably left the strongest personal mark on the appearance of the city of Rome. Favourite architect, sculptor and town-planner to three successive popes, he turned Rome into a uniquely Baroque city. This walk traces his enormous influence on the development and appearance of the centre of Rome. It starts from the busy Largo di Santa Susanna just north of Termini station, at the church of Santa Maria della Vittoria.

Quirinale. The long wing of the Palazzo del Quirinale ⑦ (see p158), nicknamed the Manica Lunga (long sleeve), is by Bernini. On the other side of the road is the facade of Sant'Andrea al Quirinale ⑧ (see p161), one of Bernini's greatest churches. When you reach the Piazza del Quirinale ⑨, note the doorway of the palazzo, attributed to Bernini. From the piazza, go up the

Facade of Santa Maria in Via ⑬

composer Donizetti lived at No. 77 and turn into Via Santa Maria in Via, where the church ⑬ has a fine Baroque

Bernini's Fontana del Tritone ②

Through Piazza Barberini

Santa Maria della Vittoria ① (see p255) houses the Cornaro Chapel, the setting for one of Bernini's most revolutionary and controversial sculptures, the *Ecstasy of St Teresa* (1646). From here take Via Barberini to Piazza Barberini. In its centre is Bernini's dramatic Fontana del Tritone ② (see p254) and at one side stands the more modest Fontana delle Api ③ (see p254). As you go up Via delle Quattro Fontane, you catch a glimpse of Palazzo Barberini ④ (see p255) built by Bernini and several other artists for Pope Urban VIII. The gateway and cornices are decorated with the bees that made up part of the Barberini family crest. Next make your way to the crossroads, decorated with Le Quattro Fontane ⑤ (see p162), to enjoy the splendid views in all four directions.

Passing the diminutive San Carlo alle Quattro Fontane ⑥ (see p161), built by Bernini's rival Borromini, take Via del

stairs to Via della Dataria, and into Vicolo Scanderbeg which leads to a small piazza with the same name ⑩. Scanderbeg was the nickname of the Albanian prince Giorgio Castriota (1403–68), the "Terror of the Turks". His portrait is preserved on the house where he lived.

The Trevi Fountain

Go along the narrow Vicolo dei Modelli ⑪, where male models waited to be chosen by artists, then turn towards the Trevi Fountain ⑫ (see p159). Its energy is clearly inspired by Bernini's work, a tribute to his lasting influence on Roman taste. Leave the piazza along Via delle Muratte where the

Neptune Fountain at the north end of Piazza Navona ⑱

facade by Bernini's follower
Carlo Rainaldi. At the top of
this street, turn left down to
Via del Corso. On the other
side of the road, you will see
the towering Column of
Marcus Aurelius ⑭ *(see p113)*
in Piazza Colonna. Beyond
this is Palazzo Montecitorio ⑮,
begun in 1650 by Bernini and
now the home of the Italian
parliament *(see p112)*.

Pantheon to Piazza Navona
Via in Aquiro leads you to the
Pantheon ⑯ *(see pp110–11)*.
Refusing Pope Urban VIII's
request for him to redecorate

Collegio Innocenziano by Bernini's rival Borromini in Piazza Navona ⑱

Fiumi *(see p120)*, was by
Bernini, though the figures
symbolic of the four rivers
were sculpted by other artists.
The central figure in the
Fontana del Moro, however, is
by Bernini himself. Bernini's
contemporaries were fascinated
by the innovative use of
shells, rocks and other natural
forms in his fountains, and his
expert handling of water to
create constant movement.

An extended walk
More energetic walkers may
like to head towards the river
to see the Ponte Sant'Angelo
and its Bernini angels; and
then on to St Peter's *(see
pp230–33)* where they can
admire Bernini's great
colonnaded piazza in front
of the church, the papal
tombs, his altar decorations
and the bronze baldacchino.

the dome,
Bernini said that
although St Peter's
had a hundred defects,
the Pantheon did not have
any. From the Pantheon,
make a small detour to Piazza
della Minerva where you can
see the bizarre Bernini obelisk,
supported by a small elephant,
by the church of Santa Maria
sopra Minerva ⑰ *(see p108)*.
Then retrace your steps and
take Salita dei Crescenzi to

reach the fabulous Piazza
Navona ⑱ *(see p120)* which
was remodelled by Bernini
for Pope Innocent X Pamphilj.
The design for the central
fountain, the Fontana dei

Angel on Ponte Sant'Angelo

KEY

— Walk route

❖ Good viewing point

Ⓜ Metro station

0 metres   250

0 yards   250

TIPS FOR WALKERS

Starting point: Largo di
Santa Susanna.
Length: 3.5 km (2 miles).
Getting there: Take Metro line A
to Repubblica or any bus to
Termini, then walk. Buses 60, 61,
62 and 137 stop in Via Barberini.
Best time for walk: Go either
between 9am and noon for good
lighting conditions in the churches,
or between 4pm and 7pm.
Stopping-off points: The
Piazza Barberini and Fontana di
Trevi areas have lots of bars and
pizzerias for tourists. The many
elegant cafés en route include
the famous Caffè Giolitti (see
p109) and there is a vast choice
of outdoor cafés and restaurants
around Piazza della Rotonda and
Piazza Navona.

A 90-Minute Walk along the Via Appia Antica

Lined with cypresses and pines as it was when the ancient Romans came here by torchlight to bury their dead, the Via Appia is wonderfully atmospheric. The fields are strewn with ruined tombs set against the picturesque background of the Alban hills to the south. Although the marble or travertine stone facings of most tombs have been plundered, a few statues and reliefs survive or have been replaced by copies.

Tomb of Sixtus Pompeus the Righteous ⑨

Capo di Bove

Start from the Tomb of Cecilia Metella ① *(see p266).* In the Middle Ages this area acquired the name Capo di Bove (ox head) from the frieze of festoons and ox heads still visible on the tomb. On the other side of the road you can see the ruined Gothic church of San Nicola ②, which, like the Tomb of Cecilia Metella, was part of the medieval fortress of the Caetani family.

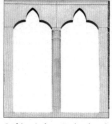

Gothic windows in the church of San Nicola ②

Proceed to the crossroads ③, where many original Roman paving slabs, huge blocks of extremely durable volcanic basalt, are still in place. Just past the next turning (Via Capo di Bove), you will see on your left the nucleus of a great mausoleum overgrown with ivy, known as the Torre di Capo di Bove ④. Beyond it,

The ruined church of San Nicola ②

on both sides of the Appia, are other tombs, some still capped with the remains of the medieval towers that were built over them. On the right after passing some private villas, you come to a military zone around the Forte Appio ⑤, one of a series of forts built around the city in the 19th century. On the left, a little further on, stand the ruins of the Tomb of Marcus Servilius ⑥, showing fragments of reliefs excavated in 1808 by the Neo-Classical sculptor Antonio Canova. He was one of the first to work on the principle that excavated tombs and their inscriptions and reliefs should be allowed to remain in situ. On the other side of the road stands a tomb with a relief of a man, naked except for a short cape, known as the

"Heroic Relief" ⑦. On the left of the road are the ruins of the so-called Tomb of Seneca ⑧. The great moralist Seneca owned a villa near here, where he committed suicide in AD 65 on the orders of Nero.

The next major tomb is that of the family of Sixtus Pompeus the Righteous, a freed slave of the 1st century AD ⑨. The verse inscription records the father's sadness at having to bury his own children, who died young.

Artist's impression of how the mausoleums and tombs lining the Via Appia looked in the 2nd century AD

Section of the Via Appia Antica, showing original Roman paving

From Via dei Lugari to Via di Tor Carbone

Just past Via dei Lugari on the right, screened by trees, is the Tomb of Pope St Urban (reigned 222–230) ⑩. Set back from the road on the left stands a large ruined podium, probably part of a Temple of Jupiter ⑪. The next stretch was excavated by the architect Luigi Canina early in the 19th century. On the right is the Tomb of Caius Licinius ⑫, followed by a smaller Doric tomb ⑬ and the imposing Tomb of Hilarius

Fuscus ⑭, with five portrait busts in relief of members of his family. Next comes the Tomb of Tiberius Claudius Secondinus ⑮, where a group of freedmen of the Imperial household were buried in the 2nd century AD.

Passing a large ruined columbarium, you reach the Tomb of Quintus Apuleius ⑯ and the reconstructed Tomb of the Rabirii freed slaves (1st century BC) ⑰. This has a frieze of three half-length figures above an inscription.

The figure on the right is a priestess of Isis. Behind her you can see the outline of a *sistrum*, the metal rattle used at ceremonies of the cult.

The majority of the tombs are little more than shapeless stacks of eroded brickwork. Two exceptions in the last stretch of this walk are the Tomb of the Festoons ⑱, with its reconstructed frieze of festive putti, and the Tomb of the Frontispiece ⑲, which has a copy of a relief with four portraits. The two central figures are holding hands.

When you reach Via di Tor Carbone, the Via Appia still stretches out ahead of you in a straight line and, if you wish to extend your walk, there are many more tombs and ruined villas to visit along the way.

KEY

— Walk route

<small>******</small> Good viewing point

Figure on the Tomb of the Heroic Relief ⑦

TIPS FOR WALKERS

Starting point: Tomb of Cecilia Metella.
Length: 3 km (2 miles).
Getting there: Take the 118 bus from San Giovanni in Laterano or the Colosseum. On the way back, the 118 goes along the Via Appia Pignatelli. Allow plenty of time for waiting for the bus.
Best time for walk: Go fairly early, before it gets too hot.
Stopping-off points: There is a bar near the church of Domine Quo Vadis?, before the start of the walk, but it is best to bring your own refreshment. There are also several well-established restaurants on the first stretch of the Appia, including the Cecilia Metella, Via Appia Antica 125/127, tel 513 67 43 (closed Mon).

TRAVELLERS' NEEDS

WHERE TO STAY

ROME HAS BEEN a major tourist centre since the Middle Ages, when pilgrims from all over Europe came to visit the home of Catholicism and its relic-packed churches. The nostalgic can still sleep in a 15th-century hotel, or stay around the Campo de' Fiori market, where visiting ecclesiastics were entertained by courtesans in the Renaissance era. Those who prefer their history a little less raffish could opt for an ex-monastery or convent, or stay in a still-functioning religious house. Romantics could sleep in the house once occupied by Keats, while stargazers could stay

Porter at the Majestic Hotel

in former palaces graced by celebrities of the past and present. Rome can offer the full range of accommodation, mostly in historical buildings, very little purpose-built. *Pensione* (guesthouse) is no longer an official category, but in practice many retain the name and more personal character that has made them so popular with travellers. Other possibilities include hostels, residential hotels and self-catering accommodation.

The 72 hotels we have selected are organized in the *Choosing a Hotel* chart *(pp294–5)* and in the listings *(pp296–301)* according to their price category and area.

WHERE TO LOOK

AROUND the Spanish Steps and Piazza di Spagna lies the traditional heartland of foreign visitors, with some of the most exclusive smaller hotels. Similar places can be found all over the centre, to the west of Via del Corso.

While moderately priced accommodation is rare in central Rome, the advantages of staying right on the doorstep of the city's many ancient sights cannot be over-estimated; you can walk to the major areas of interest and easily return at midday for a shower and siesta. If the

less expensive hotels we have recommended in the centre are full, try the Borgo – close to the Vatican – or the lively quarter of Trastevere.

Those in search of glamour should head for Via Veneto, which has many grand and luxurious hotels.

If you're looking for a peaceful retreat, try the area around the Aventine, or one of the high-class hotels next to the Villa Borghese park.

Although many of the streets immediately around Termini station are rather seedy, the area is nonetheless a convenient stopover for travellers and there's a

concentration of cheap hotels, with some decent (if basic) ones among them. The hotels recommended lie in a fairly safe area on the east side of the station. The approach to the centre from Termini has a number of good hotels that are particularly suitable for the business traveller.

HOTEL PRICES

ROME MAY STILL have more cheap accommodation than London or New York, but rates for comparable establishments have caught up. Prices are set by the state, and hotels are supposed to display the official rate on the door of each room. VAT is usually included, and has been taken into account in the price categories on p291.

It is rare, but not unheard-of, for Roman hotels to have low and high season rates, so it can be worth bargaining as you will inevitably be quoted the official rate, even in the winter months before and after Christmas, when competition is less strong. Discounts for long-stay visitors and groups are often negotiable.

Rooms without a bathroom can cost about 30% less. Single travellers are badly catered for, and though it is possible to find a single room for 60% of the price of a double, on average you'll

The Verdi Room in Via Veneto's Majestic Hotel *(see p301)*

The Plaza Minerva *(see p296)*

pay 70%, and occasionally 90%. Where breakfast is included in the quoted price, you can ask for the relevant amount to be deducted from your bill if you don't want it.

HIDDEN EXTRAS

EVEN IF the room price includes service, you are still expected to tip at least L1,000 for room service and around L2,000 for bellboys.

Hotels will often add hefty surcharges to international phone calls, and may charge extra for parking and air conditioning. The cost of drinks in minibars can be high – you can buy a cheaper supply from local shops.

FACILITIES

HOTEL STANDARDS have improved of late – you can expect air conditioning and some bathrooms with hair dryers in middle-range establishments and direct-dial phones in middle to lower price rooms, although budget travellers staying in cheaper hotels shouldn't expect much more than a clean room.

Because most hotels occupy historic buildings, room sizes can vary dramatically even within the same establishment (and this is often reflected in the

The Portoghesi Hotel *(see p296)*

pricing), so don't be afraid to ask to see your room before you check in. For the same reason, swimming pools are few and far between, but roof terraces or gardens are common across the range.

Top-class hotels will usually have some soundproofing; otherwise noise levels can be dreadful, in which case ask for a room facing away from the road. The chart on pages 294–5 indicates which hotels have a quiet location – this covers both peaceful neighbourhoods and certain quiet streets in busy areas which don't have a constant stream of traffic.

Parking in central Rome is a problem, though a few hotels have a limited number of parking spaces of their own.

Business visitors to the capital are well catered for, with hotel facilities ranging from fax machines to meeting rooms *(see pp294–5)*.

HOW TO BOOK

THE ITALIAN postal service tends to be unreliable, so it is safer to book by phone or fax. You should do this at least two months in advance if you want a particular hotel in May, June, September or October; Easter and Christmas are also busy.

If a deposit is required you can pay by credit card or international money order. Under Italian law a booking is valid as soon as the deposit is paid, so you're likely to lose money if you pull out. If you arrive by train, touts may descend on you at the station with offers of accommodation. They can be of some use if you are looking for a budget hotel, but you should exercise the usual caution. A better bet if you haven't booked anywhere in advance is to head for one of the tourist board offices. Here, staff will reserve you a room within the price range you specify.

Villa San Pio garden *(see p299)*

CHECKING IN AND OUT

ITALIAN HOTELIERS are legally obliged to register you with the police, which is the reason they always ask for your passport. They usually hold on to it for a few hours, but you need it if you're going to change money. Everyone in Italy is supposed to carry with them some sort of identification.

In some of Rome's cheaper *pensioni*, don't be surprised if you are asked to pay in advance. To speed up the checking out process, mention in advance if you intend to pay by credit card.

The Locarno *(see p297)*

TOURIST BOARDS

THE PROVINCIAL and state tourist boards can provide advice on accommodation and reserve rooms.

Rome Provincial Tourist Board (EPT)
Via Parigi 5, 00185.
(487 12 70.

EPT Leonardo da Vinci Airport, Fiumicino, 00054.
(65 01 02 55.

EPT Termini Station, Piazza dei Cinquecento, 00185.
(482 30 78.

Italian State Tourist Board (ENIT)
Via Marghera 2, 00185.
(497 11.

The reception area of the Regina Hotel Baglioni *(see p301)*

DISABLED TRAVELLERS

PROVISION for disabled travellers is very poor. Small hotels that occupy parts of buildings sometimes only start their rooms up several flights of stairs, whereas certain establishments can accommodate disabled guests on the ground floor, or only have a couple of rooms which are appropriate. Ramps, wide doorways and bathroom handrails are rare.

Our entries for wheelchair access in the listings below rely on the establishments' own assessments; any specific requirements should be checked before booking.

There is a private organization, Associazione Nazionale dei Andicappati at via Tommaso Fortifiocca 100, which gives advice to disabled travellers. They can be contacted on 781 07 72.

TRAVELLING WITH CHILDREN

ITALIANS LOVE CHILDREN and they are usually welcome across the range of hotels. Facilities, however, tend to be unimpressive on paper. Most hotels can provide cots or small beds, but high chairs, children's meals and baby-sitting services are rare. In practice, though, many establishments – especially smaller, family-run ones – go out of their way to be helpful.

Many hotels do not have any special rates for children, especially in high season, and charge a standard rate if you require an extra bed in a room, whether it's for a baby or an adult, which can add anything from a few thousand *lire* to 40% on to the price of a double room. For a family with older children, two-room suites are sometimes to be found. For hotels providing children's facilities, see Choosing a Hotel *(pp294–5)*.

SELF-CATERING

ANYONE staying in the city for more than a couple of weeks should consider renting an apartment, which can be arranged by a couple of agencies. **International Services** has a list of studios and flats; the **Landmark Trust** leases a flat (booked three years in advance) in the house where Keats died, near the Spanish Steps.

SELF-CATERING AGENCIES

International Services
Via del Babuino 79, 00187.
(36 00 00 18. **FAX** 36 00 00 37.

Landmark Trust
Shottesbrooke, Maidenhead SL6 3SW, Great Britain.
(0628-82 59 25. **FAX** 0628-82 54 17.

RESIDENTIAL HOTELS

IF YOU WANT the comfort and privacy of your own apartment coupled with the services of a hotel, you could opt to stay in a *residenza*. Prices range from around L500,000 to over L3 million for a week in a two-bedded room, though some *residenze* are only available for fortnightly or monthly lets. A full list is available from tourist board offices *(see p289)*; the following are some of the most central:

Residence Babuino
Via del Babuino 172, 00187.
(361 16 63.

Di Ripetta
Via di Ripetta 231, 00186.
(67 21 41. **FAX** 320 39 59.

In Trastevere
Vicolo Moroni 35, 00153.
(581 27 68.

Ripa
Via Orti di Trastevere 1, 00153.
(586 11.

Vittoria
Via Vittoria 60, 00187.
(679 75 33.

RELIGIOUS INSTITUTIONS

IF YOU DON'T MIND an early curfew when the rest of Rome is still swinging, quite a few religious institutions take in paying guests. You do not have to be a practising Catholic to stay in one of these, but be sure to book well in advance as all of the following places cater for groups of students and pilgrims. **Domus Mariae** and **Istituto Madri Pie** are near the Vatican; **Congregazione Suore dello Spirito Santo** is further out of town, 6 km (4 miles) west of the centre. Prices are in the same range as the cheapest hotels.

Domus Mariae
Via Aurelia 481, 00165.
(662 31 38, 662 49 04.

The Gregoriana *(see p297)*

Istituto Madri Pie
Via A. de Gasperi 4, 00165.
📞 63 19 67.

Congregazione Suore dello Spirito Santo
Via della Pineta Sacchetti 227, 00168.
📞 305 31 01.

Facade of the Excelsior *(see p301)*

BUDGET ACCOMMODATION

EVEN IF YOU'RE TRAVELLING on a shoestring, it's possible to find a clean, decent room in Rome. Dormitory accommodation can be found at rock-bottom prices in simple establishments, such as the **Ottaviano.** Youth hostels are a good option – and not just for the young. At the **Ostello del Foro Italico** bed, breakfast and shower can all be had at a very reasonable price.

Women can get single, double or triple rooms at the **Young Women's Christian Association** (YWCA). Its location near Termini is convenient but insalubrious, so those arriving at night should take care. The **Protezione della Giovane** organization has a useful

information office for women under 25; they will try to find you somewhere to stay.

HOSTEL AND DORMITORY ADDRESSES

Ottaviano
Via Ottaviano 6, 00192.
📞 370 05 33.

Associazione Italiana Alberghi per la Gioventù
(Youth Hostel Association)
Via Cavour 44, 00184.
📞 487 11 52.

Ostello del Foro Italico
Viale delle Olimpiadi 61, 00194.
📞 323 62 79.

Residenza Universitaria de Lollis
Via Cesare de Lollis 20, 00185.
Rooms in summer only. Details from Youth Hostel Association, above.

YWCA
Via C. Balbo 4, 00184.
📞 488 39 17.

Protezione della Giovane
Termini Station, Piazza dei Cinquecento, 00185.
📞 482 75 94.

CAMPING

MOST CAMPSITES are well out of town – suitable for an occasional excursion into Rome – with the exception of **Flaminio**, which is near the Olympic Village, 6 km (4 miles) north of the centre.

Flaminio
Via Flaminia Nuova 821, 00191.
📞 333 26 04.

USING THE LISTINGS
The hotels on pages 296–301 are organized according to area and price. The symbols after the hotel's address show the facilities it offers.

🛁 rooms with bath and/or shower available
1️⃣ single rate rooms available
➕ rooms for more than two people available, or an extra bed can be put in a double room
24 24-hour room service available
📺 television in all rooms
🍸 minibar in all rooms
🚭 non-smoking rooms available
🏞 rooms with good view
❄ air conditioning in all rooms
🏊 swimming pool in hotel
💼 business facilities: message-taking service, fax machine for guests, desk and telephone in each room and a meeting room within the hotel
👶 child cots and babysitting service
♿ wheelchair access (phone for details)
🛗 lift
🐾 pets allowed in bedrooms (confirm that you are bringing a pet). The majority of hotels accept guide dogs
🅿 hotel parking available
🌿 garden/terrace open to guests
🍷 bar
🍴 restaurant
ℹ tourist information
💳 credit cards accepted
AE American Express
DC Diners Club
MC Mastercard/Access
V Visa
JCB Japanese Credit Bureau

Price categories for a double room with bath or shower including breakfast, tax and service:
Ⓛ under L100,000
ⓁⓁ L100,000–L199,000
ⓁⓁⓁ L200,000–L299,000
ⓁⓁⓁⓁ L300,000–L399,000
ⓁⓁⓁⓁⓁ over L400,000

The pool in the Aldrovandi Palace garden *(see p301)*

Rome's Best: Hotels

ROMAN HOTELS RANGE from frescoed palaces and *fin-de-siècle* bastions of faded glamour, to family-run guesthouses. Most are within easy reach of restaurants, shops and transport. Whatever the price level, all the hotels shown on this map have something special to offer, whether it's a chic location, or a roof terrace with soaring views across the city. The only drawback is that these places and the others listed on pages 294–301 are exceptions to the many unremarkable hotels in the city, so you should book well in advance. The hotels shown here are the best in their particular style or price range.

Sole al Pantheon
The writers Jean Paul Sartre and Simone de Beauvoir stayed in this superbly located – and recently refurbished – 15th-century palazzo. (See p296.)

Raphael
Full of antiques and art, the Raphael offers a central location. (See p297.)

0 metres   500

0 yards   500

Vatican

Janiculum

Campo de' Fiori

Piazza Navona

Trastevere

Campo de' Fiori
Central Rome's best bargain offers small, well-furnished rooms and terrific views from the sixth-floor roof terrace. (See p298.)

Teatro di Pompeo
This guesthouse-style hotel was built on the ruins of an ancient theatre. (See p299.)

Sant'Anselmo
To be sure of getting a room you need to book well in advance at this peacefully located Roman villa. An added bonus is the lovely secluded garden. (See p299.)

Villa Borghese
*Welcoming public
rooms and a cool,
shaded courtyard,
with a leafy canopy
above, create an
unpretentious and
relaxed atmosphere
in this pleasantly
informal hotel.*
(See p301.)

Hassler
*Luxurious suites and an air
of faded grandeur remind
visitors of the Hassler's heyday.
The roof-top restaurant is
Rome's most famous.*
(See p298.)

Carriage
*The serene atmosphere
makes this city-centre
hotel a special haven.*
(See p297.)

Via Veneto

Quirinal

iol

Esquiline

Forum

Palatine

Caracalla

Lateran

ne

Grand
*Good service
and extensive
facilities are
the main
features of this
old-fashioned,
luxury hotel.*
(See p299.)

Scalinata di Spagna
*The prized location at
the top of the Spanish
Steps, and a large
private terrace, make
this hotel a popular
choice with visitors.*
(See p298.)

Inghilterra
*Sip a cocktail in the Inghilterra's club-like bar, once
frequented by Ernest Hemingway.* (See p298.)

Choosing a Hotel

THE 71 HOTELS listed in the following pages have all been inspected and assessed. This choosing chart shows some of the features which may affect your hotel choice. The hotels are listed alphabetically within their price category. For more detailed information, see pages 296–301.

Hotel	Price	Number of Rooms	Large Rooms	Business Facilities	Hotel Parking	Recommended Restaurant	Close to Shops and Restaurants	Quiet Location	24-Hour Room Service
FORUM (see p296)									
Forum	ℒℒℒℒ	76		■					●
PIAZZA DELLA ROTONDA (see p296)									
Abruzzi	ℒ	25					●		
Mimosa	ℒ	11					●	■	
Santa Chiara	ℒℒℒ	97					●		
Sole al Pantheon	ℒℒℒℒ	29					●		●
Colonna Palace	ℒℒℒℒℒ	110	●				●		
Holiday Inn Crowne Plaza Minerva	ℒℒℒℒℒ	134	●	■			●	■	●
Nazionale	ℒℒℒℒ	87	●	■			●		●
PIAZZA NAVONA (see p296)									
Navona	ℒ	26					●	■	
Due Torri	ℒℒ	26					●	■	
Portoghesi	ℒℒ	27			●		●	■	
Genio	ℒℒℒ	60					●		
Raphael	ℒℒℒℒ	63					●	■	
PIAZZA DI SPAGNA (see p297)									
Jonella	ℒ	9					●		
Firenze	ℒℒ	25	●				●		●
Homs	ℒℒ	50			●		●	■	
Locarno	ℒℒ	38		■	●		●		
Lydia	ℒℒ	17					●		
Margutta	ℒℒ	21					●	■	
Piazza di Spagna	ℒℒ	16					●		
Suisse	ℒℒ	13	●				●	■	
Carriage	ℒℒℒ	27	●				●		
Condotti	ℒℒℒ	17	●				●		●
Gregoriana	ℒℒℒ	19			●		●	■	●
Manfredi	ℒℒℒ	15		■			●	■	●
Mozart	ℒℒℒ	31					●	■	
Scalinata di Spagna	ℒℒℒ	15			●		●		●
Borgognoni	ℒℒℒℒ	50		■	●		●	■	
Hassler	ℒℒℒℒℒ	100	●	■	●	■	●	■	
Inghilterra	ℒℒℒℒℒ	105		■			●	■	●
Valadier	ℒℒℒℒ	38		■			●	■	
CAMPO DE' FIORI (see p298)									
Lunetta	ℒ	36					●	■	
Piccolo	ℒ	15					●		
Campo de' Fiori	ℒℒ	27					●	■	
Pomezia	ℒℒ	22					●		
Rinascimento	ℒℒ	19					●	■	
Smeraldo	ℒℒ	35					●		
Sole	ℒℒ	62		■	●		●	■	●
Teatro di Pompeo	ℒℒℒ	12		■	●		●	■	

Price categories for a double room per night, including breakfast, tax and service: Ⓛ under L100,000 ⓁⓁ L100,000–L199,000 ⓁⓁⓁ L200,000–L299,000 ⓁⓁⓁⓁ L300,000–L399,000 ⓁⓁⓁⓁⓁ over L400,000. **HOTEL PARKING** Car parking facilities attached to the hotel or in the hotel complex.	**CLOSE TO SHOPS AND RESTAURANTS** Within a 5-minute walk of a good area for shops, bars, cafés and restaurants. **BUSINESS FACILITIES** Message-taking service, fax machine for guest use, desk and telephone in each room and a meeting room which is available within the hotel.	NUMBER OF ROOMS	LARGE ROOMS	BUSINESS FACILITIES	HOTEL PARKING	RECOMMENDED RESTAURANT	CLOSE TO SHOPS AND RESTAURANTS	QUIET LOCATION	24-HOUR ROOM SERVICE
QUIRINAL *(see p299)*									
Grand	ⓁⓁⓁⓁⓁ	171	●	■		■			●
TERMINI *(see p299)*									
Cervia	Ⓛ	26							
Gexim	Ⓛ	9						■	
Katty	Ⓛ	11							
Mari	Ⓛ	13	●						
Restivo	Ⓛ	6							
Canada	ⓁⓁ	70	●	■	●				
AVENTINE *(see p299)*									
Aventino	ⓁⓁ	23	●	■				■	●
Sant'Anselmo	ⓁⓁ	46		■				■	●
Villa San Pio	ⓁⓁ	59	●	■	●			■	●
Domus Aventina	ⓁⓁⓁ	26	●	■	●			■	●
TRASTEVERE *(see p300)*									
Carmel	Ⓛ	10							
Manara	Ⓛ	7					●		
VATICAN *(see p300)*									
Alimandi	Ⓛ	30						■	
Amalia	ⓁⓁ	25					●		
Columbus	ⓁⓁⓁ	100		●	●				●
Atlante Star	ⓁⓁⓁⓁ	70	●	■	●		●		●
VIA VENETO *(see p300)*									
Merano	ⓁⓁ	32					●		
Alexandra	ⓁⓁⓁ	45			●		●		
Oxford	ⓁⓁⓁ	58		■	●				
Residenza	ⓁⓁⓁ	29	●				●		
Barocco	ⓁⓁⓁⓁ	28		■			●		
Imperiale	ⓁⓁⓁⓁ	95		■			●		●
Pullman Boston	ⓁⓁⓁⓁ	124	●	■			●	■	
Victoria	ⓁⓁⓁⓁ	120		■			●	■	●
Bernini Bristol	ⓁⓁⓁⓁⓁ	126	●	■			●		●
Excelsior	ⓁⓁⓁⓁⓁ	327	●	■	●		●		●
Majestic	ⓁⓁⓁⓁⓁ	96			●		●		
Regina Hotel Baglioni	ⓁⓁⓁⓁⓁ	130	●	■	●		●		
VILLA BORGHESE *(see p301)*									
Villa Borghese	ⓁⓁⓁ	31			●				●
Lord Byron	ⓁⓁⓁⓁ	37		■		■		■	●
Aldrovandi Palace	ⓁⓁⓁⓁⓁ	140		■	●				

FORUM

Forum

Via Tor de' Conti 25, 00184. **Map** 5 B5.
(679 24 46. **FAX** 678 64 79.
TX 62 25 49. **Rooms**: 76.
AE, DC, MC, V.
LLLL

Occupying a palace built out of
materials from the ruins of the
nearby Imperial Fora, the Forum
is an old-fashioned hotel, with
mellow, wood-panelled public
rooms, and a sunny roof-terrace
restaurant giving wonderful views
over the archaeological centre.

PIAZZA DELLA ROTONDA

Abruzzi

Piazza della Rotonda 69, 00186.
Map 4 F4 & 12 D3. (679 20 21.
Rooms: 25.

The Abruzzi provides clean, basic
rooms with terracotta-tiled floors
in an ochre-coloured palazzo overlooking the Pantheon. The rooms
at the back are not the best, but
quiet. No breakfast is served.

Mimosa

Via di Santa Chiara 61, 00186. **Map**
4 F4 & 12 D3. (68 80 17 53. **Rooms**:
11.

The Mimosa is a clean, if slightly
scruffy, family-run hotel close to
the Pantheon. Rooms are cool and
the five communal bathrooms and
showers are immaculate. As the
hotel is popular with groups of
visiting students, book well ahead.

Santa Chiara

Via di Santa Chiara 21, 00186.
Map 4 F4 & 12 D3. (687 29 79.
FAX 687 31 44. **Rooms**: 97.
AE, DC, MC, V,
JCB.

Conveniently located in the historic
centre, the Santa Chiara occupies
an apricot-washed palazzo. Public
rooms are cool, particularly the
marble reception area and the
lounge. Bedrooms are carpeted,
and have good-quality furnishings
and marble bathrooms. Street-
facing rooms can be noisy.

Sole al Pantheon

Piazza della Rotonda 63, 00186.
Map 4 F4 & 12 D3. (678 04 41.
FAX 684 06 89. **Rooms**: 29.
AE, DC, MC, V. LLLL

A hotel since 1467, the Sole's
illustrious list of former guests
ranges from Renaissance writer
Ariosto to Jean-Paul Sartre and
Simone de Beauvoir. Its location
opposite the Pantheon is
unbeatable, and though it has
been modernized (60% of the
rooms now have jacuzzis) there
are still bedrooms with painted,
panelled ceilings.

Colonna Palace

Piazza di Montecitorio 12, 00186.
Map 4 F4 & 12 D3. (678 13 41.
FAX 679 44 96. TX 62 14 67 CIFCOL.
Rooms: 110. AE, DC, MC, V.
LLLL

The Colonna Palace stands on the
same piazza as Italy's Chamber of
Deputies, and so attracts
politicians as well as tourists.
Bedrooms are spacious, though
the bathrooms are small. Breakfast
is served in a basement room
livened up by frescoes. There are
lovely views from the impressive
roof garden where a jacuzzi has
recently been installed.

Holiday Inn Crowne Plaza Minerva

Piazza della Minerva 69, 00186.
Map 4 F4 & 12 D3. (684 18 88.
FAX 679 41 65. TX 62 00 91 HINMIN.
Rooms: 134. AE, DC, MC, V, JCB.
LLLL

Occupying Palazzo Fonseca
behind the Pantheon, this is
Rome's newest luxury hotel. The
interior was designed by Post-
Modern architect Portoghesi, and
its centrepiece is the lounge,
canopied in semi-translucent
Venetian glass, and presided over
by a statue of Minerva. The large
bedrooms are decorated in shades
of beige and coral. Views from the
roof terrace are magnificent,
stretching over the Pantheon, St
Peter's and the Janiculum hill.

Nazionale

Piazza di Montecitorio 131, 00186.
Map 4 F3 & 12 E2. (678 92 51.
FAX 678 66 77. TX 62 14 27. **Rooms**:
87. AE, DC, MC, V, JCB.
LLLL

Home to Robert de Niro while he
was making *Godfather III*, the
Nazionale is usually frequented
by visiting tourists, businessmen
and politicians – it stands right
on the corner of the Chamber
of Deputies. Public rooms are
comfortable, particularly the
lounge, with its brocade sofas and
flower arrangements. Some of the

rooms are huge, and most are also
partially furnished with British and
Italian antiques.

PIAZZA NAVONA

Navona

Via dei Sediari 8, 00186. **Map** 4 F4 &
12 D3. (686 42 03. **Rooms**: 26.
22.

A superb location – across the
road from Piazza Navona and five
minutes' stroll from the Pantheon
– means that it's hard to find a
room here unless you book well
in advance. The hotel is run
largely by the owners' Australian
son-in-law, who is extremely
helpful. Bedrooms are basic, but
some of them have bathrooms. The
restaurant opens for groups
of 15 or more.

Due Torri

Vicolo del Leonetto 23–25, 00186.
Map 4 E3 & 11 C1. (687 69 83.
FAX 686 54 42. TX 62 20 50. **Rooms**:
26. AE, DC, MC, V. LL

This amiable hotel is a short walk
from both Piazza Navona and the
Spanish Steps, tucked into an
alleyway in the artisans' district
of the old town. Bedrooms vary:
some are stylish, others plain and
rather small. The lounge is both
elegant and homely, with swept
back drapes, statuettes, an
immense gilt-framed mirror and
pink velvet sofas.

Portoghesi

Via dei Portoghesi 1, 00186.
Map 4 E3 & 11 C2. (686 42 31.
FAX 687 69 76. **Rooms**: 27.
MC, V.

Ideally located on a cobbled street
a couple of minutes' walk from
Piazza Navona, the Portoghesi is
a fairly simple hotel, with slightly
dated bedrooms. The public
rooms, however, are elegant and
there's a roof terrace looking on
to the dome of the Portuguese
community's church next door.

Genio

Via Zanardelli 28, 00186. **Map** 4 E3 &
11 C2. (683 37 81. **FAX** 68 30 72 46.
TX 62 36 51 ORALNR. **Rooms**: 60.
AE, DC, MC, V, JCB. LLL

On a fairly busy road just behind
Piazza Navona, the Genio's
bedrooms are ordinary, though
quite comfortable. The location,
however, and a roof terrace where
you can picnic with your own
food, make it worth considering.

Raphael

Largo Febo 2, 00186. **Map** 4 E3 &
11 C2. 68 28 31. FAX 687 89 93.
TX 62 23 96 RHOTEL. **Rooms**: 63.
TV AE, DC, MC, V.

The Raphael is curtained with ivy
and situated on a cobbled street
just off Piazza Navona. The big
reception lounge has the air of
an exhibition hall, being full of
antique statues, modern sculpture
and even a painted sled. There is
a restaurant in the basement
where pride of place goes to an
ornate wine cabinet. Bedrooms are
decorated with parquet floors,
marbled walls and 18th-century-
style furniture as well as paisley
curtains. The rooms on the top
floor have terrific views.

PIAZZA DI SPAGNA

Jonella

Via della Croce 41, 00187. **Map** 4 F2.
679 79 66. **Rooms**: 9.

The Jonella occupies an orange-
coloured palazzo on one of the
most attractive shopping streets in
the Piazza di Spagna area. The
décor is somewhat down-at-heel,
but the location and low prices
make it worth considering. The
owner occasionally pops out to
shop, so if you arrive when no-
one's there, be patient and wait
for their return.

Firenze

Via Due Macelli 106, 00187. **Map** 5 A2
& 12 F1. 679 72 40. FAX 678 56 36.
Rooms: 25. AE, MC, V.

The Firenze lies a short distance
from Piazza di Spagna on a busy
main road. The owner has set her
elegant stamp on the hotel:
Chinese urns and gilt-framed
mirrors greet you in the entrance
hall, and the bedrooms are large
and beautifully decorated. There
is also a leafy terrace where you
can take breakfast.

Homs

Via della Vite 71–72, 00187.
Map 5 A3 & 12 F1. 679 29 76.
FAX 678 04 82. **Rooms**: 50.
AE, MC, V.

On one of the quieter, less
pretentious shopping streets in
the Piazza di Spagna area, the
Homs has clean, pleasant rooms with
dark-green carpets, white walls
and white bathrooms. The
breakfast room opens out on to
a pleasant terrace.

Locarno

Via della Penna 22, 00186. **Map** 4 F1.
361 08 41, 361 08 42, 361 08 43.
FAX 321 52 49. TX 62 22 51 HOTLOC.
Rooms: 38. AE, DC,
MC, V, JCB.

Situated on a small, busy side-
street near the Tiber, a brief walk
from Piazza del Popolo, the
Locarno is an attractive 1920s
hotel with an Art Nouveau door
and swags of lilac growing across
its facade. Old-fashioned touches
remain, with a grandfather clock
and Tiffany lamp in the reception,
and a marble-topped bar of
polished wood. Outside, there's a
patio packed with greenery and
kept cool by a tiny fountain.

Lydia

Via Sistina 42, 00187. **Map** 5 B2.
679 38 15. FAX 679 72 63.
TX 62 33 13. **Rooms**: 17.
AE, DC, MC, V.

The Lydia is a pleasant hotel,
popular with students, on a busy
road a few minutes' walk from the
Spanish Steps. Rooms have pale
blue walls and pastel bedcovers,
and two retain their old ceiling
frescoes. If you're not fortunate
enough to get one of these,
content yourself with breakfasting
in the chandelier-lit dining room,
which is also decorated with
beautiful frescoes. Some of the
street-facing rooms can be noisy.

Margutta

Via Laurina 34, 00187. **Rooms**: 21.
679 84 40, 322 36 74.
AE, DC, MC, V.

The Margutta sits on a quiet
cobbled street just below the
Piazza del Popolo. The scruffy
facade and slightly grubby seats in
the lobby are forgotten as soon as
you get into your room, which
has white walls and green
wrought-iron bedsteads and
candle-holders. If you wish to stay
in one of the three attic rooms
that share a pretty roof terrace, be
sure to book well in advance.

Piazza di Spagna

Via Mario de' Fiori 61, 00187.
Map 5 A2 & 12 F1. 679 30 61,
679 64 12. FAX 679 06 54. **Rooms**: 16.
AE, MC, V.

Close to the designer boutiques of
Via Condotti, this attractive, small
hotel has simple, but good-sized
rooms, with tiled floors and a
couple of bathrooms with jacuzzis.
The breakfast room and bar are
tiny, so most residents decide to
take breakfast in their own rooms.

Suisse

Via Gregoriana 54–56, 00187.
Map 5 A2 & 12 F1. 678 36 49.
FAX 678 12 58. **Rooms**: 13.
AE, DC, MC, V.

Occupying the third floor of a
dusty palazzo (the entrance is at
No. 54), the Suisse is a small,
pleasant hotel with friendly staff.
Chinese prints hang along the
corridors and in the rooms. These
also have polished floors, moulded
ceilings and marble-topped
dressers and tables. Breakfast is
served in the bedrooms.

Carriage

Via delle Carrozze 36, 00187.
Map 5 A2. 699 01 24, 679 33 12.
FAX 678 82 79. TX 62 62 46.
Rooms: 27.
AE, DC, MC, V.

Situated in a street where
noblemen used to park their
carriages, this hotel's elegance is
immediately evident in the
reception area, with its panelling,
candelabra and gilt-framed mirrors.
The rooms live up to expectations,
decorated in a serene shade of
blue, with some antique furniture.
Two rooms open on to the leafy,
terracotta tiled terrace for all
residents while two have their
own private terraces.

Condotti

Via Mario de' Fiori 37, 00187.
Map 5 A2 & 12 F1. 679 47 69.
FAX 679 04 57. **Rooms**: 17.
AE, DC, MC, V.

Close to Piazza di Spagna and in
the heart of the designer shopping
district, the Condotti is a
comfortable, welcoming hotel.
Rooms are medium to large and
well decorated. One room has its
own small terrace and three others
share one.

Gregoriana

Via Gregoriana 18, 00187. **Map** 5 A2
& 12 F1. 679 42 69. FAX 678 42 58.
Rooms: 19.

The Gregoriana is a stylish,
congenial hotel, situated close to
the Spanish Steps in a tree-lined,
quiet street of elegant palazzi.
The first- and third-floor corridors
are papered with a leopard-
spotted print, while that of the
second floor is in the style of
William Morris. The rooms are all
the same: black lacquer doors,
terracotta-coloured carpets,
flowery wallpaper and 1920s
drawings on the walls. There are
no public rooms, so breakfast and
drinks are served in the bedrooms.

Manfredi

Via Margutta 61, 00187. **Map** 5 A2.
📞 320 76 76, 320 76 95.
FAX 320 77 36. **Rooms**: 15. 🛏 1
🔢 24 TV Y 🍴 🔌 🚿 🛗 Y 🔋
🔳 AE, MC, V, JCB. ⓁⓁ

This pretty, family-run hotel is
excellently located, just off Piazza
di Spagna, in a peaceful cobbled
street of art galleries and antique
shops. The reception area and
bar-breakfast room are paved with
marble and decorated in soft
pastels. Bedrooms are peaceful –
all are soundproofed – with pale
fabric wall coverings and
co-ordinated furnishings.

Mozart

Via dei Greci 23, 00187. **Map** 4 F2.
📞 684 00 41. FAX 678 42 71.
Rooms: 31. 🛏 1 TV Y 🔌
🔋 Y 🔳 AE, DC, MC, V, JCB.
ⓁⓁ

Located in a cobbled street
between Piazza del Popolo and
Piazza di Spagna, the Mozart is
immediately appealing. Decor is
attractively worn and includes a
Venetian mirror spotted with age.
There's a small breakfast room, as
well as a bar-café, which opens
off the stone-lagged reception.
Rooms have ceramic-tiled or
parquet floors, and bathrooms
tend to be small, most having
only a shower.

Scalinata di Spagna

Piazza Trinità dei Monti 17, 00187.
Map 5 A2. 📞 684 08 96.
FAX 684 05 98. **Rooms**: 15. 🛏 1
🔢 24 TV 🔌 🚿 🔋 🛗 P
🔌 🔋 🍴 🔳 MC, V. ⓁⓁⓁ

This homely, convivial hotel
occupies a small 18th-century villa
at the top of the Spanish Steps.
Breakfast is eaten at a communal
table under the gaze of a parrot.
Some rooms retain their old
panelled ceilings. Book well ahead
if you want to stay in one of the
rooms that open out on to the
large terrace.

Borgognoni

Via del Bufalo 126, 00187. **Map** 5 A3
& 12 F1. 📞 678 00 41. FAX 684 15 01.
TX 62 30 74 BUFALO. **Rooms**: 50.
🛏 1 🔢 TV Y 🔌 🔋 🔌 P
🔌 Y 🍴 🔳 AE, DC, MC, V, JCB.
ⓁⓁⓁⓁ

This elegant hotel is just off Piazza
San Silvestro, five minutes from
the Spanish Steps. In the public
rooms, an uncluttered modern
style is coupled with traditional oil
paintings. The bedrooms – some
with terraces – are beautifully
understated.

Hassler

Piazza Trinità dei Monti 6, 00187. **Map**
5 A2. 📞 678 26 51. FAX 678 99 91.
TX 61 02 03. **Rooms**: 100. 🛏 1
🔢 24 TV Y 🔌 🚿 🔋 P 🔌
Y 🍴 🔋 🔳 AE, MC, V, JCB.
ⓁⓁⓁⓁⓁ

Standing at the top of the Spanish
Steps, with magnificent views of
Rome from its roof terrace,
restaurant *(see p313)* and suites,
the Hassler was once host to
royalty and the glitterati of Europe
and America. Its *dolce vita* days
are over, but the lounges and
bedrooms lit by Venetian glass
chandeliers, the wood-panelled
bar and marble bathrooms retain
the air of a more extravagant era.

Inghilterra

Via Bocca di Leone 14, 00187. **Map**
5 A2. 📞 67 21 61. FAX 684 08 28. TX
61 45 52. **Rooms**: 105. 🛏 1 🔢 24
TV Y 🔌 Y 🔋 🔌 🛗 🐕 🍴
🔋 🔳 AE, DC, MC, V. ⓁⓁⓁⓁⓁ

Liszt and Hemingway are among
the writers, artists and musicians
who have stayed at the Inghilterra
since it opened in 1850. In the
heart of Rome's designer shopping
area and close to the Spanish
Steps, it's still a desirable place to
stay. The bedrooms are all
individually decorated and
furnished. The bar could have
been lifted straight from a London
gentlemen's club, and the
restaurant walls, painted with
views of gardens and the sky-
frescoed ceiling create the illusion
of dining in the open.

Valadier

Via della Fontanella 15, 00187. **Map**
4 F1. 📞 361 19 98. FAX 320 15 58.
TX 62 08 73. **Rooms**: 38. 🛏 1 🔢
24 TV Y 🔌 🚿 🔌 🔋 Y 🍴 🔋
AE, DC, MC, V, JCB. ⓁⓁⓁⓁ

Slickly decorated with shiny wood
and marble, the Valadier styles
itself as an intimate hideaway for
those on a romantic visit to Rome.
Public rooms are tailor-made for
seduction, with low sofas, marble
floors and oriental rugs. If you
believe the hotel's publicity, the
bizarre art selection is there to
provide shy Casanovas with
conversation openers.

CAMPO DE' FIORI

Lunetta

Piazza del Paradiso 68, 00186.
Map 4 E4 & 11 B3. 📞 686 10 80,
686 36 87. FAX 689 20 28. **Rooms**: 36.
🛏 13. 1 🔢 🔌 Ⓛ

On a tiny, crumbling piazza,
midway between Corso Vittorio
Emanuele and Piazza Campo de'
Fiori, the Lunetta is a popular,
well-maintained little hotel with
neat, clean rooms and a courtyard.
More bathrooms are gradually
being installed and a rooftop
garden is being renovated. No
breakfast is served.

Piccolo

Via dei Chiavari 32, 00186. **Map** 4 E4
& 11 C4. 📞 68 80 25 60. **Rooms**:
15. 🛏 4. 1 🔢 🔌 Y Ⓛ

Close to Piazza Campo de' Fiori,
the Piccolo is a family-run hotel at
the cheap end of its price band.
Cool and serene, with clean,
simple rooms of various sizes, it
also has a bar-breakfast room with
a television.

Campo de' Fiori

Via del Biscione 6, 00186. **Map** 4 E4
& 11 C4. 📞 68 80 08 65. FAX 687
60 03. **Rooms**: 27. 🛏 13. 🔢 🔌 🔌
🔳 MC, V. ⓁⓁ

This very good value, mid-range
hotel occupies a well-kept house,
just off the Campo de' Fiori
market square. You enter the
tiny reception area along a
passageway, in which mirrors
intriguingly repeat a series of
columns into infinity. The small
bedrooms have beams and paisley
furnishings, or sky-painted
ceilings, lacy walls and frilly
bedcovers. On the sixth floor a
split-level roof garden gives
vertiginous views over the
Pantheon, the Victor Emmanuel
monument and St Peter's.

Pomezia

Via dei Chiavari 12, 00186. **Map** 4 E4
& 12 D4. 📞 686 13 71. **Rooms**: 22.
🛏 11. 1 🔢 Y 🔳 AE, MC, V.
ⓁⓁ

In the heart of the lively Campo
de' Fiori district, the Pomezia was
renovated recently and now has
spotless, simply decorated rooms
and a bar in the reception area.

Rinascimento

Via del Pellegrino 122, 00186.
Map 4 E4 & 11 B3. 📞 687 48 13.
FAX 683 35 18. TX 62 02 07 HTLRIN.
Rooms: 19. 🛏 1 🔢 TV Y 🔋
🔌 Y 🔋 ⓁⓁ

With an appealing location in the
Campo de' Fiori district, close to
artisans' workshops and a variety
of trattorias, the Rinascimento is
housed in an old palazzo with
stone arched windows. The
bedrooms, however, tend to be
slightly worn, and have rather
cramped bathrooms.

Smeraldo

Vicolo dei Chiodaroli 11, 00186.
Map 4 F5 & 12 D4. **(** 687 59 29.
FAX 68 80 54 95. **Rooms**: 35. 18.
🔲 ▤ ♒ 🔥 Y 🍴 AE, MC, V.
Ⓛ Ⓛ

Situated in the heart of the
bustling Campo de' Fiori quarter,
the Smeraldo offers clean, simple
rooms in an ochre-washed
building with shutters.

Sole

Via del Biscione 76, 00186. **Map** 4 E4
& 11 C4. **(** 68 80 68 73, 68 80 52 58.
FAX 689 37 87. **Rooms**: 62. 31.
🔲 24 🔥 🔲 P 🔵 Ⓛ
Possibly the oldest hotel in Rome,
this appealing establishment
occupies a palazzo just off the
central market square of Campo
de' Fiori. Rooms are furnished in a
slightly haphazard way, but with
some character. There are small
sitting areas and a leafy, sunny
terrace with a drink and snack
machine. No breakfast is served.

Teatro di Pompeo

Largo del Pallaro 8, 00186. **Map** 4 E4
& 11 C4. **(** 68 30 01 70, 687 25 66.
FAX 68 80 55 31. **Rooms**: 12. 🔲
▤ TV Y 🔥 🍴 🔥 Ⓛ
P Y 🍴 AE, DC, MC, V.
Ⓛ Ⓛ Ⓛ
This small, courteously run hotel
sits over the ruins of the first
permanent theatre in the city,
which was completed in 55 BC by
Pompey the Great. You can eat
breakfast among the original
theatre arches, and the bar has a
terracotta floor and marble tables.
Rooms have beamed ceilings.

Grand

Via V. E. Orlando 3, 00185. **Map** 5 C2.
(47 09. **FAX** 474 73 07. **TX** 61 02 10.
Rooms: 171. 🔲 🔥 24 TV Y
▤ 🔥 🍴 🔥 Y 🍴 AE, DC,
MC, V, JCB. Ⓛ Ⓛ Ⓛ Ⓛ
To step into the Grand is to enter
another world. Painted cherubs
cavort on the ceiling over the
reception area; festoons of flowers
and fruit are carved on the walls
of the lounge and rich pastel rugs
lie on the parquet floor. Facilities
also include a sauna, beauty salon,
hairdresser and a restaurant
renowned as one of the most
beautiful in the country. The
standard of bedrooms varies, but
you could be lucky enough to find
yourself sleeping in an antique
bed and reading by the light of a
genuine Venetian lamp.

Cervia

Via Palestro 55, 00185. **Map** 6 E2.
(49 10 57. **FAX** 49 10 56. **Rooms**:
26. 6. 🔲 🔥 🍴 AE, V. Ⓛ
The Cervia is a 20-room hotel
housed in the same palazzo as the
Mari and the Restivo. Some of the
rooms have been refurbished with
sponge-painted walls and private
bathrooms, and these give
excellent value. The rest, however,
tend to be a bit more basic. The
public areas are immaculate, and
there is also a pleasant up-to-date
bar-breakfast room.

Gexim

Via Palestro 34, 00185. **Map** 6 E2.
(446 02 11, 444 13 11.
FAX 444 13 11. **Closed** last 2 wks in
Aug. **Rooms**: 9. 1. 🔲 🔥 🔥 Ⓛ
Don't be put off by the shabby
exterior of the palazzo – the Gexim,
which occupies part of the third
floor, is a cut above most cheap
hotels. Pastel-painted walls are
hung with prints of Impressionist
paintings and all the bedrooms,
bathrooms and public areas are
spotless. There are plans to install
more bathrooms.

Katty

Via Palestro 35, 00185. **Map** 6 E2.
(444 12 16. **Rooms**: 11. 2.
🔲 🔥 Ⓛ
The Katty has clean, basic rooms,
some of which have an occasional
piece of antique furniture. It's
extremely popular with British
and American students, so either
book in advance or turn up early,
ideally between 8am and 9am. No
breakfast is served.

Mari

Via Palestro 55, 00185. **Map** 6 E2. **(**
446 21 37. **FAX** 482 83 13. **Rooms**:
13. 🔲 🔥 🍴 MC, V. Ⓛ
This friendly hotel run by three
women has clean, pleasant rooms
with no frills. If it's full, Mari 2
nearby at Via Calatafimi 38 (tel
474 03 71) has more rooms (half
with bathrooms) and is also good
value. There is a 5% surcharge for
paying with credit cards.

Restivo

Via Palestro 55, 00185. **Map** 6 E2.
(446 21 72. **Rooms**: 6. 🔲 🔥 Ⓛ
In the same building as the Mari,
the Restivo has six immaculately
maintained bedrooms. The elderly
lady owner has a hall full of gifts
and postcards from grateful guests
who often return again and again.

Canada

Via Vicenza 58, 00185. **Map** 6 E2. **(**
445 77 70. **FAX** 445 07 49. **TX** 61 30 37
CANADA. **Rooms**: 70. 🔲 🔲 TV
Y 🔥 ▤ 🔥 🔥 🍴 P 🔥 Y 🍴
🍴 AE, DC, MC, V, JCB. Ⓛ Ⓛ
Outside the centre, behind Termini
station, the Canada is an above-
average, mid-range hotel. Rooms
are very comfortable, and there's a
pleasant lounge-bar with attractive
cane seats and squashy sofas. The
service is courteous.

Aventino

Via San Domenico 10, 00153.
Map 8 D2. **(** 574 51 74, 578 32 14,
574 35 47. **FAX** 578 36 04. **Rooms**: 23.
🔥 🔲 🔥 24 🔥 🔥 🍴 Y
🍴 AE, MC, V. Ⓛ Ⓛ
Run by the owners of Villa San Pio
and Sant'Anselmo, the Aventino is
more modest, with large but fairly
simple rooms. However, its lush,
garden location is gorgeous, and
the breakfast room, with a
magnificent armoire and stained
glass, a reminder of headier days.

Sant'Anselmo

Piazza di Sant'Anselmo 2, 00153. **Map**
8 D2. **(** 574 51 74. **FAX** 578 36 04.
TX 62 28 12 SELMO. **Rooms**: 46. 🔥
🔲 🔥 24 🔥 🔥 🔥 Y
🍴 AE, DC, MC, V. Ⓛ Ⓛ
This pretty villa, among the
gardens of the peaceful Aventine,
is within walking distance of the
Colosseum. The entrance hall
ceiling is stencilled with flowers;
there are chandeliers and corridors
with floors of inlaid marble. The
lounge looks on to the hotel's
secluded garden. Some rooms
have antique, hand-painted
furniture. Book well in advance.

Villa San Pio

Via Sant'Anselmo 19, 00153.
Map 8 E3. **(** 578 32 14, 574 35 47.
FAX 578 36 04. **TX** 62 28 12. **Rooms**:
59. 🔥 🔲 🔥 24 🔥 🔥 🔥 P
🔥 Y 🍴 AE, DC, MC, V. Ⓛ Ⓛ
The Villa San Pio occupies a
yellow and ochre villa set in a
garden graced with statues. The
elegant entrance hall is furnished
with velvet and brocade chairs, a
painted grandfather clock and an
18th-century Venetian tapestry.
While some of the rooms are
simple, others have embroidered
bedspreads and flower-stencilled
furniture; others open on to the
garden. There are two bars.
Breakfast or drinks can also be
taken in the bedrooms or garden.

Domus Aventina

Via di Santa Prisca 11B, 00153. **Map** 8 E2. **(** 574 61 35. **FAX** 57 30 00 44. *Rooms*: 26. 🛏 **1** 📺 **24** 📺 📺 🌊 ☰ 🔥 🛗 **P** ♿ **Y** 🚹 🍴 *AE, DC, MC, V.* Ⓛ Ⓛ Ⓛ

This immaculate hotel occupies a 14th-century convent situated at the foot of the Aventine hill. Rooms are large, and simply decorated in pastel tones, and there are wonderful views of the Celian hill from many of the balconies – 18 rooms have them – and from the huge terrace.

TRASTEVERE

Carmel

Via Mameli 11, 00153. **Map** 7 C2. **(** 580 99 21. *Rooms*: 10. 🛏 9. **1** 🚹 Ⓛ

The Carmel is a few notches up from the Manara, the only other Trastevere hotel. The most appealing feature is a terrace with a leafy canopy, potted plants and garden furniture. A couple of rooms open off the terrace. All ten rooms are spotless, and most have bathrooms. The owner is not keen on having children to stay and you have to book in advance as she closes the hotel when she thinks trade will be slack.

Manara

Via Manara 25, 00153. **Map** 7 C1. **(** 581 47 13. *Rooms*: 7. 🛏 1. 🚹 Ⓛ

The Manara lies just off the main market square of Trastevere. For anyone planning to spend most of their nights in the local trattorias, bars and clubs, it's a good budget choice. All the rooms are simple and extremely clean, but only one has an en suite bathroom.

VATICAN

Alimandi

Via Tunisi 8, 00192. **Map** 3 B2. **(** 39 72 39 48. **FAX** 39 72 39 43. **TX** 61 62 19. *Rooms*: 30. 🛏 24. **1** 🚹 🌊 🔥 ☰ **Y** 🍴 *AE, DC, MC, V, JCB.* Ⓛ

On a quietish street just below the entrance to the Vatican Museums, the Alimandi is a simple *pensione* at the cheap end of its price band – hence its popularity with young travellers. Rooms are clean and adequate. The outstanding feature of this guesthouse is a lovely large roof terrace, where you can arrange to sit out and have a barbecue, if you ask in advance.

Amalia

Via Germanico 66, 00192. **Map** 3 C2. **(** 39 72 33 54, 39 72 33 56. **FAX** 39 72 33 65. *Rooms*: 25. 🛏 2. **1** 📺 🔥 **Y** 🍴 *AE, MC, V.* Ⓛ Ⓛ

Situated between the Ottaviano Metro station and the Vatican, the Amalia attracts mainly Italian visitors. It has spotless rooms ranged on three floors, a lounge with a bar and a coffee machine off the reception area.

Columbus

Via della Conciliazione 33, 00193. **Map** 3 C3. **(** 686 54 35. **FAX** 686 48 74. **TX** 62 00 96. *Rooms*: 100. 🛏 **1** 🚹 **24** 📺 **Y** 🌊 ☰ 🔥 🛗 🏠 **P** 🔌 🍴 🍴 *AE, DC, MC, V.* Ⓛ Ⓛ Ⓛ

Perfect for anyone wishing to stay near the Vatican, the Columbus occupies an austere former monastery. Heavy wrought-iron light fittings hang from the vaults in the reception hall; the magnificent upper lounge has a beamed ceiling and terracotta floor; the function room – housed in the old refectory – has kept its frescoes, and there is a walled terrace garden. The bedrooms are well-equipped, though the beds are narrow.

Atlante Star

Via Vitelleschi 34, 00193. **Map** 3 C2. **(** 687 32 33. **FAX** 687 23 00. **TX** 62 23 55. *Rooms*: 70. 🛏 **1** 🚹 **24** 📺 **Y** 🌊 ☰ 🔥 🛗 🏠 **P** 🔌 **Y** 🍴 🍴 🍴 *AE, DC, MC, V.* Ⓛ Ⓛ Ⓛ

This hotel is a good option if you're in Rome on business and need on-site office facilities. The rooftop restaurant has panoramic views of St Peter's, but both service and atmosphere leave much to be desired. Double rooms are modest in size and singles can be cramped, some of them with only a shower. Avoid street-facing rooms as they can be noisy.

VIA VENETO

Merano

Via Veneto 155, 00187. **Map** 5 B2. **(** 482 17 96. **FAX** 482 18 10. *Rooms*: 32. 🛏 **1** 🚹 🔥 **Y** 🍴 *AE, DC, MC, V.* Ⓛ Ⓛ

The Merano is a small, friendly *pensione* in a 19th-century palazzo which also houses a piano bar and hairdresser. The décor is a little dated and relatively high prices, for what is essentially a guesthouse, reflect the up-market location. The hotel's best feature is its sunny, parquet-floored breakfast room.

Alexandra

Via Veneto 18, 00187. **Map** 5 B2. **(** 488 19 43, 488 19 44. **FAX** 487 18 04. **TX** 62 26 55. *Rooms*: 45. 🛏 **1** 🚹 📺 **Y** ☰ 🔥 **P** 🍴 🍴 *AE, DC, MC, V, JCB.* Ⓛ Ⓛ Ⓛ

One of the less expensive hotels on the up-market Via Veneto, the Alexandra has a pleasant conservatory-style breakfast room and a lounge decorated with chintz and brocade. All the bedrooms are different and you could just as easily end up in a room furnished with antiques as one with splash-painted walls. If you are a light sleeper ask for an internal room, as the windows do not block out all the traffic noise.

Oxford

Via Boncompagni 89, 00187. **Map** 5 C1. **(** 482 89 52. **FAX** 481 53 49. **TX** 63 03 92. *Rooms*: 58. 🛏 **1** 📺 **Y** ☰ 🔥 🛗 🏠 **P** **Y** 🚹 🍴 *AE, DC, MC, V, JCB.* Ⓛ Ⓛ Ⓛ

On a quiet road off Piazza dei Fiumi, about ten minutes' walk from Via Veneto, the Oxford has stylish public rooms: squashy sofas of shocking-pink and modern pictures in the reception area; striped sofas and abstract art in the bar. The bedrooms are more dated, with hessian-covered walls and candlewick bedspreads.

Residenza

Via Emilia 22–24, 00187. **Map** 5 B2. **(** 488 07 89. **FAX** 48 57 21. **TX** 41 04 23 GIOTEL. *Rooms*: 29. 🛏 17. **1** 🚹 📺 **Y** ☰ **Y** 🍴 *MC, V.* Ⓛ Ⓛ Ⓛ

The Residenza is an elegant hotel that occupies a villa in a quiet road off the Via Veneto. Kilim rugs decorate the spacious lounges. There is a canopied terrace arranged with pine furniture, and a terracotta-tiled roof garden, edged with potted plants. The bedrooms are less stylish than the public rooms, but are comfortable, large and well-equipped.

Barocco

Piazza Barberini 9 (entrance on Via della Purificazione 4), 00187. **Map** 5 B3. **(** 487 20 01, 487 20 02, 487 20 03, 487 20 05. **FAX** 48 59 94. *Rooms*: 28. 🛏 **1** 🚹 📺 **Y** 🌊 ☰ 🔥 🛗 🏠 🔌 **Y** 🍴 *AE, DC, MC, V, JCB.* Ⓛ Ⓛ Ⓛ

Occupying a restored palazzo at the bottom of Via Veneto, the Barocco is ideal for anyone who prefers a small hotel. Bedrooms are pleasant with unobtrusive décor, and some have a working area. There are two small lounges (one with a bar) and a restaurant.

Imperiale

Via Veneto 24, 00187. **Map** 5 B2.
C 482 63 51. **FAX** 482 63 52.
TX 62 10 71. **Rooms**: 95. 🛏 1 🖿
24 TV 💆 🍴 🛗 🔥 📺 📶 📺 🍴 🍴
🍴 🏢 AE, DC, MC, V. Ⓛ Ⓛ Ⓛ Ⓛ

One of the more reasonably priced
Via Veneto hotels, the Imperiale
lacks the panache of its more
glamorous neighbours, but the
friendly staff make for a good
relaxed atmosphere. The lounge
is more of a place to wait than to
spend an evening, but the bar is
quite pleasant and the bedrooms
are well decorated, with pretty
co-ordinating furnishings and
small marble bathrooms.

Pullman Boston

Via Lombardia 47, 00187. **Map** 5 B2.
C 47 80 21. **FAX** 482 10 19.
TX 62 22 47. **Rooms**: 124. 🛏 120. 1
🖿 TV 💆 🗡 🛗 🔥 📺 📶 📺 🍴 🍴
🍴 🏢 AE, DC, MC, V, JCB. Ⓛ Ⓛ Ⓛ Ⓛ

Overlooking the beautifully-kept
grounds of the Villas Medici and
Ludovisi, the Boston is a quiet,
old-fashioned hotel, convenient
for both the Via Veneto and the
Spanish Steps. The rooms are
decorated in pastel shades, and
some are very large. Views from
the roof terrace stretch from the
Villa Borghese right up to St
Peter's and the Vatican City.

Victoria

Via Campania 41, 00187. **Map** 5 B1.
C 47 39 31. **FAX** 487 18 90.
TX 61 02 12. **Rooms**: 120. 🛏 1
🖿 24 TV 💆 🗡 🛗 🔥 📺 📶 📺 🍴 🍴
🍴 🔥 📺 📶 🍴 🍴 🍴 🏢 AE, DC,
MC, V. Ⓛ Ⓛ Ⓛ Ⓛ

Situated on a quiet road at the top
of Via Veneto and overlooking the
walls abutting the Porta Pinciana,
the Victoria prides itself on being
a "hotel for individuals", keeping
its personal touch by refusing large
group bookings. It is renowned for
good service. There are stylish
public rooms and an attractive roof
terrace, but the bedrooms are
rather small and uninspired.

Bernini Bristol

Piazza Barberini 23, 00187. **Map** 5 B3.
C 488 30 51. **FAX** 482 42 66.
TX 61 05 54. **Rooms**: 126. 🛏 1
🖿 24 TV 💆 🗡 🛗 🔥 📺 📶 📺 🍴 🍴
🍴 📺 📶 🍴 🍴 🏢 AE, DC, MC, V, JCB.
Ⓛ Ⓛ Ⓛ Ⓛ

This unprepossessing brick
building overlooks a busy piazza
that has Bernini's Triton fountain
as its centrepiece. The marble-
laden hotel is comfortable, with
a roof garden, but the décor is
uninspiring and the atmosphere

more conducive to work than
pleasure. The central location
and secretarial facilities ensure a
steady stream of business visitors.

Excelsior

Via Veneto 125, 00187. **Map** 5 B1.
C 47 08. **FAX** 482 62 05. **TX** 61 02 32.
Rooms: 327. 🛏 1 🖿 24 TV 💆
🔥 🗡 🛗 🔥 📺 📶 📺 🍴 🍴 🍴 🍴
🏢 AE, DC, MC, V, JCB. Ⓛ Ⓛ Ⓛ Ⓛ Ⓛ

Exotically sculpted balconies
supported by statues set the tone
for this extravagant hotel, which
houses boutiques, saunas, a
restaurant and a famous piano
bar. Public rooms are sumptuous,
with marble walls and floors, rich
carpets and brocade furnishings,
and the corridors are panelled
with silk or imitation marble. The
bedrooms are elegant and spacious
with chandeliers, painted and
gilded wooden panelling and
ornate, marble bathrooms.

Majestic

Via Veneto 50, 00187. **Map** 5 B2.
C 48 68 41, 482 80 14. **FAX** 488 09 84,
488 56 57. **TX** 62 22 62. **Rooms**: 96.
🛏 1 🖿 TV 💆 🗡 🛗 🔥 📺 📶 🔥
📺 🍴 🍴 🏢 AE, DC, V.
Ⓛ Ⓛ Ⓛ Ⓛ

Founded in 1889, the Majestic is
the oldest of Via Veneto's hotels.
Since its five-year refurbishment it
has played host to international
stars such as Madonna, Luciano
Pavarotti and Sylvester Stallone.
Most of the furniture and much of
the décor in the public rooms are
original, down to the rather
startling lime-green and gilt
lounge. Bedrooms and corridors
are decorated in a bold, bright
style, particularly on the fifth floor,
where carpets with a zig-zag
pattern provide the background to
chintz and brocade.

Regina Hotel Baglioni

Via Veneto 72, 00187. **Map** 5 B2.
C 47 64 51. **FAX** 48 54 83. **TX** 62 08 63.
Rooms: 130. 🛏 1 🖿 TV 💆 🗡
🛗 🔥 🗡 🛗 🔥 📺 📶 📺 🍴 🍴 🍴
🏢 AE, DC, MC, V. Ⓛ Ⓛ Ⓛ Ⓛ Ⓛ

The exuberance of the Baglioni's
exterior – it is painted vanilla and
strawberry pink and decorated
with grimacing masks – continues
in the reception area where a
wrought-iron staircase is guarded
by the statue of a sea god. The
bedrooms are painted in vivid
shades of coral, aqua and blue,
and many are very spacious.
Double glazing in the rooms
overlooking Via Veneto cuts down
on some of the traffic noise but
light sleepers might still prefer to
ask for a room at the back of the
hotel when booking.

VILLA BORGHESE

Villa Borghese

Via Pinciana 31, 00198. **Map** 2 F5.
C 844 0105, 854 96 48.
FAX 844 26 36. **Rooms**: 31. 🛏 1
🖿 24 TV 💆 🗡 🛗 📺 📶 📺 🍴
🏢 AE, DC, MC, V, JCB. Ⓛ Ⓛ Ⓛ

This immediately likeable hotel
occupies a villa close to Villa
Borghese. Although the hotel is on
a rather busy main road, the
atmosphere is pleasant: more that
of a private home than a hotel.
Public rooms include an intimate,
old-fashioned bar, a lounge with
comfortable sofas and floral soft
furnishings, and there is a
courtyard sheltered by a pretty
ivy-covered pergola. The rooms
are on the small side but they are
tastefully decorated.

Lord Byron

Via de Notaris 5, 00197. **Map** 2 D4.
C 361 30 41. **FAX** 322 04 05.
TX 61 12 17 HBYRON. **Closed** Sun &
last 2 wks in Aug. **Rooms**: 37. 🛏 1
🖿 24 TV 💆 🗡 🛗 🔥 📺 📶 🔥
📺 🍴 🍴 🍴 🏢 AE, DC, MC, V.
Ⓛ Ⓛ Ⓛ Ⓛ

This small, refined hotel is housed
in a dazzling white building in the
residential district of Parioli. It was
originally a monastery, but there
is nothing ascetic about its rooms
today. The lounge is lavishly
furnished with antiques and
tapestry-seated chairs and the tiny
sitting room has capacious sofas
and old-fashioned portraits. The
restaurant is decorated with plenty
of chintz and fresh flowers and
serves some of the best food in
Rome. All the bedrooms have
tapestry and floral soft furnishings
with marble coffee tables and are
provided with a full decanter of
port, which comes with the
compliments of the management.

Aldrovandi Palace

Via Aldrovandi 15, 00197. **Map** 2 E4.
C 322 39 93. **FAX** 322 14 35.
TX 61 61 41 ALDROV. **Rooms**: 140.
🛏 1 🖿 TV 💆 🗡 🛗 🔥 📺 📶
🔥 🗡 📺 📶 📺 🍴 🍴 🍴 🍴
🏢 AE, DC, MC, V, JCB. Ⓛ Ⓛ Ⓛ Ⓛ Ⓛ

Among the most restful luxury
hotels in the city, the Aldrovandi is
just outside the centre of Rome on
a fairly busy road overlooking
Villa Borghese. The reception
lounge is elegant, decorated with
rich soft furnishings, carpets,
chandeliers and lots of vases of
fresh flowers. The real highlight of
the hotel, however, is the sunny
garden with its attractive
swimming pool with is overlooked by an airy restaurant.

For key to symbols see p291

RESTAURANTS AND CAFÉS

IN ROME, eating out can be both a joy and an entertainment. On warm summer evenings tables flow out into every conceivable open space and diners dedicate long hours to the popular social activity of people watching (and of being noticed and admired themselves) in a confusion of passers-by, buskers, rose sellers and traffic. Although Romans have always loved to linger at the table, the lavish feasts of ancient Rome have slimmed down and today's cooking is based on simplicity, freshness and good quality local raw ingredients in

Waiter at
Alberto Ciarla
(see p316)

what is essentially a seasonal cuisine. Fast food is gradually arriving, but it is fundamentally alien to the Roman temperament and way of life.

The 66 restaurants reviewed in this chapter have been selected from the best that Rome can offer across all price ranges. The chart on pages 310–11 will help narrow down your selection, and the map on page 308 shows the highlights of the list. The section on *Light Meals and Snacks* featured on pages 318–21 has details of recommended cafés, pizzerias, wine bars and other places for more casual eating.

WHERE TO FIND GOOD RESTAURANTS

EVERY AREA of the city has its own culinary delights. True Roman cooking can be found in the old slaughter-house area of Testaccio and in the Jewish quarter (the Ghetto) near Campo de' Fiori. Around the university, in San Lorenzo, northeast of the city centre, you will find lots of cheap pizzerias and trattorias.

Near Termini station there's a good selection of African – particularly Ethiopian and Eritrean – restaurants. For dining outdoors, which often means in beautifully secluded piazzas, or in impressively ancient parts of the city, try the restaurants in the narrow streets of Trastevere (the old

The interior of Relais le Jardin *(see p317)*

artists' quarter), around Campo de' Fiori, or along the old Via Appia Antica.

TYPES OF RESTAURANTS

IN GENERAL, a *trattoria* is an unassuming, family-run establishment with good home cooking, while a *ristorante* is more up-market, more elegant and thus more expensive.

Many eating places – where paper tablecloths give a clue to low prices – simply have no name. They offer an open doorway and, more often than not, excellent, basic home cooking. Some of them offer a great deal more than that, and your chances of finding authentic Roman cooking are higher in the best of these establishments than in expensive restaurants.

There will probably be times when you don't want a full-blown restaurant meal, and Rome offers a huge variety of places for more casual eating *(see pp318–21)*. One type of place offering snacks or more

Fresh artichokes, a Roman speciality

substantial dishes is the *enoteca,* which doubles as a well-stocked wine shop for browsers and connoisseurs.

The sign *vino e cucina* (wine and food), sadly fast disappearing, holds the same promise. Other places for a sit-down, informal lunch or dinner are *birrerie,* which are not only for beer drinkers, but which also offer pizzas or even four-course meals.

There's plenty of interesting takeaway food on sale throughout the day – *pizza al taglio* (pizza by the slice) is available all over the city. For full-size pizzas, choose places with wood stoves *(forno a legna)* for better results than from electric ovens. Other takeaways such as whole roast chicken, potatoes or *suppli* (fried rice croquettes) can be had from *rosticcerie.* A self-service *tavola calda* will serve an impressive array of hot food and is ideal for lunchtimes.

VEGETARIAN FOOD

PURELY VEGETARIAN restaurants are largely unknown in Rome, but everywhere you'll find pasta or rice dishes (risotto) using interesting combinations of vegetables, salads, artichokes cooked in different ways, or vegetables stuffed and then baked in the oven. Most menus are very adaptable.

THE PRICE OF A MEAL

WHAT YOU PAY will clearly depend on your choice of establishment. In a *tavola calda* or Roman pizzeria, for example, you can often eat for as little as L15,000 a head. A local trattoria costs perhaps L25,000, whereas in a full-blown restaurant reckon on around L50,000 and up. Bottled wine, as opposed to a jug or carafe of house wine (*vino della casa*), commands higher prices but should offer a more interesting range of tastes (*see p306*). House wine is usually acceptable, though.

READING THE MENU

NOT EVERY restaurant automatically provides a menu – the waiter will often tell you the day's specialities (*piatti del giorno*), usually not mentioned on the standard menu but almost always worth ordering. If you are not sure about these, you can always ask for *la lista* (the menu) and then allow yourself to be guided.

A meal could begin with *antipasti* (appetizers) or *primi piatti* – the latter consisting of *pasta asciutta* (pasta with some kind of sauce), *pasta in brodo* (clear broth with pasta in it), *pasta al forno* (baked pasta), risotto or a substantial soup. You then move on to the *secondi*, the main meat or fish course, for which you'll need to order vegetables (*contorni*) separately if you would like them. Afterwards you have *formaggi* (cheeses), *frutta* (fruit) or *dolci* (desserts). Romans don't usually eat

One of many Trastevere cafés

Outdoor café life in the piazza outside Santa Maria in Trastevere

cheese as well as a sweet dish, but cheese often comes with fruit such as pears, figs or melon. Strong espresso coffee, and perhaps a liqueur (*amaro* or *digestivo*) rounds off the meal (*see p306*). You may want to skip the first course, or you may prefer to choose a salad or vegetable dish. Pasta alone tends not to be seen as a full meal.

OPENING TIMES

RESTAURANTS are generally open from about noon to 3pm and from 8pm to 11pm or much later. The busiest times tend to be 9pm–9.30pm for dinner and 1pm–1.30pm at lunchtime. Dinner is generally the preferred time for dedicated, relaxed eating, particularly in summer, when it will begin and end late as the heat of the day subsides. Bars are open all day, often from the early hours, serving all kinds of drinks (alcohol can be sold at any time of day) and snacks. The quietest month is August, when many restaurant owners take their annual holiday (shown by *chiuso per ferie* signs).

BOOKING A TABLE

BOOKING (*prenotazione*) is generally advisable. Sunday is the main lunch date of the week when you should definitely book; the same usually goes for Saturday evening. Check the weekly closing day if you don't book. Many places are closed on Mondays, and Sunday evening can also be difficult.

In summer try to book a shady table outside, since air conditioning is not universal.

WHEELCHAIR ACCESS

ROME is becoming more solicitous towards those in wheelchairs, but a call to the restaurant in advance will help secure the right table.

TAKING CHILDREN ALONG

CHILDREN are made very welcome, particularly in family-run places. You can usually order half-portions (but expect to pay more than half), or just ask for an extra plate. High chairs (*seggioline*) may also be available in some of the establishments.

USING THE LISTINGS
Key to symbols in the listings on pp312–17.

|O| fixed price menus
🚭 non-smoking area
V vegetarian dishes
fï child portions and sometimes high chairs
& wheelchair access
T jacket and tie required
🎵 live music
🏠 tables outside
P exceptional wine list
★ highly recommended
💳 credit cards accepted
AE American Express
DC Diners Club
MC Mastercard/Access
V Visa
JCB Japanese Credit Bureau

Price categories for a three-course meal for one, including a half bottle of house wine, cover charge, tax and service:
Ⓛ up to L35,000
ⓁⓁ L35,000–L55,000
ⓁⓁⓁ L55,000–L75,000
ⓁⓁⓁⓁ L75,000–L100,000
ⓁⓁⓁⓁⓁ over L100,000

What to Eat in Rome

**Bulb of
fresh garlic**

THE TRADITIONAL *cucina romanesca* has always relied on local markets full of fresh seasonal vegetables, fruit, cheese and meat from the nearby countryside plus seafood from the Mediterranean. As in the rest of Italy, pasta is an important part of the menu; one popular dish is the famous *spaghetti alla carbonara,* which was devised in Rome. Many genuinely Roman meat dishes are based on the so-called *quinto quarto* (fifth quarter) – head, innards, tail, trotters and so on. Highly flavoured with olive oil, herbs, lard, bacon *(pancetta)* or pig's cheek *(guanciale)* they become a culinary delight. Fish from the Mediterranean is excellent. In season, mushrooms and artichokes may be served in dozens of different ways. *Misticanza* is also good in season; it's a fresh mix of salad leaves including the peppery *rughetta* (rocket) and *puntarelle* (curly endive shoots, often served with anchovy dressing). For dessert you should not miss out on ice cream, or puddings like the classic *tiramisù.*

Maritozzi alla Panna
*These soft buns with raisins
and candied peel are filled
with whipped cream.*

Bruschetta
*Toasted bread is rubbed
with garlic and olive oil;
tomato can be added.*

Fresh basil

Anchovies

**Artichoke
hearts**

Roasted peppers

**Baby
octopus**

Antipasto
*Italian appetizers may include
olives, cured meats, seafood and
grilled or preserved vegetables.*

Suppli
*Fried rice croquettes are
stuffed with mozzarella
and make a tasty snack.*

**Olive Oil
and Vinegar**
*Always on the
table, these are
for dressing
salads and
flavouring
antipasto.*

Filetti di Baccalà
*A Jewish speciality, deep-
fried cod fillets are a typical
Roman snack or first course.*

Risotto alla Romana
*Liver, sweetbreads, Marsala
and pecorino cheese are
used to make this risotto.*

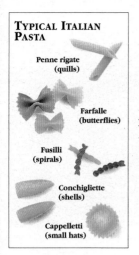

TYPICAL ITALIAN PASTA

Penne rigate (quills)

Farfalle (butterflies)

Fusilli (spirals)

Conchigliette (shells)

Cappelletti (small hats)

Bucatini all'Amatriciana
Pasta tubes are served with bacon, tomatoes and onion, with grated pecorino on top.

Spaghetti alla Carbonara
Chopped bacon, eggs and cheese are used to prepare this famous local dish.

Gnocchi alla Romana
Small potato or semolina dumplings are served with tomato or just with butter.

Fiori di Zucca e Carciofi Fritti
Courgette flowers in batter and whole artichokes deep-fried are popular antipasti.

Coda alla Vaccinara
A traditional Roman dish, this is made from braised oxtail with tomatoes.

Parmesan

Saltimbocca alla Romana
Veal with Parma ham and sage, this tasty dish is also served rolled and skewered.

Fave al Guanciale
Fresh springtime broad beans are simmered with bacon and onion.

Crostata di Ricotta
This Roman cheesecake is filled with ricotta, Marsala and lemon.

Italian Cheeses
Parmesan is the best-known Italian cheese but Rome's classic is pecorino romano, made from ewe's milk. The mature, hard version is often used grated, but fresh pecorino can be eaten as a dessert cheese. Mild buffalo-milk mozzarella is the classic one for pizza.

Mozzarella

Tiramisù
Mascarpone cheese, coffee and chocolate are combined for this wonderful dessert.

What to Drink in Rome

Roman mosaic showing bird and vines

ITALY IS ONE OF Europe's most significant wine-producing countries, keeping up a tradition started in the hills around Rome over 2,000 years ago. Today, wine is usually drunk with meals as a matter of course, and knowing the difference between *rosso* (red) and *bianco* (white) may be all the vocabulary you need to get by. Beer is widely available too, as well as good ranges of apéritifs and digestifs. Rome's drinking water, another debt to the ancient Romans, is particularly good, fresh and sweet, and in abundant supply.

The vineyards of Frascati, southeast of Rome

WHITE WINE

Orvieto   **Frascati**

VINES THRIVE in the warm climate of Lazio, the region around Rome, producing abundant supplies of inexpensive dry white wine for the city's cafés and restaurants. It is usually sold by the carafe. Of local bottled wines, Frascati is the best-known, but Castelli Romani, Marino, Colli Albani and Velletri are very similar in style. All are made from one grape variety, the Trebbiano, though better quality versions contain a dash of Malvasia for perfume and flavour. Other central Italian whites worth trying are Orvieto and Verdicchio. Quality white wines from all over Italy, including fine whites from Friuli in the northeast, are widely available in Rome.

Calcaia comes from Barberani, a reliable producer of Orvieto.

Bigi produce good quality Orvieto, especially the single-vineyard Torricella.

Casal Pilozzo is an easy-drinking white wine from Frascati producers, Colli di Catone. Choose the youngest vintage.

Colle Gaio, with its rich, fruity flavour, stands out among the dry white Frascatis.

WINE TYPE	GOOD VINTAGES	GOOD PRODUCERS
WHITE WINE		
Friuli (Pinot Bianco, Chardonnay, Pinot Grigio, Sauvignon)	The most recent	Gravner, Jermann, Puiatti, Schiopetto, Volpe Pasini
Orvieto/ Orvieto Classico	The most recent	Antinori, Barberani, Bigi, Il Palazzone
RED WINE		
Chianti/ Chianti Classico/ Chianti Rufina	90, 88, 85	Antinori, Castello di Ama, Castello di Cacchiano, Castello di Volpaia, Felsina Berardenga, Fontodi, Frescobaldi, Isole e Olena, Il Palazzino, Riecine, Rocca delle Macie, Ruffino, Vecchie Terre di Montefili, Villa Cafaggio
Brunello di Montalcino/ Vino Nobile di Montepulciano	90, 88, 85	Altesino, Avignonesi, Biondi Santi, Caparzo, Case Basse, Lisini, Il Poggione, Poliziano, Villa Banfi
Barolo/ Barbaresco	90, 89, 88, 85, 82, 78	Aldo Conterno, Altare, Ceretto, Clerico, Gaja, Giacomo Conterno, Giacosa, Mascarello, Ratti, Voerzio

Tuscan table wine   Barolo

RED WINE

THOUGH SOME local red wine is made, most of the bottled red wine in Rome comes from other parts of Italy. Regions like Tuscany and Piedmont produce very good everyday drinking as well as top-class wines like Barolo. Price should reflect quality – try Dolcetto, Rosso di Montalcino or Montepulciano for good value reds.

Montepulciano d'Abruzzo, a rich and juicy red wine, is always good value. It is produced in the Abruzzi region east of Rome.

Torre Ercolana is produced in small quantities and is generally regarded as one of Lazio's best red wines. It is made from Cesanese and Cabernet grapes and requires at least five years' ageing.

Chianti Classico Riserva is older and stronger than a normal Chianti Classico.

READING THE LABEL

ITALY has a two-tier system for labelling quality wine. DOC *(denominazione di origine controllata)* means you can be sure the wine is from the region declared on the label and is made from designated grape varieties. A higher classification – DOCG *(denominazione di origine controllata e garantita)* – is given to top wines such as the reds Barolo, Barbaresco, Chianti Classico and Brunello di Montalcino.

Chianti Classico

APÉRITIFS AND OTHER DRINKS

BITTER, herb-flavoured drinks like Martini, Campari or Aperol are the most popular apéritifs. (Ask for an *analcolico* if you prefer a non-alcoholic one.) Italians drink their apéritifs neat or with ice and soda. Strong, herby after-dinner drinks, known as *digestivi* or *amari*, are worth trying if you need to settle your stomach. Italian brandy and grappa can be very fiery. Italian beer, popular with pizza, is made in lager style.

Campari

SOFT DRINKS

ITALIAN FRUIT juices are good and most bars squeeze fresh orange juice *(spremuta)* on the spot. Iced tea and coffee are refreshing in summer, and fruit-flavoured tea, such as peach, is very popular.

Refrigerated storage for wine and beer

DRINKING WATER

Unlike many Mediterranean cities, Rome benefits from a constant supply of fresh drinking water, piped down from the hills through a system of pipes and aqueducts which has changed little from ancient Roman times. Only if there is a sign saying *acqua non potabile* is the water not safe to drink.

One of Rome's many fresh water drinking fountains

Coffee is almost more important to Roman life than wine. Take espresso for neat strong black coffee at any time of day, milky cappuccino for breakfast or mid-afternoon, caffelatte for extra milk.

Espresso   **Cappuccino**    **Caffelatte**

Rome's Best: Restaurants and Cafés

ROME IS NOT particularly known for luxury restaurants, but more for atmospheric places where the focus is on the social side of dining and on regional cooking. An amazing variety can be found. Many places specialize, often priding themselves on being the best of their kind – whether they offer superb espresso, or traditional foods like deep-fried salted cod *(baccalà)*. Other restaurants can offer especially beautiful settings or are known as the best places to see and be seen. The selection here shows some of the many highlights of a city where eating is taken very seriously.

Caffè Giolitti
This historic ice cream shop serves a variety of flavours, to eat in or take away. (See p320.)

Romolo nel Giardino della Fornarina
For romantic Roman eating, Romolo is best in the summer, with its walled garden, candlelit tables and guitar music.
(See p316.)

Vatican

Piazza Navona

Campo de' Fiori

Janiculum

Il Delfino
This snack bar at Largo Argentina sells everything from whole chickens on the spit, to salads, sandwiches and supplì *(rice croquettes): a feast for the eye.*
(See p320.)

Trastevere

Filetti di Baccalà
This small, crowded place serves tasty fried fillets of cod – one of Rome's most traditional dishes – and offers a truly Roman experience. (See p320.)

Piperno
For over a century, traditional Roman Jewish cooking has been the speciality of Piperno, in the heart of the Jewish Ghetto. (See p314.)

Babington's Tea Rooms
This old-fashioned, genteel establishment at the foot of the Spanish Steps serves English tea and cakes. (See p320.)

Caffè Greco
Famous as the haunt of writers, artists and intellectuals in the 19th century, this café still retains the faded grandeur shown in this painting. (See p320.)

Tazza d'Oro
This figure graces the wall on the outside of Tazza d'Oro, where you will find some of the best coffee in Rome – its espresso is rated highly by connoisseurs. (See p320.)

azza di pagna

Via Veneto

della nda

Quirinal

Capitol

Esquiline

Forum

Palatine

Lateran

Aventine

Caracalla

| 0 metres | 500 |
| 0 yards | 500 |

Sora Lella
This Roman trattoria is famous for its setting on the Isola Tiberina and for the fashionable crowd which it attracts. (See p314.)

Vecchia Roma
Summer is the best time to eat here and make the most of the quiet and pretty Baroque piazza. (See p314.)

Choosing a Restaurant

THE RESTAURANTS in this guide have been selected for their good value or exceptional food. This chart highlights some of the factors which may influence your choice. Entries are alphabetical within price category. For more details on the restaurants, see pages 312–17. Information on cafés and wine bars is on pages 318–21.

	Fixed Price Menu	Vegetarian Dishes	Tables Outside	Seafood Specialities	Late Opening	Air Conditioning	Attractive Setting
PIAZZA DELLA ROTONDA (see p312)							
Da Gino ℒ							
Il Buco ℒℒ	●		●		●	■	
Girone VI ℒℒℒ		■	●	■	●	■	●
Chez Albert ℒℒℒℒ	●				●	■	
La Rosetta ★ ℒℒℒℒℒ	●			■		■	
El Toulà ℒℒℒℒℒ	●	■		■		■	
PIAZZA NAVONA (see p312)							
La Taverna ℒℒ	●		●			■	●
Nel Regno del Re Ferdinando ℒℒℒ		■		■	●	■	
Il Convivio ★ ℒℒℒℒ	●			■		■	
Osteria dell'Antiquario ℒℒℒℒ	●		●			■	●
Papà Giovanni ℒℒℒℒ		■				■	
PIAZZA DI SPAGNA (see p313)							
Birreria Viennese ℒ	●				●	■	
Fiaschetteria Beltramme ℒ			■				
Mario alle Vite ℒ						■	
Al 34 ℒℒ		■		■		■	
Porto di Ripetta ℒℒℒ	●			■	●	■	
Sogo-Asahi ℒℒℒℒ	●			■		■	
Hassler Roof Restaurant ℒℒℒℒℒ	●					■	●
CAMPO DE' FIORI (see p313)							
Mekong ℒ	●	■				■	
Le Maschere ℒℒ	●	■	●		●	■	
Al Pompiere ℒℒ					●		
Taverna Giulia ℒℒ			●		●		
Il Cardinale ℒℒℒ		■		■		■	
Il Drappo ℒℒℒ	●		●		●	■	
Piperno ℒℒℒ			●	■			
Sora Lella ℒℒℒ						■	
Vecchia Roma ℒℒℒ		■	●	■		■	●
Camponeschi ℒℒℒℒℒ			●	■	●		●
Da Patrizia e Roberto del Pianeta Terra ★ ℒℒℒℒℒ	●			■		■	
QUIRINAL (see p314)							
Colline Emiliane ℒℒ						■	
Al Moro ℒℒℒ				■		■	
Il Posto Accanto ℒℒℒ		■		■		■	
Quadrifoglio ℒℒℒℒ					●	■	
TERMINI (see p314)							
Gemma alla Lupa ℒ	●	■	●			■	
Coriolano ℒℒℒℒℒ		■		■		■	

Price categories for a three-course meal for one, half a bottle of house wine, and all unavoidable extra charges such as cover, service, tax:
Ⓛ up to L35,000
ⓁⓁ L35–55,000
ⓁⓁⓁ L55–75,000
ⓁⓁⓁⓁ L75–100,000
ⓁⓁⓁⓁⓁ over L100,000.
★ Means highly recommended.

FIXED PRICE MENU
Restaurant offering *menu turistico* (tourist menu): usually three or four courses without wine or coffee, for a set price.

VEGETARIAN DISHES
Restaurant with a good selection of vegetarian dishes.

LATE OPENING
Last orders on or after 11.30pm.

ATTRACTIVE SETTING
Restaurant set in a pretty piazza or with a garden terrace, or with a lovely view.

	Price	FIXED PRICE MENU	VEGETARIAN DISHES	TABLES OUTSIDE	SEAFOOD SPECIALITIES	LATE OPENING	AIR CONDITIONING	ATTRACTIVE SETTING
ESQUILINE (see p315)								
Cicilardone	ⓁⓁ							
La Tana del Grillo	ⓁⓁ							
Trattoria Monti	ⓁⓁ	●	■					
Agata e Romeo	ⓁⓁⓁⓁ	●	■	●			●	■
LATERAN (see p315)								
Alfredo a Via Gabi	ⓁⓁ				●		■	
Cannavota	ⓁⓁⓁ	●			■		■	
Charly's Saucière	ⓁⓁⓁ					●	■	
AVENTINE (see p315)								
Perilli a Testaccio	ⓁⓁ						■	
Checchino dal 1887 ★	ⓁⓁⓁ				●			
TRASTEVERE (see p316)								
Da Lucia	Ⓛ			●				
Da Paris	ⓁⓁ			●	■			●
Romolo nel Giardino della Fornarina	ⓁⓁ	●		●		●	■	
La Taverna di Bambù	ⓁⓁ		■			●	■	
La Cornucopia	ⓁⓁⓁ	●		●	■	●	■	●
Peccati di Gola	ⓁⓁⓁ			●	■			
Cul De Sac 2 ★	ⓁⓁⓁⓁ				■		■	
Tentativo ★	ⓁⓁⓁⓁ	●				●	■	
Alberto Ciarla ★	ⓁⓁⓁⓁⓁ	●		●	■	●	■	
JANICULUM (see p316)								
Al Tocco	ⓁⓁⓁ	●	■		■	●	■	
VATICAN (see p316)								
Tavola d'Oro	Ⓛ		■		■			
San Luigi	ⓁⓁⓁ	●	■				■	
VIA VENETO (see p317)								
Cantina Cantarini	Ⓛ			●	■	●		
Giovanni	ⓁⓁⓁ	●			■		■	
Tullio	ⓁⓁⓁ				■		■	
Andrea	ⓁⓁⓁⓁ				■		■	
San Benedetto	ⓁⓁⓁⓁ	●			■		■	
George's ★	ⓁⓁⓁⓁⓁ		■	●		●	■	●
Le Sans Souci ★	ⓁⓁⓁⓁⓁ		■			●	■	
VILLA BORGHESE (see p317)								
Al Ceppo	ⓁⓁⓁ		■	●	■		■	
Relais la Piscine ★	ⓁⓁⓁⓁⓁ	●		●	■		■	●
Relais le Jardin ★	ⓁⓁⓁⓁⓁ	●			■		■	

PIAZZA DELLA ROTONDA

Da Gino

Vicolo Rosini 4 (Piazza del Parlamento). **Map** 4 F3 & 12 D1.
(687 34 34. **Open** 12.45pm–2.45pm, 8pm–10.45pm Mon–Sat.
Closed Aug. & (L)

Journalists, politicians and the initiated scramble for a seat under the kitsch, frescoed pergola of this ancient, ultra-Roman trattoria to feast upon traditional daily dishes: *gnocchi* and *osso buco* (Thursdays), *baccalà* (Fridays), tripe (Saturdays), plus classic sturdy soups, dutifully executed Roman standards and delectable homemade *tiramisù*.

Il Buco

Via di Sant'Ignazio 8. **Map** 4 F4 & 12 E3. **(** 678 32 98, 678 44 67.
Open 12.30pm–4pm, 6.30pm–midnight Tue–Sun. **Closed** 10 Aug–1 Sep. |♥| ⩙ & ▦ ⌑ AE, DC, MC, V. (L)(L)

Much has happened since the tiny *buco* (hole) opened in 1891 – the small osteria has become a large restaurant, yet the calm atmosphere, unfailing courtesy and formidable Tuscan menu remain. From the traditional *crostini* (liver pâté canapés), robust *ribollita* (thick vegetable soup) and huge Florentine steaks, to the final *tozzetti* (almond biscuits) with vin santo (dessert wine), this is a truly Tuscan experience.

Girone VI

Vicolo Sinibaldi 2. **Map** 4 F4 & 12 D3. **(** 68 80 28 31. **Open** 8pm–midnight Mon–Sat. **Closed** 20 Dec–10 Jan.
▣ ▦ ⌑ AE, DC, MC, V, JCB. (L)(L)

Visit this small, family-run Ligurian restaurant in summer, when tables line the secluded arched street. Everything shows extreme care – including the impeccable service. An imaginative combination of herbs and vegetables characterizes the menu: risotto with courgette flowers, *porcini* mushroom crêpes, stuffed truffled rabbit and lots of fresh fish. There's a good selection of French and regional wines.

Chez Albert

Vicolo della Vaccarella 11. **Map** 4 F3 & 12 D2. **(** 686 55 49. **Open** 7pm–1am Mon–Sat. **Closed** Aug. |♥| &
⌑ AE, DC, MC, V. (L)(L)(L)(L)

In this small, intimate and elegant bistro, Albert and his family conjure up dishes from their native Provence and other regions *(bouillabaisse, cassoulet, coq au vin)*, together with equally delicious classic Mediterranean standards *(couscous, paella)*. Try the light, fragrant desserts and excellent French and Italian wines.

La Rosetta

Via della Rosetta 9. **Map** 4 F4 & 12 D2. **(** 68 30 88 41. **Open** 1pm–3pm, 8pm–11.30pm Mon–Sat.
Closed 3 wks Aug, Christmas. |♥| & ⩙ ★ ⌑ AE, DC, V.
(L)(L)(L)(L)

Despite the exorbitant prices, people flock nightly (having booked in advance) for a seat in the elegant, tightly-packed rooms. Fresh fish and seafood arrive daily from Sicily and, cooked in the simplest ways, achieve culinary perfection. Enthusiastic waiters and quality French and Italian wines, particularly the Sicilian whites, do justice to the cuisine.

El Toulà

Via della Lupa 29B. **Map** 4 F3 & 12 D1. **(** 687 34 98. **Open** 1pm–3pm, 8pm–11pm Mon–Fri, 8pm–11pm Sat.
Closed Aug, Christmas. ▣ ▥ ▥
⩙ ⌑ AE, DC, MC, V. (L)(L)(L)(L)(L)

El Toulà is justly renowned as one of the most exclusive, traditional and luxurious restaurants in Rome. The Venetian-inspired cooking is serious and professional, with forays into the realms of the best classic international cuisine. In dignified, sober surroundings the service is exemplary and the selection of wines superb.

PIAZZA NAVONA

La Taverna

Via del Banco di Santo Spirito 58. **Map** 4 D3 & 11 A2. **(** 686 41 16.
Open noon–3pm, 7pm–11pm Tue–Sun. |♥| & ▤ ▥ ⌑ AE, DC, MC, V, JCB. (L)(L)

Tourists and local residents mingle in Giovanni's crowded Roman trattoria to enjoy the family atmosphere and traditional regional cooking. Particularly appreciated are the *rigatoni all'amatriciana, coda alla vaccinara* and, on Thursday, Friday and Saturday respectively, *gnocchi, baccalà* and tripe.

Nel Regno del Re Ferdinando

Via dei Banchi Nuovi 8. **Map** 4 D4 & 11 B2. **(** 68 80 11 67. **Open** 8pm–1am Mon–Sat. **Closed** Aug. ⩙ ▣
⌑ AE, MC, V. (L)(L)(L)

Reminiscent of a classic 19th-century taverna, Re Ferdinando is a rare representative in Rome of the southern Campania region. Delights include some colourful vegetable and fish antipasto, and *maccheroni*. Another speciality is *sartù di riso* (a savoury rice mould covered in tomato sauce, cheese and breadcrumbs and baked in the oven). The Neapolitan desserts are delicious. There is a separate non-smoking room. Good regional wines include many from Ischia.

Il Convivio

Via dell'Orso 44. **Map** 4 E3 & 11 C2. **(** 686 94 32. **Open** 1pm–2.30pm, 8pm–11pm Mon–Sat. **Closed** May.
|♥| ▣ ▣ ⩙ ★ ⌑ AE, DC, MC, V.
(L)(L)(L)(L)

An air of sophisticated tranquillity pervades this intimate restaurant, one of the very best specializing in modern creative cookery. Its young chef, one of the three brother-owners from the Marches, creates both subtle and unusual combinations of flavours, and the highly personalized menu evolves with the seasons. The wine list is extensive and service is discreet.

Osteria dell'Antiquario

Piazzetta San Simeone 27. **Map** 4 E3 & 11 B2. **(** 687 96 94. **Open** 12.30pm–2.30pm, 8pm–11.30pm Mon–Sat. **Closed** 15 Aug, 20 Dec–7 Jan. |♥| ▦ ▣ ⌑ AE, DC.
(L)(L)(L)

In the comfort of the elegantly restructured rooms of an old antique shop, Giorgio Nisti offers an unusual menu dictated by the whims of the chef and the daily market, with traditional dishes creatively adapted to contemporary health-conscious tastes. There is an impressive choice of regional, French and Californian wines.

Papà Giovanni

Via dei Sediari 4. **Map** 4 F4 & 12 D3.
(686 53 08. **Open** 1pm–2.30pm, 8pm–11pm Mon–Sat. **Closed** Aug, Dec. ⩙ ▣ ▣ ⌑ MC, V.
(L)(L)(L)

Nearly 60 years have passed since Papà Giovanni first sold his country wines in Rome; the bottles lining the walls are testimony to the past and to the superb cellar of Giovanni's son, Renato Sentuti. Here diners sample the best of the new lighter Roman cuisine. Classics such as *cacio e pepe*, salt cod and tripe live alongside exotic salads and truffled dishes. Desserts include ricotta soufflé with strawberry sauce, hot chocolate profiteroles and exquisite sorbets.

PIAZZA DI SPAGNA

Birreria Viennese

Via della Croce 21. **Map** 5 A2.
679 55 69. Open 11.30am–
midnight Thu–Tue. **Closed** 15 Jul–15
Aug. 🍴 🚻 🕭 AE, DC, MC, V,
JCB. ⓛ

The stained-glass entrance leads to
a long, crowded room where, for
more than 60 years, traditional
beers and Austrian specialities
have been sampled. Try sausages,
goulash, *Wienerschnitzel*,
sauerkraut, or the massive *piatto
di legno della Transilvania*
(wooden platter heaped with
delights, for two). Wine is
available, and the service is
extremely helpful and courteous.

Fiaschetteria Beltramme

Via della Croce 39. **Map** 4 F2. **Open**
12.10pm–3pm, 7.45pm–10.30pm
Mon–Sat. **Closed** 2 wks Aug. 🕭 ⓛ

This small Roman trattoria bears
witness to its glorious past; signed
photos and paintings line the long
walls, and the crowded tables
make sharing – and new
friendships – inevitable. The family
atmosphere is enhanced by
traditional basic fare – *pasta e ceci,
minestra di fagioli*, fresh fish and
typical meat dishes. Efficient,
speedy service means this is not a
place for lingering over dinner.

Mario alla Vite

Via della Vite 55. **Map** 5 A3 & 12 E1.
678 38 18. Open 12.30pm–3pm,
7.30pm–11pm Mon–Sat. **Closed**
Aug. 🕭 AE, DC, MC, V, JCB. ⓛ

Despite an exclusive address,
Mario has kept prices reasonable,
and his food is still simple, honest
Tuscan fare. Elbow-to-elbow
dining, haphazard service and
noisy confusion seem inevitable.
Nevertheless, the food is worth it –
traditional *fagioli al fiasco*
(cannellini beans in oil), *ribollita*
(thick vegetable soup), Florentine
steaks and delicious pastries are
the attractions, along with a wide
selection of wines.

Al 34

Via Mario de' Fiori 34. **Map** 5 A2.
679 50 91. Open noon–3pm,
7.30pm–11pm Tue–Sun. **Closed** Aug
🔲 🕭 🕭 AE, DC, MC, V, JCB. ⓛⓛ

For a comfortable chat or a
romantic *tête-à-tête*, Al 34 provides
the perfect setting. Predominantly
featuring southern Italian cooking,
the extensive menu offers an
esoteric choice, particularly where
vegetables and herbs are allied

with pasta, meat and fish. Given
the atmosphere and its location,
the prices are affordable.

Porto di Ripetta

Via di Ripetta 250. **Map** 4 F2.
361 23 76. Open 1pm–3pm,
8pm–midnight Mon–Sat. **Closed**
Aug. 🍴 🔲 🕭 AE, DC, MC,
V. ⓛⓛⓛ

The fame of this restaurant
depends largely on the genius of
chef Maria Romani. With the fish
that arrives daily from her native
Marches she creates inspired
combinations such as fish and
broad bean soup or giant prawns
with artichokes. It is expensive,
but worth it; the business lunch
menu is much cheaper. There's a
selection of excellent wines.

Sogo-Asahi

Via di Propaganda 22. **Map** 5 A2.
678 60 93. Open noon–3pm,
7.30pm–11.30pm Mon–Sat. 🍴 🕭
🕭 AE, DC, MC, V, JCB. ⓛⓛⓛⓛ

This luxury, top-quality restaurant
is a find for lovers of Japanese
cooking. Traditional Japanese
specialities are elegantly served by
helpful and knowledgeable
waiters: *sashimi* (raw fish) and
melt-in-the-mouth tempura are
accompanied by saké, Japanese
beer or a good Italian wine. The
special set menus are particularly
inexpensive at lunchtime. Sogo-
Asahi opens in August, when most
of Rome's restaurants are closed.

Hassler Roof Restaurant

Piazza Trinità dei Monti 6. **Map** 5 A2.
678 26 51. Open 7.30am–
11.30am, noon–3.30pm, 7.30pm–
10pm Mon–Sat. 7.30am–11.30am,
noon–3.30pm Sun. 🍴 🔲 for
dinner. 🎵 🔲 🕭 AE, MC, V, JCB.
ⓛⓛⓛⓛ

Perched on the sixth floor of the
Hotel Hassler, overlooking the
Spanish Steps, the roof restaurant
commands a breathtaking view of
Rome. Come for the gargantuan
and pricy Sunday brunch. The
wine list is excellent and the
hovering waiter service timely
and discreet. In the evening,
when prices are higher, there's
piano music.

CAMPO DE' FIORI

Mekong

Corso Vittorio Emanuele II 333.
Map 4 E4 & 11 C3. **686 16 84.
Open** noon–3pm, 7pm–11pm Wed–
Mon. 🍴 🔲 🕭 AE, MC, V. ⓛ

This cheerful Vietnamese
restaurant offers a respectable
alternative to Italian food. Eat by
candlelight in a relaxed atmosphere and try the wide selection of
relatively inexpensive dishes. A
waiter patiently explains the menu
for first-timers; recommended are
the fried ravioli starters, chicken in
foil *(pollo d'argento)* and the *tre
delizie* (three delights – beef,
chicken and prawns in a special
sauce). There are also reasonable
Italian wines, tea, ginseng liqueur
and a selection of grappas.

Le Maschere

Via Monte della Farina 29.
Map 4 F5 & 12 D4. **687 94 44.
Open** 7pm–midnight Tue–Sun.
Closed Aug. 🍴 🔲 🕭 🕭 🎵 🔲
🕭 AE, DC, MC, V, JCB. ⓛⓛ

There is an agreeable sensation of
being in the country as you cross
the spacious tiled hall and descend
to the rustic indoor terrace with its
high reed-lined ceiling, a roofed
grill and eerily-lit wall masks.
Candles on the tables, and a
subdued conversational hum, lull
you in preparation for the fiery
Calabrian food to come. Charming
service and good Calabrian house
wine (plus a short list) ensure an
enjoyable evening.

Al Pompiere

Via S. M. dei Calderari 38. **Map** 4 F5
& 12 D5. **686 83 77. Open** noon–
4pm, 7.30pm–1am Mon–Sat. **Closed**
last week Jul & all Aug. 🔲 🕭 ⓛⓛ

In the heart of the Jewish Ghetto,
Al Pompiere occupies the first
floor of the 16th-century Palazzo
Cenci-Bolognetti. Under its
frescoed and open-beamed
ceilings, in a homely atmosphere,
all the classic dishes of the
substantial Roman cuisine are
expertly served: among them
fried courgette flowers with
anchovies, *rigatoni con la pajata*,
and baby lamb.

Taverna Giulia

Vicolo dell'Oro 23. **Map** 4 D4 & 11 A2.
686 97 86, 686 40 89. Open
12.30pm–3.30pm, 7.30pm–midnight
Mon–Sat. **Closed** Aug. 🕭 🕭 🕭
🕭 AE, DC, MC, V. ⓛⓛ

Taverna Giulia's customers respect
the quiet comfort of its ancient
dining rooms and discreet service,
as much as the superb Genoese
and Ligurian food. Salmon and
mozzarella *canapés, pansoti*
(ravioli) in nut sauce, stockfish
alla genovese, and perfect *crème
brûlée* are complemented by
Ligurian wines and *Sciacchetrà*
(dessert wine) served with
almond biscuits.

For key to symbols *see p303*

Il Cardinale

Via delle Carceri 6. **Map** 4 D4 & 11 B3.
[686 93 36. **Open** 8pm–11.30pm
Mon–Sat. **Closed** Aug. Ⓥ &
🄴 AE, MC, V. ⒧⒧⒧

For genuine regional cooking,
using the best local ingredients
from the Castelli Romani, this
small, elegant yet comfortable
restaurant near Via Giulia is highly
recommended. Dishes range from
tasty robust soups, to specialities
such as zucchine alla velletrana
(baked courgettes) and crema al
cocco (coconut crème brûlée).
There are particularly good wines
from Lazio.

Il Drappo

Vicolo del Malpasso 9. **Map** 4 D4 &
11 B3. [687 73 65. **Open** noon–
3pm, 8pm–midnight Mon–Sat.
Closed Aug. 🍽 👫 & 🍴 🄴
🄴 AE. ⒧⒧⒧

A small, intimate restaurant, with
ceiling drapes (hence the name),
plants and candlelight, Il Drappo
provides an authentic taste of
Sardinia – traditional dishes
imbued with flashes of culinary
creativity. Everything is evocative
of the island, including the wines,
particularly the seada (sweet
cheese-filled ravioli) for dessert.
Try the mirtillo liqueur at the end.

Piperno

Via Monte de' Cenci. **Map** 4 F5 & 12 D5.
[68 80 66 29. **Open** 12.30pm–3pm,
8pm–11pm Tue–Sat, 12.30pm–3pm
Sun. **Closed** Aug, Christmas, Easter.
& 🍴 🄴 AE, DC, MC, V. ⒧⒧⒧

Piperno, at the heart of the Jewish
Ghetto, has been famed for over
a century for its traditional
Jewish/Roman dishes. Despite the
competition, the restaurant is still
unbeaten for lightly fried courgette
flowers, various fritto misto,
carciofi alla giudia, tripe, and
superb fish, served in plain
surroundings. Service is familiarly
attentive and timely. The house
wine is excellent Frascati. Book
well in advance.

Sora Lella

Via Ponte Quattro Capi 16, Isola
Tiberina. **Map** 8 D1. [686 16 01.
Open 1pm–2.30pm, 8pm–10.40pm
Mon–Sat. **Closed** 30 days over Aug
and Sep. & ⒧⒧⒧

Founded by the exuberant Roman
actress Sora Lella, this small, bright
trattoria is a well-known place to
people-watch. Sora Lella is now
run by Lella's son Aldo. Dishes are
based on traditional Roman
cuisine, but prices are very high
for an essentially simple style of

cooking. Go instead for the
beautiful location on the Isola
Tiberina, the often glamorous
clientele, and the good service.

Vecchia Roma

Piazza Campitelli 18. **Map** 4 F5 &
12 E5. [686 46 04. **Open** 1pm–
4pm, 8pm–11.30pm Thu–Tue.
Closed ⒲Ⓥ & 🍴 🍴 🄴 AE,
DC. ⒧⒧⒧

Set in a quiet, atmospheric piazza,
this is one of the best places for a
summer evening. Reliable Roman
cooking is on offer, with tempting
antipasto, simply-cooked fish and
grilled meats, and a connoisseur's
wine list. Specialities are summer
salads and, in winter, numerous
variations on polenta. Added
pleasures are the 18th-century
interior and the excellent service.

Camponeschi

Piazza Farnese 50. **Map** 4 E5 & 11 C4.
[687 49 27. **Open** 8pm–1am
Mon–Sat. **Closed** 10 days Aug.
🍴 🍴 🍴 🄴 AE, DC, MC, V.
⒧⒧⒧⒧

Camponeschi is set in one of the
most attractive piazzas in Rome,
especially beautiful in summer.
The extensive menu includes
modern and regional Italian
cooking, creative Mediterranean
fish and meat dishes, soufflés and
refined French specialities. There's
a varied regional, French and
Californian wine list.

Da Patrizia e Roberto del Pianeta Terra

Via Arco del Monte 94/95. **Map** 4 E5
& 11 C4. [68 80 16 63. **Open**
12.30pm–3pm, 8pm–11pm
Tue–Sun. **Closed** Aug. 🍽 👫 🍴
🍴 ★ 🄴 AE, DC, MC, V, JCB.
⒧⒧⒧⒧

On the first floor of an elegant
14th-century palazzo, this small
restaurant – offering some of the
finest creative cooking in Rome –
is the perfect choice for a relaxed
celebration. The menus show
Roberto's culinary skill and
imagination, while Patrizia, expert
sommelier, is an attentive hostess.
Superb French and Italian wines
fill the well-stocked cellar.

QUIRINAL

Colline Emiliane

Via degli Avignonesi 22.
Map 5 B3. [481 75 38. **Open**
12.30pm–2.45pm, 7.30pm–10.45pm
Sat–Thu. **Closed** Aug. & ⒧⒧

Regional dishes are the hallmarks
of this small family trattoria: one
unpretentious room presenting a

welcome haven from the nearby
Via del Tritone. Enjoy food typical
of the northern province of Emilia
Romagna – salamis and cold
meats, homemade pastas
(tagliatelle, tortellini), boiled meats
with salsa verde (spinach, onion
and anchovy sauce) and strictly
Emilian wines.

Al Moro

Vicolo delle Bollette 13. **Map** 5 A3 &
12 F2. [678 34 95. **Open** 1pm–
3.30pm, 8pm–11.30pm Mon–Sat.
Closed Aug. 🍴 ⒧⒧⒧

Franco Romagnoli's trattoria is a
reliable choice for traditional
Roman cooking, using fresh local
ingredients. Noisy and crowded,
its closely packed tables do not
encourage intimate dining. Classic
dishes are served: bucatini
all'amatriciana, spaghetti alla
Moro (special carbonara), fried
vegetables, excellent baccalà alla
Moro (salt cod), tripe, abbacchio.
There is a vast wine list.

Il Posto Accanto

Via del Boschetto 36 A. **Map** 5 B4.
[474 30 02. **Open** 12.30pm–3pm
Mon–Fri, 7.45pm–10pm Mon–Sat.
Closed Aug. Ⓥ 👫 & 🄴 AE, DC,
MC, V, JCB. ⒧⒧⒧

Tiny, intimate and elegant, this
family-run restaurant owes its
success to a short, carefully chosen
menu revolving around homemade
pasta (excellent tagliolini con
asparagi and ravioli con zenzero
– ginger), simply prepared fish
and meat, top-quality vegetables
and familiar desserts (tiramisù),
often prepared within sight of the
lucky diners. There is a range of
wines, as well as good grappas.

Quadrifoglio

Via del Boschetto 19. **Map** 5 B4.
[482 60 96. **Open** 12.30pm–3pm
Mon–Fri, 8pm–midnight Mon–Sat.
Closed Aug. 👫 🄴 AE, DC.
⒧⒧⒧

Chef Pino Forlenza has researched
diligently to reproduce authentic,
skilfully prepared dishes from
Naples, Campania and the tip of
Africa. They are tailored to modern
tastes by the carefully selected raw
ingredients. These are delivered
with southern hospitality and
courteous service. Most of the
wines are from Campania, too.

TERMINI

Gemma alla Lupa

Via Marghera 39. **Map** 6 E3.
[49 12 30. **Open** noon–3.30pm,
7pm–11pm Mon–Sat. **Closed** 20
Jul–20 Aug. 🍽 Ⓥ 👫 & 🍴 ⒧

Gemma's is a modest, family-run, typically Roman trattoria serving substantial portions of orthodox Roman cooking. The main features are its bustling atmosphere and speedy service. But it is a good choice where you eat well despite the low prices.

Coriolano

Via Ancona 14. **Map** 6 D1.
[855 11 22. **Open** noon–3pm, 8pm–11pm Mon–Sat, noon–3pm, 8pm–11pm Mon–Fri in Jul. **Closed** Aug. **V** **&** **Y** **€** AE, DC, MC, V. **LLLL**

This small restaurant aims at perfection with its lacy tablecloths and crystal glasses. The Italian menu changes with the seasons and uses only fresh raw materials, including fish. Specialities include home-made *ravioli di ricotta e spinaci*, *capretto* (kid) and creamy chocolate *zuppa del contadino*.

ESQUILINE

Cicilardone

Via Merulana 77. **Map** 6 D5.
[73 38 06. **Open** 1pm–3pm, 8pm–11.30pm Tue –Sat, 1pm–3pm Sun. **Closed** end Jul/beg Aug. **LL**

Ring at Cicilardone's door and your host – Domenico Lucia – will greet you like an old friend and converse about the gastronomic delights from the region of Basilicata. Try the *menu di assaggini* – a number of dishes to give you an idea of the regional taste, including traditional pastas and hot chocolate profiteroles. There are some unusual southern wines.

La Tana del Grillo

Via Alfieri 4. **Map** 6 E5.
[731 64 41. **Open** 12.30pm–2.30pm, 7.30pm–11pm Mon. **Closed** Aug. **Y** **&** **€** AE, DC, MC, V. **LL**

Marisa Balboni runs an elegant and characteristically hospitable Emilian restaurant. Clients are pampered, from the cushioned chairs, restful prints and attractive tableware, to the wholesome food served with courtesy and care. Particularly recommended are the *polpettone all'emiliana* (meat loaf), *salame al sugo ferrarese* (Ferrarese salami), *cappellacci con la zucca* (pumpkin-stuffed pasta).

Trattoria Monti

Via di San Vito 13A. **Map** 6 D4.
[446 65 73. **Open** 12.30pm–3pm, 7.30pm–11pm Wed–Mon. **Closed** 18 Aug–12 Sep. **¶●¶** **V** **Ÿ** **&** **€** DC, V. **LL**

This small, unpretentious local trattoria serves delicate, creative regional dishes from the Marches. Franca Camerucci cooks, while husband Mario is attentive waiter and expert *sommelier*. Specialities include fried stuffed olives, artichokes and *ciauscolo* (salami); *tortello al rosso d'uova* (fresh pasta stuffed with ricotta, spinach and tomato); and *tacchino all'aceto balsamico* (lightly vinegared turkey slices). There's good Verdicchio house wine and a commendable wine list.

Agata e Romeo

Via Carlo Alberto 45. **Map** 6 D4.
[446 61 15. **Open** noon–4pm, 7.30pm–midnight Mon–Sat. **Closed** 2 wks Aug, Christmas. **¶●¶** **V** **&** **⊞** **Y** **€** AE, DC, MC, V. **LLLL**

One of the newer trattorie-turned-restaurants, its increasing prices sadly reflect recent popular acclaim. Nevertheless, Agata's skill in producing a changing menu of predominantly Roman and southern Italian dishes, and Romeo's impeccable service and range of carefully chosen wines, are hard to beat. Well-spaced, elegantly set tables are ideal for tranquil eating. The *menu degustazione* is recommended.

LATERAN

Alfredo a Via Gabi

Via Gabi 36. **Map** 10 D3.
[77 67 92. **Open** noon–3pm, 7.30pm–11pm Wed–Mon. **Closed** Aug. **⊞** **LL**

This is a spacious local trattoria with a pavement pergola for out-door eating. Specialities from Rome and the Marches – served in ample portions – include *tonnarelli ai sapori di bosco* (pasta with mushrooms), excellent *porcini* mushrooms (in season), *straccetti all'ortica* (meat in nettle sauce), and *panna cotta* (rich crème caramel) with fruit or chocolate. Service is cheerful and friendly.

Cannavota

Piazza San Giovanni in Laterano 20. **Map** 9 C1. **[** 77 50 07. **Open** 12.30pm–4pm, 6.30pm–11pm Thu–Tue. **Closed** 1–20 Aug. **¶●¶** **€** AE, DC, MC, V. **LLL**

Join the enthusiastic regulars who crowd this friendly restaurant if you are feeling especially hungry. Portions are generous, the cooking is traditional Italian and the service swift. Seafood – prawns, in particular – is excellent, but meat also features on the menu.

Charly's Saucière

Via San Giovanni in Laterano 270. **Map** 9 B1. **[** 736 66 66. **Open** 8pm–midnight Mon–Sat. **Closed** 2 wks Aug. **&** **€** AE, MC, V. **LLL**

An old-style, unsurprising and well-established French restaurant, this has scarcely altered over the years and is especially warm and intimate on a winter evening. Diners choose from reassuring French and Swiss fare: pâtés, onion soup, cheese soufflé, fondues, *rösti*, steaks in a variety of sauces and crêpes, accompanied by a small but careful selection of wines. Service is professional and attentive.

AVENTINE

Perilli a Testaccio

Via Marmorata 39. **Map** 8 D3.
[574 24 15. **Open** 12.30pm–3pm, 7.30pm–11pm Thu–Tue. **Closed** Aug. **&** **LL**

In the heart of Testaccio, this archetypal Roman trattoria is always packed with hungry regulars (and the occasional famous face). On offer are giant-size quantities of robust traditional fare – *rigatoni alla pajata*, *spaghetti alla carbonara* (served in king-size bowls), *coda alla vaccinara*, *carciofi alla romana* – helpfully and efficiently served. Ignore the noise, lack of intimacy and hideous murals – tuck in and enjoy yourself.

Checchino dal 1887

Via di Monte Testaccio 30. **Map** 8 D4.
[574 63 18. **Open** Oct–Jun: 12.30pm–3pm, 8pm–11pm Tue–Sat, 12.30pm–3pm Sun & Mon; Jul & Sep: 12.30pm–3pm, 8pm–11pm Tue–Sat, 12.30pm–3pm Mon. **Closed** Aug, 1 wk at Christmas. **&** **Ÿ** **Y** **★** **€** AE, DC, MC, V. **LLLL**

Historic home of Roman cuisine for over 100 years, Checchino specializes in authentic dishes using the *quinto quarto* (offal, tripe, intestines and tail), originally discarded by the old slaughter-house opposite. At the old convent tables under vaulted ceilings, with an open fire in winter, Ninetta Mariani and her two *sommelier* sons offer traditional *rigatoni alla pajata*, *coda alla vaccinara*, *crostata di ricotta*, a superb cheese tray and an extraordinary wine selection. Carved into the artificial Monte de' Cocci (made from broken amphoras), its cool, natural wine cellar deserves a special visit.

TRASTEVERE

Da Lucia

Vicolo del Mattonato 2B. **Map** 7 B1.
[580 36 01. **Open** 12.30pm–3pm,
7.30pm–11.30pm Tue–Sun. **Closed**
3 weeks Aug, 1 wk Christmas. 🔥 ♿
🎴 Ⓛ

Head for this popular, well-worn
trattoria off Via Garibaldi if you
like genuine Roman cooking. You
won't be disappointed by the
*pasta e ceci, baccalà, pollo con i
peperoni* (chicken with peppers),
boiled meats and, incongruously,
Milanese risotto. The service is
take it or leave it, the wine basic.
Outdoor tables make a more
attractive dining area in summer.

Da Paris

Piazza San Calisto 7A. **Map** 7 C1.
[581 53 78. **Open** 12.30pm–3pm,
8pm–11pm Tue–Sat, 12.30pm–3pm
Sun. **Closed** Aug. 🎴 ⓨ 🄴 AE, DC,
MC, V. Ⓛ Ⓛ

This classic Roman-Jewish
restaurant is a firm favourite with
choosy diners in Trastevere. Jole
Cappellanti's homemade pasta and
traditional dishes are a must and
include *minestra di arzilla* (skate)
and *trippa* (tripe) *alla romana*.
The *fritto misto vegetale* is
extraordinary, the fish fresh. There
are good desserts and the owner's
personal choice of wines.

Romolo nel Giardino della Fornarina

Via Porta Settimiana 8. **Map** 4 D5 &
11 B5. [581 82 84. **Open** noon–
3pm, 7.30pm–midnight Tue–Sun.
Closed 3–26 Aug. 🍴Ⓞ ♿ 🎵 🄴
🄴 AE, DC, MC, V. Ⓛ Ⓛ See p210.
A Roman institution, this was said
to be the home of La Fornarina,
Raphael's celebrated mistress
and model, and is best enjoyed
for its atmosphere on a summer
evening. Eat out by candlelight
in the walled courtyard, to the
accompaniment of a melancholy
guitar. The food is Roman,
including fried *mozzarella alla
Fornarina* and *cervella e carciofi*
(brains and artichokes).

La Taverna di Bambù

Via Santa Dorotea 2 (Piazza Trilussa).
Map 4 E5. [580 60 65. **Open**
noon–3pm, 7pm–midnight Tue–Sun.
Closed Aug. Ⓥ Ⓛ Ⓛ

An intimate Chinese restaurant,
this is well known for its freshly
prepared dishes served in
abundant portions. A few
Italianate specialities, such as
pizza with onions, are offered as a
concession to the host city, but the

authentic Cantonese dishes such
as crispy beef and spare ribs in
orange sauce are excellent and
well-complemented by a selective,
extensive Italian wine list.

La Cornucopia

Piazza in Piscinula 18. **Map** 8 D1.
[580 03 80. **Open** 1pm–3.30pm,
8pm–midnight Mon–Sat. **Closed**
8 Aug–8 Sep. 🍴Ⓞ 🎵 🄴 AE DC
MC V. Ⓛ Ⓛ

One of the better fish restaurants
in Trastevere, it is particularly
recommended for its candlelight,
elegant place settings and, in
summer, comfortable tables
outside in the piazza. Dishes are
mostly Mediterranean, with
excellent antipasto, unusual pasta,
simply cooked fish such as *spigola
al vapore* (steamed sea bass) and
selected meats. The Castelli house
white will soften the bill.

Peccati di Gola

Piazza dei Ponziani 7A. **Map** 8 D1.
[581 45 29. **Open** 12.30pm–3pm,
8pm–11.30pm Tue–Sun. **Closed** 10
days Jan, 10–15 days Aug. ♿ 🎵 🄴
ⓨ 🄴 AE, DC, MC, V, JCB. Ⓛ Ⓛ Ⓛ

Situated in a quiet, ivy-clad
piazza, Peccati di Gola (literally,
"gluttony") is renowned for its
Calabrian and Mediterranean fish
cuisine successfully interpreted for
modern tastes. There is delicious
antipasto and a tantalizing choice
of fresh seafood, risotti and fish.

Cul de Sac 2

Vicolo dell'Atleta 21. **Map** 8 D1.
[581 33 24. **Open** 8pm–11pm
Tue–Fri, 8pm–11.30pm Sat,
12.30pm–2.30pm Sun. **Closed** Aug.
ⓨ ★ 🄴 AE, DC, MC, V.
Ⓛ Ⓛ Ⓛ

Cul de Sac 2 has emerged as both
a wine lover's mecca (with over
650 labels to choose from) and the
most innovative and stylish
restaurant in the capital. Guy, the
chef, creates French-inspired
flavours for pasta, fish, meat,
extraordinary game and desserts.
Trastevere's magical setting, the
elegant white rooms with their
antiques and the obliging service
complete the exceptional appeal.

Tentativo

Via della Luce 5. **Map** 8 D1.
[589 52 34. **Open** 8.30pm–1.30am
Mon–Sat. **Closed** Aug. 🍴Ⓞ 🄴 ♿
ⓨ ★ 🄴 AE, DC, MC, JCB.
Ⓛ Ⓛ Ⓛ

Its full intriguing and ambitious
name, *Tentativo di descrizione di
un banchetto a Roma* ("an attempt
to describe a Roman banquet")
gives some clue as to the

aspirations of this refined and
intimate restaurant with its
exclusive, ultra-modern decor. The
creative nouvelle cuisine combines
an adventurous but well-advised
selection of flavours. Service is
discreet, genteel and attentive.

Alberto Ciarla

Piazza San Cosimato 40. **Map** 7 C1.
[581 86 68. **Open** 1pm–3pm,
8.30pm–midnight Mon–Sat. **Closed**
15 days Aug, 15 days Jan. 🍴Ⓞ 🎴
🎵 🄴 ⓨ ★ 🄴 AE, DC, MC, V, JCB.
Ⓛ Ⓛ Ⓛ Ⓛ

This is the quintessential restaurant for fish lovers – at least, those
who are prepared to splash out.
Elegant, dramatically dark decor is
relieved by candlelight. Perfectly
executed dishes fluctuate between
the traditional and inventive,
always with an eye to what's best
in the market, ranging from simple
to elaborately creative. A few
innovatory meat dishes can be
had. Ciarla, president of the
Italian *sommeliers*, provides an
exceptional wine list, with many
French and Californian wines.

JANICULUM

Al Tocco

Via San Pancrazio 1, Piazzale Aurelio
7. **Map** 7 A1. [581 52 74. **Open**
1pm–4pm, 8pm–midnight Tue–Sun.
Closed 18–30 Aug. 🍴Ⓞ 🄴 Ⓥ ♿
🄴 AE, DC, MC, V. Ⓛ Ⓛ Ⓛ

In this attractive 15th-century, ivy-
clad restaurant, Danilo Albanesi
has succeeded in creating the
hospitable atmosphere of a tasteful
private home, complete with faded
photographs, old lace and laden
sideboards. He brings alive ancient
culinary traditions of the Tuscan
Maremma: rustic soups, fish, grills
and simple, yet mouth-watering
desserts. Try the carefully selected,
mainly Tuscan, wines.

VATICAN

Tavola d'Oro

Via Marianna Dionigi 37. **Map** 4 E2.
[321 26 01. **Open** 1pm–3pm,
7pm–11pm Mon–Sat. **Closed** mid-
Aug to mid-Sep. 🄴 Ⓥ Ⓛ

This is a tiny piece of Sicily where,
in the family atmosphere of a
small, sparse, noisy, no-frills room,
a good mix of customers eagerly
await the abundant, Sicilian fare
prepared almost under their noses.
Especially good are the *caponata*
(aubergine purée), *arancini di riso*
(rice croquettes), *pasta con le
sarde* (with sardines), swordfish
and *involtini* (meat rolls). Desserts
and wines complete the meal.

San Luigi

Via Mocenigo 10. **Map** 3 B2.
📞 39 72 07 04. **Open** 12.30pm–
3pm, 8pm–11pm Mon–Sat. **Closed**
Aug. 🍴 🗷 🗷 🔽 🎵 🖭 AE, MC, V.
Ⓛ Ⓛ Ⓛ

If you have just spent hours in the
Vatican Museums, the pleasure
of a relaxing restaurant with 19th-
century decor and soft music will
soothe your aching limbs. A set
menu is on offer at lunchtime and
a choice of traditional Neapolitan
and creative dishes in the evening.
Pastas and desserts are particularly
successful. There's a choice of
good French and Italian wines.

VIA VENETO

Cantina Cantarini

Piazza Sallustio 12. **Map** 5 C2.
📞 48 55 28. **Open** noon–3pm,
7pm–midnight Mon–Sat. **Closed**
Aug. 🖭 🖭 AE, DC, MC, V, JCB. Ⓛ

Hidden away on a small square,
this popular local trattoria is
remarkable for the good nature
of its waiters. Meat is on the menu
from Monday to Wednesday, and
fish the rest of the week. Typical
dishes are *alla marchigiana* (from
the Marches); the vegetable and
veal *fritto misto* is amazingly light.

Giovanni

Via Marche 64. **Map** 5 B1.
📞 482 18 34. **Open** 1.30pm–3pm,
7.30pm–11pm Sun–Thu, 1.30pm–
3pm Fri. **Closed** Aug. 🍴
🖭 AE, V. Ⓛ Ⓛ Ⓛ

A throng of satisfied regulars
crowd this classic, well-established
restaurant near Via Veneto. It's run
on traditional lines by the Sbrega
family, with a strong regional influence from Lazio and the Marches.
They serve fresh pasta dishes such
as *tagliolini all'amatriciana*,
vegetable soups, boned chicken
with rice, unbeatable roast lamb,
osso buco, fresh fish and *mille-
feuilles*. The house wines are good.

Tullio

Via San Nicola da Tolentino 26.
Map 5 B2. 📞 481 85 64. **Open**
12.30pm–3.30pm, 7.30pm–11pm
Mon–Sat. **Closed** Aug. 🔽 🖭
🖭 AE, DC, MC, V, JCB. Ⓛ Ⓛ Ⓛ

This genuine Tuscan restaurant
is frequented by an enthusiastic
clientele for its generous helpings
and fair prices. Typical dishes
include *porcini* mushrooms in
every possible form, *pasta e
fagioli*, grilled meat and fish
and Florentine steaks – served
in agreeable surroundings by
courteous, speedy waiters.

Andrea

Via Sardegna 26. **Map** 5 C1.
📞 482 18 91, 474 05 57. **Open**
1pm–3pm, 8pm–11pm Tue–Sat,
8pm–11pm Mon. **Closed** Aug.
🔽 🗷 🖭 🖭 AE, DC, MC, V, JCB.
Ⓛ Ⓛ Ⓛ

This congenial, refined restaurant
offers a superb array of antipasto,
ranging from humble *suppli* (rice
croquettes) to regal lobster (try
it in *insalata catalana*). Leave
room, however, for the impressive
seasonal first and second courses,
and desserts. An extensive choice
of French and Italian wines
completes the meal.

San Benedetto

Via Romagna 20–22. **Map** 5 C1.
📞 474 39 81, 488 28 20.
Open Oct–Mar: 12.30pm–4pm,
7.30pm–10.30pm Tue–Sat; Apr–Sep:
12.30pm–4pm, 7.30pm–10.30pm
Mon–Fri. **Closed** 10–22 Aug,
Christmas–New Year. 🍴 🖭
🖭 AE, DC, MC, V. Ⓛ Ⓛ Ⓛ

San Benedetto del Tronto in the
Marches is the inspiration behind
Pier Luigi Camiscioni's restaurant.
Local fish is expertly cooked *alla
marchigiana*; there are delicious
antipasti (mussels, fresh sardines),
soups and simple fried and grilled
fish. Follow these with fruity
desserts and excellent cheese and
dessert wine from the Marches.

George's

Via Marche 7. **Map** 5 B2.
📞 48 45 75 04. **Open** 12.30pm–
3pm, 7.30pm–2am Mon–Sat. **Closed**
Aug. 🔽 🖭 🎵 🖭 🖭 ★ 🖭 AE,
DC, MC, V, JCB. Ⓛ Ⓛ Ⓛ Ⓛ

Visit this slightly tarnished
survivor from the *dolce vita* era
for its nostalgic air of luxurious
elegance, softly illuminated rooms,
garden terrace, tinkling piano
music and impeccable service.
George's offers tempting and
expertly prepared international
dishes and a good selection of
French and Italian wines.

Le Sans Souci

Via Sicilia 20. **Map** 5 C1.
📞 482 18 14. **Open** 8pm–2am
Tue–Sun. **Closed** Aug. 🔽 🖭 🎵
🖭 ★ 🖭 AE, DC, MC, V.
Ⓛ Ⓛ Ⓛ Ⓛ

This restaurant has overcome a
glitzy fame to emerge as a sound
exponent of elaborate French and
Italian cuisine. The decor is black
and gold, with 17th-century gilt
mirrors and chandeliers. In the
sophisticated anteroom you can
drink an apéritif and consult the
menu and magnificent wine list.
The service is eagerly efficient.

VILLA BORGHESE

Al Ceppo

Via Panama 2. **Map** 2 F3.
📞 841 96 96. **Open** 12.30pm–3pm,
8pm–11pm Tue–Sun. **Closed** 3 wks
Aug. 🔽 🖭 🗷 🖭 🖭 AE, DC,
MC, V, JCB. Ⓛ Ⓛ Ⓛ

In 20 years, two sisters from the
Marches, Cristina and Marisella
Milozzi, have won over an
affectionate following of regulars
in this exclusive, notoriously
diffident area of Rome, attracted
by the consistently reliable food
and a hospitable yet refined family
atmosphere. The strictly seasonal
menu concentrates on traditional
dishes with a touch of daily
invention, as well as excellent
grilled meats, homemade
desserts and Italian wines.

Relais la Piscine dell'Aldrovandi Palace Hotel

Via G Mangili 6. **Map** 2 D4.
📞 321 61 26. **Open** 12.30pm–3pm,
7.30pm–11pm Mon–Sat. **Closed**
Aug. 🍴 🗷 🖭 🖭 🖭 🖭 ★
🖭 AE, DC, MC, V. Ⓛ Ⓛ Ⓛ Ⓛ Ⓛ

The autonomous restaurant of
the Aldrovandi Palace Hotel is
especially beautiful in summer
when tables are set outside on
the terrace by the pool. Jean Luc
Frenat, the young Breton chef,
produces an excellent, typically
Mediterranean nouvelle cuisine,
using prime meat and fish,
vegetables and herbs. This is
accompanied by meticulous
service, wonderful desserts and
a fully comprehensive wine list.
Business lunches are a speciality.

Relais le Jardin dell'Hotel Lord Byron

Via Giuseppe de Notaris 5.
Map 2 D4. 📞 322 45 41. **Open**
12.30pm–2.30pm, 8pm–11pm
Mon–Sat. **Closed** mid-Aug. 🍴 🗷
🖭 🎵 🖭 ★ 🖭 AE, DC, MC, V, JCB.
Ⓛ Ⓛ Ⓛ Ⓛ

For many, this is Rome's greatest
restaurant, located in the quiet,
exclusive and green area of
Parioli. Diners here are undaunted
by absolutely top prices, high-
class, impeccably correct service,
and *haute cuisine* at its finest. The
inspired chef draws predominantly
on traditional Italian regional
cooking, with exceptionally
creative combinations of fruit,
herbs and vegetables as partners
to top-quality meats and fish.
To finish, there are homemade
desserts and pastries; the list of
French, Italian and Californian
wines is outstanding.

For key to symbols *see p303*

Light Meals and Snacks

WHERE SHOULD YOU GO for a casual bite to eat? Rome has the ability to satisfy the all-important stomach at most hours of the day and night. A sound network of *gelaterie, pasticcerie,* pizzerias, wine bars, *rosticcerie* and *tavole calde* mean that good food and drink are always just around the corner.

Start with a classic breakfast at your local stand-up bar: cappuccino and a hot *cornetto* (like a croissant). A heavy morning's sightseeing may leave you ready for an apéritif in one of Rome's elegant 19th-century bars, followed by lunch at a wine bar or Roman-style fast food. In the afternoon there are plenty of opportunities for coffee and cakes at a *pasticceria,* while the late-night bars, especially those with tables outside, are a source of endless entertainment, where you can sip a drink or linger over the final ice cream of the day.

PIZZERIAS

ROMAN PIZZERIAS are the natural choice for informal eating: they are noisy, convivial and fun. Most open only at night, when the wood ovens are lit and the embers glow reassuringly up until last orders. Look for the *forno a legna* (wood-burning oven) sign – electric ovens simply don't produce the same results. In the best pizzerias you sit in view of the vast marble slabs where the *pizzaioli* flatten the dough and whip the pizzas in and out of the oven on long-handled pallets. Turnaround is fast, so you may not be encouraged to linger.

The running order is straightforward: you might have a *bruschetta* (toasted tomato or garlic bread) to start, some *supplì* (fried rice croquettes), fried courgette flowers or *filetti di baccalà* (battered cod fillets), or perhaps a plate of *cannellini* beans in oil. Follow this with a *calzone* (folded-over pizza) or the classic Roman pizza – round, thin and crunchy – with various toppings: *napoletana* (tomato, anchovies, mozza-rella), *margherita* (without the anchovies), *capricciosa* (ham, artichokes, eggs, olives) and anything else the *pizzaiolo* fancies. Draught beer is the classic thing to drink, but wine is always available. You should expect to pay around L15,000 a head for a meal.

The most representative Roman pizzerias, from all points of view, are **Da Baffetto** (look for the queue outside) and its offspring, **La Montecarlo**; also **Remo** in Testaccio and **Ivo** in Trastevere, where tables line the road in summer. **Osteria Picchioni** and restaurant-cum-pizzeria **Manuia** prepare elaborate, up-market combinations. Another place not to be missed is **Panattoni**, where a huge variety of customers patiently queue for a pavement seat on Viale Trastevere in summer, or clamour for one of the marble-topped tables (hence its well-known nickname "the mortuary") inside.

ENOTECHE (WINE BARS)

ENOTECHE offer a fine selection of wines from Italy and around the world. They are usually run by experts, keen to share their knowledge and advise on the best combinations of wine and food. Some *enoteche* are simply shops for browsing. Others like **Achilli al Parlamento** and **Bevitoria Navona** offer the traditional *mescita* – wine and cham-pagne tasting by the glass, accompanied by snacks and canapés. Their prices are reasonable: about L1,500 for a glass on tap, L3,000 upwards for a quality wine, to about L8,000 for champagne. **Vineria Reggio** in Campo

de' Fiori is a typical spot for *mescita,* especially at night. Here business people, residents and tourists alike meet for an apéritif or to share a bottle at a table.

For more substantial food for as little as L20–25,000 a head, try the bistro- or restaurant-style *enoteche,* open at lunch and until late. Particularly recommended are the innovative **Cul de Sac 1**, **Trimani Wine Bar**, the tiny **Il Tajut** serving specialities from Friuli, and **Cavour 313**.

BIRRERIE (BEER HOUSES)

ROMAN BIRRERIE had their heyday in the early years of this century. The few that have survived the competition from subsequent pizzerias and *enoteche* are some of the best: German-style beer houses where you can still enjoy beer and substantial snacks in traditional wood-panelled rooms. The quiet **Premiata Fabbrica Birra Peroni**, serving classic beer-drinkers' fare, is worth a visit for its authentic, turn-of-the-century air of decadence, as is the permanently crowded **Fratelli Tempera**. Another place which attracts Italians and foreigners alike is the **Birreria Viennese/Wiener Bierhaus** with its excellent Transylvanian specialities, which come heaped generously on a wooden plate. If you eat here, or in the **Birreria Bavarese**, you'll spend around L30–50,000. Elsewhere will be cheaper if you want to concentrate more on drinking.

FAST FOOD

ROME HAS PLENTY of homespun fast food options for when you need something quick and inexpensive to eat. Slices of freshly baked pizza are available for a couple of thousand lire from *pizza al taglio* shops. Many of these places also sell spit-roasted chickens, *supplì* and other traditional pizzeria fare. *Rosticcerie* offer deliciously tasty roast chicken and potatoes as well as ready-made pasta dishes, cooked vegetables, salads and desserts – useful for picnics or for making a complete takeaway meal. For a similarly speedy but sit-down snack, bars with a *tavola calda* (hot table) have the same kind of selection, especially at lunchtime; one of the largest and most popular is **Il Delfino** at Largo Argentina. Vegetarians should seek out the **Centro Macrobiotico** near Piazza di Spagna. The **McDonald's** in Piazza di Spagna also offers a good range of fresh mixed salads.

Most *alimentari* (grocery shops) will make you up a *panino* (filled roll). Especially delicious are **Paladini's** hot plain pizza pockets stuffed with choices from the shop's counters, where you can also have a glass of wine. Try one of the region's specialities if you see the sign *porchetta*: whole aromatic roast pig with crackling, sliced into *rosette* (rolls) or thick country-bread sandwiches – there is a good stall selling these at the tram stop in Viale Carlo Felice opposite San Giovanni in Laterano. At the hole-in-the-wall **Er Buchetto** you can even sit down in relative comfort with a glass of wine. For a really typical Roman snack, make a late-afternoon detour to **Filetti di Baccalà** serving, as the name suggests, fried cod fillets and little else.

BARS, CAFÉS AND TEA ROOMS

ROMAN BARS are the city's lifeline: they are places to meet, eat, drink, pick up milk, buy coffee, make phone calls or find a toilet. Some of them are small, stand-up, basic one-counter bars for grabbing a quick *cornetto* and cappuccino and some may be more luxurious, grandiose affairs doubling as cake shop, ice cream parlour, tea room or *tavola calda*, or all of these in one. Most open early at around 7.30am and close late, particularly at weekends, at around midnight or 2am. In summer, tables cover all the

available outdoor space, and the fight for a place in the shade begins.

Traditionally elegant – and pricy – bars for people watching are the admirably located **Rosati** and **Doney**, as well as **Caffè Greco**, the 19th-century haunt of artists, writers and composers *(see p133)*, or the carefully restored **La Caffettiera** at the Pantheon. Another popular and well-established bar is the **Antico Caffè della Pace**. **Minim's de Paris**, **Caffè Flores** (with piano music) and **Selarum** in Trastevere are recommended for late-night drinks, as is **Zodiaco** on Monte Mario for its panoramic views.

Earlier in the day Rome's favoured meeting places are its tea rooms. **Babington's** *(see p134)* is the place to go for an expensive cup of tea and cakes in genteel surroundings, while **Dolci e Doni** is more relaxed. Try a *gran caffè speciale* at the counters of **Sant'Eustachio**, or one of Rome's best espressos at **Tazza d'Oro**. **Ciampini al Café du Jardin** with its garden setting and roof-top views is unbeatable in summer, particularly at the apéritif hour, as is the **Bar Parnaso** in Parioli.

Museum cafés are seldom open, or worth visiting. A welcome exception however is the café of the **Palazzo delle Esposizioni** which is open throughout the day *(see p164)*. If you're stuck for choice, try one of the grander, larger bars such as **Alemagna** – where you can stand, sit, eat and drink at any time of the day, well into the night.

PASTICCERIE (PASTRY SHOPS)

ON SUNDAY mornings you'll often see Romans emerging from the local *pasticceria* with a beautifully wrapped package. This can contain dainty individual pastries, whole cakes or tarts, traditional Easter *colombe* (doves) or Christmas *panettoni* – huge cakes with raisins and candied peel – all

for consumption by large gatherings of friends, relatives or family after lunch. The window displays of Rome's cake shops are often fantastic. These, and the aroma of brewing coffee, might tempt you in for a hot *cornetto* or a *brioche* in the early morning, a midday *pizzetta* or savoury tart, or choux pastry or fruit tart later in the afternoon.

GELATERIE (ICE CREAM PARLOURS)

ICE CREAM *(gelato)* is one of summer's particular delights, and nowhere more so than in Rome. Every well-equipped bar has its tubs of homemade ice cream, and in the *gelaterie* the choice is endless – water-ices made with a phenomenal variety of fruit; lemon and coffee *granite* (crushed ice); as well as more exotic ice cream specialities such as rice, *zuppa inglese* (English trifle), *zabaglione, tiramisù* and After Eight. Choose as many varieties as the size of your cone or cup will hold, topped with cream *(panna)* and then go for a stroll, or else take a break and be served with an ornate creation with all the trimmings at a table. *Gelaterie* are open all day until late at night, when they become evening entertainment.

Tre Scalini in Piazza Navona is a famous spot for enjoying the pricy yet so heavenly chocolate *tartufo*, while a summer evening in EUR, especially with children, nearly always ends in a trip to **Giolitti**, a historic ice cream name; try also the strategically placed, crowded original near the Pantheon *(see p109)*, also serving coffee and pastries. In the same area is the popular **Gelateria della Palma**.

Adults may prefer to pick their night-time treat at **Chalet del Lago**, again in EUR, while sitting beside the lake. If you come across a small kiosk bearing the sign *grattachecche* (most likely in Trastevere and Testaccio), try one of Rome's oldest traditions – ice grated on the spot and enlivened with a variety of classic flavourings.

DIRECTORY

FORUM

Pizzerias
Alle Carrette
Vicolo delle Carrette 14.
Map 5 B5.

PIAZZA DELLA ROTONDA

Pizzerias
Barroccio
Via dei Pastini 13.
Map 4 F4 & 12 D2.

Er Faciolaro
Via dei Pastini 123.
Map 4 F4 & 12 D2.

Wine Bars
Achilli al Parlamento
Via dei Prefetti 15.
Map 4 F3 & 12 D1.

Corsi
Via del Gesù 88.
Map 4 F4 & 12 E3.

Spiriti
Via di Sant'Eustachio 5.
Map 4 F4 & 12 D3.

Fast Food
Fiocco di Neve
Via del Pantheon 51.
Map 4 F4 & 12 D2.

Bars, Cafés and Tea Rooms
La Caffettiera
Piazza di Pietra 65.
Map 4 F3 & 12 E2.

Camilloni
Piazza Sant'Eustachio 54.
Map 4 F4 & 12 D3.

Ciampini
Piazza S. Lorenzo in Lucina
29. **Map** 4 F3 & 12 D1.

Sant'Eustachio
Piazza Sant'Eustachio 82.
Map 4 F4 & 12 D3.

Tazza d'Oro
Via degli Orfani 82/84.
Map 4 F4 & 12 D2.

Teichner
Piazza S. Lorenzo in Lucina
17. **Map** 4 F3 & 12 E1.

Ice Cream Parlours
Gelateria della Palma
Via della Maddalena 20.
Map 4 F3 & 12 D2.

Giolitti
Via Uffici del Vicario 40.
Map 4 F3 & 12 D2.

PIAZZA NAVONA

Pizzerias
Da Baffetto (Volpetti)
Via del Governo Vecchio
114. **Map** 4 E4 & 11 B3.

Corallo
Via del Corallo 10.
Map 4 E4 & 11 B3.

La Montecarlo
Vicolo Savelli 12/13.
Map 4 E4 & 11 C3.

Wine Bars
Bevitoria Navona
Piazza Navona 72.
Map 4 E4 & 11 C2.

Cul de Sac 1
Piazza Pasquino 73.
Map 4 E4 & 11 C3.

Fast Food
Paladini
Via del Governo Vecchio
28/29. **Map** 4 E4 & 11 B3.

Bars, Cafés and Tea Rooms
Antico Caffè della Pace
Via della Pace 5.
Map 4 E4 & 11 C3.

Pastry Shops
A Bella Napoli
Corso Vittorio Emanuele II
246. **Map** 4 E4 & 11 B3.

Ice Cream Parlours
Tre Scalini
Piazza Navona 28.
Map 4 E4 & 11 C3.

PIAZZA DI SPAGNA

Pizzerias
La Capricciosa
Largo dei Lombardi 8.
Map 4 F2.

Il Leoncino
Via del Leoncino 28.
Map 4 F2.

Wine Bars
Buccone
Via di Ripetta 19.
Map 4 F1.

Roffi Isabelli
Via della Croce 76A.
Map 5 A2.

Beer Houses
Birreria Bavarese
Via Vittoria 47. **Map** 5 A2.

**Birreria Viennese/
Wiener Bierhaus**
Via della Croce 21.
Map 5 A2.

Fast Food
Centro Macrobiotico
Via della Vite 14.
Map 5 A3.

Fior Fiore
Via della Croce 17/18.
Map 5 A2.

McDonald's
Piazza di Spagna 46.
Map 5 A2.

Bars, Cafés and Tea Rooms
Alemagna
Via del Corso 181.
Map 5 A3.

Babington's Tea Rooms
Piazza di Spagna 23.
Map 5 A2.

Caffè Greco
Via Condotti 86.
Map 5 A2.

Ciampini al Café du Jardin
Piazza Trinità dei Monti.
Map 5 A2.

Dolci e Doni
Via delle Carrozze 85B.
Map 4 F2.

Rosati
Piazza del Popolo 5.
Map 4 F1.

Pastry Shops
Krechel
Via Frattina 134.
Map 5 A2.

Ice Cream Parlours
Minim's de Paris
Via di Propaganda 26A.
Map 5 A2.

CAMPO DE' FIORI

Wine Bars
Bottega del Vino da Bleve
Via Santa Maria del Pianto
9A/11.
Map 4 F5 & 12 D5.

Il Goccetto
Via dei Banchi Vecchi 14.
Map 4 D4 & 11 B3.

Vineria Reggio
Piazza Campo de' Fiori 15.
Map 4 E4 & 11 C4.

Fast Food
Il Delfino
Corso Vittorio Emanuele II
67. **Map** 4 F4 & 12 D4.

Filetti di Baccalà
Largo dei Librari 88.
Map 4 E5 & 11 C4.

Da Giovanni
Piazza Campo de' Fiori 39.
Map 4 E4 & 11 C4.

Bars, Cafés and Tea Rooms
Alberto Pica
Via della Seggiola 12.
Map 4 F5 & 12 D5.

Caffè Flores
Lungotevere dei Vallati
25/27. **Map** 4 E5 & 11 C5.

Pastry Shops
Bernasconi
Largo di Torre Argentina 1.
Map 4 F4 & 12 D4.

La Dolceroma
Via del Portico d'Ottavia
20B. **Map** 4 F5 & 12 E5.

Il Forno del Ghetto
Via del Portico d'Ottavia 2.
Map 4 F5 & 12 E5.

QUIRINAL

Pizzerias
Est! Est! Est!
Via Principe Amedeo 4A.
Map 6 D3.

I Rioni
Via dei SS. Quattro
Coronati 24. **Map** 9 B1.

Wine Bars
Cavour 313
Via Cavour 313.
Map 5 B5.

Beer Houses
Albrecht
Via Rasella 52. **Map** 5 B3.

Fratelli Tempera
Via San Marcello 19.
Map 5 A4 & 12 F3.

Fast Food
Bar del Palazzo del Yogobar
Via Mazzarino 8–10.
Map 5 B4.

Er Buchetto
Via del Viminale 2.
Map 5 C3.

McDonald's
Piazza della Repubblica
40. **Map** 5 C3.

Nadia e Davide
Via Milano 33.
Map 5 B4.

**Bars, Cafés and
Tea Rooms**
**Palazzo delle
Esposizioni**
Via Milano 9.
Map 5 B4.

TERMINI

Pizzerias
La Bruschetta
Via Ancona 35.
Map 6 D1.

Formula 1
Via degli Equi 13.
Map 6 F4.

Le Maschere
Via degli Umbri 8/14.
Map 6 F4.

Wine Bars
Trimani Wine Bar
Via Cernaia 37B.
Map 6 D2.

Beer Houses
**Premiata Fabbrica
Birra Peroni**
Via Brescia 24/32.
Map 6 D1.

Pastry Shops
La Partenopea
Via Appia Nuova 198.
Map 10 E3.

ESQUILINE

Pizzerias
Osteria Picchioni
Via del Boschetto 16.
Map 5 B4.

Beer Houses
Marconi
Via di Santa Prassede 9C.
Map 6 D4.

Fast Food
Cottini
Via Merulana 286.
Map 6 D4.

**Palazzo del Freddo di
Giovanni Fassi**
Via Principe Eugenio 65/67.
Map 6 E5.

**Bars, Cafés and
Tea Rooms**
Ristoro della Salute
Piazza del Colosseo 2.
Map 9 A1.

LATERAN

Fast Food
**Viale Carlo Felice
Porchetta Stall**
Viale Carlo Felice.
Map 10 D1.

Ice Cream Parlours
**Premiate Gelaterie
Fantasia**
Via La Spezia 100/102.
Map 10 E1.

AVENTINE

Pizzerias
Remo
Piazza Santa Maria
Liberatrice 44. **Map** 8 D3.

Taverna Cestia
Via della Piramide Cestia
67. **Map** 8 E3

Wine Bars
Palombi
Piazza Testaccio 38/41.
Map 8 D3.

TRASTEVERE

Pizzerias
Almacrì
Via F. Benaglia 3.
Map 7 B4.

Da Gildo
Via della Scala 31A.
Map 4 D5 & 11 B5.

Ivo
Via di San Francesco a
Ripa 158. **Map** 7 C1.

Panattoni
Viale Trastevere 53.
Map 7 C1.

Ar Popi Popi
Via delle Fratte di
Trastevere 45. **Map** 7 C1.

Da Vittorio
Via di San Cosimato 14A.
Map 7 C1.

Wine Bars
**Il Cantiniere di Santa
Dorotea**
Via di S. Dorotea 9.
Map 4 D5 & 11 B5.

Ferrara
Via dell'Arco di San
Calisto 36. **Map** 7 C1.

Fast Food
McDonald's
Piazza Sonnino 39/40.
Map 8 D1.

**Bars, Cafés and
Tea Rooms**
Selarum
Via dei Fienaroli 12.
Map 7 C1.

Pastry Shops
Valzani
Via del Moro 37B.
Map 7 C1.

Ice Cream Parlours
La Fonte della Salute
Via Cardinale Marmaggi
2/4/6. **Map** 7 C1.

Sacchetti
Piazza San Cosimato 62.
Map 7 C1.

VATICAN

Pizzerias
Pizzeria San Marco
Via Tacito 29.
Map 4 D2.

Il Tempio della Pizza
Viale Giulio Cesare 91.
Map 3 C1.

Wine Bars
**Il Simposio di Piero
Costantini**
Piazza Cavour 16.
Map 4 E2.

Beer Houses
Tiroler Keller
Via G. Vitelleschi 23.
Map 3 C2.

VIA VENETO

Wine Bars
Marchetti
Via Sicilia 144.
Map 5 C1.

**Bars, Cafés and
Tea Rooms**
Doney
Via Veneto 145.
Map 5 B2.

EUR

Fast Food
McDonald's
Piazzale Don Luigi Sturzo
21/22.

**Bars, Cafés and
Tea Rooms**
Chalet del Lago
Lake, EUR.

Ice Cream Parlours
Giolitti
Casina dei Tre Laghi, Viale
Oceania 90.

FURTHER AFIELD

Pizzerias
La Cicala
Via Stabia 7/9.
Map 10 E4.

Da Cocco
Circonvallazione Appia
37A. **Map** 10 E4.

Manuia
Via Gallia 107.
Map 9 C3.

Wine Bars
Guerrini
Viale Regina Margherita
205/207.

Semidivino
Via Alessandria 230.

Il Tajut
Via Albenga 44.
Map 10 E3.

Fast Food
Svizzera Siciliana
Piazza Pio XI 10/11.

**Bars, Cafés and
Tea Rooms**
Bar Parnaso
Piazza delle Muse 22.
Map 2 E2.

Il Cigno
Viale Parioli 16.
Map 2 E3.

Duse
Via Eleonora Duse 1E.
Map 2 F2.

Pannocchi
Via Bergamo 56.
Map 6 D1.

San Filippo
Via di Villa San Filippo
8/10. **Map** 2 F2.

Zodiaco
Viale Parco Mellini 90.

Pastry Shops
Euclide
Via F. Civinini 119.
Map 2 D3.

Ice Cream Parlours
**Premiate Gelaterie
Fantasia**
Via Oderisi da Gubbio 230.

SHOPS AND MARKETS

ROME HAS BEEN a thriving centre for design and cosmopolitan shopping since ancient times. In the heyday of the Empire the finest craftsmen were drawn to Rome, and artefacts and produce of all kinds, including gold, furs, wine and slaves, were imported from far-flung corners of the Empire to service the needs of the wealthy Roman population.

Shopping in Rome today in many ways reflects this diverse tradition. Italian designers have

Window shopping in Rome, an absorbing pastime

an international reputation for their luxuriously chic style in fashion, knitwear and leather goods (especially shoes and handbags) as well as in interior design, fabrics, ceramics and glass. The artisan-craftsman tradition is strong and the love of good design filters through into the smallest items. It is not a city for bargains (though often better value than Florence or Milan), but the joys of window shopping here will offer plenty of compensation.

BEST BUYS

LEATHER GOODS of all kinds, including shoes and bags, are a strong point. Ready-to-wear Italian designer clothes are not cheap, but they are certainly less expensive than in other countries. Armani jeans are a good example *(see p327)*. You are also likely to find designer lighting fixtures, for example, at lower prices here. Both modern and traditional Italian ceramics and handicrafts can be very beautifully made and, if you have time to wander around the back streets, really unusual and individual gifts can often be found.

SALES

SALE TIME *(saldi)* is from mid-July to mid-September and the period from just before Christmas to the first week in March. Top designers

(see p326) slash prices by half, but their clothes are still very expensive even then. Good bargains can be found in the young designer wear shops *(see p327)* and good-quality large shoe sizes are sold off very cheaply (most Italians have small feet). Both of the Cesari shops *(see p327 and p333)* are well-known for their sales. In general, though, sales in Rome do not offer huge discounts.

Both the original and the sale price should be quoted on each reduced item. *Liquidazioni* (closing down sales) are usually genuine and can sometimes be worth investigating. However, other signs in shop windows such as *vendite promozionali* (special introductory prices) and *sconti* (discounts) are often only lures to get you into the shop. The sign on the door saying *entrata libera* means "browsers welcome".

Antiques at Acanto *(see p336)*

WHEN TO SHOP

SHOPS ARE GENERALLY open from 9am to 1pm and from 3.30pm to 7.30pm (4pm to 8pm in the summer months). Some of the shops in the centre stay open all day from 10.30am to 7.30pm. Most shops are closed on Sunday (except immediately before Christmas). Shops are also closed on Monday morning, apart from food and technical supply stores, which close on Thursday afternoons in winter and Saturday afternoons in summer.

August brings the city to a virtual standstill as Roman families escape the heat to the sea or the mountains. Signs saying *chiuso per ferie* (closed for vacation) appear everywhere in the shops. Most shops close for at least two weeks around 15 August, the national holiday.

Flower stalls in Piazza Campo de' Fiori *(see p338)*

SHOPPING ETIQUETTE

APART FROM a few department stores, most Roman shops are small, specializing in just one field. Browsing at leisure may at first seem daunting if you are used to large shopping centres. Customers will almost always receive better attention if they dress smartly – the emphasis on *fare la bella figura* (making a good impression) is taken seriously.

Stylish leather gloves on display

Sizes are not always uniform, so it's wise to try clothes on if possible before buying, since refunds and exchanges are not usually given.

HOW TO PAY

MOST SHOPS now accept all the major credit cards, whose signs are displayed on the shop window. Some will also accept foreign currency, though the exchange rate may not be good. When you make a purchase you are bound by Italian law to leave the shop with a *ricevuta fiscale* (receipt). You can try asking for a discount if paying cash and you may be lucky, though many shops have a *prezzi fissi* (fixed prices) sign.

VAT EXEMPTION

VALUE ADDED TAX – VAT (IVA in Italy) – ranges from 12% on clothing to 35% on luxury items such as jewellery and furs. Marked or advertised prices normally include the IVA. It is possible for non-European Community citizens

Craftsmen near Piazza Navona

to obtain an IVA refund for individual purchases that exceed L650,000, but be prepared for a long and bureaucratic process. The simplest method is to shop at a place displaying the "Euro Free Tax" sign. Present your passport when you make your purchase, and fill in a form from the shop; the shop then deducts the IVA, gives you a copy of the form, and sends their copy to the Euro Free Tax Organization in Milan which will then deal with the paperwork.

If you wish to buy something from a shop which is not part of the "Euro Free Tax" scheme, you must get the Italian customs to stamp the vendor's receipt at your departure, showing them the purchased article, and then post the stamped receipt back to the shop, who should then send you a refund.

Mercato delle Stampe *(see p338)*

DEPARTMENT STORES AND SHOPPING CENTRES

DEPARTMENT STORES, known as *grandi magazzini,* are few and far between in Rome. **La Rinascente** and **Coin** are good for ready-to-wear clothes, household linens and haberdashery, and have well-stocked perfume counters. La Rinascente give 10% discount to tourists on perfumes and cosmetics if you show your passport. The Rinascente group also owns the popular **Croff** household furnishings chain *(see p333).* The **Standa** and **Upim** chain stores offer moderately-priced medium-quality clothes and household goods.

Another alternative is to head for one of Rome's two shopping centres. **Cinecittà Due Centro Commerciale**,

Bargains in Via Sannio *(see p339)*

built in 1988, offers around a 100 shops plus bars, banks and restaurants within easy reach of the centre by Metro (line A to Cinecittà). An even bigger centre, called **I Granai**, has now opened in Via Laurentina, reachable by Metro (line B to Laurentina).

Cinecittà Due Centro Commerciale
Via Tuscolana.

Coin
Piazzale Appio 7. **Map** 10 D2.
📞 708 00 20.

I Granai
Via Laurentina.

La Rinascente
Via del Corso 189. **Map** 5 A3 & 12 E2.
📞 679 76 91.

Piazza Fiume. **Map** 6 D1.
📞 884 12 31.

Standa
Via Cola di Rienzo 173. **Map** 4 D2.
📞 324 32 83.

Viale Trastevere 60. **Map** 7 C2.
📞 581 60 36.

Via Appia Nuova 181–3. **Map** 10 D2.
📞 702 48 96.

Upim
Via del Tritone 172. **Map** 5 A3.
📞 678 33 36.

Via Nazionale 211. **Map** 5 C3.
📞 48 45 02.

Piazza S. Maria Maggiore. **Map** 6 D4.
📞 446 55 79.

Rome's Best: Shopping Streets and Markets

THE MOST INTERESTING shops in Rome are in the old centre, so shopping is easy to combine with sightseeing. The shops are often housed in medieval or Renaissance buildings and their window displays can be exquisite. Just like shopkeepers in past centuries, traders tend to specialize in one type of merchandise. Street names often refer to the old tradesmen: locksmiths in Via dei Chiavari, leather jerkin makers in Via dei Giubbonari and chairs in Via dei Sediari. Today, antique merchants have taken over from the rosary sellers on Via dei Coronari. The top names in fashion and modern design dominate the Via Condotti area, and the artisan-craftsman tradition is still strong around Campo de' Fiori and Piazza Navona.

Via dei Coronari
Art Nouveau and antiques enthusiasts will love browsing in the shops that line this charming street just northwest of Piazza Navona. But be prepared for high prices as most of the items are imported.

Via Cola di Rienzo
Situated close to the Vatican Museums, this long wide street has the finest food shops and is also good for clothes, books and gifts.

Vatican

Piazza Navona

Via del Pellegrino
Book and art shops abound here next to working artisans in the historic centre. Don't miss the mirror-lined alley near Campo de' Fiori.

Janiculum

Via dei Cappellari
This narrow, medieval street is a great place for watching furniture restorers and other artisans plying their crafts in the open air.

Porta Portese
You can buy anything from antiques to a tin whistle at Trastevere's Sunday morning flea market. (See p339.)

Via Margutta
Up-market antique shops mix with genteel restaurants on this peaceful, cobbled street.

Via del Babuino
This street is renowned for designer furniture, lighting and glass, as well as interesting antique and fashion shops.

DESIGNER SHOPPING
All the well-known stars of the Italian fashion scene, plus exclusive jewellers, gift shops, shoe designers and tailors, are concentrated in this cluster of chic and stylish shopping streets by the Spanish Steps (*see pp326–31*). Romans love to stroll here in the early evening.

MISSONI
GIORGIO ARMANI
PIAZZA DI SPAGNA
VIA CONDOTTI
GUCCI
valentino
VIA BORGOGNONA
VIA DEL CORSO
FENDI
VIA FRATTINA
MaxMara

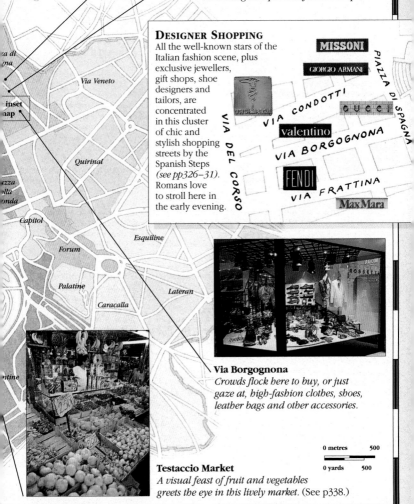

Via Borgognona
Crowds flock here to buy, or just gaze at, high-fashion clothes, shoes, leather bags and other accessories.

| 0 metres | 500 |
| 0 yards | 500 |

Testaccio Market
A visual feast of fruit and vegetables greets the eye in this lively market. (See p338.)

Men's and Women's Fashion

ITALY IS ONE of the leading lights in high-class fashion, or *alta moda*. Many of the most famous designers are based in Milan, but Rome is home to a cluster of sophisticated and internationally distinguished fashion houses. There is also a wonderful selection of *alta moda* shops. Boutiques displaying an eclectic mix of designer goods rub shoulders with showrooms devoted to single collections. But even for those of us unable to splash out on genuine designer-wear, much fun can be gained from a stroll down the exclusive streets that radiate out from the Piazza di Spagna, as some of the window displays are truly spectacular.

The "atelier" made-to-measure fashions are beyond most pockets, but the designers also offer ready-to-wear alternatives in their boutiques. These are not cheap, but cost far less than a tailor-made garment.

WOMEN'S HIGH FASHION

ROME'S MOST famous designer internationally is probably **Valentino**. However, one of the first houses to make a name for Roman fashion was **Sorelle Fontana**. This was *the* salon to be dressed by during the 1950s heyday of Rome's *dolce vita*. Sorelle Fontana has been dressing high society since the 1930s, and stocks a wide selection of ready-to-wear clothes and accessories.

Fendi occupies a large tract of the fashion street, Via Borgognona. Fendi made its name with high-fashion furs, then branched out into leather goods, accessories and ready-to-wear, collaborating with Karl Lagerfeld who designed the coveted double-F logo which emblazons its very collectable products. Third-generation family members design the younger, less expensive Fendissime line.

For well over a decade, **Laura Biagiotti** has reigned as Rome's queen of discreet, conservative couture. From her headquarters in a castle just outside Rome, she designs a range of timelessly elegant knitwear and silk separates for women who don't want to sacrifice style for comfort. She is famous for her use of cashmere and white as well as her creative use of fabrics and quality of finish. Her flagship showroom in Via Borgognona stocks her complete collection, which now includes hosiery, perfumes, swimwear and leather goods. Her scarves make wonderful presents, and are often reduced in price during sales; other items from previous collections are available in the shop all year round at very good discounts.

Other internationally known Rome-based designers include **Renato Balestra** for tailored suits and glamorous evening wear and **Roberto Capucci**, who uses wonderful textures and fabrics in classy suits. **Raniero Gattinoni** produces elegant suits and blouses for both his made-to-measure and off-the-peg showrooms. **Mila Schön**'s speciality is dramatic evening wear.

Other luminaries of Italian fashion with shops in Rome include **Giorgio Armani**, **Gianfranco Ferrè**, **Gianni Versace** and **Trussardi**. A rising star in ready-to-wear is **Genny**. Based in Ancona, the Genny design team produces some really classic, elegant and stylish collections.

If you're looking for clothes from unconventional designers, **Gente** is the place to go – its Roman showrooms have exclusive rights to the original couture collections of avant-garde stylists such as Dolce & Gabbana and Moschino, plus Europeans such as Jean-Paul Gaultier. **MaxMara** also has a number of branches here. Chic suits and separates are the mainstays of this popular label. The quality of fabric and finish is superb and, with suits available for around L1,000,000, its prices are much lower than other *alta moda* couture designers' ready-to-wear lines.

MEN'S TAILORS AND DESIGNER WEAR

ITALIAN MEN are every bit as fashion conscious as the women, and there is no shortage of choice in Rome for the well-dressed man. Suits generally begin at around L1,000,000, jackets L750,000 and trousers L250,000.

Most of the "star" designers of women's *alta moda* have a shop for men, like **Valentino Uomo** and **Versace Uomo**. The designs are less dramatic than the women's, with the accent on understated sophistication and casual sportiness. Valentino's distinctive monogrammed accessories are relatively affordable.

Battistoni is probably the most prestigious designer concentrating on menswear. Giorgio Battistoni and family's fine custom-made shirts and suits have been in demand with film stars and top society

---

VALENTINO

One of the high priests of Italian fashion, **Valentino Garavani** opened the doors of his Roman studio in 1959 to a distinguished clientele which included Sophia Loren, Audrey Hepburn and Jackie Kennedy, and has never looked back. He has created some of the most dramatic and flattering evening dresses of the last three decades. In the 1970s he began designing ready-to-wear lines for both men and women alongside his *alta moda* collections, and you can now find his very distinctive "V" logo on a wide range of accessories. Valentino's salon is in a huge palazzo in Piazza Mignanelli, and he also has a separate ready-to-wear boutique nearby (see p330).

for 50 years. **Cucci**, also on Via Condotti, provides similar-quality designer shirts (they cost around L300,000 for made-to-measure).

Carlo Palazzi's Baroque palazzo setting offers elegant ready-to-wear, and the master tailor Peppino Scarapazzi will also make to measure. **Davide Cenci** has been a mecca for those in search of the English country gentleman look since 1926. **Brioni** offers traditional tailor-made and own-label ready-to-wear men's clothing. **Trussardi** sells beautifully tailored classics, and **Polidori Uomo** offers sober classics made-to-measure or ready-to-wear from its own gorgeous tweeds and wools. **Testa** has impeccably tailored suits that appeal to younger Romans, and **Enzo Ceci** is popular for ready-to-wear *alta moda* designs. **Degli Effetti** stocks more avant-garde designers such as Romeo Gigli and Jean-Paul Gaultier.

YOUNG DESIGNER WEAR

THERE IS A HUGE choice for the young. Top designers Valentino and Armani offer their particular style translated into more affordable lines at **Oliver** and **Emporio Armani** (Armani jeans are very good value at about L100,000). Fendi has its Fendissime line, and MaxMara's Penny Black label can be found in its **Max & Co** branches. Targeted at the younger set, these are good places to pick up stylish, sporty numbers. **Henry Cottons** is another very collectable designer label. Average prices are L100,000 for a shirt, L400,000 for raincoats, L800,000 for suits.

Energie is a big hit and has two shops with some of the best window displays in Rome. Teenagers flock here for jeans and T-shirts. **Aria**, **Babilonia**, **Box 233** and **Uniform** are also very popular.

Bacillario, **Cantiere del Nord** and **Eventi** represent the more avant-garde styles – *dark*, as they call it here – fusing Gothic, New Age and punk influences, with outrageous window creations. **Luna e L'altra** offers some

unconventional designer clothes in a pleasant, friendly atmosphere.

HIGH STREET FASHION

ROME IS NOT a good place to look for everyday wear, since there is a distinct lack of mid-price shops bridging the huge gap between the dazzlingly priced *alta moda* designer exclusives and the ultra-cheap goods sold in markets (*see pp338–9*). Lower-budget shops do exist, but quality is often poor. If you have the stamina, you may find a bargain along Via del Corso, Via del Tritone, Via Nazionale, Via Cavour, Via Cola di Rienzo, Via Ottaviano or the Via dei Giubbonari.

The most convenient places to shop are department stores like La Rinascente, Standa and Upim (*see p323*). They may not sound exciting, but you can browse at leisure and find nice things. It's also worth trying shops mentioned under Young Designer Wear – particularly the *alta moda* designers' cheaper lines such as **Emporio Armani** and **Max & Co**. At **Discount dell'Alta Moda** and **Discount System** you can find end-of-season designer labels at 50% less than the boutique prices. **Scala Quattordici** is a good place to buy simple linen dresses made by the owner. And while you don't need to come to Rome to shop at **Benetton**, there are many shops here, along with the subsidiary **Sisley**.

KNITWEAR

KNITWEAR is a particular strength in Italian design, and in Rome there are plenty of specialist shops. **Laura Biagiotti** is celebrated for her luxurious cashmere separates, and **Missoni** for spectacular kaleidoscopic patterns and colours. Mariuccia Mandella creates sophisticated knitwear for **Krizia**.

Choses de Cachemire has cashmere cardigans, pullovers and knitted suits. **Miranda** offers beautiful handmade items, from wool scarves for less than L100,000 to coats for

around L500,000. Other shops, such as the **Luisa Spagnoli** outlets, offer a wider selection, including lower-priced items.

LINGERIE

THIS IS ANOTHER Italian speciality excelling in both style and quality, with lines like La Perla exported world-wide. Lingerie is traditionally sold in top household linen shops (*see p333*) – **Cesari**, for example, is La Perla's main outlet in Rome. There are also boutiques specializing in lingerie and swimwear.

Riccioli stocks swimwear, La Perla, and men's designer underwear, and makes sumptuous silk pyjamas for around L350,000. **Brighenti** is said to be where film stars go for their lingerie. **Tomassini** has original designs by Luisa Romagnoli. **Schostal** has more traditional underwear with a very good men's section.

SECOND-HAND CLOTHES

THOSE WHO are willing to browse will find a wide variety of second-hand clothes, whether inspired by a collector's interest in vintage clothes or a low budget. Apart from Via Sannio and Porta Portese markets (*see p339*), which have many second-hand clothes stalls, the mecca is Via del Governo Vecchio. Among the best shops in this ancient street off Campo de' Fiori are **Sempreverde**, which stocks clothes from the 1930s to the 1960s at low prices, and **Moon**, which has mostly 1920s dresses and some hats and jewellery.

Wilma Silvestri offers a marvellous selection of period hats and sells both second-hand and vintage clothes. At **Via dei Chiavari 40** you can find smart clothes from the 1920s onwards, and owner Solange also does some dressmaking on the spot and sells at reasonable prices. **Maga Morgana** will make reproductions of period dresses and costumes to order. Via del Pellegrino is also a good street for second-hand clothes.

Shoes and Accessories

ITALY'S LEATHER INDUSTRY is renowned all over the world, and shoes, bags and belts are a good buy in Rome. Accessories in general are not just an afterthought but an integral part of an outfit for the well-dressed Roman. The choice of stylish jewellery, scarves, ties and other accessories is excellent.

SHOES

ROME IS FULL of shoe shops, ranging from high-quality stores in the Via Condotti area (where prices tend to start at L250,000) to the more economical shops around the Trevi fountain, and every big market has its bargain shoe stalls on its fringes.

Probably the best-known shop is **Ferragamo** – one of the world's top shoe shops. It stocks classic yet fashion-conscious shoes, as well as women's clothing and leather goods – the silk signature scarves are quite a feature.

Fratelli Rossetti is a close contender for the number one position. Founded by brothers Renzo and Renato over 30 years ago, this company produces classic men's shoes and beautiful, dressy low-heeled shoes for women that reflect the most up-to-the-minute trends. Along with **Campanile** in Via Condotti it represents the epitome of elegance. Its prices, of course, are sky-high. **Bruno Magli**, Bologna's well-known star, has dressy patent-leather pumps and other classic styles.

Beltrami is an amazing shop boasting a spacious shopfront. It sells bags, as well as men's and women's shoes in classic and innovative styles. **De Bach** has colourful styles for women.

Rome's own **Raphael Salato** has three extremely elegant, high-priced shops: his shoes are genuine masterpieces of craftsmanship, and many are made of intricately embroidered leather. Neapolitan **Mario Valentino** is another Rome-based designer, with an impressive flagship shop on Via Frattina. He designs leather clothing, bags and accessories as well as shoes – all beautifully tailored and expensive.

Via Frattina also has other, more moderately-priced shoe shops such as **Pollini** and **Ramirez**. Pollini makes boots and bags for men and women in trendy and imaginative styles. **Fausto Santini** stocks original, colourful designs for younger people at more reasonable prices. The same goes for **I Cervone**, which specializes in highly colourful women's shoes. **Borino** stocks simple, low-heeled designs. The **Bata** shops concentrate more on casual shoes and boots, and stock children's shoes as well. **Albanese** and **Rampone**, at the other end of the scale, make shoes to measure; the latter also sells beautiful ready-made shoes, and bags and accessories.

Guido Pasquali is a younger designer; his boots in particular are worth looking out for.

LEATHER GOODS

THE MOST FAMOUS of Rome's leather shops is **Gucci**, selling shoes, suitcases, handbags, wallets, belts and other accessories. It has a fashion boutique for men and women and is well-known for its silk ties and scarves. **Fendi** also has exquisite leather goods as well as some lower-priced lines in synthetic materials and a range of gift items. Although their famous "stripe" line leather-finished synthetic handbags cost as much as L250,000 (and their all-leather ones start at L300,000), they are cheaper to buy here than abroad. **Valextra** has high-quality, fairly traditional briefcases, handbags, wallets and purses from Milan. **Skin**, **Ginocchi** and the more economical suede and leather factory **Pappagallo** are all in the Via Sistina area. **Mandarina Duck**'s brightly coloured fabric bags and range of

luggage are very much in fashion and make an attractive alternative to the more traditional leather styles.

There are also some great places to buy artisan leatherwork. **Sirni** is at the top end of the scale with elegant bags and briefcases made in a workshop at the back. **Ibiz** has two shops, selling handmade items which are slightly cowboy in style. Some of the smaller things are made on site but the rest come from a workshop-cum-factory elsewhere. **Anna Maria Pirozzi** makes everything – belts and handbags etc – herself, and has a tiny workshop in Via Panisperna. Prices are very reasonable and she will even make special items to order. **Joker Cuoio** also has a workshop, where bags, belts, wallets and shoes are made.

CLASSIC JEWELLERY

WHAT CARTIER is to Paris, Tiffany & Co is to New York and Asprey's is to London, **Bulgari** is to Rome. This internationally revered jeweller's has passers-by glued to the windows gazing at its large fat gemstones. These "windows" are rather curious small boxes inserted into a wall with one or two pieces of jewellery in each of them, which adds to the feeling of looking at precious items in a case at a museum. Bulgari's watches, especially the men's, are popular and very elegant, as are the famous mesh necklaces. It specializes in large, colourful stones in High Renaissance-style settings but also produces contemporary designs. This was one of Andy Warhol's favourite shops, and it is the most palatial shop on Via Condotti. Inside, the shop's atmosphere is one of almost religious awe and contemplation.

Buccellati is an offshoot of the famous Florentine dynasty, which was begun by Mario Buccellati in the 1920s and patronized by the poet Gabriele D'Annunzio. Its delicately engraved designs are inspired by the Italian Renaissance, and are real classics, displaying superb craftsmanship.

Ansuini designs are fashionable yet classic with strong, imaginative themes being introduced for each new collection. **Massoni**, founded in 1790, is one of Rome's oldest jewellery houses. Its refined one-offs and brooches are quite outstanding. At **Moroni Gioielli** you will also find imaginative, unique pieces of the highest-quality workmanship. **Petocchi**, which was jeweller to the former Italian monarchy (1861–1946), the House of Savoy, has both traditional and contemporary styles on display.

Peroso is an old-fashioned shop which has been going since 1891 and specializes in antique jewellery and silverware. **Boncompagni Sturni** sells traditional designs with the emphasis on quality and craftsmanship. You have to ring the bell to be admitted to both of these shops, and they are extremely expensive.

Ouroboros is known for less expensive handmade gold and silver items. Traditional jewellery can be bought more cheaply in the Via dei Pettinari and Piazza del Monte di Pietà.

COSTUME JEWELLERY

FOR LESS conventional tastes, there are several shops selling innovative, avant-garde pieces, often using semi-precious metals and stones. Both **Amati e Amati** and **Via dei Coronari 193** are worth trying. **Via dei Pettinari 80** has a mixture of Art Nouveau items and other types of contemporary designs.

Delettré produces bold, unique designs influenced by Art Deco styles. You are as likely to find rock crystal here as diamonds. Their logo of a crescent moon and five stars was specially designed by Karl Lagerfeld.

Tempi Moderni has an interesting collection of Art Deco and Liberty period jewellery. You can also find

some nice pieces from the 1920s and 1930s in Cose Così (see p336). **Bozart** is the place for trendy, flashy costume jewellery. **Siragusa** puts beautiful 3rd- and 4th-century BC beads and coins into handmade gold chains, in a museum-like shop just off the Piazza di Spagna.

TRADITIONAL GOLDSMITHS AND SILVERSMITHS

THE MAINSTAY of Rome's jewellery industry is still the traditional artisan goldsmith and silversmith, working to order in tiny studio workshops. These are concentrated in the old Jewish Ghetto area, Campo de' Fiori, Ponte Sisto near Via Giulia, and Montepietà (where the pawnbrokers live). Artisan jewellery can also be found in Via dei Coronari, Via dell'Orso, Via del Pellegrino. The jewellers create individual pieces to their own designs and have often learned their profession from their parents

and grandparents. They also do repair work, or take old gold jewellery, melt it down and make it into something to suit you. **Oddi e Seghetti** produces some traditional artisan jewellery and always works to customers' commissions.

GLOVES, HATS AND HOSIERY

IF YOU'RE LOOKING for top quality, you will find an expensive line of gloves and scarves at **Merola**. **Di Cori** and **Sermoneta** stock every imaginable kind of glove. **Catello d'Auria** specializes in gloves and hosiery. The **Anticoli** gloves factory is one of the oldest in Rome and has a large selection at reasonable prices. It also sells belts, scarves, ties and handbags. **Borsalino** is the place for hats. **Calza e Calze** has the best range of hosiery in Rome – the friendly staff will serve you with almost any colour or pattern of tights and stockings that you could wish for.

SIZE CHART

For Australian sizes follow British and American convention.

Children's clothing

Italian	2-3	4-5	6-7	8-9	10-11	12	14	14+ (years)
British	2-3	4-5	6-7	8-9	10-11	12	14	14+ (years)
American	2-3	4-5	6-6x	7-8	10	12	14	16 (size)

Children's shoes

Italian	24	25½	27	28	29	30	32	33	34
British	7	8	9	10	11	12	13	1	2
American	7½	8½	9½	10½	11½	12½	13½	1½	2½

Women's dresses, coats and skirts

Italian	38	40	42	44	46	48	50
British	8	10	12	14	16	18	20
American	6	8	10	12	14	16	18

Women's blouses and sweaters

Italian	81	84	87	90	93	96	99 (cms)
British	31	32	34	36	38	40	42 (inches)
American	6	8	10	12	14	16	18 (size)

Women's shoes

Italian	36	37	38	39	40	41
British	3	4	5	6	7	8
American	5	6	7	8	9	10

Men's suits

Italian	44	46	48	50	52	54	56	58 (size)
British	34	36	38	40	42	44	46	48 (inches)
American	34	36	38	40	42	44	46	48 (inches)

Men's shirts (collar size)

Italian	36	38	39	41	42	43	44	45 (cms)
British	14	15	15½	16	16½	17	17½	18 (inches)
American	14	15	15½	16	16½	17	17½	18 (inches)

Men's shoes

Italian	39	40	41	42	43	44	45	46
British	6	7	7½	8	9	10	11	12
American	7	7½	8	8½	9½	10½	11	11½

DIRECTORY

WOMEN'S HIGH FASHION

Fendi
Via Borgognona 36A/39.
Map 5 A2. **C** 679 76 41.

Genny
Piazza di Spagna 27.
Map 5 A2. **C** 679 60 74.

Gente
Via del Babuino 82.
Map 4 F1. **C** 320 76 71.
Also: Via Frattina 69.
Map 5 A2. **C** 678 91 32.
Also: Via dei Due Macelli
62. **Map** 5 A3 & 12 F1.
C 679 27 27.

Gianfranco Ferrè
Via Borgognona 42C.
Map 5 A2. **C** 679 00 50.

Gianni Versace
Via Bocca di Leone 26.
Map 5 A2. **C** 678 05 21.

Giorgio Armani
Via Condotti 77.
Map 5 A2. **C** 699 14 60.
Also: Via del Babuino 140.
Map 4 F1. **C** 679 68 98.

Laura Biagiotti
Via Borgognona 43–44.
Map 5 A2. **C** 679 12 05.

MaxMara
Via Condotti 46.
Map 5 A2. **C** 678 79 46.
Also: Via Frattina 28.
Map 5 A2. **C** 679 36 38.

Mila Schön
Via Condotti 64–65.
Map 5 A2. **C** 678 48 05.

Raniero Gattinoni
Piazza di Spagna 91.
Map 5 A2. **C** 679 53 61.

Renato Balestra
Via Sistina 36. **Map** 5 A2.
C 679 54 24.

Roberto Capucci
Via Gregoriana 56.
Map 5 A2. **C** 679 51 80.

Sorelle Fontana
Salita S. Sebastianello 6.
Map 5 A2. **C** 679 86 52.

Trussardi
Via Condotti 49.
Map 5 A2. **C** 679 21 51.

Valentino
Piazza Mignanelli 22.
Map 5 A2. **C** 673 91.

Also: Via Bocca di Leone 15.
Map 5 A2. **C** 679 58 62.
Also: Via Gregoriana 24.
Map 5 A2. **C** 673 91.

MEN'S TAILORS AND DESIGNER WEAR

Battistoni
Via Condotti 57 & 61A.
Map 5 A2. **C** 678 62 41.

Brioni
Via Barberini 79.
Map 5 C2. **C** 488 47 65.

Carlo Palazzi
Via Borgognona 7E.
Map 5 A2. **C** 678 91 43.

Cucci
Via Condotti 67.
Map 5 A2. **C** 679 18 82.

Davide Cenci
Via Campo Marzio 1–7.
Map 4 F3 & 12 D2.
C 678 45 37.

Degli Effetti
Piazza Capranica 75–79.
Map 4 F3 & 12 D2.
C 679 16 50.

Enzo Ceci
Via della Vite 52.
Map 5 A3 & 12 E1.
C 679 88 82.

Polidori Uomo
Via Borgognona 4A.
Map 5 A2. **C** 678 48 42.

Testa
Via Borgognona 13.
Map 5 A2. **C** 679 61 74.
Also: Via Frattina 104.
Map 5 A2. **C** 679 12 96.

Trussardi
See Women's High Fashion.

Valentino Uomo
Via Condotti 13.
Map 5 A2. **C** 678 36 56.

Versace Uomo
Via Borgognona 29.
Map 5 A2. **C** 679 52 92.

YOUNG DESIGNER WEAR

Aria
Via Nazionale 239.
Map 5 C3. **C** 48 44 21.

Babilonia
Via del Corso 185.
Map 4 F3 & 12 E1.
C 678 66 41.

Bacillario
Via Laurina 43. **Map** 4 F1.

Box 233
Via Nazionale 233.
Map 5 C3. **C** 481 45 18.

Cantiere del Nord
Via del Corso 187.
Map 5 A3 & 12 E2.
C 678 66 41.

Emporio Armani
Via del Babuino 140.
Map 4 F1. **C** 678 84 54.

Energie
Via del Corso 408–409.
Map 4 F2.
C 687 12 58, 687 10 04.
Also: Via del Corso
486–487. **Map** 4 F2.
C 321 49 71.

Eventi
Via dei Serpenti 134.
Map 5 B4. **C** 48 49 60.

Henry Cottons
Via del Babuino 75.
Map 4 F1. **C** 679 08 36.
Also: Via Appia Nuova 51.
Map 10 D2. **C** 700 89 87.

Luna e L'Altra
Via del Governo
Vecchio 105.
Map 4 E4 & 11 B3.
C 68 80 49 95.

Max & Co
Via Nazionale 56.
Map 5 C3.
C 48 90 31 10.
Also: Via Appia Nuova
201–203. **Map** 10 D2.
C 701 44 13.
Also: Via Salaria 59–61.
Map 6 D1. **C** 854 67 15.

Oliver
Via del Babuino 61.
Map 4 F1. **C** 679 83 14.

Uniform
Via del Corso 481.
Map 4 F2. **C** 322 71 56.

HIGH STREET FASHION

Benetton
Via Condotti 59.
Map 5 A2. **C** 679 79 82.

Discount dell'Alta Moda
Via di Gesù e Maria 16.
Map 4 F2. **C** 361 37 96.

Discount System
Via del Viminale 35.
Map 5 C3. **C** 474 65 45.

Emporio Armani
See Young Designer Wear.

Max & Co
See Young Designer Wear.

Scala Quattordici
Via della Scala 14.
Map 4 D5 & 11 B5.

Sisley
Via Condotti 19B.
Map 5 A2. **C** 684 19 50.

KNITWEAR

Choses de Cachemire
Via del Babuino 105.
Map 4 F1. **C** 679 84 88.

Krizia
Piazza di Spagna 77B.
Map 5 A2. **C** 679 34 19.

Laura Biagiotti
See Women's High Fashion.

Luisa Spagnoli
Via del Corso 385.
Map 5 A4 & 12 F3.
C 679 39 83.
Also: Via Vittorio
Veneto 130. **Map** 5 B1.
C 488 58 81.
Also: Via Frattina 116.
Map 5 A2. **C** 679 55 17.
Also: Via Barberini 84.
Map 5 C2. **C** 488 07 57.

Miranda
Via Francesco Crispi 44.
Map 5 B2. **C** 48 55 32.

Missoni Donna
Via del Babuino 97.
Map 4 F1.
C 679 79 71.

Missoni Uomo
Piazza di Spagna 78.
Map 5 A2.
C 679 25 55.

LINGERIE

Brighenti
Via Frattina 7–8.
Map 5 A2. **C** 679 14 84.

Cesari
Via Barberini 1. **Map** 5 B3.
C 488 13 82.

Riccioli
Via del Governo Vecchio 36.
Map 4 E4 & 11 C3.
C 68 80 50 35.

Schostal
Via del Corso 158.
Map 4 F3 & 12 E1.
C 679 12 40.

EMPORIO ARMANI

Emporio Armani
See Young Designer Wear.

Max & Co
See Young Designer Wear.

Tomassini
Via Sistina 119. **Map** 5 A2.
[488 19 09.

SECOND-HAND CLOTHES

Maga Morgana
Via del Governo Vecchio 27.
Map 4 E4 & 11 C3.
[687 99 95.

Moon
Via del Governo Vecchio
89A. **Map** 4 E4 & 11 B3.

Sempreverde
Via del Governo Vecchio
26. **Map** 4 E4 & 11 C3.
[68 80 13 96.

Via dei Chiavari 40
Via dei Chiavari 40.
Map 4 E4 & 11 C4.
[686 52 74.

Wilma Silvestri
Via del Boschetto 76.
Map 5 B4. [488 10 17.

SHOES

Albanese
Via Carlo Dossi 71.
[828 09 85.

Bata
Via dei Due Macelli 45.
Map 5 A2. [679 15 70.

Beltrami
Via Condotti 18–19.
Map 5 A2. [679 13 30.

Borino
Via dei Pettinari 86.
Map 4 E5 & 11 C5.
[687 56 70.

Bruno Magli
Via Vittorio Veneto 70A.
Map 5 B2. [488 43 55.
Also: Via Barberini 94.
Map 5 C2. [48 68 50.
Also: Via Cola di Rienzo
237. **Map** 4 D2.
[324 17 59.
Also: Via del Gambero
1–2. **Map** 5 A3 & 12 E1.
[679 38 02.

Campanile
Via Condotti 58.
Map 5 A2. [678 30 41.

De Bach
Via del Babuino 123.
Map 4 F1.

Fausto Santini
Via Frattina 122.
Map 5 A2. [678 41 14.

Ferragamo
Via Condotti 73–74.
Map 5 A2. [679 15 65.
Also: Via Condotti 66.
Map 5 A2. [678 11 30.

Fratelli Rossetti
Via Borgognona 5A.
Map 5 A2. [678 26 76.

Guido Pasquali
Via Bocca di Leone 5.
Map 5 A2. [679 50 23.

I Cervone
Via del Corso 99.
Map 4 F2. [678 35 22.

Mario Valentino
Via Frattina 84.
Map 5 A2 & 12 E1.
[679 12 46.

Pollini
Via Frattina 22–24.
Map 5 A2 & 12 E1.
[678 90 28.

Ramirez
Via del Corso 73.
Map 4 F3 & 12 E1.

Rampone
Piazza di Spagna 65.
Map 5 A2. [679 29 50.

Raphael Salato
Via Veneto 149.
Map 5 B1. [482 18 16.
Also: Piazza di Spagna 34.
Map 5 A2. [679 56 46.

LEATHER GOODS

Anna Maria Pirozzi
Via Panisperna 65.
Map 5 B4.

Fendi
See Women's High Fashion.

Ginocchi
Via Sistina 35. **Map** 5 B2.
[488 39 25.

Gucci
Via Condotti 8. **Map** 5 A2.
[678 93 40.

Ibiz
Via dei Chiavari 39.
Map 4 E4 & 11 C4.
[683 07 97.
Also: Via G Tamassia
42–44.
[663 06 54.

Joker Cuoio
Via del Pellegrino 11.
Map 4 E4 & 11 C4.
[686 97 03.

Mandarina Duck
Via di Propaganda 1.
Map 5 A2. [684 03 20.

Pappagallo
Via Francesco Crispi 115.
Map 5 B2. [678 30 11.

Sirni
Via della Stelletta 33.
Map 4 F3 & 12 D2.
[68 80 52 46.

Skin
Via dei Due Macelli 59 &
87–88. **Map** 5 A3 & 12 F1.
[679 58 56.

Valextra
Via del Babuino 94.
Map 4 F1. [679 23 23.

CLASSIC JEWELLERY

Ansuini
Via del Babuino 150D.
Map 4 F1. [679 58 35.

Boncompagni Sturni
Via del Babuino 115.
Map 4 F1. [678 38 47.

Buccellati
Via Condotti 31.
Map 5 A2. [679 03 29.

Bulgari
Via Condotti 10.
Map 5 A2. [679 38 76.

Massoni
Largo Carlo Goldoni 48.
Map 4 F2 & 12 E1.
[678 26 79.

Moroni Gioielli
Via Belsiana 32A.
Map 4 F2. [678 04 66.

Ouroboros
Via di Sant'Eustachio 14.
Map 4 F4 & 12 D3.
[654 45 84.

Peroso
Via Sistina 29. **Map** 5 B3.
[474 79 52.

Petocchi
Piazza di Spagna 23.
Map 5 A2. [679 39 47.

COSTUME JEWELLERY

Amati e Amati
Via dei Pianellari 21.
Map 4 E3 & 11 C2.
[686 43 16.

Bozart
Via Bocca di Leone 4.
Map 5 A2. [678 10 26.

Delettré
Via Fontanella Borghese.
Map 4 F2. [687 77 22.

Siragusa
Via delle Carrozze 64.
Map 5 A2.
[679 70 85.

Tempi Moderni
Via del Governo Vecchio
108. **Map** 4 E4 & 11 B3.
[687 70 07.

Via dei Coronari 193
Via dei Coronari 193.
Map 4 E3 & 11 B2.
[68 80 15 03.

Via dei Pettinari 80
Via dei Pettinari 80.
Map 4 E5 & 11 C5.

TRADITIONAL GOLDSMITHS AND SILVERSMITHS

Oddi e Seghetti
Via del Cancello 18.
Map 4 E3 & 11 C2.
[68 80 26 43.

GLOVES, HATS AND HOSIERY

Anticoli
Via Lombardia 4.
Map 5 B2. [488 44 82.

Borsalino
Via IV Novembre 157B.
Map 5 A4 & 12 F3.
[679 41 92.

Calza e Calze
Via della Croce 78.
Map 4 F2.

Catello d'Auria
Via dei Due Macelli 55.
Map 5 A2 & 12 F1.
[679 33 64.

Di Cori
Piazza di Spagna 53.
Map 5 A2. [678 44 39.

Merola
Via del Corso 143.
Map 4 F3 & 12 E1.
[679 19 61.

Sermoneta
Piazza di Spagna 61.
Map 5 A2.
[679 19 60.

Interior Design

ITALIAN DESIGN belongs to a long-established tradition based on the skills of the master craftsman, and some firms have a history going back hundreds of years. Rome's stylish interior design shops are worth seeking out, even if it's only to look around and enjoy the ambience. You might well pick up some design ideas for your home, as well as finding some interesting or unusual things to buy.

FURNITURE

A WORLD-FAMOUS name in furniture design is **Cassina**: here its expensive hi-tech designs can be bought for far less than abroad. Its style features stark, clean-lined tables, armchairs and sofas in glass, tubular steel and leather in the tradition of architect-designed furniture by Le Corbusier, Eileen Gray, and Vico Magistretti. It can arrange for merchandise to be shipped abroad.

Stildomus, further down the same street, has a long, narrow showroom displaying mainly very fine modern wood furniture. **Fontana Arte** has some highly original furniture and lamps made almost entirely of glass.

Take a look at the nearby **Studio Punto Tre** if you want something different: it's packed with strangely painted chests of drawers, Egyptian-style artefacts and small bits and pieces that would make good presents. **Alivar**, near the Capitol, sells impeccable reproductions of the "classics" of modern furniture, such as Aalto, Le Corbusier and Mackintosh, at accessible prices.

Spazio Sette, near Largo Argentina, has a spectacular showroom on three levels in the Palazzo Lazzaroni, a former cardinal's palace. It is one of Rome's premier home furnishing stores and, apart from furniture, it stocks items that would make interesting gifts. The furniture – modern, laminated, stack-up chairs and so forth, vases, glass, bowls, and kitchen equipment – is jumbled together in a fascinating display.

Magazzini Forma & Memoria is in a cleverly converted old printing works on the edge of the Tiber, not far from St Peter's. It has four levels of display space for the latest in furniture and design items from Italy and elsewhere. In the basement there is a reading area, a health-food bar, and an exhibition space. All this and panoramic views at the top make it a fascinating place to visit.

LIGHTING FIXTURES

LIGHTING FIXTURES are one of the most popular and more easily transportable items, and there are a number of superb showrooms to visit. **Flos Arteluce** is a merger of two design houses whose Roman showroom displays its lights as if they were museum exhibits. The design style is minimalist – plenty of black and white, chrome and steel.

Nearby **Artemide** is, like Flos Arteluce, a design house in its own right, and is similarly well-known abroad. Its Rome showroom is elegant, with expensive, hi-tech lighting design similar to Flos Arteluce. **Borghini** sells less famous names, and so is more economical.

Italian lighting and other electrical equipment is designed for 220–240 volts. If you are going to use it in countries with lower voltages always ask the shop whether the product needs a transformer, as this can depend on the model. Lighting fixtures generally take screw-bulbs, although bayonet-bulbs of some designer models may be ordered.

KITCHENS AND BATHROOMS

ALTHOUGH YOU won't be able to take one home with you, you may like to look at a few of the ultra-modern hi-tech kitchens sold in Rome. For an overview of the latest designs, visit **La Residenza**, which has a selection of about 15 kitchen sets from about nine different Italian manufacturers. **Coas Tradizione Casa** in Piazza Cardelli has some interesting combinations in a centrally located showroom.

Italian bathroom shops concentrate almost entirely on modern design. **Odorisio** is the equivalent of La Residenza for bathrooms, and has some luxurious examples. **Ravasini**, nearby, has very decorative floral fixtures with some matching accessories. **Andreucci** also has a bathroom shop which sells all the latest styles.

TILES

THE ITALIAN ceramic tile tradition is an ancient one. A great variety of tiles is displayed in kitchen and bathroom showrooms, but there are also specialist shops. The most beautiful and the most expensive is **Farnese**, looking ancient Roman in style with its mosaic tables. Di Donato uses old-fashioned methods to design and produce the tiles – hence the cost. He is influenced by Roman and Pompeian art but also produces modern one-off designs.

Ceramiche Musa specializes in modern tiles with decorative floral and ancient Roman motifs, which are popular with visitors. **Via Giulia** sells period tiles, in limited editions. You can become owner of an Art Nouveau tile for around L30,000–L60,000 but older or rarer examples can cost more.

GLASS

GLASS is fashionable again, and when it comes to modern design and spectacular display **Venini** is hard to beat. The beautiful shop window and interior highlight very expensive products – splendid plates, vases and bowls. The ostentatious **Vetreria Murano Veneto**, behind the Excelsior Hotel, offers a lavish collection of blown glass from the famous glass-blowing workshops at Murano, near Venice. **Archimede Seguso** also specializes in Murano glass but includes smaller pieces and gift-sized items.

Tupini, the Roman equivalent of the Harrods china department, has quality glass, china and silverware. **Richard Ginori** is a famous name in modern ceramics. Its products include the award-winning designs of Giò Ponti and Giovanni Garibaldi. **Arteque** is a very beautiful shop, with a more traditional flavour. For less expensive gifts, try **Stilvetro**. It is the ideal place for pasta bowls, glass and ceramics.

Shipment home can usually be arranged at any of these glass establishments.

FABRICS

SUMPTUOUS furnishing fabrics are what **Cesari** in Via del Babuino is renowned for. It also has a linen and lingerie shop (see p327). **Il Sigillo** offers fabrics and wallpapers to order from a rich assortment of samples. At **Galtrucco** you can choose material for a suit which they will make to measure. **Bises** has two shops in Via del Gesù, No. 91 for silks and fashion fabrics and No. 63 for furnishing materials.

If you are looking for worthwhile bargains, wander round the old Jewish quarter that runs from Largo Argentina down to the Tiber; it is full of cheaper fabric shops such as **Paganini**. At sale time, remnants (scampoli) can be really good value.

HOUSEHOLD LINENS AND KITCHENWARE

A SELECTION of lovely sheets can be found at **Frette**. For brightly coloured cottons and towels at reasonable prices, try **Croff (Centro Casa)**, a subsidiary of the Rinascente group (see p323), which has a good linen department as well as designer objects, glass and furniture along the lines of stores like Habitat and Ikea.

If you enjoy designer kitchenware, don't miss **C.u.c.i.n.a.** in the cellars of No. 118 Via del Babuino. It stocks kitchen utensils, pots and pans, in both rustic and hi-tech styles. **Single** specializes in stainless steel designs like Alessi, and also sells wooden breadboards and assorted containers.

Books and Gifts

Rome offers huge scope for gift buying. There are products from all over Italy as well as locally-produced artisan wares. Seeking out the smaller shops can be an adventure in itself, as many are in attractive parts of the city that you might not otherwise visit.

Some of the artisan ceramics are very unusual; there are beautiful books on Italian art and architecture, and there are wonderful paper products. Foodie gifts and drinks are always welcome – especially if it is something really special such as a 20-year-old balsamic vinegar. As well as the usual souvenirs, there is an abundance of religious artefacts – for obvious reasons – and Michelangelo masterpieces are the number one icon for T-shirts, statuettes and postcards.

BOOKSHOPS

Rome is rich in bookshops, from the encyclopedic to the very specialized. Italian books, both hardback and softback, are generally very attractive but also tend to be quite expensive.

Rizzoli, Rome's largest bookshop, has a wide selection on art and cookery among other subjects, and many books in English and other foreign languages. **Feltrinelli** has three shops in the capital. The most important is situated in Via del Babuino and offers a wide selection of contemporary literature. Milanese **Franco Maria Ricci** offers very beautiful art books, as well as its own glossy magazine *FMR*. **Libreria Godel** is also good for browsing – it has a lot of books on Rome, great postcards, art calendars and some second-hand art books. **Libreria San Silvestro** has half-price bargains and sells games for children too. There are lots of cut-price bargains as well as second-hand book stalls in Via delle Terme di Diocleziano and in Largo della Fontanella di Borghese.

MULTIMEDIA AND MUSIC

Rome's biggest music store is **Ricordi**. As well as records, cassettes and CDs, it sells musical instruments and musical scores in its four central outlets. By contrast, **Discoteca Frattina** is quite a small, handy music shop that also sells video cassettes. The multimedia shop **Mondadori** sells greetings cards, posters and videos, and has good map and music departments as well as stocking books.

STATIONERY AND PAPER CRAFTS

The delightful **Papirus** sells papercraft, boxes, obelisks, picture frames and other desk items. **Laboratorio Scatole** offers pretty marbled notebooks, writing paper, files and boxes in various sizes.

Pineider, stationery suppliers to the Roman gentry, will print exquisite visiting cards for you. They also sell handsome leather-bound desk diaries. Just as classy, though less traditional, **Vertecchi** is filled with original paper gifts: boxes of every size and shape, paper tablecloths and napkins, wrapping paper and dazzling Christmas decorations.

ARTISAN HANDICRAFTS

Spacious and artistically rustic, **La Galleria** is filled with authentic artisan wares, including hand-woven textiles and beautiful ceramics that owner Clotilde Sambuco chooses from all parts of Italy. Domenico and Lavinia Sarti's **Bottega Artigiana** nearby is a small shop with ceramics made by the couple in their Anzio studio. You can buy vases and urns in unglazed terracotta and some attractive terracotta wall-light fittings. **Arti e Mestieri** is the workshop of a friendly mother and daughter who make original articles in wood and terracotta. For a really original gift, go to **Opificio Romano**, a workshop that reproduces ancient Roman and Pompeian mosaics, where they will recreate any design you choose to order.

SOUVENIRS AND RELIGIOUS ARTEFACTS

Most of the tobacconists in central Rome sell postcards, stamps and a variety of souvenirs, and many cheap and sometimes appealingly kitsch souvenirs are sold by the mobile stalls around the major tourist attractions.

Bookshops near the main basilicas, such as **Libreria Belardetti**, sell souvenirs and religious mementos. Other shops specialize in religious articles for both the clergy and the layman. Facing the Vatican gates in Via di Porta Angelica there are several shops, such as **Al Pellegrino Cattolico**, selling mementos to visiting pilgrims.

FOOD

One of the unusual things about shopping in Rome is the absence of large-scale supermarkets in the centre. It has been local government policy to keep them out in order to protect the little *alimentari* or delicatessens. There are hundreds of these, not on the main shopping streets, but in small side streets running off them or in the "village" districts such as Monti, Trastevere, the Ghetto, Borgo and Campo de' Fiori. They are often crammed from floor to ceiling with all the irresistible delicacies that are typical of Italy.

Here you can buy, the day before your departure, your supply of parmesan and pecorino romano cheese *(see p305)*, Parma ham or prosciutto di montagna, attractive bottles of dark-green, extra-virgin unfiltered olive oil, dried porcini mushrooms and sun-dried tomatoes to take home (but check customs restrictions first). Food is by no means cheap, and most of the above are considered luxury items.

Pietro Franchi is without doubt the most exclusive delicatessen in the city, and its windows are a visual feast of seafood platters, pâtés, cheeses and cold meats. Next door is the famous coffee shop **Castroni**, which has Rome's largest selection of imported products from all over the world. It also stocks Italian olive oils, balsamic vinegars, honeys and preserves, and of course coffee.

Via della Croce deserves a special mention for its good selection of well-stocked *alimentari* like **Fratelli Fabbi**. Specialist food shops like **Fior Fiore** sell exquisite little almond and orange peel cakes, ricotta cheese, and piles of artichoke-, spinach- and tomato-flavoured pasta, as well as thin, crispy pizza straight from the oven.

The **Azienda Agricola** is a tiny shop selling specialist products. Enjoy the display of beautifully packaged bottles of olive oil flavoured with garlic or herbs, pâtés made of black or green olives, small jars of truffles, asparagus and artichokes, and their own pre-serves. They all make ideal and much-appreciated gifts.

Cheese-lovers can usually find lots of Italian varieties in any of the small *alimentari* in the city, but it's also worth trying the local cow, sheep and buffalo milk cheeses that are sold at the **Cisternino Cooperativa fra Produttori di Latte di Lazio** near Piazza Campo de' Fiori.

Boxes of chocolates and traditional confectionery and cakes such as *torrone* and *panettone* can be bought from good-quality bars. **L'Albero del Pane** sells wonderful wholemeal and rye flour breads and other health foods.

WINE

WINE IS GENERALLY sold in *alimentari* and also in supermarkets. There are, however, many specialist shops (look for the sign *Enoteca*) with a huge stock of wines and spirits. They invariably have a little bar where they serve wine and light snacks or canapés. Here you can find Italian wines, and usually local wines, mostly white, from the nearby Frascati, Colli Albani and Marino vineyards, on tap. One of the most select is **Enoteca Buccone**, which is housed in an old coach-house. Another well-known one is **Roffi Isabelli** which has an old-world feeling to it. The **Enoteca del Corso** is more modern, with a good selection of Italian grappa and jars of marinated fruits. **Enoteca Corsi** in Via del Gesù is also worth a visit.

Art and Antiques

Rome's ART and antique shops range from exclusive establishments to contemporary art galleries. In response to a fashion for collecting early-20th-century artefacts, new dealers and galleries are springing up throughout Rome – Venini's Murano glass is popular, as are lighting and furniture. Many more sell more general bric-a-brac and jewellery. Copies of antique prints can be picked up for a fraction of the originals' price. Rome is not good for antique bargains, but it's worth looking in shops along Via dei Cappellari and Via del Pellegrino or going to the Porta Portese Sunday market *(see p339)*.

ANTIQUES AND OLD MASTER PAINTINGS

THERE ARE antique shops dotted all over the centre of Rome, though the cream tend to be concentrated in distinct areas. Discreet haggling in the shops is accepted practice, but make sure the dealer provides the relevant export documents.

The famous Via del Babuino, and to a lesser extent Via Margutta, which is more famous for its art galleries, are home to around 30 of Rome's grandest showrooms for antique furniture, Old Master paintings and *objets d'art*.

W Apolloni is one of the city's most respected and prestigious shops, attracting museums and professional collectors with fine 17th-century paintings, furniture and rare silver.

Cesare Lampronti, aided by his partner Carlo Peruzzi, is a top dealer in 16th- to 18th-century European paintings, with an emphasis on Roman and Italian works in general.

Amedeo di Castro, apparently no relation to the other four di Castros on this street, is a fourth-generation dealer in bas-relief sculptures and exquisite pieces from the 18th and early 19th centuries.

At the **Granmercato Antiquario Babuino**, also known as GAB, you will find silver, porcelain, scientific instruments and other small-scale collectors' pieces from the 17th century onwards.

Via Giulia *(see p153)* has over 20 high-quality antique shops to choose from.

Definitely worth a visit is **La Chimera**, which is a temple to owner Paola Cipriani's love of simply elegant Neo-Classical furniture and paintings. She also sells the occasional modern piece. Another shop not to miss on Via Giulia is **Antiquariato Valligiano**. It's the only place in Rome where you can find 19th-century Italian country furniture; a rustic antidote for those overpowered by the grandiose Baroque.

Via Monserrato, running parallel, is worth scouring for slightly lower-quality pieces at more attainable prices.

Via dei Coronari is almost exclusively devoted to antiques, with over 40 shops lining both sides of this picturesque street. Quality is very high – as are the prices. It is a good place for Baroque and Empire elaborate inlaid vases, secretaries and consoles.

L'Art Nouveau specializes in high-quality Art Nouveau (usually called *Liberty* here). The **Art Deco Gallery** sells furniture and sculpture from that period.

Piero Talone has a superb collection of lighting fixtures from the Baroque through to Art Deco periods.

Slightly further away lies Via della Stelletta, which is home to a handful of unusual and fascinating shops.

Acanto is an inexpensively priced Aladdin's cave with an eclectic mix of *objets d'art*. It is the perfect place to search for religious memorabilia, Italian curiosities and prints.

Bilenchi is yet another specialist, but in exquisite, turn-of-the-century lamps.

Another relatively undiscovered area is Via del Boschetto and Via Panisperna. Shops here tend to specialize in early-20th-century artefacts, with some English Victorian pieces thrown in.

Retrospettiva is strong on top designers and craftsmen selling furniture, Murano glass and Faenza pottery from 1900–50. **Passato Prossimo** has some more curious bygones, including a collection of Bakelite and plastic jewellery of the 1940s and 1950s. And **Antichità di Antonella e Maria Teresa** offers a dazzling collection of Art Deco and Liberty lamps.

Of course there are many perennial favourites apart from these streets. The best way to discover them is through word of mouth or just by chance as you stroll along. **Cose Così** is a charming little shop full of small decorative pieces from 1800–1940 (watches, silver, glass, frames, vases and jewellery). **Manasse** is the best place to head for if you're after antique jewellery, icons and Fabergé eggs.

Anticaja e Petrella has an eccentric collection of used junk and printed ephemera stored under Sant'Andrea della Valle *(see p123)*.

MODERN ART

Rome is RICH in avant-garde galleries exhibiting paintings by recognized Modern Masters through to the up-and-coming generation of young, mainly Italian, artists.

Rome's art galleries are usually open 10am–1pm and 5pm–8pm Tue–Sat. Some open only in the afternoon; others also stay open on Monday afternoon. The best times to visit are afternoons and early evenings.

As with Rome's antique shops, the art galleries tend to be concentrated in a couple of distinct areas. The largest of these covers the triangle area between Via del Babuino and Via di Ripetta and adjoining streets, known locally as the Trident.

The pioneering **Agenzia d'Arte Moderna**, founded in 1913, promoted Futurism from the start and other modern art movements as well. There are works by Burri and Kounellis always on show.

Il Millennio is strong on abstract art, and is particularly interested in promoting women artists. **Sperone**, under the owner-directorship of Gian Enzo Sperone who has a similar gallery in New York, shows works by American artists like Ray Smith, Julio Galan, and Jonathan Lasker. Also on view are Italian artists like Gallo, Bianchi, Dessi, Paladino and Merzi.

Apollodoro, which is halfway between a gallery and a design shop, has an entrance modelled on Borromini's illusionistic perspective in the garden gallery of Palazzo Spada (see p147).

One of this area's highlights is the Via Margutta art fair (see p339), which usually takes place around Christmas and in springtime.

Via Giulia and its surroundings is the next area to investigate: **Galleria Giulia** is a gallery-cum-bookshop with work on display by artists such as Argeles, Boille, Cano, Cascella, Echaurren, Erba and Lionni, as well as works by Bauhaus artists and German Expressionists.

Fabio Sargentini at **L'Attico** follows the latest trends in Italian art from Del Giudice to Corsini and Fabiani.

Trastevere is possibly better for more innovative ventures: The **Alessandra Bonomo** gallery, which opened in 1987, spotlights young Italian and foreign painters such as Schifano, Boetti, Twombly, Nunzio, Tremlett, LeWitt, Dokoupil. **Immart** is a new venue for contemporary painting and sculpture.

ANTIQUE PRINTS AND PHOTOGRAPHS

THE JUSTIFIABLY celebrated **Nardecchia**, named after its cultivated owner Plinio, is the cream of Rome's print dealers. Look out for originals by the 18th-century engraver, Piranesi, and views of the city and ancient Roman life.

Another Roman institution, **Casali**, has been trading for over 100 years. The family now runs two shops specializing in 16th- to 19th-century drawings and engravings of Roman scenes from museum-standard Piranesi down to relatively inexpensive unknown and decorative floral scenes.

The Florence-based **Alinari** family is renowned for its old sepia photographs of Italy from 1890 onwards, including shots of Rome at the turn of the century. At its Roman outlet, prices of photographs from the original plates start at around L30,000 and mounted prints at L500,000. Larger sizes can be mounted on wood or card.

Another place definitely worth heading for in search of that perfect print of old Rome and some enjoyable browsing is the **Mercato delle Stampe** (see p338).

DIRECTORY

ANTIQUES AND OLD MASTER PAINTINGS

Acanto
Via della Stelletta 10.
Map 4 F3 & 12 D2.
📞 686 54 81.

Amedeo di Castro
Via del Babuino 77–78.
Map 4 F1. 📞 320 76 50.

Anticaja e Petrella
Via Monte della Farina 62.
Map 4 F5 & 12 D4.

Antichità di Antonella e Maria Teresa
Via Panisperna 51.
Map 5 B4. 📞 488 54 11.

Antiquariato Valligiano
Via Giulia 193.
Map 4 E5 & 11 B5.
📞 686 95 05.

Art Deco Gallery
Via dei Coronari 14.
Map 4 E3 & 11 C2.
📞 686 53 30.

L'Art Nouveau
Via dei Coronari 221.
Map 4 E3 & 11 C2.
📞 68 80 52 30.

Bilenchi
Via della Stelletta 17.
Map 4 F3 & 12 D2.
📞 687 52 22.

Cesare Lampronti
Via del Babuino 67.
Map 4 F1. 📞 679 58 00.

La Chimera
Via Giulia 122.
Map 4 D4 & 11 A3.
📞 68 30 83 44.

Cose Così
Via del Governo Vecchio 89.
Map 4 E4 & 11 C3.
📞 68 80 53 63.

Granmercato Antiquario Babuino
Via del Babuino 150.
Map 4 F1.
📞 323 56 86.

Manasse
Via Campo Marzio 44.
Map 4 F3 & 12 D2.
📞 687 10 07.

Passato Prossimo
Via del Boschetto 1B.
Map 5 B4. 📞 482 62 57.

Piero Talone
Via dei Coronari 135.
Map 4 E3 & 11 B2.
📞 687 54 50.

Retrospettiva
Via del Boschetto 77A.
Map 5 B4. 📞 474 55 28.

W Apolloni
Via del Babuino 132–134.
Map 4 F1. 📞 679 24 29.

MODERN ART

Agenzia d'Arte Moderna
Piazza del Popolo 3.
Map 4 F1. 📞 361 09 75.

Alessandra Bonomo
Piazza di Sant'Apollonia 3.
Map 7 C1. 📞 581 05 79.

Apollodoro
Piazza Mignanelli 17.
Map 5 A2. 📞 678 75 57.

L'Attico
Via del Paradiso 41.
Map 4 E4 & 11 C4.
📞 686 98 46.

Galleria Giulia
Via Giulia 148.
Map 4 D4 & 11 B4.
📞 68 80 20 61.

Immart Gallery
Vicolo del Cinque 24B.
Map 4 E5.
📞 588 43 09.

Il Millennio
Via Margutta 51.
Map 4 F1.
📞 322 44 89.

Sperone
Via di Pallacorda 15.
Map 4 F3 & 12 D1.
📞 689 35 25.

ANTIQUE PRINTS AND PHOTOGRAPHS

Alinari
Via Alibert 16A. **Map** 5 A2.
📞 679 29 73.

Casali
Piazza della Rotonda 81A.
Map 4 F4 & 12 D3.
📞 678 35 15.

Nardecchia
Piazza Navona 25.
Map 4 E4 & 11 C3.
📞 656 93 18.

Street Markets

ROME'S OPEN-AIR MARKETS are essential to visit if you're interested in soaking up the bubbling exuberance and earthiness for which Romans are renowned. They are wonderfully vivid experiences too, as Italian stallholders have raised the display of even the humblest vegetable to an art form.

The city is dotted with popular, small local food markets, and there are several fascinating well-established markets near the centre, along with the famous flea market over in Trastevere.

It is important to keep your wits about you in markets because pickpockets work with lightning speed in the bustling crowds. But this said, Roman markets provide a vibrant source of entertainment and it would be a shame to let such caveats deter you from joining in the fun.

The street fairs that take place throughout the year are fun to go to, if they coincide with your visit, as they normally sell a good variety of local produce, handicrafts and clothes. Seasonal fairs also occur, especially around Christmas, when you can stock up on Italian specialities.

Campo de' Fiori

Piazza Campo de' Fiori. **Map** 4 E4 & 11 C4. ▥ *44, 46, 62, 64, 70, 81, 90, 90b, 492.* **Open** 7am–1.30pm Mon–Sat. See p146.

Right in the heart of the old city, Rome's most picturesque market is also its most historical. Its name, Campo de' Fiori, which translates as field of flowers, sometimes misleads people into expecting a flower market. In fact the name is said to derive from Campus Florae (Flora's square) – Flora being the lover of the great Roman general Pompey. A market has actually been held in this now rather shabby, but still beautiful, piazza for many centuries.

Every morning, except Sunday, the piazza is transformed by an array of stalls selling colourful fruit and vegetables, meat, poultry and fish. One or two stalls specialize in pulses, rice, dried fruit and nuts and there are also flower stalls situated near the fountain. But the huge open baskets of ready-stripped broccoli and spinach, chopped vegetables for minestrone and freshly prepared green salad mixes are the main attraction for visitors. They provide a real visual display as well as an edible feast.

The excellent delicatessen shops on the square, and bread shops nearby, complement the market. They make it a great place to stock up for an impromptu picnic if the weather turns out fine and you're tempted to do some *al fresco* dining in one of Rome's many attractive parks.

Mercato delle Stampe

Largo della Fontanella di Borghese. **Map** 4 F3 & 12 D1. ▥ *119, also routes to Via Tomacelli.* **Open** 7am–1pm Mon–Sat.

This market is a veritable haven for lovers of old prints, books (both genuine antiquarian and less-exalted second-hand), magazines and other printed ephemera. The quality varies, but it is a good deal more specialized than the *banche* or stalls near Termini station which are a more obvious tourist trap. Italian-speaking collectors can enjoy a field day leafing through back issues of specialist magazines. Other visitors might prefer the wonderful selection of illustrated art books and old prints of Rome. It is a good place to pick up that Piranesi print of your favourite Roman vista, ruin or church – but be prepared to bargain hard.

Mercato dei Fiori

Via Trionfale. **Map** 3 B1. Ⓜ *Ottaviano.* ▥ *23, 70.* **Open** 10.30am–1pm Tue.

Essentially a trade market, the Flower Market, just north of Via Andrea Doria, is open to the public only on Tuesdays. Housed in a covered hall, it has two floors brimming over with cut flowers upstairs and all kinds of pot plants on the lower floor. Anyone who has an interest in flowers will enjoy this wonderful array of Mediterranean blooms, which are on sale at giveaway prices.

Mercato Andrea Doria

Via Andrea Doria. **Map** 3 B1. Ⓜ *Ottaviano.* ▥ *23, 70.* **Open** 7am–1pm Mon–Sat.

The market used to stretch the whole length of this wide avenue. It has now been reorganized on to a huge square of open ground between Via Santamaura and Via Tunisi. Apart from the magnificent displays of fruit and vegetables, it has numerous stalls selling meat, poultry, fish and groceries, as well as an interesting clothes and shoe section. Situated northwest of the Vatican Museums, it is a little off the normal beaten track and has remained very much a Roman market that caters for the needs of the large local population.

Mercato di Piazza Vittorio

Piazza Vittorio Emanuele II. **Map** 6 E5. Ⓜ *Vittorio Emanuele.* ▥ *4, 9.* **Open** 7am–2pm Mon–Sat. See p174.

Bustling Piazza Vittorio was, until recently, perhaps the most Roman of the city's larger markets.

Organized as a cramped corridor of stalls around a central garden, it is the place where bargain-hunting *popolari*, Rome's bustling shoppers, buy their food. Stallholders offer cheap prices if you buy by the kilo, but watch out for bad fruit.

Lately it has become more international and now features African and Asian food stalls.

Sadly, the market's days are numbered, as the city council says that it defaces the 19th-century square. Some stalls have moved to the new site in Via Giolitti; others won't go. The battle is on, but make a visit before a splash of Roman colour is lost for ever.

Mercato di Testaccio

Piazza Testaccio. **Map** 8 D3. Ⓜ *Piramide.* ▥ *11, 27.* **Open** 7.30am–1.30pm Mon–Sat.

The covered market at Testaccio occupies the central area of its eponymous piazza. The few cheap clothing and shoe stalls skirting the outside are unremarkable, but the inside is well worth a visit. Lined with butchers, grocers and fishmongers, the whole central area is given over to fruit and vegetables – a theatre-set array of seductive colours and textures. Very popular with local residents, it offers super-fresh, high-quality produce and reasonable prices. Much of this market's charm for visitors lies in its compact size and relaxed, friendly atmosphere.

Porta Portese

Via Portuense & Via Ippolito Nievo.
Map 7 C3. ▪ 170, 280, 718, 719.
Open 6.30am–2pm Sun.

The *mercato delle pulci* or flea market is a relatively new market in Roman terms. Established shortly after the end of World War II, it is said to have grown out of the thriving black market that operated at Tor di Nona opposite Castel Sant'Angelo during those lean years. Stallholders come from as far away as Naples and set up shop in the early hours of the morning – if you are strolling in that direction after a late night in Trastevere, it's well worth pausing just to watch them.

Anything and everything seems to be for sale, piled high on stalls in carefully arranged disorder – clothes, shoes, bags, luggage, camping equipment, linen, towels, pots, pans, kitchen utensils, plants, pets, spare parts, cassettes and CDs, old LPs and 78s.

Furniture stalls tend to be concentrated around Piazza Ippolito Nievo along with what they call "antiques", though you may have to sort through an awful lot of junk before finding a real one. And then you will have to bargain for it. The technique is to offer them half the asked price and then walk away. A lot of people go just for the fun of it and always end up buying something.

There are also second-hand clothes – leather or sheepskin coats and jackets go for L10,000 – with many of the Via Sannio stall holders relocating here for the Sunday trade. The stretch along Via Ippolito Nievo is monopolized by "*i Russi di Porta Portese*", immigrant Russian stallholders selling caviar, icons (authenticity uncertain), lace, other ethnic handicrafts, old cameras and binoculars. A must if you have a Sunday morning to spare.

Mercato di Via Sannio

Via Sannio. **Map** 9 C2.
Ⓜ *San Giovanni.* ▪ 16, 81, 87.
Open 8am–1pm Mon–Sat.

In the 1960s and 1970s this used to be Italy's answer to Carnaby Street. Today, at first glance, it doesn't seem to have anything very special to offer – random stalls selling inexpensive casual clothes, shoes, bags, belts, jewellery, toys, kitchen utensils and music cassettes. But towards the end of the street there is a large covered section which extends back to the Aurelian Wall *(see p196)* with many stalls piled high with second-hand clothes at very low prices for those who like to rummage. There is also a

section that sells military-style goods plus some camping and fishing equipment.

Some of these stalls move their wares to Porta Portese on a Sunday morning.

Local markets

Generally open 7am–1pm Mon–Sat.

Piazza delle Coppelle (map 4 F3 & 12 D2), near the Pantheon, is probably the most picturesque of the food markets sprinkled around the city. A tiny market devoted to food and fruit and flowers, it offers a charming splash of colour in the heart of the city.

Piazza San Cosimato (map 7 C1) in Trastevere hosts another lively local market with some tempting cheeses and salami.

There is a fairly big market on **Via Alessandria** (map 6 D1) in Nomentana, and other smaller ones in **Via della Pace** (map 4 E4 & 11 C3) near Piazza Navona, and in **Via Balbo** (map 5 C4) and **Via Milazzo** (map 6 E3) near Termini station. You can also visit the trade market, the **Mercato Generale**, (map 8 D5), in Via Ostiense, which is open to the public after 10am.

STREET FAIRS

A special and interesting feature of shopping in Rome is the street fair:

The **Expo Tevere** exhibition starts each year between mid-June and mid-July on both sides of the river bank between the Sant'Angelo and Cavour bridges. Its stalls display Italian regional arts and crafts and also sell pasta, jam, olive oil, wines and liqueurs. Most items are cheaper than in the shops. The exhibition opens in the evening (6pm–1am). The entrance fee is minimal and also includes ferry transport across the Tiber.

There are two antiques fairs, both known as the **Fiera dell'Antiquariato**, that take place in Via dei Coronari. The first starts in the second half of May, 10am–1pm and 4pm–11pm daily. It makes a memorable event at night when lighted torches line the carpeted street. The second goes along Via dell'Orso as well and normally occurs in mid-October (but has also started in late September), Mon–Thu 3pm–11pm & Fri–Sun 10am–11pm. Stalls also sell leatherwork, jewellery and gifts.

The **Via Margutta Art Fair** usually takes place around Christmas and in springtime. Set in one of the most charming and exclusive streets of the city, it's an event not to be missed, although it's more for browsing as prices are very high.

The utterly glamorous **Spanish Steps Alta Moda Fashion Show** is a fairly new event and doesn't have a set date. The limited seating space is filled by invitation only. However, the public can squeeze in behind to enjoy this display of all-Italian designer fashion. So far it has been held mid- to late July.

Befana, the traditional Epiphany fair in Piazza Navona (mid-December until 6 January) is now rather down-at-heel, but still fascinating for those who have never seen it or for children. Stalls selling clay statues for nativities and sweets that look like pieces of coal are the main attraction.

Natale Oggi is a well-established event taking place near Christmas in the Fiera di Roma at EUR, and worth visiting to have a look at the special Italian Christmas treats.

Via Giulia hosts art fairs now and then, and open evenings when the antique and art galleries stay open late offering food and wine to all visitors.

Every year Trastevere hosts its very own carnival, known as the **Noantri** festival, around late July, when Viale Trastevere becomes overrun with the typical *porchetta* stalls *(see p341)*, party lights, gift stalls and people.

The details given here may change, so check the local listings or at the tourist office *(see p359)*.

ENTERTAINMENT IN ROME

THERE'S A PARTICULAR excitement attached to Roman entertainment. Football and opera, for example, are both worth experiencing for sheer atmosphere alone, whether or not you are a fan. The jazz scene is especially good with international stars appearing alongside local talent. And concerts and films take on an added dimension when performances take place beneath the stars in the many open-air arenas spread across the city. Unexpectedly, given the general shutdown among shops, restaurants and museums, the summer remains Rome's liveliest time for live music and other cultural events. Rome's graceful Renaissance squares, vast parks, villa gardens, Classical ruins and other open spaces host various major arts festivals. If you prefer sport, or want to try out some Roman nightclubs, there's plenty on offer too.

Gregory Peck and Audrey Hepburn in *Roman Holiday*

PRACTICAL INFORMATION

THE HANDIEST source of information about what's on is *Trovaroma*, the weekly Thursday supplement to *La Repubblica* newspaper. It has a day-by-day rundown of what's on and where, and covers music, exhibitions,

Saxophonist at Alpheus *(see p344)*

theatre, cinemas, guided tours, restaurants and children's entertainment. There is also a monthly listings publication, *Info Rome*, which is written in English and Italian. Daily newspapers like *Il Messaggero*, *Il Manifesto*, *Paese Sera* and *La Repubblica* usually give the evening's entertainment listings.

Two fortnightly magazines, *Wanted in Rome* and *Metropolitan*, provide less detailed listings in English. They can be found in Via Veneto newsagents or at English bookshops. Also worth getting hold of is *Carnet di Roma*, available at the beginning of each month from the EPT *(see p359)*, which gives details in English

of classical music, festivals, theatre and exhibitions in the city and surroundings.

Punctuality is not what Italians are renowned for, so don't be surprised if some events start slightly later than advertised in listings.

BOOKING TICKETS

BOOKING in advance is not part of Italian lifestyle. Two ticket agencies that will book theatre tickets for you (for a small fee) are **Gesman** and **Box Office**. As a rule, theatres themselves do not accept telephone bookings – you have to visit the box office in person. They will charge you a *prevendita* supplement (about 10% of the normal price) for any tickets sold in advance. The price of a theatre ticket can be anything between L10,000 and L70,000.

Tickets for classical concerts are usually sold on the spot, and are sometimes for that night only, an arrangement that favours the last-minute

decision to go. Opera is the exception. Tickets are sold months in advance, with just a few held back until two days before the performance.

Stage at Caffè Latino *(see pp344-5)*

It is usually easier (and also cheaper) to get tickets for the Caracalla Festival which takes place in the summer.

The **Teatro dell'Opera** box office *(see p343)* handles sales for both summer and winter seasons, and they have a high-tech booking system, with a computer which colour-codes unsold seats.

Tickets for most big rock and jazz events can be bought at **Orbis**, **Prontospettacolo** and at larger record shops such as **Rinascita**.

Remember that if you're trying to get hold of a ticket for a particular performance that has already sold out, you're extremely unlikely to be able to obtain one from

Member of contemporary dance group Momix *(see p343)*

unofficial sources – there are very few ticket touts in Rome, except at major football matches such as important finals.

REDUCED-PRICE TICKETS

THEATRES and concert venues tend not to offer discounts on tickets since performances are so often over-subscribed. Cinemas, however, offer people aged over 60 and disabled people a 30% reduction on weekdays. In recent years the Comune di Roma has sponsored reduced-price cinema tickets on one day per week (usually Wednesday) but this may be discontinued. Some clubs at the beach resorts such as Fregene offer reductions: look out for *due per uno* coupons in local bars that allow two people entrance for the price of one.

FACILITIES FOR THE DISABLED

FEW ROMAN venues provide easy access for people with restricted mobility, and any disabled visitors and their companions are likely to find the lack of provision for them very frustrating.

The situation does improve a little in summer, however, when a great many performances in the city are held at open-air venues. The Baths of Caracalla have wheelchair access, as do the classical concerts held in the beautiful gardens of Villa Giulia *(see pp262–3)*. For more general information on provision for the disabled, see page 359.

Performance in the Classical setting of the Baths of Caracalla *(see p342)*

OPEN-AIR ENTERTAINMENT

OPEN-AIR OPERA, cinema, classical music and jazz concerts fill the calendar from late June until the end of September. These performances outdoors can be wonderful, with spectacular settings and enthusiastic audiences. Some of them are grand affairs, but small events may be just as evocative – a guitar recital in the cloisters of Santa Maria della Pace *(see p342)*, for example, or jazz in the beautiful gardens of Villa Doria Pamphilj *(see p344)*.

Singers performing the *Barber of Seville*

Many cinemas roll back their ceilings in summer for open-air screenings, or else move to outdoor arenas, and there are also annual open-air cinema festivals. The Cineporto along the Tiber and the Festival di Massenzio offer films, food and small exhibitions in July and August. Theatre, too, moves outside in summer. Greek and Roman plays are staged at Ostia Antica *(see p270)* and other shows take place at the Anfiteatro del Tasso *(see p347)*.

Rome's most important, month-long summer festival is RomaEuropa, with main performances in the grounds of the Villa Medici. There are other, smaller festivals too, but times and venues change from year to year, so it's best to watch for posters around

the city for the most up-to-date information. More traditional is Trastevere's community festival, Festa de Noantri *(see p59)*, with music, fireworks and processions. This religious festival is on the Saturday after 16 July but celebrations continue well into August. The Festa dell'Unità, run by the PDS (the former Communist Party), but not limited to politics, is generally held in September. The programme includes games, stalls, food and drink.

Finally, if you like your entertainment less structured, you can always do as the Romans do and take part in the *passeggiata* (early evening stroll) – the city's favourite spots are Piazza Navona *(see p120)* and along Via del Corso.

TICKET AGENCIES

Gesman
Via Angelo Emo 65.
Map 3 A2. ⟮ 63 18 03.

Box Office
Viale Giulio Cesare 88. **Map** 3 C1.
Box office tickets for classical music, rock, pop and jazz concerts and some sporting events.
⟮ 372 02 15, 372 02 16 or 568 16 23.

Orbis
Piazza dell'Esquilino 37.
Map 6 D4. ⟮ 47 44 76.

Prontospettacolo
Telephone bookings only.
⟮ 39 38 72 97 or 39 38 74 40.

Rinascita
Via delle Botteghe Oscure 1–3.
Map 4 F5 & 12 E4.
⟮ 679 74 60 or 679 76 36.

The Teatro dell'Opera *(see p342)*

Classical Music and Dance

CLASSICAL CONCERTS take place in a surprising number of venues: tickets for opera premières may be hard to get, but soloists, groups or orchestras playing in gardens, churches, villas or ancient ruins are more accessible. World-renowned soloists and orchestras make appearances throughout the year; past visitors have included Luciano Pavarotti and Placido Domingo, Catherine Malfitano and prima ballerina Sylvie Guillem.

Programmes are generally international in scope but sometimes you will find a festival dedicated to one of Italy's own, like Palestrina, the great 16th-century master of polyphonic church music, or Arcangelo Corelli, inventor of the Baroque *concerto grosso*.

MUSIC IN CHURCHES

ONE OF ROME'S main attractions for classical music lovers is the rich repertoire that can be heard in the city's churches. Always sacred in theme (by decree of Pope John Paul II), music is mainly performed as concerts rather than during services.

Programmes are posted around the city and outside the churches. You will often find very good musicians playing in the main churches, while the smaller, out-of-the-way churches frequently play host to young musicians and amateur choirs as well.

St Peter's *(see p230)* hosts one major RAI (national broadcasting company) concert on 5 December attended by the pope and free for the general public. It has two established choirs. The Coro della Cappella Giulia sing at the 10.30am mass and 5pm vespers on Sunday. The Coro della Cappella Sistina sing whenever the pope celebrates mass here, as on 29 June (St Peter and St Paul's day).

Important choral masses also take place on 25 January in **San Paolo fuori le Mura** *(see p267)*, when the pope attends, on 24 June in **San Giovanni in Laterano** *(p182)* and on 31 December at the **Gesù** *(pp114–5)* where the *Te Deum* is sung. The church of **Sant'Ignazio di Loyola** *(p106)* is another favourite venue for choral concerts.

Gregorian chant can be heard in **Sant'Apollinare** *(p127)* at 11am on Sundays and religious festivals.

Easter and the Christmas festivities are a great time for cheap and chilly concerts: there is usually neither entrance fee nor heating!

ORCHESTRAL, CHAMBER AND CHORAL MUSIC

THE **Auditorium di Santa Cecilia**, the national broadcasting company's **Foro Italico** and **Teatro dell' Opera** are Rome's three main auditoriums, with their own resident orchestras and choirs. The Orchestra e Coro dell' Accademia di Santa Cecilia is the top orchestra but the Orchestra e Coro di Roma della RAI is also good. All three offer interestingly varied seasons which include visiting groups and soloists from all over the world.

The season at the **Teatro Olimpico** usually offers very good chamber music, some orchestral concerts and ballet with at least one concert a week. They are advertised on large yellow posters with red borders, easily identifiable in the streets and a hallmark for high-level performances.

The Concerti del Tempietto concert series Festival Musicale delle Nazioni concentrates on the composers of a different country each month on Saturdays (9pm) and Sundays (5.45pm) between November and June at the **Sala Baldini**.

Ticket prices for classical concerts depend a lot on performers and venue. The **Auditorium del Foro Italico** sells tickets for most concerts for under L20,000; a ticket for the **Teatro Olimpico** costs

between L25,000–L40,000, but seats for an important concert at **Teatro dell'Opera** may cost as much as L150,000.

The Associazione Musicale Romana organizes three annual festivals in the **Palazzo della Cancelleria** *(see p149)*: the Festival Internazionale di Cembalo (harpsichord festival) in March; Musica al Palazzo in May; and the Festival Internazionale di Organo in September.

It's always worth checking who's playing at the **Teatro Ghione**, the **Oratorio del Gonfalone**, the **Auditorio di San Leone Magno**, or the **Sala Accademica di Via dei Greci**.

OPEN-AIR SUMMER CONCERTS

IN THE SUMMER music lovers can enjoy concerts in cloisters, palazzo courtyards and ancient ruins. Concerts can be one-offs or part of a festival programme, regular fixtures or impromptu. Do as the Romans do, don't plan until the last moment and keep an eye on the posters and listings pages *(see p340)* for the latest details.

Open-air opera and dance have their home in the majestic **Baths of Caracalla**. Classical concerts are often part of festivals like RomaEuropa *(see p341)* but there are also a number of open-air festivals and concert series dedicated specifically to classical music. Among the more interesting is the Stagione Estiva dell'Orchestra dell'Accademia di Santa Cecilia held at the Ninfeo *(nympheum)* in the grounds of **Villa Giulia** *(see p263)*. Also listed as the Concerti a Villa Giulia, the concerts begin in July and tickets are under L20,000.

The Associazione Musicale Romana organizes Serenate in Chiostro – a lively and varied programme of concerts during July in the cloisters of **Santa Maria della Pace** *(see p121)* with tickets on sale for under L20,000.

Estate al Tempietto (listed also as Concerti del Tempietto)

is the Tempietto orchestra's summer treat with concerts every evening from July to September in the **Area Archeologica del Teatro di Marcello** (see p151). They're held in the adjacent basilica of San Nicola in Carcere if it rains.

Festival Villa Pamphilj in Musica, in July, is a series of concerts in the gardens of **Villa Doria Pamphilj** (see p267). Programmes range from comic opera to jazz and 20th-century classical music.

Brass bands can be heard in the **Pincio Gardens** (see p136) on Sunday mornings from the end of April until mid-July – they usually strike up at around 10.30am.

CONTEMPORARY MUSIC

THE **Auditorium del Foro Italico**, the **Auditorium di Santa Cecilia** and the Accademia Filarmonica Romana (usually at the **Teatro Olimpico**) sometimes include modern pieces in their programmes but these are generally less popular than the classics and there is no set venue with a regular contemporary programme.

International names appear on festival programmes and at one-off concerts. The most interesting festivals are Nuovi Spazi Musicali (now part of RomaEuropa) in the summer,

with free concerts transmitted on Italian radio, and the Festival Nuova Consonanza in the autumn. Modern Italian composers are performed in the Rassegna Nuova Musica Italiana concert series two or three times a year. It's also worth keeping an eye out for performances by scholars of the French Academy at **Villa Medici** (see p135).

OPERA

ITALY AND OPERA are to many people synonymous. Critics will tell you (justifiably) that Rome's opera is nowhere near the standard of Milan's La Scala, Naples's San Carlo or Venice's La Fenice. But that doesn't mean it's not worth visiting – world-class singers do appear here (see p38), mainly in premières or solo recitals. In summertime the visual spectacle of *Aida*, say, performed outside, is simply magnificent.

The season starts late at **Teatro dell'Opera**, between November and January. In recent years programmes have concentrated on the great popular operas, rather than staging experimental productions or historical recoveries. Tickets range from L25,000 to L250,000.

In July and August, the Teatro dell'Opera traditionally moves outdoors to the ancient

Baths of Caracalla. Tickets are ranging from L10,000 to L120,000, and they can be obtained in advance from the box office at the Teatro dell'Opera. On the evening of the performance, tickets may also be bought on the door. The cheapest seats require exceptionally good hearing.

BALLET AND DANCE

OPPORTUNITIES to watch ballet or contemporary dance are fairly limited in Rome. The opera house's resident company Corpo di Ballo del Teatro dell'Opera di Roma performs the great classics as well as Roland Petit-style modern choreographies. Performances are staged at **Teatro dell'Opera**, the **Baths of Caracalla** (in summer) or **Teatro Brancaccio**.

Contemporary dance is best served during the summer festivals but foreign companies often perform at **Teatro Olimpico** as well. American modern dance groups of the Moses Pendleton school – Pilobolus, Momix, ISO and Daniel Ezralow – are popular visitors. Traditional folk dancers and acrobats from China and companies such as the Moscow circus and Moisseiev Dance Company usually perform at the **Teatro Tenda a Strisce**.

Rock, Jazz, Folk and World Music

ROME'S NON-CLASSICAL MUSIC SCENE is unpredictable, but if you have the patience, you'll come across a huge variety of music at the many clubs, as well as open-air events with foreign stars such as Madonna, Michael Jackson and Dire Straits. Publicity is often disorganized, but the "Music Box" section of *Trovaroma (see p340)* gives an idea of what's on.

It's not possible to book tickets in advance at the smaller venues – just turn up with everyone else. You will need to buy a *tessera* (membership card) though, costing anything from L1,000 to L20,000. Well-known musicians may mean a further entrance fee, but local groups are generally included in the membership.

ROCK MUSIC

BIG ROCK CONCERTS are held at EUR in the **Palazzo dello Sport**, or in a stadium: the **Stadio Flaminio**, the **Stadio Olimpico**, or in out-of-the-way **Ippodromo Capannelle**. Get there at least an hour before the gates open for a good seat. Testaccio's **Villaggio Globale Il Mattatoio** (a converted abattoir) is a large-scale, stand-up venue for concerts and other events. The facilities are basic, and again, over-crowding means you should turn up early.

Rome also has several lively clubs and discos which play rock music. Loyal devotees head for the good clubs in large numbers. Some are unpretentious and friendly and some, which are rather sumptuous and stylish, are frequented by the rich and famous. Entrance for the top spots can cost up to to L40,000. A venue to be aware of is **Osiris**, near Campo de' Fiori, which puts on rock, mainstream pop and world music. Check what's on, too, at the **Antica Carboneria**, **Black Out**, with concerts held on Thursdays, or at the **Piper '90**, and, in the Vatican area, **Il Castello**, a converted cinema housing rock and jazz festivals and a club.

Forte Prenestino is an interesting venue – a former prison, it was taken over by squatters a few years ago, and turned into a social centre housing rock concerts, debates and art exhibitions. Nearer the centre are more traditional establishments. **Big Mama**, the trendy **Palladium** and **Caffè Caruso** are well-known, popular venues for a great variety of live bands.

JAZZ

ROME'S TASTE for jazz has developed over the years as a result of visits from American and other foreign musicians. Miles Davis played one of his last concerts at the **Roma Jazz Festival**, for instance, and guitarist Pat Metheny, Sonny Rollins, Gil Evans' Band, the Lounge Lizards, Spyrogyra, and Joe Zawinul's Syndicate are frequent visitors. Roma Jazz takes place every year, generally in July, with performances at the **Foro Italico** *(see p351)*, sometimes listed as the Stadio del Tennis in *Trovaroma*. Tickets, which cost around L35,000–40,000, are obtainable from Orbis *(see p341)* and other agents.

Outside festival times, the best jazz musicians play at **Palladium**, near San Paolo fuori le Mura, or at **Il Castello** and **Alpheus**. **Alpheus** is unique in offering separate concert halls and interesting festivals featuring high-quality jazz ensembles every night. Other, smaller venues, some of which encourage budding talent, are **Vicolo 49** (where you are welcome to join in) and **Caffè les Folies**. Some of Rome's music schools also double as showcases for new performers – these include **Mississippi Blues**, **Saint Louis Music City**, **Ciac Musica** and **Alexanderplatz**.

In summer, many of the music festivals take place outdoors at night. Jazz has featured in the Festival Villa Pamphilj in Musica in recent years, held every July and organized by I Concerti nel Parco. Tickets, costing around L15,000, are available from the Villa Pamphilj itself.

In winter, try two pub-style venues open until late: **La Finestra sul Cortile** and **Stardust** – the latter offers jazz on Tuesdays, and a pianist on other nights. Or check what's on at **Caffè Latino**, **Caffè Caruso**, **Fonclea**, **Melvyn's** and **Antica Carboneria**.

There's a wide range of artists to look out for. Pianist Antonello Salis plays a mix of jazz and Caribbean rhythms. Crystal White and the Supernaturals are a resident Roman jazz funk formation. Guitar lovers may enjoy Eddie Palermo's fusion, and the major names to be aware of in jazz groups are Roberto Gatto, Maurizio Gianmarco, Massimo Moriconi and Massimo Urbani. Rome's other well-known bands include Orizzonte degli Eventi (fusion), Sestetto Swing di Roma (swing) and Area 2 (not strictly Roman) who play jazz-rock.

FOLK MUSIC

AT THE FOREFRONT of folk music in Rome for 30 years, **Folkstudio** in Trastevere is well worth a visit. Founded back in the 1960s, its cramped rooms have an informal, friendly, participatory atmosphere which welcomed up-and-coming stars such as Bob Dylan – a fact which is fondly remembered here. Irish folk music, and American country and western are much in demand, as well as the regional strains of Italian folk music. No drinks are sold, so bring your own. You'll need to buy a membership card to enter, costing around L10,000.

A recent arrival on Rome's folk music scene is the **Shamrock** in the Colosseum area offering country and blue-grass music. If you want to eat too, head for **Fonclea** near St Peter's, but check in *Trovaroma* to see who's playing – country music only features on some nights.

Visit some of Rome's Irish pubs and you may be lucky to find some spontaneous music-making going on. Places to try are the **Fiddler's Elbow** and **Druid's Den**, both in the Santa Maria Maggiore area. Also look out for where the Kay McCarthy Ensemble, or Square Dance are performing.

WORLD MUSIC

A STRONG Latin American colony has made its home in Rome since the 1970s. Latin American music is no passing fad here; Romans dance the night away together with the many Brazilian, Argentinian and Peruvian residents and merengue, salsa and soca are all very popular. For the last few years an open-air summer Caribe festival has taken place in Villa Borghese with live music and other attractions. It's by no means a certain annual event, but worth keeping an eye out for.

Many venues offer similar opportunities to enjoy Latin American music throughout the year: **El Charango** offers South American food as well as music and a small dance area. At **Yes Brazil** the owner and beautiful long-legged waitresses sway with the clientele to the bossa nova. Various musicians alternate way into the night: watch out for the guitarist Giovanna Marinuzzi, who plays Brazilian music, and take care to book front tables ahead of time. Also look out for resident Brazilian musicians Brenazil, Carlos de Lima and Alvinho, and local salsa band Xenaya, or check what's on at the **Caffè Latino**, **Mambo** and **Blatumba Amazons** in the Ghetto, at **Caffè Caruso** in Testaccio and the **Bossa Nova** or **Melvyn's** in Trastevere.

Other regional musical styles have less of a presence, but exist nevertheless. Arab food and music are available on alternate days at **Taverna Negma**, and lovers of African music should look out for performances by Sanganà or Akwaba. African and Italian musicians play together with Pietro dall'Oglio's group at various venues in the city.

DIRECTORY

Akab
Via di Monte Testaccio 69.
Map 8 D4.
℡ 5730 03 09.

Alexanderplatz
Via Ostia 9. **Map** 3 B1.
℡ 372 93 98.

Alpheus
Via del Commercio 36–8.
Map 8 D5.
℡ 574 77 47, 574 98 26.

Antica Carboneria
Via Cagliari 23. **Map** 6 E1.
℡ 841 19 88.

Big Mama
Vicolo S. Francesco a Ripa 18. **Map** 7 C2.
℡ 581 25 51.

Black Out
Via Saturnia 18.
Map 9 C3.
℡ 70 49 67 91.

Blatumba Amazons
Piazza in Piscinula 20.
Map 8 D1.
℡ 589 64 21.

Bossa Nova
Via degli Orti di Trastevere 23. **Map** 7 C2.
℡ 581 61 21.

Caffè Caruso
Via di Monte Testaccio 36.
Map 8 D4.
℡ 574 50 19.

Caffè les Folies
Via S. Francesco a Ripa 165. **Map** 7 C1.
℡ 588 59 08.

Caffè Latino
Via di Monte Testaccio 96.
Map 8 D4.
℡ 574 40 20.

Il Castello
Via di Porta Castello 44.
Map 4 D3.
℡ 686 83 28.

El Charango
Via di Sant'Onofrio 28.
Map 3 C4.
℡ 687 99 08.

Ciac Musica
Via Tripoli 60.
℡ 831 94 18.

Druid's Den
Via S. Martino ai Monti 28.
Map 6 D4.

Fiddler's Elbow
Via dell'Olmata 43.
Map 6 D4.

La Finestra sul Cortile
Via in Publicolis 45.
Map 4 F5 & 12 D5.
℡ 683 24 97.

Folkstudio
Via Frangipane 42.
Map 5 B5.
℡ 487 10 63.

Fonclea
Via Crescenzio 82 A.
Map 3 C2. ℡ 689 63 02.

Forte Prenestino
Via F. del Pino.

Frankie Go
Via Schiaparelli 29.
Map 2 D3. ℡ 322 1251.

Ippodromo Capannelle
Via Appia Nuova km.12.
℡ 718 31 43.

Mambo
Via dei Fienaroli 30 A.
Map 7 C1.
℡ 589 71 96.

Melvyn's
Via del Politeama 8.
Map 4 E5 & 11 C5.
℡ 580 30 77.

Mississippi Blues
Via del Mascherino 65.
Map 3 C2.

Osiris
Largo dei Librari 82 A.
Map 4 E5 & 11 C4.
℡ 68 80 63 72.

Palazzo dello Sport
Viale dell'Umanesimo.
℡ 592 51 07.

Palladium
Piazza B. Romano 8.
℡ 511 02 03.

Piper '90
Via Tagliamento 9.
℡ 855 53 98.

Roma Jazz Festival
℡ 70 49 78 51.

Saint Louis Music City
Via del Cardello 13.
Map 5 B5.
℡ 47 45 07.

Shamrock
Via Capo d'Africa 26 D.
Map 9 A1.
℡ 700 25 83.

Stadio Flaminio
Viale Pilsudski.
Map 1 B2.
℡ 323 65 39.

Stadio Olimpico
Viale dei Gladiatori.

Stardust
Vicolo de Renzi 4.
Map 7 C1.
℡ 580 53 37.

Taverna Negma
Borgo Vittorio 92.
Map 3 C3.
℡ 686 51 43.

Vicolo 49
Vicolo dei Soldati 47.
Map 4 E3 & 11 C2.
℡ 687 54 40.

Villaggio Globale Il Mattatoio
Lungotevere Testaccio.
Map 8 D4.
℡ 57 30 03 29.

Yes Brazil
Via S. Francesco a Ripa 103.
Map 7 C2.
℡ 581 62 67.

Cinema and Theatre

CINEMA-GOING IS A POPULAR pastime in Rome, with around 40 films on show on an average weekday, while theatre-goers have far less choice.

The great majority of Roman cinemas are *prima visione* (first run) and show the latest international films in dubbed version. The smaller art cinemas are more likely to show subtitled versions of foreign films.

Theatre productions are performed in Italian whether the plays are national classics or by foreign playwrights. The main theatres offer a selection by great Italian playwrights. There are also performances of traditional cabaret, avant-garde theatre and dance theatre. Theatre tickets cost between L10,000 and L70,000 and can generally only be booked in advance by visiting the theatre box office in person, or through agencies such as **Gesman** and **Box Office** *(see p341)*.

PRIMA VISIONE

THERE ARE OVER 80 *prima visione* cinemas in the city. The best cinemas in Rome in terms of decor and comfort are the **Fiamma** (two screens), **Barberini** (three screens) and **Rivoli**.

As a rule, foreign films are dubbed into Italian rather than subtitled (Italian dubbers are considered among the best in the world) but the **Alcazar** has showings in the original language – mainly English – on Mondays.

Tickets for new films generally cost around L10,000 but a few cinemas listed as *prima visione* charge less, namely **Capranichetta**, **Diamante** and **Cinema Esperia**. Over 60s and disabled people are normally entitled to a 30% reduction on weekdays. The Comune di Roma sponsors a reduced ticket day (normally it's Wednesday). Check the newspaper or *Trovaroma* for accurate details *(see p340)*.

ART CINEMAS

THERE ARE TWO main types of art cinema in Rome: the *cine-clubs* and the *cinema d'essai*. Both of these are good if you're interested in catching older classics and new foreign films as well as films by some of the contemporary Italian directors.

The *d'essai* cinemas now and then show films in the original language (indicated by *v.o.* for *versione originale* in the listings). Try the **Azzurro Scipioni** (one of the few to remain open throughout summer) or the **Nuovo Sacher**. Some of the smaller cinemas like the **Labirinto** are called *cine-clubs* and require membership.

The multi-media arts centre **Palazzo delle Esposizioni** usually shows interesting series of international films in the Sala Rossellini (prior booking is advised).

Cartoons and children's favourites are shown at **Dei Piccoli**. The evening showings for adults, often in the original language, are listed as Dei Piccoli Sera.

The **Tibur** is a small cinema with a varied programme and one of the few places where students get a reduction.

ENGLISH-LANGUAGE FILMS

IN ADDITION TO occasional undubbed showings of British, American and Australasian films in art cinemas and the **Alcazar**, Rome has its own English-language cinema, the **Pasquino**, in Trastevere. Titles change every few days (tickets cost around L7,000).

SUMMER CINEMA

MANY ROMAN cinemas have roll-back ceilings which are in use during the summer, while the others close down. The **Nuovo Sacher** has an outdoor arena which also is used for summer screenings.

Rome also has two summer cinema festivals: Cineporto and Massenzio. These show several films each night from 9pm until the small hours, with food and drinks on sale and often live music during the intervals. Cineporto (every night, July–September) has a fixed venue in the Parco della Farnesina but Massenzio moves around (see listings).

It's also worth keeping an eye on the listings pages *(see p340)* for retrospectives or avant-garde film seasons at the **Azzurro Scipioni** and the open-air arts festivals like RomaEuropa *(see p341)* and Festa dell'Unità *(see p341)*. Sci-fi enthusiasts should keep an eye out for the Fantafestival (early June), a science fiction, fantasy and horror film festival.

MAINSTREAM THEATRE

THE BACKBONE of Rome's theatrical repertoire are Luigi Pirandello's dramas and comedies by 18th-century Venetian Carlo Goldoni and 20th-century Neapolitan Eduardo de Filippo. Major foreign playwrights are also performed from time to time.

The best classic productions are staged at the **Teatro Argentina**, **Teatro Quirino**, **Teatro Valle**, **Teatro Eliseo** and **Teatro Piccolo Eliseo**. **Teatro Argentina**, originally an opera house, is state-owned and home of Rome's permanent theatre company. The **Quirino** and **Valle** host productions from other Italian cities. The **Valle** alternates between productions of great Italian classics by famous companies and lesser known modernist works. Plays at the **Quirino** often feature famous Italian actors. The **Eliseo** and **Piccolo Eliseo** are among the best of the private theatres. Agatha Christie and Alfred Hitchcock are often on at the **Teatro Stabile del Giallo** which specializes in crime and detective thrillers, while **Teatro Vittoria** goes in for Noël Coward or Raymond Queneau. The programme at

Teatro Sistina usually includes musicals by visiting foreign companies and shows by popular Italian actors.

CONTEMPORARY THEATRE

THE HOME OF contemporary theatre is the **Tordinona**, **Politecnico**, **Ateneo** (inside the university) and in a host of small theatres, ingeniously rigged up in cellars, garages, small apartments or tents. The **Colosseo** and **La Scaletta** host some alternative fringe-type productions (known here as *teatro off*) while the **Tordinona**, the **Politecnico** and the **Ateneo** tend to stage contemporary authors and occasional avant-garde productions. Some of them, like the **Teatro dei Cocci**, put on drama school productions.

FOLK, CABARET AND PUPPET THEATRE

ROMAN AND Neapolitan folk songs and cabaret can be enjoyed in one of Trastevere's traditional cabaret restaurants like **Ciceruacchio**, **Fantasie di Trastevere**, **Fieramosca** or **Meo Patacca**.

Puppet theatre is another tradition. Shows generally take place early in the evening at weekends and sometimes during the week at **Teatro Verde**, **Teatro Villa Lazzaroni**, **Teatro Mongiovino** and the **English Puppet Theatre** where puppeteers will recite in English if there is enough demand. In the summer, travelling Neapolitan and Sicilian marionette companies give one-off performances.

OPEN-AIR THEATRE

THE OPEN-AIR summer theatre season usually features Greek and Roman plays at **Ostia Antica** (*see pp270–71*).

The **Anfiteatro Quercia del Tasso** in the Janiculum park takes its name from the oak tree under which 16th-century poet Tasso used to sit. The theatre has no fixed genre (both Plato and Noël Coward were on recently, for instance), and tickets cost around L20,000.

Nearby is a permanent Neapolitan street puppet theatre booth featuring *Pulcinella* (the Italian original of Punch). Shows are usually on in the afternoons, with morning shows on Sundays; children love them.

DIRECTORY

PRIMA VISIONE

Alcazar
Via Card. Merry del Val 14.
Map 7 C1. 588 00 99.

Barberini
Piazza Barberini 52.
Map 5 B3. 482 77 07.

Capranichetta
Piazza di Montecitorio 125.
Map 4 F3 & 12 E2.
679 69 57.

Cinema Esperia
Piazza Sonnino 37.
Map 7 C1. 581 28 84.

Diamante
Via Prenestina 232.
29 56 06.

Fiamma
Via Bissolati 45.
Map 5 C2. 482 71 00.

Rivoli
Via Lombardia 23.
Map 5 B2. 488 08 83.

ART CINEMAS

Azzurro Scipioni
Via degli Scipioni 82.
Map 3 C2. 370 10 94.

Dei Piccoli
Viale della Pineta 15.
Map 5 B1. 855 34 85.

Labirinto
Via di Pompeo Magno 27.
Map 4 D1. 321 62 83.

Nuovo Sacher
Largo Ascianghi 1.
Map 7 C2. 581 81 16.

Palazzo delle Esposizioni
Via Milano 9A. **Map** 5 B4.
488 54 65.

Tibur
Via degli Etruschi 40.
495 77 62.

ENGLISH-LANGUAGE FILMS

Alcazar
See left.

Pasquino
Vicolo del Piede 19.
Map 7 C1. 580 36 22.

MAINSTREAM THEATRE

Teatro Argentina
Largo Argentina 56.
Map 4 F4 & 12 D4.
68 80 46 01.

Teatro Eliseo
Via Nazionale 183.
Map 5 B4. 488 21 14.

Teatro Piccolo Eliseo
Via Nazionale 183.
Map 5 B4. 48 85 95.

Teatro Quirino
Piazza dell'Oratorio 73.
Map 5 A4 & 12 F2.
679 45 85.

Teatro Sistina
Via Sistina 129.
Map 5 B2. 482 68 41.

Teatro Stabile del Giallo
Via Cassia 871.
30 31 10 78.

Teatro Valle
Via Teatro Valle 23A.
Map 4 F4 & 12 D3.
68 80 37 94.

Teatro Vittoria
Piazza S. Maria Liberatrice 8.
Map 8 D3. 574 01 70.

CONTEMPORARY THEATRE

Teatro Ateneo
Viale delle Scienze 3.
Map 6 F3. 49 91 44 35.

Teatro Colosseo
Via Capo d'Africa 5A.
Map 9 A1. 700 49 32.

Teatro dei Cocci
Via Galvani 69.
Map 8 D3. 578 35 02.

Teatro La Scaletta
Via del Collegio Romano 1.
Map 5 A4 & 12 E3.
678 31 48.

Teatro Politecnico
Via Tiepolo 13A.
Map 1 B3. 321 98 91.

Teatro Tordinona
Via degli Acquasparta 16.
Map 4 E3 & 11 C2.
68 80 58 90.

FOLK, CABARET, PUPPET THEATRE

Ciceruacchio
Via del Porto 1. **Map** 8 D2.
580 60 46.

English Puppet Theatre
Via di Grotta Pinta 2.
Map 4 E5 & 11 C4.
589 62 01.

Fantasie di Trastevere
Via di Santa Dorotea 6.
Map 4 D5. 588 16 71.

Fieramosca
Piazza dei Mercanti 3A.
Map 8 D1. 581 42 89.

Meo Patacca
Piazza dei Mercanti 30.
Map 8 D1. 581 61 98.

Teatro Mongiovino
Via Genocchi 15.
513 94 05.

Teatro Verde
Circonvall. Gianicolense 10.
Map 7 B4. 588 20 34.

Teatro Villa Lazzaroni
Via Appia Nuova 522.
Map 10 F5. 78 77 91.

OPEN-AIR THEATRE

Anfiteatro Quercia del Tasso
Viale Aldo Fabrizi.
Map 3 C5. 575 08 27.

Nightclubs

THE CENTRE OF ROMAN NIGHT LIFE used to be the Via Veneto area so effectively portrayed by Fellini in his film *La Dolce Vita*. The place still offers plenty of venues, but new, less formal and more affordable clubs have emerged, with a more vibrant atmosphere and appealing to a younger and more diverse crowd.

With the new clubs come new areas. The picturesque narrow streets in Trastevere, the Piazza Navona and the Pantheon areas are becoming more popular. Testaccio too has become a new mecca for Roman clubbers.

WHAT'S ON

AS IN ANY OTHER major city, Rome's nightlife is constantly changing. Roman club-goers are an extremely varied group and most clubs arrange different nights to appeal to different tastes – so it's essential to keep up-to-date on what's happening by checking in a magazine like *Trovaroma (see p340)*.

For a more direct source of information, head for the bars around the Piazza Navona and Campo de' Fiori areas. At about 10.30pm the narrow streets and piazzas swarm with people and any interesting event will soon become common knowledge. *Buoni* (free or reduced price tickets) may be handed out.

PRACTICALITIES

PREFERRED CLUBBING nights for Romans are Thursday, Friday and, of course, Saturday, when you should expect to pay around L35,000 for entrance. Queues for the most popular places can be long but provided you arrive before midnight you'll avoid the crush.

Some clubs require a *tessera* (membership card) which you can buy on the spot and which usually replaces the entrance fee. Your ticket or *tessera* usually includes a free first drink; your second could well be expensive – as much as L20,000 in some of the plusher clubs.

In these smarter places how you look is all important: a jacket and tie are a must and usually you need an invitation or a personal introduction to get in. It should not be difficult to gain entrance to the traditional discos as long as you dress in designer casual wear, but watch out! A black T-shirt could make you too *alternativo*. All-male groups are never welcome, and in more exclusive clubs neither are unaccompanied men.

CLUBS AND BARS

AN ELEGANT NIGHT out could start in one of the refined piano bars such as the **Blue Bar**, the **Little Bar** frequented by the English-speaking community, or the intimate **Tartarughino**, popular with politicians and financiers. Livelier places are the American-style bars such as **Hemingway** and **Jeff Blynn's**. If you prefer the arts world, head for **Zelig**, **Bar della Pace**, **Le Cornacchie**, **La Vetrina** and **Picasso**.

To continue, head for **Gilda**, a favourite with the Roman jet set, with two elegant restaurants, a large glitzy dancefloor and many VIPs. The famous nightclub of the 1960s, **Jackie O**, has been revamped in lavish style, with a lush interior and expensive restaurant. In a similar vein, and not to be missed, are **Open Gate**, **Divina** and **Notorious**.

The hottest club among the younger and trendier is **Alien**. This club offers house, techno and hip-hop, along with stages, wild lighting effects and "happenings". A smaller dance floor offers a more mellow music selection. Equally funky is the relatively new **Tatum** which also offers soul and dance music.

The best places for dancing are **Soul II Soul**, one of the few truly mixed black and white clubs, which offers great music; or **Radio Londra**, designed to look like a World War II bunker, where hard dance music and free entrance attract huge crowds. On **Argonauta**, a moored paddle steamer on the Tiber, you can dance to anything from techno to reggae on Fridays and Saturdays.

The more traditional disco is at its best at **Piper '90**, the oldest and biggest Roman disco which totally revamps its interior every season. It's especially popular with the younger crowd, as are **Veleno** and **New Life**. **New York, New York** offers music from the 1940s and 1950s on some nights, jazz funk on others. There are some disco bars worth noting too, like **Battello Ubriaco** and **Fandango**.

To find out about events in the more unusual Roman venues, start the evening at the **Vineria**. The old abattoir *(il Mattatoio)* at Testaccio is the setting for **Villaggio Globale**, a social centre hosting concerts, shows, discos and parties. **Circolo degli Artisti** is another social centre with a large dance floor, bar, theatre and video room, situated in the old milk centre. Two converted cinemas, **Castello** in the Vatican area and **Palladium** in the southern suburbs, provide a variety of concerts and events.

GAY

THE GAY SCENE is well served. Many clubs have fixed gay nights and one-offs are arranged, especially during the Maratona Gay festival in May. The most famous gay club is **Alibi**, where music is a mixture of underground and 1970s hits. **Angelo Azzurro** offers hi-energy and house in Post-Modern surroundings. Listen out for events organized by **Circolo Mario Mieli di Cultura Omosessuale**, or go to bars such as **Hangar** for ideas of what's on. For gay women there is less choice; try **Panico** on a Sunday evening. Women-only nights take place at **Galaxia**, Friday and Sunday.

JAZZ, SALSA AND AFRICAN

THERE ARE many jazz venues *(see p344)*. The following mix live music with dancing and drinking. **Caffè Latino** (membership club) is best at the weekend. For South American music try **Yes Brazil** and **Drink Music** with live bands and lots of people, or **Caffè Caruso** (membership club) for salsa. **Alpheus** is a four-roomed venue where different kinds of music events take place simultaneously.

African clubs like **Fantasy** (free on Fridays) and **Safari** are lively, friendly and cheap.

CLUBBING IN SUMMER

IN SUMMER when everything closes down in the city, head for the Roman seaside resorts. At Fregene, for instance, there are 13 clubs; all pretty much the same, with a dress-code of designer-label casuals. Take along your swimsuit too as much of the fun takes place in and around the pools. Names include **Gilda on the Beach**, **Tattou** and **Miraggio** – the latter two popular with a younger crowd. **Sogno del Mare** features live concerts by well-known bands, a swimming pool and a spacious, pleasant

environment. Most of these seaside clubs have restaurants attached to them as well.

LATE CLUBS

MOST ROMAN clubs stay open until 3am or 4am, but the informal and lively **Blue Zone** (a club that, un-usually, is open on Mondays) and the smarter **Le Stelle** both stay open until dawn.

Before heading off to bed, join other die-hard clubbers at any of the city's 24-hour bars for a final drink and make for one of the early-morning bakers to buy sweet *cornetti* hot from the oven.

DIRECTORY

Alibi
Via di Monte Testaccio 44.
Map 8 D4. 574 34 48.

Alien
Via Velletri 13. **Map** 6 D1.
841 22 12.

Alpheus
Via del Commercio 36/8.
Map 8 D5. 574 77 47.

Angelo Azzurro
Via Card. Merry del Val 13.
Map 7 C1. 580 04 72.

Antico Caffè della Pace
Via della Pace 2/5.
Map 4 E4 & 11 C2.

Argonauta
Lungotevere degli Artigiani.
Map 7 C4. 556 54 40.

Battello Ubriaco
Via dei Leutari 34.
68 30 05 35.

Blue Bar
Via dei Soldati 25.
Map 4 E3 & 11 C2.

Blue Zone
Via Campania 37 A.
Map 5 B1. 482 18 90.

Caffè Caruso
Via di Monte Testaccio 36.
Map 8 D4. 574 50 19.

Caffè Latino
Via di Monte Testaccio 96.
Map 8 D4. 574 40 20.

Il Castello
Via di Porta Castello 44.
Map 4 D3. 686 83 28.

Circolo degli Artisti
Via Lamarmora 28.
Map 6 E5. 446 49 68.

Le Cornacchie
Piazza Rondanini 53.
Map 4 F4 & 12 D2.

Divina
Via Romagnosi 11 A.
Map 4 E1. 361 13 48.

Drink Music
Via Natale del Grande 4.
Map 7 C1. 580 02 86.

Fandango
Corso Vittorio Emanuele
286. **Map** 4 D3 & 11 B3.

Fantasy
Via Alba 42. **Map** 10 F3.
701 67 41.

Galaxia
Piazza Bulgarelli 41.
881 10 43.

Gilda
Via Mario de' Fiori 97.
Map 5 A2 & 12 F1.
678 48 38.

Hangar
Via in Selci 69. **Map** 5 C5.

Hemingway
Piazza delle Coppelle 10.
Map 4 F3 & 12 D2.

Jackie O
Via Boncompagni 11.
Map 5 B2. 488 54 57.

Jeff Blynn's
Via Zanardelli 12. **Map** 4 E3
& 11 C2. 686 19 90.

Little Bar
Via Gregoriana 54 A.
Map 5 A2.

Circolo Mario Mieli di Cultura Omosessuale
Via Ostiense 202.
541 39 85.

New Life
Via XX Settembre 90.
Map 6 D1. 474 09 97.

New York, New York
Via Ostia 29. **Map** 3 B1.
372 40 61.

Notorious
Via San Nicola da
Tolentino 22. **Map** 5 B2.
474 68 88.

Open Gate
Via San Nicola da
Tolentino 4. **Map** 5 C2.
482 44 64.

Palladium
Piazza B. Romano 8.
511 02 03.

Panico
Via di Panico 13. **Map** 4 D3
& 11 B2. 68 30 07 49.

Picasso
Piazza della Pigna 23.
Map 4 F4 & 12 E3.
678 82 11.

Piper '90
Via Tagliamento 9.
855 53 98.

Radio Londra
Via Monte Testaccio 67.
Map 8 D4.

Safari
Via Aurelia 601.
66 41 63 09.

Soul II Soul
Via dei Fienaroli 30 A.
Map 7 C1. 581 32 49.

Le Stelle
Via C. Beccaria 22.
Map 4 E1. 361 12 40.

Tartarughino
Via della Scrofa 1.
Map 4 F3 & 12 D2.

Tatum
Via Luciani 52. **Map** 2 D3.
322 12 51.

Veleno
Via Sardegna 27.
Map 5 B1. 482 18 38.

La Vetrina
Via della Vetrina 20.
Map 4 E3 & 11 B2.

Villaggio Globale
Lungotevere Testaccio. **Map** 8 D4. 57 30 03 29.

Vineria
Campo de' Fiori 5.
Map 4 E4 & 11 C4.

Yes Brazil
Via S. Francesco a Ripa 103.
Map 7 C2. 581 62 67.

Zelig
Via Monterone 74.
Map 4 F4 & 12 D3.
687 92 09.

SUMMER CLUBS

Gilda on the Beach
Lungomare di Ponente 11.
665 06 49.

Miraggio
Lungomare di Ponente 95.
646 39 50.

Sogno del Mare
Lungomare di Ponente 25.
66 56 05 40.

Tattou
Via Francavilla a Mare.
646 38 38.

Sport

DON'T BE SURPRISED if the peace of a Sunday afternoon in Rome is interrupted by the honking of cars and people shouting. It simply means that one of the home football teams has won at the stadium and the whole town will vibrate with the excitement.

Football is Italy's national sport but other sports also manage to attract a large following and Roman sports fans are never at a loss for varied and well organized events and activities.

You'll find times and venues for most spectator sports listed in *Trovaroma (see p340)*, as well as the local sections of *La Gazzetta dello Sport* or *Corriere dello Sport*.

FOOTBALL

AN ITALIAN SOCCER MATCH is an experience not to be missed for the quality of the play, the excitable crowds and fun atmosphere. Football hooligans are rare.

Rome has two teams, Roma and Lazio, and they take it in turns to play at the **Stadio Olimpico** on a Sunday afternoon at 3pm, in the Campionato Italiano (Italian championship league). Seats can be scarce so get tickets in advance from the stadium (L15,000 to L150,000). The cheapest tickets are in the La Tribuna stand; middle-range and most expensive are in Le Catinate and Le Curve respectively.

On Wednesday evenings there are international competitions – the Coppa delle Coppe (European Cup Winners' Cup), the UEFA cup and the Coppa dei Campioni (European Championship Cup). In between these, teams battle it out for the national Coppa Italia.

TENNIS

A MAJOR EVENT, the International Championships go on at **Foro Italico** for two weeks in May. The world's top tennis stars thrash it out on clay courts at 1pm and 8.30pm from Tuesday to Friday, and at 1pm only at weekends. Buy tickets in advance either directly from the Foro Italico or from a ticket agency.

If you wish to play yourself, there are now over 350 tennis clubs in Rome. It is often essential to book at least a week in advance and there's usually a moderate court fee.

Clubs where membership is not required are the **Centro Sportivo Italiano** and the **Circolo Stampa** in northern Rome and the **Oasis di Pace**, just off the Via Appia Antica. The big hotels offer tennis for a reasonable price. **St Peter's Holiday Inn** requires a small annual membership fee on top of the court price, which includes the gym and the pool (in the summer).

HORSE-RACING, TROTTING AND LEISURE-RIDING

IMPORTANT RACES include the Derby in June and the Premio Roma in November. There are trotting races at the **Ippodromo di Tor di Valle** and flat races and steeple chases at **Ippodromo delle Capannelle**.

The International Horse Show is held at the end of April and the beginning of May in Piazza di Siena, Villa Borghese *(see p258)*. It is one of the most important social and sporting events in the calendar, and the setting makes it a great attraction.

For a hack in the countryside around Rome, try the **Centro Ippico Fiano Romano**. Most riding clubs in the city do not accept short-term members.

GOLF

EVEN THE MOST ELITE golf clubs will accept a touring golfer with a home membership and handicap. Most clubs are shut on Mondays and at the weekend when they host competitions, and when guests cannot play. Prices range from L50,000–80,000.

The **Olgiata Golf Club** is open to everybody from Tuesday to Thursday, and to guests accompanied by a member Friday to Sunday. **Country Club Castel Gandolfo** is the newest club and **Circolo Golf Roma** the oldest and most prestigious. Within the city ring road is the course at the **Sheraton Hotel** (closed Tuesday).

Two of the many important competitions taking place on the various golf courses in and around Rome are the National Championships in October and the Rome Masters in April.

CAR AND MOTORBIKE RACING

FORMULA 1 and Formula 3 races take place on Sundays at **Valle Lunga**; be prepared for some relatively expensive entrance fees. Frequently on Saturdays official trials are open to spectators, and on some non-racing Sundays Italy's car designers show new models.

GREYHOUND RACING

THE **Cinodromo** track has shed its sleazy image, and the entrance fee and bets are inexpensive. There is usually a lively, animated crowd of all ages in attendance. Races are run every Wednesday and Thursday at 6.30pm and on Sundays at 10.15am.

ROWING

IN MID-JUNE an Oxbridge crew challenges the historic Aniene crew to a race taking place alternately on the Thames and the Tiber. The best place to view this from is between the Margherita and the Sant'Angelo bridges. The race usually starts at around 6pm. Another event is the battle between the Roma and Lazio crews, from Ponte Milvio to Ponte Flaminio, on the same variable date as the Roma-Lazio football Derby.

SWIMMING

SWIMMING POOLS are few and definitely not geared to the short-term visitor. You often have to pay an expensive membership and on top of that a monthly tariff. It's also essential, in most pools, to produce a medical certificate assuring your good health.

The state-owned pools can be slightly cheaper, but you still have to pay an initial membership fee.

It's better to try the outdoor pools, often part of the big hotels. The **Shangri-La Hotel** opens its pool to non-residents from July to September. For a higher entrance fee, swim at the **Hilton** which also opens its pool in summer. Best deal is on a Sunday when the sports club and swimming pool **La Margherita** opens to non-members 10am–1pm, for a reasonable entrance charge. **Piscina delle Rose** in EUR is an Olympic-sized pool (often deserted in the morning) open from June to September 9am–5.30pm during the week, 9am–7pm at weekends.

HEALTH CLUBS

JUST AS THE swimming pools, Roman health clubs usually require both a membership and monthly payments. For just a short stay in Rome, try the hotel facilities, or, if you are willing to pay, head for one of the private clubs. Use of club facilities may be negotiable – you could be lucky and find that you are waved through for the price of a guest pass.

The **Roman Sports Centre** welcomes daily members for a reasonable price and you can use the swimming pools, the gym and the sauna. The facilities are open 9am–10pm. Wear lycra, as normal shorts are not allowed. The **Centro Internazionale di Danza** (Sep–Jul) offers cheap aerobic and dance classes for non-members on Mondays, Wednesdays and Fridays at 6.30pm; you don't need to book.

JOGGING AND CYCLING

ROME'S PERFECT climate and stunning scenery attract thousands of well-dressed joggers and cyclists into the city's many parks. Early in the morning or on a Sunday you'll find the more popular locations looking rather like a high-speed fashion show than sweat tracks.

Villa Doria Pamphilj (see p267) is an extensive park situated above the Janiculum, where you can choose among three tracks, plenty of open spaces and a network of paths. **Villa Borghese** (see p258) is another vast popular place with a running track.

Alternatively, jog under the acacia trees and palms at Villa Torlonia, on the spot-lit track at Villa Glori, or combine sport with culture, by running the **Via Appia Antica** (see p265) branching off into Parco Caffarella. Other favourites are Viale delle Terme di Caracalla, Circo Massimo, Parco degli Aquedotti and Parco di Colle Oppio.

All of the above are also ideal for cyclists, and you can hire bikes from many places including **Collalti**, **Via del Corso** and **I Bike Roma**.

Organized bike trips are advertised in *Trovaroma*.

DIRECTORY		
FOOTBALL	**HORSE-RACING AND RIDING**	**Sheraton Golf Hotel** Viale Parco dei Medici 22. (655 34 77.
Stadio Olimpico Viale dei Gladiatori. (36 85 75 20.	**Centro Ippico Fiano Romano** Between Via Tiberina and Capena. (0765 45 50 19.	**MOTOR RACING**
TENNIS	**Ippodromo delle Capannelle** Via Appia Nuova 1255. (718 31 43, 34 56.	**Valle Lunga** Autodromo di Roma, Via Cassia km.32. (904 10 27.
Circolo Stampa Piazza Mancini 19. **Map** 1 A2. (323 24 52.	**Ippodromo di Tor di Valle** Via del Mare km.9. (592 02 69.	**GREYHOUND RACING**
Centro Sportivo Italiano Lungotevere Flaminio 55. **Map** 1 A3. (322 48 42.	**GOLF**	**Cinodromo** Via della Vasca Navale 6. (556 62 58.
Foro Italico Viale dei Gladiatori 31. (321 90 64.	**Circolo Golf Roma** Via Acqua Santa 3. (780 34 07.	**SWIMMING**
Oasis di Pace Via degli Eugenii 2. (718 45 50.	**Country Club Castel Gandolfo** Via di Santo Spirito 13. (931 23 01, 30 84.	**Hilton Hotel** Via Cadlolo 101. (31 51.
St Peter's Holiday Inn Via Aurelia Antica 415. (66 42.	**Olgiata Golf Club** Largo dell'Olgiata 15. (378 91 41.	**La Margherita** Via Monti Tiburtini 511. (451 05 52.

	Shangri-La Hotel Viale Algeria 141. (591 64 41.
Piscina delle Rose Viale America 20. (592 67 17.	**HEALTH CLUBS**
	Centro Internazionale di Danza Via San Francesco di Sales 14. **Map** 4 D5 & 11 A4. (588 55 28.
	Roman Sports Centre Viale del Galoppatoio 33. **Map** 5 A1. (320 16 67.
	CYCLING
	I Bike Roma Villa Borghese car park. **Map** 5 A1. (322 52 40.
	Collalti Via del Pellegrino 82. **Map** 4 E4 & 11 B3. (68 80 10 84.
	Via del Corso Piazza S. Lorenzo in Lucina. **Map** 4 F3 & 12 E1.

CHILDREN'S ROME

ITALIANS LOVE HAVING children around, and you can be sure yours will be made welcome wherever they go. But there are few special facilities for children, and the heat, crowds and lack of clean public loos mean that Rome is not an ideal city for a holiday with babies or under-sevens. It does, however, have plenty to offer slightly older children, especially those who are keen on

Renaissance cherub from the Villa Farnesina

history or art. The temptation may be to wear yourself and your children out by packing too many sights into one day. Plan in advance and leave plenty of time to wander around the city: looking at the quirkier fountains and monuments, watching knife-grinders at work in the markets, and spending hours agonizing over the choice of ice cream flavours and special pizza toppings.

PRACTICAL ADVICE

IF YOU ARE bringing your children to Rome, try to come in early spring or late autumn, when the weather is good, but not too hot. Easter is best avoided, as the city is more crowded than usual, and you're constantly jostled on packed buses and streets. Where you stay is crucial. A hotel near the Villa Borghese park will give your children plenty of chance to relax and let off steam, though you may end up spending a lot of time and money to get to and from the town centre. A hotel in the old centre is ideal, as you can easily pop back during the day for a rest and a clean bathroom.

Jogging in Villa Borghese

As hygienic toilets and changing facilities are rare within the city, it is really not advisable to bring a baby to Rome unless you are visiting friends or family. As with many historic cities, Rome may not instantly appeal to all children, but there is plenty to inspire their imaginations. Use this book to make the buildings and history come alive. Children might also enjoy learning a few Italian words and phrases so they can order food and buy things by themselves.

If lingering over drinks on the café terraces is what you enjoy best, bring your offspring something to keep them busy once they have finished with their treat: crayons and paper, a computer game or a Walkman. Alternatively, most other adults are very tolerant of children running around and making a noise while they

relax and, if yours are reasonably outgoing, they could join in with the local children playing ball games in early evenings on piazzas like Campo de' Fiori.

If you feel the need for a total break, most hotels will be able to provide a babysitter or help you to contact a qualified childminding agency.

In the event of bad luck, see pages 360–61 for information on what to do and a list of emergency numbers.

Fairground in the Villa Borghese park

GETTING AROUND

BUMPY COBBLES, narrow streets without pavements and overcrowded buses make pushing children around in pushchairs tiring work. You will, however, inevitably find some people willing to help you haul a pram up steps in a Metro station or on to a bus. Mothers with young children are usually allowed to jump queues, and may even be offered seats on buses. The Metro is often less crowded. Kids under 1 m (3 ft 3 in) tall travel free on public transport.

Although the city is not good for cyclists, families with older children could hire bikes to ride along the Via Appia Antica, or to take on a regional train into the country. The bike hire hut in the Pincio gardens has free baby seats.

Anyone over the age of 14 can hire a scooter under 50 cc, although Rome is not the best place for novices *(see p378).*

A hire bike with free baby seat

Pony-pulled trains in the Villa Borghese park

EATING OUT

CHILDREN ARE normally warmly welcomed in neighbourhood pizzerias and trattorias, and high chairs are often available for toddlers and babies. If there's no high chair, be prepared for the waiters to improvise for you with armloads of cushions or telephone directories. Most places are perfectly happy to serve half portions, or to let children share meals.

In trattorias it can sometimes be difficult to be exactly sure what a certain dish contains (especially when there is no menu and the dishes of the day are reeled off, usually at top speed, by the waiter), so faddy eaters are likely to be happier in pizzerias *(see pp318–21).* Here they can choose their own topping (remember that *prosciutto,* which is usually translated in menus as ham, is cured). The most entertaining pizzerias for kids are the old-fashioned ones where they can watch the chefs pound, stretch and flip the pizza dough. The best places get busy from around 7.30pm, so it is wise to go early to avoid having to queue. If all else fails, there are three branches of McDonald's.

PICNICS

PICNICS IN THE parks are ideal, and shopping for the food is often half the fun. There's no problem finding small cartons of fruit juice and branded canned drinks, but except in supermarkets (the branch of Standa on Viale Trastevere is the most convenient) they are extremely expensive. The water from drinking fountains is safe, so it's worth carrying plastic cups around.

As well as picnic food from bakeries and markets, there are lots of scrumptious takeaway foods. Many of them are appealingly messy, so it's wise to bring paper tissues. Try deep-fried fruit and vegetables from Cose Fritte on Via di Ripetta and *suppli al telefono,* rice croquettes with a gooey string of mozzarella inside, from *pizza al taglio* outlets. A *tramezzino* comes quite close to an English sandwich and if your kids are miserable without Marmite or peanut butter, you can find them (and other foreign foods) at Ruggieri on Campo de' Fiori.

Feeding pigeons on Piazza Navona

ICE CREAM

ROME, OF COURSE, is famous for ice cream; you and your children are likely to be tempted at every turn. Real ice cream fans may even want to plan their day's sight-seeing round one of the best gelaterie *(see pp319–21).* It's far cheaper to buy either a cone or tub of ice cream to eat in the street, but in some of the more traditional places it's worth paying to sit down. At Fassi, they have an old-fashioned ice cream-making machine on display and at Giolitti, you can enjoy gargantuan sundaes in the elegant parlour *(see p109).*

Investigating some of the hundreds of Italian ice cream flavours

Sightseeing with Children

Entrance to the Villa Borghese Zoo

GENERAL TIPS

ROME DOES NOT have many museums with the sort of hands-on exhibits and activities that many other cities lay on for children. Instead, it has other things to entertain visitors. Bernini's marble elephant *(see p108)* and the fat *facchino*, or porter, *(p107)* appeal to children. The Capuchin cemetery at Santa Maria della Concezione *(p254)*, the catacombs *(pp264–7)* and the Mamertine Prison *(p91)* will grab more ghoulish, young imaginations.

Look for details like the dirty toenails on figures in Caravaggio's paintings, the Etruscan votives, which were offered to the gods, at the Villa Giulia *(pp262–3)*, and the illusory collapsing ceiling in the Chiesa Nuova as well

as the fake dome of Sant' Ignazio di Loyola *(see p106)*.

Museums your children will enjoy include the Museo delle Arti e Tradizioni Popolari at EUR, with its antique toys, potty and crib scene *(p267)*, and the Museo delle Mura, which explores the length of the Aurelian Wall *(p196)*.

Among the churches, St Peter's, where they can climb to the top of the dome *(see p230)*, and San Clemente, where they can descend to the underground mithreum *(see pp186–7)*, are most fun.

At the Vatican most children will like the statues and mosaics of animals in the Animal Gallery and also the Sistine Ceiling *(p246)*, especially when they get to know that Michelangelo had to paint it hunched up on a scaffolding platform.

ANCIENT RUINS

THE ANCIENT RUINS best appreciated by children are the Colosseum *(see pp92–5)*, and Trajan's Markets *(see pp 88–9)*. You can still make out what both these buildings looked like from their remains. The scant ruins of the Forum and Palatine, on the other hand, may not appeal so strongly. Ostia Antica, where the remains include a theatre, shop and 20-seater public toilet, is much more likely to interest them *(see pp270–71)*.

Mosaic from the Vatican

MOSAICS

THERE ARE SCORES of vivid, sometimes quirky, mosaics in buildings all over Rome. Many of these are particularly appealing to children. Details in the mosaics range from brilliantly coloured flowers, leaves, animals and buildings (in the churches of San Clemente, Santa Prassede and Santa Maria in Trastevere, *see p186, p171 and pp212–13*) to the debris of a banquet (in the Vatican's Museo Gregorio Profano, *see pp234–5*).

Model trains in Villa Borghese

ENTERTAINMENT

Rome's cultural offerings for children are pretty sparse. To find out what's on, scour the cinema pages of the newspapers and the listings in *Trovaroma* (*see p340*). Most theatres and cinemas have reduced entrance tickets for children, although these are only useful if your children are able to speak Italian.

Language is not a barrier in cartoons and puppet shows. There are cartoons at Villa Borghese's Cinema dei Piccoli and traditional puppet shows every afternoon, except Wednesday, up on the Janiculum hill. If your hotel has a TV, you'll find plenty of cartoons there to keep your kids entertained.

Stall at the Befana Christmas toy fair on Piazza Navona

Resting on the kerb side

One of the most appealing times for children to be in Rome is over Christmas, when Piazza Navona hosts the Befana toy fair, where stalls sell toys and sweets.

PARKS

Villa Borghese (*see p258*) has rowing boats to hire and ducks to feed; pony and pony-cart rides; bikes to rent; a mini cinema; a small fun fair; and a zoo. Villa Celimontana (*see p193*) has bike trails, and open-air theatre performances in the summer. The amusement park LUNEUR at EUR (*see p267*) is old-fashioned but can be good fun. The Bomarzo Monster Park, 95 km (60 miles) north of Rome, was built in the 16th century for a mad duke. Children can clamber over its giant stone monsters.

TOYS

A visit to a Roman toyshop can be fun. **Menasci** sells wooden toys, **Città del Sole** has delightful educational toys and games, and **Al Sogno** is a dream for stuffed animals.

Città del Sole
Via della Scrofa 65. **Map** 4 F3 & 12 D2.
687 54 04.

Menasci
Via Napoleone III 72. **Map** 5 A3 & 12 F2. 678 19 81.

Al Sogno
Piazza Navona 53. **Map** 4 E4 & 11 C3.
686 41 98.

CHILDREN'S CLOTHES

Italians adore dressing their children up, and on Sunday afternoons in particular, you are likely to encounter young children dressed as if they had walked straight out of a costume drama: girls in frills and flounces and boys in velvet breeches or knee-length shorts.

Many shops sell beautifully hand-crafted children's shoes and clothes – the downside is that they can often be expensive and impractical: dry-clean-only clothes are common and shoes are not made for mud.

Lavori Artigianili Femminili sells handmade silk and wool clothes for children up to eight. **Succo d'Arancio** sells smart casuals and **Children's Club** offers Italian styles made from classic Liberty fabrics.

Lavori Artigianili Femminili
Via Capo le Case 6. **Map** 5 A3 & 12 F1.
679 29 92.

Succo d'Arancio
Via dell'Arancio 36. **Map** 4 F2 & 12 D1.
687 62 52.

Children's Club
Via della Frezza 61–2. **Map** 4 F2.
322 18 98.

SURVIVAL
GUIDE

PRACTICAL INFORMATION

ROMANS OFTEN SEEM unconcerned by the priceless art treasures and ancient ruins which lie casually among the buildings and workings of their hectic 20th-century city. Visitors nearly always find these wonders very exciting, but it's not always easy to make the most of them. Relaxed local attitudes make for hundreds of variations on opening hours. Most places close for several hours over lunch and reopen in the late afternoon; some museums are open in the mornings only. Bank and shop hours can be just as difficult to pin down. On a more positive note, many of the main sights are within easy walking distance of one another. Start your day early and wear comfortable shoes for the Roman cobblestones. It can be a delightfully informal city to visit; but remember to observe dress rules to cover up in churches, as this is one area where the Italians are very strict.

MUSEUMS AND MONUMENTS

MANY MUSEUMS open only in the mornings and close all day on Mondays. If you are particularly keen to see a specific monument or museum, make sure it's open before you set out. There is usually an admission charge for museums and monuments, though some are free on Sundays. All churches are free, and many contain works of art that are worthy of the world's greatest museums. Some of Rome's sights are accessible only on personal application or by written appointment. Examples include Nero's Aqueduct or the gardens at the Vatican. The *Area by Area* section of this guide gives opening times for each sight and tells you whether there is an admission charge. The **EPT** publishes a useful leaflet called *Musei e Monumenti di Roma* which gives details of current exhibitions at Rome's main museums and galleries.

EPT's guide to current exhibitions

Museum entry cards are available from museums, tourist offices, or by writing in advance to **L'Associazione Nazionale Museidon**. The cards admit you without extra charge to most museums, galleries and exhibition centres in the city. They are valid for two, four or seven consecutive days and cost from around L15,000 to L50,000.

Typical traffic congestion in Via delle Quattro Fontane

TOURIST INFORMATION

THE SERVICE at the main provincial tourist office (**EPT**) is better than at the crowded station. You should be able to pick up details of special tours here. EPT also help with accommodation *(see p289)*. Besides the official tourist offices, good travel agents such as **CIT**, **Wagons Lits** or the **American Express** office can also be helpful to visitors. For information on Italian cities and areas outside Rome, contact **ENIT** (the National Tourist Board), who have offices in all the main cities.

A word of warning: any information you obtain in Italy should be regarded as only approximate; prices and opening times change often, without warning. Even sights which are normally open for regular hours can be closed for what seem to be unbelievably long periods of restoration *(chiuso per restauro)* or because of a sudden strike *(sciopero)*.

ENTE NAZIONALE ITALIANO PER IL TURISMO
ENIT logo

The 119 electric minibus: useful for the historic centre

ENTERTAINMENT INFORMATION

THE WEEKLY *Trovaroma*, in *La Repubblica*, is the main guide to what's on. The bilingual fortnightly *Un Ospite a Roma* (A Guest in Rome) also has entertainment listings and is available free from newsagents. Listings in English are also in *Metropolitan* and *Wanted in Rome*. Full entertainment information is on page 340.

Trovaroma

GUIDED TOURS

SEVERAL COMPANIES offer tours of Rome with English-speaking guides; these include **CIT**, **American Express**, **Green Line Tours** and **Carrani Tours**. Full-day city tours including lunch cost around L95,000–110,000; half-day tours around L40,000–50,000. Alternatively the No. 110 ATAC bus passes many of the main sights in Rome on a three-hour circuit. The journey will cost you around L6,000. Tour guides can be hired at many of the major sights, such as the Roman Forum (*see pp78–87*). Employ only the official guides and make sure you establish the fee in advance; on average they charge around L100,000 for a half-day's tour.

ATAC, the Rome bus company

VISITING CHURCHES

MANY OF ITALY'S churches are very dark, but they usually have light meters to illuminate chapels and works of art. The meters are coin-operated (L100, L200 or L500 coins accepted). Recorded information in several languages is often available at coin-operated machines. Dress codes are firmly upheld in Roman churches; St Peter's (*see pp230–33*) is especially strict.

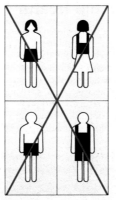

Unacceptable dress in church: both sexes should cover torsos and upper arms

ETIQUETTE

PEOPLE IN ROME are generally courteous and friendly to foreign visitors. Remember to show consideration for local residents and workers.

Italians are delighted at any effort to speak their language, so it's worth learning a few phrases (*see p431*). Italians tend to drink only with meals and are unlikely to be seen drunk – obvious drunkenness is frowned upon. Smoking is common in bars, restaurants and on streets, but banned on public transport.

Roman style

TIPPING

FOREIGNERS ARE expected to tip, although Italians themselves don't often do so. Leave a few coins in bars or cafés; in restaurants where service is not included, leave around 10%. Keep L1,000 or L2,000 notes and coins handy for taxi drivers, sacristans, chambermaids, doormen, porters and usherettes.

ROME FOR THE DISABLED

ROME'S UNEVEN cobbles and crowded pavements aren't suitable for disabled visitors and even the most agile must be alert when crossing the busy roads. Look before crossing at traffic lights and pedestrian crossings – not all vehicles stop when you expect. The seriously disabled will need to organize help getting around. Ramps, lifts and modified WCs exist in a few places, including Termini station and the Colosseum. If you have no escort, consider a specially-designed package tour, or contact an organization for disabled travellers before you set off. The Vatican Museums, Sistine Chapel and St Peter's are all accessible by wheelchair. The Vatican Museums recently received an EC award for improving accessibility for the disabled, and offer staff help if needed.

WCs

PUBLIC TOILETS are few and far between. There are clean ones by the Colosseum (with facilities for the disabled), at St Peter's and in the Rinascente store (*see p323*). Most cafés let you use theirs if you ask. Take your own paper.

USEFUL ADDRESSES

American Express
Piazza di Spagna 38. **Map** 5 A2.
[676 41.

Associazione Nazionale Museidon
Via A. Silvani 23, 00139 Rome.

Carrani Tours
Via V. E. Orlando 95. **Map** 5 C3.
[474 25 01.

CIT
Piazza della Repubblica 64.
Map 5 C3. [479 41.

ENIT
Via Marghera 2. **Map** 6 E3.
[497 11.

EPT
Via Parigi 5. **Map** 5 C2.
[487 12 70. **Open** 9am–1.30pm, 2pm–7pm Mon–Sat.

Green Line Tours
Via Farini 5A. **Map** 6 D4.
[474 48 57.

Wagons Lits
Via Boncompagni 25. **Map** 5 C2.
[481 75 45.

Personal Security and Health

O**N THE WHOLE**, Rome is a safe, unthreatening place for visitors, but petty street crime is a problem. Don't carry more money than you'll need for the day and leave other valuables or documents in a hotel safe. Cameras are less likely to be snatched if they're in a carrier bag rather than an obvious case. Take particular care in crowded places, such as stations, or on full buses, and steer clear of bands of innocent-looking children – they may be skilful professional pickpockets.

Pharmacy sign

ADVICE FOR VISITORS

T**AKE OUT ADEQUATE** property insurance before you travel (it is difficult to arrange once you are in Italy), and look after your belongings while you're in Rome. Some hotels now have personal safes in the bedrooms. You can programme these with your own memorable number. (Don't use your date of birth; it's on your passport and registration slip.) To be prepared for all eventualities, keep a separate photocopy of vital documents, such as your passport, to minimize the problem of replacing them, and take a spare photograph or two. Traveller's cheques are the safest way to carry large amounts of cash. Keep the receipts separate from the cheques for a refund in case they do go missing.

Be wary of bag-snatchers on mopeds who operate in quiet streets. You might want to take a discreet money belt or a securely-fastened, long-strapped shoulder bag, while

Mounted police

equipment like video cameras should be disguised. Pickpockets (sometimes children) adopt highly sophisticated distraction techniques with pieces of card or newspaper while they deftly sever you from your possessions in seconds. Take particular care of your valuables in market places or on public transport. Bus route No. 64, which runs between Termini station and the Vatican, is notorious for pickpockets. Thefts from cars

are also rife. Nothing portable like a jacket or bag should be left visible inside a car on Rome's streets, and don't carry luggage on a roof rack. The streets to the east and south of Termini station and around the Colosseum are well-known for prostitution and drug-peddling, and are unsavoury at night.

Women travelling alone (or even in small groups) may need to take extra care. Italian society is male-dominated, and women who are out without male escorts attract more attention than they do in much of the rest of Europe and Northern America.

Beware of unauthorized minicab drivers who are probably not insured and frequently overcharge. They operate in particular near the airport, waiting to profit from

Distinctive *carabinieri* motorcycle

Carabiniere – a member of the military police

Carabiniere in traffic police uniform

Municipal policeman directing traffic

new arrivals. Hotel touts and unofficial tour guides are also best avoided; instead stick to the official tourist agencies *(see p289 and pp358–9)*.

POLICE

Police car

THE VIGILI URBANI, or municipal police, wear blue uniforms in winter and white in summer, and can most often be seen regulating traffic. The *carabinieri* are the military police, in red striped trousers. They deal with everything from fine art thefts to speeding offences. *La polizia* (the state police) wear blue uniforms with white belts and berets, and they specialize in serious crime. Any of these should be able to help you.

Green cross ambulance

Italian fire engine

MEDICAL MATTERS

NO INOCULATIONS are required for Rome, but take mosquito repellent and sun screen in the summer. The Tiber is polluted but the water from the taps and from many street fountains is piped straight from the hills, and is fresh and palatable. EC residents are officially entitled to reciprocal medical care, but the bureaucracy involved can be daunting. Before you travel, pick up form E111 from a post office. This covers you for emergencies – you'll need medical insurance for other needs. Form E111

comes with a booklet of health advice and information on the procedure for claiming free medical treatment. It has to be stamped by a post office to be valid abroad.

Non-EC visitors should take out insurance to cover everything, including emergencies.

If you need urgent medical attention, contact the First Aid *(Pronto Soccorso)* department of a main hospital such as **Policlinico Umberto I**, or check the Yellow Pages *(Pagine Gialle)* for a doctor *(medico)* or dentist *(dentista)*. Pharmacists post late-opening rosters on their doors (several stay open all night), and can usually supply the local equivalent of foreign medicines. **Farmacia Internazionale Capranica** and **Farmacia Internazionale Barberini** stock American and British pharmaceutical products.

Farmacia Internazionale Barberini
Piazza Barberini 49. **Map** 5 B3.
(482 54 56.

Farmacia Internazionale Capranica
Piazza Capranica 96. **Map** 4 F3 & 12 D2. (679 46 80.

Policlinico Umberto I
Viale del Policlinico 1. **Map** 6 F2.
(44 70 18 07.

LOST PROPERTY

IF YOU WANT to make an insurance claim, report your loss to any police station, and get a signed form. For lost passports, go to your embassy or consulate; for lost traveller's cheques, go to the issuing company's office *(see p362)*.

Termini station has a police office on platform 1. Or contact the **Ufficio Stranieri**.

Lost Property on Buses
(581 60 40. **Open** 9am–11am.

Lost Property on the Metro
(73 89 58.

Ufficio Stranieri
Via Genova 2. **Map** 5 B3.
(46 86 29 87 (24 hrs), English spoken.

Commissariato di Polizia – a police station

EMERGENCY TELEPHONE NUMBERS

Ambulance
(51 00.

Automobile Club d'Italia
Car accidents and breakdowns.
Until Dec 1995, the ACI is offering free breakdown assistance to all cars with foreign plates, whether or not they are members of the AA or RAC.
(116.

Fire
(115.

General SOS
(113. (Free from any telephone).

Police
(112. (Carabinieri) or 46 86 (La Polizia).

Samaritans
(70 45 44 44.
Line open 1pm–10pm daily.

Traffic Police
(676 91.

Carabinieri in dress uniform

Banking and Local Currency

MONEY SERVICES are not always fast in Rome. Transactions can involve considerable paperwork and a lot of waiting around. On the whole, bank exchange rates are more favourable than those in travel agents and hotels – the deal just takes longer to complete. Small change is indispensable – especially the L100, L200 or L500 coins needed for telephones, tips and for illuminating works of art and chapels in churches *(see p359)*.

Eagle sculpture on the Ministry of Finance

CHANGING MONEY

IT'S BEST to have at least some local currency when you arrive, so you won't have to change money immediately. However, there are increasing numbers of convenient electronic exchange machines at arrival points. There are now several throughout the city too. Multilingual instructions are available. You simply feed in up to 14 notes of the same foreign currency, and should get some lire back. Exchange rates vary from place to place. The Banco di Santo Spirito office at Fiumicino airport offers reasonable rates.

For the best rates, change money at a bank (look for the sign *Cambio*). Hotels tend to give poor rates, even if they charge modest commissions. At the Vatican Museums *(see p235)*, you aren't charged any commission. The American Express office *(see p359)* gives good rates and is open on Saturday mornings. Cardholders may withdraw up to $1,000 (or £500) a week from the cash machine, but you have to pay a fee for this service and need to organize a PIN (personal identification number) linked to your account before you travel.

Automatic exchange machine

CREDIT CARDS

CREDIT CARDS, which used to be regarded with great suspicion in Italy, are now much more widely accepted in larger hotels, shops and restaurants in Rome. Some places, however, prefer Eurocheques, which can be cleared faster. All major credit and charge cards (American Express, Access/Mastercard, Visa, Diners Card) are well known. Banks and cash dispensers are more likely to accept Visa cards for cash advances, but Access (Mastercard) is accepted by more retail outlets in Italy. Take both if you have them. Paying for anything in foreign currency will almost always be expensive.

TRAVELLER'S CHEQUES

IF YOU OPT for traveller's cheques, choose a well-known name such as Thomas Cook or American Express, or take those issued through a major bank. Most issuers charge a 1% commission on traveller's cheques. Get some small denominations, so you won't be left with huge amounts of Italian currency at the end of your trip. But don't forget that the minimum commission charged for each transaction (and the amount of time involved) may make changing small amounts of money uneconomical. Always record the traveller's cheque numbers and refund addresses separately from the cheques themselves in case they are stolen. Some places will charge you for each cheque.

Check the exchange rates before you travel and decide whether lire, dollar or sterling cheques are more appropriate. Lire cheques are issued only by Italian banks, and may be more difficult to cash in Italy than dollar or sterling ones.

OPENING HOURS

BANKS ARE USUALLY open 8.30am–1.20pm Mon–Fri. Some larger branches also open from about 3pm to 4.30pm, but opening times vary and banks are closed for public holidays and at weekends. Bureaux de Change have more generous opening times, similar to shop hours. The exchange office at Termini station *(see p372)* is open on Sunday mornings.

USING BANKS

QUEUES IN BANKS can be long and the form-filling involved in changing money can take up a lot of time. You usually have to queue first at the *cambio,* then at the *cassa* to obtain your cash. Take some form of identity with you, such as a passport. Metal objects may set off emergency detectors as you enter.

Exchange office at one of the Italian national banks

One of the major Italian banks

Credito Italiano
One of the major Italian banks

BANCA DI ROMA
The Bank of Rome, which has branches in other Italian cities

CURRENCY

Italy's currency unit is the *lira* (plural *lire*) and is usually abbreviated L or £. It became the national currency during the unification process in the mid-19th century.

Lira means pound and the English pound is referred to as *lira sterlina* to distinguish it.

Telephone tokens *(gettoni)* are worth L200 and you may get some *gettoni* in your change instead of coins.

Shops and bars are usually not very keen on giving change for a high-value note, so ask for smaller denominations of bank notes when you change money. Coins are often in short supply.

The prospect of carrying around millions of units of currency may at first seem alarming. Plans to alter the basic unit have still not been realized, but you'll find in practice that the last three noughts are often ignored in spoken Italian: *sessanta* will usually mean L60,000 and not, as one may think, L60.

Bank Notes

Italian bank notes come in denominations of L100,000, L50,000, L10,000, L5,000, L2,000 and L1,000, which are easily identifiable by their colours and the historic people portrayed. Notes increase in size progressively according to their value. The lira is never divided into smaller units.

1,000 lire

2,000 lire

5,000 lire

10,000 lire

50,000 lire

100,000 lire

Coins

Coins, shown here at actual size, are in denominations of L500, L200, L100 and L50. Old L100 and L50 coins are still in use and there are L10 and L20 coins of minute value. Telephone gettoni are worth L200.

50 lire (new)

100 lire (new)

500 lire

50 lire (old)

100 lire (old)

200 lire

Gettone (200 lire)

Using Rome's Telephones

THE ROME TELEPHONE SYSTEM has recently undergone a major upheaval. Many numbers have been changed and new equipment has been installed alongside older machinery. Until the overhaul is complete you may need a degree of patience when using the phone. At present, telephone numbers can have any number of digits from four to about nine.

Telephone company logo

TELEPHONE OFFICES

TELEPHONE OFFICES *(Telefoni)* are run by the Italian telecom companies (SIP or ASST) and offer a convenient way of making long-distance or private calls. At the *Telefono* there will be several metered telephones, each in its own sound-proofed booth. An assistant will **Telephone sign** assign you a booth, and meter your call once you have been connected to the number you want. You pay on your way out. No premium is charged on this service, but *Telefoni* opening hours rarely coincide with Italy's cheapest-rate calling times. The one at the **Palazzo delle Poste** on Piazza San Silvestro is an exception – it stays open 24 hours a day. There are other *Telefoni* through-out Rome, including ones at Fiumicino airport, Termini railway station, other major post offices and in the underground car park at Villa Borghese. To send international telegrams, go to a post office or call **Italcable**.

Useful information Italcable 573 41; Palazzo delle Poste, Piazza San Silvestro 20. **Map** 5 A3 & 12 E1.

CALL CHARGES

THE CHEAPEST times to phone within Italy are 10pm–8am from Monday to Saturday and all day Sunday. If this is inconvenient, it is also relatively inexpensive to call during weekday evenings between 6.30pm and 10pm, or after 1pm on Saturday. But check what time is best if you are making international calls: time variations throughout the world make a difference to cheap rates. Telephoning from hotel rooms is usually expensive and is sometimes marked up by several hundred per cent. In general, telephone calls cost more from Italy than they do from the UK or North America.

USING A SIP COIN AND CARD TELEPHONE

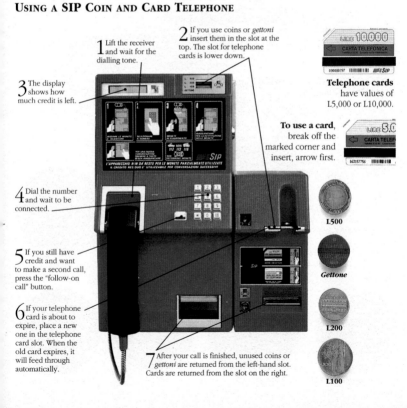

1 Lift the receiver and wait for the dialling tone.

2 If you use coins or *gettoni* insert them in the slot at the top. The slot for telephone cards is lower down.

3 The display shows how much credit is left.

4 Dial the number and wait to be connected.

5 If you still have credit and want to make a second call, press the "follow-on call" button.

6 If your telephone card is about to expire, place a new one in the telephone card slot. When the old card expires, it will feed through automatically.

7 After your call is finished, unused coins or *gettoni* are returned from the left-hand slot. Cards are returned from the slot on the right.

Telephone cards have values of L5,000 or L10,000.

To use a card, break off the marked corner and insert, arrow first.

L500

Gettone

L200

L100

USING PUBLIC TELEPHONES

New sign

Old sign for telephone

Newer SIP PAYPHONES, or *interurbani*, are orange, and from these you can dial long-distance and some international calls direct. Payphones take L100, L200 and L500 coins. For long-distance direct-dial calls, have at least L2,000 of change ready. If you don't put enough coins in to start with, the telephone simply retains your money and disconnects you. After a successful call, however, any unused coins are usually returned.

The most up-to-date payphones (pictured opposite) take SIP telephone cards (ask for a *scheda* or *carta telefonica*), costing L5,000 or L10,000, as well as coins. Some payphones will now only accept cards. Cards are available from shops, bars

REACHING THE RIGHT NUMBER

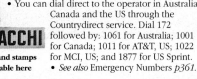

Gettoni and stamps are available here

- The telephone code for Rome is 06.
- General information on calls within Europe is on 176. Reverse charge and credit card-holder calls are also accepted.
- European operator assistance is on 15.
- Intercontinental operator assistance is on 170.
- General telephone information is on 180.
- You can dial direct to the operator in Australia, Canada and the US through the Countrydirect service. Dial 172 followed by: 1061 for Australia; 1001 for Canada; 1011 for AT&T, US; 1022 for MCI, US; and 1877 for US Sprint.
- *See also* Emergency Numbers *p361*.

and tobacconists displaying the black and white T sign. Break off the marked corner, insert the card arrow first, and the value of the unexpired units will show on a display window. After your call, the card can be retrieved and reused until its value expires.

Older-style phones tend to be found in bars and cafés. These phones will only accept tokens *(gettoni)*, costing L200, which can be purchased at shops, bars,

newsagents, post offices or special vending machines. To use these phones insert the *gettone*, dial, wait for an answer and then push the knob to make the token drop; this connects you.

For long-distance calls on older telephones, it is much easier to seek out a *telefono a scatti*, or metered phone. Ask the bar owner if you can phone and the call will be metered. You pay him or her when you have finished.

Sending Letters

The ITALIAN postal service is not especially efficient and it is said that letters travelled faster in the days of the old Roman Empire than they do today, in spite of modern technology. For leisurely postcards, the service is usually fine but expect anything sent abroad to take its

Rome letters   Other destinations

Italian state post box

Post Office sign

time; the Italian postal service is particularly slow in August when it can take up to a month for a postcard to reach the UK. For anything urgent or important, it's better to use the more expensive express system, which knocks a day or two off the delivery time, or registered post. Otherwise, you can buy ordinary stamps *(francobolli)* at tobacconists with the black and white T sign as well as in post offices. Sub-post office hours are generally from around 8.30am

until 2pm (8.30am–noon on Saturdays and the last day of the month), but main offices stay open 24 hours a day or well into the evening for some services (such as registered post). Among the 24-hour ones are Piazza San Silvestro, at Termini and at the airport. Italian post boxes are red.

POSTE RESTANTE

Letters and parcels which are to be picked up at the post office are sent care of *(c/o)* Palazzo delle Poste, Roma, *Fermo Posta*. Print the surname clearly in block capitals and underline it to make sure the letters are filed correctly. To collect your post, you have to show your passport and pay a small charge. American Express *poste restante* is free to clients.

VATICAN POST

Vatican post office sign

The Vatican postal service costs the same as the state post, but is faster. Buy cards and stamps at the post office near the Vatican Museums entrance, or in Piazza San Pietro. Letters bearing Vatican stamps can only be posted in blue Vatican post boxes.

Vatican postage stamps

Postage stamps

Airmail sticker

Additional Information

Fiumicino airport, point of arrival for most visitors to Rome

CUSTOMS AND IMMIGRATION

C ITIZENS OF the United States, Canada, Australia, New Zealand or the UK do not need visas for stays of up to three months, but all non-European Community (non-EC) residents require full passports. British citizens may use a Visitor's Card. For longer stays, a visa should be obtained from your nearest Italian embassy or consulate before you travel. You won't usually need any vaccination certificates, but you should check if you have stopped over in tropical or Middle Eastern zones. Duty-free allowances are as follows:

Non-European Community residents are allowed to bring in 400 cigarettes, 100 cigars, 200 cigarillos or 500 grams of tobacco; 1 litre of spirits or 2 litres of wine; 50 grams of perfume. Goods such as watches and cameras may be imported freely for personal or professional use. EC residents no longer have to "declare" goods but random checks are made to guard against the likes of drug traffickers.

The refund system for Value Added Tax (IVA in Italy) for non-EC residents is very complex (see p323) and it is only worth reclaiming if you have spent a lot of money in a single outlet.

Strictly speaking, all visitors to Italy have to register with the police, presenting a passport within three days of their arrival. In practice, the vast majority of visitors have this procedure taken care of for them by their hotels, when they first register. If you are

Confession box, Gesù

staying elsewhere, contact a local police department for advice, or telephone the **Questura** (police station).

Questura
 46 86 ext 2102 or 2876.

CATHOLIC SERVICES

F OR MANY CATHOLICS, a visit to Rome means an audience with the pope. General audiences are usually held every Wednesday at 11am (10am in hot weather) in St Peter's square, the Audiences room, or at the summer residence at Castel Gandolfo. To attend an audience, apply to the **Prefettura della Casa Pontificia** before your visit. (Rome travel agencies may be able to arrange an audience as part of a coach tour during your stay.) There is no charge. Mass is held daily in the main churches of Rome (High Mass is on Sunday). Churches where confession is heard include St Peter's (see pp230–33), San Giovanni in Laterano (pp182–3), San Paolo fuori le Mura (p264), Santa Maria Maggiore (pp172–3), the Gesù (pp114–15), Santa Sabina (p204) and Sant'Ignazio (p106). English-speaking Catholic churches include San Silvestro (Piazza San Silvestro) and San Tommaso di Canterbury (Via di Monserrato 45).

Prefettura della Casa Pontificia
Città del Vaticano, 00120. **Map** 3 B3.
 69 82.

STUDENT INFORMATION

A N INTERNATIONAL Student Identity Card (ISIC) or a Youth International Educational Exchange Card (YIEE) are worth having for reductions on museum and other charges.

Students on the steps of Santa Maria Maggiore

Contact the **Centro Turistico Studentesco** for information. The **Associazione Italiana Alberghi per la Gioventù** (the Italian YHA) has four hostels in the city. **Casa dello Studente** lists student hostels. **Trans-alpino** is for rail discounts.

ISIC card

Associazione Italiana Alberghi per la Gioventù
Via Cavour 44, 00184. **Map** 3 D3.
 487 11 52.

Casa dello Studente
Viale Ministero degli Affari Esteri 6.

Centro Turistico Studentesco
Via Genova 16. **Map** 5 C3. 44 67 91. (Branches at Via Appia Nuova 434 and Corso Vittorio Emanuele 297.)

Transalpino
Piazza Esquilino 8A. **Map** 6 D4.
 487 08 70. (Branch at Stazione Termini, platform 6.)

The pope on his balcony at St Peter's

Newspapers available in Rome

NEWSPAPERS, TV, RADIO

ROME'S MAIN newspapers are *La Repubblica* and *Il Messaggero*. British and American newspapers are readily available, and the *International Herald Tribune* is sold on the day of issue. The state TV channels are RAI Uno, Due and Tre; all of them are politically aligned. The advent of satellite and cable TV means there are European channels in many languages, plus sport and CNN news in English. The BBC World Service is broadcast on radio on 15.070MHz (short wave) in the mornings and 648KHz (medium wave) at night. Vatican Radio on 93.3MHz and 105MHz (FM) broadcasts news in English.

EMBASSIES AND CONSULATES

IF YOU LOSE your passport, or need other help, contact your national embassy or consulate as listed below.

Australia
Via Alessandria 215. **Map** 6 E1.
[854 27 21

Canada
Via G.B. De Rossi 27.
[841 53 41.

New Zealand
Via Zara 28.
[440 29 28.

United Kingdom
Via XX Settembre 80A. **Map** 6 D2.
[482 54 41.

United States
Via Veneto 119A/121. **Map** 5 B2.
[467 41.

ELECTRICAL ADAPTORS

ELECTRIC CURRENT in Italy is 220V AC, with two-pin round-pronged plugs. Adaptors can be purchased in most countries. In most hotels of three or more stars, there are hair dryers and shaving points in all the bedrooms.

Shaving point in hotel bedroom for 110V or 220V

Standard Italian plug

ROME TIME

ROME IS ONE HOUR ahead of Greenwich Mean Time (GMT). Examples of the time difference with Rome for other major cities are as follows: London: -1 hour; New York: -6 hours; Dallas: -7 hours; Los Angeles: -9 hours; Perth: +7 hours; Sydney: +9 hours; Auckland: +11 hours; Tokyo: +8 hours. These figures can vary slightly for brief periods with local changes in summer. For all official purposes, the Italians use the 24-hour clock.

CONVERSION TABLE

Imperial to Metric
1 inch	= 2.54 centimetres
1 foot	= 30 centimetres
1 mile	= 1.6 kilometres
1 ounce	= 28 grams
1 pound	= 454 grams
1 pint	= 0.57 litres
1 gallon	= 4.6 litres

Metric to Imperial
1 centimetre	= 0.4 inches
1 metre	= 3 feet 3 inches
1 kilometre	= 0.6 miles
1 gram	= 0.04 ounces
1 kilogram	= 2.2 pounds
1 litre	= 1.8 pints

SIGHTSEEING PERMITS

TO VISIT certain sights in Rome, you need to obtain a written permit and book the time of your visit in advance. This applies particularly to archaeological sites, which may sometimes be closed during excavations. Write to:

Comune di Roma Ripartizione X
Piazza Campitelli 7. **Map** 4 F5 & 12 E5.
[67 10 30 64. FAX 67 10 31 18.

To speed things up, deliver your application in person to the *protocollo* on the third floor. Once your application has been received, fix a time for your visit by calling Signor Natale of the:

Ufficio Monumenti Antichi e Scavi, Via del Portico d'Ottavia 29. **Map** 4 F5 & 12 E5. **Map** 4 F5 & 12 E5.
[67 10 38 19, 67 10 20 71 or 67 10 24 75. FAX 67 10 31 18.

OTHER RELIGIOUS SERVICES

Anglican
All Saints, Via del Babuino 153.
Map 4 F2. [323 54 93.

American Episcopal
St Paul's, Via Napoli 58. **Map** 5 C3.
[488 33 39.

Jewish
Sinagoga, Lungotevere Cenci.
Map 4 F5 & 12 D5. [687 50 51.

Methodist
Via Firenze 38. **Map** 5 C3.
[481 48 11.

Mosque
Viale della Moschea (Parioli district).
Map 2 F1. [808 21 67.

Presbyterian
St Andrew's, Via XX Settembre 7.
Map 5 C3. [482 76 27.

The Mosque in Parioli

GETTING TO ROME

MANY NATIONAL AIRLINES, including Italy's Alitalia, fly direct to Rome from most European cities and several in North America and Australia. There are no direct flights from New Zealand, but passengers can catch connections from either Frankfurt or London.

Alitalia aircraft

Rome also has train and coach links with the rest of Europe. These take a lot longer than flights (about 24 hours from London, compared with about three), but tend to cost about the same, so are only really worthwhile if you want to travel overland. The trains are often crowded in summer.

Part of the new extension to Fiumicino airport

BY AIR

IF YOU'RE FLYING from the United States, **TWA**, Delta and United Airlines operate regular direct scheduled flights to Rome, with services from about half a dozen cities (including New York, Boston, Washington, Los Angeles and Chicago). Flying time from New York is about eight and a half hours and it's about 13 hours from Los Angeles. **Canadian Airlines** flies from Montreal and Toronto; **Qantas** from

Alitalia flight tickets

The new ticket hall at Ostiense

Melbourne and Sydney. The Italian state airline, **Alitalia**, also flies between Rome and New York, San Francisco, Philadelphia, Boston, Chicago, Detroit, Washington, Montreal, Toronto and Sydney. It may, however, be considerably cheaper for intercontinental travellers to take a budget flight to London, Paris, Frankfurt or Amsterdam and continue the journey to Rome from there.

British Airways and Alitalia operate direct scheduled flights from London Heathrow to Rome, and you can fly from Manchester. Among the airlines using Rome as an intercontinental transit point are **Philippine Airlines**, Sudan Airways and Ethiopian Airlines: fares are cheaper, but flights tend to be less frequent and are sometimes subject to long delays.

APEX, PEX, or SuperPEX fares generally offer the best value in scheduled flights, but you must purchase them well in advance (for example, 7 or 14 days ahead in the UK; 21 days in the US). They are subject to penalty clauses if you cancel, so it's advisable to take out insurance as soon as you buy your ticket.

If you're based in the UK, it's worth looking in the small ads of newspapers for cut-price charters (though even in low season these are becoming increasingly rare). Regular charters run all year round. Most leave from Gatwick and Luton, but there are a couple of flights a week from Manchester and it's usually possible to fly from Glasgow and Birmingham. Fares vary greatly, peaking in summer, and in Holy Week for the Pope's Easter blessing.

If you want to book flights during your stay in Rome, travel agents, such as the **American Express** office, should be able to help.

> ↖ 🚉 Stazione 🚆 – Railway Station
>
> ↖ Ⓜ Metropolitana per Termini Underground to Termini
>
> ↖ Piazzale dei Partigiani
>
> 🚌🚐 P ⓒ Centro

Easy-to-follow signs at Ostiense

AIRLINE NUMBERS

Alitalia
📞 656 21 or 656 01.

American Express
📞 676 41.

British Airways
📞 47 99 91 or 65 01 15 13.

Canadian Airlines
📞 48 20 96 or 650 14 62 .

Philippine Airlines
📞 481 89 39.

Qantas
📞 488 64 57 or 65 01 01 46.

TWA
📞 472 11 or 60 12 49 36.

PACKAGE HOLIDAYS

PACKAGE HOLIDAYS to Rome can be much better value than travelling independently. For European visitors there are weekend packages and two- or three-centre holidays; Rome is frequently packaged with Florence and Venice. Those from further afield can visit the city during Europe-wide tours. Most package companies transport you free of charge from the airport to your hotel in Rome. Many, especially the more expensive ones, include a tour guide.

AIRPORTS

ROME HAS TWO international airports. Leonardo da Vinci – commonly known as Fiumicino – handles most

Ciampino, a more basic airport used by most charter flights

scheduled flights, and is about 30 km (18 miles) south-west of the city. The other airport is Ciampino, about 15 km (9 miles) southeast and used by the majority of charter flights. Major car hire firms have rental offices at both airports, though you may find it less harrowing to get into the city centre on public transport or by taxi.

Shuttle bus to car-hire lots at Fiumicino

From Fiumicino there's a train to Ostiense station (5.40am–midnight; 25 min journey). If you are lucky the ticket office (which also sells Metro tickets) will be open; if not, you'll have to tackle the automatic ticket machine *(see p373)*. Ostiense is linked with Piramide Metro by what seems to be an endless series of escalators, flyovers and moving pavements. At Piramide Metro you can catch an underground train to the city centre. This Metro line stops running at 9pm on weekdays and at 11.30pm on Saturdays and Sundays, though. Taxis can be difficult to find at Ostiense after 9pm, but there's a bus (the No. 95) to Piazza Venezia.

The swiftest way to get to the centre from Ciampino is by bus to Anagnina Metro station, where you can catch an underground train to Termini. Taxis from both airports are expensive; only use official cabs and, although most taxi drivers are honest, make sure that the fare meter is switched on and showing only the minimum charge before you leave.

One of the overhead walkways linking the air terminal at Ostiense station with Piramide Metro station

KEY

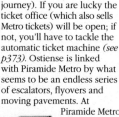

🚌	Coach to Termini
FS	Railway to Ostiense
P	Multistorey car park
– – –	Future extension
——	New ring road

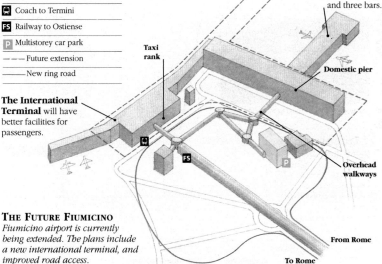

The Domestic Terminal has a restaurant, shops and three bars.

Domestic pier

Taxi rank

The International Terminal will have better facilities for passengers.

Overhead walkways

From Rome

To Rome

THE FUTURE FIUMICINO

Fiumicino airport is currently being extended. The plans include a new international terminal, and improved road access.

Arriving in Rome

THIS MAP shows the main bus, rail and Metro links used by travellers arriving in Rome. The connections between Rome's two airports and the city centre are shown, as well as links between Rome and the rest of Italy and the international rail routes from neighbouring European countries. Travel information, including details of journey times and service frequency, is listed separately in each box.

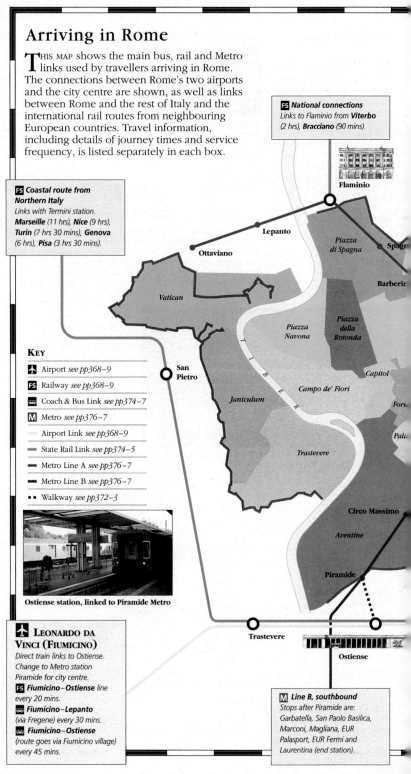

FS *National connections*
Links to Flaminio from Viterbo (2 hrs), Bracciano (90 mins).

Flaminio

FS *Coastal route from Northern Italy*
Links with Termini station.
Marseille *(11 hrs),* **Nice** *(9 hrs),* **Turin** *(7 hrs 30 mins),* **Genova** *(6 hrs),* **Pisa** *(3 hrs 30 mins).*

Lepanto

Ottaviano

Piazza di Spagna

Spagn

Vatican

Barberin

Piazza Navona

Piazza della Rotonda

KEY

✈	Airport *see pp368–9*
FS	Railway *see pp368–9*
🚌	Coach & Bus Link *see pp374–7*
M	Metro *see pp376–7*
	Airport Link *see pp368–9*
	State Rail Link *see pp374–5*
	Metro Line A *see pp376–7*
	Metro Line B *see pp376–7*
• •	Walkway *see pp372–3*

San Pietro

Janiculum

Campo de' Fiori

Capitol

Fori

Pala

Trastevere

Circo Massimo

Aventine

Ostiense station, linked to Piramide Metro

Piramide

✈ LEONARDO DA VINCI (FIUMICINO)

Direct train links to Ostiense.
Change to Metro station
Piramide for city centre.
FS *Fiumicino–Ostiense line*
every 20 mins.
🚌 *Fiumicino–Lepanto*
(via Fregene) every 30 mins.
🚌 *Fiumicino–Ostiense*
(route goes via Fiumicino village)
every 45 mins.

Trastevere

Ostiense

M *Line B, southbound*
Stops after Piramide are: Garbatella, San Paolo Basilica, Marconi, Magliana, EUR Palasport, EUR Fermi and Laurentina (end station).

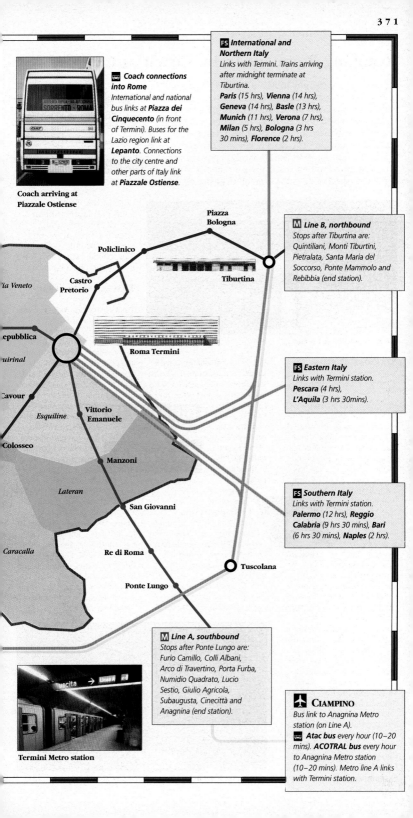

🚌 Coach connections into Rome
International and national bus links at **Piazza dei Cinquecento** (in front of Termini). Buses for the Lazio region link at **Lepanto**. Connections to the city centre and other parts of Italy link at **Piazzale Ostiense**.

Coach arriving at Piazzale Ostiense

FS International and Northern Italy
Links with Termini. Trains arriving after midnight terminate at Tiburtina.
Paris (15 hrs), **Vienna** (14 hrs), **Geneva** (14 hrs), **Basle** (13 hrs), **Munich** (11 hrs), **Verona** (7 hrs), **Milan** (5 hrs), **Bologna** (3 hrs 30 mins), **Florence** (2 hrs).

M Line B, northbound
Stops after Tiburtina are: Quintiliani, Monti Tiburtini, Pietralata, Santa Maria del Soccorso, Ponte Mammolo and Rebibbia (end station).

Piazza Bologna

Policlinico

Castro Pretorio

Tiburtina

ia Veneto

epubblica

uirinal

Roma Termini

FS Eastern Italy
Links with Termini station.
Pescara (4 hrs), **L'Aquila** (3 hrs 30mins).

Cavour

Esquiline

Vittorio Emanuele

Colosseo

Manzoni

Lateran

San Giovanni

FS Southern Italy
Links with Termini station.
Palermo (12 hrs), **Reggio Calabria** (9 hrs 30 mins), **Bari** (6 hrs 30 mins), **Naples** (2 hrs).

Caracalla

Re di Roma

Tuscolana

Ponte Lungo

M Line A, southbound
Stops after Ponte Lungo are: Furio Camillo, Colli Albani, Arco di Travertino, Porta Furba, Numidio Quadrato, Lucio Sestio, Giulio Agricola, Subaugusta, Cinecittà and Anagnina (end station).

Termini Metro station

🛬 CIAMPINO
Bus link to Anagnina Metro station (on Line A).
🚌 **Atac bus** every hour (10–20 mins). **ACOTRAL bus** every hour to Anagnina Metro station (10–20 mins). Metro line A links with Termini station.

Reaching Rome by Train, Coach or Car

Aᴺʸ ᴏᴠᴇʀʟᴀɴᴅ journey to Rome is fastest by train, though there are coach connections to most major European cities. Within Italy, journeys between large cities are usually also best done by train, but when travelling from towns which are not on the main Intercity rail routes, coaches can be quicker. For drivers, the Italian Automobile Club *(see p361)* provides free assistance and excellent maps to members of affiliated automobile clubs from all over the world.

A Pendolino – Italy's fastest train

The foyer of Stazione Termini

Stazione Termini

Sᴛᴀᴢɪᴏɴᴇ ᴛᴇʀᴍɪɴɪ, Rome's main train station, is also the hub of the urban transport system. Beneath it is the only interchange between the city's two Metro lines, and directly outside, on Piazza dei Cinquecento, is the central bus terminus. Though it is one of Rome's most stunning 20th-century buildings, it also has many unsavoury aspects, so it is unwise to linger longer than necessary.

FS logo

If you arrive late, aim to leave the neighbourhood as swiftly as you can. There are usually taxis (go to the official queue), even in the small hours, and most of the city's night buses start at Termini.

In summer the station gets very crowded, and you can expect long queues at ticket booths, bureaux de change and at both the transport and tourist information offices. There's a left luggage office, a police station where you should report anything lost or stolen on a train or in the station; and a small Citalia office where you can exchange money as well as

get travel information. In the foyer, there is an international telephone office *(see p364)*, a bookshop, a post office and a tobacconist (where you can stock up on bus and Metro tickets). Other facilities at the station include a burger bar, a café, a ticket office for Transalpino and, downstairs in the gloomy Metro subway, a hairdresser and an *albergo diurno* (day hotel), where, for a price, you can freshen up with a bath or shower.

Of Rome's other stations, four are most likely to be of interest to tourists. They are

BINARIO 17

Platform sign

← uscita

Exit sign

Ostiense and Trastevere, for trains to Fiumicino airport and Viterbo *(see p271)*; Tiburtina, for some of the trains on the north-south line through Italy; and Roma Nord for trains to Prima Porta.

Travelling by Train

Iᴛᴀʟɪᴀɴ ꜱᴛᴀᴛᴇ ʀᴀɪʟᴡᴀʏꜱ (Ferrovie dello Stato or FS) have several levels of service, from Locale trains which stop at every station, to the Pendolino, a super-fast and extremely luxurious train, which offers first- and second-class service. The Pendolino runs between Rome and Milan, Turin, Genoa, Bari, Naples and Venice. You have to reserve and you're charged hefty supplements for the privileges of speed, hostess service and free newspapers. You also pay a supplement on Intercity trains. These trains are for fast long distance journeys and have both first- and second-class carriages. They run from Rome to Venice, Milan, Florence and Naples. You should book in high season and at weekends. Booking is obligatory on some services,

Termini, the heart of Italy's rail network and Rome's transport system

An international Eurocity train

which are marked in the timetable by a black R on a white background. Some staff at the **Booking Office** speak English, but it may be easier to go in person to the station, or to a travel agent displaying the FS symbol.

From Rome you can also take international or Eurocity (EC) trains to destinations all over Europe. It's worth reserving a seat, especially during the summer when trains become crowded.

Stazione Termini
Booking Office
Via Giolitti 22. 🎧 *47 30.*

MACHINES FOR FS RAIL TICKETS

These self-service machines are easy to use, and most have instructions in four languages on a printed panel.

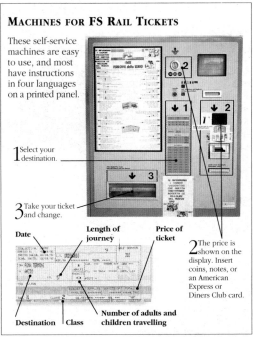

1 Select your destination.

3 Take your ticket and change.

2 The price is shown on the display. Insert coins, notes, or an American Express or Diners Club card.

Date

Length of journey

Price of ticket

Destination   Class

Number of adults and children travelling

COACH TRAVEL

Most regional and long-distance coaches are blue

MANY long-distance coaches terminate at Piazza dei Cinquecento outside Termini station, or in streets nearby. Information and tickets for Euroline coaches to European cities are available from **Lazzi Express**. The **Appian Line** offers regular services within Italy. Its itineraries include Florence, Naples, Capri, Sorrento, Pompei, Venice and Assisi. Local buses, serving villages and towns within the Lazio region, are run by **COTRAL**. All bus stations used by COTRAL are linked

to Metro stations. Tickets for COTRAL services are bought on the spot and cannot be booked in advance. Some day trips from Rome by bus are described on pages 268–71.

Appian Line
Via Barberini 109. 🎧 *488 41 51.*

COTRAL
🎧 *591 55 51.*

Lazzi Express
Via Tagliamento 27. 🎧 *884 08 40.*

TRAVELLING BY CAR

TO DRIVE YOUR own car in Italy you need an international Green Card (for insurance purposes) and the vehicle registration document. A translation of your driving licence, available at Italian tourist offices abroad, is also useful. Wearing seatbelts is

Blue signs showing A roads and green signs showing motorways

compulsory in Italy. You must also carry a warning triangle in case of breakdown. Main routes to Rome connect with the Grande Raccordo Anulare (GRA), Rome's ringroad.

Tolls are charged on all Italian motorways. You can buy petrol coupons and magnetic motorway toll cards from motoring organizations before entering Italy.

Euroline coach running between Rome and the rest of Europe

GETTING AROUND ROME

Rome's centre is compact and, although walking absolutely everywhere would be over-ambitious, it is a city in which you can spend much of your time on foot. As the main streets in the centre are usually clogged with traffic, driving and cycling cannot be recommended, but courageous motorbike or scooter riders can have great fun buzzing around on a rented Vespa. Travelling by bus and tram can be very slow, so use overland public transport only when you have a long way to go. The Metro, designed to connect the suburbs with the centre, has no stops in the historic city centre near the Pantheon or Piazza Navona, though it is certainly the swiftest way of crossing the city.

A Roman family's solution to very heavy traffic

WALKING

Wandering through Rome's old centre is one of the most enjoyable aspects of being in the city. You can take in the architectural details, absorb the streetlife, make diversions at will, and peek into any church, shop or bar that catches your interest. And you can easily visit, or at least see, several of the main tourist sights in a few hours. The Colosseum, for example, is only about 2.5 km (1.5 miles) from the Spanish Steps. Your route could pass by the Forum, Piazza Venezia and several churches; other sights, such as the Trevi Fountain, the Galleria Doria Pamphilj and the Pantheon, are just a short detour away.

Explore the city area by area, using public transport when distances are too far.

Directions for walkers

Avanti: go! Pedestrians have right of way

Alt: stop! Traffic has right of way

Only very small patches of central Rome are pedestrianized, and a street which is closed to cars will still be used by cyclists and scooter riders. There have been many plans to create more traffic-free zones, and even to ban anything on wheels from some parts of the city – but imposing such measures on a population as insubordinate as Rome's is not easily done.

If you find the summer heat hard to bear, remember that the narrow cobbled streets get little sunlight and remain relatively cool, while walking into an open piazza can be like stepping into a furnace.

During the height of summer, you'll have a more enjoyable time if you follow the example of the Italians. Walk slowly on the shady side of the street; have a long lunch followed by a siesta in the hottest part of the day. You can continue exploring in the late afternoon, when churches and shops reopen and the streets are at their liveliest. Wandering at night is worthwhile, as the streets are cool and many facades floodlit.

Pedestrian crossing   **Watch out for children**

Pedestrian crossing: only slightly safer than the open road

CROSSING ROADS

First impressions suggest there can be only two sorts of pedestrian in Rome: the quick and the dead. Even if you cross roads by sets of traffic lights and pedestrian crossings strictly in your favour, there is sure to be some van or Vespa hurtling towards you with apparently homicidal intent. Fortunately, Roman drivers have quick reactions. The pious would attribute this to the protection of Santa Francesca Romana (*see p87*), cynics to the fact that according to Italian insurance law, drivers are responsible for any road accident. Whatever the inspiration, accidents are quite rare. The best tactic is to be as alert and confident as Romans. The roads are very busy. When crossing, try to leave as large a gap as possible between yourself and oncoming traffic. Step purposefully into the road, facing approaching motorists with a determined glare. The trick now is to keep going steadily: don't hesitate, or change your course, and don't run. As long as a driver can see you, he or she should stop, or at least swerve, albeit at the last moment.

Pedestrians and drivers must both take particular care at night, when the traffic lights are switched to a constantly flashing amber, turning the crossings into free-for-alls.

STREET SIGNS

THEORETICALLY, although it may not always seem to be the case, pedestrians have right of way at crossings when the green *avanti* sign is lit up. The red sign *alt* means you must wait. Underground crossings are indicated by a sign reading *sottopassaggio*.

It is easy to get lost in the maze of streets and piazzas that comprise the historic centre. Until you know your way around, you can follow the yellow signs marking routes between the sights and piazzas of particular interest to tourists. Routes leading to general landmarks are indicated by signs on a silver-grey background.

No stopping   **No parking**

One-way street

No through road

DRIVING

DRIVING IN CENTRAL Rome can be an extremely intimidating experience for visitors. The flamboyant aggression of Italian drivers is notorious, pedestrians step out into the roads without warning, and the one-way system operating in much of the centre makes retaining a sense of direction impossible. You'll also find motorists overtaking on the

wrong side, while scooters and Vespas zoom among the lanes of traffic and go the wrong way down one-way streets. One rule to remember is to give way to the right. Unless you are accustomed to driving in Italian cities, leave your car at home – or failing that, in a guarded car park.

Car thefts are rife in Rome, so never leave anything of value in your car, even out of sight: areas such as Campo de' Fiori are patrolled by gangs on the lookout for anyone leaving cameras, fur coats and other costly items in their boots. You should also remove your car radio – you won't be the only person carrying one into a bar, restaurant or disco.

Take extra care if driving late at night. Not only do traffic lights switch to flashing amber, but many Italians are astonishingly cavalier about driving under the influence of drink or drugs.

PARKING

THE MOST convenient car park is below the Villa Borghese. Much of the city centre is reserved for residents with permits and there are thousands of drivers with fake permits, which exacerbates the problem. If you do find a legal place to park, you may return and find you've been hemmed in by double parked cars. Locations of some of the most useful car parks are listed on page 379.

Directions to parking areas

PETROL

PETROL IS very expensive. It can be bought from roadside petrol pumps throughout the city, as well as from regular garages, though the former don't always sell lead-free petrol *(senza piombo)*. In the afternoon and at night many pumps are self-service, operated by banknotes or credit cards. Late-night petrol stations are listed on page 379.

The state petrol company logo

ILLEGAL PARKING

Rome's traffic police are vigilant. If you've parked illegally, your car may be clamped or (if it's causing an obstruction) towed away, so phone 676 98 38 or 676 98 37 to check before reporting it stolen. No-parking zones should be clearly marked, but look carefully, in case the sign is hidden by a tree.

Signpost for a tow away area *(zona rimozione)*

A tow truck at work

Travelling by Bus, Tram and Metro

ROME'S PUBLIC TRANSPORT system is comparatively cheap, comprehensive and as efficient as the busy streets allow. Priests, nuns, tourists, pilgrims, business-men and pickpockets all pile aboard, transforming the buses and trams into mobile saunas during the summer. Short distances are better covered on foot, because heavy traffic often blocks the roads. Getting off at the right stop can be difficult, but other passengers will usually help if you ask for directions. Always keep a tight hold on your valuables.

Monthly pass

BUSES AND TRAMS

ROME'S PUBLIC bus and tram company is called **ATAC** (Azienda Tramvie e Autobus del Comune di Roma). Scores of its orange buses and a handful of rattling trams cover most parts of the city. They run from early morning until about midnight. There are also a few night buses.

Apart from one electric minibus (No. 119), no buses can run through the narrow streets of the historic centre. But there are plenty of bus routes to take you within a short walk of the main sights *(see map inside back cover)*.

Rome's new yellow bus stops comprehensively list the details of routes taken by all the buses using that stop. There are, however, still a number of old-style bus stops left. These list only a few of the streets and piazzas that the buses pass and are mystifying until you know Rome well.

BIG ticket for one day's unlimited travel

USING BUSES AND TRAMS

THE MAIN TERMINUS is on Piazza dei Cinquecento outside Termini station, but there are other major route hubs throughout the city, most usefully those at Largo Argentina, Piazza Venezia and Piazza del Risorgimento. You can get information and tickets from ATAC kiosks, but these are not always staffed, even during official opening hours, so it is not always wise to depend on them.

Most day buses have only a driver; night buses usually also have a conductor who issues tickets. (You can't buy tickets on day buses.)

During the day, if you have a normal ticket, you should board the bus at the back. There will be an orange machine there to timestamp your ticket. If you have a bus pass, or have already made at least one other journey on the same ticket (within the past 90 minutes), you can board the bus at the front. It's not usually any faster since that's where passengers get off the bus. You can also leave from the centre doors.

TRANSPORT INFORMATION

ATAC
Piazza dei Cinquecento.
Map 6 D3.
📞 46 95 44 44.
Open 7.30am-7pm daily

Metro ticket   **90-minute bus ticket**

ATAC bus No. 64

Rome–Gubbio bus

New-style bus stop listing details of routes served

TICKETS

TICKETS FOR CITY buses, trams and Metros have to be bought before you travel. You can buy them at bars, news-stands and tobacconists, as well as at Metro stations and bus termini. Look out for places displaying ATAC (bus and tram) and COTRAL (Metro) stickers. Most of the outlets selling tickets close by mid-evening, so it's wise to buy several tickets at a time. Also, don't count on buying tickets at a Metro station, as staffing problems mean that booths are often closed, while the automatic ticket machines, which take coins only and do not give change, are very often out of order.

Bus and tram tickets are valid for 90 minutes, during which time you can hop on and off as many buses

A Roman tram in the orange livery of ATAC

and trams as you like. Tickets for Metros are valid for one single journey only. If you are going to make five or more journeys in one day, it's worth buying a BIG ticket. These give you a day's travel on the buses, trams and the Metros. Weekly tourist passes are only valid for buses and trams, but there are monthly passes valid on all transport. Fare-dodging is common, but incurs a hefty on-the-spot fine.

METROPOLITANA

ROME's underground system, the Metropolitana, has two lines (A and B) which cross the city in a rough X-shape, converging at Termini station *(see inside back cover and pp370-71).* Line A (red) leads from Ottaviano near the Vatican to Anagnina in the southeast of the city,

where buses go to Ciampino airport. Line B (blue) runs from Rebibbia in the northeast, where you can catch a bus to Tivoli, down to EUR in the southwest, where buses leave for the coast. Stations are clearly marked by the Metro logo, a large white M on a red background.

The system was designed to ferry commuters in from the suburbs, so is not very useful within the centre, but the Metro is a relatively speedy way of crossing the city and there are stops near some of the main sights. Useful stations are Colosseo, Spagna, San Giovanni, Ottaviano and Piramide (for trains to Fiumicino). Line A runs from about 5.30am until around midnight, Line B until 9pm from Monday to Friday.

Metro logo

USEFUL BUS AND TRAM ROUTES

This map shows a selection of buses that go through interesting parts of the city with good views of major sights. The 64 is always full of tourists, since it is the one route from Termini to St Peter's. The other routes are likely to be less crowded. The 30b tram follows a long leisurely route around the southeast of the city, while 23 goes along the Tiber.

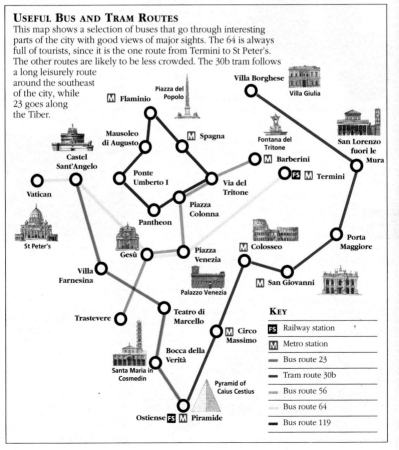

KEY

FS	Railway station
M	Metro station
—	Bus route 23
—	Tram route 30b
—	Bus route 56
—	Bus route 64
—	Bus route 119

BIKE AND MOPED HIRE

ROME'S NARROW streets and heavy traffic, combined with the seven steep hills on which it was built, make it a challenging place for even the most serious of cyclists. However, there are a few areas, such as the Villa Borghese, the banks of the Tiber and some pockets in the historic centre (around the Pantheon and Piazza Navona), where cycling can be a relaxing way to see the city. Make sure that you have a loud bell though – places that are good for cyclists tend to be popular with walkers and strollers too.

Mopeds (motorini) and scooters, called Vespas or

A Vespa scooter and helmet

Horse-drawn carriages outside the Pantheon

wasps in Italy because of the buzzing noise they make, are an efficient way of getting through the traffic. You may want to stick to quiet streets to begin with, though.

Although motorcyclists have to wear helmets by law, moped riders over 18 don't. However, you can hire helmets from most hire shops in Rome.

Bikes and mopeds can be hired from **Collalti**, **Roma Rent**, **Scoot-a-Long**, **St Peter Moto** and **Scooters for Rent**. **Biciroma** rents from several spots in the old centre and a **telephone hire service** operates in the summer and autumn.

You may have to leave a credit card as deposit when you pick up the bike.

HORSE-DRAWN CARRIAGES

THESE ARE NOT as popular in Rome as in Florence, but you can hire horse-drawn caleches (carrozzelle) for a gentle tour of the historic centre. Carriages carry up to five people and can be hired from many points: Piazza di Spagna, the Colosseum, Trevi Fountain, St Peter's, Via Veneto, Villa Borghese, Piazza Venezia and Piazza Navona. Trips last half an hour, an hour, half a day or a day. They tend to be expensive, but prices for longer rides are negotiable; establish the price before you set off and make sure you understand whether the rate is per person, or for the whole carriage.

TAXIS

OFFICIAL TAXIS in Rome are yellow and must bear the "taxi" sign on the roof. Only use these taxis, not the ones offered by touts at stations and tourist spots; official taxi drivers do not tout for customers. Yellow taxis can be hailed either at specially marked stands or on the street (drivers are not meant to stop in the street but many of them do). You can nearly always find them at the main tourist sights, at

Taxi stand signpost

airports and stations (including Termini and Ostiense). Roman taxi drivers are not renowned for their friendliness and may even refuse to take you too far from the lucrative city centre.

Taxis aren't a particularly cheap way of getting about, so, unless you have heavy luggage or screaming toddlers, public transport is usually a better option. Taxi drivers always charge supplements for baggage, night journeys (10pm–7am) and journeys on Sundays or public holidays. As with taxis elsewhere, the fare meter continues running while you're at a standstill so traffic jams can

Taxis lining up at Fiumicino

become expensive. Drivers may also take suspiciously circuitous routes to your destination. Taxi drivers in Rome expect tips from visitors. Native Romans generally give small amounts or nothing at all, but you'll be expected to give at least 10% of the fare.

You can book in advance from **Cosmos Radio Taxi**, **Società Cooperativa Autoradiotaxi Roma** or **Società la Capitale Radio Taxi**. There is a surcharge for taxis booked in advance.

Official yellow taxi

CAR HIRE

IN ITALY car hire is generally expensive, while petrol is among the highest-priced in Europe. Major international companies (**Avis**, **Europcar**, **Hertz** and **Eurodollar**) have rental offices at airports and within the city centre. However, you may get a better deal by booking a car ahead through a travel agent or tour operator before you leave. Local firms (such as **Maggiore**) are generally a lot cheaper, but check that breakdown service and collision damage waiver are included in the hire price.

Prospective renters should be aged 21 or over and have held a driving licence for at least one year. Theoretically you should also hold an international licence (available from your national automobile association) but most car rental firms do not usually insist on this.

Accident rates on Italian roads are very high, so insure yourself to the hilt. It's also a good idea to join an internationally affiliated auto-mobile association (such as the AA in Britain or the AAA in the US). If you break down in Italy, phone for **ACI** (Italian Automobile Club) assistance. They will tow anyone without charge, but only members of affiliated associations get free repairs. There is also a Roman auto-mobile club (**AC Roma**) with its own assistance centre.

Details of current road and traffic conditions (in Italian) are available from a special **Road Conditions** number. You'll find more information on driving and parking in Rome on page 375.

Roman car number plate

Car rental offices at Fiumicino airport

DIRECTORY

BIKE AND MOPED HIRE ADDRESSES

Biciroma
Piazza del Popolo.
Map 4 F1.
Also: Piazza di Spagna.
Map 5 A2.
Also: Piazza San Lorenzo in Lucina.
Map 4 F3 & 11 E1.
Also: Piazza SS. Apostoli.
Map 5 A4.

Collalti
Via del Pellegrino 82.
Map 4 E4 & 11 C4.
(68 80 10 84 (bikes).

Roma Rent
Via Vespasiano 32.
Map 3 B2.
(31 09 41 (bikes).

St Peter Moto
Via di Porta Castello 43.
Map 4 D3. **(** 687 57 14 (mopeds).

Scoot-a-Long
Via Cavour 302.
Map 5 B5.
(678 02 06 (mopeds).

Scooters for Rent
Via della Purificazione 66.
(488 54 85 (bikes and mopeds).

Telephone hire service
Lungotevere Marzio 3.
Map 4 E3 & 11 C1.
(68 80 33 94 (bikes).

TAXI BOOKING NUMBERS

Cosmos Radio Taxi
(881 77.

Società la Capitale Radio Taxi
(49 94.

Società Cooperativa Autoradiotaxi Roma
(35 70.

CAR HIRE ADDRESSES

Avis
Ciampino airport.
(724 01 95.
Also: Fiumicino airport.
(65 01 15 76.
Also: Piazza Esquilino 1.
Map 6 D4.
(470 12 16.
Also: Via Sardegna 38A.
Map 5 C1.
(470 12 28.

Eurodollar
Via Ludovisi 60.
Map 5 B2.
(487 20 98.

Europcar
Fiumicino airport.
(65 01 08 79.
Also: Via del Fiume Giallo 196.
(529 04 06.
Also: Via Lombardia 7.
Map 5 B2.
(482 43 81.

Hertz
Via Gregorio VII, 115/7.
(39 37 88 07.
Also: Stazione Termini.
Map 6 D3.
(474 03 89.
Also: Fiumicino.
(65 01 14 48.

Maggiore
Stazione Termini.
Map 6 D3.
(488 37 15.
Also: Via Po 8. **Map** 5 C1.
(854 86 98.

CAR BREAKDOWN SERVICES

ACI
Via Marsala 8.
(499 81.
Also: Via Fiume delle Perle.
(57 00 31.

ACI Breakdown
(116.

AC Roma
Via Cristoforo Colombo 261. **(** 51 49 71.

AC Roma Assistance Centre
(44 77.

Autosoccorso CARA
Via Trinchese 27.
(33 62 58 56.
(24-hour rescue service.)

Road Conditions
Via Magenta 5. **Map** 6 E3.
(44 77.

MAIN CAR PARKS

Acqua Acetosa station.
Map 2 E1.
Also: Lepanto Metro station. **Map** 4 D1.
Also: Piazza del Popolo.
Map 4 F1.
Also: EUR Palasport Metro station.

USEFUL 24-HOUR PETROL STATIONS

Trastevere
Lungotevere Ripa.
Map 8 D1.

Portuense
Piazza della Radio.
Map 7 B5.

STREET FINDER

MAP REFERENCES given with sights, restaurants, hotels, shops and entertainment venues refer to the maps in this section (*see* How the Map References Work *opposite*). A complete index of the street names and places of interest marked on the maps follows on pages 382–91. The key map below shows the area of Rome covered by the *Street Finder*. This includes the sightseeing areas (which are colour-coded) as well as the whole of central Rome with all the districts important for restaurants, hotels and entertainment venues. Because the historic centre is so packed with sights, there is a large-scale map of this area on pages 11 and 12.

0 kilometres   2

0 miles   1

HOW THE MAP REFERENCES WORK

The first figure tells you which Street Finder map to turn to.

Trevi Fountain ⑦

Fontana di Trevi. **Map 5 A3** & **12 F2** 🚌 52, 53, 58, 60, 61, 62, 71, 95, 492 and many other routes.

The letter and number are a grid reference. You will find the letters at the top and bottom of the map and the numbers at the sides.

The second reference refers to the large-scale maps of central Rome (11 & 12). It is read in exactly the same way as the first.

The map continues on map 8 of the Street Finder.

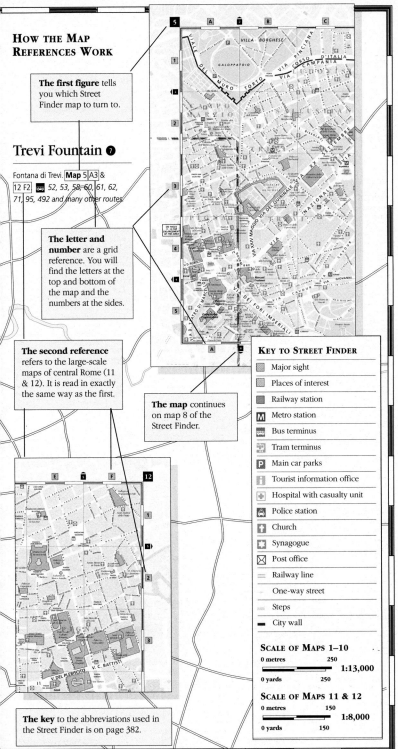

KEY TO STREET FINDER

	Major sight
	Places of interest
	Railway station
M	Metro station
🚌	Bus terminus
🚊	Tram terminus
P	Main car parks
🛈	Tourist information office
✚	Hospital with casualty unit
🚓	Police station
🕆	Church
✡	Synagogue
⊠	Post office
═	Railway line
—	One-way street
⋯	Steps
▬	City wall

SCALE OF MAPS 1–10

0 metres	250	
0 yards	250	**1:13,000**

SCALE OF MAPS 11 & 12

0 metres	150	
0 yards	150	**1:8,000**

The key to the abbreviations used in the Street Finder is on page 382.

Street Finder Index

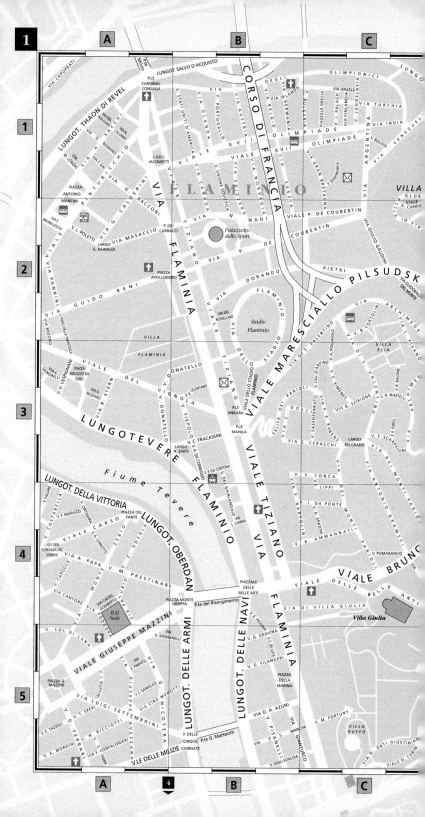

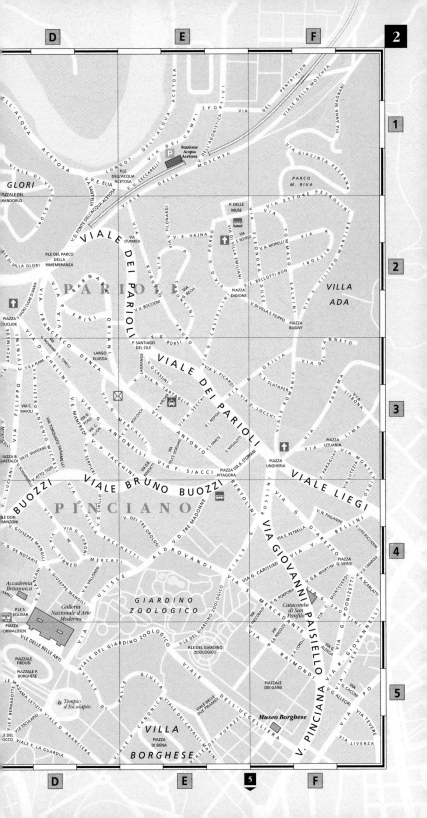

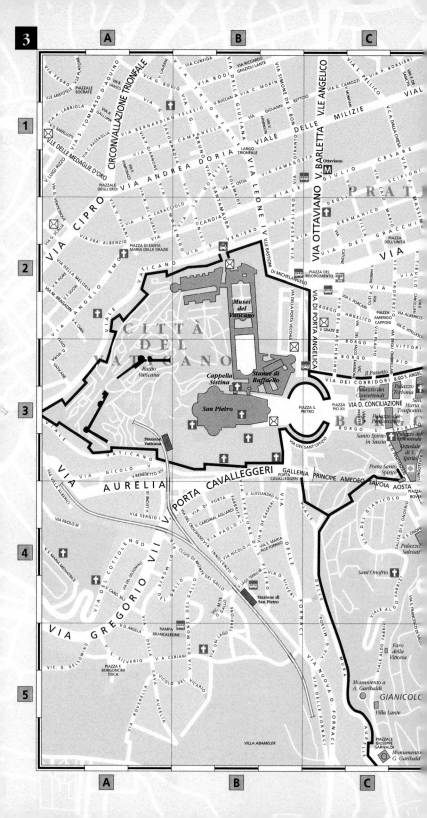

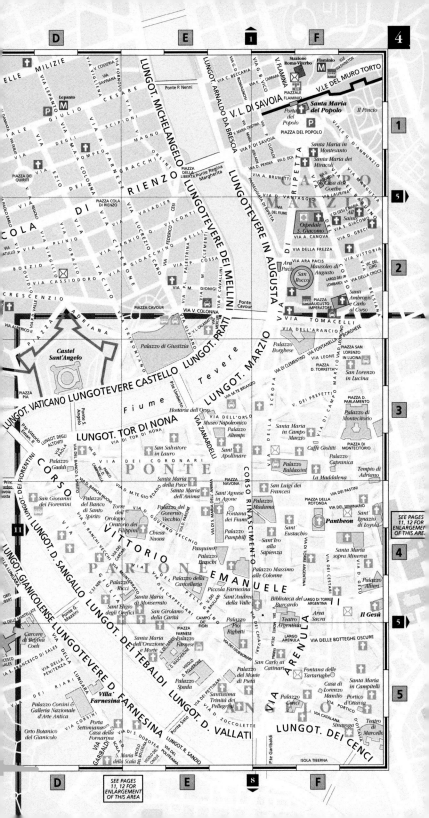

SEE PAGES 11, 12 FOR ENLARGEMENT OF THIS AREA.

SEE PAGES 11, 12 FOR ENLARGEMENT OF THIS AREA.

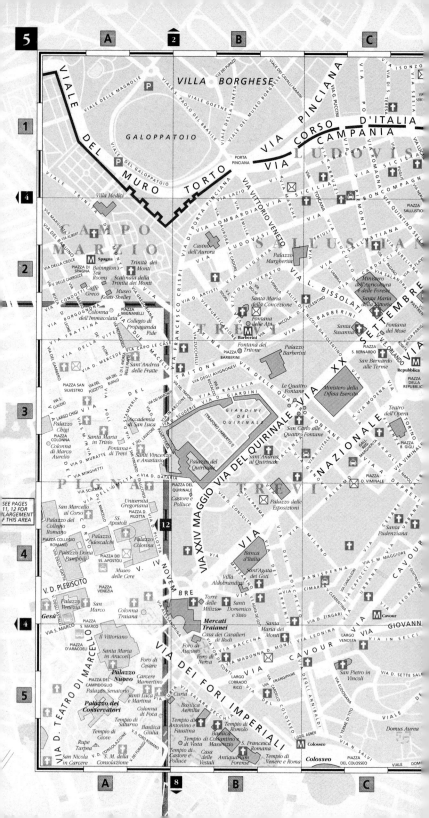

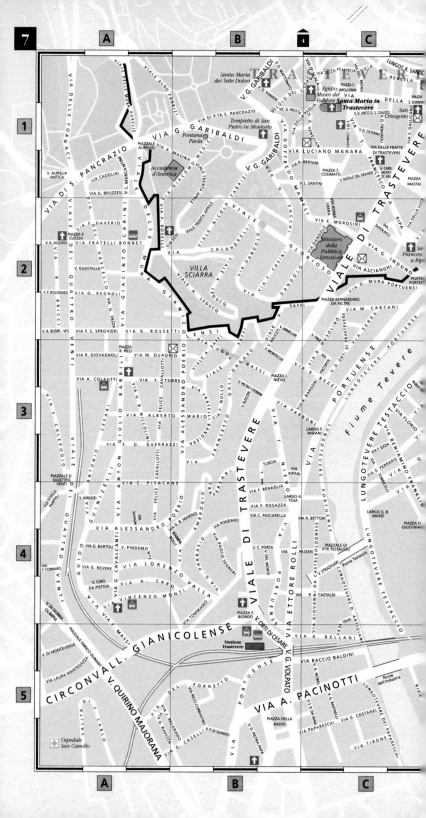

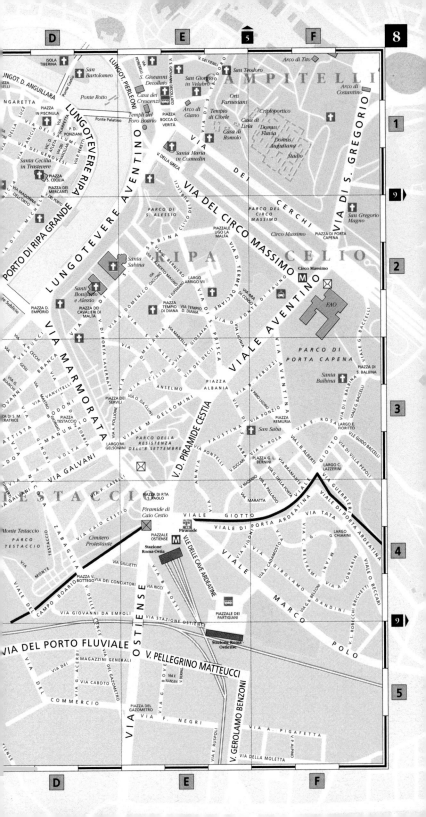

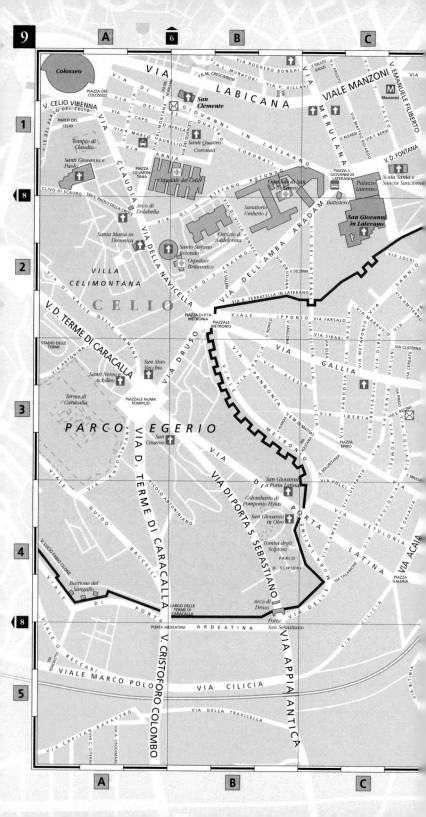

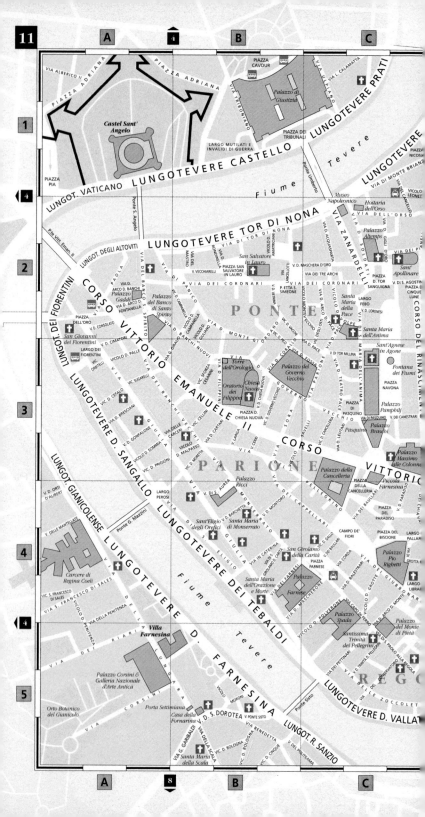

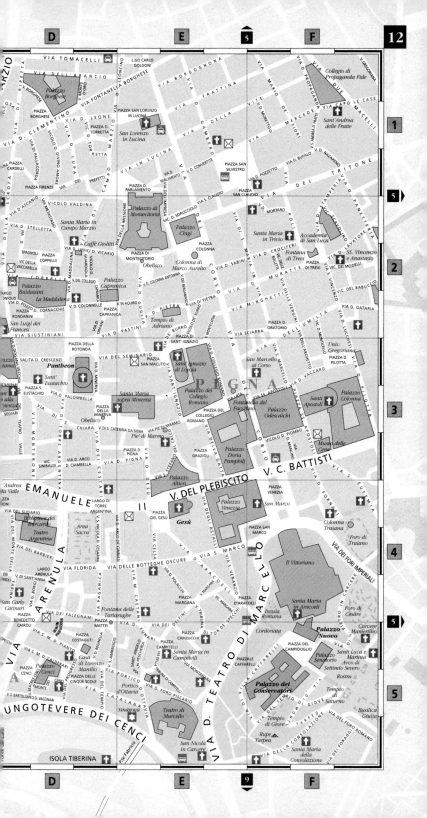

General Index

Acknowledgments

DORLING KINDERSLEY would like to thank the following people whose contributions and assistance have made the preparation of this book possible.

MAIN CONTRIBUTORS

Olivia Ercoli is an art historian and tour guide, who has lived all her life in Rome. Bilingual in English and Italian, she lectures on art history and writes on a range of subjects for English and Italian publications.

Travel writer Ros Belford conceived the idea of the Virago Woman's Guides, of which she is now series editor, and wrote the *Virago Woman's Guide to Rome*. She has travelled widely in Europe and as well as writing guide books contributes to a variety of publications including *The Guardian*.

Roberta Mitchell heads the editorial section of the UN's Publishing Division in Rome, where she has lived for many years. An experienced writer and editor with extensive knowledge of the city, she has contributed to a number of guides to Rome including the *American Express Guide to Rome*.

CONTRIBUTORS

Sam Cole, Mary Jane Cryan Pancani, Daphne Wilson Ercoli, Laura Ercoli, Lindsay Hunt, Adrian James, Christopher McDowall, Davina Palmer, Rodney Palmer, Debra Shipley.

DORLING KINDERSLEY wishes to thank the following editors and researchers at Websters International Publishers: Sandy Carr, Matthew Barrell, Siobhan Bremner, Serena Cross, Valeria Fabbri, Annie Galpin, Gemma Hancock, Celia Woolfrey.

ADDITIONAL PHOTOGRAPHY

Andy Crawford, Philip Enticknap, Steve Gorton, Neil Mersh, Poppy, David Sutherland.

ADDITIONAL ILLUSTRATIONS

Anne Bowes, Robin Carter, Gillie Newman, Chris D Orr.

ADDITIONAL PICTURE RESEARCH

Sharon Buckley.

CARTOGRAPHY

Advanced Illustration (Cheshire), Contour Publishing (Derby), Euromap Limited (Berkshire). Street Finder maps: ERA Maptec Ltd (Dublin) adapted with permission from original survey and mapping from Shobunsha (Japan).

CARTOGRAPHIC RESEARCH

James Anderson, Donna Rispoli, Joan Russell.

RESEARCH ASSISTANCE

Janet Abbott, Flaminia Allvin, Licia Bronzin, Lupus Sabene.

DESIGN AND EDITORIAL ASSISTANCE

Hilary Bird, Vanessa Courtier, Claire Edwards, Simon Farbrother, Vanessa Hamilton, Marcus Hardy, Sasha Heseltine, Sally Ann Hibbard, Stephanie Jackson, Steve Knowlden, Mary Lambert, Janette Leung, Jane Middleton, Fiona Morgan, Helen Partington, Naomi Peck, Carolyn Pyrah, Salim Qurashi, Jane Shaw, Clare Sullivan, Andrew Szudek, Daphne Trotter, Diana Vowles.

SPECIAL ASSISTANCE

Dottore Riccardo Baldini, Signor Mario di Bartolomeo of the Soprintendenza dei Beni Artistici e Storici di Roma, Belloni, Dorling Kindersley picture department, David Gleave MW, Debbie Harris, Emma Hutton and Cooling Brown Partnership, Dottoressa Todaro and Signora Camimiti at the Ministero dell'Interno, Trestini.

PHOTOGRAPHY PERMISSIONS

DORLING KINDERSLEY would like to thank the following for their kind permission to photograph at their establishments: Bathsheba Abse at the Keats-Shelley Memorial House, Accademia dei Lincei, Accanto, Aeroporti di Roma, Aldrovandi Palace, Alpheus, Banco di Santo Spirito at Palazzo del Monte di Pietà, Rory Bruck at Babington's, Caffè Giolitti, Caffè Latino, Comune di Roma (Ripartizione X), Comunità Ebraica di Roma, Guido Cornini at Monumenti Musei e Gallerie Ponteficie, Direzione Sanitaria Ospedale di Santo Spirito, Dottoressa Laura Falsini at the

Soprintendenza Archeologica di Etruria Meridionale, Hotel Gregoriana, Hotel Majestic, Hotel Regina Baglioni, Marco Marchetti at Ente EUR, Dottoressa Mercalli at the Museo Nazionale di Castel Sant'Angelo, Ministero dell'Interno, Plaza Minerva, Ristorante Alberto Ciarla, Ristorante Filetti di Baccalà, Ristorante Romolo, Signor Rulli and Signor Angeli at the Soprintendenza Archeologica di Roma, Soprintendenza Archeologica per il Lazio, Soprintendenza per i Beni Ambientali e Architettonici, Soprintendenza per i Beni Artistici e Storici di Roma, Daniela Tabo at the Musei Capitolini, Villa d'Este, Villa San Pio, Mrs Marjorie Weeke at St Peter's.

PICTURE CREDITS

t = top; tl = top left; tc = top centre; tr = top right; cla = centre left above; ca = centre above; cra = centre right above; cl = centre left; c = centre; cr = centre right; clb = centre left below; cb = centre below; crb = centre right below; bl = bottom left; b = bottom; bc = bottom centre; br = bottom right.

Every effort has been made to trace the copyright holders and we apologize in advance for any unintentional omissions. We would be pleased to insert the appropriate acknowledgments in any subsequent edition of this publication.

Works of art have been reproduced with the permission of the following copyright holders: © DACS: Città con Cattedrale Gotica, 1925 by Paul Klee 241b.

The publishers are grateful to the following individuals, companies and picture libraries for permission to reproduce their photographs:

ACCADEMIA NAZIONALE DI SAN LUCA, Rome: 160b; AFE: 57b, 61cr; Sandro Battaglia 59c, 61clb, 61br, 324br; Louise Goldman 157t; G La Malfa 251t; AGENZIA SINTESI: Fabio Fiorani 360br, 361t, 361b; Antonella di Girolamo 361c; Marco Marcotulli 360bc; R Venturi 360bl; ALITALIA: 368t, 369cl; ALLSPORT: David Cannon 39br; ANCIENT ART AND ARCHITECTURE: 16bl, 20tl, 21tl, 25bc, 34crb, 35tc, 44cl; ARTOTHEK, Stadelsches Kunstinstitut Frankfurt, Goethe in the Roman Campagna by JHW Tischbein 136t.

BIBLIOTECA REALE, Torino: 28–29c; BRIDGEMAN ART LIBRARY: 18br, 37tr; Agnew & Sons, London 51tr; Antikenmuseum Staatliches Museum, Berlin 19bl; Biblioteca Publica Episcopal, Barcelona/Index 114bl; Bibliothèque da la Sorbonne 28c, British Museum, London 27ctr; Chateau de Versailles, France/Giraudon 33tr, 54cl; Christie's, London 40, 55tr, 68b, 95t; The Fine Art Society, London 151tr, 279tl; Galleria degli Uffizi, Florence 31bl; Greek Museum, University of Newcastle-upon-Tyne 16br; King Street Galleries, London 33br; Louvre, Paris/Lauros-Giraudon 56br; Louvre, Paris/Giraudon 26br; Roy Miles Gallery, 29 Bruton St, London 228t; Musée des Beaux-Arts, Nantes 53t; Museo e Gallerie Nazionali di Capodimonte, Naples, Detail from the predella of San Ludovico by Simone Martini 26tr; Musée Condé, Chantilly f.71v Très Riches Heures, 26tc; Museum of Fine Arts, Budapest 110bl; Museo Archeologico di Villa Giulia 48cl; Museo Poldi Pezzoli, Milan 54tr; Palazzo Doria Pamphilj, Rome 107b; Piacenza Town Hall, Italy/Index 27br; Private Collection 19br, 22bl, 24br, 27tr, 178b; Pushkin Museum, Moscow 111t; Sotheby's, London 18bl; Spink & Son Ltd., London 163b; Vatican Museums & Galleries 41ca, 237tr.

CEPHAS PICTURE LIBRARY: Mick Rock 306tr; VANESSA COURTIER: 355t.

CM DIXON: 17bl, 24c, 268b, 269t, 269b.

ECOLE NATIONALE SUPERIEURE DES BEAUX-ARTS: 21cr, 22–23, 248t, 284–285bs; ENTE NAZIONALE ITALIANO PER IL TURISMO: 358cl, cr; ET ARCHIVE: 14, 17tr, 17clb, 18tr, 19tc, 23t, 27cl, 28tl, 31br, 32br, 37br, 48tl, 306tl; MARY EVANS PICTURE LIBRARY: 9, 18cl, 23cl, 24cl, 29br, 30cb, 30b, 31t, 34tl, 34cr, 34bl, 54tl, 56tl, 67bl, 74t, 81b, 91t, 92b, 94bl, 127c, 135t, 135b, 213b.

CORALDO FALSINI: 38–39c, 340b, 341t, 341c; WERNER FORMAN ARCHIVE: 17cr, 20bl, 22tl, 23cr, 23bl, 23br, 47tr, 155t, 163tr, 175c; FOLKLORE MUSEUM, Rome: 210br.

GARDEN PICTURE LIBRARY: Bob Challinor 172cb; GIRAUDON: 15b, 28br, 36br, 55tl; RONALD GRANT: 52br, 340t.

SONIA HALLIDAY: 19c, 22br, 25cl; Laura Lushington 24bl; ROBERT HARDING PICTURE LIBRARY: 23cra, 32bl, 79cr, 177t, 268c, 353c; Mario Carrieri 35tr; Caffè Greco, Rome by

Ludwig Passini 309tr; John G Ross 38tl, 59cl, 341b; Sheila Terry 39cl; G White 59br; MICHAEL HOLFORD: 70b; HULTON DEUTSCH: 36tl, 38bc, 57cr, 63, 175b, 287c, 357c.

MAGNUM: Erich Lessing 15t, 17tl, 89br; MANSELL COLLECTION: 19tr, 25bl, 26bc, 31cl, 54bc, 55tc, 56cl, 57cl, 75cl, 75cr, 78tc, 93b, 112c, 122t, 125tr, 126tl, 132br, 133cr, 136bl, 139bl, 139br, 162tr, 172bl, 172 br, 183br, 192bl, 196bl, 210c, 220bl, 227cr, 229cr; Alinari 80br, 141bl, 160tl, 174t, 254b; Anderson 78cr, 138bl, 163tl, 228b; MORO ROMA: 36cl, 37cl, 38br, 39tr, 39bl.

NATIONAL PORTRAIT GALLERY, London: 55cr, 55b, 56tr, 57tr; © NIPPON TELEVISION NETWORK CORPORATION, Tokyo 1992: 244t, 245t, 245bl, 245br.

LA REPUBBLICA TROVAROMA: 359tl; REX FEATURES: Sipa 366br; Today 39cr.

SCALA: 94t, 278cl, Casa di Augusto 97t, Chiesa del Gesù 115t, Galleria Borghese 32cla, 260tr, Galleria Colonna 157b, Galleria Doria Pamphilj 46br, 105cr, Galleria Spada 46cl, Galleria degli Uffizi 16–17, 27bl, Museo d'Arte Orientale 174t, 174br, Musei Capitolini 47bl, Museo della Civiltà Romana 48tr, 48b, Museo delle Terme 21tr, Museo Napoleonico 49cr, Museo Nazionale, Napoli 21cl, Museo Nazionale, Ravenna 22cl, Museo del Risorgimento, Milano 36clb, 36–37c, Museo del Risorgimento, Roma 37tl, Museo di San Marco 54bl, Palazzo Barberini 253bl, Palazzo Ducale 8, 19tr, Palazzo della Farnesina 220ct, Palazzo Madama 20cl, Palazzo Venezia 47cr, 66bl, San Carlo alle Quattro Fontane 33cl, 33cr, Santa Cecilia in Trastevere 32tl, San Clemente 35bl, Santa Costanza 24–25c, Santa Maria Antiqua 24tl, Santa Maria dell'Anima 121t, Santa Maria Maggiore 43tr, Santa Maria del Popolo 139tr, 139c, Santa Prassede 26bl, 28bl, Santa Sabina 25tc, 29cl, Vatican Museums 19bc, 25t, 25cr, 25cra, 27cr, 29tl, 29cr, 30tl, 30ct, 31cr, 31bc, 32cr, 32clb, 41tr, 46tl, 48cr, 49bl, 224bl, 225cr, 235t, 238tl, 238br, 240t, 240b, 241t, 241c, 241b, 242tl, 242c, 242b, 243t, 243c, 243b, 244–245c, 246cl, 246cr, 246b, 247tl, 247c, 247cr, 247b; TONY STONE: Richard Passmore 1c.

TOPHAM PICTURE SOURCE: 38cl.

ZEFA: 2, 39tl, 230cl, 231br, 356–7, 358t, 372t; Eric Carle 58t; Kohlhas 231t.

Thanks also to Dottoressa Giulia De Marchi of L'ACCADEMIA NAZIONALE DI SAN LUCA, Rome for 160b, Rettore Padre Libianchi of LA CHIESA DI SANT'IGNAZIO DI LOYOLA for 106t, ENTE NAZIONALE PER IL TURISMO, HASSLER HOTEL, Rome for 293tl, GRAND HOTEL, Rome for 293crb and to LA REPUBBLICA TROVAROMA.

Phrase Book

IN EMERGENCY

Help!	**Aiuto!**	*eye-yoo*-toh
Stop!	**Fermate!**	*fair-mah*-teh
Call a doctor	**Chiama un medico**	*kee-ah-mah oon meh-dee-koh*
Call an ambulance	**Chiama un' ambulanza**	*kee-ah-mah oon am-boo-lan-tsa*
Call the police	**Chiama la polizia**	*kee-ah-mah lah pol-ee-tsee-ah*
Call the fire brigade	**Chiama i pompieri**	*kee-ah-mah ee pom-pee-air-ee*
Where is the telephone?	**Dov'è il telefono?**	*dov-eh eel tel-leh-foh-noh?*
The nearest hospital?	**L'ospedale più vicino?**	*loss-peh-dah-leh pee-oo vee-chee-noh?*

COMMUNICATION ESSENTIALS

Yes/No	**Sì/No**	*see/noh*
Please	**Per favore**	*pair fah-vor-eh*
Thank you	**Grazie**	*grah-tsee-eh*
Excuse me	**Mi scusi**	*mee skoo-zee*
Hello	**Buon giorno**	*bwon jor-noh*
Good bye	**Arrivederci**	*ah-ree-veh-dair-chee*
Good evening	**Buona sera**	*bwon-ah sair-ah*
morning	**la mattina**	*lah mah-tee-nah*
afternoon	**il pomeriggio**	*eel poh-meh-ree-joh*
evening	**la sera**	*lah sair-ah*
yesterday	**ieri**	*ee-air-ee*
today	**oggi**	*oh-jee*
tomorrow	**domani**	*doh-mah-nee*
here	**qui**	*kwee*
there	**la**	*lah*
What?	**Quale?**	*kwah-leh?*
When?	**Quando?**	*kwan-doh?*
Why?	**Perchè?**	*pair-keh?*
Where?	**Dove?**	*doh-veh*

USEFUL PHRASES

How are you?	**Come sta?**	*koh-meh stah?*
Very well, thank you.	**Molto bene, grazie.**	*moll-toh beh-neh grah-tsee-eh*
Pleased to meet you.	**Piacere di conoscerla.**	*pee-ah-chair-eh dee cob-noh-shair-lah*
See you soon.	**A più tardi.**	*ah pee-oo tar-dee*
That's fine.	**Va bene.**	*va beh-neh*
Where is/are ...?	**Dov'è/Dove sono ...?**	*dov-eh/doveh soh-noh?*
How long does it take to get to ...?	**Quanto tempo ci vuole per andare a ...?**	*kwan-toh tem-poh chee voo-oh-leh pair an-dar-eh ah...?*
How do I get to ...?	**Come faccio per arrivare a ...?**	*koh-meh fah-choh pair arri-var-eh ah...?*
Do you speak English?	**Parla inglese?**	*par-lah een-gleh-zeh?*
I don't understand.	**Non capisco.**	*non ka-pee-skoh*
Could you speak more slowly, please?	**Può parlare più lentamente, per favore?**	*pwoh par-lah-reh pee-oo len-ta-men-teh pair fah-vor-eh*
I'm sorry.	**Mi dispiace.**	*mee dee-spee-ah-cheh*

USEFUL WORDS

big	**grande**	*gran-deh*
small	**piccolo**	*pee-koh-loh*
hot	**caldo**	*kal-doh*
cold	**freddo**	*fred-doh*
good	**buono**	*bwoh-noh*
bad	**cattivo**	*kat-tee-voh*
enough	**basta**	*bas-tah*
well	**bene**	*beh-neh*
open	**aperto**	*ah-pair-toh*
closed	**chiuso**	*kee-oo-zoh*
left	**a sinistra**	*ah see-nee-strah*
right	**a destra**	*ah dess-trah*
straight on	**sempre dritto**	*sem-preh dree-toh*
near	**vicino**	*vee-chee-noh*
far	**lontano**	*lon-tah-noh*
up	**su**	*soo*
down	**giù**	*joo*
early	**presto**	*press-toh*
late	**tardi**	*tar-dee*
entrance	**entrata**	*en-trah-tah*
exit	**uscita**	*oo-shee-ta*
toilet	**il gabinetto**	*eel gah-bee-net-toh*
free, unoccupied	**libero**	*lee-bair-oh*
free, no charge	**gratuito**	*grah-too-ee-toh*

MAKING A TELEPHONE CALL

I'd like to place a long-distance call.	**Vorrei fare una interurbana.**	*vor-ray far-eh oona in-tair-oor-bah-nah*
I'd like to make a reverse-charge call.	**Vorrei fare una telefonata a carico del destinatario.**	*vor-ray far-eh oona teb-leh-fon-ah-tah ah kar-ee-koh dell dess-tee-nah-tar-ree-oh*
I'll try again later.	**Ritelefono più tardi.**	*ree-teb-leh-foh-noh pee-oo tar-dee*
Can I leave a message?	**Posso lasciare un messaggio?**	*poss-oh lash-ah-reh oon mess-sah-joh?*
Hold on	**Un attimo, per favore**	*oon ah-tee-moh, pair fah-vor-eh*
Could you speak up a little please?	**Può parlare più forte, per favore?**	*pwoh par-lah-reh pee-oo for-teb, pair fah-vor-eh?*
local call	**la telefonata locale**	*lah teb-leh-fon-ah-ta loh-kah-leh*

SHOPPING

How much does this cost?	**Quant'è, per favore?**	*kwan-teb, pair fah-vor-eh?*
I would like ...	**Vorrei ...**	*vor-ray*
Do you have ...?	**Avete ...?**	*ah-veh-teh...?*
I'm just looking.	**Sto soltanto guardando.**	*stoh sol-tan-toh gwar-dan-doh*
Do you take credit cards?	**Accettate carte di credito?**	*ah-chet-tah-teh kar-teb dee creb-dee-toh?*
What time do you open/close?	**A che ora apre/ chiude?**	*ah keh or-ah ah-preh/kee-oo-deh?*
this one	**questo**	*kweb-stoh*
that one	**quello**	*kwell-oh*
expensive	**caro**	*kar-oh*
cheap	**a buon prezzo**	*ah bwon pret-soh*
size, clothes	**la taglia**	*lah tab-lee-ah*
size, shoes	**il numero**	*eel noo-mair-oh*
white	**bianco**	*bee-ang-koh*
black	**nero**	*neh-roh*
red	**rosso**	*ross-oh*
yellow	**giallo**	*jal-loh*
green	**verde**	*vair-deh*
blue	**blu**	*bloo*
brown	**marrone**	*mar-roh-neh*

TYPES OF SHOP

antique dealer	**l'antiquario**	*lan-tee-kwah-ree-oh*
bakery	**la panetteria**	*lah pah-net-tair-ree-ah*
bank	**la banca**	*lah bang-kah*
bookshop	**la libreria**	*lah lee-breh-ree-ah*
butcher's	**la macelleria**	*lah mah-chell-eh-ree-ah*
cake shop	**la pasticceria**	*lah pass-tee-chair-ee-ah*
chemist's	**la farmacia**	*lah far-mah-chee-ah*
department store	**il grande magazzino**	*eel gran-deh mag-gad-zee-noh*
delicatessen	**la salumeria**	*lah sah-loo-meb-ree-ah*
fishmonger's	**la pescheria**	*lah pess-keb-ree-ah*
florist	**il fioraio**	*eel fee-or-eye-oh*
greengrocer	**il fruttivendolo**	*eel froo-tee-ven-doh-loh*
grocery	**alimentari**	*ah-lee-men-tah-ree*
hairdresser	**il parrucchiere**	*eel par-oo-kee-air-eh*
ice cream parlour	**la gelateria**	*lah jel-lah-tair-ree-ah*
market	**il mercato**	*eel mair-kah-toh*
news-stand	**l'edicola**	*leh-dee-koh-lah*
post office	**l'ufficio postale**	*loo-fee-choh pos-tah-leh*
shoe shop	**il negozio di scarpe**	*eel neb-goh-tsioh dee skar-peh*
supermarket	**il supermercato**	*su-pair-mair-kah-toh*
tobacconist	**il tabaccaio**	*eel tah-bak-eye-oh*
travel agency	**l'agenzia di viaggi**	*lah-jen-tsee-ah dee vee-ad-jee*

SIGHTSEEING

art gallery	**la pinacoteca**	*lah peena-koh-teb-kah*
bus stop	**la fermata dell'autobus**	*lah fair-mah-tah dell ow-toh-booss*
church	**la chiesa**	*lah kee-eb-zah*
	la basilica	*lah bah-seel-i-kah*
garden	**il giardino**	*eel jar-dee-no*
library	**la biblioteca**	*lah beeb-lee-oh-teb-kah*
museum	**il museo**	*eel moo-zeb-oh*
railway station	**la stazione**	*lah stah-tsee-oh-neh*
tourist information	**l'ufficio turistico**	*loo-fee-choh too-ree-stee-koh*
closed for the public holiday	**chiuso per la festa**	*kee-oo-zoh pair lah fess-tah*

STAYING IN A HOTEL

Do you have any vacant rooms?	**Avete camere libere?**	*ah-**veb**-teb kab-mair-eb lee-bair-eb?*
double room	**una camera doppia**	*oona **kab**-mair-ab **dob**-pee-ab*
with double bed	**con letto matrimoniale**	*kon **let**-tob mab-tree-mob-nee-**ab**-leb*
twin room	**una camera con due letti**	*oona **kab**-mair-ab kon **doo**-eb **let**-tee*
single room	**una camera singola**	*oona **kab**-mair-ab **sing**-gob-lab*
room with a bath, shower	**una camera con bagno, con doccia**	*oona **kab**-mair-ab kon **ban**-yob, kon **dot**-cbab*
porter	**il facchino**	*eel fab-**kee**-nob*
key	**la chiave**	*lab kee-**ab**-veb*
I have a reservation.	**Ho fatto una prenotazione.**	*ob **fat**-tob oona preb-nob-tab-tsee-**ob**-neb*

EATING OUT

Have you got a table for ...?	**Avete una tavola per ... ?**	*ah-**veb**-teb oona **tab**-vob-lab pair ...?*
I'd like to reserve a table.	**Vorrei riservare una tavola.**	*vor-**ray** ree-sair-**vab**-reb oona **tab**-vob-lab*
breakfast	**colazione**	*kob-lab-tsee-**ob**-neb*
lunch	**pranzo**	***pran**-tsob*
dinner	**cena**	***cheb**-nah*
The bill, please.	**Il conto, per favore.**	*eel **kon**-tob pair fab-**vor**-eb*
I am a vegetarian.	**Sono vegetariano/a.**	*sob-nob veb-jeb-tar-ee-ab-nob/nah*
waitress	**cameriera**	*kah-mair-ee-**air**-ab*
waiter	**cameriere**	*kah-mair-ee-**air**-eb*
fixed price menu	**il menù a prezzo fisso**	*eel meb-**noo** ab **pret**-tso **fee**-sob*
dish of the day	**piatto del giorno**	*pee-**ab**-tob dell **jor**-no*
starter	**antipasto**	*an-tee-**pass**-tob*
first course	**il primo**	*eel **pree**-mob*
main course	**il secondo**	*eel seb-**kon**-dob*
vegetables	**il contorno**	*eel kon-**tor**-nob*
dessert	**il dolce**	*eel **doll**-cheb*
cover charge	**il coperto**	*eel kob-**pair**-tob*
wine list	**la lista dei vini**	*lab **lee**-stab day **vee**-nee*
rare	**al sangue**	*al **sang**-gweb*
medium	**al puntino**	*al poon-**tee**-nob*
well done	**ben cotto**	*ben **kot**-tob*
glass	**il bicchiere**	*eel bee-kee-**air**-eb*
bottle	**la bottiglia**	*lab bot-**teel**-yab*
knife	**il coltello**	*eel kol-**tell**-ob*
fork	**la forchetta**	*lab for-**ket**-tab*
spoon	**il cucchiaio**	*eel koo-kee-**eye**-ob*

MENU DECODER

apple	**la mela**	*lab **meb**-lab*
artichoke	**il carciofo**	*eel kar-**choff**-ob*
aubergine	**la melanzana**	*lab meb-lan-**tsah**-nab*
baked	**al forno**	*al **for**-nob*
beans	**i fagioli**	*ee fab-**job**-lee*
beef	**il manzo**	*eel **man**-tsob*
beer	**la birra**	*lab **beer**-rab*
boiled	**lesso**	***less**-ob*
bread	**il pane**	*eel **pab**-neb*
broth	**il brodo**	*eel **brob**-dob*
butter	**il burro**	*eel **boor**-ob*
cake	**la torta**	*lab **tor**-tab*
cheese	**il formaggio**	*eel for-**mad**-job*
chicken	**il pollo**	*eel **poll**-ob*
chips	**patatine fritte**	*pab-tab-**teen**-eb **free**-teb*
baby clams	**le vongole**	*leb **von**-gob-leb*
coffee	**il caffè**	*eel kab-**feb***
courgettes	**gli zucchini**	*lyee dzoo-**kee**-nee*
dry	**secco**	***sek**-kob*
duck	**l'anatra**	***lab**-nab-trab*
egg	**l'uovo**	*loo-**ob**-vob*
fish	**il pesce**	*eel **pesh**-eb*
fresh fruit	**frutta fresca**	***froo**-tab **fress**-kab*
garlic	**l'aglio**	***labl**-yob*
grapes	**l'uva**	***loo**-vab*
grilled	**alla griglia**	*ab-lab **greel**-yab*
ham	**il prosciutto**	*eel pro-**shoo**-tob*
cooked/cured	**cotto/crudo**	***kot**-tob/**kroo**-dob*
ice cream	**il gelato**	*eel jel-**lab**-tob*
lamb	**l'abbacchio**	*lab-**back**-kee-ob*
lobster	**l'aragosta**	*lab-rab-**goss**-tab*
meat	**la carne**	*lab **kar**-neb*

milk	**il latte**	*eel **labt**-teb*
mineral water	**l'acqua minerale**	*lab-kwah mee-nair-ab-leb*
fizzy/still	**gasata/naturale**	*gab-**zab**-tab/nab-too-**rab**-leb*
mushrooms	**i funghi**	*ee **foon**-gee*
oil	**l'olio**	***loll**-yob*
olive	**l'oliva**	*lob-**lee**-vab*
onion	**la cipolla**	*lab cbee-**poll**-ab*
orange	**l'arancia**	*lab-ran-chab*
orange/lemon juice	**succo d'arancia/ di limone**	*soo-kob dab-**ran**-cbab/ dee lee-**mob**-neb*
peach	**la pesca**	*lab **pess**-kab*
pepper	**il pepe**	*eel **peb**-beb*
pork	**carne di maiale**	***kar**-neb dee mab-**yah**-leb*
potatoes	**le patate**	*leb pab-**tab**-teb*
prawns	**i gamberi**	*ee **gam**-bair-ee*
rice	**il riso**	*eel **ree**-zob*
roast	**arrosto**	*ar-**ross**-tob*
roll	**il panino**	*eel pab-**nee**-nob*
salad	**l'insalata**	*leen-sab-**lab**-tab*
salt	**il sale**	*eel **sab**-leb*
sausage	**la salsiccia**	*lab sal-**see**-cbab*
seafood	**frutti di mare**	***froo**-tee dee **mab**-reb*
soup	**la zuppa,**	*lab **tsoo**-pab,*
	la minestra	*lab mee-**ness**-trab*
steak	**la bistecca**	*lab bee-**stek**-kab*
strawberries	**le fragole**	*leb **frah**-gob-leb*
sugar	**lo zucchero**	*lob **zoo**-kair-ob*
tea	**il tè**	*eel **teb***
herb tea	**la tisana**	*lab tee-**zab**-nab*
tomato	**il pomodoro**	*eel pob-mob-**dor**-ob*
tuna	**il tonno**	***ton**-nob*
veal	**il vitello**	*vee-**tell**-ob*
vegetables	**i legumi**	*ee leb-**goo**-mee*
vinegar	**l'aceto**	*lab-**cheb**-tob*
water	**l'acqua**	***lab**-kwah*
red wine	**vino rosso**	***vee**-nob **ross**-ob*
white wine	**vino bianco**	***vee**-nob bee-**ang**-kob*

NUMBERS

1	**uno**	***oo**-nob*
2	**due**	***doo**-eb*
3	**tre**	*treb*
4	**quattro**	***kwat**-rob*
5	**cinque**	***ching**-kweb*
6	**sei**	***say**-ee*
7	**sette**	***set**-teb*
8	**otto**	***ot**-tob*
9	**nove**	***nob**-veb*
10	**dieci**	*dee-**eb**-chee*
11	**undici**	***oon**-dee-cbee*
12	**dodici**	***dob**-dee-cbee*
13	**tredici**	***tray**-dee-cbee*
14	**quattordici**	*kwat-**tor**-dee-chee*
15	**quindici**	***kwin**-dee-chee*
16	**sedici**	***say**-dee-chee*
17	**diciassette**	*dee-cbab-**set**-teb*
18	**diciotto**	*dee-**cbot**-tob*
19	**diciannove**	*dee-cbab-**nob**-veb*
20	**venti**	***ven**-tee*
30	**trenta**	***tren**-tab*
40	**quaranta**	*kwab-**ran**-tab*
50	**cinquanta**	*ching-**kwan**-tab*
60	**sessanta**	*sess-**an**-tab*
70	**settanta**	*set-**tan**-tab*
80	**ottanta**	*ot-**tan**-tab*
90	**novanta**	*nob-**van**-tab*
100	**cento**	***chen**-tob*
1,000	**mille**	***mee**-leb*
2,000	**duemila**	***doo**-eb **mee**-lab*
5,000	**cinquemila**	***ching**-kweb mee-**lab***
1,000,000	**un milione**	*oon meel-**yob**-neb*

TIME

one minute	**un minuto**	*oon mee-**noo**-tob*
one hour	**un'ora**	*oon or-ab*
half an hour	**mezz'ora**	*medz-**or**-ab*
a day	**un giorno**	*oon **jor**-nob*
a week	**una settimana**	*oona set-tee-**mab**-nab*
Monday	**lunedì**	*loo-neb-**dee***
Tuesday	**martedì**	*mar-teb-**dee***
Wednesday	**mercoledì**	*mair-koh-leb-**dee***
Thursday	**giovedì**	*job-veb-**dee***
Friday	**venerdì**	*ven-air-**dee***
Saturday	**sabato**	***sab**-bab-tob*
Sunday	**domenica**	*doh-**meb**-nee-kab*